T0336721

Serious Games and Virtual Worlds in Education, Professional Development, and Healthcare

Klaus Bredl
Department of Media and Educational Technology at Augsburg University, Germany

Wolfgang Bösche
University of Education Karlsruhe, Germany

Information Science
REFERENCE

Managing Director:	Lindsay Johnston
Editorial Director:	Joel Gamon
Book Production Manager:	Jennifer Yoder
Publishing Systems Analyst:	Adrienne Freeland
Development Editor:	Christine Smith
Assistant Acquisitions Editor:	Kayla Wolfe
Typesetter:	Christina Henning
Cover Design:	Jason Mull

Published in the United States of America by
Information Science Reference (an imprint of IGI Global)
701 E. Chocolate Avenue
Hershey PA 17033
Tel: 717-533-8845
Fax: 717-533-8661
E-mail: cust@igi-global.com
Web site: http://www.igi-global.com

Library of Congress Cataloging-in-Publication Data

Serious games and virtual worlds in education, professional development, and healthcare / Klaus Bredl and Wolfgang, editors.
     pages cm
 Includes bibliographical references and index.
 Summary: "This book explains how digital environments can easily become familiar and beneficial for educational and professional development, with the implementation of games into various aspects of our environment"--Provided by publisher.
  ISBN 978-1-4666-3673-6 (hardcover) -- ISBN 978-1-4666-3674-3 (ebook) -- ISBN 978-1-4666-3675-0 (print & perpetual access) 1. Virtual reality in education. 2. Shared virtual environments. 3. Computer games--Design. 4. Career development--Computer simulation. 5. Medical care--Computer simulation. I. Bredl, Klaus, editor of compilation. II. B?sche, Wolfgang, editor of compilation.
 LB1044.87.S48 2013
 371.33'44678--dc23
                    2012048460

British Cataloguing in Publication Data
A Cataloguing in Publication record for this book is available from the British Library.

All work contributed to this book is new, previously-unpublished material. The views expressed in this book are those of the authors, but not necessarily of the publisher.

List of Reviewers

Alke Martens, *University of Education Schwäbisch Gmünd, Germany*

Andreas Hebbel-Seeger, *MHMK Macromedia University for Media and Communication, Germany*

Christian Reuter, *Technische Universität Darmstadt, Germany*

Christopher J. Ferguson, *Texas A&M International University, USA*

Daniel Schultheiss, *Ilmenau University of Technology, Germany*

Dennis Maciuszek, *University of Rostock, Germany*

Dick Davies, *Ambient Performance, UK*

Elizabeth Dean, *RTI International, USA*

Florian Mehm, *Technische Universität Darmstadt, Germany*

Hannah R. Marston, *German Sport University,Germany*

Hein de Graaf, *Social Psychologist, The Netherlands*

Inesita Soares de Araújo, *Oswaldo Cruz Foundation, Brazil*

Jana Birkenbusch, *Technische Universität Darmstadt, Germany*

Joe Murphy, *RTI International, USA*

Johannes Konert, *Technische Universität Darmstadt, Germany*

Josef Wiemeyer, *Technische Unversität Darmstadt, Germany*

Klaus Hauer, *Agaplesion Bethanien-Hospital Heidelberg, Germany*

Kristina Richter, *Technische Universität Darmstadt, Germany*

LeRoy Heinrichs, *Stanford University, USA*

Li Fellander-Tsai, *Karolinska Institutet, Sweden*

Maike Helm, *Ilmenau University of Technology, Germany*

Marcelo Simão de Vasconcellos, *Oswaldo Cruz Foundation, Brazil*

Michael Brach, *University of Muenster, Germany*

Michael Gutjahr, *Technische Universität Darmstadt, Germany*

Oliver Christ, *Technische Universität Darmstadt, Germany*

Oliver Korn, *KORION Simulation and Assistive Technology GmbH, Germany*

Patrick Felicia, *Waterford Institute of Technology, Ireland*

Philip A. McClenaghan, *Augsburg University, Germany*

Richard (Dick) Schoech, *University of Texas at Arlington, USA*

Sandro Hardy, *Technische Universität Darmstadt, Germany*

Sarah Cook, *RTI International, USA*

Stefan Göbel, *Technische Universität Darmstadt, Germany*

Steffen Winny, *University of Augsburg, Germany*

Sue Gregory, *University of New England, Australia*

Sven Unkauf, *Wohlfahrtswerk für Baden-Württemberg, Germany*

Viktor Wendel, *Technische Universität Darmstadt, Germany*

Table of Contents

Section 3
Games and Virtual Worlds in Education

Section 4
Games and Virtual Worlds in Health Care

Detailed Table of Contents

Section 1
Factors and Key Components of Serious Games and Multi-User Virtual Environments

Jana Birkenbusch, Technische Universität Darmstadt, Germany
Oliver Christ, Technische Universität Darmstadt, Germany

In the area of health care, dynamic changes and improvements of computer-based methods of intervention are more and more observable. This tendency is, amongst other reasons, caused by the implementation of theoretical constructs and psychological phenomena, such as flow, immersion, and presence, because they are able to explain processes and effects of medical interventions and thereby provide helpful hints to the enhancement of rehabilitation technology. This chapter provides an overview of the definitions of constructs related to computer-based technology, how these constructs are related to each other, and how they can be measured. Furthermore, practical aspects of improvement, possible areas of application, and potential benefits of implementing these constructs are discussed.

Alke Martens, University of Education Schwäbisch Gmünd, Germany
Dennis Maciuszek, University of Rostock, Germany

In game-based learning and in teaching using virtual worlds, designers creating the products and teachers providing them to students are both faced with a dualism between instruction and construction. Open-ended virtual worlds may provide authentic settings and inspire experimentation; on the other hand a lack of guidance may result in learners losing direction. The chapter conducts a narrative review of concepts across disciplines that describe the dilemma and imply certain instructional design strategies. Many authors advocate constructivist learning, but with instructional elements added. The authors collect their recommendations and apply and refine them in their own ideas: adaptivity inspired by Cognitive Apprenticeship, guidance on the basis of Cognitive Task Analysis, and immersive, interactive quest journals. Study setups and first results from ongoing projects illustrate the theoretical considerations.

Chapter 3

Christopher J. Ferguson, Texas A&M International University, USA

It has been recognized that video games may function well as a platform for education. However, educators may be reluctant to use such games, particularly those with violent content, given controversies over games in recent years. Yet recent data suggests that these controversies over video games may have been misplaced. The current chapter examines the controversies over video games, data to support and refute these controversies, and how the public debates on video games may have influenced educator's decisions about the use of video games in their classrooms. It is argued that it is time to acknowledge that the alleged harmfulness of video games was far overrated and that educators may wish to consider how games, even those with mildly violent content, can contribute to education.

Section 2
Authoring, Control, and Evaluation in Serious Games for Education

Chapter 4

Florian Mehm, Technische Universität Darmstadt, Germany
Christian Reuter, Technische Universität Darmstadt, Germany
Stefan Göbel, Technische Universität Darmstadt, Germany

Serious Games (SG) place requirements on all members of a development team, from the designers and domain experts to artists and programmers. In order to support the collaborative work required in serious game production, authoring tools can be introduced in the development process. They allow members of the team to work in one common environment and to have one uniform vision of the project, as opposed to a work environment in which each group uses some software tools exclusively and multiple visions of the finished game do exist simultaneously. Presenting a range of examples including the authoring framework StoryTec, the use of authoring tools for the development of SG is explained in this chapter.

Chapter 5

Stefan Göbel, Technische Universität Darmstadt, Germany
Florian Mehm, Technische Universität Darmstadt, Germany

Storytelling and gaming approaches are used as motivational instruments for suspenseful, engaging learning. This chapter describes the concept of Narrative Game-Based Learning Objects (NGLOB), providing a model of how to combine these different axes (narration, gaming, and learning) and how to apply it within personalized, adaptive Digital Educational Games (DEG). From a research perspective, this results in one of the main technical challenges of Serious Games (SG): personalization and adaptation. Here, the central question might be summarized with "How does one create and control a game during play considering the game context and characteristics of individual users or user groups?" This question and the use of NGLOBs are illustrated through the example of "Save the Earth" for teaching and learning geography.

The purpose of the chapter is to provide a state of the art survey addressing research and development aspects for the control of multiplayer Serious Games for collaborative learning scenarios. Hereby, several facets of multiplayer scenarios are addressed: synchronous and asynchronous gameplay and the role of an instructor as Game Master, supervisor, and provider of individual feedback as well as individual feedback among learners in the process of continuous adaptation of the on-going gameplay. Existing approaches and best-practice examples focus on digital educational games for pupils and collaborative learning environments for students. The theoretical foundations of instructional support as well as the implications and technical approaches are discussed. They include some aspects of authoring Serious Games (as already covered in chapter "Authoring Serious Games").

Comprehensive evaluation studies are necessary to "prove" the benefit of Serious Games (SG). This is also extremely important for the commercial success of SG: Best practice examples with profound, well-recorded positive effects will provide relevant arguments to invest into SG for training/education, sports and health, and other application domains. On the other hand, it is not easy to prove the benefit of SG and to measure its effects (e.g. learning effects or medical effects) and affects (user experience factors such as fun during play). Evaluation methodologies might be split into observation, self-evaluation (e.g. questionnaires, interviews), associative methods, performance analyses, and psychophysiology measurement. Technology-enhanced evaluation methods, for instance, facing expression measurement are in the centre of attention. This chapter provides an overview of these methods and describes current interdisciplinary research and technology development achievements in that field.

Section 3
Games and Virtual Worlds in Education

Social presence varies from low, to moderate, to high in self-administered, telephone, and face-to-face survey interviews. New communication technologies add another layer of survey modes that can be understood along the same spectrum of social presence. Virtual worlds like Second Life are rapidly becoming popular environments for testing theories of social and economic behavior. Researchers who use

Second Life as a data collection platform must consider the extent to which existing social theories hold in virtual environments. This study tests the hypothesis that indicators of interviewers' social presence observed in real world survey environments persist in virtual environments with avatar interviewers and respondents. Results from data quality indicators provide tentative support for the hypothesis.

Chapter 9

Sue Gregory, University of New England, Australia

Virtual worlds, such as Second Life, are multi-user, interactive computer-simulated environments created for users to inhabit and interact via avatars, which are graphical representations of a person that can be personalised and used in the virtual world. In this research, 239 off-campus (distance) education students chose to attend weekly sessions in Second Life from 2008 to 2011. These sessions catered for a diverse group of students. It is internationally claimed that virtual worlds are engaging for distance education students. Engagement is the combination of student's feelings, observable actions or performance, perceptions, and beliefs. This mixed-methods research sought to investigate whether virtual worlds were engaging for adult student learners. Recorded in-world (in the virtual world) conversations and the completion of a survey by university students provide data from which the findings are made. In-world discussion found that the virtual world, in this case Second Life, is an engaging environment in which to learn. These findings indicate the need for further research in using a virtual world as an educational resource.

Chapter 10

Daniel Schultheiss, Ilmenau University of Technology, Germany
Maike Helm, Ilmenau University of Technology, Germany

As the impact of media on society steadily increases, schools need to teach their students media skills. In this regard, the usage of computers is an inherent part of everyday school life. The recent integration of serious games and their future potential in Middle German general educational schools is the subject of this chapter. With the aid of interviews held with experts the usage and potential of serious games in Middle German schools are examined, and the barriers to integrate computers and serious games into lessons are discussed. Serious game usage has clear potential for development. Games are applied in different subjects and for different age groups, but not all teachers are aware of their existence. The interviewees disagree about factors hindering integration of computers and serious games in school. As a qualitative study, this chapter constitutes a basis for further research and enlarges knowledge about serious games in schools.

Chapter 11

Michael Gutjahr, Technische Universität Darmstadt, Germany
Wolfgang Bösche, University of Education Karlsruhe, Germany

To investigate the possibilities that are offered to improve teaching within a virtual environment, chat recordings from a paper presentation seminar in a virtual world were analyzed. A total of 9 sessions with more than 500 minutes of recordings from 19 participants were classified in diverse categories by two independent coders. The channel used (voice or keyboard) as well as other attributes of the contributions, the contributors, and the sessions were coded. Results show that the voice channel was mainly used for relevant contributions, while the keyboard channel contained mainly irrelevant contributions. The longer a session was the lower was the percentage of irrelevant contributions, $p < .05$. Gender and previous experience with digital games are both highly correlated with the percentage of irrelevant contributions, $p < .01$. Technical and personal factors are related to the rate of irrelevant contributions, while situational and relational factors seem to have a minor impact.

This chapter contains a systematic overview of various didactic designs, which are used to provide learning experiences via the Internet. Using the example of renewable energy, the development and status quo of Web-didactic offers is reconstructed on the basis of concrete cases ranging from simple replication of classical teaching materials to different kinds of serious games. This bottom-up approach provides a practical introduction on how to evaluate serious games or other digital learning offers by identifying the most essential criteria for a didactic game analysis, but can also be used for benchmarking as some of the examples might also be inspiring for actual game design. Furthermore, this review indicates a significant gap between the high didactic standards for designing self-administrated learning environments and the factual realization as it is shown in most of the examined cases. A basic understanding of the requirements of different learning settings is given in the introduction.

Section 4
Games and Virtual Worlds in Health Care

Digital games in general require fine motor skills, i.e., operating the computer mouse, the keyboard, the touch-screen, or a joystick. With the development of new gaming interfaces, the performance of whole-body movements became possible to control a game. This opens up new lines of application, e.g. improving motor skills and motor abilities. The most important question is whether and how virtual game-based perceptual-motor training transfers to real motor tasks. Theory distinguishes between specific motor skill learning and generic motor ability improvement. Existing evidence shows that the improvement of motor abilities (e.g., balance) is possible by particular exergames while the improvement of motor skills (e.g., basketball throw) depends on several moderators like accuracy of the interface and correspondence of virtual and real tasks. The authors conclude that there are two mechanisms of transfer, located at the elementary and fundamental perceptual-motor level and at the cognitive level. Current issues for technology comprise adaptivity, personalization, game mastering, accuracy of interfaces and sensors, activity recognition, and error detection.

Chapter 14

LeRoy Heinrichs, Stanford University, USA

Li Fellander-Tsai, Karolinska Institutet, Sweden

Dick Davies, Ambient Performance, UK

The deployment of virtual worlds into clinical practice is gradually becoming an accepted if innovative approach. This chapter offers an overview of the application of virtual worlds in a healthcare settings with specific focus on the application of virtual worlds in clinical practice. When combined with dynamic patient data models, facilitators are able to customize and deliver real time immersive clinical training experiences in a range of contexts. Given that virtual worlds are now being implemented in some of the more complex areas of healthcare, this chapter then explores how the lessons being learnt in this context could be applied more widely to other areas of professional development in the healthcare sector and concludes that direct and valuable lessons from mainstream clinical practice with virtual worlds are ready to be applied now more widely in the healthcare sector.

Chapter 15

Hannah R. Marston, German Sport University,Germany

Philip A. McClenaghan, Augsburg University, Germany

Exergames and Exergaming have become a new phenomenon in recent years due to the release of the Nintendo Wii console and more recently the Microsoft Kinect. Videogames are categorized into genres based upon the actions that gamers are expected to execute to achieve goals and overcome challenges. However, with the development of new technology, and this notion of exergaming, is it actually activity or gameplay that defines the notion of exergames as a genre into current categories? This chapter reviews several genre/taxonomy theories to gain a greater understanding of exergames within the serious games arena, with several facets proposed by the authors to provide a more succinct progress within this sector.

Chapter 16

Oliver Korn, KORION Simulation and Assistive Technology GmbH, Germany

Michael Brach, University of Muenster, Germany

Klaus Hauer, Agaplesion Bethanien-Hospital Heidelberg, Germany

Sven Unkauf, Wohlfahrtswerk für Baden-Württemberg, Germany

This chapter introduces the prototype of a software developed to assist elderly persons in performing physical exercises to prevent falls. The result—a combination of sport exercises and gaming—is also called "exergame." The software is based on research and development conducted within the motivotion60+ research project as part of the AAL-program (Ambient Assisted Living). The authors outline the use of motion recognition and analysis to promote physical activity among elderly people: it allows Natural Interaction (NI) and takes away the conventional controller, which represented a hurdle for the acceptance of technical solutions in the target group; it allows the real-time scaling of the exergame's difficulty to adjust to the user's individual fitness level and thus keep motivation up. The authors' experiences with the design of the exergame and the first results from its evaluation regarding space, interaction, design, effort, and fun, as well as human factors, are portrayed. The authors also give an outlook on what future exergames using motion recognition should look like.

In this chapter, the theoretical foundation of the use of virtual worlds (3D environments) to strengthen the personal social network of people who are challenged in that area, especially the elderly, is described. The psychological (bordering on sociological and anthropological) aspects of "living" in a virtual "world," such as Second Life, are described. Opportunities and threats of those aspects regarding the possibilities of strengthening the personal network and quality of life are indicated. The chapter is based on a 5-year research project. The concrete outcome of which is translated into real life projects under the name VayaV. VayaV is described in this chapter as a case study. The Dutch municipalities all agree that the main social problems facing their citizens are exclusion, feeling lonely, passivity, and lack of friends and an adequate personal social network. In the latest figures, more than a third of the people who were interviewed (a cross section of the whole Dutch population) said: I am often lonely and I am suffering because of it. With their consent, a virtual environment is developed based on the research project in Second Life, in such a way that people who do not like computers and know nothing about digital social networks can meet and have fun and form a community of friends and acquaintances. In this case, there is more to the VayaV approach than playing a game in which someone has set the rules and goals for you. It is more like everyday life where people set their own goals and rules, according to their own values and norms.

Chapter 18

Video games' potential for gathering interest from children and adults originated many serious games to communicate, inform, teach, and train. MMORPGs may have even more potential, since they create a shared communication space where players can interact with each other. In Brazil, public Health Communication is a major area of concern, since there is a large population who needs information about health. Much of the communication initiatives come from dated models and are too normative, unable to attend population adequately. This chapter presents first reflections about the main advantages of applying MMORPGs for public Health Communication, using Mediations Theory as a starting point to look into these games' characteristics. This perspective reveals that, in addition to engagement created by their interactive nature, MMORPGs' social characteristics are particularly useful for building Brazilian Health Communication current aspirations: creating instances for hearing population, granting them active voice and enhancing their participation in developing public health policies.

Preface

The incorporation of digital games in adult education, specifically health education, counseling, and therapy appears to be a complex venture at first sight, especially because empirical evidence and evaluation is still lacking in this area. The aim of this book is to show that digital games can be easily implemented as tools to motivate teaching, learning, health education, and communication through single-player digital games, as well as Multi-User Virtual Environments (MUVE), Massive Multiplayer Online Games (MMORPG), and virtual worlds for adults.

The education community has certainly seen an increase in interest for teaching in already existing and popular virtual worlds like Second Life or World of Warcraft, just to name a few. However, the idea of using digital games, MMORPGs, and virtual worlds for teaching is often met with general skepticism and objections from traditionally-oriented instructors. Many consider these tools as too technically complicated for present students who do not have experience in this particular area. The idea of importing and transforming traditional classroom materials into this new medium also seems challenging. In contrast and in reference to therapeutic uses of virtual environments, the plasticity of these digital games offers the opportunity to create simulations that allow students to effectively immerse themselves in a particular subject, and can also serve as a general platform for online education. Through the use of this innovative technology we can both help "digital immigrants" familiarize themselves with the games, as well as finally reach a new generation of learners.

In the field of therapy and health promotion, the idea of using virtual environments for treating anxiety disorders via systematic desensitization or promoting healthy behavior by presenting information in a single-player digital game is nothing new. However, multi-user online approaches are rare in this field. Applying education community concepts could add the motivational benefits for learning and therapy in groups to this approach.

This book aims to offer a key component to any technology-oriented education or health promotion wishing to include virtual environments in its curriculum, or use these as a method of delivering content. We present a combination of up-to-date research projects, small case studies, examples, as well as comprehensive reviews. Both positive as well as negative aspects and experiences are described and analyzed, along with "best practice" and "lessons learned" about the different tasks and methods, so that the reader is sufficiently informed and able to decide on a method of endeavor.

We intend to reach a balance between the theoretical, empirical, and practical chapters. The book includes both essential theoretical and empirical works, and presents applications in Education and Healthcare.

Therefore, the chapters are arranged in four sections:

Section 1: Factors and Key Components of Serious Games and Multi-User Virtual Environments
Section 2: Authoring, Control, and Evaluation in Serious Games for Education
Section 3: Games and Virtual Worlds in Education
Section 4: Games and Virtual Worlds in Health Care

The first, more theoretically oriented section starts with the chapter of Jana Birkenbusch and Oliver Christ who give deep insight into theoretical constructs and phenomena such as flow, immersion, and presence connected to the technological possibilities in games and virtual worlds, especially in the area of health care. Apart from the definitions, the focus lays in the exposition of the relation between the constructs and the methods of measuring. Furthermore, they discuss the questions to improve, apply, and implement these theoretical approaches.

The subject of Alke Martens and Dennis Maciuszek is about the balance of instruction and construction in virtual world learning. They present this dualism between situated learning contexts and instructional guidance in a review of interdisciplinary concepts and instructional challenges. The chapter ends with studies that combine constructivist with instructional elements.

The third and closing chapter of the first section of the book comes from Christopher J. Ferguson. He concentrates on the lively and controversial discussion of the harmfulness of video games, which caused a public debate that influences potentially interested educators a lot when deciding if they should or should not use digital games in their classrooms. Ferguson deconstructs the debate by data-driven arguments to relativize the meaning and impact of violence and aggressive behavior in video games, and demonstrates the potential for education.

The second section of the book presents chapters that describe vital parts of the cycle of building and enhancing Serious Games for education. From authoring and control to adaption, how to foster collaborative learning, and finally how to evaluate Serious Games, these themes are all discussed using best practice examples. Florian Mehm, Christian Reuter, and Stefan Göbel open this section with the presentation of several authoring tools that allow educators, domain experts, designers, artists, and programmers to collaborate interdisciplinarily in the production of Serious Games. Stefan Göbel and Florian Mehm present a model for combing narrative, gaming, and learning components that highlights personalization and adapting as critical aspects. They illustrate the concept by presenting an Educational Game that incorporates that concept both in the authoring process as well as in optimizing the learning process by using adaptive algorithms that change game parameters. Johannes Konert, Viktor Wendel, Kristina Richter, and Stefan Göbel focus on the control of multiplayer games to foster collaborative learning. They clarify certain important concepts of a multiplayer situation, explicate the current research on the phenomena and challenges arousing in peer education including the role and purpose of a Game Master demonstrating feedback, synchronous and asynchronous processes, and suggest how these can be accounted for in the authoring process. Finally, Stefan Göbel, Michael Gutjahr, and Sandro Hardy review classical and current approaches to evaluate the user experience in (Serious) Games, and present newer approaches that also include sensor-based measurements that use psychophysiological data.

The chapters of the third and fourth sections—although still driven by a theoretical background—focus more on empirical findings. They present, analyze, and interpret data collected in various projects in education, professional development, and healthcare. Lessons learned and implications are given both for future research and more refined projects.

The section focused on Education opens with Elizabeth Dean, Joe Murphy, and Sarah Cook showing an example for effects and correlations translating real world processes into virtual environments. The conditions and their effects on behavior, like filling out a survey in a real world interview, are applicable to an interview in a virtual world, in this case Second Life.

Sue Gregory presents her observations, made over four years, of how students are actually engaged in Second life sessions. She measured engagement using a variety of measures, different categories, subsumed into affective, behavioral, and cognitive components. Her results, based on more than 50,000 lines of in-world conversations, show that all students contributed to the discussions and went beyond what was asked of them.

Daniel Schultheiss and Maike Helm assess the potential of the integration of serious games in general educational schools in Germany. While serious games have a clear potential for development in nearly all fields, some factors hinder their integration. The authors discuss the potentially hindering roles of time consummation, general aversion to computer use, the effort to change teaching plans, and the association of violence with digital games.

Gutjahr and Bösche analyze chat behavior in a paper presentation seminar that was held in a virtual world and point out the advantages of parallel communication channels. Their data of over 500 minutes of recordings show that substantially relevant topics and content was discussed within the virtual world, while at the same time irrelevant contributions happened frequently. They analyze which technical, personal, and situational factors might influence the occurrence of such irrelevant communications, and that—even though they are irrelevant to the seminar topic—could be helpful for an atmosphere of respecting the students.

Steffen Winny closes this section with a review and an analysis of websites dedicated to renewable energy. He delivers a good overview of existing learning offers on the World Wide Web, starting from simple websites up to complex and elaborate games. His review indicates a gap between didactic standards and the factual realizations, and comments on possible enhancements needed.

The fourth section has a focus on the domain of healthcare. Josef Wiemeyer and Sandro Hardy present their research on concepts, evidence, and technology of serious games and motor learning. The new possibilities of whole-body movements to control a game implicate the improvement of motor skills and motor abilities. The authors study how virtual game-based perceptual-motor training transfers to real motor tasks. The chapter presents interesting findings on the mechanisms of transfer at the perceptual-motor level and at the cognitive level.

LeRoy Heinrichs, Li Fellander-Tsai, and Dick Davies show the wider implications for professional development in clinical virtual worlds. The chapter gives an overview of the application of virtual worlds in immersive clinical training. The core of the study are the lessons learned by implementing virtual worlds in clinical settings and the potential of applying it in the whole healthcare sector.

Hannah R. Marston and Philip McClenaghan write about the subject of Exergames, which have gained more importance by the development of new interfaces and technologies. The authors review related theories for a better understanding of the concept of exergames.

The next chapter of the section comes from Oliver Korn, Michael Brach, Klaus Hauer, and Sven Unkauf. It is about the connection of Gamification with the concept of Ambient Assisted Living. They illustrate the role of Exergames for Elderly Persons. By using a prototype, the project group outlines the use of motion recognition and portrays the first results of an analysis to promote physical activity among elderly people. At the end, the chapter gives insight in the future developments of exergames.

The following chapter of Hein de Graaf deals with social inclusion via virtual worlds. Hein de Graf, who is a social psychologist and active inhabitant of Second Live, gives the theoretical foundation for the use of virtual worlds to strengthen the social network—especially of elderly people. Furthermore, the project VayaV is described as a case study for avatar-based communication, socializing, and community building.

Marcelo Simão de Vasconcellos and Inesita Soares de Araújo give us an insight of Massively Multiplayer Online Role Playing Games (MMORPG) for Health Communication in Brazil. The situation in Brazil is special because there is a need for information about the health of a large population. An approach is to use less normative public Health Communication like MMORPGs. The potential in the area of interactivity, social characteristics, and participation of such games is discussed.

This book should reach researchers, lecturers, therapists, teachers, students, and people working in healthcare who are interested in using new media forms as serious digital games and multi-user virtual environments in their daily work. We would like to refer to university-level courses as well as instructional technologies, distance learning, computer science, instructional design, health promotion, and behavior therapy, just to name a few. We wish to offer practical guidelines and applications of concepts in combination with case studies and reports on state of the art research. To ensure this, the editors integrated a review process between the authors.

The book is an anthology; the chapters describe different themes of the topic, but they are not based on one another.

Klaus Bredl
Department of Media and Educational Technology at Augsburg University, Germany

Wolfgang Bösche
University of Education Karlsruhe, Germany

Acknowledgment

We would like to thank Anika Bonitz, Sandra Junger, and Verena Reger for their support in organizing and finalizing the documents for this edited book.

Section 1
Factors and Key Components of Serious Games and Multi-User Virtual Environments

Chapter 1
Concepts behind Serious Games and Computer-Based Trainings in Health Care:
Immersion, Presence, Flow

Jana Birkenbusch
Technische Universität Darmstadt, Germany

Oliver Christ
Technische Universität Darmstadt, Germany

ABSTRACT

In the area of health care, dynamic changes and improvements of computer-based methods of intervention are more and more observable. This tendency is, amongst other reasons, caused by the implementation of theoretical constructs and psychological phenomena, such as flow, immersion, and presence, because they are able to explain processes and effects of medical interventions and thereby provide helpful hints to the enhancement of rehabilitation technology. This chapter provides an overview of the definitions of constructs related to computer-based technology, how these constructs are related to each other, and how they can be measured. Furthermore, practical aspects of improvement, possible areas of application, and potential benefits of implementing these constructs are discussed.

INTRODUCTION

Regarding the new developments in therapy and health care, the application of software containing virtual reality settings is an observable tendency (Gamberini, Barresi, Majer, & Scarpetta, 2008; Ma & Zheng, 2011). To ease the theory to praxis transfer and understanding of individual processes occurring when persons are interacting with virtual environment interventions, it is necessary to regard theoretically related constructs, especially immersion, presence, and flow. For example, there are individual differences in the fitting and the success of certain clinical interventions because of different levels of immersive tendencies or technology acceptance, so there constructs, which are

DOI: 10.4018/978-1-4666-3673-6.ch001

related to technical or personal issues. To explain the individual differences and to improve the effects of technology driven intervention strategies, it should be possible to assess these constructs.

There are different reasons and goals that motivate the improvement of technology used in clinical settings (Reinkensmeyer & Boninger, 2012). Besides the improvement of the rehabilitations' cost-benefit ratio, advances in therapy software may reduce extensive diagnostic and therapeutic processes and, in addition to that, are able to provide helpful hints on clinical decision-making. Furthermore, the assessment of accurate data of the mentioned constructs leads to a better prediction of therapy success and thereby has a positive impact on the motivation of the individual participating in the intervention. In addition to that, the consideration theoretically related constructs might lead to the improvement of already established as well as the creation of new intervention methods.

Literature describing the enhancement of use- and user-dependent adaptability shows technical improvements in virtual reality, robotics, orthotics, computer gaming, computer vision, electrical stimulation and wearable sensors (Adamovich, Fluet, Tunik, & Merians, 2009; Brewer, McDowell, & Worthen-Chandari, 2007; Brochard, Robertson, Médée, & Rémy-Néris, 2010; Burke et al., 2009; Burridge & Hughes, 2010). Within those new technologies, constructs like immersion, presence and flow are directly related to the well-being of the therapies' participants as well as to the effect of the intervention (Zimmerli, Duschau-Wicke, Riener, Mayr, & Lunenburger, 2009). Thus the goal of this paper is to describe how these constructs are defined, how they are related to each other and what kinds of methods are used for measurement.

PRESENCE, IMMERSION, AND FLOW

The term *presence* developed from *telepresence* (Minsky, 1980), which described teleoperators' sense of being physically present at a remote lo-

cation even if only interacting with the system's human interface. Steuer (1992) redefined presence as "closely related to the phenomenon of distal attribution or externalization, which refers to the referencing of our perceptions to an external space beyond the limits of the sensory organs themselves." He argues that whenever "perception is mediated by a communication technology, one is forced to perceive two separate environments simultaneously", so that one experiences presence in the natural environment and telepresence in the computer-mediated environment.

Nowadays, the terms presence and telepresence are used synonymously, because a cross environment comparison of everyday life and Virtual Environment (VE) seems to be invalid (Usoh, Catena, Arman, & Slater, 2000). Slater (2004) argues that people have varying degrees of attention in different real situations, but do not doubt their presence in these situations. So presence is defined as "the subjective experience of being in one place or environment, even when one is physically situated in another" (Witmer & Singer, 1998). When talking about presence, other related terms like immersion, flow, or involvement are often mentioned. These constructs are related to presence, but do not describe the same phenomenon, so they have to be distinguished in their definitions.

Concerning the term *immersion*, there is a general discussion how to distinguish *presence* and *immersion*. Witmer and Singer (1998) describe immersion as "a psychological state characterized by perceiving oneself enveloped by, included in, and interacting with an environment that provides a continuous stream of stimuli and experiences" and this means as a response to the VE system. This definition seems to be very similar to the concept of presence itself. Other researchers like Schubert, Friedmann, and Regenbrecht (2001) regard presence as a direct function or the outcome of immersion. In contrast to that, Slater (1999) states that immersion is just an objective description of the VE system and its technology. Kawalsky (2000) supports this view and describes immersion as referring to the physical extend of the sensory information provided by the system and thus as a function of the applied technology. Immersion can be caused by pictorial realism (Welch, Blackman, Liu, Mellers, & Stark, 1996), frame rate (Barfield & Hendrix, 1995), extend of the display (Kawalsky, 2000), dynamic shadows (Slater, Usoh, & Chrysanthou, 1995), and Field of View (Prothero & Hoffman, 1995). Steuer (1992) summarizes these technological factors producing a sensory rich mediate environment in the term vividness.

Flow is a term introduced by Csikszentmihalyi (2004) describing a state of an ideal balance between the perceived level of challenge and the skills of a person. The components of flow are in some ways similar to the observations on presence: Sense of personal control and intrinsic reward, balance between ability level and challenge, direct and immediate feedback, distorted sense of time, loss of feeling of self-consciousness and high degree of concentration. It is obvious that flow and presence both lead to an absorption into the current activity, so that a person loses awareness of the real world and instead shifts all his attention to the happenings of the current activity. The fundamental difference between flow and presence is that flow requires a balance between ability level and challenge which causes a positive experience, whereas a person can be present in an emotionally either positive or negative setting and unrelated to his personal abilities (Jennett, et al., 2008).

Involvement is a "psychological state experienced as a consequence of focusing one's energy and attention on a coherent set of stimuli or meaningfully related activities and events" (Witmer & Singer, 1998). It is highly related to how well the activities and events in the VE attract and hold the participant's attention. Thornson et al. (2009) suppose involvement to be a determinant to experience presence and distinguish between passive and active cognitive involvement:

Passive cognitive involvement is defined as a state in which a person is fully engaged in his activities, "characterized by a feeling of energized focus and full involvement" in this activity and thus related to absorption, a tendency to become involved or immersed in everyday's events (Banos et al., 1999; Murray, Fox, & Pettifer, 2007).

In contrast to that, active cognitive involvement describes the participant's involvement in the VE concerning decision making and judgment, "where the user intentionally (actively) tunes out distractions (internal and external) in order to focus attention" on the experiences in VE. This definition is related to the findings of Ijsselsteijn (2002), who claims interactivity to be an important determinant for participants to experience presence.

DETERMINANTS OF PRESENCE

There are several different concepts of presence, which more or less differ from each other concerning the determinants of presence. With regards to the further descriptions, some of these concepts will be explained in the following section.

Presence, as Sheridan (1992) defines it, is determined by *external objective determinants*, called *media characteristics* and *internal subjective determinants*, called *user characteristics*. Media characteristics are subdivided into *media form* and *media content*. Media form contains the extend of sensory information presented, the degree of control a participant has over positioning his sensors, e.g. turning his head, and the user's ability to modify aspects of the VE. Media content is described as the overall theme, narrative and the story. User characteristics are perceptual, cognitive and motor abilities, personality traits, sex and age.

Witmer and Singer (1998) state that involvement and immersion are necessary to experience presence. According to their research, determinants for involvement and immersion and thereby determinants for presence are *control factors*, *sensory factors*, *distraction factors* and *realism factors*. The control factors are defined by the amount of control the user has on the events in the VE. The sensory factors are related to the quality, number and consistency of displays. The distraction factors are defined by the degree of distraction by objects and events in the real world. While these three factors affect both involvement and immersion, the realism factors, which are related to the degree of realism of the portrayed VE, only affect involvement.

Slater and Wilbur (1997) state that presence includes the three aspects the sense of being there, the extent to which the VE becomes the dominant one and the extent to which participants, after the VE experience, remember it as having visited a place rather than just having seen images generated by a computer. These aspects result from Sheridan's notion of presence (1992) and from results and observations of many different experimental studies.

Another concept of presence based on a factor analytic study by Schubert et al. (2001) extracted three factors, *presence experience*, *immersion*, and *interaction*. The presence factor consists of the distinct components *spatial presence*, *involvement*, and *judgment of realness*, which are concerned with presence itself. The other two factors immersion and interaction which contain the five distinct components, *quality of immersion*, *drama*, *interface awareness*, *exploration of VE* and *predictability*, do not measure presence experiences, but subjective evaluations of its contributing factors and thus can be used to predict presence nonetheless. This solution supports the distinction between spatial-constructive and attention components which was earlier postulated by Witmer and Singer (1998). According to these findings, Schubert et al. (2001) constructed the Ingroup Presence Questionnaire (IPQ) containing 75 items with an internal consistency of about Cronbach's coefficient $\alpha = .85$.

Lessiter, Freeman, Keogh, and Davidoff (2000) stated that the experience of presence is determined by the four factors *physical space*, *engagement*, *naturalness*, and *negative effects*. These factors were found by carrying out a factor analysis in terms of the construction of the cross-media ITC Sense of Presence Inventory (ITC-SOPI) and are similar to the factors found by Schubert et al. (2001). In a validation study, it was found that the factors of the ITC-SOPI load on the same factors as those of a presence questionnaire by Slater et al. (1995) and that both questionnaires are able to discriminate between different media.

CONSEQUENCES OF PRESENCE

The subjective sense of *being there* (Slater, Usoh, & Steed, 1994) or *being-in-the-world* (Zahorik & Jenison, 1998) is an often referred term in matters of effectiveness of VEs. The potential relevance of the concept of presence for the design and evaluation of both interactive and non-interactive media and the specific usage of VE demands for detailed understanding of the results of presence. There are different areas of application for presence such as medicine, e.g. the virtual reality exposure therapy, memory training, computer based education, training and learning, serious games, and entertainment.

Subjective Sensation

The usually described feeling of *being there* is not the only subjective sensation when interacting with VEs. Subjects often report on the VE as if they were visiting a place instead of being in a laboratory in front of a display (Slater, 1999). Instead of remembering a computer-generated environment, subjects describe their interaction with the VE as if they made real experiences and generated memories of a real place they had been to.

Task Performance

Concerning the coherence of presence and task performance, different controversial findings were made. While Kim and Biocca (1997) found a significant correlation between presence and average recognition speed as well as factual memory, other researchers found no (Mania & Chalmers, 2000) or even negative correlations (Ellis, 1996) between presence and task performance. Slater, Linakis, Usoh, and Kooper (1996) found a significant influence of immersion on presence and performance, but no significant correlation between the latter.

Responses and Emotions

One of the most interesting applications of presence is its effect on emotions and behavior. Especially in the field of phobia and anxiety treatment, many studies were conducted, that revealed significant correlations between presence and fear (Schuemi et al., 2000). Alsina-Jurnet, Gutierrez-Maldonado, and Rangel-Gomez (2011) found a relationship between presence and anxiety, which was stronger for high test anxiety students than for low test anxiety students, whereas Krijn et al. (2004) found no significant relationship between presence and anxiety concerning the treatment of acrophobia. So there has more research to be done to clarify the relationships between presence and the treatment of anxiety disorders.

Simulator Sickness

Cyber sickness is a kind of motion-sickness with nausea and dizziness caused by movement experience or moving scenes in virtual reality. Slater, Steed, and Usoh (1993) and Kim, Kim, Kim, and Ko (2005) found a positive correlation between presence, cyber sickness and physiological variables such as eye blink rate, heart period and EEG delta wave, whereas Witmer and Singer (1998) claimed a negative relationship between the experience of presence and the score of the Simulator Sickness Questionnaire (Kennedy, Lane, Berbaum, & Lilienthal, 1993).

MEASURING PRESENCE

Scientific research was still not able to develop a systematic method for the assessment of presence to evaluate media containing user-centered design (Ijsselsteijn, Ridder, Freeman, & Avons, 2000). Reasons therefore might be the lack of a consistent definition of presence as well as the large difference between the laboratory settings in which presence is measured. The different methods of measuring presence can be subdivided into two main categories: subjective and objective measures.

Subjective Measures

There are several methods for subjective estimation of presence, mostly in the form of questionnaires (Slater et al., 1994; Witmer & Singer, 1998). Questionnaires are usually presented to the participants as post-test rating scales, so the experience with the VE does not need to be interrupted and data collected from questionnaires can easily be interpreted. Although most of the questionnaires are reliable and valid, their results are often confounded. For example, Slater (1999) criticizes that the Presence Questionnaire (PQ), which was developed by Witmer and Singer (1998) according to their concept of presence, consists of merely theoretical factors. He states that the PQ is not able to measure presence, because it cannot separate between individual differences in the experience of presence and the system characteristics of the VE and that none of the questions is directly about presence. Additionally, subjects have different understandings of the term 'presence', so that the subjective reports are often unstable and dependent from prior experience. The temporal variation of presence during the exposure to the VE is another limitation of post-test ratings.

Another approach to the subjective measuring of presence is the continuous presence assessment. Participants make a judgment of presence by moving a hand-held slider in a position in accordant with their perceived level of presence during their exposure to the VE. Although this method compensates some of the limitations of questionnaires, such as anchoring effects and inaccurate recall, it interrupts the participant's attention towards the VE and shifts it to the real world in which the slider should be moved into the correct position.

Objective Measures

The benefits of the objective measurement are obvious: There are no inconsistencies and insta-bilities across different raters and situations and the ratings are not biased by subjects' previous experiences, their individual understanding of presence. They are independent from the sub-ject's attention, because objective variables are measured automatically. In addition to that, the subjects do not get in conflict between their ex-perience of being in the VE and the knowledge of being in a laboratory, because they do not know that presence is measured during their interaction with the VE (Freeman, Avons, Meddis, Pearson, & Ijsselsteijn, 2000).

An often discussed measure of presence is per-formance, but the relationship between presence and performance still remains unclear (Slater et al., 1996; Kim & Biocca, 1997) and additionally could only be used in tasks with interactive, but not with non-interactive media.

The analysis of physiological variables to measure presence is not investigated sufficiently. Some physiological measures such as heart rate, skin conductance response, respiration rate and peripheral skin temperature have been suggested to be substitutes for subjective presence ratings,

but did not reveal any significant correlations with presence. The interaction with a VE often implicates a change of arousal, emotion, and he-donic valence, so measuring presence with these physiological variables is difficult, because they are known to be related with these emotional responses (Wiederhold, Davis, & Wiederhold, 1998).

Another method to assess presence in VE is the implication of dual tasks or shadowing tasks. Because the allocation of attention is one of the main determinants of presence (Witmer & Singer, 1998), an increasing reaction time and more errors in a secondary task could show a higher level of presence in the primary task (Norman & Bobrow, 1975). The integration of stimuli from the real world into the setting of the VE could also be a corroborative measure to estimate presence (Slater, et al., 1995), but it would be necessary to select distractors that potentially fit into the setting of the VE, such as a telephone ring or a talking col-league in a VE office setting.

Postural responses, such as participants' auto-matic postural adjustments, which were collected by a magnetic tracking device, can be used as group corroborative measures of presence, but cannot substitute subjective presence ratings, because they were not correlated across participants (Freeman et al., 2000).

Social responses and behavior such as facial expressions, gestures, head and body movements, eye contact, or eye blinking have a potential to be used to assess presence, but have not been investigated yet in the case of being predictors.

PERSONAL CHARACTERISTICS

Because presence is a cognitive state, not only system characteristics are determinants for the level of experienced presence, but also many different individual personality variables. Several research approaches revealed that many different personality variables are positively correlated with the tendency to experience presence.

Weibel, Wissmath, and Mast (2010) investigated in a large-scale survey study the relationship between Big Five personality traits, measured by the NEO FF-I (Costa & McCrae, 1992), and presence and showed that openness to experience, neuroticism, and extraversion were positively related to immersive tendencies. In another study, Weibel, Wissmath, and Stricker (2011) showed that individuals scoring high on neuroticism experienced significantly more presence when watching a movie sequence. Laarni, Ravaja, Saari, and Hartmann (2004) showed that high levels of extraversion, impulsivity, and self-transcendence are attended by a higher subjective sensation of presence.

Imagination, the ability to have a perceptual experience in the absence of the external stimuli triggering this perception, is according to Sas and O'Hare (2003) also a personality variable significantly correlated with the experience of presence.

Banos et al. (1999) found a relationship between dissociation, a "disruption in the normally integrated functions of consciousness, memory, identity or perception of the environment," and presence, as well as between absorption, the ability to get lost in a task, and presence. Murray et al. (2007) also found significant correlations between dissociation and the participants experienced presence, but not between absorption and presence. Absorption was therefore correlated with the score of the Immersive Tendencies Questionnaire (Witmer & Singer, 1998) measuring person's immersive tendency towards presence. This result can be explained by the similarity between the ITQ items and the items of the Tellegen Absorption Scale (Tellegen & Atkinson, 1974) which was applied to assess participants' subjective absorption.

Additionally, Murray et al. (2007) found a relationship between locus of control, the degree to which a person perceives a personal control on the events of his life (Rotter, 1966), and presence. Persons who think that the events in their lives are influenced by outside forces, such as chance or fortune, have, according to Rotter, an external locus of control and report a higher sense of presence.

Another variable having an impact on presence is empathy. Nicovic, Boller, and Cornwell (2005) as well as Sas and O'Hare (2003) found significant correlations between both constructs. A high score on empathy, defined as the ability to experience affective reactions to the observed experiences of others and the ability to adopt their psychological points of view, is related to a high score of experienced presence.

One of the most interesting personality factors determining the experience of presence is the participant's immersive tendency or his or her so called tendency towards presence. The tendency towards presence is a trait and therefore a theoretical construct that relates to the tendency to behave playfully and to become involved in a continuous stream of stimuli (Wallach, Safir, & Samana, 2010). Immersive tendencies have a significant main effect in predicting presence (Johns et al., 2000; Laarni et al., 2004). To assess the participant's personal tendency towards presence, different questionnaires like the TPI (Thornson et al., 2009) or the ITQ (Witmer & Singer, 1998) can be used.

ITQ

The Immersive Tendencies Questionnaire (ITQ) is a questionnaire developed by Witmer and Singer (1998) to measure the differences in the personal tendencies of individuals to experience presence. It contains the subscales *Focus, Involvement,* and *Games.* The subscale Focus describes the tendency to maintain focus on current activities, but also asks about the subjects' mental alertness, their ability to concentrate on enjoyable activities, and their ability to block out distractions from the real environment. The subscale Involvement is defined as the subjects' propensity to get involved passively in some activity, such as reading books, watching television, or viewing movies. The subscale Games assesses the tendency to play video games.

Some of the items assess persons' immersive tendencies and abilities to focus or redirect their attention and thereby immersive tendencies as a

7

trait, while others measure participants' current fitness or alertness, and thereby immersive tendencies as a state. In its original version, the ITQ contained 29 items. In the revised version after the item analysis, the questionnaire consists of 16 items, although 23 of the items were significantly correlated with the ITQ total score.

Responses are made on a 7-point scale with different anchors, such as 1 = *never*, 4 = *sometimes* and 7 = *very often*. The range of possible scores is 16 - 112. None of the items was reverse-coded.

The ITQ has an internal reliability of Cronbach's $\alpha = .81$, but validity was not examined. The mean score on the 16 item ITQ scale is $M = 76.66$ with a standard deviation of $SD = 13.61$.

Witmer and Singer also examined the relationship between the ITQ and their Presence Questionnaire (PQ) and found a significant correlation between ITQ und PQ scores in two of four experiments. Slater (1999) criticized the conceptual design of the PQ, because it would not be able to separate individual characteristics and the characteristics of the virtual environment, what might be an explanation for the missing correlations between ITQ and PQ score in the other two experiments of Witmer and Singer. Johns et al. (2000) used the ITQ and the PQ in their study and found correlations between the total scores only in so-called *high-presence* settings and also stated that these results might be explained by the conceptual design of the PQ, but not by an inappropriate measurement of immersive tendencies by means of the ITQ. Other researchers (Renaud et al., 2007; Robillard, Bouchard, Fournier, & Renaud, 2003) found significant positive correlations between the ITQ and the subjects' experienced presence in their investigations. Slater (1999) stated that he would use the ITQ, since it stands alone as an attempt to measure important psychological characteristics of individuals.

The ITQ also exists in Hebrew and in German language. The Hebrew ITQ version has an internal reliability of Cronbach's $\alpha = .69$ (Wallach et al.,

2010), while the internal consistency of the German version is Cronbach's $\alpha = .75$ (Birkenbusch, 2012).

TPI

The tendency Towards Presence Inventory (TPI) is a questionnaire constructed by Thornson et al. (2009) to predict a person's tendency to experience the cognitive state of presence. It contains the factors *Active Cognitive Involvement, Spatial Orientation, Introversion, Passive Cognitive Involvement, Ability to Construct Mental Models* and *Empathy*.

The factor Active Cognitive Involvement describes the tendency to become involved and immersed in tasks that demand for decision making and judgment. The factor Spatial Orientation refers to the natural ability to maintain body orientation and/or posture in relation to the surrounding environment at rest and during motion. The factor Introversion describes the tendency to prefer solitary activities or spending time with one or two others with whom they feel an affinity. The factor Passive Cognitive Involvement refers to a cognitive state in which the person is fully engaged with in what he or she is doing, characterized by a feeling of energized focus and full involvement in the activity. The factor Ability to Construct Mental Models describes the person's capability to develop an internal scale-model representation of an external reality. The factor Empathy is related to the ability to adopt another's psychological point of view and to experience the emotions observed in the experience of others.

The TPI is, in contrast to the ITQ, a cross media inventory and does not respond to specific types of technology. The factors of the TPI are related to the user him- or herself, his or her tendency to experience presence, but not to his or her tendency to use certain media or to solve certain types of tasks.

In its original version, the TPI contained 105 items. In the revised version after the item analysis, the questionnaire consists of 42 items with 8 items on the factor active cognitive involvement, 10 items on the factor spatial orientation, 8 items on the factor introversion, 7 items on the factor passive cognitive involvement, 5 items on the factor ability to construct mental models and 4 items on the factor empathy.

Responses are made on a 5-point Likert scale with the anchors 1 = *completely disagree* and 5 = *completely agree*. The range of possible scores is 42 - 210. To avoid participants' random responding, several items are reverse-coded.

The TPI factors were extracted by an Exploratory Factor Analysis (EFA) and items were screened on the basis of their rotated factor matrices (Varimax rotation). Afterwards, a Confirmatory Factor Analysis (CFA) was carried out to confirm the factor structure and to reselect the items. The TPI has an internal consistency ranging from Cronbach's $\alpha = .61$ to $.91$ for the different factors. Criterion and predictive validities need to be explored in further studies.

The TPI was translated and evaluated in German language. The analysis revealed the same factor structure like the English version and an overall internal consistency of Cronbach's $\alpha = .80$ (Birkenbusch, 2012)

DISCUSSION

The consideration of theoretical constructs which are related to the success of the application of software in clinical settings and health care seems to be an appropriate way to improve therapeutic arrangements. Especially the individual adaption of VEs might be a promising method to enhance the effect of rehabilitation measures as well as other elements contained in clinical settings.

With regards to the occurrence of flow, it might be possible to adapt the difficulties of the VE setting to the individual skills of the participant, so the participant is more likely to experience flow

and thereby gets in a higher level of absorption and in a positive state of mind. This might result in a higher motivation and thereby in a higher success of the therapy. In addition to that, a well-balanced ratio between experienced challenge and skills may enhance the level of self-confidence in handling of technology, which is an important determinant for the acceptance of technology (Schaar & Ziefle, 2011). The acceptance of technology, which is highly related to technical expertise with its components interest in technology, technical literacy, handling competence and distrust in technology (Venkatesh, 2000; Venkatesh & Davis, 2000), also turned out to have an impact on the acceptance of medical technologies containing virtual reality and thus influences the success of the therapy. So in technology orientated rehabilitation processes, measures to assess the changing of the acceptance of the implemented technology should be applied (Neyer, Felbert, & Gebhardt, 2012).

In addition to that, more attention should be paid to the improvement of the technical characteristics of the medical setting to enhance its immersion. For example, bigger screens, other types of presentation via head mounted displays or the reduction of disturbing factors from the medical surrounding area might be implemented to create a more real and convincing environment and thereby to enhance the experience of presence. This is important, because immersion seems to be a moderator between flow and presence, because it influences psychological experiences in interaction with VEs (Weibel & Wissmath, 2011).

The experience of presence itself seems to be one of the most important factors influencing the success of software in clinical settings, especially of the effect of virtual reality exposure therapy (Krijn et al., 2004; Regenbrecht, Schubert, & Friedman, 1998). Besides the technical characteristics and the characteristics of the VE itself, the individual's characteristics are an important determinant for the level of experienced presence. Thus, the level of individual immersive tendency measured by TPI or ITQ might be a good predictor for the required duration of a successful intervention. If it is possible to adapt the configuration of the characteristics of the VE used in the therapy, the analysis of the determinants of an individual's immersive tendency respectively the level of the different factors might be a helpful criterion to design an environment exactly fitting to the individual and thus produce a maximum level of presence and a maximum success of intervention.

Furthermore, newer reviews conclude that not only technological issues are important predictors of presence, but that also the degree to which the interaction with the VE satisfies motivational needs (Przybylski, Ryan, & Rigby, 2010). If it is possible to satisfy personal needs within the interaction with the VE, individuals are phenomenologically more embedded in the emotional, physical, and narrative elements of the virtual world independent from its content (Przybylski, Ryan, & Rigby, 2009).

The understanding and measurement of immersion, flow and presence, especially the individual's tendency towards presence, are therefore indispensable, because they allow an adaption and thereby an improvement of medical technology, which would not be well founded and conducive.

CONCLUSION

The aim of this chapter was to explain how constructs like presence, immersion and flow are defined, how they are related to each other and what kind of methods are used for their measurement. Although it is additional work to assess and to interpret individuals' characteristics determining the perception of computer-based interventions, the implementation of the results in general, but also for individual application is a helpful method to enhance interventions' effects. However, this process demands for more detailed fundamental research on the one hand and for a better transfer to practical application on the other hand, but

as an ambitious result, the design of innovative medical methods according to new findings and conclusions on personal user characteristics provides a promising further step in health care development and therapy.

REFERENCES

Adamovich, S., Fluet, G., Tunik, E., & Merians, A. (2009). Sensorimotor training in virtual reality: A review. *NeuroRehabilitation*, *25*, 29–44. PMID:19713617.

Alsina-Jurnet, I., Gutierrez-Maldonado, J., & Rangel-Gomez, M. (2011). The role of presence in the level of anxiety experienced in clinical virtual environments. *Computers in Human Behavior*, *27*, 504–512. doi:10.1016/j.chb.2010.09.018.

Banos, R., Botella, C., Garcia-Palacious, A., Villa, H., Perpina, C., & Gallardo, M. (1999). Psychological variables and reality judgements in virtual environments: The role of absorption and dissociation. *Cyberpsychology & Behavior*, *2*, 135–142. doi:10.1089/cpb.1999.2.143 PMID:19178249.

Barfield, W., & Hendrix, C. (1995). The effect of update rate on the sense of presence within virtual environments. *Virtual Reality: The Journal of the Virtual Reality Society*, *1*, 3–16. doi:10.1007/BF02009709.

Birkenbusch, J. (2012). *Measuring immersive tendencies: Conception of a German language questionnaire*. (Unpublished Master Thesis). Technische Universität Darmstadt. Darmstadt, Germany.

Brewer, B., McDowell, S., & Worthen-Chaudhari, L. (2007). Poststroke upper extremity rehabilitation: A review of robotic systems and clinical results. *Topics in Stroke Rehabilitation*, *14*, 22–44. doi:10.1310/tsr1406-22 PMID:18174114.

Brochard, S., Robertson, J., Médée, B., & Rémy-Néris, O. (2010). What's new in new technologies for upper extremity rehabilitation? *Current Opinion in Neurology, 23,* 683–687. doi:10.1097/WCO.0b013e32833f61ce PMID:20852420.

Burke, J., McNeill, M., Charles, D., Morrow, P., Crosbie, J., & McDonough, S. (2009). Optimising engagement for stroke rehabilitation using serious games. *The Visual Computer, 25,* 1085–1099. doi:10.1007/s00371-009-0387-4.

Burridge, J., & Hughes, A. (2010). Potential for new technologies in clinical practice. *Current Opinion in Neurology, 23,* 671–677. doi:10.1097/WCO.0b013e3283402af5 PMID:20962639.

Costa, P., & McCrae, R. (1992). *Revised NEO personality inventory (NEO-PI-R) and NEO five- factor inventory (NEO-FFI) professional manual.* New York, NY: Psychological Assessment Resources

Csikszentmihalyi, M. (2004). *Flow: The psychology of optimal experience.* Paris, France: Robert Laffont.

Dyer, R., Matthews, J., Stulac, J., Wright, C., & Yudowitch, K. (1976). *Questionnaire construction manual, annex literature survey and bibliography.* Palo Alto, CA: Operations Research Associates.

Ellis, S. (1996). Presence of mind: A reaction to Thomas Sheridan's "further musing on the psychology of presence". *Presence (Cambridge, Mass.), 5,* 247–259. PMID:11539412.

Freeman, J., Avons, S., Meddis, R., Pearson, D., & IJsselsteijn, W. (2000). Using behavioral realism to estimate presence: A study of the utility of postural responses to motion stimuli. *Presence (Cambridge, Mass.), 9,* 149–164. doi:10.1162/105474600566691.

Gamberini, L., Barresi, G., Majer, A., & Scarpetta, F. (2008). A game a day keeps the doctor away: A short review of computer games in mental health-care. *Journal of Cyber Therapy & Rehabilitation, 1,* 127–145.

Ijsselsteijn, W. (2002). *Elements of a multi-level theory of presence: Phenomenology, mental processing and neural correlates.* Paper presented at Presence 2002: International Workshop on Presence. Porto, Portugal.

Ijsselsteijn, W., de Ridder, H., Freeman, J., & Avons, S. (2000). Presence: Concept, determinants and measurement. In *Proceedings of the SPIE, Human Vision and Electronic Imaging,* (pp. 520-529). SPIE.

Jennett, C., Cox, A., Cairns, P., Dhoparee, S., Epps, A., Tijs, T., & Walton, A. (2008). Measuring and defining the experience of immersion in games. *International Journal of Human-Computer Studies, 66,* 641–661. doi:10.1016/j.ijhcs.2008.04.004.

Johns, C., Nunez, D., Daya, M., Sellars, D., Casanueva, J., & Blake, E. (2000). The interaction between individuals' immersive tendencies and the sensation of presence in virtual environments. In J. Mulder & R. van Liere (Eds.), *Virtual Environments 2000: Proceedings of the Eurographics Workshop.* London, UK: Springer.

Kawalsky, R. (2000). *The validity of presence as a reliable human performance metric in immersive environments.* Paper presented at Presence 2000: International Workshop on Presence. Delft, The Netherlands.

Kennedy, R., Lane, N., Berbaum, K., & Lilienthal, M. (1993). Simulator sickness questionnaire: An enhanced method for quantifying simulator sickness. *The International Journal of Aviation Psychology, 3,* 203–220. doi:10.1207/s15327108ijap0303_3.

Kim, T., & Biocca, F. (1997). Telepresence via television: Two dimensions of telepresence may have different connections to memory and persuasion. *International Journal of Computer-Mediated Communication, 3.*

Kim, Y., Kim, H., Kim, E., & Ko, H. (2005). Characteristic changes in the physiological components of cybersickness. *Psychophysiology, 42,* 616–625. PMID:16176385.

Krijn, M., Emmelkamp, P., Biemond, R., & Ligny, C., de Wilde, Schuemi, M., & van der Mast, C. (2004). Treatment of acrophobia in virtual reality: The role of immersion and presence. *Behaviour Research and Therapy, 42,* 299–239. doi:10.1016/S0005-7967(03)00139-6 PMID:14975783.

Laarni, J., Ravaja, N., Saari, T., & Hartmann, T. (2004). Personality-related differences in subjective presence. In Alcaniz Raya, M., & Rey Solaz, B. (Eds.), *Proceedings of Presence 2004* (pp. 88–95). Valencia, Spain: Presence.

Lessiter, J., Freeman, J., Keogh, E., & Davidoff, J. (2000). *Development of a cross-media presence questionnaire: The ITC-sense of presence.* Paper presented at Presence 2000: International Workshop on Presence. Delft, The Netherlands.

Ma, M., & Zheng, H. (2011). Virtual reality and serious games in healthcare. In Brahnam, S., & Jain, L. C. (Eds.), *Advanced Computational Intelligence Paradigms in Healthcare* (pp. 169–192). Berlin, Germany: Springer. doi:10.1007/978-3-642-17824-5_9.

Mania, K., & Chalmers, A. (2000). *A user-centered methodology for investigating presence and task performance.* Paper presented at Presence 2000: International Workshop on Presence. Delft, The Netherlands.

Minsky, M. (1980). Telepresence. *Omni (New York, N.Y.), 2,* 45–51.

Murray, C., Fox, J., & Pettifer, S. (2007). Absorption, dissociation, locus of control and presence in virtual reality. *Computers in Human Behavior, 23,* 1347–1354. doi:10.1016/j.chb.2004.12.010.

Neyer, F., Felber, J., & Gebhardt, C. (2012). Entwicklung und validierung einer kurzskala zur erfassung von technikbereitschaft. *Diagnostica, 58,* 87–99. doi:10.1026/0012-1924/a000067.

Nicovic, S., Boller, G., & Cornwell, T. (2005). Experienced presence within computer-mediated communications: Initial explorations on the effects of gender with respect to empathy and immersion. *Journal of Computer-Mediated Communication, 10,* 1–17.

Norman, D., & Bobrow, D. (1975). On data-limited and resource-limited processes. *Cognitive Psychology, 7,* 44–64. doi:10.1016/0010-0285(75)90004-3.

Prothero, J., & Hoffman, H. (1995). *Widening the field-of-view increases the sense of presence within immersive virtual environments.* Human Interface Technology Laboratory Technical Report R-95-4. Seattle, WA: University of Washington.

Przybylski, A., Ryan, R., & Rigby, C. (2009). The motivating role of violence in video games. *Personality and Social Psychology Bulletin, 35,* 243–259. doi:10.1177/0146167208327216 PMID:19141627.

Przybylski, A., Ryan, R., & Rigby, C. (2011). A motivational model of video game engagement. *Review of General Psychology, 14,* 154–166. doi:10.1037/a0019440.

Regenbrecht, H., Schubert, T., & Friedman, F. (1998). Measuring sense of presence and its relation to fear of heights in virtual environments. *International Journal of Human-Computer Interaction, 10,* 233–249. doi:10.1207/s15327590ijhc1003_2.

Reinkensmeyer, D., & Boninger, M. (2012). Technologies and combination therapies for enhancing movement training for people with a disability. *Journal of Neuroengineering and Rehabilitation, 9*, 17. doi:10.1186/1743-0003-9-17 PMID:22463132.

Renaud, P., Chartier, S., Albert, G., Décarie, J., Cournoyer, L.-G., & Bouchard, S. (2007). Presence as determined by fractal perceptual-motor dynamics. *Cyberpsychology & Behavior, 10*, 122–130. doi:10.1089/cpb.2006.9983 PMID:17305458.

Robillard, G., Bouchard, S., Fournier, T., & Renaud, P. (2003). Anxiety and presence during VR immersion: A comparative study of the reactions of phobic and non-phobic participants in therapeutic virtual environments derived from computer games. *Cyberpsychology & Behavior, 6*, 467–476. doi:10.1089/109493103769710497 PMID:14583122.

Rotter, J. (1966). Generalized expectancies for internal versus external locus of reinforcement. *Psychological Monographs, 33*, 300–303.

Sas, C., & O'Hare, G. (2003). Presence equation: A investigation into cognitive factors underlying presence. *Presence (Cambridge, Mass.), 12*, 523–537. doi:10.1162/105474603322761315.

Schaar, A., & Ziefle, M. (2011). What determines the public perception of implantable medical technology: Insights in cognitive and affective factors. In Holzinger, H., & Simonic, K.-M. (Eds.), *Human-Computer Interaction: Information Quality in eHealth* (pp. 513–532). Berlin, Germany: Springer. doi:10.1007/978-3-642-25364-5_36.

Schubert, T., Friedmann, F., & Regenbrecht, H. (2001). The experience of presence: factor analytic insights. *Presence (Cambridge, Mass.), 10*, 266–281. doi:10.1162/105474601300343603.

Schuemi, T., Bruynzeel, M., Drost, L., Brinckman, M., de Haan, G., Emmelkamp, P., et al. (2000). Treatment of acrophobia in virtual reality: A pilot study. In F. Broeckx & L. Pauwels (Eds.), *Conference Proceedings Euromedia 2000,* (pp. 271-275). Antwerp, Belgium: Euromedia.

Sheridan, T. (1992). Musings on telepresence and virtual presence. *Presence (Cambridge, Mass.), 1*, 120–125.

Slater, M. (1999). Measuring presence: A response to the Witmer and Singer presence questionnaire. *Presence (Cambridge, Mass.), 3*, 130–144.

Slater, M. (2004). How colorful was your day? Why questionnaires cannot assess presence in virtual environments. *Presence (Cambridge, Mass.), 13*, 484–493. doi:10.1162/1054746041944849.

Slater, M., Linakis, V., Usoh, M., & Kooper, R. (1996). *Immersion, presence and performance in virtual environments: An experiment with tridimensional chess.* Paper presented at the 1996 Virtual Reality and Software and Technology Conference. Hong Kong, Hong Kong.

Slater, M., Steed, A., & Usoh, M. (1993). The virtual treadmill: A naturalistic metaphor for navigation in immersive virtual environments. In M. Goebel (Ed.), *First Eurographic Workshop on Virtual Reality Environments,* (p. 71-83). Barcelona, Spain: IEEE.

Slater, M., Usoh, M., & Chrysanthou, Y. (1995). The influence of dynamic shadows on presence in immersive virtual environments. In Goebel, M. (Ed.), *Virtual Environments* (pp. 8–21). New York, NY: Springer Computer Science. doi:10.1007/978-3-7091-9433-1_2.

Slater, M., Usoh, M., & Steed, A. (1994). Depth of presence in virtual environments. *Presence (Cambridge, Mass.), 6*, 130–144.

Slater, M., & Wilbur, S. (1997). A framework for immersive virtual environments (five): Speculations on the role of presence in virtual environments. *Presence (Cambridge, Mass.), 6*, 603–616.

Steuer, J. (1992). Defining virtual reality: Dimensions determining telepresence. *The Journal of Communication, 42*, 73–93. doi:10.1111/j.1460-2466.1992.tb00812.x.

Tellegen, A., & Atkinson, G. (1974). Openness to absorption and self-altering experiences ("absorption"), a trait related to hypnotic susceptibility. *Journal of Abnormal Psychology, 83*, 267–277. doi:10.1037/h0036681 PMID:4844914.

Thornson, C., Goldiez, B., & Le, H. (2009). Predicting presence: Constructing a tendency towards presence inventory. *International Journal of Human-Computer Studies, 67*, 62–78. doi:10.1016/j.ijhcs.2008.08.006.

Usoh, M., Catena, E., Arman, S., & Slater, M. (2000). Using presence questionnaires in reality. *Presence (Cambridge, Mass.), 9*, 497–503. doi:10.1162/105474600566989.

Venkatesh, V. (2000). Determinants of perceived ease of use: Integrating control, intrinsic motivation, and emotion into the technology acceptance model. *Information Systems Research, 11*, 342–365. doi:10.1287/isre.11.4.342.11872.

Venkatesh, V., & Davis, F. (2012). A theoretical extension of the technology acceptance model: Four longitudinal field studies. *Management Science, 46*, 186–204. doi:10.1287/mnsc.46.2.186.11926.

Wallach, H., Safir, M., & Samana, R. (2010). Personality variables and presence. *Virtual Reality (Waltham Cross), 14*, 3–13. doi:10.1007/s10055-009-0124-3.

Weibel, D., & Wissmath, B. (2011). Immersion in computer games: The role of spatial presence and flow. *International Journal of Computer Games Technology*. Retrieved from http://www.hindawi.com/journals/ijcgt/2011/282345/

Weibel, D., Wissmath, B., & Mast, F. (2010). Immersion in mediated environments: The role of personality traits. *Cyberpsychology, Behavior, and Social Networking, 13*, 251–256. doi:10.1089/cyber.2009.0171 PMID:20557243.

Weibel, D., Wissmath, B., & Stricker, D. (2011). The influence of neuroticism on spatial presence and enjoyment in films. *Personality and Individual Differences, 51*, 866–869. doi:10.1016/j.paid.2011.07.011.

Welch, R., Blackman, T., Liu, A., Mellers, B., & Stark, L. (1996). The effects of pictorial realism, delay of visual feedback and observer interactivity on the subjective sense of presence. *Presence (Cambridge, Mass.), 5*, 263–273.

Wiederhold, B., Davis, R., & Wiederhold, M. (1998). The effects of immersiveness on physiology. In Riva, G., Wiederhold, B., & Molinari, E. (Eds.), *Virtual Environments in Clinical Psychology and Neuroscience*. Amsterdam, The Netherlands: IOS Press.

Witmer, B., & Singer, M. (1998). Measuring presence in virtual environments: A presence questionnaire. *Presence (Cambridge, Mass.), 7*, 225–240. doi:10.1162/105474698565686.

Zahorik, P., & Jenison, R. (1998). Presence as being-in-the-world. *Presence (Cambridge, Mass.), 7*, 78–89. doi:10.1162/105474698565541.

Zimmerli, L., Duschau-Wicke, A., Riener, R., Mayr, A., & Lunenburger, L. (2009). Virtual reality and gait rehabilitation: Augmented feedback for the Lokomat. In *Proceedings of the IEEE Virtual Rehabilitation International Conference*, (pp. 150-153). IEEE.

Chapter 2
Balancing Instruction and Construction in Virtual World Learning

Alke Martens
University of Education Schwäbisch Gmünd, Germany

Dennis Maciuszek
University of Rostock, Germany

ABSTRACT

In game-based learning and in teaching using virtual worlds, designers creating the products and teachers providing them to students are both faced with a dualism between instruction and construction. Open-ended virtual worlds may provide authentic settings and inspire experimentation; on the other hand a lack of guidance may result in learners losing direction. The chapter conducts a narrative review of concepts across disciplines that describe the dilemma and imply certain instructional design strategies. Many authors advocate constructivist learning, but with instructional elements added. The authors collect their recommendations and apply and refine them in their own ideas: adaptivity inspired by Cognitive Apprenticeship, guidance on the basis of Cognitive Task Analysis, and immersive, interactive quest journals. Study setups and first results from ongoing projects illustrate the theoretical considerations.

INTRODUCTION

Fifteen years ago, the first author became involved in an ambitious project: to create a virtual hospital for training students of medicine. Two years later, *Docs 'n Drugs: The Virtual Polyclinic* (Martens, 2004) was made available to the first students at the University of Ulm, Germany, through a Web page. Behind it was an Intelligent Tutoring System (ITS). Already then, we were thinking in terms of constructivist learning and digital storytelling, employing a case-oriented approach. The learner meets virtual patients who narrate their health problems. Students may try out different forms of diagnosis and treatment – without hurting anyone. The idea of setting up the hospital as a virtual world

DOI: 10.4018/978-1-4666-3673-6.ch002

was already there, but at the time technologies like Java 3D proved to be cumbersome and inefficient. Nowadays, virtual world technology has become more easily accessible to designers. A number of 3D hospitals have appeared in *Second Life* (e.g. Toro-Troconis et al., 2008), even in entertainment computer games (*E.R.*).

Virtual worlds in teaching open up a range of possibilities. We can bring a rainforest, a power plant, an ancient civilization, or life in a far-away country to the classroom or students' homes. Different from a book, photos, or a video, students may interact with the content, have meaningful experiences and try out lots of things. In multiuser scenarios, students may communicate and cooperate with teachers or peers—even people in that far-away country—from any place. Virtual classrooms, labs, factories, or theater stages have the potential of stimulating imagination, creativity, and personal expression, thus helping realize the vision of constructivist, third-generation game-based learning (cf. Egenfeldt-Nielsen, 2007).

It starts already with the customization of one's avatar. Once this is done, the student may explore the virtual surroundings and experiment with them to gain insight about the subject matter. What happens, if I push this button? Does the balance of the ecosystem change, if I introduce this new species? Can I place an order in a restaurant in France? What if Hamlet had treated his girlfriend better? But then, the underlying model of the ecosystem may be too complicated for a student to grasp through experimentation. Who helps out with missing vocabulary? If there are too many buttons to push, with which might the student start? Will they learn the technical concepts behind the machine, or just in which sequence to press differently colored buttons?

Virtual worlds in education do not succeed by themselves. Designers creating the technology and teachers implementing them in their curricula need to make informed decisions based on insights from learning theory and media design. If we disregard the aspect of human cooperation

for a moment, educational virtual worlds can be seen as microworlds, i.e. closed environments with well-defined rules that make up the behavior of the world, allowing the learner to interfere via a set of actions, to construct mental models, and thus to discover the rules by experiencing them.

Papert (1980) introduced microworlds for experiencing and experimenting with Newtonian laws of motion in the early 1980s, at the time realizing them through turtle graphics in his programming language for kids, *Logo*. Today, 3D worlds like *Second Life* already come with an implemented, interactive Newtonian physics engine.

If executing actions results in meaningful or joyful activities for the learner, he or she may reach a state of transportation (switching focus from the real to the virtual world), presence (feeling as if being in the virtual world), engagement (feeling involved in what happens in the virtual world), immersion (experiencing actions and activities in the virtual world as one's own), and/or even flow (experiencing intense intrinsic motivation during the activities, 'losing' oneself in a task). These are desirable effects of game design and virtual worlds. Achieving immersion etc. in the users will not automatically mean, though, that construction of knowledge related to the learning goals will take place. For instance, the learner might 'lose' him- or herself in the subject matter as intended, but not draw types of intended conclusions. They might lose track of the many possibilities and digress, constructing some knowledge, but not related to the goals. They might learn how to customize their avatar, or, better, to actually operate the virtual devices provided, yet they might not be able to formulate and validate hypotheses about a simulated phenomenon.

Discovery learning (also inquiry learning) is a typical form of constructivist learning in science domains where the student is expected to formulate hypotheses and to validate them in a lab environment — be it virtual or real. In their literature review, de Jong and van Joolingen (1998) point out that discovery learning is hard. They cite a range of empirical studies identifying common difficulties students have with hypothesis generation, design of experiments, interpretation of data, and regulation of discovery learning. Learning by experimentation will still require a human teacher to guide and structure the learning activity, or, alternatively, sophisticated cognitive tools or an intelligent tutoring mechanism. de Jong and van Joolingen (1998) discuss a number of suggested tools (with fewer empirical evidence than for the problems).

Guidance may support knowledge acquisition, yet minimizing guidance might enhance creativity. When is it good to lead the student, and when not? When does guidance become restrictive and ruin the individual discovery experience?

Many virtual-world projects start out with an open-ended environment, but end up with presenting closed exercises (multiple choice, sequence tasks, etc.). The *Sloodle* project does a good job in connecting the learning management system *Moodle* to the multi-user virtual environment *Second Life*. But if such a connection means basing one's instructional design on looking at PDFs, reading Web forums, or leaving a vote in an online poll, then the experience of free experimentation in an artificial world will be inhibited. Some game-based-learning projects present a role-playing-game-style world, such as a 3D dungeon, but populate it with traditional quizzes that leave little space for individual knowledge creation (cf. Maciuszek & Martens, 2011c, pp. 665–666).

In *Global Conflicts: Palestine*, the learner composes an online newspaper article about his or her experiences in a virtual Jerusalem. An empirical study (Harr, Buch, & Hanghøj, 2008), however, found the multiple-choice approach too restrictive for expressing critical thinking. In their study of *Global Conflicts: Latin America*, Magnussen and Holm Sørensen (2010) had participating students write newspaper articles offline instead. The main problem, though, was that the players experienced it as a separate activity. Guidance need not only be there, but must be designed and implemented in a pedagogically sound way.

The intricate conflict between closed instruction and open-ended construction support is difficult to deal with and in fact much larger than just affecting learning in virtual worlds. Works from various disciplines describe the conflict, each for their own field. To benefit from these insights in answering the question of how to balance instruction and construction in designing virtual world learning activities, this paper integrates the different views by presenting a narrative, dialectic review and discussion of concepts and related publications across disciplines. Having arrived at an extraction of the core problems, we then present our own solutions toward bridging the gap.

BACKGROUND: CONSTRUCTIVISM

The foundation of open-ended learning environments favoring free experimentation and individual construction of knowledge is constructivist learning theory. It contrasts behaviorist learning theory (the brain as a black box, since around 1913 with Watson; Lieberman, 1992, pp. 397–400) and cognitivist learning theory (the brain as an information processor, since around 1950; Lieberman, 1992, pp. 431–434). The cognitivist view of learning evolved into concepts like situated cognition (thinking and learning in application contexts; e.g. Brown, Collins, & Duguid, 1989) and social cognition (learning by and for communication with others; e.g. Tomasello, 2003).

Constructivism, as an epistemological set of theories, emphasizes the individual learner's active role in transforming information to knowledge. Everybody constructs their own version of the truth—if there is a truth at all—or at least finds their own way toward it. Constructivist teaching does not convey stimulus-response associations or fixed facts-rules systems upon the learner. Instead, it creates authentic, complex situations in which learners' own experiences inspire the construction of their own explanations of the world. New knowledge is born by anchoring newly acquired information in previous personal experience.

Constructivism-inspired design of e-learning software would favor simulation and hypermedia environments over intelligent tutoring approaches (Schanda, 1995, p. 65).

Although constructivist teaching became popular—and relevant for e-learning—around the 1980s and 90s, related learning theories and teaching approaches have evolved for much longer, building on movements like active learning and progressive education as well as pioneering work by Vygotsky and Piaget, centering round teaching methods such as learning by teaching (by helping each other, students consolidate their own knowledge), problem-based learning (faced with a real-world problem, students collect knowledge that might help solve it), or discovery learning. It connects to advanced cognitivist theories, e.g. situated cognition, and carries on the 'learning by doing' idea (students master a skill by practicing it rather than reading about it; e.g. Dewey & Dewey, 1915).

As a philosophical way of thinking, constructivism originated in the 1970s, first in Neurobiology (*Biology of Cognition*; Maturana, 1970), but was influenced and/or spread to Philosophy, Psychology (Kelly, 1955), Cybernetics, and Sociology (social constructivism) (see the review in Pörksen, 2011). Common elements are 'how' questions instead of 'what' questions, the observer as the creator of knowledge, neglection of an absolute truth, acknowledgment of a multitude of truths, transformation of external control into self regulation (or the appearance thereof), and circular and recursive thinking (output feeds back into the system as new input) (Pörksen, 2011).

In essence, there are two schools of constructivism. Radical constructivism (e.g. von Glaserfield in Mietzel, 2007) believes that there is no absolute, true knowledge of the world—only the interpretation of each individual. As a consequence, teachers cannot test student knowledge and basically lose the possibility of providing pedagogical guidance toward certain learning goals. Moderate con-

structivism, on the other hand, allows for shared construction—including teaching—of cognitive structures.

Mietzel (2007) lists a number of instructional design or teaching strategies resulting from this. In short, (1) show students that there are flaws and gaps in their previously constructed knowledge; (2) provide authentic environments fostering situated learning experiences without having to fear negative consequences; (3) teach meta-cognitive skills.

Notice that educational games should be particularly suited for realizing the second requirement: They can illustrate situations in visualizations, and provide interactive simulations for free experimentation. Still, the other two requirements demand a form of guidance. Mietzel points out that constructivist learners may build their own constructions, yet there is still need for a teacher to hand them the bricks. Sometimes, students will not even know where to put a brick and drop or misplace it (Mietzel, 2007, p. 43).

But, is handing bricks not, after all, a form of instruction that might limit construction to those constructs one can build with those particular bricks? This would not pose a problem for Reich (2005), who splits up constructivist learning into processes of construction, reconstruction, and deconstruction. It makes perfect sense to gain an own understanding of how somebody else—an inventor or a teacher—constructed certain knowledge before, as well as being able to question and—in one's own understanding—correct previous constructions. As Reich (2005) emphasizes, such learning requires imagination, which, according to him, has long been suppressed by prevalent symbolic (i.e. analytical) systems. Encouraging imagination would be another potential strength of virtual-world and game-based teaching.

Summing up, a seminar at university in which students perform their own literature studies and then present their results in a talk or in writing would constitute a typical case of constructivism-inspired teaching. Everybody compiles their own constructions of their topic. The opposite case would be a professor lecturing, presenting only his or her own version to the recipients. Yet, is it really that simple? The seminar-form of teaching forces the students to seek certain knowledge and to present it in a certain form to pass their course. On the other hand, a broad lecture covering a range of issues, supplemented by lists of recommended reading, constitutes a pool of possible traces an individual student can choose to follow – or not. The distinction between construction and instruction is not a trivial one, after all.

Teachers and instructional designers, though, must be able to make informed decisions on how to create inspiring educational scenarios. Which teaching approach suits different types of knowledge and different target groups best? In designing educational activities in virtual worlds or game-based learning environments, what are possible options and their consequences? Educational games have the potential of encouraging experimentation and individual knowledge construction. But what degree of instructional guidance do players need, so they do not lose themselves in infinite possibilities?

As it appears, the question on where to position oneself in this freedom vs. guidance debate is bigger than just covering virtual-world, serious-game, or technology-enhanced-learning design. The debate hints at a fundamental philosophical dualism. It is the eternal struggle between the forces of law and the forces of chaos in the works of fantasy author Michael Moorcock. It is the question whether one believes in the power of autopoiesis (self-organization) that emerges from chaos. But it is also a question of how to raise your kids—the strict or the lenient way? It is a philosophical question, yet one with very practical implications for teaching and instructional design.

The following sections provide a review of related concepts in literature relevant to game-based and virtual world learning. They gather insights from a range of disciplines, before incorporating them in a set of ideas and recommendations for educational game design.

Note that a comprehensive review of empirical findings—like that of de Jong and van Joolingen (1998) for the case of scientific discovery learning—is beyond the scope of this broad conceptual review. A review of studies would require a chapter of its own and have to distinguish between application domains, concrete constructivist teaching methods, and, possibly most important, types of taught knowledge (declarative vs. procedural, cognitive vs. affective vs. psychomotor). For instance, not every biological insight may require an experiment. Walking through the forest listening to the teacher pointing out plants and animals has its merits as well.

INSTRUCTION VS. CONSTRUCTION

Concepts in Learning Theory

In theories of learning and instruction found within educational studies, psychology, and, in combination, educational psychology, the central dualism seems to be teaching-centered learning (external control, i.e. instruction) vs. self-regulated learning (internal control, i.e. construction). According to Schiefele and Pekrun's (1996) summary, there is no 'either-or.' Most educational activities will contain certain degrees of teaching and self-regulation.

In their review, the authors find that self-regulated learning includes activities like self-observation, self-assessment, and self-reinforcement. Those activities require that a learner can assess their own behavior, can recognize deficits, knows reinforcement strategies, and can motivate themselves on their own. A self-regulated (or regulating) learner applies certain cognitive strategies—repetition, elaboration, and organization—as well as meta-cognitive strategies, namely understanding oneself, understanding the tasks, and knowing required learning strategies. They plan, monitor, and regulate cognitive acts on their own. Another requirement is managing internal (e.g. allocating time) and external (e.g. finding the right environment) resources. Finally, there are aspects of volition and motivation, e.g. being able to immerse oneself in a learning task and showing an interest or having intrinsic goals.

Interestingly, these would be aspects ascribed to the prospects of game-based learning. Hence, educational games should—in theory—suit self-regulated learning, and thus construction. On the other hand, does every learner have the learning skills compiled by Schiefele and Pekrun? An instructor may have to supplement unfulfilled requirements. Learning journals (or learning logs) as a way of reflecting on one's learning process and outcomes are an exemplary tool for encouraging self-regulated learning. They benefit from instructional prompts on what to write (Hübner, Nückles & Renkl, 2007). Empirical studies have shown that prompted learners apply a larger variety of learning strategies (Nückles, Hübner & Renkl, 2008; Glogger et al., 2009).

By means of cluster analysis, Walber (2007) found that a disposition toward teaching-centered or self-regulated learning in professional training may be described as a personality trait. The study identified five types: self-regulating learners, learners regulating goals and content, learners choosing an education by themselves, learners not restricted by time and space, and learners preferring to be taught.

This might be related to individual cognitive styles (Sternberg & Grigorenko, 1997), such as legislative (creative) and executive (following rules) learners.

Dreyfus and Dreyfus (1986) relate a disposition toward different degrees of self-regulation in learning to the level of experience. A novice learner gains knowledge through direct instruction. Learners at subsequent levels—advanced beginner, competence, proficiency, and expertise—acquire situation-awareness, learn more intuitively, and are more independent. For instance, a competent nurse will not visit patients according to scheduled routine, but self-regulate her attention on a basis of intuitively diagnosed needs. Dreyfus and Dreyfus later (2004) questioned whether their abstract model was applicable to domains that cannot

be described from an intellectualist perspective only. In ethical judgment, new situations come up where experts fall back to earlier stages. Two experts may find conflicting solutions to the same problem, e.g. assuming a "justice" or a "caring" position. The model may require a next stage or alternative paths. This argumentation is interesting for constructivist e-learning, as it may demand instructional assistance that is quite flexible in terms of adaptation to levels of expertise or accepted solutions. The designer may not be able to anticipate all solutions, still the system should understand them to some degree.

Cognitive Apprenticeship (Collins, Brown & Newman, 1987) is a classic situated-cognition set of teaching strategies intended to address different levels of learner expertise. In the beginning, the master instructs the apprentice, but gradually instruction fades and makes way for more and more self-regulated construction. Keeping in mind Dreyfus and Dreyfus (2004), it should also be made possible to return to stronger instructional assistance in face of new situations.

According to Winteler (2004, p. 17), even teachers may gain more and more trust in students' self-regulation—within another five-level model – as they gain more teaching experience.

At this point, we omit the discussion whether different kinds of knowledge relate to different degrees of self-regulation and construction. But certainly, particular types of learning goals in Bloom's taxonomy of learning objectives (Bloom et al., 1956), like "synthesis" ("compose", "construct"...), may suit construction-oriented approaches better than others.

Summing up, learning theory regards construction-oriented approaches as progressive when compared to behaviorist instruction, however pointing out that self-regulation requires certain skills, that it benefits from prompts, that learners may have a personality bias toward or against it, and that construction may work better for advanced learners and teachers. Teachers can adjust the degree of instruction to learners' experience and to learning goals.

Concepts in Technology-Enhanced Learning

Early work in the field of 'e-learning' (electronically enhanced learning) was very much teaching-centered. The ideal of an artificial teacher evolved from behaviorist teaching machines that could tell whether an answer to a multiple-choice or fill-in-the gaps exercise was correct or not to cognitivist ITS. These artificial-intelligence-powered systems used either exercises or natural language input and analyzed the learner's thought process to provide according feedback, in the end to help him or her reach one of the prepared solutions. Unfortunately, ITS rarely made the step from research prototypes to off-the-shelf products. Instead, the 1980s and 90s introduced a range of commercial products that combined graphics-rich hypermedia environments with traditional right/wrong multiple choice, categorization, sequence, or fill-in-the-gaps exercises. These were criticized, however, as being too linear and not exploiting the interactive potential of the personal computer.

In his early handbook on e-learning design and application, Schanda (1995) condemns author-controlled educational software, and lays out different strategies for putting the learner in control. An analysis from around 1989 had identified three ways of breaking linear course design: giving more differentiated feedback, including help mechanisms, and branching into side paths. Thinking this further, it was possible in Schanda's approach to dissect a linear course altogether into smaller units: lessons related to single learning goals, exemplary cases, exercises, additional information, a glossary, etc. An individual learner would choose on his or her own in which sequence to access the different units, or in fact which units to select at all. Interestingly, although the author puts so much faith in a learner's self-regulation, his design model includes instructional parts as well. There is a learning path recommendation mechanism and the idea of providing a number of prefabricated modes of interaction: exam mode, drill mode, exercise mode, info mode, feedback mode, info-on-demand mode, multiple choice mode (instead of single choice), hint mode etc. (Schanda, 1995, p. 74). Schanda's approach continues to count on traditional exercises, but on a macro level he advocates nonlinear, interactive sequencing of exercises (and other units), whereas on a micro level he seeks to improve feedback.

Later on, Schulmeister (2003) proposed a taxonomy of multimedia components that formalizes 'more freedom' in interaction, thus deconstructing traditional exercises and offering the tools for creating a wider range of activities. In his scheme, a designer may create interactive elements on a six-level scale of control: (1) viewing objects and receiving, (2) watching and receiving multiple representations, (3) varying the form of representation, (4) manipulating the component content, (5) constructing the object or representation contents, (6) constructing the object or contents of the representation and receiving intelligent feedback from the system through manipulative action. Interestingly, Schulmeister advocates the highest degree of freedom or construction support (level 6) decidedly for applications in maths and science domains.

de Jong and van Joolingen (1998) discuss self-directed, constructivist learning in science domains. They contrast discovery learning, i.e. free experimentation aimed at forming constructions of domain concepts, with experiential learning, i.e. focusing on the operations (tasks) a learner is instructed to perform. They follow the free, discovery learning approach, and review related psychological studies. As it appears, learning by hypothesis validation on the basis of changing parameters in simulated environments is difficult, and they recommend a number of instructional mechanisms—from various cognitive tools to intelligent tutoring—to help the young scientist.

Rather than focusing on a specific domain, Martens (2004) investigates the specific teaching method of the case study. In designing the virtual hospital, her group made the design decision to differentiate between guided, partially guided, and unguided cases. Guidance is applied in working with linear, narrated cases. Partial guidance is applied in working with unstructured cases including correct facts, correct/false facts, or correct/false facts with different results. There is no guidance in free exploration cases (cf. learning theories in Einsiedler, 1981). Martens' ITS adapts to learner experience. Guided, linear cases are intended for beginners. Partially guided, unstructured cases are for three levels of advanced learners, while unguided experiments are for experts.

Mandl and Kopp (2006) point out that a balance between construction and instruction (as described by Linn, 1990) is also needed in blended learning scenarios (e-learning blended with face-to-face sessions). Their compromise is called a problem-oriented learning environment. Following this design philosophy, students would learn to solve authentic problems in multiple contexts and from multiple perspectives, in collaboration with other students. This is the constructivist part. Unlike in the case of ITS, a human advisor would supplement instruction, assistance, rules, and feedback for the group. Mandl and Kopp point out that learning in problem-oriented environments requires certain self-regulation, media-literacy, and cooperation competencies.

To sum up, e-learning approaches to the instruction-construction dualism are often rooted in design experience. Designers aim for high degrees of self-regulated navigation and interaction, but recognize that, although the learning outcome may be greater, increased freedom may make the actual learning process more difficult. They propose adding instructional elements to their software in the form of cognitive tools, artificial-intelligence tutors, or human advisors. Alternatively, adaptation techniques applied by ITS may present content in different degrees of freedom, corresponding to an individual learner's level of expertise.

Concepts in Virtual Worlds Research

One of the reasons why Papert (1980) invented the concept of microworlds was his criticism of instructivist teaching that does nothing but present one correct bit of information after the other. In his opinion, learners must be allowed to make mistakes before they can understand what is correct. This is what virtual worlds provide: an environment in which to try out all kinds of strange ideas, before realizing what leads to an insight. Whether they are virtual worlds for the purpose of learning (Schwan & Buder, 2002) or for experiencing stories (or virtual drama; Trogemann, 2002), open virtual worlds are sources for emergence (Trogemann, 2002)—that magical phenomenon when something unexpected, but meaningful comes out of nothing but the mechanisms of the system. It is a quality of virtual worlds, and also the basis for human creativity—the source of insights.

This is why virtual worlds have the potential of supporting creative processes (Trogemann, 2002). In his book on creativity, Hinz (2001) lays out his view of people engaging in co-creative processes with the universe. While this may sound far-fetched in our daily lives, it makes perfect sense in the context of virtual worlds.

Still, uncontrolled fantasizing and exploration may lead to confusion, and nothing will emerge at all. That is why Schwan and Buder (2002) recommend the structuring of learning processes, a careful design of repertoires of potential actions, and finding appropriate help mechanisms. Strategies for defining actions include providing alternative (realistic and artificial) views of the exploration space, providing natural (i.e. authentic) actions to minimize cognitive load and the risk of choosing dysfunctional actions, but also to provide metaphoric actions that exploit the potential of the virtual world.

Investigating virtual worlds of contemporary video games, Wesener (2004) makes a distinction between micro-, meso-, and macro-virtual worlds. Micro-virtual worlds include e.g. first- or third-person role-playing games like *Gothic* in which the player manipulates the environment through an avatar. Meso-virtual worlds include e.g. isometric real-time strategy games like *Empire Earth* in which the player controls or commands a population or an army. Macro-virtual worlds include e.g. turn-based strategy games like *Civilization*, in which the world is seen from high above and the player assumes a more or less god-like role. Wesener's point is that macro-virtual worlds are the most open-ended and micro-virtual worlds the most linear type of virtual worlds.

The distinction makes sense: A macro-virtual world allows the manipulation of complex economies or ecosystems, whereas micro-virtual worlds tend to feature the most author-initiated storytelling. Wesener relates this to different kinds of transfer that can happen between the virtual and the real world. His study is limited to games, though. What about multi-user virtual environments? *Second Life* can be experienced through a third-person view. The avatar interacts with the simulated environment—the micro perspective. But it is also possible to build and modify the environment.

Rieber (1992) continued the early work of Papert on microworlds. Even though virtual worlds did not center round avatars at that time, one could, in fact, situate Rieber's description of microworlds at the "micro" end of virtual worlds in Wesener's categorization. This is because of two striking features that, according to Rieber, make microworlds, originally a constructivist invention, a bridge between construction support and instruction—or "guided discovery" (Rieber, 1992, p. 94). First, educational microworlds are simulations, but they rstrict the complexity of models to the minimum needed, e.g. by reducing the number of variables. Second, the constructivist simulation can be extended with guiding missions: "The purpose of the 'missions' is to induce and encourage the fantasy in a series of structured activities."—"Fantasy entails providing learners with a meaningful context for learning which is easy to augment with [users'] imaginations"

(Rieber, 1992, p. 99). Missions are thus more than learning paths toward the learning goal in an educational microworld. As an instructional method, they can inspire processes of construction. Experienced learners can actually modify mission conditions, which would, in Wesener's terminology, turn micro- into meso- or macro-worlds. The gaming community would call this "modding."

Rieber illustrates the ideas with examples from an early *Logo*-based space shuttle simulator. As an instructional part, it features simulation-based flight lessons, as a construction part it adds story-based missions (Rieber, 1992, 96). Today, we have to translate the ideas of 1980s' microworld pioneers to immersive 3D environments and virtual realities.

Summing up, simulated, interactive virtual worlds show emergent behavior, and thereby can support emergent construction of knowledge. Micro-virtual worlds are the closest compromise between instruction and construction support, as they augment simplified simulations and well-defined sets of actions with integrated narrative missions that can even be modified by experienced users.

Concepts in Interactive Storytelling

As addressed in the previous section, educational virtual worlds can be enhanced by stories (there called missions). Interactive stories are very much tied to virtual worlds, as a world is a part of a story (and of a game, for that matter). Worlds, however, are rather open-ended, whereas plots, which are often discussed in the context of interactive storytelling, are a structuring element. The most important part of stories, though, according to Crawford (2005, pp. 15-16), are the characters.

Trogemann (2002) addresses interactive storytelling in relation to virtual worlds, artificially intelligent characters, and the dualism as a conflict in this area. He calls it control vs. autonomy. He agrees with Szilas (1999) that autonomous characters should first of all serve the story.

Storytelling has always been interactive. Think of elders telling stories to a responsive audience in the village square, or a bedtime story that a child interrupts with questions. Aristotle (335 BC) was among the first to formalize storytelling, introducing narrative structures and story components. A tragedy consists of plot, character, thought, diction, melody, and spectacle (Wikipedia, 2012).

Books and plays evolved through time. The twentieth century saw a renaissance of interactive storytelling, still in analog form. Choose-your-own-adventure books that came up in the 1970s are branching stories that leave the reader different options at the end of a page to continue reading the story on other pages. In fact, the concept of branching brooks had existed before, for educational texts (e.g. Crowder & Martin, 1960). Another, more open-ended form of analog interactive storytelling are pen-and-paper role-playing games. In these, human gamemasters structure the creative chaos of interacting players, and provide plot and non-player characters.

Digital interactive storytelling does not need a gamemaster; the software assumes this role. In comparison to interactive books, multimedia presentations of stories (e.g. animations) are now possible, but also increased interaction. Different forms include narrative games (especially adventure games) and virtual drama (like *Façade*), interactive fiction (text adventures with natural language input) and hyperfiction (branching stories in hypertext form), hypervideo (links in the video lead to other scenes) and interactive movies (different sorts of interactivity, most often navigation through the plot).

Crawford (2005) wrote a textbook on interactive storytelling that also treats the problem of the dualism. Here, the 'constructing' part is the reader or player that makes choices. The 'instructing' part is the author who wants to tell a story, with an artistic intention. Crawford calls the constructivist perspective agency or interactivity, the instructivist perspective narrativity, storiness, or plot (Crawford, 2005, p. 49). In resolving the

issue, he rejects the various narration-oriented branching models (see reviews in Crawford, 2005, pp. 123–134; Handler Miller, 2004, pp. 124–133; Trogemann, 2002, pp. 293–295), advocating intelligent, rule-based drama managers (which can be found, e.g., in the virtual drama *Façade* or in the Virtual Storyteller research project by Swartjes & Theune, 2006). The latter approach seeks emergence through increased nonlinearity and interactive choices. Writers would compose rules instead of fixed texts.

In education, branching models would suit experiential learning that is based on operations or tasks, whereas emergence engines might be suitable for the discovery learning view (cf. Rieber, 1992; de Jong and van Joolingen, 1998).

Anyhow, researchers and practitioners seem to agree that some form of nonlinear plot is the fundamental basis for an interactive story. Sander (2008), however, lays out a vision of linear interactive storytelling that leaves the reader or user of a virtual world little choices, yet still creates a meaningful interactive experience by relying on psychological theories for predicting or influencing behavior and decision-making.

In the context of education, these ideas relate to Bopp's (2005) concept of immersive instruction (German: "Immersive Didaktik"). Bopp analyzed game tutorials, and collected strategies for 'sneaking in' educational content in game activities in a natural, meaningful way.

Summing up, storytellers and literary theorists and critics have been looking for structure since the time of Aristotle. Nonlinear structures enabling interactive storytelling have been around for a while now, and they can be divided into (1) rather closed branching approaches and (2) rather open-ended drama engines aiming for emergence in the system and the experience. The second view requires quite advanced artificial intelligence programming, whereas the first view may be too simple to create a feeling of controlling the narrative.

As it appears, many still believe that this conflict is unsolvable. This view is evident in labels like the "narrative paradox" or the "interactive dilemma". Already the existence of these two expressions—one including "narration," the other "interaction"—marks the conflict. Louchart and Aylett (2003) and Peinado, Gómez-Martín and Gómez-Martín (2005), respectively, among others, are trying to resolve these postulated problems despite prevailing skepticism.

Another version of the paradox, or dilemma, manifests itself in two rivaling groups: narratologists and ludologists. In a nutshell, the first regard all interactive media for entertainment as stories, and the latter as games.

Concepts in Game Design

Maybe the most important tool of a game designer is to know and make use of genre conventions. This does not mean crime or fantasy, but, for instance, knowing the essential game mechanisms of an adventure game. Especially designers of educational games should make sure they know

how entertainment games work, so they do not have to have to reinvent what people like and can identify with. Of course, rules may be broken for artistic or didactical purposes, once one has understood them.

Rollings and Adams (2003) as well as Bates (2004) have published introductory books documenting established video game genres and their conventions. The dualism between simulation (construction support) and story (instruction) is reflected in two opposing genres: simulation games and adventure games, respectively. On the x-axis, Figure 1 shows that adventure games build on scripted (authored) narratives, whereas simulation games lead to emergent narratives (Maciuszek & Martens, 2011c). See Sweetser (2005) and Kickmeier-Rust (2009) on the scripted-emergent dualism, as well as Dormans (2011) discussing progression versus emergence.

Some simulation games do use a narrative frame in the form of missions or a career mode (Maciuszek & Martens, 2009). At the same time, some adventures add mini-games. Dormans (2011) argues though that an integration of both has failed

Figure 1. Adventure genre vs. simulation genre

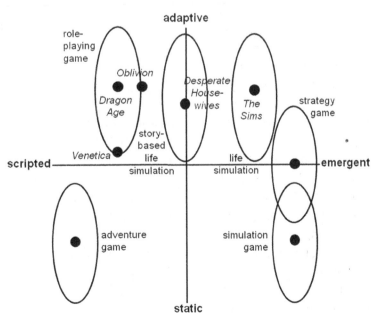

so far, largely because progressing stories are not being modeled as well as emergence mechanisms are. He proposes to treat story progress as a quantifiable resource in game mechanics.

From the perspective of genre, a comprise between the two poles does exist in Computer Role-Playing Games (CRPG) like the *Dragon Age* games or the *Elder Scrolls* series as well as life simulations like *The Sims*. CRPG provide a virtual world with simulated activities like Crafting or Conversations (Maciuszek & Martens, 2011b), each comprised of a number of player actions (cf. Schwan & Buder, 2002 in the Virtual Worlds section above). CRPG structure open-ended simulations through scripted quests (missions), dialogs (for Conversation), and recipes (for Crafting).

Notice in Figure 1 that CRPG and life simulations add another quality. Like an ITS in the e-learning field, they are user-adaptive. Before playing, the player creates their own avatar. During play, the game adapts by choosing appropriate enemies or handing out suitable quests, as the avatar gains (virtual) experience.

In pen-and-paper role-playing, there is an eternal debate whether players prefer a 'sandbox' or a 'railroading' style of storytelling. 'Plot point campaigns' in *Savage Worlds* are a compromise: short, linear scenarios may be composed sequentially in multiple ways. This discussion extends to the digital domain: Whereas the open-world *Elder Scrolls* games have been described as sandboxes supporting construction of very individual playing experiences, *Dragon Age* is quite linear, offering small parts of the world divided up into chapters. These, however, span up a story of epic proportions immersing the player through the storytelling.

Even in activities, the dualism becomes visible. Often, Crafting in an otherwise 3D virtual world simply involves choosing a scripted recipe via a 2D window interface and hitting a 'create' button (e.g. *Dragon Age*, *Drakensang*). This is not very interesting if it is to be used for experimentation or interactive demonstration of work processes in education. Smithery in *Gothic* is actually a

virtual hands-on exercise in which the avatar is directed to apply virtual tools to objects in the 3D environment. Conversations usually employ scripted dialog trees for single-choice interaction (sometimes with a strong impact on the evolving story, as in the *Global Conflicts* educational games). Some games use hypertext models (*Elder Scrolls*) or even free text input (*Galatea*, *Façade*).

All in all, many of the more advanced educational games borrow from the adventure and simulation game genres, thereby placing themselves on extreme ends of the instruction-construction scale. In the future, CRPG may prove to be a worthwhile compromise—especially since adaptivity is a genre-immanent trait.

Concepts in Automation

The essence of the discussion is: How much freedom do we grant the learner? Or, vice versa, how much control should the teacher apply. In the e-learning case, this would rephrase as: how much control should the designer apply? Or, assuming that we have a proactive intelligent tutor: how much automation should it apply?

This is an issue discussed by cognitive systems engineers. Sheridan (2002) published a book on *Humans and Automation*. It does discuss virtual reality for training and entertainment (Sheridan, 2002, pp. 36–39) as well as education (Sheridan, 2002, pp. 48–49), but also automation in many other areas. He arrives at a conflict between allocating functions to either human or machine. That discussion results in a two-dimensional model (Sheridan, 2002, pp. 61–63). In joined cognitive systems, four operations can be performed: acquire information, analyze and display, decide action, and implement action. Each of these can be allocated to the human user or the machine—or both—on an eight-degrees scale: (1) The computer offers no assistance; the human must do it all. (2) The computer suggests alternative ways to do the task. (3) The computer selects one way to do the task and (4) executes that suggestion if the human approves, or (5) allows the human a restricted time to veto before automatic execution, or (6) executes automatically, then necessarily informs the human, or (7) executes automatically, then informs the human only if asked. Finally, (8) the computer selects the method, executes the task, and ignores the human. This works as a design space in which to make design decisions, but automation may also adapt to a user's workload dynamically (Sheridan, 2002, pp. 64–65).

This model relates to the insights from the disciplines in the sections above. It takes into account inter-individual, even intra-individual differences (cf. Learning Theories). It proposes automated adaptation to these different needs, similar to the idea of ITS (cf. Technology-enhanced Learning). It offers a design space like a set of different genre conventions (cf. Game Design).

We may interpret Schulmeister's model (cf. Technology-enhanced Learning)—which is similar, but aimed at learners and multimedia interaction—in a similar way as Sheridan's design space by applying it to different elements of

instructional stories (cf. Interactive Storytelling) and construction-oriented virtual environments (cf. Virtual Worlds). As a result, we arrive at a taxonomy of interactive stories and microworlds for different learners and learning situations: Table 1.

Towards Balancing Instruction and Construction

How can we support self-regulatory creative processes in computer-based educational games and virtual worlds with fully or partially automated teaching? In previous work, we have argued that instruction and construction are no 'either-ors', but in fact extreme poles between which teaching/ learning processes swing back and forth, oscillating around a center of gravity. The poles of this dualism are dialectic opposites that exclude, at the same time require each other (Hellmig & Martens, 2010).

In Sheridan's (2002) model, the pendulum would swing between no assistance (1) and complete automation (8), either at design time

Table 1. Design and adaptivity space for storytelling in virtual worlds

Instruction ⇨ Construction	Characters	Perspective	Virtual world	Plot	Mise-en-scène	Language
1. View objects and receive	Fixed avatar	Fixed perspective	Restricted to current level	Linear plot	Fixed presentation	Fixed, prewritten text
2. Multiple representations	Choice of avatar	Change of view (first vs. third person, 2D/3D)	Visit places on a map	Branching	Choice of scenes	Single-choice dialogues
3. Vary form of representation	Variation of avatar appearance	Free camera operation in 3D	Change weather etc.	Play missions/ quests within linear frame	Avatar appears in cut scenes, changed clothing visible	Text changes to fit avatar
4. Manipulate content	Assignment of characteristics	Switch protagonist	Move objects, crafting	Missions/quests affect a nonlinear frame	Effects of interaction with environment visible	Choice of wording or additional options based on skills
5. Construct object/content	Creation of avatar	Become author	Building	Write missions/ quests	Creation of environments	Free text input, keywords
6. Construct object/content and receive intelligent feedback	Creation of avatar, world responds to characteristics	Become author, share creations	Building, other players visit	Write missions/ quests, share, others play or extend them	Creation of environments affects gameplay/story	Free text input, parsing of phrases or sentences, feedback

or adaptively. In our game-based-learning version (Table 1) inspired by Schulmeister (2003), the pendulum swings between passive reception (1) and active construction with intelligent feedback (6), independently for at least six aspects of storytelling in virtual worlds. Even parts of the world may differ, e.g. one can swing weapons, cast spells, or kick objects in the 3D worlds of the *Elder Scrolls* games (mise-en-scène level 4), but lockpicking, trading, or crafting happens in a separate 2D window (level 1, as the virtual world 'freezes'). One can switch between first-person and third-person view (perspective level 2), but not between 2D and 3D (perspective level 1).

One way of traversing the in-between levels of the design space is to start out with an experiential learning view and linear task models (plot level 1) and from that on extend them with more and more branches (plot level 2), including alternative solutions and possible errors that can happen during experimentation (Weicht, Maciuszek & Martens, 2012).

Moreover, instead of modeling a multitude of solutions, one could stick to one expert model, but accept variations. In a student thesis (Leitert, 2011), we examined the matching of graph-based learner solutions to sample solutions. The investigated graph matching algorithms identify omitted and added nodes or edges. Maybe some error patterns are actually creative modeling solutions, e.g. a 'detour' or a 'shortcut'? Assessing this should already be difficult for a human teacher, though.

Our review has shown that designers, researchers, and theorists often argue the other way round. Many favor construction environments amended with instruction mechanisms. Those include prompts, cognitive tools, intelligent feedback, and human help. In deciding how much instruction to apply, designers need to attend to inter-individual and intra-individual differences. Whether we have a human teacher in a blended-learning scenario or a virtual tutor, this may be adapted dynamically to the current needs.

Some entertainment game genres are inherently adaptive. CRPG and life sims allow the player to customize their avatar, initially and in the course of the experience. Gameplay adapts dynamically (characters level 6). CRPG happen in micro-virtual worlds, which is the closest constructivist game environments come to instruction. Via their avatars, players can manipulate the world in a lifelike fashion, e.g. when crafting items (virtual world level 4) or conversing with non-player characters (language levels 2–5). Graphical representations of actions and activities relevant for education still need to reach a similar standard as combat or casting spells, though. Smithery in *Gothic* is a positive example (as is potion brewing in the *Harry Potter* action adventures). CRPG embed such virtual world construction in instructional, guiding quests (plot level 4). This may solve the narrative paradox! However, very few educational CRPG have been made so far (Maciuszek & Martens, 2011b). Among off-the-shelf products, the *Global Conflicts* series probably comes closest.

In three current instructional design projects, we examine the idea of educational CRPG. All of them start out with a virtual world with simulated activities as an environment for construction (virtual world 4). Following the idea of immersive didactics (Bopp 2005), each project maps a constructivist teaching method from face-to-face learning to a CRPG activity (Maciuszek & Martens, 2011b). Project 1 maps discovery learning in computer science to Crafting in a virtual factory. In the role of an inventor, students assemble virtual robots and program their behavior. Project 2 maps discovery learning in marine science to Crafting in a virtual lab. In the role of a scientist, students manipulate an ecosystem and model biogeochemical and physical processes. Project 3 maps interpretative writing in literature class to Conversations and an interactive journal in a virtual theater. In the role of a detective, students construct author's intentions behind a classic drama. After the world is established, each study tries out a different strategy of adding instruction by exploiting and extending CRPG genre conventions. The idea is to use Table 1 as a design space to choose from (Projects 2 and 3), but also as a template for adaptive instruction along the levels (Project 1).

Propositions for Virtual Factories

In Project 1, we teach applied artificial intelligence to high school students aged 15 to 18 in the context of a computer science course. To this end, we have built a virtual factory in *Second Life*: Figure 2.

In four 90-minute sessions, students assemble virtual robots and program their behavior, particularly autonomous steering (Reynolds, 1999). Applying an engineering-oriented discovery learning approach, we provide a variety of robot parts and have students understand and change the robots' movement strategies when they respond to stimuli. In a first pilot course with university students, we noticed that the *Linden Scripting Language* and its effects on the physics engine were difficult to grasp just by lecturing and subsequent experimentation already for this group. After the painful learning phase though, they obtained astonishing results, e.g. inventing a surveillance system with virtual cameras and a robot swarm pursuing the player on the basis of planning by graph search (Maciuszek et al., 2013).

In order to reach the learning goals and come up with creative ideas themselves, school students would certainly need more guidance. To balance instruction and construction better with learners' experiences, we formalized our teaching approach by applying a version of Collins, Brown, and Newman's (1987) Cognitive Apprenticeship. Their approach comprises six teaching strategies. Modeling is the most instructional strategy: A teacher (or e-learning software) demonstrates something, and the learner copies the procedure. Coaching means that the teacher observes the learner, and provides hints when they get stuck. In Scaffolding, the teacher does some of the tasks where the student is still weak. Yet, bit by bit the teacher withdraws, as learner knowledge fortifies. This is called Fading, and it appears to be a suitable model for a learner-adaptive process. Exploration is the advanced learning method of free experimentation. Articulation and reflection are supplementary in that they ask the learner to express gained knowledge and discuss it with peers.

So far, our virtual factory expects the coach to be a human teacher, but after we have understood the processes enough, we would like to implement it as an intelligent tutor. In the first session, the teacher presents the virtual world. Students can find out how to navigate and operate it through their avatars (Modeling and Coaching). From then on, we have built in Scaffolding and Fading in tasks (exercise sheets) handed out to the students. Tasks of low difficulty have students craft robots

Figure 2. Student crafting a virtual robot

with a desired behavior from prefabricated, communicating pieces ("manipulate content" in Table 1). Tasks of medium difficulty involve studying program code in the pieces. Tasks of high difficulty have students write their own code, beginning with manipulating parameters, to achieve a different behavior ("construct object/content" in Table 1).

The list of second-session tasks reads $Seek_1$, $Seek_2$, $Seek_3$, $Flee_1$, $Flee_2$, $Flee_3$, $Arrive_1$, $Arrive_2$, $Arrive_3$. Having completed $Seek_1$, a student may continue with $Seek_2$ or $Flee_1$. The teacher decides what is most appropriate. It is also possible to move backwards when a task was too difficult (from $Flee_2$ to $Flee_1$). Adaptively, the teacher guides the student through the construction space. Sessions 3 and 4 add more advanced learning goals, each in three versions, ultimately expecting creative solutions (Exploration).

The students write down their insights on their worksheets, which act as pages of a learning journal (Articulation). Thus, each student works on a construction manual, reading more in the earlier tasks, writing more later. The hypothesis is that by this approach, students get used to the possibilities of a constructivist environment bit by bit, at their own speed, paving individual learning paths.

We are currently in the midst of evaluating this proposition. The idea is to use the worksheets as a cultural probe capturing individual learning processes. We will perform a content analysis on the written explanations, analyze the learning paths, and match them with collected self-assessments: how difficult was each task and how much fun (on scales from 1 to 5). Preliminary results from a trial with two students indicate that we managed to adapt to their abilities. We observed self-regulative, inquiry, creative, and cooperative behaviors. The main study will show whether this will hold for a larger group.

Summing up, our proposition for Crafting activities in virtual factories—at least in computer science domains—is to pave a space of individual learning paths. These traverse the educational domain, but are also capable of expressing a flexible level of instruction and construction for each learning goal: Table 2. The teacher or intelligent tutor moves on a Scaffolding-Fading scale dynamically by picking the appropriate next task—leaning towards crafting or building—and assisting the student in solving it.

Propositions for Virtual Labs

Project 2 is part of an e-learning module within the EU-funded project *South Baltic WebLab* (www.southbalticweblab.eu), which aims at raising an interest in marine sciences among students aged 15 to 18. A first demo was made using the virtual world software *OpenSim* (Figure 3; Maciuszek & Martens, 2011c), while current Web-based experiments are being implemented in *Flash*.

Applying a science-oriented discovery learning approach, we provide a simulation of an ecosystem. Students may manipulate parameters of the simulation using virtual tools as metaphors—in Figure 3 a fishing rod to decrease a certain fish population or a fodder tube to increase it, there in order to produce and validate hypotheses about predator-prey dynamics.

In the Web-based experiment currently under development, students interact with biogeochemical and physical processes using tools for viewing species and molecules (magnifying glasses), sampling (a water sampler), measuring (an oxygen meter, a disk for measuring water transparency), and changing nutrient concentrations (advancing/rewinding time, choosing scenarios). The learn-

Table 2. Balancing crafting and building

Instruction ⇔ Construction	Virtual factory	Articulation/ Reflection
4. Manipulate content	Crafting: Connect robot parts	Read construction manual
⇕		
5. Construct object/content	Building: Program robot parts	Write construction manual

Figure 3. Manipulating simulation parameters through virtual tools

ing goal is to understand eutrophication (over-fertilization) in the Baltic Sea and in the end to sketch a qualitative model.

A first prototype evaluation (10 respondents) using again worksheets as reflection tools and cultural probes for data collection showed that students were able to complete individual tasks. Some were easier, in others comparison of measurements was difficult. Yet, nobody put together their results in a model. Besides clearer missions, more instructional assistance is needed, which we plan to include as an intelligent tutor.

While experimenting, the student may ask the tutor for subsequent meaningful actions that might lead them toward a goal given the current state of the experiment (Maciuszek & Martens, 2011a).

'Good' sequences for an ITS knowledge base—corresponding to Crafting recipes in a CRPG—are gained by querying experts and by analyzing successful student behavior. For an application of Cognitive Task Analysis in educational games design, see e.g. Wouters, van Oostendorp, and van der Spek (2010). In our prototype study, we had asked students what sequences had helped them solve a task. Answers included *measure water transparency*; *view phytoplankton*; *understand the connection* (more light means more algae growth) or *sample water*; *measure oxygen*;

compare measurements (to understand changes in oxygen concentration over the year). Thus, whenever a student has taken a water sample, but hesitates how to proceed, the tutor might consult its knowledge base and remind them to measure oxygen. The next step is to enrich the activity with quests for the different scenarios and to record action sequences in tests at schools.

There will be a drawing tool for visualizing mental models, with tutorial help as well. To gain an understanding of how students construct knowledge in a lab environment and how reflection tools can support Crafting, we performed an additional, small-scale study with a group of 3 university students. These went through a real-world physics experiment—crafting a boat that enables marbles to float on water—and wrote a live learning journal in the form of a blog. We are still at the stage of exploratory qualitative studies, so what we did was a quick content analysis of the blog entries. The students did produce and apply hypotheses (one falsified, one verified), as expected in scientific discovery learning. Basically the tutor needs to prompt for those steps.

Summing up, our proposition for an instructional addition to the constructivist scenario is in this case to extend a level-4 virtual world ("manipulate content," "crafting") with a level-2 branching plot. Cognitive task models are often formulated as branching structures defining in each state possible next actions. The Petri net in Figure 4 is our task analysis of a Crafting recipe in the entertainment CRPG *Drakensang* (Maciuszek & Martens, 2011a, p. 271).

A guiding tutor would assist in solving a task by traversing branches in the expert model and suggesting actions leading toward meaningful goals. When augmenting the nonlinear lab with missions or quests that structure scenarios (Rieber, 1992), we add level-4 plots. This is what every CRPG does, but also simulation games with missions. Table 3 sums up the suggestions.

Propositions for Virtual Theaters

Interpretative writing is a constructivist teaching method from literature studies in which students analyze classic or contemporary texts by producing related fiction themselves. Howard (2008, pp. 139–146) showed how this works through creating and playing CRPG quests based on the literary material.

Our third project aims at setting up virtual theater stages for students aged 15 and up. By playing a game adaptation of a classic piece, they would assume the role of one of the characters (this might even follow an assessment: which *Hamlet* character are you?). They would interact with the other characters and story, and at the same time write about what they have learned, in-game.

Journals that chronicle the proceeding of quests are a genre convention of CRPG. Normally, entries have been scripted by the designer, yet in *Neverwinter Nights (NWN)*, for instance, the player may add his or her own thoughts and memories in free-text form. Our idea is that these will form the student's essay. The problem is that *NWN* completely lacks instruction such as prompts (cf. Learning Theory above), leaving players on their own. Some detective games (*CSI: Dark Motives*) do provide a structure, but lack the free text input. Games in the educational *Global Conflicts* series offer at least some drag-and-drop interaction with the journal when its comes to feeding collected clues back into the climax scene (e.g. in *Sweatshops*). Our proposition is thus to increase construction in literature games by mapping interpretative writing to free-text writing of quest journals, while supporting this reflection process through instructional prompts, guiding the student toward types of intended learning goals.

In a focus group interview with seven humanities researchers using a *Hamlet* prototype (made with the *NWN* toolset) as a focus (Figure 5), we

Figure 4. Branching task model

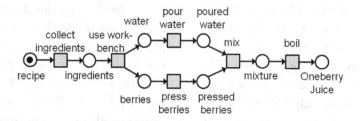

Table 3. Adding linear narratives to nonlinear simulations

Instruction ⇨ Construction	Virtual lab		+ Plot/Guidance
2. Multiple representations		⇨	+ Branching task models
4. Manipulate content	Move objects, crafting		+ Missions/quests

identified a Whodunit (or murder mystery) plot employing the CRPG activity Conversation as a suitable quest. Playing Ophelia in a dinner scene at Castle Elsinore, the player would act as a detective, interviewing the other characters and taking notes in order to track down the killer of the late king (Maciuszek & Martens, 2011b).

In order to gather requirements on game-based reading logs, we had a group of university students play a few turns of an analog, text-based detective game (*Sherlock Holmes Consulting Detective*). They were to collect clues in a Wiki, which we had pre-structured with categories. The result was that the students made use of only one of our instructional prompts, "People." In addition, they created a new category in which they could store theories about suspects. Interestingly, the process of problem solving and reflecting on read information was not all that different from hypothesis validation in virtual labs (Maciuszek & Martens, 2011b) and thus might be supported in a similar fashion.

The main study underway seeks to find evidence for the applicability of Conversation-based games as a game-based version of interpretative writing. In a participatory design setup, we invited three 9th grade students to be design partners (Druin, 2002, pp. 12–18) in creating an interactive adaptation of Schiller's *Kabale und Liebe* for German class. To support creativity and structured thinking, we employ textbooks on game design and the piece itself, content design patterns (Maciuszek, Ladhoff, & Martens, 2011), a developing script, and the actual authoring tool, the *NWN* toolset (cf. Howard, 2008). We are especially interested in the journal entries our young designers will prepare for the player, as this will provide insight towards working with free-text entries in the future. After the first brainstorming and writing sessions, the students seem highly motivated, and it will be interesting to perform a content analysis on their finished script, as well as using the final product in class.

Summing up, typical in-game journals are language level 1 in Table 1. We suggest to design those for entering own reflective thoughts more freely, aiming for level 4 at least: Table 4. Ideally, instructional designers would come up with the right prompts that would elicit parts of written essays for assessment by the human teacher (level 5) or even ways of feeding text input back into Conversations (level 6). A first Conversation-journal model is in the works (Langer, 2012).

FUTURE RESEARCH DIRECTIONS

In our work, we will conduct three evaluative studies, understand learning processes in constructivist virtual environments, and refine our approaches of adding instruction. In general, the game-based learning and virtual world education

Figure 5. In-game journal in an NWN-based literature game prototype

Table 4. Encouraging and supporting journal writing

Instruction ⇨ Construction	Journal entries (player)	Journal prompts (game)
1. View objects and receive	Fixed, prewritten text in CRPG	Fixed, prewritten prompts
	⇩	⇧
4. Manipulate content	Choice of wording	
5. Construct object/content	Free text input	Empty text field in *NWN*
6. Construct object/content and receive intelligent feedback	Free text input, parsing of phrases or sentences, feedback	

field is in need of more ideas on balancing the dualism. Inspiration is out there – a lot has been envisioned already in the 1980s (Papert, 1980) or 90s (Rieber, 1992), but those visions require translation to the case of immersive 3D environments, a re-evaluation, and an extension.

For example, our discussion has so far omitted the issue of physical experiences in virtual worlds and the complexity of sensory-motor interaction. In another small-scale pilot study, we found indications that manual operations might benefit knowledge construction in a virtual factory. Students who had trained in an environment where they could move and rotate building blocks showed better transfer to a real-world Lego task than students who trained using a drag-and-drop interface.

We encourage researchers to play lots of entertainment games. Many concepts and possible solutions, e.g. adaptivity in CRPG are out there already. CRPG design conventions have been documented by Hallford and Hallford (2001). Howard (2008) discusses how to design quests, and Bates (2004, pp. 119–127) has produced a catalog of typical puzzles found in adventure games. This leads to the issue of design patterns. Once researchers have analyzed a corpus of games, they can document best practices: what are successful design options, and how can we make use of those for educational purposes (Maciuszek & Martens, 2011b; Maciuszek, Ladhoff & Martens, 2011)?

CONCLUSION

The chapter has provided a narrative review of concepts relevant for instructional design of digital educational games and virtual world learning. Many authors seem to agree that open-ended, constructivist learning environments are desirable, as they have the potential of encouraging experimentation and initiating creative processes. In order for learners not to get lost in infinite possibilities of the virtual space, they recommend the addition of instructional elements.

We have presented three suggestions from our own work. Scaffolding and Fading, task-based guidance in simulations, and free-text in-game journals are promising approaches, but need to be worked out further in our qualitative, exploratory studies, and then be evaluated quantitatively with larger groups.

It would be interesting to re-build our virtual hospital in 3D, supplying virtual devices the student can operate, and then to try out the strategies. Moreover, constructivist virtual-world learning in the health care domain need not be limited to future doctors. One recent trend is to use virtual worlds in psychotherapy, representing the patient as an avatar. As Bredl and Groß (2012) point out, certain forms of therapy are not that different from constructivist learning. The question will be again: when and to what extent should the therapist intervene?

REFERENCES

Bates, B. (2004). *Game design* (2nd ed.). Boston, MA: Thomson Course Technology.

Bloom, B. S., Engelhart, M. D., Furst, E. J., Hill, W. H., & Krathwohl, D. R. (1956). Taxonomy of educational objectives: The classification of educational goals. In Handbook, I. (Ed.), *Cognitive Domain*. New York, NY: McKay.

Bopp, M. (2005). Immersive didaktik: Verdeckte lernhilfen und framingprozesse in computerspielen. *kommunikation@gesellschaft, 6*.

Bredl, K., & Groß, A. (2012). Gestaltung und bewertung von lernszenarien in immersiven virtuellen welten. *Zeitschrift für E-Learning, 7*(1), 36–46.

Brown, J. S., Collins, A., & Duguid, P. (1989). Situated cognition and the culture of learning. *Educational Researcher, 18*(1), 32–42.

Collins, A., Brown, J. S., & Newman, S. E. (1987). *Cognitive apprenticeship: Teaching the craft of reading, writing, and mathematics* (Tech. Rep. No. 403). Urbana-Champaign, IL: Center for the Study of Reading, University of Illinois.

Crawford, C. (2005). *Chris Crawford on interactive storytelling*. Berkeley, CA: New Riders Games.

Crowder, N. A., & Martin, G. C. (1960). *Adventures in algebra*. Garden City, NY: Doubleday.

de Jong, T., & van Joolingen, W. R. (1998). Scientific discovery learning with computer simulations of conceptual domains. *Review of Educational Research, 68*(2), 179–201.

Dewey, J., & Dewey, E. (1915). *Schools of tomorrow*. New York, NY: Dutton.

Dormans, J. (2011). *Integrating emergence and progression*. Paper presented at the 5th DiGRA Conference on Games and Play. Utrecht, The Netherlands.

Dreyfus, H. L., & Dreyfus, S. E. (1986). *Mind over machine*. New York, NY: The Free Press.

Dreyfus, H. L., & Dreyfus, S. E. (2004). The ethical implications of the five-stage skill-acquisition model. *Bulletin of Science, Technology & Society, 24*(3), 251–264. doi:10.1177/0270467604265023.

Druin, A. (2002). The role of children in the design of new technology. *Behaviour & Information Technology, 21*(1), 1–25. doi:10.1080/01449290110108659.

Egenfeldt-Nielsen, S. (2007). Third generation educational use of computer games. *Journal of Educational Multimedia and Hypermedia, 16*(3), 263–281.

Einsiedler, W. (1981). *Lehrmethoden*. Baltimore, MD: Urban & Schwarzenberg.

Glogger, I., Holzäpfel, L., Schwonke, R., Nückles, M., & Renkl, A. (2009). Activation of learning strategies in writing learning journals. *Zeitschrift fur Padagogische Psychologie, 23*(2), 95–104. doi:10.1024/1010-0652.23.2.95.

Hallford, N., & Hallford, J. (2001). *Sword & circuitry: A designer's guide to computer role-playing games*. Roseville, CA: Prima Tech.

Handler Miller, C. (2004). *Digital storytelling: A creator's guide to interactive entertainment*. Burlington, MA: Focal Press.

Harr, R., Buch, T., & Hanghøj, T. (2008). Exploring the discrepancy between educational goals and educational game design. In *Proceedings of the 2nd European Conference on Games Based Learning (ECGBL 2008)*, (pp. 165–174). Reading, UK: Academic Publishing.

Hellmig, L., & Martens, A. (2010). Blended learning– Ein sinnloser begriff? In S. Hambach, A. Martens, D. Tavangarian, & B. Urban (Eds.), *eLearning Baltics 2010: Proceedings of the 3rd International eLBa Science Conference*, (pp. 215–224). Stuttgart, Germany: Fraunhofer.

Hinz, J. (2001). *Facetten der kreativität: Entwicklungsprozesse in natur, kultur und persönlichkeit* (2nd ed.). Aachen, Germany: Shaker.

Howard, J. (2008). Quests: Design, theory, and history in games and narratives. Wellesley, MA: A K Peters.

Hübner, S., Nückles, M., & Renkl, A. (2007). Lerntagebücher als medium des selbstgesteuerten lernens: Wie viel instruktionale unterstützung ist sinnvoll? *Empirische Pädagogik, 21*(2), 119–137.

Kelly, G. A. (1955). *The psychology of personal constructs*. New York, NY: Norton.

Kickmeier-Rust, M. D. (2009). Talking digital educational games. In M. D. Kickmeier-Rust (Ed.), *Proceedings of the First International Open Workshop on Intelligent Personalization and Adaptation in Digital Educational Games,* (pp. 7–16). Graz.

Langer, H. (2012). *Entwicklung eines gesprächsmodells für interactive geschichten in computerspielen*. (Bachelor's Thesis). University of Rostock, Rostock, Germany.

Leitert, A. (2011). *Graphenbasierte überprüfung unvollständiger lösungen in modellierungsaufgaben*. (Student Thesis). University of Rostock, Rostock, Germany.

Lieberman, D. A. (1992). *Learning: Behavior and cognition*. Pacific Grove, CA: Brooks/Cole.

Linn, M. C. (1990). Summary: Establishing a science and engineering of science education. In Gardner, M., Greeno, J. G., Reif, F., Schoenfeld, A. H., diSessa, A., & Stage, E. (Eds.), *Toward a Scientific Practice of Science Education* (pp. 323–341). Hillsdale, NJ: Lawrence Erlbaum.

Louchart, S., & Aylett, R. (2003). Solving the narrative paradox in VEs – Lessons from RPGs. In T. Rist, R. Aylett, D. Bellin, & J. Rickel (Eds.), *Intelligent Virtual Agents: 4th International Workshop, IVA 2003, Proceedings,* (pp. 244–248). Berlin, Germany: Springer.

Maciuszek, D., Ladhoff, S., & Martens, A. (2011). Content design patterns for game-based learning. *International Journal of Game-Based Learning, 1*(3), 65–82. doi:10.4018/ijgbl.2011070105.

Maciuszek, D., & Martens, A. (2009). Virtuelle labore als simulationsspiele. In S. Fischer, E. Maehle, & R. Reischuk (Eds.), INFORMATIK 2009 – Im Focus das Leben: Beiträge der 39. Jahrestagung der Gesellschaft für Informatik, (pp. 1965–1979). Bonn, Germany: GI.

Maciuszek, D., & Martens, A. (2011a). Cognitive tasks and collaborative agents for microadaptive game activities. In A. Dittmar & P. Forbrig (Eds.), *Designing Collaborative Activities. ECCE 2011: European Conference on Cognitive Ergonomics 2011,* (pp. 271–272). Rostock, Germany: Universitätsdruckerei Rostock.

Maciuszek, D., & Martens, A. (2011b). Computer role-playing games as an educational game genre: Activities and reflection. In D. Gouscos & M. Meimaris (Eds.), *Proceedings of the 5th International Conference on Games-Based Learning (ECGBL 2011),* (pp. 368–377). Reading, MA: Academic Publishing.

Maciuszek, D., & Martens, A. (2011c). A reference architecture for game-based intelligent tutoring. In Felicia, P. (Ed.), *Handbook of Research on Improving Learning and Motivation through Educational Games: Multidisciplinary Approaches* (pp. 658–682). Hershey, PA: IGI Global. doi:10.4018/978-1-60960-495-0.ch031.

Maciuszek, D., Martens, A., Lucke, U., Zender, R., & Keil, T. (2013). Second life as a virtual lab environment. In Hebbel-Seeger, A., Reiners, T., & Schäffer, D. (Eds.), *Synthetic Worlds: Emerging Technologies in Education and Economics*. Berlin, Germany: Springer.

Magnussen, R., & Holm Sørensen, B. (2010). Designing intervention in educational game research: Developing methodological approaches for design-based participatory research. In B. Meyer (Ed.), *Proceedings of the 4th European Conference on Games-Based Learning (ECGBL 2010)*, (pp. 218–225). Reading, MA: Academic Publishing.

Mandl, H., & Kopp, B. (2006). *Blended learning: Forschungsfragen und perspektiven* (Tech. Rep. No. 182). München, Germany: Department Psychologie, Institut für Pädagogische Psychologie, Ludwig-Maximilians-Universität.

Martens, A. (2004). *Ein tutoring prozess modell für fallbasierte intelligente tutoring systeme*. Berlin, Germany: Aka.

Maturana, H. R. (1970). *Biology of cognition (Tech. Rep. No. BCL 9.0)*. Urbana, IL: Biological Computer Laboratory, University of Illinois.

Mietzel, G. (2007). *Pädagogische psychologie des lehrens und lernens* (8th ed.). Göttingen, Germany: Hogrefe.

Nückles, M., Hübner, S., & Renkl, A. (2008). Enhancing self-regulated learning by writing learning protocols. *Learning and Instruction, 19*, 259–271. doi:10.1016/j.learninstruc.2008.05.002.

Papert, S. (1980). *Mindstorms: Children, computer and powerful ideas*. New York, NY: Basic Books.

Peinado, F., Gómez-Martín, P. P., & Gómez-Martín, M. A. (2005). A game architecture for emergent story-puzzles in a persistent world. In *Proceedings of DiGRA 2005 Conference: Changing Views – Worlds in Play*. Vancouver, Canada: DiGRA.

Pörksen, B. (2011). Schlüsselwerke des konstruktivismus: Eine einführung. In Pörksen, B. (Ed.), *Schlüsselwerke des Konstruktivismus* (pp. 13–28). Wiesbaden, Germany: VS-Verlag. doi:10.1007/978-3-531-93069-5_1.

Reich, K. (2005). *Systemisch-konstruktivistische Pädagogik* (5th ed.). Weinheim, Germany: Beltz.

Reynolds, C. W. (1999). Steering behaviors for autonomous characters. In *Proceedings of Game Developers Conference 1999*, (pp. 763–782). San Francisco, CA: Miller Freeman Game Group.

Rieber, L. R. (1992). Computer-based microworlds: A bridge between constructivism and direct instruction. *Educational Technology Research and Development, 40*(1), 93–106. doi:10.1007/BF02296709.

Rollings, A., & Adams, E. (2003). *Andrew Rollings and Ernest Adams on game design*. Berkeley, CA: New Riders Games.

Sander, F. N. (2008). *Linear interactive storytelling*. (Master's Thesis). Stuttgart Media University. Stuttgart, Germany.

Schanda, F. (1995). *Computer-lernprogramme*. Weinheim, Germany: Beltz.

Schiefele, U., & Pekrun, R. (1996). Psychologische modelle des fremdgesteuerten und selbstgesteuerten lernens. In Weinert, F. E. (Ed.), *Psychologie des Lernens und der Instruktion* (pp. 249–278). Göttingen, Germany: Hogrefe.

Schulmeister, R. (2003). Taxonomy of multimedia component interactivity: A contribution to the current metadata debate. *Studies in Communication Sciences, 3*(3), 61–80.

Schwan, S., & Buder, J. (2002). Lernen und wissenserwerb in virtuellen realitäten. In Bente, G., Krämer, N. C., & Petersen, A. (Eds.), *Virtuelle Realitäten* (pp. 109–132). Göttingen, Germany: Hogrefe.

Sheridan, T. B. (2002). *Humans and automation: System design and research issues.* Hoboken, NJ: Wiley.

Sternberg, R. J., & Grigorenko, E. L. (1997). Are cognitive styles still in style? *The American Psychologist, 52*(7), 700–712. doi:10.1037/0003-066X.52.7.700.

Swartjes, I., & Theune, M. (2006). A fabula model for emergent narrative. In S. Göbel, R. Malkewitz, & I. Iurgel (Eds.), *Technologies for Interactive Digital Storytelling and Entertainment, Third International Conference, TIDSE 2006,* (pp. 49–60). Berlin, Germany: Springer.

Sweetser, P. (2005). *An emergent approach to game design – Development and play.* (Dissertation). University of Queensland. Brisbane, Australia.

Szilas, N. (1999). *Interactive drama on computer: Beyond linear narrative.* Paper presented at AAAI 1999 Fall Symposium on Narrative Intelligence. Cape Cod, MA.

Tomasello, M. (2003). The key is social cognition. In Gentner, D., & Goldin-Meadow, S. (Eds.), *Language in Mind: Advances in the Study of Language and Thought* (pp. 47–57). Cambridge, MA: MIT Press.

Toro-Troconis, M. et al. (2008). Designing game-based learning activities for virtual patients in second life. *Journal of Cyber Therapy & Rehabilitation, 1*(3), 225–238.

Trogemann, G. (2002). Augmenting human creativity: Virtuelle realitäten als design-aufgabe. In Bente, G., Krämer, N. C., & Petersen, A. (Eds.), *Virtuelle Realitäten* (pp. 275–297). Göttingen, Germany: Hogrefe.

Walber, M. (2007). *Selbststeuerung im lernprozess und erkenntniskonstruktion: Eine empirische studie in der weiterbildung.* Münster, Germany: Waxmann.

Weicht, M., Maciuszek, D., & Martens, A. (2012). Designing virtual experiments in the context of marine sciences. In *Proceedings of the 2012 12th IEEE International Conference on Advanced Learning Technologies (ICALT 2012), Workshop Go-Lab.* Rome, Italy: ICALT.

Wesener, S. (2004). *Spielen in virtuellen welten: Eine untersuchung von transferprozessen in bildschirmspielen.* Wiesbaden, Germany: VS-Verlag. doi:10.1007/978-3-322-80655-0.

Wikipedia. (2012). *Poetics.* Retrieved May 2, 2012, from http://en.wikipedia.org/wiki/Poetics_(Aristotle)

Winteler, A. (2004). *Professionell lehren und lernen: Ein praxisbuch.* Darmstadt, Germany: Wissenschaftliche Buchgesellschaft.

Wouters, P., van Oostendorp, H., & van der Spek, E. D. (2010). Game design: The mapping of cognitive task analysis and game discourse analysis in creating effective and entertaining serious games. In M. Neerincx & W.-P. Brinkman (Eds.), *Proceedings of the 28th Annual European Conference on Cognitive Ergonomics (ECCE 2010),* (pp. 287–293). New York, NY: ACM.

ADDITIONAL READING

Barton, M. (2008). Dungeons & desktops: The history of computer role-playing games. Wellesley, MA: A K Peters.

Carbonaro, M., Cutumisu, M., Duff, H., Gillis, S., Onuczko, C., & Schaeffer, J. Waugh, K. (2006). Adapting a commercial role-playing game for educational computer game production. In *Proceedings of the 2nd International North American Simulation and AI in Computer Games Conference (GAME'ON-NA'2006),* (pp. 54–61). Monterey, CA: GAME ON.

Carron, T., & Marty, J.-C. (2009). User modelling in learning games. In M. Pivec (Ed.), *3rd European Conference on Games-Based Learning (ECGBL 2009),* (pp. 86–94). Reading, MA: Academic Publishing.

Charles, D., & McNeill, M. (2009). Virtual learning landscapes to enhance the student learning experience. In M. Pivec (Ed.), *3rd European Conference on Games-Based Learning (ECGBL 2009),* (pp. 95–102). Reading, MA: Academic Publishing.

Cobb, P., & Bowers, J. (1999). Cognitive and situated learning perspectives in theory and practice. *Educational Researcher, 28*(2), 4–15.

Connolly, T., Stansfield, M., & Boyle, L. (Eds.). (2009). *Games-based learning advancements for multi-sensory human computer interfaces.* Hershey, PA: IGI Global. doi:10.4018/978-1-60566-360-9.

Csikszentmihalyi, M. (1975). *Beyond boredom and anxiety – The experience of play in work and games.* San Francisco, CA: Jossey-Bass.

Edvarsen, F., & Kulle, H. (Eds.). (2010). *Educational games: Design, learning and applications.* Hauppauge, NY: Nova.

Felicia, P. (Ed.). (2011). *Handbook of research on improving learning and motivation through educational games: Multidisciplinary approaches.* Hershey, PA: IGI Global. doi:10.4018/978-1-60960-495-0.

Felicia, P., & Pitt, I. (2009). Profiling users in educational games. In Connolly, T., Stansfield, M., & Boyle, L. (Eds.), *Games-Based Learning Advancements for Multi-Sensory Human Computer Interfaces* (pp. 131–156). Hershey, PA: IGI Global. doi:10.4018/978-1-60566-360-9.ch009.

Kickmeier-Rust, M. D., Göbel, S., & Albert, D. (2008). 80 days: Melding adaptive educational technology and adaptive and interactive storytelling in digital educational games. In R. Klamma, N., Sharda, B. Fernández-Manjón, H., Kosch, & M. Spaniol (Eds.), *Proceedings of the First International Workshop on Story-Telling and Educational Games (STEG '08) – The Power of Narration and Imagination in Technology Enhanced Learning.* Maastricht, Germany: STEG.

Maciuszek, D., & Martens, A. (2012). Integrating cognitive tasks in game activities. In *Proceedings of the 2012 12th IEEE International Conference on Advanced Learning Technologies (ICALT 2012).* Rome, Italy: ICALT.

Marty, J.-C., Carron, T., & Heraud, J.-M. (2009). Observation as a requisite for game-based learning environments. In Connolly, T., Stansfield, M., & Boyle, L. (Eds.), *Games-Based Learning Advancements for Multi-Sensory Human Computer Interfaces* (pp. 51–71). Hershey, PA: IGI Global. doi:10.4018/978-1-60566-360-9.ch004.

Schank, R. C. (1995). *Tell me a story: Narrative and intelligence.* Evanston, IL: Northwestern University Press.

Schank, R. C., & Cleary, C. (1995). *Engines for education.* Hillsdale, NJ: Lawrence Erlbaum.

Spring-Keller, F., & Schauer, H. (2009). The autopilot – A personalized pathfinder in open games for learning. In M. D. Kickmeier-Rust (Ed.), *Proceedings of the 1st International Open Workshop on Intelligent Personalization and Adaptation in Digital Educational Games,* (pp. 105–112). Graz.

KEY TERMS AND DEFINITIONS

Adaptivity: Adjusting the choice and presentation of learning content to each student's individual needs.

Construction: Gaining knowledge by finding one's own explanation of a phenomenon.

Constructivism: In education the belief that a student needs to experience developing their own explanations in order to gain knowledge.

Discovery Learning: Obtaining knowledge by validating hypotheses through experiments.

Immersion: Having the feeling of actually being, acting, and making experiences in a virtual world.

Instruction: Gaining knowledge by adopting what the teacher says.

Interpretative Writing: Analyzing literature and documenting the results in one's own fictional texts.

Learning Journal: Writing entries in a book that reflect one's learning process and outcomes.

Chapter 3

Not in My Class You Don't!:
The Naive Association of Video Games with Aggression as a Hindrance to Their Use in Education

Christopher J. Ferguson
Texas A&M International University, USA

ABSTRACT

It has been recognized that video games may function well as a platform for education. However, educators may be reluctant to use such games, particularly those with violent content, given controversies over games in recent years. Yet recent data suggests that these controversies over video games may have been misplaced. The current chapter examines the controversies over video games, data to support and refute these controversies, and how the public debates on video games may have influenced educators' decisions about the use of video games in their classrooms. It is argued that it is time to acknowledge that the alleged harmfulness of video games was far overrated and that educators may wish to consider how games, even those with mildly violent content, can contribute to education.

INTRODUCTION

In November of 2010, the Sacramento Public Library decided to host a video game tournament featuring the game "Black Ops," a first-person shooter game with an M-rating for mature violent themes. The library had been motivated by the goal of attracting young people to the library. The tournament was limited to those 17 and up, due to the M-rating of the game (which suggests the game be limited to those aged 17 and older). Nonetheless, the library's effort became the focus of a vocal protest by a few, including the local chapter of the Veterans for Peace, who did not feel it appropriate that the library use a violent video game to attract young people.

DOI: 10.4018/978-1-4666-3673-6.ch003

Black Ops is a war game, part of the Call of Duty series. Put briefly, the game takes place during the 1960s and involves taking on missions as a special forces/covert ops soldier during this time period. The game has a gritty, 'is it all worth it' feel to it; fun to play, but presenting war as a dark experience. In this sense it has similarities to Apocalypse Now, a movie both entertaining to watch as a war movie despite being condemnatory toward war itself.

The protests were led, in part by a group called the Veterans for Peace, mainly US war veterans who campaign against war and violence in all forms. Video games are not a typical element of their platform, although in this case they felt that the use of Black Ops potentially glorified war. Interestingly the protestors seemed to take no offense to the myriad of war themed books or movies contained within the same library, not the least of these Apocalypse Now and Hearts of Darkness, the book on which the movie was based.

Given my interest in video game violence, I contacted the organizer of the Veterans for Peace protests, named John Reiger. I found him to be a very cordial man, but also passionate about his opposition to violence in all forms. He was gracious enough to discuss, even debate the issue with me a bit, although neither of us convinced the other. However, toward the end of our exchange I thought to ask him whether he had played the game Black Ops, which he was protesting. He responded that he had not, in fact had not played any electronic games other than solitaire. I had almost been embarrassed to ask the question as it is something of a cliché for someone to protest a form of media to which they had no exposure, no understanding. But in this case the cliché happened to be accurate.

It is not my intent to be overly critical of Mr. Reiger, who I found to be quite sincere and passionate. Indeed the issue of video games at the Sacramento Library was only a small part of an otherwise worthy agenda. However, I do suspect this case illustrates an ongoing issue for the debate of video game violence: so much of it is bred from ignorance, fear and misunderstanding. So much of the rhetoric over video game violence has focused on the notion that they "award points for antisocial behavior" or that their "interactive" nature makes them more harmful. These sorts of portrayals are incredibly simplistic and do more to illustrate the speaker's unfamiliarity with games or personal biases than they do an objective understanding of the phenomenology of video game use. Of course in previous generations, older adults said the same basic things about everything from waltz music to comic books to dime novels to Dungeons and Dragons.

This chapter concerns itself with the debate over video game violence and how this debate is both related to historical cultural processes involving the introduction of new media in psychology and also may have fostered misunderstanding and reluctance to incorporate video games, including those with violent content, into educational pedagogy. I begin by presenting evidence regarding the utility of video games in learning environments before moving to the issue of violent video games and aggression and the "urban legends" that surfaced during that debate. Finally, I will discuss how misinformation regarding the effects of violent video games ultimately impacted the educational system and the willingness to incorporate games into pedagogy.

VIDEO GAMES IN EDUCATION

Violent Video Games as Blazing Angels

In discussing the issue of video game violence, we first must try to understand what a violent video game is. Most often when talking about violent video games today people imagine the ultraviolent shooters, most often typified by the *Grand Theft Auto* series in which players could take on the role of a thug and shoot police officers or run over innocent pedestrians (although contrary to claims such games "award points" for such behavior, in fact the game world tended to respond much like the real world, with increasingly police response usually ultimately resulting in the character's death). However, this was not always the case. Video games were controversial right from their inception as commercial media in the mid 1970s. So long as one set of blips appeared to be trying destroy another set of blips it was possible to label some games as "violent." Indeed, in early research video games such as *Space Invaders* (Silvern & Williamson, 1987), *Centipede* and *Zaxxon* (Anderson & Ford, 1987) were labelled as "violent video games" although arguably such video games would likely illicit little concern from most parents or policy makers today. However, such research was taken very seriously at the time, and many scholars today do not distinguish from the alleged "harm" done by games such as Centipede as from Grand Theft Auto. For instance during the recent Brown v EMA Supreme Court case in the United States (2011) the fact that some scholars asserted that the harmful effects of games such as Centipede did not differ from ultraviolent games (or poignantly, Bugs Bunny cartoons) was all but ridiculed by the majority decision of the court. However at the time of these primitive games, no less than the Surgeon General of the United States, C. Everett Koop, claimed that video games were one of the leading causes of family violence (Cooper & Mackie, 1986).

So the concept of a "violent video game" has itself been a slippery one over time. Today most people would likely scoff at the idea that Centipede or Zaxxon constituted "harmful" games. However the increasing sophistication of video game technology has allowed video game producers to progressively ramp up the gore, potentially perpetuating new concerns about video games even as old ones may have seemed absurd.

Violence in educational games itself is nothing particularly new. The famous math game "math blasters" for instance was technically a "violent"

video game by the definitions of scholars at the time although of course a very mild one. But such content in educational games has always been controversial as well, since such games may be used for young audiences.

Interest in using video games in education has been expanding since the time of Math Blasters (Annetta, 2010). There are multiple reasons for this. First there is the simple observation that video games draw in attention and thus may serve as useful platforms for education. Indeed advocates for the notion of *gamification* (e.g. McGonigal, 2011) suggest that real-life social tasks such as school or work should be remade so as to resemble video games in regards to reward structure. Simply using video games would fit well within such a structure. Given that almost all children now play at least some video games (Lenhart et al., 2008) the appeal to using video games in education is rather obvious. Similarly, given that violent video games are particularly popular among boys (Kutner & Olson, 2008) and boys tend to lag behind girls in regards to educational achievement, the appeal in using violent video games is also apparent.

A second issue is the observation that students of today are going to need to be increasingly proficient in new technology in order to succeed in the evolving job market (Schrader & Lawless, 2011). This does not necessarily mean there is a large market for video game players of course (although those of us who do research on video games are happy there is a market at all!) but that video games and computers may provide one particular platform for building technical knowledge.

As one remarkable example of a working serious game, *Re-Mission* is a game which has been used in health psychology with such success it has been singled out by President Obama as a positive use of technology for education. A third-person shooter game, *Re-Mission* improved self-efficacy, cancer knowledge, and treatment adherence in teen and young adult cancer patients (Kato, Cole, Bradlyn, & Pollock, 2008). In the game *Re-Mission* players play as a microscopic female robot who is injected into the bodies of cancer patients and blasts cancer cells and infections with a variety of weapons. Arguably the game succeeds because it presents a lively action-oriented platform that holds players' attention, allowing the educational components of the game greater opportunity for impact. *Re-Mission* takes advantage of the existing, popular first-person shooter format and applies this format for a pro-social purpose.

It might be reasonable to ask whether a non-violent game would not be just as successful. Indeed, violence in a game is probably tangential to any educational content (except perhaps in military or police simulators). However, the strategic nature of using violent games for educational purposes is in drawing in video game audiences who intrinsically prefer violent games. Given that boys particularly seem to prefer violent games (Lenhart et al., 2008; Olson, 2010; Olson, Kutner, Warner et al., 2007), ignoring the use of this medium out of hand may be shortsighted. To be direct, educational games are inherently at a disadvantage regarding the time demands of potential child and teen players, vis-à-vis commercial games. To refuse to incorporate design elements that make commercial games successful, at times including violence, places educational games at further disadvantage.

Not surprisingly, given the controversy over violent video games, there have been many educational games that have been developed with minimal violent content (e.g. Lim, 2008; United Nations World Food Program, 2008). Those that include violence such as *Re-Mission* tend to include relatively mild levels of violence. Both non-violent and mildly violent educational games have demonstrated short-term efficacy for specific educational goals in controlled settings (Asakawa & Gilbert, 2003; Reiber, Smith, & Noah, 1998), yet little research has expanded outcomes to longer-term, global, and ecologically valid results. It is not well understood how non-violent games and violent games compare in regards to their potential educational value. One challenge for any

educational video game is that it must complete with commercially available games in a medium where short shelf lives are quite common.

The use of video games directly in educational settings faces several practical constraints, including time commitment limitations and teacher prejudices against video games (Rice, 2007 see also Ceranoglu, 2010 for a discussion of similar issues in play therapy). However, the use of violent video games in informal settings may also promote some cognitive development, although this is usually an unintended element of game play. For instance research in this area has typically focused on *World of Warcraft* (WoW) a MMORPG that has enjoyed an unusually long active life. WoW is a fantasy role-playing game with violent content, for which many players actively participate in message boards and blogs related to the game (Barnett & Coulson, 2010). There has been speculation about the potential education benefit of WoW for some years (Squire, 2006). Some early research has suggested that WoW may promote reading and writing achievement, including among boys who previously had little interest in such activities (Steinkuehler, in press; Steinkuehler & Duncan, 2008; Steinkuehler & Williams, 2006). Similarly VanDeventer and White (2002) found that children who displayed expertise at mildly violent games were likely to display higher-ordered thinking skills.

There is, thus, a fair amount of scholarship and interest regarding the use of video games in education. However, there has historically been resistance to the inclusion of video games in education as well. It's important to understand the controversies that surrounded video games, particularly those with violence, and how these controversies themselves did more harm than good.

Media Based Moral Panics

Attempts by schools to introduce video games into educational curriculum are often met with controversy and complains by politicians or parents. Curiously, controversies may erupt over video games despite the same schools or libraries teaching or providing children with access to violent literature such as *Lord of the Flies*, *Antigone* or *Heart of Darkness*. Indeed, particularly in later middle and high school grades, youth are increasingly expected to be able to cognitively process and analyze controversial material. Why is it so often assumed that youth are capable of processing controversial material in literature but not in video games?

It helps, perhaps, to understand that all new media go through a cycle called *moral panic* in which new media are blamed for all manner of social ills. Thinking back to our own childhoods it is probably possible to remember such incidents, whether over Rock and Roll, gangsta rap, waltz music, jazz music, Harry Potter, comic books, etc., etc. Many books regularly taught to children in school such as *1984* or *The Adventures of Huckleberry Finn* once experienced attempts to ban them due to presumed harms they might cause (and many books including Huckleberry Finn still endure attempts at banning from school and public libraries). During my day it was Dungeons and Dragons, a role-playing game in which players take on the persona of fantasy characters (D&D as it is called is, in fact, far more interactive than even video games). At the time of its inception there was much hue and cry that D&D might lead to violence, suicide and psychosis in players, claims which ultimately proved to be ephemeral. The moral panic in this case was itself enshrined in the television movie *Mazes and Monsters* in which Tom Hanks plays a college student driven to psychosis by a role playing game based on D&D. Ultimately no evidence emerged that D&D caused any harm and the case of the fears over D&D are now generally regarded as a warning regarding media based moral panics.

In many cases the moral panics may look embarrassing in hindsight. Notions that the Harry Potter series would lead children into Satanism and witchcraft are one such example. Thus, although taken very seriously at the time, moral panics do not need to be grounded in any careful reasoning of the facts regarding actual risk presented by the new media. Indeed the idea that media can cause harm may be discussed as if "common sense" and disconfirmatory evidence simply ignored or repudiated.

The case of comic books in the United States presents a further dramatic example of media based moral panics. By the 1950s comic books involving violence and even gory depictions of decapitations and implied sexual violence had become very common. Not surprisingly such controversial content evoked a strong moral response, particularly given that comic book use was readily associated with children. The panic reached the US congress which held hearings on the topic. By this time some academics had also become mired in claims that comic books could be harmful (e.g. Wertham & Legman, 1948) leading to not only delinquency but also homosexuality (because some comic book characters such as Batman and Robin were apparently living secretly homosexual lifestyles). In the case of comic books, the typical moral panic cycle is typified. Before data is available, politicians and advocates begin making statements of considerable alarm regarding the presumed harmfulness of the media. Once the powerbrokers of society have essentially settled upon the conclusion, they then call for "research" to support the pre-existing conclusion. It is one unfortunate aspect of the social sciences that it is typically not difficult to find some scholars willing to make extreme or exaggerated claims about the harmfulness of some new media. Claims by psychiatrists that comic books were the cause of juvenile delinquency or homosexuality (which in 1950s US were outcomes likely considered on par with each other) are clearly absurd in hindsight, yet the same pattern is identifiable with video games in contemporary times.

Video Game Violence: The Scourge that Was Not

As mentioned earlier, politicians and anti-media advocacy groups had been making alarmist claims about video games long before research caught up with them. Indeed prior to the year 2000, most of the research on video games was inconsistent at best and most scholars acknowledged this (Sherry, 2001). These inconsistent findings cannot be blamed on differing qualities of the video games, as video games of that era included games such as *Street Fighter, Doom,* and *Mortal Kombat,* which were both very bloody and controversial. Scientific discourse about video games changed very suddenly around the year 2000. The Columbine massacre in 1999 in which two youth killed a number of teens and a teacher at their high school may have been one element to add emphasis to this issue in the scientific community. Perhaps more importantly, scholars who had been heavily invested in social cognitive models of aggression which emphasized learning of aggression though violent media began to enter the field. Very quickly these scholars began to inject language indicating far greater certitude about harmful effects than had previously been the norm (e.g. Anderson, 2004; Anderson & Bushman, 2001). Scholars such as these began now to readily invoke school shootings and other examples of violence as anecdotal "evidence" of their causal beliefs, and compare the effects of video game violence to important medical findings such as smoking and lung cancer. It's important to note that the research data had not suddenly changed from one year to the next, rather it was the rhetoric which had changed.

Indeed often those authors' own data remained as inconsistent as previous research had been. As one somewhat "classic" example of this problem, in their experimental study Anderson and Dill (2001) present four aggression outcomes based on the "noise blast" test of aggression (in which participants give another player bursts of non-painful noise as punishment for losing a reaction

time test). Of the four, only one was significant and even this last would not have been significant had proper statistical controls been used. Yet the authors focus on the significant finding and ignore the other three when interpreting their results.

Across the decade of the 2000s a core group of scholars who invested their reputations heavily in the "harm" view increasingly pushed the rhetoric of what video games might do to youth. Thus statements equating video game violence research with smoking or lung cancer, or claiming the military used video games to desensitize soldiers to killing, or that the interactive nature of video games made them more harmful than other media began to circulate, coming even into the public consciousness. Ironically, during this same period more and more research was produced which concluded video games did NOT cause aggression in players (e.g. Adachi & Willoughby, 2011; Colwell & Kato, 2003; Desai et al., 2010; Ferguson et al., 2008; Ferguson, 2001; Kutner & Olson, 2008; von Salisch et al., 2011). This began to push the scholarly community further apart into camps of optimists and pessimists, who disagreed fundamentally.

This polarization of scholars reached its nadir during the Brown v EMA US Supreme Court case. During Brown v EMA the US state of California sought to ban the sale of violent video games to minors. Two sets of scholars filed amicus briefs supporting or opposing California's efforts. During the time the Supreme Court was deliberating, several scholars who signed the brief supporting California (Pollard-Sacks, Bushman, & Anderson, 2011) published an article engaging in little more than ad hominem attacks against their opponents who they attempted to label as having less expertise. The Pollard-Sacks article was later evaluated by independent scholars who were not involved in either amicus brief; the arguments of Pollard-Sacks were deemed to be non-credible and self-serving (Hall, Day & Hall, 2011). As for the Brown v EMA case, the majority opinion of the court also found fault with the "evidence" California tried to use to support its case, largely ridiculing the research as deeply flawed. Ultimately the case was decided against California based both on First Amendment issues as well as lack of research evidence to support the "harm" position.

During the same period it also became increasingly recognized that during the video game epoch, despite increasing sales of video games the majority of which some scholars argued had violent content, youth violence rates cross nationally plummeted to lowest levels in 40 years (see Ferguson, 2010). Figure 1 presents the corresponding data for video game sales and youth violence rates in the United States for the years for which both sets of data were available (childstats.gov, 2012; NPD Group, 2012).

As can be seen, youth violence rates correspond almost perfectly with video game sales, but in the inverse manner expected by the "harm" perspective. As video game sales have increased since the mid-1990s, youth violence rates have decreased precipitously. This is not to say that violent games are responsible for this decline in youth violence of course, rather that this data contradicts the extreme claims of some scholars, politicians and advocates who had attempted to link violent games with youth violence.

The "harm" position gave voice to certain "scientific urban legends" that have since been discredited, but nonetheless continue to be repeated. That, in essence, is the definition of a scientific urban legend, an urban legend which is presented as a scientific fact and continues to be repeated despite having actually been discredited in the scientific literature. Several of these commonly reported but false urban legends are discussed next. For some claims the origin is clearer than for others, but all have been unfortunately repeated within the scholarly community.

Perhaps the first of the video game urban legends was the belief violent games were "linked" with school shooting incidents. This was a com-

Figure 1. Video game sales and youth violence rates in the United States

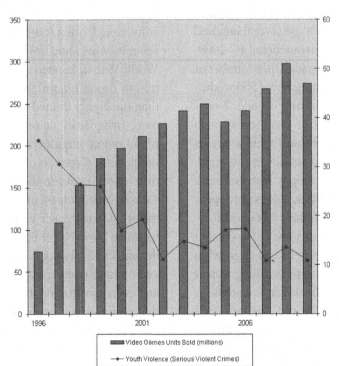

mon refrain following the 1999 Columbine High Massacre, indulged regularly by politicians and pressure groups. Unfortunately, some scholars also joined in this litany, making claims that many school shootings were "linked" to violent games (e.g. Anderson, 2004). Of course almost all young men play violent games at least occasionally so making such "links" are not difficult. Despite that older adults commit as many if not more mass shootings as teenagers, it is interesting to observe that the issue of violent games never arises when an older adult commits mass homicide (tenure was the boogeyman in the recent case of a female biology professor in Alabama). The supposed video game link was laid to rest in 2002 by the US Secret Service, which found no evidence for such a link. Yet it continues to be resurrected.

Another curious and somewhat apocryphal claim was the statistic that 3500 studies of media violence existed as far back as the late 1990s, with only 18 not finding evidence for harmful effects. This statistic was repeated by no less than the American Academy of Pediatrics (AAP; Cook, 2000), although it has since been revealed as utterly false and of uncertain origin (Freedman, 2002). There appear in fact to be several hundred studies with wildly divergent outcomes. By 2009, the AAP had quietly downgraded then number of studies to 2000, not explaining how 1500 studies had vanished in the intervening decade. Nonetheless, the quoted number of 2000 studies also appears to be in error, with most meta-analyses finding only a few hundred studies in this field. Given the AAP has been so sloppy with as basic a figure as the number of studies, it does not appear they have been careful with their fact checking.

Arguably more pernicious is the argument that the effects of video game violence on aggression are similar to those for smoking and lung cancer or similar medical effects (Bushman & Anderson, 2001). Such a wild claim should have attracted great scrutiny, but instead has been uncritically repeated by politicians and some scholars. Unlike

the school shooting claim, the 3500 studies claim, and the interactivity claim discussed later, the lung cancer urban legend is clearly attributed to Bushman and Anderson (2001) who used some dubious statistics to make this claim. These statistics have since been debunked in the published literature (Block & Crain, 2007; Ferguson, 2009). Nonetheless, politicians and some scholars continue to repeat this claim *without making any mention of the debunking articles*. Of course any comparison between the dubious outcome measures used in most aggression studies and the unquestionable validity of death is fraught with error. However, even taken at face value the two bodies of research and the research results they produce are not remotely similar.

Another common urban legend is that the US military uses video games to desensitize soldiers so that they will kill more reliably. The origins of this particular idea seem to lay with David Grossman (1996), although he references some earlier US Army work comparing the rates at which US soldiers in World War II fired at the enemy with those of modern US infantrymen such as during the first Gulf War. Results indicating that the conscripted, often rudimentarily trained farmers, schoolteachers and lawyers called to duty during World War II, handed a semi-automatic M1 and told to fire at identifiable targets shot less often than the highly trained volunteer career infantrymen, firing fully automatic M-16s while using night-vision goggles and instructed to fire in the general direction of the enemy. With all the differences between the two groups, Grossman focused on the advent of simulations in training as the crucial difference and hence an urban legend has been born. Never mind that the US Army has denied these claims (video games are used for vehicle and team training and decision making and even recruitment, but not desensitization) or that police organizations use similar simulations to *reduce* impulsive "bad" shootings. Nor does it seem to matter that today's youth, consuming far greater amounts of violent games than any past generation possibly could are the least violent youth in 40 years. The sound byte is repeated often, presumably given its emotional appeal.

Lastly I address the claim that the interactivity of video games makes them more harmful than other media. This argument was one basis for California's recent anti-game law. However, though it is often repeated as speculation, by now the evidence is clear that, even taken at face value, media violence research finds no evidence for an increased effect for video games (Ferguson & Kilburn, 2009; Sherry, 2001). Politicians and even some scholars nonetheless repeat this claim ad infinitum, despite that it's long past time to lay it to rest. One gets the sense that the motivation for repeating this belief is that it *must be true* according to those that proposed the theory. Unfortunately the research evidence has not lined up to support it.

Why Did the Scholarly Persist in Anti-Game Claims?

In understanding what went wrong, it helps to deconstruct the social processes that led to the scholarly (and primarily pediatrics and psychology) community's persistence in adhering to the "harm" view of video games even as disconfirmatory evidence rolled in. It is almost certainly not the case that there was any wide-scale intention to misrepresent data; indeed I work from the assumption that even the most alarmist and extreme statements were made in good faith. Rather, the scholarly community fell victim to pre-existing dogma, incentives from society produced by the moral panic, and poor oversight and peer review of alarmist claims. Or put more simply, the scholarly community persisted in making alarmist but incorrect claims because, for a time, the scholarly community had no incentives to do otherwise and, indeed, plenty of incentives to stay the course.

A big part of the issue is that, during a period of moral panic, the social environment can become such as to incentivize and select scholars who are more willing to make extreme and exaggerated claims of harm. When we consider video games, people have a full range of opinions. Some people consider video games to, quite literally, be among the most harmful things ever to happen to children, at least behaviourally. On the other side, some people advocate that the entire society should be rebuilt so as to more closely resemble video games (e.g. McGonigal, 2011) and video games are, therefore, much more a net plus than negative. Scholars are not much different in this respect. The notion that the scholarly community is unified in condemning video games was put to the lie during the US Brown v EMA Supreme Court when nearly equal numbers of scholar signed opposing amicus briefs supporting and condemning efforts to regulate violent video games.

In a moral panic, the society very quickly makes a decision about the truthiness of a particular concern. As noted, with the video game violence issue, politicians and activists were already decrying the great harm caused by violent video games (by which they meant Pac Man, Space Invaders and Zaxxon at that time) before any research existed. Once such an environment has developed, even if we have a range of scholars making a range of claims in good faith, it is very easy for society to pick and choose from among those messages those which best fit with the pre-existing moral panic. New outlets cite research or get quotes only from scholars willing to make the most extreme claims. Grants are of course always easier to get while proclaiming an issue of pressing societal concern. Imagine you were a member of a grant organization deciding whether to give me a million dollars to study the effects of video games. Now if I come to you and say, "I don't think video games do much of anything. They neither harm people nor particularly help them. Can I have a million dollars to study that?" that obviously is not a very effective pitch to convince you to spend a million dollars, possibly of taxpayer money. On the other hand if I claim, "Increasingly evidence suggests that video games lead to youth violence and damage the brains of minors! Can I have a million dollars to study that?" well, now we're talking.

As noted, in almost every past moral panic, it has been possible to find scholars willing to make very extreme claims. In retrospect they often seem almost comical (as will claims about video games in future generations), but were always taken very seriously at the time. They are often joined by professional organizations, who are advocacy organizations of their own, themselves often incentivized to make more extreme rather than careful claims. For instance the American Academy of Pediatrics (AAP) has a history of making extreme claims about media that have been demonstrated to be blatantly wrong when fact checked by other scholars (e.g. Freedman, 2002; Magid, 2011). For instance the AAP's claims of the existence of a 'Facebook depression' have proven to be fantastical (Magid, 2011), and the AAP has made wild, factually incorrect claims about even basic issues such as the number of media violence studies, by which they were off by a factor of 10 (Freedman, 2001).

Many of the claims made by groups such as the AAP were, in fact, authored by committees comprised of scholars who had the most invested in anti-media claims, not representative groups of scholars. Such scholars then turn around and claim that professional groups have backed up their claims, failing to note that they themselves wrote or helped write the statements made by these professional groups, a process called "echo attribution" (Rosen & Davison, 2001). Echo attribution is misleading in that it implies independent verification where none exists.

As advocacy groups, groups such as the AAP and APA may be under their own pressure to identify pressing social problems and offer their own organizations as experts with the potential

to solve those problems. The problem, however, as highlighting these issues as pressing social concerns comes at a credibility cost. That is to say, once groups such as the AAP or APA make extreme claims about the harmfulness of a particular media, it becomes very difficult for them to back away from such claims once the data or research evidence begins to change. Thus professional groups may appear recalcitrant even as the society at large begins to accept that the new media was *not* a pressing social concern and move along to other matters. In this sense, the professional groups and individual scholars who, at one point, had been reinforced for making extreme claims of harm, now are left, in essence, holding the bag, becoming the objects of ridicule and criticism as happened to Dr. Wertham with the comic book panic and which happened to the scientific community as a consequence of Brown v EMA.

Not in My Classroom You Don't

We are probably reaching a point in which the science has tipped back to noting the negligible impact of video games on human behaviour. More bluntly, perhaps, society is probably reaching a point where it recognizes the absurdity of claims regarding the harmfulness of video games, particularly when phrased in their more extreme forms such as in the scientific urban legends listed previously. Nonetheless, some teachers and school administrators may feel some lingering doubts over the utility of video games for educational purposes. Such lingering fears are likely the aftershocks of the video game moral panic particularly (as with the case of the Sacramento Public Library) driven by individuals who are either unfamiliar with video games or do not value them as an entertainment medium.

The work of James Ivory, a communications professor at Virginia Tech is probably illustrative (Ivory, & Kalyanaraman, 2009). Dr. Ivory has found that people tend to be suspicious of violent video games in the abstract. That is to say, when people are asked whether violent video games can contribute to violent behavior, many say they can… so long as they have no exposure to any particular game. Once they are invited to play a particular violent game and then asked if that *particular* game contributes to violent behavior, people are much less likely to endorse such a belief. In other words, much of the fear of violent games stems from unfamiliarity and ignorance of the content of such games. Keeping in mind that much of the scholarly community, political community and activist community constitutes older adults who are less likely to be familiar with video games, and thus more likely to be suspicious of them. Although the declining fear of video games is likely do to many phenomena, not least the absence of relation between video game violence and youth violence in the real world, gamers aging into segments of the "elder elite" of society is likely one factor that extreme claims about their harmfulness are being less common.

As one example of this, following a mass shooting in Norway by Anders Breivik in 2011. Although Breivik claimed to have been motivated mainly by his belief that Muslims were bent on world domination, he created some stir when he claimed to have improved his aim with weapons by training on video games. Although Breivik did not claim video games motivated him to commit homicide, ten years prior this link, however tangential, would have provoked comments among politicians and scholars alike that such claims provided further "evidence" for the harmfulness of video games. By 2011, Breivik's claims were noted, but did not lead to widespread claims that video games were thusly "linked" to violent video games (see Anderson, 2004 for comparison). In fact, the government Australia, which had been moving to introduce an R18+ rating for the most violent video games, expressly declined the invitation to find a link between violent games and violence in the wake of the Breivik shooting (e.g. Moses, 2011).

Nonetheless, it remains possible that past furor over video games, even if subsequently debunked as largely the product of moral panic and poorly construed science, may create blocks for the implementation of video game technology in classrooms. This reluctance may ironically do more harm than good to the extent that a viable pedagogical approach to education is not implemented and youth are not properly prepared for the challenges of an increasingly technological society (Pew Research Center, 2012).

Solutions and Recommendations

Although the moral panic over video games was not created by the scholarly community, the scholarly community bears responsibility for providing the fuel to allow the panic to continue for as long as it did and for giving it a veneer of credibility for a time. Ultimately that veneer of credibility came back to haunt the scholarly community in the form of damage to its own credibility (Hall, Day, & Hall, 2011). As noted before, although certainly well-intentioned, the scholarly community may have been incentivized to identify a "problem" that they could presumably offer a "solution" for in the form of their own expertise. As a consequence, careful peer review and scrutiny of some of the more extreme claims about video games was lacking. This is perhaps most evident in the error-ridden policy statements by the AAP, which fail an even cursory fact checking, but was an endemic problem among scholarly statements in the first decade of the 21st century.

This scenario highlights the need both for greater rigor within the scholarly community and, potentially, a need for reform in the peer-review system. As to the point about rigor, the dogma on video game (and television) effects appears to have been well-identified as the product of a rigid and moralistic scientific ideology (Grimes, Anderson, & Bergen, 2008) that misconstrued some pieces of evidence as more conclusive than they were

(Freedman, 2002) and simply ignored other pieces of disconfirmatory evidence that could not simply be misconstrued (Ferguson, 2010). As observed by Bennerstedt, Ivarsson, and Linderoth (2012), the hypodermic needle approach to video game effects was largely a situation in which the cart was put before the horse. That is to say, scholars began with the conclusion that video games were harmful. They then began construing data to fit the pre-ordained conclusion, rather than carefully and neutrally collecting and interpreting data. This was aided by a wider problem increasingly identified in psychological science broadly of *methodological flexibility* or the ability for social scientists to manipulate (even unconsciously) data analysis techniques so as to get almost any result from a particularly dataset (Lebel & Peters, 2011; Simons et al., 2011). Or put more directly, social science's support of the "harm" view of video games was the product of hard-line ideology coupled with slippery data analysis problems that are endemic to social science.

Related to this is one of the weaknesses of peer-review. Churchill once said of Democracy that democracy is the worst form of government... except for all the other forms of government. The same could be said of the peer-review process. No viable alternative has been raised to peer-review, yet it has weaknesses that must be considered. Chiefly among them, when a particularly field becomes focused on a small number of scholars who are insular and publish together, peer-review can be used to protect their collective ideology, effectively squashing disconfirmatory data, while letting pass poor-quality research from their own insular group. Imagine that scholars A, B, C, and D are all experts in a narrow field, work together, publish together, are close colleagues who share an ideological perspective. At one point in time scholars A and B write a paper together. When it is sent out for peer review it is sent to reviewers C and D...their close colleagues who can probably identify the writing (and in some cases journals do not mask authors anyway). When B and C

later write a paper it is reviewed by A and D, and so on. Later, scholars E and F, who are not part of that consortium write up results challenging the perspective of scholars A, B, C, and D. However, the journal sends it out to those same scholars (A through D) for peer review. Since the new data threatens the perspective in which they have invested their professional reputation, they recommend rejection. This has been a problem for this field, which had been dominated by advocates of hypodermic needle approaches during the mid-2000s. This issue with peer review (and echo attribution as discussed earlier) highlights the need for the scientific community to more carefully monitor statements made by scholars and to solicit a careful, wide range of scholarly opinions before weighing in on controversial issues. Otherwise, the scholarly community may do more damage than good, particularly to their own credibility (Hall, Day, & Hall, 2011).

Outside in the community it likely helps to put current fears of media (whether over video games, social media, or whatever comes next) into a historical context. We know that new media typically go through a cycle of moral panic with exaggerated claims by politicians and scholars that often appear comical with the benefit of hindsight (Ferguson, 2010). As the maxim goes, failing to understand history makes us doomed to repeat it. It may help for people in the community, including leaders in education, to understand that new media are likely to be greeted with exaggerated claims of their harmfulness (and even some apparent scholarship to that effect, although often of poor quality). Leaders in education would do well to take a cautious stance when presented with such claims, knowing they have proven to be ephemeral so often in the past. This does not mean it is impossible for any media to have any effect on behaviour. Advertising seems to genuinely influence children's food choices for instance (Ferguson, Munoz & Medrano, 2012). One of the interesting research questions to explore in the near future is why advertising is able to influence us, whereas fictional media does not. Are there different mechanisms at play? Does advertising circumvent "fiction detectors" in our brain we use to not be influenced by fantastical stories?

Thus, in equal measure, the solution to the problems of the video game controversies is for the scholarly community to exhibit far greater caution in the analysis of data and in public communications regarding that data and far greater scepticism on the part of the general public when presented with alarmist claims about media and supposed effects. Or put another way, both the scholarly community and general public need to be more vigilant about alarmist claims and learn from the mistakes of the past.

FUTURE RESEARCH DIRECTIONS

As for future research directions, I offer three main thoughts. First, I observe that inevitably research will shift away from video games onto newer media. As hinted at earlier in this chapter, it seems evident that Facebook and other social media outlets are next in the crosshairs. The "Facebook depression" debacle (Magid, 2011) already serves as a warning that we have to be careful about the potential for moral panics regarding this new media as well (Feinstein et al., 2012). Thus examining the influence of social media on youth will likely be the immediate next media related research direction, and our first opportunity to apply caution to how we examine these influences. Unfortunately, if the statements by the AAP are an indication, it appears the scholarly community is disinclined to take seriously lessons from the past.

Second, an intriguing avenue for research would be in examining the "fiction detectors" that develop in children's brains and how these are used to process media messages. As noted prior advertising effects appear to be very different from fictional media. It is probably time to abandon notions that all media should be treated similarly, with all media potentially having effects on consumers (this was one criticism of

the field by the US Supreme Court in Brown v EMA). Research indicates that children begin to distinguish fantasy from reality messages early on in life (Wooley and van Reet, 2006). Thus, it would be fruitful for research to consider how media influences children at different ages and how children's brains process certain media messages and disregard some as fictional. Further examining how advertising may function to circumvent these "fiction detectors" would also be worthwhile.

Lastly, I suggest that the time has come to move away from hypodermic needle models of media effects (Gill, 2012) including social cognitive theories in favour of those that examine more active consumer participation in media as well as more subtle potential effects for media use. Chief among these is the "uses and gratifications" approach to media use (Sherry et al., 2006) which suggests, briefly, that media consumers actively select media to consume based on what they hope to get from it. From such a perspective, the media consumer is far more active in guiding media selection, quite possibly with a particular emotional or motivational goal already in mind. This view is consistent with Self-Determination Theory in psychology (Przybylski, Rigby, & Ryan, 2010) which suggests media consumers use media to meet basic human motivations or the Catalyst Model (Ferguson et al., 2008) which suggests that biological predispositions and early life events shape personality and personality shapes media preferences. I submit that use of these more sophisticated theoretical models, replacing social cognitive models, will help in providing a more nuanced and valid science of media effects, while subsequently avoiding some of the common ideologically based errors of the past.

CONCLUSION

In closing, the current chapter examined the phenomenon of educator's potential reluctance to use video games in the classroom as well as the potential origins of this reluctance. As discussed, a combination of societal moral panic and poor quality science allowed for the promulgation of alarmist claims about video games, claims which have failed to materialize. The time has come to set these claims aside and examine ways in which video games may provide positive platforms for educational content.

REFERENCES

Adachi, P. C., & Willoughby, T. (2011). The effect of video game competition and violence on aggressive behavior: Which characteristic has the greatest influence? *Psychology Of Violence, 1*(4), 259–274. doi:10.1037/a0024908.

Anderson, C. (2004). An update on the effects of playing violent video games. *Journal of Adolescence, 27*, 113–122. doi:10.1016/j.adolescence.2003.10.009 PMID:15013264.

Anderson, C., & Dill, K. (2000). Video games and aggressive thoughts, feelings and behavior in the laboratory and in life. *Journal of Personality and Social Psychology, 78*, 772–790. doi:10.1037/0022-3514.78.4.772 PMID:10794380.

Anderson, C., & Ford, C. (1987). Affect of the game player: Short term effects of highly and mildly aggressive video games. *Personality and Social Psychology Bulletin, 12*(4), 390–402. doi:10.1177/0146167286124002.

Anderson, C. A., & Bushman, B. J. (2001). Effects of violent video games on aggressive behavior, aggressive cognition, aggressive affect, physiological arousal, and prosocial behavior: A meta-analytic review of the scientific literature. *Psychological Science, 12*(5), 353–359. doi:10.1111/1467-9280.00366 PMID:11554666.

Annetta, L. (2010). The "I's" have it: A framework for serious educational game design. *Review of General Psychology, 14*(2), 105–112. doi:10.1037/a0018985.

Bennerstedt, U., Ivarsson, J., & Linderoth, J. (2012). How gamers manage aggression: Situating skills in collaborative computer games. *Computer Supported Collaborative Learning, 7*, 43–61. doi:10.1007/s11412-011-9136-6.

Block, J., & Crain, B. (2007). Omissions and errors in media violence and the American public. *The American Psychologist, 62*, 252–253. doi:10.1037/0003-066X.62.3.252 PMID:17469907.

Brown v EMA. (2011). *Website.* Retrieved 7/1/11 from http://www.supremecourt.gov/opinions/10pdf/08-1448.pdf

Bushman, B., & Anderson, C. (2001). Media violence and the American public. *The American Psychologist, 56*, 477–489. doi:10.1037/0003-066X.56.6-7.477 PMID:11413871.

Ceranoglu, T. (2010). Video games in psychotherapy. *Review of General Psychology, 14*(2), 141–146. doi:10.1037/a0019439.

Childstats.gov. (2012). *America's children: Key national indicators of wellbeing.* Retrieved 9/26/12 from http://www.childstats.gov/americaschildren/beh.asp

Colwell, J., & Kato, M. (2003). Investigation of the relationship between social isolation, self-esteem, aggression and computer game play in Japanese adolescents. *Asian Journal of Social Psychology, 6*, 149–158. doi:10.1111/1467-839X.t01-1-00017.

Cook, D. (2000). *Testimony of the American academy of pediatrics on media violence before the U.S. senate commerce committee.* Elk Grove Village, IL: American Academy of Pediatrics. Retrieved from http://www.aap.org/advocacy/releases/mediaviolencetestimony.pdf

Cooper, J., & Mackie, D. (1986). Video games and aggression in children. *Journal of Applied Social Psychology, 16*, 726–744. doi:10.1111/j.1559-1816.1986.tb01755.x.

Desai, R., Krishnan-Sarin, S., Cavallo, D., & Potenza, M. (2010). Video-gaming among high school students: health correlates, gender differences, and problematic gaming. *Pediatrics, 126*(6), e1414–e1424. doi:10.1542/peds.2009-2706 PMID:21078729.

Durkin, K. (2010). Videogames and young people with developmental disorders. *Review of General Psychology, 14*(2), 122–140. doi:10.1037/a0019438.

Feinstein, B. A., Bhatia, V., Hershenberg, R., & Davila, J. (2012). Another venue for problematic interpersonal behavior: The effects of depressive and anxious symptoms on social networking experience. *Journal of Social and Clinical Psychology, 31*(4), 356–382. doi:10.1521/jscp.2012.31.4.356.

Ferguson, C. J. (2009). Is psychological research really as good as medical research? Effect size comparisons between psychology and medicine. *Review of General Psychology, 13*(2), 130–136. doi:10.1037/a0015103.

Ferguson, C. J. (2010). Blazing angels or resident evil? Can violent video games be a force for good? *Review of General Psychology, 14*(2), 68–81. doi:10.1037/a0018941.

Ferguson, C. J. (2011). Video games and youth violence: A prospective analysis in adolescents. *Journal of Youth and Adolescence, 40*(4), 377–391. doi:10.1007/s10964-010-9610-x PMID:21161351.

Ferguson, C. J., Munoz, M. E., & Medrano, M. R. (2012). Advertising influences on young children's food choices are only marginally reduced by parental influence: A randomized controlled experiment. *The Journal of Pediatrics, 160*(3), 452–455. doi:10.1016/j.jpeds.2011.08.023 PMID:21983204.

Ferguson, C. J., Rueda, S., Cruz, A., Ferguson, D., Fritz, S., & Smith, S. (2008). Violent video games and aggression: Causal relationship or by-product of family violence and intrinsic violence motivation? *Criminal Justice and Behavior, 35*, 311–332. doi:10.1177/0093854807311719.

Grossman, D. (1996). *On killing: The psychological cost of learning to kill in war and society.* Boston, MA: Back Bay Books.

Group, N. P. D. (2012). *Research shows $2.88 billion spent on video game content in the US for second quarter, 2012.* Retrieved 9/26/12 from https://www.npd.com/wps/portal/npd/us/news/press-releases/pr_120809/

Hall, R., Day, T., & Hall, R. (2011). Reply to Murray et al. (2011) and Ferguson (2011). *Mayo Clinic Proceedings, 86*(6), 821–823. doi:10.4065/mcp.2011.0357.

Ivory, J., & Kalyanaraman, S. (2009). Video games make people violent - Well, maybe not that game: Effects of content and person abstraction on perceptions of violent video games' effects and support of censorship. *Communication Reports, 22*(1), 1–12. doi:10.1080/08934210902798536.

Kato, P., Cole, S., Bradlyn, A., & Pollock, B. (2008). A video game improves behavioral outcomes in adolescents and young adults with cancer: A randomized trial. *Pediatrics, 122,* e305-e317. Retrieved 10/6/08 from http://pediatrics.aappublications.org/cgi/content/full/122/2/e305

Kutner, L., & Olson, C. (2008). *Grand theft childhood: The surprising truth about violent video games and what parents can do.* New York, NY: Simon & Schuster.

LeBel, E. P., & Peters, K. R. (2011). Fearing the future of empirical psychology: Bem's (2011) evidence of psi as a case study of deficiencies in modal research practice. *Review of General Psychology, 15*(4), 371–379. doi:10.1037/a0025172.

Lenhart, A., Kahne, J., Middaugh, E., MacGill, A., Evans, C., & Mitak, J. (2008). *Teens, video games and civics: Teens gaming experiences are diverse and include significant social interaction and civic engagement.* Retrieved 10/2/08 from http://www.pewinternet.org/PPF/r/263/report_display.asp

Lim, Q. (2008). Global citizenship education, school curriculum and games: Learning mathematics, English and science as a global citizen. *Computers & Education, 51*, 1073–1093. doi:10.1016/j.compedu.2007.10.005.

Magic, L. (2011). *Facebook depression: A nonexistent condition.* Retrieved 5/20/12 from http://www.huffingtonpost.com/larry-magid/facebook-depression-nonexistent_b_842733.html

McGonigal, J. (2011). *Reality is broken: Why games make us better and how they can change the world.* New York, NY: Penguin Press.

Moses, A. (2011). *From fantasy to lethal reality: Breivik trained on modern warfare game.* Retrieved 5/22/12 from http://m.smh.com.au/digital-life/games/from-fantasy-to-lethal-reality-breivik-trained-on-modern-warfare-game-20110725-1hw41.html

Olson, C., Kutner, L., Warner, D., Almerigi, J., Baer, L., Nicholi, A., & Beresin, E. (2007). Factors correlated with violent video game use by adolescent boys and girls. *The Journal of Adolescent Health, 41*, 77–83. doi:10.1016/j.jadohealth.2007.01.001 PMID:17577537.

Olson, C. K. (2010). Children's motivations for video game play in the context of normal development. *Review of General Psychology, 14*(2), 180–187. doi:10.1037/a0018984.

Pew Research Center. (2012). *Digital divides and bridges: Technology use among youth.* Retrieved 5/22/12 from http://pewinternet.org/Presentations/2012/Apr/Digital-Divides-and-Bridges-Technology-Use-Among-Youth.aspx

Pollard Sacks, D., Bushman, B. J., & Anderson, C. A. (2011). Do violent video games harm children? Comparing the scientific amicus curiae "experts" in Brown v. Entertainment Merchants Association. *Northwestern University Law Review: Colloquy, 106*, 1-12.

Przybylski, A. K., Rigby, C. S., & Ryan, R. M. (2010). A motivational model of video game engagement. *Review of General Psychology, 14*(2), 154–166. doi:10.1037/a0019440.

Rice, J. (2007). New media resistance: Barriers to implementation of computer video games in the classroom. *Journal of Educational Multimedia and Hypermedia, 16*, 249–261.

Rosen, G. M., & Davison, G. C. (2001). Echo attributions and other risks when publishing on novel therapies without peer review. *Journal of Clinical Psychology, 57*(10), 1245–1250. doi:10.1002/jclp.1092 PMID:11526612.

Schrader, P. G., & Lawless, K. A. (2011). Research on immersive environments and 21st century skills: An introduction to the special issue. *Journal of Educational Computing Research, 44*(4), 385–390. doi:10.2190/EC.44.4.a.

Sherry, J. (2001). The effects of violent video games on aggression: A meta-analysis. *Human Communication Research, 27*, 409–431.

Sherry, J. L., Lucas, K., Greenberg, B. S., & Lachlan, K. (2006). Video game uses and gratifications as predicators of use and game preference. In Vorderer, P., Bryant, J., Vorderer, P., & Bryant, J. (Eds.), *Playing Video Games: Motives, Responses, and Consequences* (pp. 213–224). Hoboken, NJ: Lawrence Erlbaum.

Silvern, S. B., & Williamson, P. A. (1987). The effects of video game play on young children's aggression, fantasy and prosocial behavior. *Journal of Applied Developmental Psychology, 8,* 453–462. doi:10.1016/0193-3973(87)90033-5.

Simmons, J. P., Nelson, L. D., & Simonsohn, U. (2011). False-positive psychology: Undisclosed flexibility in data collection and analysis allows presenting anything as significant. *Psychological Science, 22*(11), 1359–1366. doi:10.1177/0956797611417632 PMID:22006061.

Squire, K. D. (2006). From content to context: Videogames as designed experience. *Educational Researcher, 35,* 19–29. doi:10.3102/0013189X035008019.

Steinkuehler, C., & Duncan, S. (2008). Scientific habits of mind in virtual worlds. *Journal of Science Education and Technology.* doi:10.1007/s10956-008-9120-8.

Steinkuehler, C., & Williams, D. (2006). Where everybody knows your (screen) name: Online games as "third places". *Journal of Computer-Mediated Communication, 11*(4). doi:10.1111/j.1083-6101.2006.00300.x.

Steinkuehler, C. A. (2013). Cognition and literacy in massively multiplayer online games. In Leu, D., Coiro, J., Lankshear, C., & Knobel, K. (Eds.), *Handbook of Research on New Literacies.* Mahwah, NJ: Erlbaum.

United Nations World Food Program. (2008). *Food force.* Retrieved 10/7/08 from http://www.food-force.com/

VanDeventer, S., & White, J. (2002). Expert behavior in children's video game play. *Simulation & Gaming, 33*(1), 28–48. doi:10.1177/1046878 102033001002.

von Salisch, M., Vogelgesang, J., Kristen, A., & Oppl, C. (2011). Preference for violent electronic games and aggressive behavior among children: The beginning of the downward spiral? *Media Psychology, 14*(3), 233–258. doi:10.1080/1521 3269.2011.596468.

Wertham, F., & Legman, G. (1948). The psychopathology of comic books. *American Journal of Psychotherapy, 2*(3), 472–490. PMID:18883856.

Woolley, J., & Van Reet, J. (2006). Effects of context on judgments concerning the reality status of novel entities. *Child Development, 77,* 1778–1793. doi:10.1111/j.1467-8624.2006.00973.x PMID:17107460.

ADDITIONAL READING

Ferguson, C. J. (in press). Violent video games and the Supreme Court: Lessons for the scientific community in the wake of Brown v EMA. *The American Psychologist.*

Ferguson, C. J., Garza, A., Jerabeck, J., Ramos, R., & Galindo, M. (in press). Not worth the fuss after all? Cross-sectional and prospective data on violent video game influences on aggression, visuospatial cognition and mathematics ability in a sample of youth. *Journal of Youth and Adolescence.* PMID:22875464.

Ferguson, C. J., & Heene, M. (in press). A vast graveyard of undead theories: Publication bias and psychological science's aversion to the null. *Perspectives on Psychological Science.*

Grimes, T., Anderson, J., & Bergen, L. (2008). *Media violence and aggression: Science and ideology.* Thousand Oaks, CA: Sage.

Gunter, W. D., & Daly, K. (2012). Causal or spurious: Using propensity score matching to detangle the relationship between violent video games and violent behavior. *Computers in Human Behavior, 28*(4), 1348–1355. doi:10.1016/j.chb.2012.02.020.

Hall, R., Day, T., & Hall, R. (2011). A plea for caution: Violent video games, the supreme court, and the role of science. *Mayo Clinic Proceedings, 86*(4), 315–321. doi:10.4065/mcp.2010.0762 PMID:21454733.

Lancet. (2008). Is exposure to media violence a public health risk? *Lancet, 371,* 1137. doi:10.1016/S0140-6736(08)60495-X PMID:18395556.

Nature. (2003). A calm view of video violence. *Nature, 424,* 355.

Ramos, R. A., Ferguson, C. J., Frailing, K., & Romero-Ramirez, M. (in press). Comfortably numb or just yet another movie? Media violence exposure does not reduce viewer empathy for victims of real violence among primarily Hispanic viewers. *Psychology of Popular Media Culture.*.

Sherry, J. (2007). Violent video games and aggression: Why can't we find links? In Preiss, R., Gayle, B., Burrell, N., Allen, M., & Bryant, J. (Eds.), *Mass Media Effects Research: Advances Through Meta-Analysis* (pp. 231–248). Mahwah, NJ: L. Erlbaum.

Section 2
Authoring, Control, and Evaluation in Serious Games for Education

Chapter 4
Authoring of Serious Games for Education

Florian Mehm
Technische Universität Darmstadt, Germany

Christian Reuter
Technische Universität Darmstadt, Germany

Stefan Göbel
Technische Universität Darmstadt, Germany

ABSTRACT

Serious Games (SG) place requirements on all members of a development team, from the designers and domain experts to artists and programmers. In order to support the collaborative work required in serious game production, authoring tools can be introduced in the development process. They allow members of the team to work in one common environment and to have one uniform vision of the project, as opposed to a work environment in which each group uses some software tools exclusively and multiple visions of the finished game do exist simultaneously. Presenting a range of examples including the authoring framework StoryTec, the use of authoring tools for the development of SG is explained in this chapter.

INTRODUCTION

The development of games as well as Serious Games is cost-intensive and requires a development team with a range of different skills. For the development of SG this includes the expertise of subject matter experts and pedagogues in addition to game designers, content producers and game programmers. Research aspects include mechanisms to support authors (domain experts such as teachers, coaches and trainers as well as game designer and game developer) in the collaborative, interdisciplinary authoring and development process and to enable personalization and adaptation

DOI: 10.4018/978-1-4666-3673-6.ch004

of single and multiplayer scenarios considering the characteristics of individual users (players, learners) and user groups (e.g. a school class).

Whereas this chapter concentrates on the authoring process, the next chapter focuses on personalisation and adaptation issues of SG. The mechanisms and research and technology development principles are presented in the context of the best-practice examples (projects) 80Days (EU, FP7, Technology-enhanced Learning—providing a single player learning experience for geography) and StoryTec (technology transfer project in the field of authoring SG funded by the State of Hesse in the frame of the LOEWE program for economic and scientific excellence).

BACKGROUND

The development of a SG in general is similar to the development of a regular entertainment digital game, with the additional challenges of providing appropriate content for the game's serious purpose. Traditional roles found in game development include game designers, who are tasked with setting up the game's story, game world, characters, and gameplay. Technicians, i.e. game programmers and associated roles, are then tasked with creating the technical infrastructure of the game and realizing the gameplay, while artists (graphical artists, sound artists, etc.) create the necessary assets such as 3D models, images, or sounds for the game. Finally, the game's quality is assured by game testers (typical gamers testing the functionality, feasibility, usability, and user/game experience) before being released.

In the creation and testing of a SG, the previously user groups receive new tasks and simultaneously new groups are added. This already indicates the increased complexity compared to entertainment-only games. The development team is augmented with domain experts, who introduce specialized knowledge about the target domain, as well as – in the case of digital educa-

tion games – pedagogues in order to establish an educational design of the game. Common tasks for these groups include the creation of exercises or exercise pools, whereby in practice commonly general purpose tools are used for the creation and dissemination of the created content to the rest of the team. Further, the subject matter experts are responsible to check the content-related correctness and the fulfillment of intended goals beyond entertainment before deployment of the SG.

The core game development team, as mentioned before, also receives more tasks as compared to the development of an entertainment-only game. Since one major purpose of the SG is the presentation of domain-or purpose-specific content, the game design has to be adjusted for this, either by providing possibilities for placing this content in the game or by adapting the gameplay itself in such a way as to be beneficial to the SG's purpose. An example for the former could be an adventure game placing educational content in the dialogue with a character, while an example for the latter is a physics game involving actual simulated physics-based puzzles the player has to solve by means of interacting with a simulation.

It is necessary to closely link the content production and programming of the game with the serious purpose. The art production has to be managed to create assets which conform to the content of the game, and programming tasks have to be carried out keeping the serious aspect of the game in view by providing the necessary features.

Authoring Frameworks for Serious Games

SG Authoring Frameworks for interactive experiences might be placed in the middle ground between Authoring Tools in the eLearning field and the tools used by professional game developers (See Figure 1). E-Learning Authoring Tools are in place at a multitude of educational institutions as well as companies, and can be used to create educational courses which are presented to users

Figure 1. Left: the interface of the hot potatoes e-learning authoring tool; right: the graphical user interface of the unity 3D game editor

for example via the internet as Web-Based Training. An overview of tools is given in (Horton & Horton, 2003). This category also encompasses tools such as the docendo LCMS (http://www.docendo.org/) developed at TU Darmstadt, which are used for non-interactive content or content with very little and clearly structured interaction such as multiple choice quizzes. In the latter category, we find specialized and complex game engines and associated tools/editors.

Authoring Tools for SG offer additional instruments with regard to the purpose of the game to be created. For example, Authoring Tools for educational games can provide specialized functionality for building the knowledge transported by the game or for assisting in the instructional design of the game. In the field of SG for Health, doctors and therapists are supported to create and configure training programs for prevention and rehabilitation.

Game authoring and production tools are often of commercial nature. These tools can be sorted into a spectrum ranging from very complete tools which allow the creation of any kind of game (for example, the Unity game creation suite, see http://www.unity3d.org) to tools linked to one genre (e.g. Adventure Game Studio for adventure games, see http://www.adventuregamestudio.co.uk) or even

only one game (for example the Portal 2 in-game editor, http://www.thinkwithportals.com/blog.php?id=7853&p=1), which are typically more restrictive. On the academic side, the e-Adventure system (Torrente, del Blanco, Marchiori, Moreno-Ger, & Fernandez-Manjón, 2008) represents a scientific approach for authoring Story-based digital educational games.

Another area interlinked with the creation of interactive experiences is the field of Interactive Storytelling, where systems provide users with renditions of stories and allow them to alter the course of the presented story. Of importance to the research undertaken in authoring related to storytelling (especially in the multiplayer experience environment) are the findings of the IRIS Network of Excellence (Cavazza, Champagnat, & Leonardi, 2009) which has the study of authoring systems for interactive storytelling as one of its core objectives (see overview of authoring tools from Interactive Storytelling at http://iris.interactive-storytelling.de/AuthoringToolDescriptions).

Integrating the beneficial aspects of eLearning Authoring Tools such as the clean separation between content and presentation and the structured process of authoring with the highly interactive nature of computer games requires efforts in several directions.

Visual Programming Support for Authors without Programming Skills

Since Authoring Frameworks as described prior are aimed at non-technicians, the use of complicated concepts such as programming languages has to be avoided. Instead, one can turn towards alternative approaches such as natural language-inspired programming languages such as the authoring language Inform 7 for interactive fiction or visual programming languages as that used in the storytelling editor "Storytelling Alice" (See left part of Figure 2). Instead of a programming language, the Authoring Tool StoryTec (Göbel, Mehm, & Wendel, 2012; Mehm, 2010) (see also dedicated section) utilizes visual approaches to authoring in several key areas (See Figure 2, right part). The structure of the game (i.e. the individual scenes in the game) is edited in the form of a graph, with boxes representing scenes and arrows representing the transitions between scenes. Instead of using a programming language, authors can set up the interactions and events in the game by using a visual programming approach, which is realized by a branching tree structure.

In principle, an Authoring Framework is required to give various user groups access to the contents of the games to be developed. These user groups can all be characterized as non-professional game developers with different background knowledge (programming languages, multimedia skills, teaching experience) and different time constraints for their work. This leads to the requirement of providing different means to work with an Authoring Tool for this purpose. On the lower end, this can result in an authoring process where an author can only fill out open fields, for example for integrating a video or text into a multimedia presentation. For this task, templates/metadata formats will be developed which can be used to create simple presentations. This – basically Web-based – approach for authoring can be used by persons only able to invest a minimal amount of time for learning about the Authoring Tool. On the other hand, persons able to invest more time can use a less restricted interface to the Authoring Tool, resulting in more freedom for creativity and more interactivity in the resulting game or presentation. As a result of different access for different authoring groups, collaborative authoring is supported and encouraged, as each user group has a way of working with the framework in the way benefitting their role and their connections with other users/author groups best (Mehm, Hardy, Göbel, & Steinmetz, 2011).

Figure 2. Visual programming approaches: left: the storytelling alice tool with the visual programming language approach visible; right: the visual programming model of StoryTec

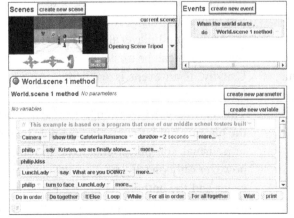
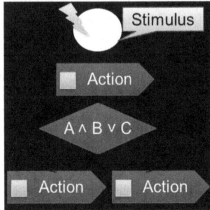

Authoring Template Mechanisms and Encapsulation of Functionality

A major aspect that can be exploited for providing both authoring approaches described previously is the separation between the game's implementation or presentation and the content of the game, leading to a level of abstraction for the authors. This means that the intricacies of digital games are hidden from the user, who is only tasked with configuring the game itself. Furthermore, this increases the extensibility of the system. Simple changes to authored experiences are possible directly in the authoring tool. More complex changes such as the provision of new templates for authors can be made centrally in the authoring framework and are subsequently available to all authors.

This concept is similar to the definition of Frame Games (Stolovitch & Thiagarajan, 1980), which refer to games in which the structure of the game (e.g. rules, level concept) can be separated from the content, thereby allowing the introduction of different content into the same game. Game templates as described before can be realized by utilizing the Component-Based Software Engineering paradigm. An example for this in the case of interactive simulations in eLearning can be seen in the work of El Saddik (2001). Such game templates can provide detailed information about their use, ranging from providing descriptions about the possible means to integrate content (e.g. fields for images, videos etc.) to the provision of wizard dialogues which lead the author through the correct usage of the game template (Zimmermann, Rensing, & Steinmetz, 2008). Similar to this, StoryTec was recently extended in order to support additional minigame-components (Mehm, Göbel, & Steinmetz, 2011).

Authoring Multiplayer Serious Games

Another dimension implying further requirements does exist with respect to the Authoring of multiplayer games. Hereby, the major challenge is that the players interact among themselves, which lies outside of the author's control. On the one side this increases the so called *narrative paradox* – the conflict between the story tightly defined by an author and the freedom of the players' actions (Louchart & Aylett, 2003). But since every player is an active entity, which may act at any given moment in time, further problems may arise (Zagal, Nussbaum, & Rosas, 2000). It is possible that players create conflicts even between themselves, i.e. when they try to drag the same object in different directions. In this case there have to be available clearly defined rules on how the game will react. This question is even more important on a story level, if the players are able to influence the course of the narrative (see section on Personalized, Adaptive Digital Educational Games using Narrative Game-based Learning Objects). Here the author can choose to regulate decision finding, for example by providing a voting mechanism. Another approach would let the players shape their social skills by trusting on their ability to decide based on discussion without external help. Respecting each player's preferences in the case of conflicting choices however is not possible in this case.

These players may be also differently skilled. This is especially relevant in SG with learning content, where the players might have varying pre-existing knowledge and may even represent different learning types. Regardless, every player in a group should be equally challenged without missing some learning content or distributing effort unevenly (Zagal, Rick, & Hsi, 2006).

Adding multiplayer also violates some assumptions, which can be made in single player games. Usually, if an event is triggered at a specified location, the player must be located at this place. This can be used to change something outside the player's field of view, for example the arrival of a virtual non-player character. In multiplayer however only one player may have triggered the event and the author has to take extra measures to make either sure that all other players are there as well or explicitly check where each player is located in this moment. This is easily overlooked by authors who use this assumption regularly and are not familiar with creating multiplayer games. Therefore this case is an appropriate application for support by authoring tools.

The complexity of authoring games is also increased immensely, when multiple players are involved. Let's take the possibilities on how the player(s) can be located in a world consisting of m rooms as a simple example. While there are m possible states in a single player game, in a multiplayer game there are m^n possibilities for n players. Since the author must respect each possible state and make sure that the game works under each condition, creating a multiplayer game is much more complex. It would be beneficial if some of this complexity could be reduced by automatically checking if every possibility was respected in the author's scripts or by even generating new ones based on a blueprint given by the author.

Finally, testing the game becomes also more difficult, since the author cannot start the game by himself and simply start playing. Instead he needs some additional players to test how the game reacts when others are involved or, depending on the type of game, even has to set up a network connection between multiple instances of the application.

Authoring Framework StoryTec

StoryTec (Göbel et al., 2012; Mehm, 2010; Mehm, Göbel, Radke, & Steinmetz, 2009) has been elaborated and continuously further cultivated by the Serious Gaming group at TU Darmstadt within a set of projects, e.g. INSCAPE – Interactive Storytelling for Creative People (FP6, IST, IP), U-CREATE – Creative Authoring Tools for Edutainment Applications (FP6, CRAFT), 80Days (FP7, STREP, see http://www.eightydays.eu/), and StoryTec (funded in the framework of Hessen ModellProjekte, financed with funds of LEWE – state offensive for the development of scientific and economic excellence, see also http://www.storytec.de) in direct cooperation with game producers (developers, designer) and

subject matter experts. In the INSCAPE project (Stefan Göbel, Becker, & Feix, 2005), the focus of the authoring tool was providing an interface for creative authors (e.g., artists, writers) in order to allow them to build interactive storytelling applications. U-CREATE (Göbel, Konrad, Salvatore, Sauer, & Osswald, 2007) aimed at the efficient content creation for new technologies, in particular interactive setups, Mixed Reality experiences and location-based services. A graphical authoring tool was developed to allow the creation of elaborated content in a fast and easy way.

StoryTec incorporates the workflows and processes found in game development as outlined. The main user interface of StoryTec as seen in Figure 3 is the principal interface for all user groups collaborating directly in the authoring tool, including game designers, artists, and domain experts. Therefore, all important information is provided visually in the interface, and all functions for editing the game rely on simple concepts instead of programming languages or other more technical systems.

The main overview of the whole project is the Story Editor, in which scene hierarchies (game levels, leaning units, etc.), objects (e.g. virtual characters and game assets like images) and transitions are created and visualized. Authors create the structure of the game in this editor or re-use a provided structural template. The basic unit they use at this stage is the Scene, similar to a theater play. Connections between Scenes are referred to in the system as Transitions. For providing adaptivity, Scenes can be annotated with metadata concerning their adaptive features in order to become Narrative Game-Based Learning Objects. The resulting adaptive system including "free" (adaptive) transitions and scene pools are available directly in the Story Editor, allowing all collaborating users to see and manipulate them.

For each scene created in the Story Editor, the users utilize the Stage Editor for setting up the content of individual scenes, i.e. adding and organizing objects in the scene. This process relies on the interaction templates included in StoryTec

Figure 3. The graphical user interface of StoryTec: from top left in clockwise order: story editor, objects browser, property editor, story editor

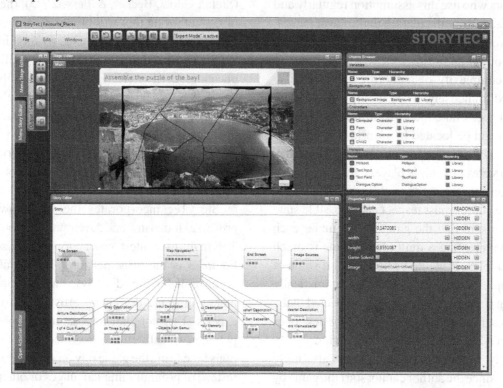

or added by game programmers for a specific game (genre). Therefore, this allows quick editing of the content of the game, since each scene is equipped with an interaction template handling the details of gameplay implementation in the game, only requiring the input of the necessary content and settings. Since this approach of encapsulating gameplay allows the creation of several games in the same genre, it can lower the costs of production by fostering re-use and more rapid development cycles. Creating variations of scenes for allowing adaptivity by multiple paths through the game is supported by copying the required scenes and changing the relevant content or parameters.

The two other user interface elements in the standard configuration of StoryTec are the Objects Browser and Property Editor. The former is used for providing an overview of all available content objects and for adding them to any scene via drag & drop, while the latter is used to change parameters for objects and scenes.

Interactivity on a low level (graphics rendering, sound playback, camera control in 3D games) is intended to be handled by the game engine and the interaction templates. This is due to the inherent complexity of these tasks, which would result in very complex and unusable programs in visual programming languages. For high-level concepts, authors are empowered to configure them themselves by using the ActionSet Editor, which connects each Stimulus (See Figure 2, right part) with a set of actions that should be applied in the game at runtime. Boolean conditions allow branching, thereby reacting to the current state of the game (cf. StoryTec Condition Editor in Figure 9). Additional Actions are provided for assessment purposes, i.e. to update the user models for adaptivity. These actions are to be used whenever a Stimulus can be interpreted to indicate a change in a user model (e.g. a player solving a task that requires understanding a certain piece of knowledge, c.f. section "Control"). Since this system again is available to all collaborating users and does not require previous knowledge in game programming, it can increase collaboration and support rapid prototyping by allowing designers to quickly test game prototypes without waiting for a programmed prototype.

The StoryTec authoring tool has been evaluated in several user studies with larger user bases and in small-scale expert focus group tests. The resulting feedback has been incorporated into several redesigns of the user interface in order to increase the usability of the tool and lower the threshold for novice users and non-programmers.

Specific support for the creation of educational games is offered in the Skill Tree Editor. This editor assists in modeling the knowledge domain the game is based on by visualizing competencies and facts and the dependencies between them as a graph of boxes and arrows. A dependency here indicates that a certain competency A has to be understood before competency B can be addressed, a notion found in Competency-Based Knowledge Space Theory (Albert & Lukas, 1999). Authors can first model the domain in the Skill Tree Editor during the design phase and later on use the resulting data directly by annotating scenes with competencies from the created structure for indicating prerequisite skills.

This task is directly linked to the creation of ontologies, a common task in all fields of computing with knowledge (e.g. artificial intelligence).

For this purpose, a multitude of editors have been created to support the editing of ontologies. One of those with the most widespread use is the Protégé ontology editor (Gennari et al., 2003) developed at Stanford University, allowing users to work visually with an ontology represented as a graph structure (See Figure 4).

StoryTec Framework with Run-Time System and Players

The complete StoryTec version also includes a full runtime environment for playing games created with the authoring tool. This includes, on the one hand, a player application intended to be used for evaluation purposes and as a rapid prototyping tool, and a multi-platform player application on the other hand.

As a basis for all provided player applications, several components are important to mention. The projects which are created by StoryTec are interpreted by a component referred to as Story Engine, which is linked to the game engine. The Story Engine acts as a high-level command instance, dispatching commands to the game engine and other components based on the parameters and actions the authors have set up in StoryTec. It relays all gameplay commands to the game engine and the interaction template implementations included in the game engine and receives stimuli back from the game engine. For adaptivity purposes

Figure 4. Skill tree editor of the StoryTec authoring tool

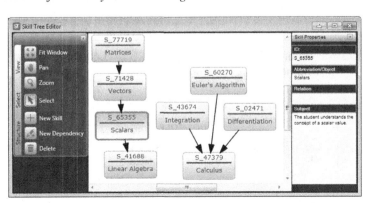

it includes the user models of the players whose updates it carries out based on information from the game as well as the algorithms for choosing how to continue in the game. Whenever an update in the game calls for an adaptive choice, all possible variations are considered (all free transitions or all scenes in a scene pool) and assigned a numerical value indicating their appropriateness when seen from a narrative, learning or play perspective. Depending on the overall goal of the play session, these values are then weighted in order to result in a choice of next scene. The chosen scene is that which yields the highest weighted sum of all values and conforms to all further constraints (e.g. not visiting the same scene again in a scene pool).

The result of the authoring process are ICML-encoded stories. These ICML files are loaded into the run-time environment of the 80Days framework in form of an executable story graph in the Story Engine. Then, the story starts and unfolds according to the user/player/learners´ interactions, behavior, rules and application logic provided by the author, and context information. The context information of NGLOB is hold within the content layer (repository, see lower part in Figure 5) and the modeling part (See upper part in Figure 5).

As described in Figure 6, this basic architecture is realized in two player applications:

"StoryPlay" (Mehm, Wendel, Göbel, & Steinmetz, 2010 - previously referred to as "Bat Cave") features a two-part user interface. One part is reserved for the gameplay and is therefore similar to StoryPublish. The second part (which can be hidden by the user) visualizes current information such as the state of the user models, the history of previous choices by the adaptation algorithms as well as the state of variables. This tool can therefore aid authors in evaluating the games they created concerning the effects of adaptivity by allowing to check the results of annotations and user models early during development. A slider allows quick tuning of the weights associated with the adaptive choices along the narrative, educational and play adaptivity axes. Furthermore, the player allows authors to quickly export a game from StoryTec even though it is not finished yet and test it using the current state of the game.

The "StoryPublish" player is intended for cross-platform publishing a finished game. Based on Java, it can be built for Java on desktop computers, Android as a mobile platform and HTML 5 for Web (See Figure 7).

Figure 5. StoryTec framework with conceptual layer (models, top), run-time components (engines, middle), and content layer (repository with game and story assets, etc.)

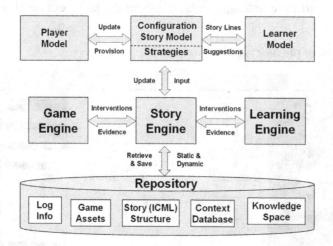

Figure 6. StoryTec player "StoryPlay"

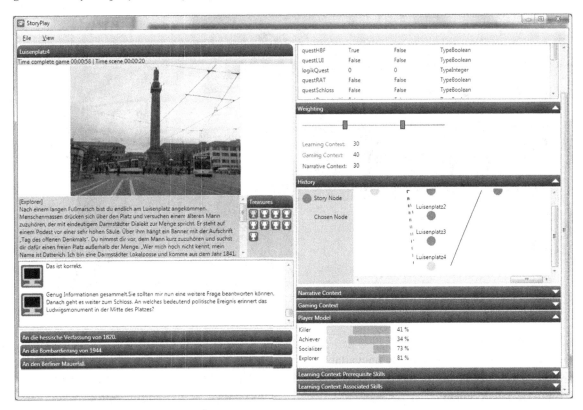

Cross-Platform Publishing in StoryTec

One goal of the development of StoryTec is the deployment of games on various game platforms. This increases the target audience by offering more ways to access the generated content without increasing the cost. It also enables use cases where the games should be deployed in schools where the pupils are only granted limited access to the computers (i.e. are forbidden to install programs). Another benefit is the use in online learning platforms.

The technical realization of this feature on the game platform side was carried out in cooperation with KTX Software Development (http://www.ktx-software.com/) and allows the deployment of games on the platforms Nintendo DS, Apple iOS and Browser platforms (See Figure 8). The version of StoryTec available to the public allows deploy-

ment on Android devices, HTML5-compatible browsers and Java-capable desktop devices due to legal constraints. Especially the newly formed web standard HTML 5 is very appealing due to the standardized plugin-less possibilities for in-

Figure 7. StoryTec player "StoryPublish"

Figure 8. Cross-platform publishing using StoryTec

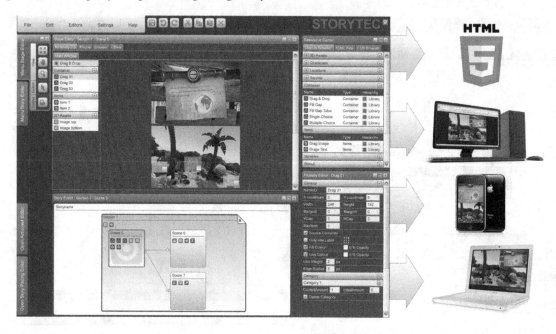

teraction and multimedia previously unavailable to browser-based applications and is therefore in the centre of development.

The portability of games is made possible by the design of StoryTec and leveraging the used xml-based description language ICML (Göbel et al., 2012) as a platform-independent intermediate format. For porting purposes, it is therefore only necessary to port the configurable interaction templates described previously onto the target hardware/software. The basic structure and control remain the same across platforms. Necessary steps for adapting the game's content to the peculiarities of the target platform (such as scaling of images to the display resolution) are carried out by a set of tools realizing a pipeline for the creation of platform-specific version.

Multiplayer-Support in StoryTec

Although StoryTec mostly focused on Singleplayer Games in the past, Multiplayer-Support will be added in the next version of the authoring tool. A first prototype (Reuter, Wendel, Göbel, & Stein-

metz, 2012a, 2012b) offers basic functions like defining the number of players needed to play a specific story. New conditions allow ActionSets to react differently for every user, allowing authors to enforce team play by distributing responsibilities between the players. It is also possible to have players moving independently or to call them together in one place. Likewise, sounds can be set to be heard by every player or only by players in the same location as the one who triggered it.

Figure 9. Multiplayer-prototype of StoryPlay with text chat and avatars

StoryPlay (See Figure 9) was extended as well. It was given a text chat and a simple avatar system in order to help users coordinate themselves. In order to support adaptivity in a multiplayer setting, the Story Engine is now able to process multiple player models. This is done by assessing each player individually and then combining their player models (e.g. by averaging) when an adaptive decision is made.

This Prototype of StoryTec has already been used to create a short Multiplayer Adventure Game. A basic evaluation showed that this game as well as the enhanced Authoring Environment was perceived well by users.

FUTURE RESEARCH DIRECTIONS

In the future, authoring tools will undergo several changes and improvements. Some of the beneficial concepts and methods we see are procedural content generation for the automatic generation of game content to be used in an authoring tool, new authoring paradigms, for example inspired by the extremely simple 3D editing found in games like Minecraft (http://www.minecraft.net/) and also the possibility of in-game editing, where the authoring tool and the game itself are melded into one, allowing changes directly in the game environment.

CONCLUSION

Authoring tools for Serious Games support the collaborative task of creating a Serious Game, establishing a common tool for working on the game and providing a uniform vision of the game for all team members. By integrating easy to use, visual editors such as the Story Editor or Knowledge Space Editor of StoryTec, authoring tools allow non-programmers to work on the structure, logic, and content of a game. Especially the creation of multiplayer games is a novel field and can lead to many challenges, many of which can be addressed in an authoring tool for multiplayer games. By using authoring tools and working detached from any specific target platform, the portability of the resulting game is increased, which was demonstrated by the cross-platform publishing aspect of StoryTec.

REFERENCES

Albert, D., & Lukas, J. (1999). *Knowledge spaces: Theories, empirical research, and applications.* London, UK: Routledge.

Cavazza, M., Champagnat, R., & Leonardi, R. (2009). The IRIS network of excellence: Future directions in interactive storytelling. In *Proceedings of the 2nd Joint International Conference on Interactive Digital Storytelling: Interactive Storytelling* (pp. 8-13). ICIDS.

El Saddik, A. (2001). *Interactive multimedia learning - Shared reusable visualization-based modules.* Heidelberg, Germany: Springer.

Gennari, J. H., Musen, M. A., Fergerson, R. W., Grosso, W. E., Crubezy, M., & Eriksson, H. et al. (2003). The evolution of Protege: An environment for knowledge-based systems development. *International Journal of Human-Computer Studies*, *58*(1), 89–123. doi:10.1016/S1071-5819(02)00127-1.

Göbel, S., Becker, F., & Feix, A. (2005). IN-SCAPE: Storymodels for interactive storytelling and edutainment applications. In *Proceedings of Virtual Storytelling - Using Virtual Reality Technologies for Storytelling* (pp. 168–171). Berlin, Germany: Springer. doi:10.1007/11590361_19.

Göbel, S., Konrad, R., Salvatore, L., Sauer, S., & Osswald, K. (2007). U-CREATE: Authoring tool for the creation of interactive storytelling based edutainment applications. In *Proceedings of Eva 2007 Florence: Electronic Imaging and the Visual Arts: Conference, Training and Exhibition* (pp. 53–58). Bologna, Italy: Pitagora Editrice.

Göbel, S., Mehm, F., & Wendel, V. (2012). Adaptive digital storytelling for digital educational games. In Kickmeier-Rust, M. D., & Albert, D. (Eds.), *An Alien's Guide to Multi-Adaptive Educational Computer Games* (pp. 89–104). Santa Rosa, CA: Informing Science Press.

Horton, W., & Horton, K. (2003). *E-learning tools and technologies: A consumer's guide for trainers, teachers, educators, and instructional designers*. Hoboken, NJ: Wiley.

Louchart, S., & Aylett, R. (2003). Solving the narrative paradox in VEs – Lessons from RPGs. In Rist, T., Aylett, R., Ballin, D., & Rickel, J. (Eds.), *Intelligent Virtual Agents* (Vol. 2792, pp. 244–248). Berlin, Germany: Springer. doi:10.1007/978-3-540-39396-2_41.

Mehm, F. (2010). Authoring serious games. [New York, NY: ACM.]. *Proceedings of Foundations of Digital Games, 2010*, 271–273.

Mehm, F., Göbel, S., Radke, S., & Steinmetz, R. (2009). Authoring environment for story-based digital educational games. In M. D. Kickmeier-Rust (Ed.), *Proceedings of the 1st International Open Workshop on Intelligent Personalization and Adaptation in Digital Educational Games*, (pp. 113–124). IEEE.

Mehm, F., Göbel, S., & Steinmetz, R. (2011). Introducing component-based templates into a game authoring tool. In M. M. Dimitris Gouscos (Ed.), *5th European Conference on Games Based Learning*, (pp. 395–403). Reading, UK: Academic Conferences Limited.

Mehm, F., Hardy, S., Göbel, S., & Steinmetz, R. (2011). Collaborative authoring of serious games for health. In *Proceedings of the 19th ACM International Conference on Multimedia*, (pp. 807–808). New York, NY: ACM.

Mehm, F., Wendel, V., Göbel, S., & Steinmetz, R. (2010). Bat cave: A testing and evaluation platform for digital educational games. In B. Meyer (Ed.), *Proceedings of the 3rd European Conference on Games Based Learning*, (pp. 251–260). Reading, UK: Academic Conferences International.

Reuter, C., Wendel, V., Göbel, S., & Steinmetz, R. (2012a). Multiplayer adventures for collaborative learning with serious games. In *Proceedings of the 6th European Conference on Games Based Learning*, (pp. 416–423). Reading, UK: Academic Conferences International.

Reuter, C., Wendel, V., Göbel, S., & Steinmetz, R. (2012b). Towards puzzle templates for multiplayer adventures. In S. Göbel, W. Müller, B. Urban, & J. Wiemeyer (Eds.), *3rd International Conference on Serious Games for Training, Education and Health*, (pp. 161–163). Berlin, Germany: Springer.

Stolovitch, H. D., & Thiagarajan, S. (1980). *Frame games*. Englewood Cliffs, NJ: Educational Technology Publications.

Torrente, J., Blanco, Á. D., Cañizal, G., Moreno-Ger, P., & Fernandéz-Manjón, B. (2008). <e-Adventure3D>: An open source authoring environment for 3D adventure games in education. In *Proceedings of the 2008 International Conference on Advances in Computer Entertainment Technology*, (pp. 191-194). New York, NY: ACM.

Zagal, J. P., Nussbaum, M., & Rosas, R. (2000). A model to support the design of multiplayer games. *Presence: Teleoperating Virtual Environments*, 9(5), 448–462. doi:10.1162/105474600566943.

Zagal, J. P., Rick, J., & Hsi, I. (2006). Collaborative games: Lessons learned from board games. *Simulation & Gaming*, 37(1), 24–40. doi:10.1177/1046878105282279.

Zimmermann, B., Rensing, C., & Steinmetz, R. (2008). Experiences in using patterns to support process experts in wizard creation. In Proceedings of EuroPLoP 2008. EuroPLoP.

ADDITIONAL READING

Kickmeier-Rust, M. D., & Albert, D. (Eds.). (2012). *An alien's guide to multi-adaptive educational computer games*. Santa Rosa, CA: Informing Science Press.

KEY TERMS AND DEFINITIONS

Authoring Framework: By the term "Authoring Framework" we are referring to systems which allow non-specialist users (e.g. users without a programming or professional game development background) to create an interactive experience. As they thereby require less specialist knowledge and can decrease the number of people working on and the resources used by a project, their use can lead to lower costs or make the creation of an interactive experience affordable in the first place.

Interaction Template: An interaction template is a structure encapsulating the interaction for a game or a part of game. For authors in an authoring tool, it abstracts from implementation details, allowing configuration without requiring programming. In a game, it defines the interaction patterns including interaction metaphors (point & click, drag & drop, enter text, etc.) users use to interact with the game. Common examples are so-called "minigames" such as Puzzle or Memory.

Chapter 5
Personalized, Adaptive Digital Educational Games using Narrative Game–Based Learning Objects

Stefan Göbel
Technische Universität Darmstadt, Germany

Florian Mehm
Technische Universität Darmstadt, Germany

ABSTRACT

Storytelling and gaming approaches are used as motivational instruments for suspenseful, engaging learning. This chapter describes the concept of Narrative Game-Based Learning Objects (NGLOB), providing a model of how to combine these different axes (narration, gaming, and learning) and how to apply it within personalized, adaptive Digital Educational Games (DEG). From a research perspective, this results in one of the main technical challenges of Serious Games (SG): personalization and adaptation. Here, the central question might be summarized with "How does one create and control a game during play considering the game context and characteristics of individual users or user groups?" This question and the use of NGLOBs are illustrated through the example of "Save the Earth" for teaching and learning geography.

INTRODUCTION

Regarding educational games, the motivation to learn is proportional to the fun of the game. Thus, it is desirable to adapt such a game to the player's preferences. While some prefer action games, others prefer story-based adventures or Role-Play Games (RPGs). It is certainly not possible to create an own game for each type of player but it would be a great advance if an educational game was flexible and customizable enough to be able to adapt to the heterogeneous needs of

DOI: 10.4018/978-1-4666-3673-6.ch005

different players preferences by using adaptive technologies. Hereby, adaptation and adaptivity should consider the selection of appropriate content and presentation forms to teach subjects and skills of a curriculum as well as the speed and order of learning units in order neither to bore nor overstrain students. Furthermore, what people like to play depends on various non-static factors, like skills, mood, etc., which can change during play. Consequently, the game ideally would keep track of these factors and adapt accordingly during play. Concerning motivational aspects, the game should contain an interesting, suspenseful, and entertaining story, and be challenging, but not too stressing. Providing a good and suspenseful story however, is often a restricting factor to the variability of a game. This chapter wants to discuss these aspects and describe the concept of *Narrative Game-based Learning Objects* (*NGLOB*'s) combining these elements. As example to illustrate the NGLOB concept, the *Digital Educational Game* (DEG) 'Save the Earth' for teaching and learning geography –elaborated within the context of the EU project 80Days – is considered.

BACKGROUND

For adaptation to the player's preferences, a player model is necessary. A lot of research in the field of player modeling has been done up to now. One of the first player models was designed by Bartle (1996). Houlette (2004) introduced a player model which keeps track of several player traits to create a model which can be used to adapt the behavior of *Non-Player Characters* (*NPCs*). In this context, Yannakakis and Maragoudakis (2005) showed how to improve a player's experience during a Pacman game by an adaptation of the opponents' behavior according to the player's skill by use of an adaptive player modeling. Magerko, Heeter, Fitzgerald and Medler (2008) designed a game for teaching microbiology concepts called S.C.R.U.B., which can be personalized according

to a player type chosen at the beginning by answering a questionnaire. The chosen model however is static for the whole game and does not consider adaptation based on the learning context. Cowley, Charles, Black and Hickey (2008) propose a game adaptation mechanism based on a continuously updated factorial player modeling with varying factors for different game genres. In the context of storytelling, the system Passage (Thue & Bulitko, 2008) uses player modeling to adapt the game's story individually to the type of player. In Façade (Mateas & Stern, 2005) the player can join an interactive story which adapts its agents' behavior according to the players`s actions.

For adaptation to storytelling metaphors, a story model is necessary. Here, the basic idea is to use well-proven story structures in order to 'guarantee' suspenseful stories. The most prominent examples for story structures in that context of story-based edutainment applications (and entertainment genre in general) represent the Writer's journey (Vogler, 1992) respectively Hero's Journey (Campbell, 1949) as well as the Hollywood film model (Field, 2005) (See Figure 1).

From a Storytelling perspective the narrative paradox and the question how a Story-based DEG continues during run-time (→ macro adaptation, sequencing) has been at core of research within the first period of the 80Days project and previous work of the authors of this chapter (Hoffmann, Göbel, Schneider, & Iurgel, 2005; Kickmeier-Rust, Göbel, & Albert, 2008). As outcome of comprehensive analytic studies and conceptual work, a compromise between plot-based Storytelling and non-linear, interactive gaming approaches has been identified (Göbel, Malkewitz, & Becker, 2006; Göbel, Mehm, & Radke, 2009) and built the conceptual basis for the overall story structure of the demonstrator 1: The Hero's Journey (Campbell, 1949; Vogler, 1992) which is well-proven especially in the domain of adventure games, was used as underlying (in major parts linear) story model in order to 'guarantee' a suspenseful story.

Figure 1. Story model of the hero's journey (left); linear and modular story units (right)

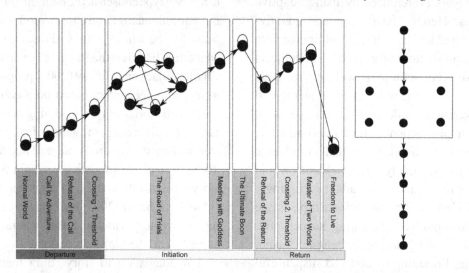

Hereby, the middle part with the dramatic step 'The Road of Trials' is very flexible and provides the possibility to integrate as many story units (→ so-called 'micro missions' in 80Days – similar to levels in a DEG) as the author wishes. Then, during run-time, the story and sequence of micro missions evolves based on the player interaction respectively a mixture of (1) pre-defined rules by the author, (2) player/learner model and (3) learning, gaming and storytelling context.

Third, for adaptation to (teaching and) learning by means of DEG's, the use of a learner model is necessary, because an adaptive DEG must track the player's state of knowledge and adapt the learning content and its difficulty according to it. The *Knowledge Space Theory* (*KST*), as originally proposed by Doignon and Falmagne (1985) and adapted by Albert and Lukas (1999), is designated to be used for modeling and for the assessment of a learner's knowledge. ALEKS (http://www.aleks.com) for example provides a commercial adaptive learning system based on Knowledge Spaces. Hereby, KST deduces the learners actual knowledge from his ability to solve problems associated to learning objects but not from his/her existing competences. Korossy (1999) provided an extension of KST called *Competence based Knowledge Spaces* (*CbKST*). Projects like

ELEKTRA (www.elektra-project.org) already successfully utilized CbKST to provide adaptive interventions relying on a well-designed, cognition based logic (Kickmeier-Rust & Albert, 2007).

Storytelling, Learning, and Gaming

The major challenge was to harmonize the different characteristics and objectives of the storytelling, learning and gaming approaches. In simple words, key aspects and aims of these approaches might be summarized as:

- **Storytelling:** Use of stories as instrument for suspenseful knowledge transfer. Keywords include dramaturgy, suspense or emotion and immersion.
- **Gaming:** Provision of a playful learning environment. As slogan 'Learning by playing' might serve. Fun, motivation, exploration and interaction are dominant.
- **Learning:** Most relevant is the knowledge transfer. Emphasis is set on assessment, learning success and effectiveness or methodic-didactic aspects. Mechanisms to motivate and engage users are welcome (See Figure 2).

Figure 2. Technology-enhanced learning with storytelling and gaming

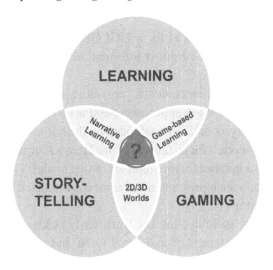

In major parts, these aspects and characteristics are complementary, for instance both storytelling and gaming concepts are used to increase the motivation of users in digital educational games. On the other hand—especially with respect to a technical implementation and integration of the concepts—the so-called "narrative paradox" (Louchart & Aylett, 2003) indicates a conflict between storytelling (narratology; linear, non-interactive, plot-based approach) and gaming (ludology; interaction, non-linear gaming approach). Consequently, the role of the author is different: Whereby in storytelling approaches the author has full control over the DEG run-time scenario (everything is pre-scripted, no interaction, no choice to choose among learning paths → '*aura of the author*'), in gaming approaches the player more or less has full control and decides how a Story-based DEG continues (the story evolves during gameplay → '*emergent narrative*' (Kriegel & Aylett, 2008; Louchart & Aylett, 2004).

Similar conflicts occur between learning and gaming (How should the learning content be presented? Is it worth to create playful learning environments/DEG with learning tasks directly included into gameplay?) as well as learning

and storytelling (a storymodel foresees some dramatic function to increase the suspense of a learner/gamer, but the curriculum or knowledge space simply says 'the next learning topic should deal with.').

Therefore, a comprehensive concept is necessary to combine the different aspects of storytelling, learning and gaming.

Narrative, Learning, and Gaming Context: Narrative Game-Based Learning Objects

From a Storytelling perspective, *Narrative Objects* (*NOB*) represent the smallest, atomic units of Story-based DEG. In 80Days, NOB are implemented as storytelling situations and technically implemented as cut scenes (without any interaction) or as speech acts and additional actions of virtual characters (animations, gestures, etc.). For the formalization of NOB and narrative contexts, the idea is –as far as applicable– to map and annotate NOB corresponding to the steps and dramaturgic functions of underlying story models such as the Hero's Journey.

With respect to learning issues, formal models for *Learning Objects* (*LOB*) and its use within courseware (Computer and Web-Based Training) have been researched for a long time in the field of E-Learning (for instance with a focus on data storage (Hoermann, Hildebrandt, Rensing, & Steinmetz, 2005) and standards are already available: Whilst SCORM (Sharable Content Object Reference Model, see http://www.adlnet. org/Technologies/scorm) focuses on the definition of the overall structure of online courses and provides mechanisms for sequencing LOB (part 'Sequencing and Navigation', available since version SCORM 2004), LOM provides a set of metadata elements for the description of LOB and to facilitate search, evaluation, acquisition, and use of LOB.

For the conceptualisation and formalization of LOB in the context of Story-based DEG it is not the aim to rebuild the LOM standard. Contrary, the approach is to use existing learning resources and to reference on it within the content section of the overall story format ICML (INSCAPE Markup Language, elaborated within the Integrated Project INSCAPE[1]). Additionally, the idea is to formalize the learning and learner context and to provide machine-readable information about associated and prerequisite skills of a LOB respectively learning situation based on the Competency-based Knowledge Space Theory (CbKST) provided by Albert and Lukas (1999). Thus, for sequencing purposes—presumed an open, modular, emergent (narrative) environment is available without hard-coded transitions as in pure linear approaches—it is possible to decide whether a learning situation is appropriate for a specific learner (the learner does have the prerequisite skills) or not (the learner would be overstrained).

Opposite to the learning context, unfortunately, there are no well-known, elaborated definitions, standards or formats for the gaming context and *Gaming Objects* (*GOB*). However, different generic descriptions of games à la '*What makes a good game?*' indicate relevant characteristics and criteria: Apart from graphic and audio/sound, especially gameplay, interaction concepts and a good story decide about success or failure of a game. With respect to the formalization of NGLOB and its use in educational games, the interaction concept in form of interaction templates (e.g. drag-and-drop, multiple-choice and puzzle templates in classic courseware or an explorative 3D environment such as a flight mission) provides useful attributive information.

Second, similar to the learning context, the idea is to build a correlation between gaming situations/GOB and the users (i.e. players in the gaming context) and underlying player models. Hence, all gaming situations are set into context with player types and annotated with appropriateness factors.

Model and Technical Implementation of NGLOBs

In sum, the model for a NGLOB is built by a composition of context information resulting in a triple vector $C_N \times C_G \times C_L$.

The narrative context C_N provides a list of tuples (storymodelStep, appropriatenessFactor) whereby the storymodelStep is encoded by the initials of a storymodel (for instance 'HJ' for Hero's Journey) plus a number for the step/part of that model. The parameter appropriatenessFactor is normalized in the range [0…1].

The gaming context C_G primarily tackles the appropriateness of individual GOB and gaming situations for different players and player types. Analogue to the narrative context C_N, the gaming context C_G also provides a list of tuples (playerAttribute, appropriatenessFactor). Here, 'PA_B$_x$' describes the player type based on the classification of Bartle (1996). For example, 'PA_B1, 0.9' indicates that the GOB is very appropriate for the player type 'Explorer' according to Bartle (1996).

The model for the learning context C_L provides a vector composed out of two parts listing all associated and prerequisite skills for a specific learning situation/LOB. In the example, 'A1$_{xyz}$' and 'B2$_{xyz}$' skills represent identifiers for learning topics of the 80Days´ demonstrator 1 DEG being extracted out of the curriculum for teaching geography in the 6th to 8th grade at school (See Figure 3).

Apart from that quantifiable part described previously, the model for NGLOB contains further descriptive elements such as short texts/abstracts summarizing the synopsis of narrative, gaming and learning functions of a specific NGLOB.

In order to use NGLOB in Story-based DEG such as 80Days, the authoring tool StoryTec (http://www.storytec.de) has been enhanced both in the authoring tool and run-time components: In the authoring tool, the Property Editor provides fields to enter context information of NGLOB. The Condition Editor is used to enter application logic and define conditions for transitions

Figure 3. Quantifiable part of the model for narrative game-based learning objects

$$\left(\left\langle \begin{matrix} (HJ\_2, 0.1), \\ (HJ\_4, 0), \\ (HJ\_4\_1, 0.2), \\ (HJ\_5, 0.85), \\ \vdots \end{matrix} \right\rangle, \left\langle \begin{matrix} (PA\_B1, 0.15), \\ (PA\_B2, 0.4), \\ (PA\_B3, 0.2), \\ (PA\_B4, 0.9) \end{matrix} \right\rangle, \left\langle \begin{matrix} \langle A1030, A1033 \rangle \\ \langle B2122, B2297 \rangle \end{matrix} \right\rangle \right)$$

among story units (→ sequencing of story units in Story-based DEG, see also (Göbel et al., 2006) describing an algorithm for selecting a "best next scene" based on appropriateness factors of scenes and external constraints such as limited time for a learning experience) (See Figure 4).

More detailed descriptions of the concept of NGLOB's and its technical implementation are provided by Göbel, Wendel, Ritter, and Steinmetz (2010).

Best-Practice DEG "Save the Earth" for Teaching and Learning Geography

To demonstrate the concept and mechanisms of NGLOB, we describe the best-practice example of the game elaborated in the course of the EU-funded project 80Days. The DEG created during 80Days included a curriculum of topics related to geography assembled from national curricula of several European countries.

The target user group, 12-14 year old children, required a game with fun gameplay that is embedded in a suspenseful narrative that captures and motivates the players. The final game was a 3D in which players are able to fly a spaceship over Europe, exploring geographical locations along the way. In a second stage, players simulate the effects of human geographical interventions (e.g. re-routing rivers or clearing forests). This game-

Figure 4. Condition editor (left) and property editor (right)

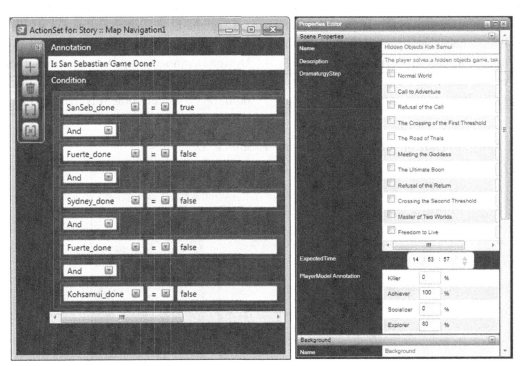

play is interwoven with a story in which the player is approached by an alien life form to help with mapping the Earth's surface.

In order to structure the narrative of the game, the Hero's Journey model shown prior was used (c.f. Figure 5). Parts of the game's story are told in the form of cinematic cut scenes to make sure no interaction interferes with the dramatic arc of the story. After an introduction showing the game's protagonist in his "ordinary world" of dreaming of UFOs and science at night, the protagonist and the player are given a call to adventure by being approached by an alien. This alien, Feon, then turns into the protagonist's mentor by providing a space ship to fly around and by helping out when the player is stuck. The "Road of Trials" stage is then realized by a set of micro-missions with individual story lines and various geographical topics that are taught.

The design of the game utilized the NGLOB concept, i.e. each situation of the game was seen as having storytelling, learning, and gaming aspects. As can be seen in Tables 1 and 2, the initial story was drafted by providing general descriptions (in terms of narrative, this is the objective through-line, stating what happens in the situation) along with the narrative, learning and gaming purpose of this situation. Each micro mission or the Cinematic Intro provide an unique ID and a

short description/synopsis, optionally a visual representation (e.g. a sketch) and it is split into *Storytelling Situations* (*StS*), *Learning Situations* (*LeS*) and *Gaming/Gameplay Situations* (*GpS*) on a narrower level.

For allowing adaptivity, several variations of situations or parts of the situation (e.g. concerning dialogues, music, …) were created. For example, if the adaptive algorithm of the game decided that a player required more exciting gameplay, the background music of the situation could be exchanged from a normal musical background to a more energetic one. Similarly, feedback and content for different stages of learning and for adaptation of narrative were created. For organizing these situations and their annotation concerning their appropriateness for the player types and learning paths, the authoring tool StoryTec was used.

The situations themselves vary in its emphasis on either one specific context (e.g. a pure story-driven situation without any gameplay and minor/nor learning effects, see situation *CI_scene1* in Table 1) or a combination of contexts (e.g. *LeS 1.3* as game-based learning situation, see Table 2).

In summary, that kind of style for a Game Design Document might be useful for authors and serve as compact storyboard, but from a technical point of view the problem is the lack of metric,

Figure 5. Story structure of 80Days' demonstrator 1 (Source: Uni Graz)

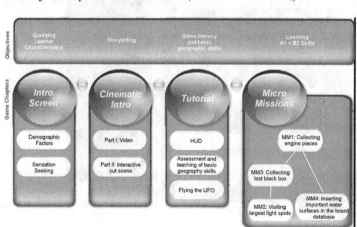

Table 1. Extract out of the game design document for the cinematic intro of 80Days' demonstrator 1

Game Chapter	Cinematric Intro			
Situation	*Short description*	*Function for Story*	*Function for Learning*	*Function for Gameplay*
CI_scene 1	We see the original NASA film footage of the Apollo 8 mission..	Create the beginning of a mystery story; set the mood and frame of the story..	This is a visual metaphor for our philosophy for teaching Geography..	--

Table 2. Extract out of the game design document for learning unit 1 of demonstrator 1

Game Chapter	Learning Unit 1 (LU1): B2 Skills European Capitals & Countries			
Situation	*Short description*	*Function for Story*	*Function for Learning*	*Function for Gameplay*
LeS 1.1 Pre-test of existing knowledge	Alien asks boy: "You know what cities are these?" The boy now can link illuminated spots and city names on a desk. ..	Now, Mr. Jackanapes has to struggle a first time to keep up his blarney of being an all-knowing earthling.	Reflection on and pre-test of existing knowledge without immediate feedback. ..	Introduction: Game play mode "Global view/ Map desk" in simplified 2D view.
LeS 1.3 Position of cities without known names	The gamer can fly above Europe in the UFO and the 2D night map in the HUD gives him his precise position and supports him in deciding to which city (light spot) he wants to fly next.		The player can freely explore Europe while having the learning goals on a map in front of him (cities shown as light spots).	To verify the cities´ names the player has to fly there and to stay paused above them (logging).

quantifiable information being necessary to be interpreted and processed by computer systems – e.g. in order to determine whether a situation is appropriate to fulfill a specific dramaturgic step within the story model of the Hero's Journey or not.

For that, the concept of Narrative Game-Based Learning Objects with measurable, quantitative and qualitative elements and annotations for the narrative, gaming and learning contexts has been elaborated.

During runtime, the game was linked to two external engines, a Story Engine for controlling the narrative and a Learning Engine for updating and managing a learner model. These engines collaborated in matching the current state of the player with the next optimal scene as described.

The 80Days game was evaluated in-depth in schools in England and Austria. The evaluation showed a beneficial effect on the participants. However, the overall cost incurred by the adaptive approach of 80Days has to be mentioned as

well. As automatic content production is not (yet) feasible, a larger amount of content (voice recordings, 3D models, ...) than for a non-adaptive game had to be created.

CONCLUSION

For the provision of personalized, adaptive DEG the conceptual model of NGLOB has been elaborated. NGLOB's consider both the narrative, gaming and learning contexts. To implement the NGLOB concept, two steps are necessary: In the first phase, during the authoring process, all scenes (game units) are annotated with appropriateness factors for its use for specific narrative functions (story models), gaming functions (player models) and learning functions (learning topics with skills and prerequisite skills). Then, during play, it is decided how the DEG continues by selecting (computation) a best 'next scene' based on the match between the actual (learning, gaming and narrative) context and the appropriateness of all possible next scenes (candidates). The NGLOB concept has been elaborated and prototypically implemented in the course of the 80Days project. First feasibility studies are promising. Though, more sophisticated evaluation studies based on comprehensive DEG providing a wealth of content (with many scenes, different peculiarities of scenes and many possible game paths) are necessary in order to determine the benefit of NGLOB for Story-based DEG – by means of learning effects and user experience.

ACKNOWLEDGMENT

The research and development presented in this work is funded by the European Commission under the seventh framework programme in the ICT research priority, contract number 215918 (80Days, www.eightydays.eu).

REFERENCES

Albert, D., & Lukas, J. (1999). *Knowledge spaces: Theories, empirical research, and applications.* London, UK: Routledge.

Bartle, R. (1996). Hearts, clubs, diamonds, spades: Players who suit MUDS. *Journal of Virtual Environments, 1*(1), 19.

Campbell, J. (1949). *The hero with a thousand faces.* London, UK: Bollingen Foundation.

Cowley, B., Charles, D., Black, M., & Hickey, R. (2008). Toward an understanding of flow in video games. *Computers in Entertainment, 6*(2), 1. doi:10.1145/1371216.1371223.

Doignon, J.-P., & Falmagne, J.-C. (1985). Spaces for the assessment of knowledge. *International Journal of Man-Machine Studies, 23*(2), 175–196. doi:10.1016/S0020-7373(85)80031-6.

Field, S. (2005). *Screenplay.* New York, NY: Delta.

Göbel, S., Malkewitz, R., & Becker, F. (2006). *Story pacing in interactive storytelling. Technologies for E-Learning and Digital Entertainment* (*Vol. 3942,* pp. 419–428). Heidelberg, Germany: Springer. doi:10.1007/11736639_53.

Göbel, S., Mehm, F., & Radke, S. (2009). 80Days: Adaptive digital storytelling for digital educational games. In Y. Cao, A. Hannemann, & B. F. Manjon (Eds.), *International Workshop on Story-Telling and Educational Games: CEUR Workshop Proceedings.* CEUR.

Göbel, S., Wendel, V., Ritter, C., & Steinmetz, R. (2010). Personalized, adaptive digital educational games using narrative game-based learning objects. In Proceedings of Entertainment for Education: Digital Techniques and Systems, (pp. 438–445). IEEE.

Hoermann, S., Hildebrandt, T., Rensing, C., & Steinmetz, R. (2005). Resource center - A digital learning object repository with an integrated authoring tool set. In P. Kommers & G. Richards (Eds.), *World Conference on Educational Multimedia, Hypermedia and Telecommunications,* (pp. 3453–3460). IEEE.

Hoffmann, A., Göbel, S., Schneider, O., & Iurgel, I. (2005). Storytelling-based edutainment applications. In Tan, L., & Subramaniam, R. (Eds.), *E-Learning and Virtual Science Centers* (pp. 190–212). Hershey, PA: IGI Global. doi:10.4018/978-1-59140-591-7.ch009.

Houlette, R. (2004). Player modelling for adaptive games. [IEEE.]. *Proceedings of AI Game Programming Wisdom, II,* 557–566.

Kickmeier-Rust, M., & Albert, D. (2007). The ELEKTRA ontology model: a learner-centered approach to resource description. In *Advances in Web Based Learning–ICWL 2007* (pp. 78–89). Springer.

Kickmeier-Rust, M., Göbel, S., & Albert, D. (2008). 80Days: Melding adaptive educational technology and adaptive and interactive storytelling in digital educational games. In R. Klamma Nalin, N. Sharda, B. Fernández-Manjón, H. Kosch, & M. Spaniol (Eds.), *Proceedings of the First International Workshop on Story-Telling and Educational Games (STEG'08),* (p. 8). STEG.

Korossy, K. (1999). Modelling knowledge as competence and performance. In Albert, D., & Lukas, J. (Eds.), *Knowledge Spaces Theories Empirical Research Applications* (pp. 103–132). Springer.

Kriegel, M., & Aylett, R. (2008). Emergent narrative as a novel framework for massively collaborative authoring. In *Intelligent Virtual Agents* (pp. 73–80). Berlin, Germany: Springer. doi:10.1007/978-3-540-85483-8_7.

Louchart, S., & Aylett, R. (2003). Solving the narrative paradox in VEs – Lessons from RPGs. In Rist, T., Aylett, R., Ballin, D., & Rickel, J. (Eds.), *Intelligent Virtual Agents* (Vol. 2792, pp. 244–248). Springer. doi:10.1007/978-3-540-39396-2_41.

Louchart, S., & Aylett, R. (2004). Narrative theory and emergent interactive narrative. *International Journal of Continuing Engineering Education and Lifelong Learning, 14,* 506–518. doi:10.1504/IJCEELL.2004.006017.

Magerko, B., Heeter, C., Fitzgerald, J., & Medler, B. (2008). Intelligent adaptation of digital game-based learning. In *Proceedings of the 2008 Conference on Future Play: Research, Play, Share,* (pp. 200–203). New York, NY: ACM.

Mateas, M., & Stern, A. (2005). Structuring content in the Facade interactive drama architecture. In M. Young & J. Laird (Eds.), *Proceedings of the First Artificial Intelligence and Interactive Digital Entertainment Conference,* (pp. 93-98). Palo Alto, CA: AAAI Press

Thue, D., & Bulitko, V. (2008). PaSSAGE: A demonstration of player modeling in interactive storytelling. In *Proceedings of the Fourth Artificial Intelligence and Interactive Digital Entertainment Conference,* (pp. 226–227). IEEE.

Vogler, C. (1992). *The writer's journey: Mythic structures for storytellers and screenwriters.* New York, NY: M. Wiese Productions.

Yannakakis, G. N., & Maragoudakis, M. (2005). Player modeling impact on player's entertainment in computer games. [Springer.]. *Proceedings of User Modeling, 2005,* 74–78.

KEY TERMS AND DEFINITIONS

Digital Educational Game: An educational game realized on a digital platform, combining the respective strengths of educational technology and digital games.

Gaming Object: A basic unit of a game or game-like application.

Learning Object: An atomar and re-usable unit of learning content. By combining learning objects on similar topics, a learning application can be composed.

Narrative Game-Based Learning Object: Based on Learning Objects (LOB), NGLOB's consider not only the learning context, but also the narrative and gaming context. In the authoring phase of Serious Games, game units (scenes) are annotated with appropriateness factors to serve as learning/gaming/storytelling situations regarding dedicated story and player models as well as learning contexts (skills). During play, the most appropriate NGLOB is selected based on the computation (matching) between the actual context (story, player and learner model/behavior) and the annotated NGLOBs in order to decide how a story-based Digital Educational Game continues.

Narrative Object: A basic unit of a narrative-driven application, that has a specific function in a story model (e.g. introduce the protagonist or serve as the climax of the story).

ENDNOTES

[1] INSCAPE – Interactive Storytelling for Creative People, Integrated Project, European Commission, FP7.

Chapter 6
Collaborative Learning and Game Mastering in Multiplayer Games

Johannes Konert
Technische Universität Darmstadt, Germany

Kristina Richter
Technische Universität Darmstadt, Germany

Viktor Wendel
Technische Universität Darmstadt, Germany

Stefan Göbel
Technische Universität Darmstadt, Germany

ABSTRACT

The purpose of the chapter is to provide a state of the art survey addressing research and development aspects for the control of multiplayer Serious Games for collaborative learning scenarios. Hereby, several facets of multiplayer scenarios are addressed: synchronous and asynchronous gameplay and the role of an instructor as Game Master, supervisor, and provider of individual feedback as well as individual feedback among learners in the process of continuous adaptation of the on-going gameplay. Existing approaches and best-practice examples focus on digital educational games for pupils and collaborative learning environments for students. The theoretical foundations of instructional support as well as the implications and technical approaches are discussed. They include some aspects of authoring Serious Games (as already covered in chapter "Authoring Serious Games").

INTRODUCTION

Collaborative learning is a concept which has been researched for many decades and is an established method of teaching in today's classes. Serious Games (SG) show a similar trend from single to multi player, just like the gaming world did during the last ten years with more and more focus on social interaction between players in the last years. In recent years, first approaches appeared which try to combine the collaborative learning paradigm with SG technology. In the focus are collaborative learning scenarios and social interaction between players.

DOI: 10.4018/978-1-4666-3673-6.ch006

Compared to single player SG, multiplayer SG provide additional challenges during authoring, control, and validation.

In terms of authoring, concurrent gaming in one game world/level has to be considered. How can the game be designed to enable players/learners to interact in the game (world) in a way such that they profit most from the presence of other players? This includes design of collaborative challenges, division of labour or knowledge sharing.

During runtime, adaptation multiplayer scenarios considering the characteristics of individual users (players, learners) and heterogeneous user groups (e.g. a school class) and supporting knowledge sharing and peer education (tutoring and assessment) among learners during play is vital. The concept of Narrative Game-Based Learning Objects (NGLOBs) as presented in the previous chapter is only partly usable in multiplayer scenarios. Therefore, new concepts for adaptation of multiplayer games to the needs of learner groups will have to be developed. One focus is set on the Game Master concepts. These domain experts use software tools to monitor, control, and influence the game scenarios with their individual instructional support. A key challenge is to optimize their view on the game during runtime so that they can analyse and control the group's learning process inside the game in an optimal way.

In terms of validation, one major challenge is to assess learning progress of groups in multiplayer Serious Games. Although assessment of (collaborative) learner groups is being researched for several decades, up to today it is still not entirely clear, how these mechanisms can be adapted in order to be used for the assessment of groups of learners in games.

The proposed mechanisms and RTD principles are presented in the context of the best-practice examples (projects) Genius (technology transfer projects in the field of Serious Games authoring and combining Serious Games with social networks; funded by the State of Hessen in the frame of the LOEWE program for economic and scientific excellence), PEDALE (strategic interdisciplinary research at TU Darmstadt addressing collaborative math learning supported by peer education), Woodment and Escape from Wilson Island (strategic research at the Serious Gaming group offering multiplayer learning scenarios enhanced by game mastering principles to support coaches/tutors).

COLLABORATIVE LEARNING

Whereas the proposed NGLOB concept serves for single player SG, other mechanisms are required for the control of multiplayer environments: Multiplayer games offer a whole new range of applications for Serious Games. With Multiplayer games, inter-personal skills like communication, teamwork, or other soft skills may be trained. Multiplayer Serious Games are also especially well fit to be used for game-based collaborative learning scenarios.

The concept of collaborative learning is being discussed among educators for decades. Collaborative learning is used in schools today in various forms, like joint problem solving in teams, debates, or other team activities. According to Pierre Dillenbourg (1999, one definition for collaborative learning is "*a situation in which two or more people learn or attempt to learn something together.*" Roschelle and Teasley (1995) define collaboration as "*a coordinated, synchronous activity that is the result of a continued attempt to construct and maintain a shared conception of a problem.*" Compared to Dillenbourg's definition of cooperation, "*In cooperation, partners split the work, solve sub-tasks individually and then assemble the partial results into the final output,*" this is much more than just cooperation. Dillenbourg defines collaboration as follows: "*In collaboration, partners do the work 'together.'*" The idea of collaborative learning is to make learners interact in particular ways such that certain learning mechanisms are triggered. Therefore, several mechanisms to enhance the probability of these interactions to occur are currently being researched. These are according to Pierre Dillenbourg (1999):

- **Setup of Initial Conditions:** Group size, gender, same viewpoint vs. opposing viewpoint.
- **Role-Based Scenario:** problems which cannot be solved with one type of knowledge.
- **Interaction Rules:** Free communication vs. predefined communication patterns, see also Baker and Lund (1997).
- **Monitoring and Regulation of Interactions:** Need for specific tools for the teacher.

Johnson and Johnson (1988) identified five essential elements which foster cooperative work in Face-to-Face groups. These are often cited as *"five components that are essential for collaborative learning"* (Zea, Sanchez, & Gutierrez, 2009):

- **Positive Interdependence:** Knowing to be linked with other players in a way so that one cannot succeed unless they do.
- **Individual Accountability:** Individual assessment of each student's performance and giving back the results to both the group and the individual.
- **Face-to-Face Promotive Interaction:** Promoting each other's success by e.g. helping, encouraging and praising.
- **Social Skills:** Interpersonal and small group skills are vital for the success of a cooperative effort.
- **Group Processing:** Group members discussing their progress and working relationships.

For the success of collaborative learning, both with or without the use of a computer, it is essential that the collaborative learning environment enables and fosters those elements.

The idea of using computers to support learning arose in the 1980s, with computers as tools mainly for writing, and organizing. In the 1990s, with the Internet and network technologies arising, new ways of communication and collaboration emerged. Intelligent tutoring systems were designed. However, the main task for a computer was being a medium for communication, in form of email, chat, forums, etc. (Stahl, Koschmann, & Suthers, 2006). In recent years, many forms of Computer-Supported Collaborative Learning (CSCL) have been designed and used in curricula at schools. Collaborative writing (Onrubia & Engel, 2009) is one such form, where learners collaboratively create a document using computer technologies. Furthermore, today many web technologies are used for CSCL, like Forums or Wikis (Larusson & Alterman, 2009).

With the upcoming of Virtual Worlds like Second Life or private virtual worlds like IBM Virtual Collaboration for Lotus Sametime, research also focused on using those as collaborative learning environments (Nelson & Ketelhut, 2008). As they are very popular and often freely available, also Massively Multiplayer Online Games (MMOG) have been used as environments for collaborative learning scenarios. Delwiche (2006) held online courses in the MMOG Everquest and Second Life teaching about videogame design and criticism. Hämäläinen, Manninen, Järvelä, and Häkkinen (2006) tried to find out whether the characteristic features of 3D-games can be used to create meaningful virtual collaborative learning environments. Zea et al. (2009) presented design guidelines enabling incorporation of features of collaborative learning in the videogame development process based on the five essential elements for collaborative learning stated by Johnson and

Johnson. Voulgari and Komis (2008) investigated the design of effective collaborative problem solving tasks within MMOGs, and Rauterberg (2002) performed a test about collaboration in MMOGs finding out that communication is essential for effective collaboration.

An approach for a 3D collaborative multiplayer Serious Game for learning with freely definable learning content is presented in Wendel et al. (2010). Woodment is a collaborative game in which two opposing teams fight about a common resource: wood. The game world is restricted in a natural way by the use of an island setting. The teams both have to lead a logging company in which each player has a unique position with unique duties and options. This way, it is not possible for one player to decide the game alone. The team members rather need to coordinate their actions in order to be successful. In order to be successful at gathering resources like food for their workers, the players need to answer questions, which are triggered by entering special orbs placed all around the island. Players can ask their team about their opinion when answering a question. Only if it is correct, the team receives the resource, otherwise they receive background information necessary to answer the question. A question answered wrongly will be triggered with a higher probability in the future until it is answered correctly.

Another approach by Wendel, Gutjahr, Göbel, and Steinmetz (2012) is called Escape From Wilson Island. It is a multiplayer Serious Game focussing on collaboration among team members with a focus on soft skills like communication, coordination, teamwork, etc. Players are placed in a Robinson Crusoe-like setting and need to collaborate effectively in order to flee from an island. As the players have heterogeneous resources, they need to interact and help each other in order to succeed, e.g. only the player possessing the axe is able to fell palms which are necessary to create a raft or a log hut. However, to carry palms, three players are needed. To move a palm, they need to coordinate their movements very accurately, so that they do not drop the palm (See Figure 1).

However, whereas Adaptation and Personalization (A&P) is a challenging task in single player settings, it becomes even more challenging in multiplayer settings. Where A&P in single player can focus on the player and adapt the game in terms of learning, gaming, or narration to the skill level, knowledge, or preferences of the player, in a multiplayer setting, all players have to be taken into account. It is still an open question, how a multiplayer game can be adapted automatically to the needs, skill levels and preferences of a group of players in such a way that each individual's needs are satisfied as well as the group's needs.

Figure 1. Multiplayer learning environment 'Woodment' (left); game mastering for multiplayer SG 'Escape from Wilson Island' (right)

GAME MASTERING

One approach to solve this problem is Game Mastering (GM) or Game Orchestration by a real person. The term 'Game Master' is taken from pen and paper role-play games. In these games, it is the Game Master's task to tell a story in which the other players are actively taking part, thus taking influence on the story through their actions. The GM's most challenging task is balancing between telling a good story while taking the players' actions into account. As players' acting is often unpredictable, the GM will have to improvise very often in order to keep the story running and not to give players the feeling that their actions do not matter.

Transferring the GM concept to Serious Games means enabling instructors (e.g. teachers/trainers) to orchestrate/control/adapt a Serious Game at runtime in a way such that it takes into account singleplayers' needs as well as group needs. Still it is not clear, which information about a multiplayer Serious Game needs to be provided to the GM and which control options need to be available.

Recently, first approaches have been designed for supporting a real person in a GM-like role at orchestrating games for collaborative learning. (Hämäläinen, 2006) for example designed an environment for computer-supported learning for vocational learning. Their findings suggest that game-based learning "may enrich learning and the pedagogical use of technology" but they also point out many remaining challenges.

One of these challenges is the fact that instructors are usually only insufficiently integrated when using game-based approaches for learning in groups or classes and are not able to orchestrate collaborative learning processes properly (Hämäläinen & Oksanen 2012). It has been argued (Dillenbourg, Järvelä, & Fischer, 2009), (Kollar 2012) that real-time orchestration is vital for collaborative learning scenarios to be successful. Also, Azevedo et al. (2005) argue that externally-facilitated regulated learning (using a human tutor)

is more effective than self-regulated learning when using hypermedia. Kreijns, Kirschner, Jochems and Van Buuren (2007) state that technological environments can support teachers' abilities to foster productive knowledge construction by helping them to control and assess learning activities. Tychsen, Hitchens, Brolund, and Kavakli (2005) proposed an approach for a virtual Game Master based on the idea of the Game Master role in pen-and-paper roleplay games. Hämäläinen and Oksanen (2012) developed a scripted 3D learning game for vocational learning with real-time teacher orchestration. Their findings indicate that the teacher plays a vital role in knowledge construction processes.

One approach (Wendel et al., 2012) (See Figure 2) describes collaborative 3D multiplayer Serious games as a set of three elements: The Game World, the Players, and (Inter-)Actions. Players are modelled using a group model to summarize the learning, gaming, and social interaction features of the group of players. The group model is updated according to actions and interactions of its members. The group model, as well as game relevant parameters are collected in the GM interface and toolset, which provides the GM with

1. A complete overview over all necessary actions and events in the game. The GM can view the group model, thus having insight into the players' actions and interactions, their learning progress and gaming behaviour.

2. The necessary mechanism to adapt/control these happenings according to his/her professional opinion. The GM is provided with a set of tools for adaptation of gaming mechanisms for him/her to be able to control/adapt the game ad hoc. Adaptable parts of such games can generically be described as the Terrain+static 3D objects, NPCs, and interactable objects, which together form the Game World.

Figure 2. Conceptual approach towards game-mastering in multiplayer serious games

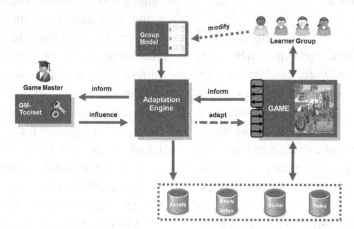

This approach is being used in the above-mentioned 3D multiplayer Serious Games for collaborative learning and training: Woodment and Escape from Wilson Island.

Woodment: A GM is provided with the necessary observation and control tools based on the approach mentioned above. The GM is able to adjust difficulty parameters whenever players are over-challenged or bored, he/she can provide help or trigger specific questions. Furthermore, the GM can control chat options for training of communication among team members.

Escape from Wilson Island: Again, a GM is provided with the necessary tools for observation and adaptation of the game. The GM can alter difficulty related parameters, use an NPC for communication with the players, or place/remove 3D objects to alter the degree of difficulty.

KNOWLEDGE SHARING IN SERIOUS GAMES USING PEER EDUCATION

The knowledge exchange among peers playing a Serious Game for Learning can be supported by inter-connecting the players. Beside the teacher who is supervising the scenario as a Game Master and giving individual instructional support, the peers can help each other with hints or identification of mistakes (Peer Tutoring). Even though immersion into the story and adaptation to the player's abilities are pedagogically well designed in Serious Games for Learning, players can have misconceptions or get stuck with game quests. Then they seek for assistance from friends or online. Accessing hints, solutions and help of others directly in the gaming context can improve the game play and learning experience.

Furthermore the use of open-format quest(ion)s is most valuable for diagnosis of learners' misconceptions. As approaches and solutions to these tasks are creative and manifold it is still a challenge for computer algorithms to interpret and assess such content thoroughly. Instead, peers of the player can assess and rate the created solutions (Peer Assessment). On the one side, this concept helps players in learning by teaching and analysis of the solutions and on the other side it allows the use of open-format-quests in Serious Games.

Additionally the users from *Online Social Networks* can be connected to the game as a valuable resource of experience knowledge if they are provided with participation possibilities.

In summary the concept of *Peer Education (Peer Tutoring and Peer Assessment)* is valuable for teaching and assessment among peers with similar learning targets in Serious Games. Thus this chapter provides an overview over the interconnection of players for knowledge exchange, the technical solution approach and related research projects.

State of the Art Research on Peer Education

E-Learning environments that can serve diagnostic purposes are in the scope of different research interests. *Intelligent Tutoring Systems* try to keep track of the student's input and are predefined in a very elaborate way (Ritter, Anderson, Koedinger, & Corbett, 2007). They are proved to be useful providing feedback in time of the problem solutions. In addition didactic research proved the advantages of methods like learning by teaching, collaborative learning and the benefits of social exchange for motivation (Gillies, 2004).

Sociological analysis of interactions of individuals in their organizational and private social networks have shown the benefit of information exchange among peers; especially if they are not closely but weakly tied. From the field of computer science the *Social Network Analysis* (SNA) has carried out extensive research to investigate the phenomenon of knowledge sharing over weak ties between users not closely related (Fetter, Berlanga, & Sloep, 2009; Granovetter, 1973; Petróczi, Nepusz, & Bazsó, 2006). That indeed weakly tied 'strangers' are willing to contribute information, assistance and help, depends on the consciously belonging to the same social group or having the same, non-competitive goals (Constant, Sproull, & Kiesler, 1996).

From a pedagogical point of view fostering the knowledge transfer between peers of a social group (e.g. classroom peers or players of the same game) is valued beneficial for personality and social competency development, learning by teaching, additional supplement to instructors teaching and provides individualized learning ex-

periences (Damon, 1984); highlighting the positive effects like raising interest for challenging tasks and fostering pro-social behavior. The potential of *Peer Education* (Tutoring and Assessment) has been investigated in the field of web-based collaboration and online tutoring. Beside a general interest of students in examining peer work (Stepanyan, Mather, Jones, & Lusuardi, 2009) better knowledge acquisition has been shown for computer-supported collaborative work as well (Mohammad, Guetl, & Kappe, 2009; Westera & Wagemans, 2007). Results show the motivational benefits and improved social and knowledge skills.

Group dynamics and individuals role adaption in groups (leaders, followers) has been highly investigated for team communication processes and collaborative, learning-oriented groupwork (Lisak & Erez, 2009; Mohan, Lemenager, & McCracken, 2006). These studies result in the importance of an individual commitment or shared goals and identify several more (cultural) factors influencing the performance of groups. Thus, it is the focus and target of the suggested Peer Education concepts of this chapter, *not* to establish groupwork or teamwork where individuals are tied together to reach a common (learning) target, but to build on the mentioned findings from Social Network Analysis and from the field of computer-supported collaboration as mentioned above. In these scenarios, the individuals are loosely coupled and give individual feedback or assess individual solutions in a structured computer-mediated communication process. That a structured, formalized feedback process for issue-focussed communication increases the quality of hints (and knowledge transferred) has been shown by Baker for a school class scenario (Baker & Lund, 1997). Consequently such a formalization may lower the social issues (like group dynamics, leadership, etc.), too.

The connection of Serious Games to Social Media is inspired by the interaction types that are used by players of *Social Casual Games* which are connected to *Online Social Networks*. Loreto and Gouaïch (2004) identify *Asynchronous Play* as one important characteristic of such games. Players interact by e.g. exchanging items or favors, but do not have to be online or in the game at the same time. As stated by O'Neill (2008) in his criteria list about Social Games, these games are mostly *turn-based* and *casual games* connected to Online Social Networks, but still Multiplayer in a sense that there is an awareness of others' actions in games. We summarize these four criteria as *Casual Multiplayer*, which means a singleplayer game pay, but multiplayer atmosphere due to asynchronous play and awareness – and thus interplay – of the activities of others. Asynchronous Play and Casual Multiplayer are a basis to create so called *Social Serious Games* (Konert, Göbel, & Steinmetz, 2012).

A broader view to *Social Media* interaction patterns in general is given by Crumlish and Malone (2009). A somewhat simplified list focusing the interaction types between users of *Social Media* applications can be found at Julien (2011) and will be used in this chapter later on.

Computer Diagnosis Problem

Processing and interpreting free text answers, drawings and different solutions of open format questions is still a challenge for computer systems. Advances in text and language processing are made continuously, especially if the context can be narrowed to a specific field. Nonetheless, the matching of semantic meaning in a student's reply to the desired answer remains as a research field. Thus diagnostic software tools widely use multiple-choice, gap text or sorting rather than open format test questions (Ritter et al., 2007). Unfortunately open format test questions are the most important ones for teachers from a diagnostic point of view as they reveal misconceptions or partial understanding of students (Prediger, Selter, & Dortmund, 2008). We call this the *Computer Diagnosis Problem.*

Individual Group Assessment Problem

Diagnosis is usually conducted on an individual level. This prevents students from working collaboratively, sharing knowledge and giving hints. At the same time the benefits of group learning has been reported in many studies (Gillies, 2004; Klawe & Phillips, 1995). More precisely classroom research shows advantages for learning when feedback is given by peers as well rather than by teachers only (Gillies, 2004). Peer tutoring helps students to understand their misconceptions better, if they are explained by other students as they use the same language and share a common background for communication (Damon, 1984). We call the fact, that for individual diagnosis students need to be assessed individually, but for learning knowledge sharing in the peer group is favored the *Individual Group Assessment Problem*. It is desired to allow the knowledge sharing without risking precise individual students' assessment.

Peer Matching Problem

When students have to choose their peers in the classroom for a group work they usually feel obliged to choose their friends or peers of a similar proficiency level in the subject (Cohen, 1994). Both lead to a suboptimal, homogeneous group formation concerning instead of heterogeneous groups for optimal knowledge exchange and learning outcome for every group member. In secondary schools with classes that usually contain around 30 students a teacher has not the time to establish an optimal grouping for group work in pairs or triples as this would mean an intensive preparation to mix the students with different proficiency levels. Additionally learning styles should be taken into account for peer matching as it influences the perceived suitability of the group members and learning effects. Unfortunately students "will be rebellious if they are forced to work in groups that are not of their own choosing" (Mitchell, Reilly,

Bramwell, & Lilly, 2012, p. 21). We call the fact that a mix of proficiency level is desired and learning styles should be considered for optimal knowledge exchange, but actually friendship and similar proficiency levels are matched the *Peer Matching Problem*.

Diagnosis Adaptation Problem

The main goal of diagnosis is to provide a standardized and comparable result of individuals (Schleicher, 1999). A student's motivation for participation (i.e. using the tools provided) increases significantly, if the questions provided fit her individual skills and prevent situations of boredom or anxiety (Buchanan & Csikszentmihalyi, 1991; Chen, 2007). We call the fact that a suitable level of diagnostic task difficulty increases the motivation and performance of a student while diagnosis needs to be inter-individually comparable the *Diagnosis Adaptation Problem*.

Teacher's Supervision Problem

The peer-learning scenario where each student has his own pace and different tasks while sharing knowledge through feedback to each other by means of a computer-based environment is much more dynamic than traditional classroom setups. In order to keep control of the guidance and support of the class as a whole and each individual student at once, the teacher needs to have a tool at hand to supervise and influence the scenario in order to give the individual instructional support and have a diagnostic overview. The requirements concerning the teacher supervision can be summarized as the *Teacher's Supervision Problem*.

A SOCIAL SERIOUS GAMING APPROACH

The focus of the proposed architectural concept (framework) named GENIUS is the enhancement of (existing) Serious Games with content-centered functionality for *Knowledge Sharing* among peers (players) using existing *Online Social Networks*. Even though the approach is extendable to any computer game or content-related software application the focus is on Serious Games for Learning that are mostly designed as adventure games where learners explore the learning content in a story-based game environment. The following three enhancing components are designed as the *Social Serious Game Middleware*:

User-Generated Content Exchange

When tasks (quests) in such games have to be solved, complex games allow several approaches to reach this aim. Even so the game has been thoroughly designed and help is available in the game by descriptions and dialogs with e.g. Non-Person Characters (NPCs), players do have misconceptions about the rules or goals related to the task leading to frustration because the game does not provide proper feedback. In this case players are forced to pause the game, search in forums or ask other players for hints. The found results might be misleading, to detailed or to brief and players might read more of the solution as they need, because the content generated by other players is not tight detailed enough to the game level, quest and context of play.

In GENIUS-enhanced Serious Games the players can save game-play related content (text, image, video) enriched with meta-data into the middleware database. Such a storage can as well be done by the game engine automatically and transparent to the user. The content is then used for recommendations in case (other) players need hints. The provision of content can be done automatically or on request by the player. The content itself is categorized as question, information, hint or solution for a specific game's quest. Additionally to the game-integrated storage and retrieval of user-generated content a web-frontend allows the browsing, rating and commenting, too. Thus players can share their knowledge in a bulletin board-like structure and explore other players' approaches, opinions and (best) solutions (*Peer Tutoring* concept and *Learning by Example*). For games that allow open solutions to quests that challenge the creativity and lead to solutions not easily assessable by computer-algorithms the community-based structure allows other players to assess the solutions (*Peer Assessment* concept and *Learning by Teaching*). By combining the judgment of several other players a thorough result can be calculated and the game engine can integrate the resulted rating into further game flow. In brief, the difference to the commonly available bulletin board systems is the automatic synchronization and organization of content according to the levels and quest-structure of the computer game that as well has access to the content, rating and comments.

Game Influencing

The above mentioned sharing of content to increase game-play experience and knowledge acquisition primarily connects players already using the game. Beside this, the *Game Influencing* component of the middleware focusses on connecting a game player with his social network around. Thus two effects can be achieved:

First, the awareness for the Serious Game can be increased as the news posts spread in social networks directly affect viral propagation; especially if it is not only a posted message, but a call for participation (as described in the next effect).

Second, knowledge from outside the game community can be drawn into the game play. Therefore the middleware provides the possibility to spread news (posts) to befriended social network users and offers an interface to ask the receivers of posted messages to participate in votes or content uploads. Game designers using the middleware create and enable such a *Game Influence* instance via the provided Application Programming Interface (API), select type of influence (e.g. multiple choice, gap text, image upload), timeout and scope. The middleware spreads the news according to the scope, e.g. to former players or non-player friends. The participation results can then be pulled by the computer game and be integrated in further game play. These influence kinds are manifold. To the best of our knowledge no taxonomy of game influence kinds from online social networks to one's personal game play and vice versa does exist. Thus, one currently ongoing aspect of the research is the creation of such a structure (See Figure 3).

Peer Matching

Fostering the knowledge exchange between players (peers in the social network of currently playing individuals) is a promising way of increasing each individual learning outcomes and achievement of the learning targets related to the computer game.

The usefulness of comments, hints, solutions, or approaches of peers for one individual player is assumed to depend on the divergence or similarity of level of expertise, personal traits, learner type, and player type. The middleware therefore continuously maintains player profiles accounting the mentioned attributes to provide recommendations of (temporarily) suitable learning partners or small groups of peers to exchange knowledge related to the game. Additionally the matching algorithms can be used to order multiple available hints or solutions in the component called *User-generated Content Exchange*. The combination and relevance of such personal attributes for Peer Matching to enhance learning outcomes in Serious Games is part of the research focus.

KNOWLEDGE SHARING IN ENCLOSED SOCIAL NETWORKS

It can be seen that all components of the described middleware benefit from a connection to existing Online Social Networks like Facebook, but are not necessarily need this connection. It can be substituted by the ad-hoc community network

Figure 3. Middleware design for social serious game middleware. <def> for definition, <use> for usage (access).

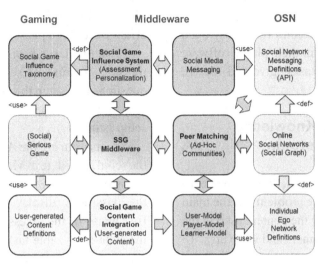

of players playing the same Serious Game or the existing enclosed social network of classmates in a school classroom, as focused in the now described implementation.

The previously-mentioned problems have been addressed by combining diagnosis and learning together with social networking principles using the described middleware concept (GENIUS) for peer assessment and knowledge sharing between students in a classroom math learning environment where all students and the teacher(s) form the underlying social network. In order to address the problems, the system will use a carefully reviewed and empirically validated didactic model of competence development and diagnosis (Bayrhuber, Leuders, Bruder, & Wirtz, 2010). Hence, the system in this scenario aims to be highly valuable for diagnosis (teacher's perspective) and understanding the own learning progress (students' perspective).

The proposed system, called PEDALE (Peer Education Diagnostic And Learning Environment), will be used by teachers during classroom instruction to get a detailed diagnosis about their students' competencies. The students are instructed to use the software within a fixed time period

(e.g. 40 minutes, depending on test configuration) to solve the diagnostic tasks, each student at an individual computer. During the time the students work with the software the teacher can monitor as well as participate in the process. With the help of a specific control panel that is activated if a teacher logs into the scenario the teacher can get an overview about the whole classes' progress as well as over certain events. It provides a filter-based search interface to see answers in the database by student or by task, with or without feedbacks. The teacher can select a particular solution to be displayed like the feedback giving students see it. The teacher can simply look at the given feedbacks as well as give individual feedback to specific students himself. The control panel can slide up and down to overcome overlapping due to screen size restrictions.

Role Model

The users of PEDALE belong to two user groups: teachers and students in secondary schools. The teachers have the role of editing, changing, and storing the scenario setups with the appropriate authoring software. In the player software they have a 'bird's eye view' over the scenario and can see which student has solved which tasks, given which feedback and so on (see next).

The students are the second role. They open the configured scenario in their player software and solve the prepared tasks, give and receive feedback.

3-Phase Model for Knowledge Sharing in the Classroom

Beside other application areas, the design of educational software faces the problem that the main experts (e.g. teachers) for the content used in the software are not programmers and vice versa. To decouple the dependencies during development a feasible approach is to provide authoring software for teachers to create content and configure the application behavior independently from programmers who otherwise would need to implement this. A second component is a player that displays the configured test interface and content to the students. The authoring tool will be used for the setup of diagnostic tests and the input of test questions fitting the used diagnostic model. The corresponding player has to be capable of displaying the new interface elements and will adapt the test course (See Figure 4). For further details about the functionality of authoring tool and player see chapter *StoryTec Framework*.

A diagram of the software components with their key functionality and the data flow are displayed in Figure 5. The work with the software is arranged in three phases:

First, the *Assessment Setup* with teachers authoring, creating or selecting the desired test questions and setup the characteristics like duration, amount of peer assessment and the class setup (students).

Second, during the *Assessment* students load the configured test via their player software and work through the diagnostic assessment in the classroom (displayed as Student A). In the first phase of the assessment the students solve machine-analyzable tasks. On the base of these tasks a first diagnosis is generated automatically and returned to the students after they went through all the tasks of the first part. The second part of the assessment asks the students to evaluate solved problems regarding the correctness and the solution process. The answers to these solved problems are open test questions and are displayed to peer students (e.g. student B gets a solved problem of student A and vice versa). The solved problems are retrieved from the tool's data repository and the player decides which of the related solved problems matches best to be displayed. A Peer Matching Algorithm will be developed that takes into account students' current skill competence profiles and test performance.

Figure 4. StoryTec (left) and StoryPlay (right) displaying the same math task scene (texts in German)

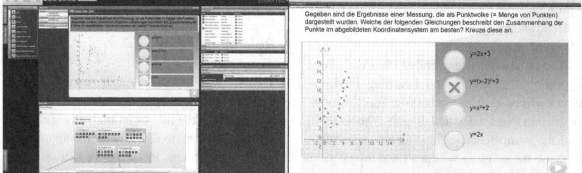

Figure 5. Phases (1-3) of diagnosis and learning with peer assessment

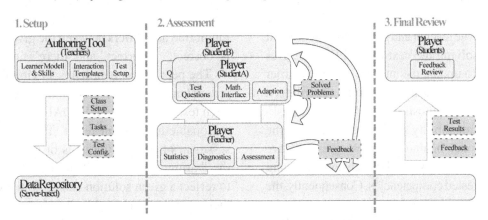

The given peer feedback is then stored for later review. Additionally, a second player version is provided to teachers for monitoring the students' progress and for final review of all solved problems.

In a final *Feedback* phase, the students are provided with all their assessment results and peer feedback, as well as a feedback from the teacher.

Adaptive Diagnostic Model

As a sound diagnosis of the students' current state of knowledge is required for effective and individual learning, we use the diagnostic instrument developed in the 3-year project HEUREKO (Bayrhuber-Habeck, 2009). Within the project a competence model for the mathematical domain "functions and graphs" for lower secondary level students was developed. Focus of the model is the heuristic use and change between the fundamental mathematical representations (numerical, graphic, symbolic, verbal) what can be considered as a significant competence of mathematical problem-solving and modelling (Bayrhuber et al., 2010). Theoretical didactic models of ability that have proven successful at a national as well as an international level were operationalized and empirically assessed in order to provide an empirically grounded instrument for diagnosis and instruction that can be applied to school practice. The Rasch

analyses (Rasch, 1981) proved a four-dimensional model to be the best predictor. Furthermore, the separateness of these dimensions could be shown. Latent class analyses indicate that seven typical competence profiles can be identified empirically across the model dimensions (Bayrhuber et al., 2010). The resulting competency model here provides the basis for a diagnostic instrument for mathematical competencies in the domain "functions and graphs", while at the same time offering approaches to instructional support. The underlying model maps four dimensions of competencies on three levels of mastery. The first two levels comprise tasks that require a predefined input like multiple choice, decisions and numerical solutions, plotting points, intercepts or intersections. The highest level comprises open format replies like describing and reasoning.

We are transfering the paper-based tests about the understanding of mathematical functional dependencies into a software-represenation and provide an user-interface that allows students to choose between and produce verbal expressions, to draw graphs, to develop algebraic terms and to note and complete numerical representations.

About 75% of the questions can be assessed automatically by the software as the solutions and results are definite. Variants of correct and incorrect students' solutions are taken from the results of the HEUREKO Research Project. The questions that ask for open text input and the corresponding given answers (Solved Problems) are assessed by the teacher and peers while the student continues solving the next tasks. PEDALE uses the results to update the internal didactic learner model and select further questions accordingly. This adaptive diagnosis is possible without risking the comparability of the results due to the didactic model behind. The test questions are all categorized into several dimensions mapping exactly the tested competencies. Consequently, the use of the appropriate didactic model avoids the *Diagnosis Adaptation Problem* stated above. Still it can utilize the findings of flow theory research and adaptation (Buchanan & Csikszentmihalyi, 1991; Chen, 2007).

Peer Assessment

The test itself will be organized into several parts, each containing questions for specific dimensions of the model. With the completion of one part of the underlying diagnostic model a student (Student B) is asked to review so called solved problems of this domain. These are questions that display the approach and/or solution of another student (Student A) and that ask student B:

- To decide whether or not the approach is correct and to rate the confidence of the given evaluation on a five-point-Likert-scale.
- Give qualitative feedback on where things were done well, which mistakes can be identified or where insufficiencies were found.
- Give hints and advice how the solution could be improved or solved alternatively and finally.
- Self-evaluate how helpful the given feedback might be for the addressed peer on a five-point-Likert-scale.

In order to give a constructive and helpful feedback each student has a feedback guide at his desk which contains guiding questions for

writing a good feedback. The feedback guide is structured by what sort of solutions the students might find and differs between the given solution is 'correct,' 'incorrect,' and 'there's no solution.'

The peer assessment helps solving the *Computer Diagnosis Problem*. It enables us to provide open test questions with PEDALE and still get a reasonable assessment result. The learners' assessment of peer solutions is of great value for the learning process as it prompts the students to reflect a given solution and set it in relation to their own approach and knowledge. In doing so students are encountered with 1) real solutions and (2) approaches and mistakes of students with same social and learning background (Hilbert, Renkl, Schworm, Kessler, & Reiss, 2008).

For peer assessment, the effects of social networks have to be taken into account. Conflictive forces influence the student's motivation to invest time and energy in providing a good or average feedback to peers. Research in Social Network Analysis shows complex interdependencies between individuals in a social network. Studies show for settings in which people feel themselves as part of a common organizational team (like a school or class) a strong motivation to help each other with constructive and qualitative feedback (Constant et al., 1996). However, in a classroom environment a competitive situation and complex social interdependencies can exist. The influence on the peer feedback in this scenario remains an open research question. It has to be investigated, whether students provide more appropriate feedback to peer students when names are displayed or when the solution and feedbacks are displayed in an anonymous way. It is expected that students in general have the desire to see and comment other students' solutions as research for computer-supported collaborative learning environments indicates (Stepanyan et al., 2009). The proposed peer assessment setup is expected to support group learning aspects with knowledge sharing through feedback and to prevent the *Individual Group Assessment Problem*, because the students still carry out the test parts independently from each other.

Provision of Feedback

When the assessment time is over students are provided with a direct feedback. The tool returns an evaluation of the machine-analyzable questions as well as the feedback given by peers and the teacher. As Social Network Analyses indicate, the level of trust plays a major role for giving advise and critics (Golbeck, 2005; Petróczi et al., 2006). The transferability of effects of trust and closeness for classroom settings remains to be explored. As students share a more similar cultural background, language and interests with their peers as they do with the teacher, it is expected that feedback of other students is valued as a positive additional learning source. As the overall feedback is displayed after the test, it does not raise the *Individual Group Assessment Problem*.

Peer Matching Model

For each student the actual performance in the scenario (correct and incorrect solutions to tasks), the current math proficiency level (last math mark), gender and age are stored in the role model. In an extra questionnaire the learning style preferences are investigated and added to the model afterwards (see evaluation). As it remains uncertain which criteria should be considered to which degree for matching the peers for feedback provision and

receiving, the model will store the mentioned parameters, but not use them for matching in our model so far. The authors expect to find indicators for optimal matching by analyzing statistically dependencies between the described criteria and the perceived usefulness of received feedback (rated by the students individually). Currently the model will be optimized to take criteria into account for distributing the matching randomly among all participating students that each student gives and receives a balanced amount of feedbacks. By matching the students automatically by computer-algorithms PEDALE helps solving the Peer Matching Problem as teachers do not need to match the students manually.

Supervision

While the students are working with the software the teacher can monitor the classes' overall progress as well as individual student's solutions and feedbacks (see as well chapter *Game Mastering in Multiplayer Games* for further aspects of supervision). Teachers can monitor the task solutions through a teacher supervision panel which allows them to filter the collected information according to their diagnostic or instructional interest. They can supervise all solutions to a specific task, all feedbacks to a specific solution or to a specific task, all solutions and feedbacks a specific students

Figure 6. Left: a student working on a task solution using a digital pen; right: a provided feedback and readers own handwriting in a popup

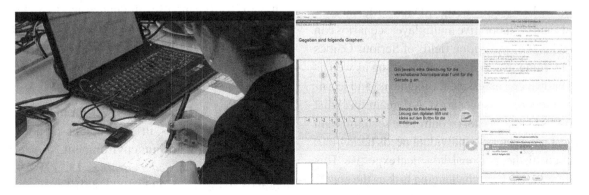

has submitted or received or watch the number of solved tasks in a general overview. Additional to monitoring the student's work, the teachers can intervene by writing feedbacks to a particular student's solution themselves or give hints how to solve the task when a student is stuck with a particular task. If desired, teachers can intervene as well when an incorrect or inadequate feedback is given (See Figure 6).

FUTURE RESEARCH DIRECTIONS

Open Research questions include the design of collaborative multiplayer Serious Games for heterogeneous learner groups. Also, one focus will be orchestration of learning groups in multiplayer SG scenarios with one focus on the concept of a human Game Master and another focus on an AI-based Game Mastering approach. Furthermore, it is an open aspect how Knowledge Sharing processes in games (Peer Education) and Game Mastering can add to each other conceptual. Furthermore, the algorithmic group forming of learners to build learning groups for an optimal learning outcome towards the learning targets in collaborative Serious Games is not yet thoroughly explored.

CONCLUSION

A structured approach towards individual support and control of one's gaming and learning experience is a huge improvement to the field of Serious Games. Thoroughly designed Game Master concepts and collaborative multiplayer scenarios can broaden the application fields of Serious Games for learning in simulation and training as well as for knowledge assessment (diagnosis) and learning in school class scenarios. A domain specialist can – as Game Master – control the scenarios and adjust parameters to individual needs taking into account his/her personal didactical expertise. This is, however, a very challenging task as the cognitive load on the Game Master is very high during

the process of mastering the game. Furthermore, it requires various skills (multitasking, computer skills, etc.). As one cannot assume that every domain expert has these skills, the design of tools to support the Game Master in his tasks is vital. Moreover, with individual instructional support learners gain more from Serious Games if they are enhanced with such components for Game Mastering and Knowledge Sharing among peers.

Thus, Game Designers get tools at hand to influence the learning impact of such Serious Games in several ways:

1. First, with parameters available to instructors as Game Masters for adaptation before a game is played.
2. Second, by paying attention to a thorough embedding of appropriate learning and diagnosis models as well as the appropriate support and visualization for Game Masters to control collaborative learning scenarios during the play.
3. Third, by enabling the exchange of content among the players for knowledge transfer to foster mutual support and assessment of open-format task solutions.

REFERENCES

Azevedo, R., Moos, D., Winters, F., Greene, J., Cromley, J., Olson, E., & Godbole Chaudhuri, P. (2005). Why is externally-regulated learning more effective than self-regulated learning with hypermedia? In *Proceeding of the 2005 Conference on Artificial Intelligence in Education: Supporting Learning through Intelligent and Socially Informed Technology,* (pp. 41–48). IEEE.

Baker, M., & Lund, K. (1997). Promoting reflective interactions in a computer-supported collaborative learning environment. *Journal of Computer Assisted Learning*, *13*, 175–193. doi:10.1046/j.1365-2729.1997.00019.x.

Bayrhuber, M., Leuders, T., Bruder, R., & Wirtz, M. (2010). *Pedocs - Repräsentationswechsel beim umgang mit funktionen – Identifikation von kompetenzprofilen auf der basis eines kompetenzstrukturmodells: Projekt HEUREKO.* BELTZ Pädagogik.

Bayrhuber-Habeck, M. (2009). *Konstruktion und evaluation eines kompetenzstrukturmodells im bereich mathematischer repräsentationen: Psychologie schweizerische zeitschrift für psychologie und ihre andwendungen.* PH Freiburg.

Buchanan, R., & Csikszentmihalyi, M. (1991). Flow: The psychology of optimal experience. *Design Issues, 8*(1), 80. doi:10.2307/1511458.

Chen, J. (2007). Flow in games (and everything else). *Communications of the ACM, 50*(4), 31–34. doi:10.1145/1232743.1232769.

Cohen, G. E. (1994). *Designing groupwork: Strategies for the heterogeneous classroom* (2nd ed.). New York, NY: Teachers College Press.

Constant, D., Sproull, L., & Kiesler, S. (1996). The kindness of strangers: The usefulness of electronic weak ties for technical advice. *Organization Science, 7*(2), 119–135. Retrieved from http://www-2.cs.cmu.edu/~kiesler/publications/PDFs/Constantkindness.pdf doi:10.1287/orsc.7.2.119.

Crumlish, C., & Malone, E. (2009). *Designing social interfaces: Principles, patterns, and practices for improving the user experience (animal guide)* (p. 520). New York, NY: Yahoo Press.

Damon, W. (1984). Peer education: The untapped potential. *Journal of Applied Developmental Psychology, 5*(4), 331–343. doi:10.1016/0193-3973(84)90006-6.

Delwiche, A. (2006). Massively multiplayer online games (MMOs) in the new media classroom. *Journal of Educational Technology & Society, 9*(3), 160–172.

Dillenbourg, P. (1999). What do you mean by collaborative learning? In Dillenbourg, P. (Ed.), *Collaborative-Learning: Cognitive and Computational Approaches* (pp. 1–19). Oxford, UK: Elsevier.

Dillenbourg, P., Järvelä, S., & Fischer, F. (2009). The evolution of research on computer-supported collaborative learning. *Technology-Enhanced Learning*, 3–19.

Fetter, S., Berlanga, A., & Sloep, P. (2009). Enhancing the social capital of learning communities by using an ad hoc transient communities service. *Advances in Web Based Learning*, (1), 150–157. doi:10.1007/978-3-642-03426-8_19

Gillies, R. (2004). The effects of cooperative learning on junior high school students during small group learning. *Learning and Instruction, 14*(2), 197–213. doi:10.1016/S0959-4752(03)00068-9.

Golbeck, J. A. (2005). *Computing and applying trust in web-based social networks.* University Park, MD: University of Maryland.

Granovetter, M. S. (1973). The strength-of-weak-ties perspective on creativity: A comprehensive examination and extension. *American Journal of Sociology, 78*(6), 1360–1380. doi:10.1086/225469.

Hämäläinen, R. (2006). Designing and evaluating collaboration in a virtual game environment for vocational learning. *Computers & Education, 50*(1), 98–109. doi:10.1016/j.compedu.2006.04.001.

Hämäläinen, R., Manninen, T., Järvelä, S., & Häkkinen, P. (2006). Learning to collaborate: Designing collaboration in a 3-D game environment. *The Internet and Higher Education, 9*(1), 47–61. doi:10.1016/j.iheduc.2005.12.004.

Hämäläinen, R., & Oksanen, K. (2012). Challenge of supporting vocational learning: Empowering collaboration in a scripted 3D game - How does teachers' real-time orchestration make a difference? *Computers & Education, 59,* 281–293. doi:10.1016/j.compedu.2012.01.002.

Hilbert, T., Renkl, A., Schworm, S., Kessler, S., & Reiss, K. (2008). Learning to teach with worked-out examples: A computer-based learning environment for teachers. *Journal of Computer Assisted Learning, 24*(4), 316–332. doi:10.1111/j.1365-2729.2007.00266.x.

Johnson, R. T., & Johnson, D. W. (1988). Co-operative learning: Two heads learn better than one. *Transforming Education: In Context, 18,* 34. Retrieved from http://www.context.org/ICLIB/IC18/Johnson.htm

Julien, J. (2011). Social media interaction pattern library. *The Jordan Rules.* Retrieved May 8, 2012, from http://thejordanrules.posterous.com/social-media-interaction-pattern-library

Klawe, M., & Phillips, E. (1995). A classroom study : Electronic games engage children as researchers. In *Proceedings of the First International Conference on Computer Support for Collaborative Learning,* (pp. 209–213). doi:10.1.1.47.9799

Kollar, I. (2012). *The classroom of the future: Orchestrating collaborative learning spaces.* Sense.

Konert, J., Göbel, S., & Steinmetz, R. (2012). Towards social serious games. In T. Connolly, P. Felicia, G. Neville, & S. Tabirca (Eds.), *Proceedings of the 6th European Conference on Games Based Learning (ECGBL),* (Vol. 1). Cork, Ireland: Academic Bookshop.

Kreijns, K., Kirschner, P. A., Jochems, W., & Van Buuren, H. (2007). Measuring perceived sociability of computer-supported collaborative learning environments. *Computers & Education, 49*(2), 176–192. doi:10.1016/j.compedu.2005.05.004.

Larusson, J. A., & Alterman, R. (2009). Wikis to support the "collaborative" part of collaborative learning. *International Journal of Computer-Supported Collaborative Learning, 4*(4), 371–402. doi:10.1007/s11412-009-9076-6.

Lisak, A., & Erez, M. (2009). Leaders and followers in multi-cultural teams. In *Proceeding of the 2009 International Workshop on Intercultural Collaboration - IWIC '09,* (p. 81). New York, NY: ACM Press. doi:10.1145/1499224.1499238

Loreto, I. D., & Gouaïch, A. (2004). *Social casual games success is not so casual.* Word Journal of the International Linguistic Association.

Mitchell, S. N., Reilly, R., Bramwell, F. G., & Lilly, F. (2012). Friendship and choosing groupmates: Preferences for teacher-selected vs. student-selected groupings in high school science classes. *Journal of Instructional Psychology, 31*(1), 1–6.

Mohammad, A. L. S., Guetl, C., & Kappe, F. (2009). PASS: Peer-assessment approach for modern learning settings. In *Proceedings of the Advances in Web Based Learning-ICWL 2009: 8th International Conference,* (p. 44). Springer-Verlag. doi:10.1007/978-3-642-03426-8_5

Mohan, A., Lemenager, E., & McCracken, M. (2006). Targeting areas of improvement in intra-group dynamics using a participative approach - A case study. In *Proceedings of the 2006 IEEE International Engineering Management Conference,* (pp. 110–115). IEEE. doi:10.1109/IEMC.2006.4279828

Nelson, B., & Ketelhut, D. (2008). Exploring embedded guidance and self-efficacy in educational multi-user virtual environments. *International Journal of Computer-Supported Collaborative Learning, 3*(4), 413–427. Retrieved fromhttp://dx.doi.org/10.1007/s11412-008-9049-1

O'Neill, N. (2008). What exactly are social games? *Social Times.* Retrieved January 18, 2011, from http://www.socialtimes.com/2008/07/social-games/

Onrubia, J., & Engel, A. (2009). Strategies for collaborative writing and phases of knowledge construction in CSCL environments. *Computers & Education, 53*(4), 1256–1265. doi:10.1016/j.compedu.2009.06.008.

Petróczi, A., Nepusz, T., & Bazsó, F. (2006). Measuring tie-strength in virtual social networks. *Connections, 27*(2), 39–52.

Prediger, S., Selter, C., & Dortmund, U. (2008). Diagnose als grundlage für individuelle förderung im mathematikunterricht. *Schule NRW, 6*(3), 113–116.

Rasch, G. (1981). *Probabilistic models for some intelligence and attainment tests.* Chicago, IL: University of Chicago Print (Tx). Retrieved from http://www.amazon.com/Probabilistic-Models-Intelligence-Attainment-Tests/dp/0226705544

Rauterberg, G. W. M. (2002). Determinantes for collaboration in networked multi-user games. In *Proceedings of Entertainment Computing: Technologies and Applications.* IEEE.

Ritter, S., Anderson, J. R., Koedinger, K. R., & Corbett, A. (2007). Cognitive tutor: Applied research in mathematics education. *Psychonomic Bulletin & Review, 14*(2), 249–255. doi:10.3758/BF03194060 PMID:17694909.

Roschelle, J., & Teasley, S. (1995). The construction of shared knowledge in collaborative problem solving. In O'Malley, C. (Ed.), *Computer-Supported Collaborative Learning* (pp. 69–97). Berlin, Germany: Springer-Verlag. doi:10.1007/978-3-642-85098-1_5.

Schleicher, A. (1999). *Measuring student knowledge and skills: A new framework for assessment.* Organization for Economic.

Stahl, G., Koschmann, T., & Suthers, D. (2006). *Cambridge handbook of the learning sciences.* Cambridge, UK: Cambridge University Press.

Stepanyan, K., Mather, R., Jones, H., & Lusuardi, C. (2009). Student engagement with peer assessment: A review of pedagogical design and technologies. In *Proceedings of the Advances in Web Based Learning–ICWL 2009,* (pp. 367–375). ICWL. doi:10.1007/978-3-642-03426-8_44

Tychsen, A., Hitchens, M., Brolund, T., & Kavakli, M. (2005). The game master. In *Proceedings of the Second Australasian Conference on Interactive Entertainment,* (pp. 215–222). IEEE.

Voulgari, I., & Komis, V. (2008). Massively multiuser online games: The emergence of effective collaborative activities for learning. In *Proceedings of the 2008 Second IEEE International Conference on Digital Game and Intelligent Toy Enhanced Learning,* (pp. 132–134). IEEE Computer Society. doi:http://dx.doi.org/10.1109/DIGITEL.2008.20

Wendel, V., Babarinow, M., Hörl, T., Kolmogorov, S., Göbel, S., & Steinmetz, R. (2010). *Transactions on edutainment IV.* Springer.

Wendel, V., Gutjahr, M., Göbel, S., & Steinmetz, R. (2012). Designing collaborative multiplayer serious games for collaborative learning. In *Proceedings of the CSEDU 2012.* CSEDU.

Westera, W., & Wagemans, L. (2007). Help me! Online learner support through the self- organised allocation of peer tutors. *Abstracts of the 13th International Conference on Technology Supported Learning & Training,* (pp. 105–107). Berlin, Germany: ICEW GmbH. Retrieved from http://hdl.handle.net/1820/2075

Zea, N. P., Sanchez, J. L. G., & Gutierrez, F. L. (2009). Collaborative learning by means of video games: An entertainment system in the learning processes. In *Proceedings of the 2009 Ninth IEEE International Conference on Advanced Learning Technologies,* (pp. 215–217). Washington, DC: IEEE Computer Society. doi:http://dx.doi.org/10.1109/ICALT.2009.95

ADDITIONAL READING

Harteveld, C. (2011). *Triadic game design: Balancing reality, meaning and play*. Berlin, Germany: Springer. doi:10.1007/978-1-84996-157-8.

Kaplan, A. M., & Haenlein, M. (2010). Users of the world, unite! The challenges and opportunities of social media. *Business Horizons, 53*(1), 59–68. doi:10.1016/j.bushor.2009.09.003.

Ritterfeld, U., Cody, M. J., Vorderer, P., & MyiLibrary. (2009). *Serious games: Mechanisms and effects* (1st ed.). New York, NY: Routledge.

Salen, K., & Zimmerman, E. (2003). *Rules of play: Game design fundamentals*. Cambridge, MA: The MIT Press.

KEY TERMS AND DEFINITIONS

Application Programming Interface (API): An constant and documented scheme or pattern that allows independent software components to access the API-providing software component. The specification allows communication and exchange of data without any further needed knowledge about components' internal implementation.

Collaborative Learning: Collaborative learning describes a process in which a group of learners learn together in a previously defined setting such that they profit from each other.

Computer-Supported Collaborative Learning (CSCL): Computer-supported Collaborative Learning is a concept in which collaborative learning is enhanced by computers and computer-supported technology like email, messengers, visual presentations, or special e-learning tools.

Game Mastering: The term Game Mastering describes authoring, assessing, and controlling a Serious Game at runtime by a human person with the goal of optimizing the players' experience in terms of learning and gaming.

Knowledge Sharing: When an individual externalizes accumulated knowledge into an explicit transferable form that enables interaction concerning the knowledge content and this explicit form is made available to other individuals, then we call this process Knowledge Sharing.

Narrative Game-Based Learning Object (NGLOB): A Narrative game-based Learning Object is a used as an attribution of scenes or scene-like parts of games in order to explain their function in terms if story (narration), gaming, and learning. An NGLOB contains information about what should be learned in the scene, how the scene does continue the game's story, and for which player type the scene fits best.

Peer Education: Peer Education is the superordinate term for all peer-based educational processes. These are mainly Peer Tutoring and Peer Assessment. In Peer Tutoring students help each other with hints, support and mentoring (Learning by Teaching) whereas in Peer Assessment they evaluate, assess, rate and give feedback to solutions and approaches of their peers (Learning by Example). All concepts have in common that they foster the knowledge exchange between individuals on a same level of expertise in contrast to traditional teacher-student interactions.

Social Network Analysis (SNA): Originating from social sciences, SNA investigates (dynamic) data of (large) social networks, i.e. interactions and relations among individuals (mostly humans) to derive, by mathematical means, metrics to describe the structural roles and characteristics of a network as a whole and individual nodes.

Social Serious Games: By the term Social Serious Game, we are referring a Serious Game with all components mandatory for a Social Game. This includes the use of Social Media interaction for Peer Education accounting the concepts of Casual Multiplayer and Asynchronous Play.

Chapter 7
Evaluation of Serious Games

Stefan Göbel
Technische Universität Darmstadt, Germany

Michael Gutjahr
Technische Universität Darmstadt, Germany

Sandro Hardy
Technische Universität Darmstadt, Germany

ABSTRACT

Comprehensive evaluation studies are necessary to "prove" the benefit of Serious Games (SG). This is also extremely important for the commercial success of SG: Best practice examples with profound, well-recorded positive effects will provide relevant arguments to invest into SG for training/education, sports and health, and other application domains. On the other hand, it is not easy to prove the benefit of SG and to measure its effects (e.g. learning effects or medical effects) and affects (user experience factors such as fun during play). Evaluation methodologies might be split into observation, self-evaluation (e.g. questionnaires, interviews), associative methods, performance analyses, and psychophysiology measurement. Technology-enhanced evaluation methods, for instance, facing expression measurement are in the centre of attention. This chapter provides an overview of these methods and describes current interdisciplinary research and technology development achievements in that field.

INTRODUCTION

The main target of an evaluation study for Serious Games is to prove an impact of a SG (fulfillment of overall serious goal plus entertainment factors). Therefore, two important questions have to be addressed: *What* effects and affects are going to be measured? And *How* is it done? "What" defines the target of the game "what are the main effects and affects the game should fulfill and be proved by an evaluation study?" (e.g. improvement of knowledge, performance, well-being). "How"

DOI: 10.4018/978-1-4666-3673-6.ch007

defines the method, includes aspects of evaluation methods design and instruments. "How has the study to be designed (setting)" and "how can the effects been measured (instrument)".

To decide what to measure, a first classification can be conducted by dividing the "impact" of a game in three categories: emotion, cognition, and performance. Emotions are all variables that can be used to draw a conclusion of the emotional state of the user and its experience of the game. But the term "user experience" (Lennart Nacke, 2009) represents a complex construct including aspects of positive emotions, negative emotions, effectance, motivation, immersion, flow, arousal, curiosity, usability and not at last cognitive load. Cognition includes all variables showing some changes in cognition and its structure like problem solving, decision making, memory and available knowledge. Performance includes all variables indicating an advancement in the person's ability to conduct a task like reaction time, persistence, strength.

Concerning 'what to measure', a lot of research has been done to show effects and to prove the benefit of Serious Games in particular application domains. Examples include work in the field of game-based learning, e.g. Egenfeldt-Nielsen (2005) conducted a study at a Danish high-school involving 72 students and two teachers. In this study the use of Europa Universalis II, a commercial historical strategy game was examined. De Freitas and Oliver (2006) introduced a framework for helping tutors evaluating the potential of using games- and simulation-based learning and applied their framework to two Serious Games. Mitchell, Savill-Smith, and Britain (2004) provide a comprehensive overview over the use of computer and video games for learning. They argue to use those games for learning as they engage players and draw them into virtual worlds, because they are fun and provide a challenge and immediate feedback, and because they handle huge amounts of content and can be instantly updated and customized. Law, Kickmeier-Rust, Albert, and Holzinger

(2008) provide an evaluation framework based on a holistic understanding and a formal ontological representation of interacting processes involved in active and dynamic learning processes, which is able to measure performance outcomes, attitude outcomes, and programmatic outcomes. Shen, Wang, and Ritterfeld (2009) performed a study about the entertainment value of Serious Games. Their findings reveal that Serious Games can be reasonably enjoyable compared to non-serious games. Further work in the field of game-based learning comes from Malone and Lepper (1987), Klabbers (2003), and Prensky (2003). Work in the field of games for health and sport shows some effectiveness of games e.g. a reduction of "diabetes-related urgent and emergency visits by 77 percent after diabetic youngsters had the game at home for six months, compared to [...] a control group" (Lieberman, 2001). Whitehead, Johnston, Nixon and Welch (2010) "survey a number of quantitative exergame studies to define a general set of elements that make exergames effective from a physical standpoint", Kato, Cole, Bradlyn and Pollock (2008) evaluated the effectiveness of a game, Re-Mission, for cancer therapy and lined out that "the video-game intervention significantly improved treatment adherence and indicators of cancer-related self-efficacy and knowledge". Further work in the field of games for health and sport comes from Baranowski, Buday, Thompson and Baranowski (2008), Papastergiou (2009) and Kretschmann, Dittus, Lutz, and Meier (2010).

But *how* can emotion, cognition and performance be measured? Here it is necessary to differ between the *method* (the setting/the design of a study) and the *instrument* (tool) that should be used. The method is the design of the study (the setting in which the data are collected). Most important for the possibility to interpret empirical data is the methodical design of the research study. An experimental design with a control group allows a causal interpretation and therefore is mostly desirable. Conducting a pretest and a posttest in both groups (the experimental group and the control group) ensures to compare only the changes caused by the treatment. But often there can be gathered information by field inquiry, preliminary one group studies or case reports. The instrument is the tool that is used to collect data (e.g. a questionnaire or a blood pressure monitor). Classical instruments to measure the impact of a game represent user-centred questionnaires, interviews, observations and expert testimonies or logfile analyses and video analyses on the technical side. A first classification of instruments that can be used to measure user experience may divide the instruments in five categories of tests, depending on the source of information these tests are using: Observation (e.g. video analysis), self-report (e.g. questionnaire, interview), association (e.g. responsiveness), performance analysis (e.g. log-file) and psycho-physiology (e.g. blood pressure, EEG).

Figure 1 summarizes and categorizes a number of possible evaluation methodologies and instruments. The main differences cover the complexity (effort) of the methods and instruments and the proposed quality of the evaluation results in terms of subjective versus technology driven, objective results. In the literature of psychology, quality criteria of testing/evaluation processes are classified into objectivity, validity, and reliability. These aspects are considered, but not further elaborated within the rough schema in Figure 1. For instance, the involvement of experts may be highly appreciated – though it is still of subjective nature. Compared to that, log-file analyses can be very objective and easily to be implemented, but are not appropriate to evaluate affects/user experience factors such as emotion, usability etc. For that, cost-intensive evaluation studies and technology-enhanced setups with sensor technologies (e.g. with facial expression systems or bio signals) are required. In that context, Nacke, Drachen and Göbel (2010) describe methods for assessing individual player experience (psychophysiological player testing via Electromyography (EMG) – allowing a mapping of emotions in the valence dimensions of the circumplex model of affect – with Electrodermal Activity (EDA)

Figure 1. A fist approach to classify research- and evaluation-methods. An ideal method should be highly objective, but low in efforts.

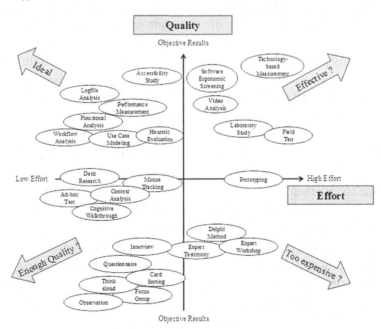

directly related to physical arousal or via Electro-encephalography (EEG), eye tracking, qualitative interviews and questionnaires or parid interative testing and evaluation) and player context experience (taking into account ethnographic and cultural issues, playability heuristics or multiplayer game metrics).

Empirical Evaluation with Questionnaires

A very traditional way to measure emotion is a questionnaire asking for different aspects of user experience.

A questionnaire, measuring a multifarious constructs (like user experience), usually contains different subscales (e.g. positive emotion and negative emotion) which describe the different, multifarious aspects of this construct. To provide a reliable and valid measurement for the overall scale as well as for each of these subscales the subscales themselves consist of diverse items (e.g. items for the subscale "positive emotion" are "fun" and "competence").

The analysis of the overall scale (e.g. user experience) as well as the analysis of each subscale is usually conducted by taking the mean of the (numerical) answers to the diverse items of the scales.

To evidence the quality of the scales the reliability of the scale is stated by using Cronbach's alpha. This value ranges from "0.0" to "1.0" and estimates if the items used to calculate the score of the scale are measuring the same construct (e.g. user experience). The higher the value is the higher is the reliability. A reliable score should hold a reliability of an alpha no less than .80.

Nacke (2009) provides a related work, which also has been considered in the conceptualization of our own questionnaire. Based on the analysis of the usability standards ISO 9241-10/-11, ISO 14915-1 and ISO 13407 (ISO 9241 is a guide line of human computer interaction focusing on aspects like usability. ISO 13407 is a standard specifica-

tion for designing interactive systems) and user experience research by Mandryk, Aktins, and Inkpen (2006) and Nacke (2009), a questionnaire for the evaluation of Serious Games in an interdisciplinary study at TU Darmstadt between the Multimedia Communications Lab and the faculty for psychology has been elaborated. Hereby, the main idea was to create a simple tool (in form of a questionnaire) in order to measure the (individual) user experience of a gamer in addition to relevant usability aspects (such as interface and control). Further, individual feedback concerning possible game design improvements should be collected in order to figure out correlations between game aspects and the user experience of players. The questionnaire is structured into two main parts: A user (experience) part with 7 subscales – positive emotion, negative emotion, cognitive load, motivation, immersion, flow and arousal – and a game (design) part with ten subscales: Quest, Environment, Effectance, Curiosity, Personalization, Interface, Feedback, Social Needs, Storytelling and Structure. For each subscale, three questions are provided resulting in a total amount of 51 questions for the questionnaire. Each item has an evaluation scale between 1 and 10 points; average scores are built per dimension and for the two main parts (user experience and game design), an overall score is used.

To evaluate the reliability of the questionnaire different games has been rated in diverse studies. So the games as well as the settings vary a lot. The games been rated are commercial games as well as self-made games. The games have been rated under different experimental conditions by different participants as well as paired in comparison by the same participant. All in all 145 questionnaires have been evaluated. Evaluation studies show a Cronbach's alpha of .93 for the overall user experience score, which implies that the user experience scale of the questionnaire measures **one** homogeneous construct. The full questionnaire is provided in the Appendix of this chapter.

Showing a satisfying reliability for the user experience score the questionnaire is used to evaluate the user experience of games in order to improve the process of game construction, to conduct scientific studies using the questionnaire as a dependent measurement of user experience and to compare subjective ratings with psycho-physiological data (Wendel, Gutjahr, Göbel, & Steinmetz, 2012) (See Figure 2).

But today sensor-based measurement of emotional states of the user is in the focus of interest in order to objectify user-centered evaluation. Hence, nowadays psycho-physiological data (like blood pressure, pulse, Electrodermal Activity (EDA), Galvanic Skin Response (GSR), Skin Conductance (SC), Electrocardiography (ECG), Electromyography (EMG), Electroencephalography (EEG)) and changes in the facial expression are used more and more to measure user experience. For that, current research efforts are investigated to find appropriate reliable metrics for sensor-based measurement of use experience.

Technology-Enhanced Evaluation and Validation

Further scientific studies of (Brumels, Blasius, Cortright, Oumedian, & Solberg, 2008) or (Wiemeyer & Kliem, 2012) already show the impact of commercial games such as Wii Fit or Dance Dance Revolution in the field of Games for Health, with an emphasis on movement-based digital sports games (exergames). Here, training effects (higher energy expenditure, balance improvement) could be proven. Compared to classical training exercises these effects are small, which is not surprising since the examined games are not optimized to provide adequate training results. Other studies (Baranowski, Buday, Thompson, & Baranowski, 2008, investigated the impact of behaviour change video games. Behaviour change games create an impression by knowledge transfer and changing the attitude towards something, for example a dietic treatment or a medical therapy. One of

Figure 2. By comparing the subscales of the two questionnaires (left: Nacke; right: Gutjahr) it becomes clear, that both analysis of 'what user experience a good game should trigger' are coming to a very similar answer. Even if both questionnaires focus on other aspects of this constructs and the questions to measure this constructs differ, the main idea of 'what is part of good user experience?' is not falling apart.

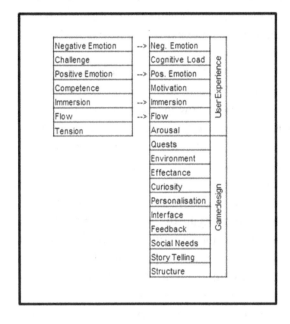

the most prominent examples for such a game is Re-Mission. Re-Mission has been developed especially for adolescents and young adults who suffer from cancer. It shows impressively that it is possible to develop high-quality serious games for the health sector, which are motivating and effective if a sufficient budget is available. In the game Re-Mission the player controls a tiny female nano robot called Roxxi through the body of 19 virtual cancer patients. During her journey, Roxxi learns how to fight against cancer cells using the appropriate medicine. She also learns how to cope with the side effects of the medicine she needs to use. A scientific study examined the impact of Re-Mission on the health-related behaviour of the players and the success of the cancer therapy. The multi-centric, controlled, and randomized trial was conducted at 34 medical centres in the United States, Canada, and Australia. A total of 375 patients aged 13 to 29 played remission for a total period of 3 months for 1h a week or in the comparison group another video game. The patients who played Re-Mission had a significantly higher treatment adherence, and improved their cancer-related knowledge which increased the chance of a successful therapy. These positive effects are mainly caused by the mediation of knowledge in the game and the changed attitude towards the therapy.

However, the effects of these games have been evaluated in pre- and post-measurements, the games did not allow any real-time measurements or an adaptation of the game according to the actual context or health status of the player. Likewise, the user experience of these games (motivation, immersion, fun) – relevant for the acceptance of the games – had been measured with questionnaires after playing the games. Accordingly, these studies lack meaningful predictions about the effects of single game aspects and elements on e.g. emotions, motivation and health-related (sub-) effects. First results of scientific studies about the usage of sensors to take into account physiological parameters to identify emotions show the general possibility of technology-enhanced user experience measurements.

Qualitative interviews and questionnaires neither allow real-time or event-related measurements nor allow an adaptation of the evaluated games to the measured results. Psychophysiological player testing is the controlled measure of gameplay experience, usually deployed in a laboratory by using e.g. electromyography, electrodermal activity, electrocardiograms, or electroencephalograms, which require attaching electrodes directly to the skin of the player. Electromyography is a technology to measure the electrical activation of muscles, which well reflects basic emotions. By putting electrodes on defined points in the players face the reactions (smile, surprise, sadness) can be estimated based on the electric impulse mea-

sured in the face muscles. A second possibility to measure the same emotions (with less accuracy but contactless) are digital video image processing algorithms. Different available technologies (e.g. Facelab, see Figure 3) use different kinds of hardware and differ in accuracy and detection scope.

The measurement of Electrodermal Activity (EDA) is, because of its easiness, one of the most commonly used methods. The measured sweat gland activity is directly related to physical arousal, but gives no hints by what this arousal is caused – similar to electrocardiograms allowing to identify an unspecific excitation. Electroencephalograms theoretically provide the biggest potential, but it still lacks adequate methods to analyse the measured values in this context.

The objective, sensor-based impact measurement of serious games is probably one of the most relevant research questions and could pave the way for a broad application of serious games. Lead by the Serious Gaming group at the Multimedia Communications Lab, different faculties of TU Darmstadt (psychology, sport science, computer science, etc.) tackle that issue within its interdisciplinary activities in the key research area on Serious Games. As outlined in Figure 4, one of the objectives is to get insights about effects and affects – caused by individual gameplay parameters. The technical basis for these studies represents the prototype ErgoActive, an adaptive cardio training system based on the adaptation model for exergames provided by Hardy, Göbel, Gutjahr, Wiemeyer, and Steinmetz (2011). For objective, technology-enhanced evaluation, physiological sensors and eye-tracking technology is going to be used.

CONCLUSION

For a good serious game, two basic impacts have to be proved by an evaluation: The game should trigger a good user experience and reach a defined purpose. While the purpose follows a special defi-

Figure 3. Sensor-based measurement of affects in serious games using Facelab

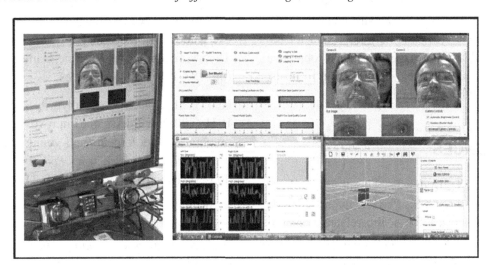

nition in addiction of the game (e.g. loss of weight, growth of knowledge or improvement of skill) the user's experience is a complex construct mixed of motional, cognitive, and psychophysiological components. Hence, methods of user experience measurement differ from classical questionnaires to technology-enhanced evaluation methodologies, such as facial expression analysis, EDA/GSR, ECG, or EEG. The technology-enhanced, objective evaluation of Serious Games would pave the path for the acceptance of Serious Games in a broad application field such as training/education as well as health and sports.

In general, recently a lot of research effort has been spent into the analysis (and development) of SG, but research in SG is still at its beginning. For example, there is still no common, globally accepted clear definition of Serious Games. For that, Göbel, Gutjahr, and Steinmetz (2011) provided a first conceptual approach towards a metadata format for the description and evaluation of Serious Games. This will be continuously enhanced in order to serve as foundation for a roadmap for the evaluation of SG respectively a quality label for SG as well.

Figure 4. Technology-enhanced evaluation of effects and affects in serious games for health (source: interdisciplinary research for serious games at TU Darmstadt)

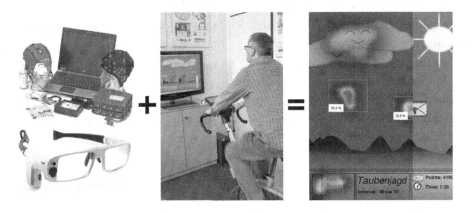

Further, comprehensive evaluation studies are necessary to 'prove' the sustainable benefit of SG. This is also extremely important for the commercial success of SG. As soon as objective evaluations are available, the decision to invest into SG will be much higher.

REFERENCES

Baranowski, T., Buday, R., Thompson, D. I., & Baranowski, J. (2008). Playing for real: Video games and stories for health-related behavior change. *American Journal of Preventive Medicine*, *34*(1), 74–82. doi:10.1016/j.amepre.2007.09.027 PMID:18083454.

Brumels, K. A., Blasius, T., Cortright, T., Oumedian, D., & Solberg, B. (2008). Comparison of efficacy between traditional and video game based balance programs. *Clinical Kinesiology: Journal of the American Kinesiotherapy Association*, *62*(4), 26–31.

de Freitas, S., & Oliver, M. (2006). How can exploratory learning with games and simulations within the curriculum can be most effectively evaluated. *Computers & Education*, *46*(3), 249–264. doi:10.1016/j.compedu.2005.11.007.

Egenfeldt-Nielsen, S. (2005). *Beyond edutainment: Exploring the educational potential of computer games*. Copenhagen, Denmark: IT-University Copenhagen.

Göbel, S., Gutjahr, M., & Steinmetz, R. (2011). What makes a good serious game - Conceptual approach towards a metadata format for the description and evaluation of serious games. In D. Gouscous & M. Meimaris (Eds.), *5th European Conference on Games Based Learning*, (pp. 202-210). Reading, UK: Academic Conferences Limited.

Hardy, S., Göbel, S., Gutjahr, M., Wiemeyer, J., & Steinmetz, R. (2011). Adaptation model for indoor exergames. In Proceedings of Serious Games - Theory, Technology & Practice, GameDays 2011, (pp. 183-196). Serious Games.

Kato, P. M., Cole, S. W., Bradlyn, A. S., & Pollock, B. H. (2008). A video game improves behavioural outcomes in adolescents and young adults with cancer: A randomized trial. *Pediatrics*, *122*(2), 305–317. doi:10.1542/peds.2007-3134.

Klabbers, J. H. G. (2003). Gaming and simulation: Principles of a science of design. *Simulation & Gaming*, *34*(4), 569–591. doi:10.1177/1046878103258205.

Kretschmann, R., Dittus, I., Lutz, I., & Meier, C. (2010). Nintendo Wii sports: Simple gadget or serious "measure" for health promotion? A pilot study according to the energy expenditure, movement extent, and student perceptions. In *Proceedings of the GameDays 2010 – Serious Games for Sports and Health*, (pp. 147-159). GameDays.

Law, E. L.-C., Kickmeier-Rust, M., Albert, D., & Holzinger, A. (2008). Challenges in the development and evaluation of immersive digital educational games. *Lecture Notes in Computer Science*, 5289.

Lieberman, D. A. (2001). Management of chronic pediatric diseases with interactive health games: Theory and research findings. *The Journal of Ambulatory Care Management*, *24*(1), 26–38. PMID:11189794.

Malone, T. W., & Lepper, M. R. (1987). Making learning fun: A taxonomy of intrinsic motivations for learning. In Snow, R. E., & Farr, M. J. (Eds.), *Aptitude, Learning and Instruction: Conative and Affective Process Analyses* (pp. 223–253). Hillsdale, NJ: Erlbaum.

Mandryk, R. L., Aktins, M. S., & Inkpen, K. M. (2006). A continuous and objective evaluation of emotional experience with interactive play environments. In *Proceedings of CHI'06*. ACM.

Mitchell, A., Savill-Smith, C., & Britain, G. (2004). *The use of computer and video games for learning: A review of the literature*. London, UK: Learning and Skills Development Agency.

Nacke, L. (2009). *Affective ludology: Scientific measurement of user experience in interactive entertainment*. Karlskrona, Sweden: Blekinge Institute of Technology.

Nacke, L., Drachen, A., & Göbel, S. (2010). Methods for evaluating gameplay experience in a serious gaming context. *International Journal of Computer Science in Sport, 9*.

Papastergiou, M. (2009). Exploring the potential of computer and video games for health and physical education: A literature review. *Computers & Education, 53*(3), 603–622. doi:10.1016/j.compedu.2009.04.001.

Prensky, M. (2003). Digital game-based learning. *Computer Entertainment, 1*(1), 21. doi:10.1145/950566.950596.

Shen, C., Wang, H., & Ritterfeld, U. (2009). Serious games and seriously fun games. In Ritterfeld, U., Cody, M., & Vorderer, P. (Eds.), *Serious Games: Mechanisms and Effects*. New York, NY: Routledge.

Wendel, V., Gutjahr, M., Göbel, S., & Steinmetz, R. (2012). *Designing collaborative multiplayer serious games for collaborative learning*. Paper presented at the 4th International Conference on Computer Supported Education. Porto, Portugal.

Whitehead, A., Johnston, H., Nixon, N., & Welch, C. (2010). *Exergame effectiveness: What the numbers can tell us*. New York, NY: Academic Press. doi:10.1145/1836135.1836144.

Wiemeyer, J., & Kliem, A. (2012). Serious games and ageing - A new panacea? *European Review of Aging and Physical Activity, 9*(1), 41–50. doi:10.1007/s11556-011-0093-x.

ADDITIONAL READING

Nacke, L. E. (2009). *Affective ludology: Scientific measurement of user experience in interactive entertainment*. Karlskrona, Sweden: Blekinge Institute of Technology.

Schandry, R. (1989). *Lehrbuch psychophysiologie*. München, Germany: Psychologie-Verl.-Union.

KEY TERMS AND DEFINITIONS

Affects: Affects means the emotional impact of the game on the user. This includes positive emotion (e.g. fun) as well as negative emotion (frustration).

Effects: Effects include all impacts of the game on the user other than his/her subjective (user) experience (e.g. loss of weight, growth of knowledge, or improvement of skill).

Game Experience: User Experience (UX) means the entity of the experience a user undergo by playing a game. This includes e.g. emotional (fun, frustration), cognitive (boredom), and physiological (arousal) components.

APPENDIX

QUESTIONNAIRE FOR MEASURING USER EXPERIENCE

1. The game avoided boredom.
2. The game avoided frustration.
3. The game only sometimes made me angry.
4. The game challenged me in a pleasant way.
5. The story engaged my fantasy.
6. I was able to keep track of tasks, impressions, information and possibilities of the game and was neither overstrained nor overloaded.
7. The game was fun.
8. The game made me feel self-determined and competent.
9. I found the game's design to be aesthetically pleasing.
10. The game was at times so engaging that I had the need to know how it continued.
11. Realizing a process of progression strongly motivated me to continue playing.
12. At times I played only for the sake of playing.
13. At times I felt like a part of the game world.
14. I felt like I was the game's protagonist while playing.
15. The game offered the possibility of developing an individual concept that was fun to follow.
16. The game was so exciting that it captured my whole attention during play.
17. The game was so interesting that I lost all track of time.
18. At times the game was so enthralling that I was completely engaged in the game.
19. After some points of the game I was very relieved since I had expected a failure.
20. I noticed that I was at times strongly emotionally involved (excitement, sadness, relief, joy, anger).
21. I was in a pleasant state due to playing the game.
22. The game allowed me to choose between different tasks and to decide if and when I would complete them.
23. The game offered many small and interesting tasks on the way to the ultimate goal.
24. The game's ultimate goal was clear from the beginning.
25. The game offered a world with varied experiences and rich impressions.
26. The game created an individual and complete world using a unique history, time lapses.
27. The game allows free (not tied to tasks) exploration of the game world and trial of existing interaction choices.
28. During play, I had the feeling of being completely in control of the actions of the game's protagonist.
29. My actions had lasting effects on the game environment.
30. The game gave feedback whether my actions were successful or not.
31. The game includes problems that encourage their solution.
32. I wanted to follow the destinies of the characters in the game.
33. There were places in the game I was keen on seeing or learning their history.
34. The game offered the possibility of creating an individual identity.
35. The game offered the possibility of developing an individual style of play.
36. The music in the game supported the development of emotions.

37. Possible actions were easy to recognize and clearly laid out.

38. The controls of the game were easy to understand.

39. The game displayed the current game state at all times.

40. The game offered clear goals and feedback on my progress of reaching them.

41. The tasks in the game were rewarded based on their difficulty.

42. The design of the tasks allowed me to have a good overview of how close I was to their completion at any time.

43. The game allowed me to achieve recognition and status.

44. The game allowed a progression.

45. The game kept coming back to established knowledge or acquired skills.

46. The game included interesting characters.

47. The game's story was good.

48. The story was narrated in an interesting way.

49. The game allowed to choose among tasks of different difficulty.

50. The game supported the acquisition of necessary skills.

51. The game offered optional tasks that lead to interesting subplots and diversified areas.

Note: All questions are supposed to be answered within a scale from 1 (not at all) to 10 (extremely).

This questionnaire has been used to evaluate the user experience in different prototypically implemented Serious Games. Additionally, users (players, learners) were pleased to provide some information about their background (age, gender, experience and attitude in gameplay: How many hours do you play computer games per week? and What is the adequate price for that Serious Game in your opinion?) in order to support the analysis and interpretation of their answers and to get a feeling about the value (price, success vs. failure) of a SG.

Section 3
Games and Virtual Worlds in Education

Chapter 8
Social Presence in Virtual World Interviews

Elizabeth Dean
RTI International, USA

Joe Murphy
RTI International, USA

Sarah Cook
RTI International, USA

ABSTRACT

Social presence varies from low, to moderate, to high in self-administered, telephone, and face-to-face survey interviews. New communication technologies add another layer of survey modes that can be understood along the same spectrum of social presence. Virtual worlds like Second Life are rapidly becoming popular environments for testing theories of social and economic behavior. Researchers who use Second Life as a data collection platform must consider the extent to which existing social theories hold in virtual environments. This study tests the hypothesis that indicators of interviewers' social presence observed in real world survey environments persist in virtual environments with avatar interviewers and respondents. Results from data quality indicators provide tentative support for the hypothesis.

INTRODUCTION

Survey modes vary according to communication technology and presentation format. Surveys are administered via paper, telephone, and web, and can be self-administered or interviewer-administered, or a combination of both. All of the types of technology listed above have been used to present surveys in visual, auditory, or mixed format. Additionally, surveys vary by the extent of social presence in the interview setting from no social presence in a self-administered

DOI: 10.4018/978-1-4666-3673-6.ch008

survey to high social presence in an in-person interviewer-administered survey. A persistent question in survey research is the extent to which social presence in the interview setting is desired.

The concept of social presence, a type of presence, or telepresence, has been the subject of much exploration (Lombard & Jones, 2007). It has been defined broadly as "a sense of being with another" (Biocca, Harms, & Burgoon, 2003, p. 456) and more specifically as "a psychological state in which virtual (para-authentic or artificial) social actors are experienced as actual social actors in either sensory or nonsensory ways" (Lee, 2004, p. 37). Biocca, Harms, and Burgoon (2003) assert that the internet is an inherently social place where applications and environments are designed to increase social presence.

Social Presence and Survey Modes

The amount of social presence in a survey can have biasing effects on study results. For example, some respondents may report less honest answers to sensitive questions when an interviewer is present (Tourangeau & Smith, 1996; Turner et. al, 1998). The use of telephone interviewing gives way to less candid reporting of sensitive information as well, because respondents are speaking directly to another person (de Leeuw & Van der Zouwen, 1998; Tourangeau & Yan, 2007). Respondents may also be influenced by the visual appearance of the interviewer. An interviewer's race, gender or perceived attractiveness has been found to not only influence the respondent's trust, but also the respondent's belief of what is a desirable response (Couper, 2008).

While these findings may encourage moving towards a self-administered surveying universe, there are advantages to using interviewers in survey research that cannot be ignored. Interviewers are not only helpful in persuading people to participate in surveys and keep them motivated to continue, but they are also useful for probing

respondents for accurate reporting and clarifying questions respondents may ask unpredictably. Respondents have been known to be more participatory and involved in the survey when an interviewer is involved than when there is no interviewer (Couper, 2008). The use of interviewers can also reduce item non-response compared to self-administered surveys. Interviewers can hide answer options such as "Don't Know" and "Refuse," whereas self-administered surveys have those options ready for the respondent to choose (Dillman, 2000).

Survey modes vary along a spectrum of social presence. Low social presence surveys include self-administered mail surveys and web surveys. Extremely low social presence surveys are mail and web surveys with text only. Somewhat higher social presence can be found in web surveys with pictures of individuals or with reactive communication technologies. High social presence surveys include face-to-face surveys, where the interviewer conveys presence through tone of voice, along with facial expressions, eye movement, body language and other visual cues. Telephone surveys have moderate social presence.

Developments in communication technologies add additional layers of survey modes to apply to the social presence spectrum. Telephone surveys can be administered by interactive voice response (IVR), maintaining the voice interaction that allows some social presence, but decreasing the personality behind the voice. Face-to-face interviews can be enhanced with components where the respondent listens to or watches an audio or video recording and enters answers privately into a computer. Web surveys may include avatars or other interviewer agents to encourage and provide feedback on respondents' answers.

For the most part, new modes of survey research are attempting to combine the benefits of both interviewer and self-administered surveying, minus all of the disadvantages. That is, emergent survey technologies are applied in the hopes of providing enough social distance to encourage respondents to report honestly and without fear of judgment, but with enough social presence to guarantee respondent engagement and attentiveness.

The "computers as social actors" or CASA paradigm states that people react to computers as social actors providing a social presence, not as inorganic machines. Some research has found that, when using Interactive Voice Response (IVR) to administer automated telephone interviews, respondents sometimes even stereotyped the "interviewer" based on the sex of the recorded voice (Nass, Moon, & Green, 1997).

On the other hand, a series of experiments conducted in surveys, rather than in a laboratory environment, did not reveal strong support for the CASA paradigm (Couper, 2008). Their results did not show the effects of interviewer presence on sensitive questions as the CASA paradigm would suggest using ACASI, virtual interviewers (via video), IVR and images on a web survey. However, other research has found that adding the humanizing feature of dialogue with question clarification to web surveys increases accuracy of responses. Furthermore, respondents preferred the option to seek clarification (Conrad, Shober, & Coiner, 2007).

This research suggests that there may be some personal presence perceived by respondents through a virtual interviewer interaction, but not with the magnitude of a real interviewer and not enough to hinder truthful responses to sensitive questions. Using interviewers in a virtual setting, as opposed to face-to-face, telephone or self-administered modes, may lead researchers to be able to obtain sensitive information accurately while still keeping the benefits of an interviewer's presence. As technology advances and as we learn more about interviewing with voices, videos, and other types of "distanced interviewers," survey research moves closer to the age of researching in virtual worlds.

Surveys in Virtual Worlds

A virtual world is an "electronic environment that visually mimics complex physical spaces, where people can interact with each other and virtual objects, and where people are represented by animated characters" (Bainbridge, 2007, p. 472). Virtual worlds enhance interpersonal communication across distances beyond what telephone and text communication have to offer. Virtual reality places respondents in a common environment. Respondents in virtual meetings are able to examine the same digital object—for example, a medical assessment or procedure or a design project—and discuss it and interact with it despite their physical distance (Hindmarsh, Heath, & Fraser, 2006).

Virtual world users experience a quasi-realistic 3D graphical environment, and can walk, talk, fly, live, work, and play in the virtual environment. Some online virtual worlds, such as World of Warcraft™, are actual games. Others are Multi-User Virtual Environments (MUVEs) for socialization and gaming. The earliest research in virtual worlds is still emerging. Schroeder and Bailenson (2008) identify four types of research conducted in virtual worlds, including social psychological experiments studying online behavior (Bailenson et al., 2005), participant observation or ethnography of virtual world users (Becker & Mark, 2002; Boellstorff, 2008), unobtrusive data capture and analysis of online behaviors (Yee et al., 2007), and experimental manipulation of virtual settings (Williams, Caplan, & Xiong, 2007). Blascovich et al. (2002) argue that virtual environments are a boon for social psychology, enabling both high experimental control and environmental realism. Virtual worlds offer tremendous resource to social science research because they offer a safe, minimal-risk environment for macro-level manipulation and analysis (Castronova & Falk, 2008).

Preliminary research in the virtual world of Second Life has shown that social norms from interpersonal communication apply, suggesting that social presence does exist in the virtual community. A study of gender, distance, and talking behaviors in-world found that male-male dyads maintain larger interpersonal distance than female-female dyads, males maintain less eye contact with each other, and decreases in interpersonal distance between avatars are associated with an increase in eye avoidance (Yee et al., 2007). All of these observations replicate behaviors between and within genders in real life. However, earlier research posited that virtual social environments foster "transformed social interaction"—that is, a set of behaviors that diverge from in-person interactive behaviors as users become more experienced in virtual worlds (Bailenson & Yee, 2006).

Although few results from Second Life surveys have been published, surveys are common in Second Life. Surveys are conducted in Second Life through links to Web surveys, "survey bots" (programs that administer questionnaires), and through e-mail invitation to members of Web panels recruited through Second Life avatars. The Virtual Assisted Survey Interview, or VASI, has been used to interview over 2000 respondents in Second Life (Bell, Castronova, & Wagner, 2009).

A 2006 survey of 246 Second Life users (de Nood & Attema) recruited through in-person avatar intercept methods in-world revealed that on average, Second Life users:

- Are more affluent than the general population,
- Spend 30+ hours on average each week in Second Life,
- Maintain their same gender for their avatars,
- Have a university degree, and
- Work in information technology or creative professions.

In separate research, use of Second Life's virtual currency, Linden dollars, resulted in a 29% response rate. Researchers theorized that using the virtual currency discouraged participation of professional Web survey respondents. Professional respondents tend to be more responsive to dollar incentives. There is doubt about the quality and accuracy of Web surveys when professional survey response is rampant. Answers obtained by respondents who were given virtual currency were longer and more deliberative than the researchers had previously experienced from Web survey respondents (Neff & Klaasen, 2007).

Second Life easily lends itself to researchers as a data collection environment. Residents are primarily in the world for socialization, and are willing to answer survey questions, especially to receive Linden dollar incentives. Much as web surveys exploded in popularity as a mode as the internet expanded in accessibility, Second Life or another online virtual environment like it is likely to do the same thing as it grows. A virtual world offers the opportunity for researchers to test hypotheses about social and economic behavior with significantly less costs than real world lab tests (Bainbridge, 2007). The low costs of data collection will drive the usage of the mode. This necessitates attention to how data are collected and whether or not virtual survey modes are reliable and valid.

STUDY DESIGN

The purpose of this study was to compare indicators of social presence across two survey data collection modes in Second Life. Two surveys were conducted with avatars in Second Life. The first used a kiosk to test self-administered data collection. The second employed an avatar-interviewer to interact with respondents in mimicking a face to face interview.

Survey 1: Self-Administered Interviewing

A convenience sample of respondents was recruited, via Second Life classifieds, message boards, and word of mouth within the virtual world, to visit the virtual facility of the not-for-profit research institute RTI International to complete a brief interview. The interior of the RTI facility, depicting the survey kiosk, an RTI employee, and the keypad used for accessing private interviewing rooms is pictured in Figure 1. If a respondent was interested in participating in the RTI survey, he/she would click on the SLURL (Second Life URL) linking to the RTI facility in our recruitment text. Respondents were directed to the kiosk, where an object administered the survey.

The survey was administered in individual SL "notecards," blue boxes that popped up on screen, one per question. The user clicked on the appropriate button in the notecard, much like in a web survey, to answer each question. There were 404 avatar respondents to the self-administered survey.

Survey 2: In-Avatar Interviewing

Using the same recruitment methods, a second convenience sample of respondents was selected to complete the in-avatar (virtual face-to-face) interview. Interested residents were invited to contact an interviewer via Instant Message (IM) in Second Life. In this study, to reduce potential error due to unanticipated translation and cross-cultural issues, eligibility was restricted to only United States residents. Eligible respondents were invited to enter a secure private room in our Second Life facility. There they met with an interviewer, who conducted a brief survey via text chat. Each interview took about 10 minutes. Sixty respondents completed the in-avatar interview.

Hypothesis

We hypothesized that social presence is replicated in virtual survey modes as in real life survey modes. That is, in-avatar interviews were expected to exhibit greater social presence than self-administered interviews. We expected respondents to the in-avatar survey to react to survey questions differently

Figure 1. RTI facility in Second Life

than those completing the kiosk survey based on the presence of the interviewer. The interviewer could control the pace of the survey and develop rapport with the respondent. This would result in an engaged respondent who took the survey task seriously and did not simply "breeze through" the interview, also known as satisficing. Further, we expected the respondents to the in-avatar survey to be more compliant with the survey request and have a lower rate of item nonresponse compared to the kiosk survey respondents.

Results

We first compared the rate of "straightlining," or providing the same response option to multiple consecutive questions which would indicate probable satisficing behavior. Looking at just the first four questions of the survey, there was no evidence that respondents in the in-avatar survey demonstrated straightlining behavior—no respondents provided the same response option for all four questions. For the kiosk survey, 37 of 404 respondents (9.2%) provided the same response option to the first four questions of the survey (95% CI [0.07, 0.12]). As further evidence of straightlining, 22 (5.5%) provided the same response option for the first eight questions of the survey (95% CI (0.04, 0.08)).

Another indicator of satisficing, or shortcutting, is interview administration time. In the in-avatar survey, the interviewer controlled the pace of the survey and none of the 20-question surveys were completed in fewer than 30 seconds. While the kiosk survey had only 18 questions, it was unlikely that a respondent could reasonably read, think through, and answer all questions in 30 seconds. However, 75 respondents (18.6%) did in fact complete the kiosk interview in 30 seconds (95% CI (0.15, 0.23)); 20% of these respondents also demonstrated straightlining behavior. This suggests that respondents to the kiosk survey were not as engaged in the task as those responding to an avatar interviewer.

Regarding item nonresponse, there were only two questions in the entire in-avatar survey for which one respondent failed to supply a response. In the kiosk survey, rates of item nonresponse among all questions ranged from 0.3% to 1.5%. This suggests several possibilities: (1) respondents were perhaps more willing or comfortable providing answers in the in-avatar survey; (2) the presence of the interviewer allowed the respondent to seek clarification on confusing questions; and/or (3) the presence of the interviewer had a positive effect on respondents' level of compliance with the survey task. It should be noted that respondents to the in-avatar survey were provided a higher incentive for completion compared to the kiosk survey respondents. This is a confounding factor that limits our ability to draw conclusions from these findings.

Finally, the last question in each survey asked respondents to indicate whether they would be willing to let us retain their avatar name: "We would like to keep your avatar name on record in case there are other research opportunities. May we keep your avatar name?" In the in-avatar survey, 96.7% of respondents consented while only 75.8% from the kiosk survey consented. This difference of 21 percentage points is statistically significant at the 95% confidence level (95% CI (0.15, 0.27)) and suggests that respondents either felt more comfortable with the in-avatar survey experience and would be open to repeating it, or were more compliant in the presence of an interviewer. Again, the incentive difference could have been a confounding factor here.

CONCLUSION

Our results show indications of increased social presence along the dimensions of more attentiveness (less straightlining and less satisficing) and higher data quality (fewer "Don't Know" and "Refuse" answers) on the part of the respondents and improved data quality in the in-avatar interview. These results are not an ideal test, because the surveys, though similar, were not identical. The incentive amount varied in the two surveys. Despite these limitations, particularly the straight-lining behavior and the item nonresponse results suggest that the increased social presence of the in-avatar survey does contribute to better quality survey data. More testing should be conducted with a controlled incentive amount and with a control for social influence or social obligation. It is possible that social influence is the factor defining these results. A more precise test would operationalize social presence without social influence. However, as a preliminary study, these results are an indicator that the avatar-interviewer's presence (or influence) may be required to ensure quality of data collected in virtual worlds.

REFERENCES

Bailenson, J. N., Beall, A. C., Blascovich, J., Loomis, J., & Turk, M. (2005). Transformed social interaction, augmented gaze, and social influence in immersive virtual environments. *Human Communication Research*, *31*, 511–537. doi:10.1111/j.1468-2958.2005.tb00881.x.

Bailenson, J. N., & Yee, N. (2006). A longitudinal study of task performance, head movements, subjective report, simulator sickness, and transformed social interaction in collaborative virtual environments. *Presence (Cambridge, Mass.)*, *15*(6), 699–716. doi:10.1162/pres.15.6.699.

Bainbridge, W. S. (2007). The scientific research potential of virtual worlds. *Science*, *317*(5837), 472–476. doi:10.1126/science.1146930 PMID:17656715.

Becker, B., & Mark, G. (2002). Social conventions in computer-mediated communication: a comparison of three online shared virtual environments. In Schroeder, R. (Ed.), *The Social Life of Avatars: Presence and Interaction in Shared Virtual Environments* (pp. 19–39). London, UK: Springer. doi:10.1007/978-1-4471-0277-9_2.

Bell, M. W., Castronova, E., & Wagner, G. G. (2009). *Surveying the virtual world - A large scale survey in second life using the virtual data collection interface (VDCI)*. German Council for Social and Economic Data (RatSWD) Research Notes No. 40. Retrieved from http://ssrn.com/abstract=1480254

Biocca, F., Harms, C., & Burgoon, J. (2003). Towards a more robust theory and measure of social presence: Review and suggested criteria. *Presence (Cambridge, Mass.)*, *12*(5), 456–480. doi:10.1162/105474603322761270.

Blascovich, J., Loomis, J., Beall, A. C., Swinth, K. R., Hoyt, C. L., & Bailenson, J. (2002). Immersive virtual environment technology as a methodological tool for social psychology. *Psychological Inquiry*, *13*(2), 103–124. doi:10.1207/S15327965PLI1302_01.

Boellstorff, T. (2008). *Coming of age in second life*. Princeton, NJ: Princeton University Press.

Castronova, E., & Falk, M. (2008). *Virtual worlds as petri dishes for the social and behavioral sciences*. Retrieved from http://ssrn.com/abstract=1313161

Conrad, F. G., Shober, M. F., & Coiner, T. (2007). Bringing features of human dialogue to web surveys. *Applied Cognitive Psychology*, *21*, 165–187. doi:10.1002/acp.1335.

Couper, M. P. (2008). Technology and the survey interview/questionnaire. In Conrad, F. G., & Schober, M. F. (Eds.), *Envisioning the Survey Interview of the Future* (pp. 58–76). Hoboken, NJ: John Wiley & Sons, Inc..

de Leeuw, E., & Van der Zouwen, J. (1988). Data quality in telephone and face-to-face surveys: A comparative meta-analysis. In Groves, R., Biemer, P., Lyberg, L., Massey, J., Nicholls, W. II, & Waksberg, J. (Eds.), *Telephone Survey Methodology* (pp. 283–300). New York, NY: John Wiley.

de Nood, D., & Attema, J. (2006). *Second life, the second life of virtual reality*. The Hague, The Netherlands: Electronic Highway Platform. Retrieved from: http://www.epn.net/interrealiteit/EPN-REPORT-The_Second_Life_of_VR.pdf

Dillman, D. A. (2000). *Mail and internet surveys: The tailored design method* (2nd ed.). New York, NY: John Wiley & Sons.

Hindmarsh, J., Heath, C., & Fraser, M. (2006). (Im)materiality, virtual reality and interaction: Grounding the 'virtual' in studies of technology in action. *The Sociological Review*, *54*(4), 795–817. doi:10.1111/j.1467-954X.2006.00672.x.

Lee, K. M. (2004). Presence, explicated. *Communication Theory*, *14*(1), 27–50. doi:10.1111/j.1468-2885.2004.tb00302.x.

Lombard, M., & Jones, M. T. (2007). Identifying the (tele)presence literature. *PsychNology Journal*, *5*(2), 197–206.

Nass, C., Moon, Y., & Green, N. (1997). Are machines gender neutral? Gender-stereotypic responses to computers with voices. *Journal of Applied Social Psychology*, *27*(10), 864–876. doi:10.1111/j.1559-1816.1997.tb00275.x.

Neff, J., & Klaassen, A. (2007). Web research could gain clout via virtual currency. *Advertising Age*, *78*(50), 4–34.

Schroeder, R., & Bailenson, J. (2008). Research uses of multi-user virtual environments. In Fielding, N., Lee, R. M., & Blank, G. (Eds.), *The SAGE Handbook of Online Research Methods*. Thousand Oaks, CA: SAGE. doi:10.4135/9780857020055.n18.

Tourangeau, R., & Smith, T. W. (1996). Asking sensitive questions: The impact of data collection mode, question format and question context. *Public Opinion Quarterly*, *60*, 275–304. doi:10.1086/297751.

Tourangeau, R., & Yan, T. (2007). Sensitive questions in surveys. *Psychological Bulletin*, *133*(5), 859–883. doi:10.1037/0033-2909.133.5.859 PMID:17723033.

Turner, C. F., Forsyth, B. H., O'Reilly, J. M., Cooley, P. C., Smith, T. K., Rogers, S. M., & Miller, H. G. (1998). Automated self-interviewing and the survey measurement of sensitive behaviors. In Couper, M. P., Baker, R. P., Bethlehem, J., Clark, C. Z. F., Martin, J., Nichols, W. L. II, & O'Reilly, J. M. (Eds.), *Computer Assisted Survey Information Collection* (pp. 455–474). New York, NY: Wiley and Sons.

Williams, D., Caplan, S., & Xiong, L. (2007). Can you hear me now? The impact of voice in an online gaming community. *Human Communication Research*, *33*, 427–449. doi:10.1111/j.1468-2958.2007.00306.x.

Yee, N., Bailenson, J. N., Urbanek, M., Chang, F., & Merget, D. (2007). The unbearable likeness of being digital: The persistence of nonverbal social norms in online virtual environments. *Cyberpsychology & Behavior*, *10*(1), 115–121. doi:10.1089/cpb.2006.9984 PMID:17305457.

KEY TERMS AND DEFINITIONS

Avatar: Graphical representation of a person used in an online environment. An avatar could be a still image or a moving 3D identity, and can human or non-human.

Second Life: An online virtual world, developed by Linden Lab in 2003 and accessed by millions of users. See http://secondlife.com/.

Social Presence: The extent to which a user experiences the presence of another human in any form of mediated communication.

Survey Mode: The communication tool used for a survey, typically: web, phone, mail, or face-to-face, but can also be email, text message, or mobile app.

Survey Research: The use of questionnaires to systematically collect data about respondents' thoughts, opinions and behaviors.

Telepresence: The extent to which a user experiences online or virtual social interaction as real social interaction.

Virtual World: A quasirealistic 3D graphical, interactive online environment where users play games, socialize, work, learn and buy and sell virtual commodities.

Chapter 9
Engaging Classes in a Virtual World

Sue Gregory
University of New England, Australia

ABSTRACT

Virtual worlds, such as Second Life, are multi-user, interactive computer-simulated environments created for users to inhabit and interact via avatars, which are graphical representations of a person that can be personalised and used in the virtual world. In this research, 239 off-campus (distance) education students chose to attend weekly sessions in Second Life from 2008 to 2011. These sessions catered for a diverse group of students. It is internationally claimed that virtual worlds are engaging for distance education students. Engagement is the combination of student's feelings, observable actions or performance, perceptions, and beliefs. This mixed-methods research sought to investigate whether virtual worlds were engaging for adult student learners. Recorded in-world (in the virtual world) conversations and the completion of a survey by university students provide data from which the findings are made. In-world discussion found that the virtual world, in this case Second Life, is an engaging environment in which to learn. These findings indicate the need for further research in using a virtual world as an educational resource.

INTRODUCTION

Research was conducted with voluntary students at the University of New England (UNE) in Australia. These students were enrolled in Information Communication Technology (ICT) Education or Teaching and Learning units (subjects) in an off-campus mode from 2008 to 2011. The research was to determine whether a virtual world, such as Second Life, was engaging for the students who participated in the sessions. Over the semester students attended weekly sessions where they spent the first part of the session in a space created for them discussing topics relevant to education using

DOI: 10.4018/978-1-4666-3673-6.ch009

virtual worlds. The second part of the session was spent attending virtual lectures from educators around the world or going on virtual excursions, tours, simulations, role-plays and web quests. At the end of each session, students regrouped to reflect on their experiences in the virtual world. Students were engaged during these sessions and this research demonstrates this.

Second Life is a virtual world, which is a low cost computer-based simulation with features of real and fantasy life and can be a substitute for many real world activities (Gregory, 2007). Second Life is one of over 200 virtual worlds (Campbell, 2009; Farley & Steel, 2009; Honey, Diener, Connor, Veltman, & Bodily, 2009; Lemon & Kelly, 2009). People enter a virtual world via their avatar, which is an electronic presence that imitates real life in the form of personal presence and can be personalized (Gregory & Smith, 2008). In the virtual world an avatar can interact virtually by talking (through text and audio, complete with lip sync), walking, running, sitting, dancing, flying, driving, riding, teleporting (moving locations), making gestures (such as clapping or waving), changing appearance (such as clothing, gender, hair and skin colour), interacting with other avatars and the environment including land formations, (Gregory & Smith, 2008), ie if the avatar walks into a wall, they cannot go through it, they have to go through doors that open, just like real life.

This chapter discussed research undertaken from 2008 to 2011 and firstly provides context of the study. This is followed by a discussion of three adult learning theories and how they relate to adults learning in a virtual world. Outlined is why the virtual world of Second Life was chosen for the research and how engagement was measured by students participating in virtual world activities. Methods of data collection and findings were discussed followed by ideas of future research and concluding remarks.

BACKGROUND

When students are not on campus, a virtual world provides flexibility so students can connect through a highly interactive, immersive, multimodal learning environment (Wood & Hopkins, 2008). For adults to learn and be engaged in a virtual learning environment, adult learning theories of transformative, constructivist and connectivism theories all need to be taken into consideration, using andragogy as an approach to teaching. A combination of learning theories contributes to one's learning in the virtual environment. The research presented here is an analysis of students' engagement in their learning via virtual world sessions over a four year period – 2008 to 2011. The students were studying education ICT or Teaching and Learning units UNE. They were either undergraduate or postgraduate students. Theories of how adults learn in a virtual world were explored by examining student's engagement in their learning. The result of this research is presented in this chapter.

ADULT LEARNING THEORIES

Contemporary Adult Learning

Theories surrounding the way in which adults learn is relatively new and have only bandied around since the time of Ivan Illich, in the mid 1950's. Adults predominantly learn by symbolic interactionism which is one's ability to manipulate symbols (Finger & Asun, 2001). There is no objective reality when it comes to human interaction. The meanings things have result from social interaction. Three learning theories, transformative, constructivist and connectivism, with andragogy as an approach to teaching, provide context to how adults learn in a virtual world.

Andragogy

The term andragogy was coined by Knowles (Knowles, 1984) to encompass the methods used to teach adults as opposed to pedagogy that are the techniques used to teach children. Learning, for many adults, is a means to an end, not an end in itself and adults often learn something to make a change for the better. There are four characteristics of adult learners (Knowles, 1984, p. 12):

- Adults need to know why they need to learn something;
- Adults need to learn experientially;
- Adults approach learning as problem solving; and
- Adults learn best when the topic is of immediate value.

With this approach to learning, virtual worlds can assist adults to know why they are learning using problem solving techniques through experimentation so they can see the value of what they are learning.

Transformative Learning

Transformative learning, according Mezirow, is the process of reflection and action (Cranton, 1992). It is "freeing oneself from psychological distortions acquired during infancy as well as throughout their whole life [where] true adult learning occurs when meaning perspectives are transformed through critical reflection" (Finger & Asun, 2001, p. 55). Transformation occurs when one critically reflects actions and pays particular attention to when these critical reflections take place. Values and beliefs are challenged and self-concepts are threatened (Cranton, 1992). Transformative learning theory is based on critical self reflection and is a largely cognitive, rational process (Cranton & Tisdell, 2008). There are two kinds of learning; instrumental (focusing on learning through task-oriented problem solving

and determining cause and effect relationships) and communicative learning (communicating individual feelings, needs and desires) (Kearsley, 2009a). Virtual worlds are an ideal learning environment for learners to reflect on their learning after attending a session in the virtual world.

Constructivism

The constructivist learning theory was established by Bruner in 1986 where "learning is an active and explicit cognitive process in which learners construct new concepts based upon their current knowledge" (Chesnevar, Maguitman, Gonzalez, & Cobo, 2004, p. 92). Virtual worlds are suitable learning environments if the student experience is underpinned by a constructivist approach to learning (Butler, 2008). Students actively construction their knowledge, not passively absorb it from lectures and textbooks (Chesnevar et al., 2004). Virtual worlds encourage student interaction and are learning-centred constructivist environments (Beldarrain, 2006) that promote student-driven learning experiences (Calonge, 2007). They can be an alternate learning space for interaction and engagement. Virtual worlds combine synchronous (at the same time, such as a chat room) and asynchronous (at different times, such as email) activities for collaboration and simulation that emulate the learning environment in context (Gregory & Smith, 2008). Activities can be designed to enable students to explore understandings of concepts demonstrating constructivist pedagogy in a virtual world (Gregory, Reiners, & Tynan, 2010). A variety of tools can be used within the environment to enhance student construction of knowledge.

Connectivism

Siemens (2004, para 1) states, "knowledge is growing exponentially" and developed a new theory for the digital age. Information is continually being acquired and is driven by the understanding that decisions are based on rapidly altering foundations. This notion is supported by Vygotsky in that people develop psychological tools to gain mastery over one's own behaviour and cognition (Dahms, Geonnotti, Passalacqua, Schilk, & Wetzel, 2008). The connectivism theory comes from the concept of artificial intelligence, connectionism, cognitive neuroscience, conceptual learning and social network analysis contributing to validate learning in networks (Siemens, 2008).

Adults Learning in a Virtual World

Second Life can be used as an enhancement to the andragogy that educators already use if using a full and diverse range of pedagogical approaches (Hollins & Robbins, 2008). In their repertoire of pedagogical practices, educators need to re-think how they use virtual worlds. They need to claim these spaces for social and educational purposes (Schutt & Martino, 2008). It can assist the educational needs of students using methods which they can identify with (Carr, Oliver, & Burn, 2008). Variation will occur amongst educators depending on their level of experience with a virtual world (Gregory, Reiners, Tynan, 2010). There are new models of andragogy required to meet the new generation of learners who need greater autonomy, connectivity and opportunities for socio-experiential learning (McLoughlin & Lee, 2008). Non-player characters in a virtual world, such as academics, "require a knowledge model, a dialogue model and a user-performance model in addition to any physical and behavioural traits necessary to make them interesting and credible members of the environment" (Jeffery, 2008, p. 181).

Adults learn differently than children because they have different reasons for learning. Adults require problem-oriented instruction such as case studies, simulations, problem solving and group work, which a virtual world lends itself to. Adults need to know why they need to learn something, they learn experientially, they approach learning as problem-solving and learn best if the topic is of immediate value (Kearsley, 2009b). Virtual worlds have been designed for adult learning and there are many examples of simulations, problem solving and group work that occur within the environment.

WHY WAS SECOND LIFE CHOSEN FOR THE RESEARCH?

Second Life was chosen for the research because it was readily available. It is a tested educational environment that Linden Lab, the proprietors of Second Life, released to the public in 2003 (Gregory, et al., 2011; Gregory, et al., 2010; Hearns, et al., 2011). Registered members (residents) can inhabit and build their own 3D world (Collins, 2008a) and when they create something they own the Intellectual Property of that item (Linden Lab, 2008). Many institutions have created content that is freely available for other users, thus making Second Life an appropriate space for conducting sessions with students. At any one time, there are approximately, on average, 45,000 residents online at the one time (Tateru, 2012). There are now over 29,000,000 residents (Tateru, 2012) however, many residents are not active users of Second Life, some do not return after their first visit and there are some users with several avatars (residents).

Lester (2008), former Academic Program Manager of Linden Lab, stated that there were (approximately) 1,000 educational institutions using Second Life, although it is difficult to actually state accurately. Educators can create their own avatar to use in Second Life that can be altered according to the educator's needs. As an educator, this is important as they may wish to change their avatar's appearance to demonstrate a technique, in context, such as an avatar created for a history lesson and therefore in a historical garment. Once someone has registered, no one else can use the same name. This is important for educators so that their avatar's name can be the same as their real name, if available. Educators can easily create their own educational space to use with their students. They can create a space that is in context with the learning that they wish their students to experience.

The researcher's avatar is Jass Easterman or, depending on which viewer (software) someone is using, it may be Sue Gregory. In 2007 when the researcher's avatar was first created, personal names were not available and surnames were selected from a list. This has since changed and the selection of one's own name is now available. Hence, the researcher's avatar is Jass Easterman, but has been changed to Sue Gregory. If someone is using an older viewer, Jass Easterman is displayed. If they are on a new viewer, Sue Gregory is displayed. Students have to search for both.

In the Australian context, the most number of people online is on a Sunday and the general peaks are 10 am AEST and 10 pm AEST (Australian Eastern Standard Time) Collins (2008b). Australia has the ninth most users of Second Life with the 9.00 am to 5.00 pm usage of Second Life increasing as people are using the environment more for educational and business purposes. As most of the researcher's students were working during the day, evenings were the best time for everyone to meet. Sundays were not a viable meeting time for students and they decided to meet on a Wednesday evening. They have been meeting on a Wednesday evening since 2008, with only an occasional change. The middle of the week appears to suite off-campus students as a time to meet inworld.

What is Engagement?

Engagement is multidimensional and can be divided into three categories: affective, behavioural and cognitive. It is a combination of student's feelings (affective), observable actions or performance (behavioural), perceptions and beliefs (cognitive) (Jimerson, Campos, & Greif, 2003; Russell, Ainley, & Frydenberg, 2005). This re-

search incorporated a variety of ways to measure engagement in the virtual world through student's perceived ability, observations and achievement. Engagement can be measured through teacher and student reporting and observation (Reading, 2008). A study by Hu & Kuht (2002) found that engagement is a function of the interaction of the student and institutional characteristics. Greene & Miller (1996) report that achievement in the classroom is determined by a student's perceived ability and learning goals that influence meaningful cognitive engagement. If someone is engaged they "have a sense of energetic and effective connection with the activities they are undertaking" (Schaufeli, Bakker, & Salanova, 2006, p. 702). Whilst undertaking activities in the virtual world, students "learned the skills for seeking out the required knowledge as the changing situation demanded" which "facilitated active student engagement in authentic learning activities designed to achieve desired learning outcomes" (Raeburn et al., 2009, p. 821). Engagement refers to the "time, energy and resources students devote to activities designed to enhance learning" (Krause, 2005, p. 3). This research demonstrates student engagement in their virtual world activities as measured by a variety of data collection techniques.

THE AVATAR AS RESEARCHER

An avatar is an electronic graphical representation of a person's alter ego that can be used when in the virtual world (Gregory & Smith, 2008). Jass was created in 2007 (See Figure 1) and always looks the same so that students will immediately recognise her. This is important when there are many students (up to 50 at a time) at a session. Students need to be able to recognize their educator quickly and easily.

A meeting place called Education Online Headquarters was initially created for student to use when they were online together. The meeting place is secure and private. It was only open to

Figure 1. Jass Easterman the researcher's avatar

Jass and her students. When there, students knew they were the only people that could go there. This was so that could talk privately and knew that anyone else that was there was a student of Jass. Figure 2 is an example of a discussion underway at Australis 4 Learning, the other space that Jass has created for her students to learn in. Several areas have been created for group discussions, but the place in this image and another round table conference area were the most popular. When given a choice, this is where students congregated, perhaps it was because of the round-table enabling everyone to see each other properly, which is important for new users when they are unfamiliar with how to do this easily. Australis 4 Learning was created when Education Online Head Quarters became too small for the growing number of students opting to participate in this learning. Australis 4 Learning is an open space. That means that anyone can visit. When students require a private space, they can go to Education Online Headquarters.

METHODOLOGY

Students were enrolled in one of five ICT Education or two Teaching and Learning units. The learning objectives were: to integrate social computing technologies as tools for learning in an educational setting; use and evaluate software suitable for classroom use, including social networking and computing tools; construct and present a personal philosophy for uses of social computing tools in an educational setting; and discuss the use of emerging tools in the context of technology development, educational paradigms, usage by various social

Figure 2. Jass in discussions with students

groups, innovation and adoption by social groups. They were able to achieve these objectives in their Second Life sessions. Students were studying by off-campus mode on a voluntary basis and were located at various locations around Australia with some from overseas. It was compulsory for on-campus students to participate. The research reported here on engagement only gathered data from off-campus students.

University Ethics was approved to gather the data. The research triangulated data collection methodologies (both quantitative and qualitative) through various formats, including: surveys, recording of online dialogue, observation and questioning. The interpretations of the analysis were strengthened based on more available evidence when undertaking the research this way. The impact of potential biases were reduced across data sets where they can exist in a single study (University of Southern California, 2007). This research provided data to support the notion that a virtual world engages education students and was therefore an effective teaching and learning resource.

Engagement was measured by:

- Asking how students felt (questioning/ survey);
- Observing students (through their actions whilst answering questions, contributing to discussions, participation and monitoring whether they stayed on task); and
- Discovering students' attitudes, perceptions and beliefs (discussions/questions/ surveys).

Off-campus students elected to attend weekly sessions over the teaching period to learn how to use Second Life as an educational tool. Not all students started at week one, with students able join part way through. Each week students gathered inworld, for round table discussions at either Education Online Headquarters or Australis 4 Learning. After discussions, they would then venture on to participate in virtual excursions and tours, demonstrations of virtual educational tools, web quests, role-plays, basic building and scripting and attend inworld lectures by academics from other institutions worldwide to see how they were using virtual worlds with their students.

Data was collected by recording of discussions in the virtual world, email, discussion board and blog postings. Students completed a survey seeking both quantitative and qualitative answers. Direct questioning of the students, recording and observations of how long students were logged on, how often students participated, student's opinions of what they wanted to do when attending Second Life sessions and their contribution to discussions were all gathered and recorded for analysis.

FINDINGS

The average age on Second Life is 36 (Korolov, 2011). In 2008, Collins stated that the average age was 33 years. With the merging of TeenLife with Second Life, it would have been thought that the average age would have gone down. Collins suggested that the demographic was getting younger as there had been a big increase in the past year of 18-20 year olds (Collins, 2008a). However, according to research from (Kzero, 2008) the average age for users of Second Life is over 30. As mentioned, it now stands at 36 years of age.

Figure 3 outlines the age distribution of students attending Second Life sessions with the researcher. The age categories were changed in 2010 to cater for a younger demographic being offered sessions inworld. The graphs indicate that in the years 2008 and 2009, most of the users who took up the option to study using Second Life were in the 30 to 45 age range. 2010 was the first year the pre-service teacher education unit began offering study in off-campus mode. This unit, two Masters units and two Teaching and Learning units also offered the option of studying using a virtual world as part of their assessment in 2010. The introduction of these five units, one being a large undergraduate unit of approximately 200 students, meant that the number of younger students taking up this offer increased. Figure 3 demonstrates that most of the users were in the 30-45 age range, with the younger users following closely behind due to the introduction of first year undergraduate students in off-campus mode in later year sessions.

As outlined previously, engagement is described as affective, behavioural or cognitive. Fifty-two thousand lines of text were analysed through Leximancer which is a software package designed to identify themes. After analysis of the words spoken (written through text chat) in the virtual world, common themes linked from the concept words of "Second Life" and "Jass" are as follows: time, space, voice, people, real life, school, computer, place, interesting, found and tonight as outlined in Figure 4. Whilst not all these words demonstrate engagement, they are the core words behind the conversations and are all positive words that can contribute to students feeling engaged in the sessions. When students referred to time, they often mentioned the time spent in the virtual world or the fact that time moved at a faster pace. Students voiced their perceptions of their learning depending on the context that they were experiencing at the time. This could be that they were comparing the virtual world learning to real life, schools, use of computers or the

people they were interacting and engaging with. "Computer" would have been a prominent word spoken as this is the medium in which the virtual world experiences were undertaken. It should also be stated that if the word "computer" was mentioned in the chat text, the student was possibly voicing concerns about the technology. Over the years, the technology has improved to be able to support a virtual world as a learning space better. However, on occasion, students have voiced concerns about the technology and that they were experiencing slowness (lag) or that it was taking time for images to rezz (come into focus). Tonight was a word mentioned regularly as it was of an evening that the sessions took place. Students also mentioned place and space regularly as a different word for virtual world or Second Life.

Of the quotations that presented a form of affective, behavioural or cognitive engagement 73% were affective engagement, 4% behavioural engagement and 23% cognitive engagement. However, not all engagement from this study was analysed from the student quotations. Other forms of data collection demonstrated engagement such as surveys and observations. Following are ways in which engagement was measured via student quotes through inworld text, discussion board, wiki and blog postings and images that capture what students were doing whilst in the virtual world of Second Life. Also, engagement was

Figure 3. Age distribution of students who completed surveys and attended second life sessions with Jass on a voluntary basis (2008/2009 n= 21, 2010/2011 n=77)

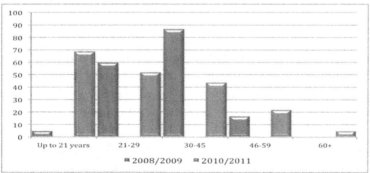

Figure 4. Themes occurring from the inworld discussions using Leximancer for theme analysis

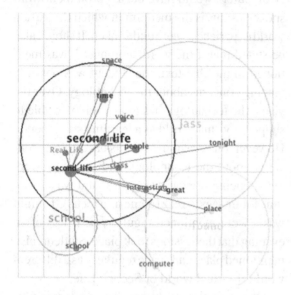

measured by observing student's inworld actions. Words in bold and italics are engagement words, corresponding to the type of engagement – affective (feelings), behavioural (observable actions or performance) or cognitive (perceptions and beliefs). Analysis of the data was via several modes: establishment of themes using Leximancer; manual sorting of inworld text into themes; observations of time spent inworld; statistical analysis of demographic data from surveys such as location and age, the unit the students were studying, student results (grades) of their studies; and analysis of surveys questions which included a selection of both quantitative and qualitative questions.

Affective: Feelings

Students demonstrated how they felt about their inworld sessions with the following quotes, which depict affective engagement – their feelings of their experiences.

- Students will be having *so much fun*, that they will *not even realise* they are learning.

Figure 5 encapsulates this statement – the students went to a Tai Chi lesson and then on to meditate. This was undertaken with Jass was not able to be online for a short period. The students invited Jass to participate once she arrived.

- I'm only sorry I missed so much - the weeks since I finally got here have been *amazing* - a *highlight* of my uni week.
- I am so *glad* we are finally out of the classroom!
- Wow this is *great*. Wow, what a *buzz*, phew, that was *exhausting*. I feel a little *motion sick*.... (smiles) That was *amazing*.
- I *feel* very *excited*, I have so many ideas.... Seeing something like that makes them *seem* possible.
- I *love* these discussions Jass! I am going to *miss* them.
- It has been one of the *highlights* of my entire uni life! This is my 7th year of uni.... and only performing in operas has been better. This has been a *life-changing experience*.
- The lecturer made the learning environment very comfortable therefore my *first impression was 'wow'*. Along with the special guests that Jass brought in to speak with us, I *felt it enriched my personal learning*.
- In a virtual world you *learn through play*. Everything is *fun*! I *believe strongly* in the educational value of virtual worlds and can't wait for the opportunity to be able to use it in a school context.

Figure 6 displays images of students engaged in discussions with guest lecturers. Many students expressed their feelings whilst undertaking their learning in Second Life as depicted in the quotes above. Figure 6a is at the University of Torino in Italy, where students were given a lecture followed by a tour. Figure 6b is at St Joseph's school in Australia where students were provided with ideas

Figure 5. Meditation being undertaken in world

Figure 6. Students engaged in conversations with guest academics: (6a) University of Torino, Italy, (6b) St Josephs School, Australia, (6c) Griffith University, Australia

on how they could use a virtual world with their future school students. Figure 6c shows students attending Griffith University, Australia, where they learnt how this university was using virtual worlds in their teaching of education students.

Behavioural: Observable Actions or Performance

A statistical comparison of students across the four years demonstrated student engagement in their sessions in the virtual world. There were large numbers of pages written by the students. All conversations were in text. Recordings were made of the inworld chat. The numbers of pages were the recordings of all student conversations during the sessions. Sometimes these were just one word, such as lol (laugh out loud) or a line. However, many times they were as long as several lines in a paragraph. Over 52,000 lines of conversations were recorded over the duration of the research. Table 1 outlines the number of students who participated on a voluntary basis in each year of the research, the average time spent inworld over the semester and the number of pages of conversation recorded.

Table 1 indicates that students were so immersed and engaged in what they were doing that they lost track of time or wanted to learn more, as depicted in the two quotes below. Sessions were advertised to go for two hours in 2008 and 2009. In 2008, on average they stayed for two hours fifty-one minutes and on two (2) occasions stayed for over three (3) hours. In 2009, students stayed on average three hours twenty minutes and on three (3) occasions they stayed over four (4) hours. What some of the students said were:

… so much for not staying the full 2 hours! (lol)

… wow time flies in here

In 2010, students spent, on average, two hours twenty-seven minutes inworld and on four occasions they spent over three (3) hours. In 2011,

students spent, on average, two hours thirty-four minutes inworld and on two occasions they stayed over three (3) hours. In 2010 and 2011, the advertised time for inworld sessions was one hour. Figure 7 shows a group of students in discussions where many students often lost track of time.

Cognitive: Perceptions and Beliefs

Students' perceptions and beliefs about their learning in the virtual world are depicted in the following quotes. These quotes demonstrate how students believe that their learning in the virtual world was engaging or used words that depict that they were engaged in their learning.

- I had my first visit to Second Life on Wednesday and it was a blast. I can *see* the *students engaged* in this environment and developing understanding in life skills and applying these to real life.
- They are the *highlight* of my degree.
- This is great … love the change *almost like face to face* with lecturer.
- Your … work … doesn't just recreate classrooms and lecture halls but *seriously uses the creative potential* of Second Life of teaching.
- Firstly though I can see me using a virtual world environment in a classroom because I *believe* it is a great way to *inspire learning* in all students. It is a way of *engaging* the digital natives giving them a sense of freedom and individuality in their learning.
- You could use the environment for music students who had *performance anxiety*. They could *practice here before performing live*.
- I had a *defining experience* last week when we sat down in that open air lecture space and I sat on one side and the rest of you sat on the other side. Suddenly I felt *lonely* and without thinking got up and moved to where you were all sitting. And then I thought that felt so *real*!

Table 1. Statistical comparison of student attendance in second life sessions

	2008	2009	2010	2011
Students signed up to attend	12	18	99	110
Average number of students in attendance	6.5	9.2	19.4	20.1
Average time spent inworld each session	2 hours 51 minutes (advertised two hour sessions)	3 hours 20 minutes (advertised two hour sessions)	2 hours 27 minutes (advertised one hour session)	2 hours 34 minutes (advertised one hour session)
Number of A4 pages recorded of inworld conversations	190	306	194	174

- In a strange way I think exploring a virtual world can actually make that *world more real* than say looking at pictures or reading texts or even viewing a video.

- Virtual worlds are an *outstanding educational tool*. They are *exciting and empowering*. They enable students to *take control of their own learning*, thus *creating deeper learning experiences*.

- I *believe so strongly* in the educational uses of SL that, after working with Jass, I have been considering doing a PhD in this area.

Figure 8 is a student performing in Second Life as part of an assessment task. This student was studying to become a music teacher and was demonstrating how someone could perform, via their avatar, in Second Life, to overcome performance anxiety. They were anonymous in the virtual world and felt the freedom of being able to perform without "stage fright." The student used audio, keyboard, dance and lighting to create her demonstration. This student stated that her own music students were often overcome by performance anxiety. However, performing in the virtual world alleviated these feelings as they were only performing to a computer and were unaware of the audience listening to their performance until the end when they received the audience feedback of clapping and cheering, thus increasing their confidence and alleviating their feelings of anxiety.

These statements are of what the student's believed, thought and did and demonstrate that they were engaged whilst learning in Second Life.

Figure 7. Discussions at education online headquarters

Figure 8. Student performing in second life

Because the sessions felt so real to the students, like they were actually there, demonstrated how immersed and engaged they were in their learning in the virtual world.

This is presented by the various quotations indicating that the students were immersed in their learning. They lost track of time, they wrote (spoke) large quantities of text and talked about their feelings and perceptions of their learning taking place.

FUTURE RESEARCH DIRECTIONS

We do not know what the future holds in terms of technology. There has been an enormous change over the past decade in terms of interactivity from web based, social networking tools and virtual worlds. There is a need for academics to understand how these tools can be used undertaking good pedagogical or andragogy practices. More research is required on immersive tools being used to educate students to ascertain whether they are engaging and most importantly, educational. Virtual worlds have developed over the four years of this research with the advent of new ways in which to teach students. The incorporation of bots (non-player characters) has provided a different avenue in which students can learn. Students can

now undertake their learning asynchronously with bots to practise their teaching skills at Australis 4 Learning (see http://www.virtualprex.com). They can also learn languages using bots at Chinese Island. These are two ways in which virtual worlds have changed and improved to assist students with their learning. Virtual worlds are continuously developing and educators are exploring new ways in which to engage their students in their learning. Augmented reality and haptic sensors are directions in which virtual worlds are able to provide very real experiences for students. Learning and teaching in a virtual world is still relatively new and as technology is continuously changing, students will be able to undertake their learning in ways we are yet to imagine.

CONCLUSION

Students are engaged when attending inworld activities in Second Life. All students contributed to the discussions and went beyond what was asked of them in terms of time, depth and satisfying their learning outcomes. The students would ask questions and put their point of view across. They contributed to other's queries. Students did not want to leave at the end of the evening and only did so when it was getting late. Many students asked if they could participate in the discussions when they were next being offered (even if they were not enrolled at university). This demonstrated that the students valued the sessions that they received in Second Life and were engaged in their learning. A final quote from a student demonstrates their perception of how engaging learning in Second Life could be for students and would be a valuable tool to use in the classroom "Because it is more game-like students will engage more. And higher engagement means more learning and less behaviour issues." This chapter has demonstrated that by analyzing student comments, perceptions, and actions when participating in their learning in the virtual world they are engaged in their learning. They are engaged from an affective, behavioural or cognitive perspective. Fifty-two thousand lines of inworld conversations, surveys, observations and online posts were analysed to provide data to make this claim.

REFERENCES

Beldarrain, Y. (2006). Distance education trends: Integrating new technologies to foster student interaction and collaboration. *Distance Education, 27*(2), 139–153. doi:http://dx.doi.org/10.1080/01587910600789498

Butler, D. (2008). *Air gondwana: Teaching negotiation skills by utilising virtual worlds for an authentic learning experience.* Paper presented at the ascilite 2008. Melbourne, Australia. Retrieved from http://www.ascilite.org.au/conferences/melbourne08/procs/butler-d-poster.pdf

Calonge, C. (2007). *A view from second life's trenches: Are you a pioneer or a settler?* Paper presented at the New Media Consortium. Berkeley, CA.

Campbell, M. (2009). *Using 3D-virtual worlds to teach decision-making.* Retrieved from http://www.ascilite.org.au/conferences/auckland09/procs/filename.pdf

Carr, D., Oliver, M., & Burn, A. (2008). *Learning, teaching and ambiguity in virtual worlds.* Retrieved from http://www.open.ac.uk/relive08/

Chesnevar, C. I., Maguitman, A. G., Gonzalez, M. P., & Cobo, M. L. (2004). Teaching fundamentals of computing theory: A constructivist approach. *Journal of Computer Science & Technology, 4*(2), 91-97.

Collins, C. (2008). *AVWW 2008 program: Australasian Virtual worlds workshop.* Retrieved from http://slenz.wordpress.com/2008/11/12/the-slenz-update-no-24-november-12-2008/

Cranton, P. (1992). *Working with adult learners.* Montreal, Canada: Wall & Emerson, Inc..

Cranton, P., & Tisdell, E. J. (2008). Transformative learning. In J. Athanasou (Ed.), Adult Education and Training, (pp. 35–50). Terrigal: David Barlow Publishing.

Dahms, M., Geonnotti, K., Passalacqua, D., Schilk, J. N., & Wetzel, A. (2008). *The educational theory of Lev Semenovich Vygotsky: An analysis.* Retrieved April 24, 2009, from http://www.newfoundations.com/GALLERY/Vygotsky.html

Farley, H., & Steel, C. (2009). *A quest for the holy grail: Tactile precision, natural movement and haptic feedback in 3D virtual spaces.* Retrieved from http://www.ascilite.org.au/conferences/auckland09/procs/farley.pdf

Finger, M., & Asun, J. M. (2001). *Adult education at the crossroads: Learning our way out.* New York, NY: Zed Books Ltd..

Green, J. (1998). Andragogy: Teaching adults. *Encyclopedia of Educational Technology.* Retrieved April 7, 2009, from http://coe.sdsu.edu/eet/Articles/andragogy/index.htm

Greene, B., A., & Miller, R., B. (1996). Influences on achievement: Goals, perceived ability and cognitive engagement. *Contemporary Educational Psychology, 21*(15), 181–192. doi:10.1006/ceps.1996.0015.

Gregory, B., Gregory, S., Wood, D., Masters, Y., Hillier, M., Stokes-Thompson, F., et al. (2011). How are Australian higher education institutions contributing to change through innovative teaching and learning in virtual worlds? Retrieved from http://www.leishman-associates.com.au/ascilite2011/downloads/papers/Gregory-full.pdf

Gregory, S. (2007). *Virtual classrooms: Learning in a virtual environment*. Retrieved October 9, 2007, from http://www.virtualclassrooms.info

Gregory, S., Lee, M. J. W., Ellis, A., Gregory, B., Wood, D., Hillier, M., et al. (2010). Australian higher education institutions transforming the future of teaching and learning through virtual worlds. In C. Steel, M. J. Keppell, & P. Gerbic (Eds.), *Curriculum, Technology & Transformation for an Unknown Future,* (pp. 399–415). Retrieved from http://www.ascilite.org.au/conferences/sydney10/Ascilite%20conference%20proceedings%202010/Gregory-full.pdf

Gregory, S., Reiners, T., & Tynan, B. (2010). Alternative realities: Immersive learning for and with students. In Song, H. (Ed.), *Distance Learning Technology, Current Instruction, and the Future of Education: Applications of Today, Practices of Tomorrow* (pp. 245–271). Hershey, PA: IGI Global.

Gregory, S., & Smith, H. (2008). *How virtual classrooms are changing the face of education: Using virtual classrooms in today's university environment*. Paper presented at the ISTE. Armidale, Australia.

Hearns, M., Diener, S., Honey, M., Cockeram, J., Parsons, D., Champion, E., et al. (2011). He ara hou ka tū mai: NZ institutions of higher learning unpacking demands and facilitating change. In G. Williams, P. Statham, N. Brown, & B. Cleland (Eds.), *Changing Demands, Changing Directions: Proceedings Ascilite Hobart 2011,* (pp. 571–579). Retrieved from http://www.leishman-associates.com.au/ascilite2011/downloads/papers/Hearns-concise.pdf

Hollins, P., & Robbins, S. (2008). *The educational affordances of multi user virtual environments (MUVE)*. Retrieved from http://www.open.ac.uk/relive08/

Honey, M., Diener, S., Connor, K., Veltman, M., & Bodily, D. (2009). *Teaching in virtual space: An interactive session demonstrating second life simulation for haemorrhage management*. Retrieved from http://www.ascilite.org.au/conferences/auckland09/procs/honey-interactivesession.pdf.

Hu, S., & Kuht, G., D. (2002). Being (dis)engaged in educationally purposeful activities: The influences of student and institutional characteristics. *Research in Higher Education, 43*(5), 555–575. doi:10.1023/A:1020114231387.

Jeffery, C. (2008). *Using non-player characters as tutors in virtual environments*. Retrieved from http://www.open.ac.uk/relive08/

Jimerson, S. R., Campos, E., & Greif, J. L. (2003). Toward an understanding of definitions and measures of school engagement and related terms. *California School Psychologist, 8*, 7–27.

Kearsley, G. (2009a). *Explorations in learning & instruction: The theory into practice database; transformative learning (J. Mezirow)*. Retrieved September 8, 2009, from http://tip.psychology.org/bruner.html

Kearsley, G. (2009b). *Explorations in learning & instruction: The theory into practice database; andragogy (M.Knowles)*. Retrieved September 8, 2009, from http://tip.psychology.org/knowles.html

Knowles, M. S. (1984). *Andragogy in action: Applying modern principles of adult learning.* San Francisco, CA: Jossey-Bass.

Korolov, M. (2011). Virtual world usage accelerates. *Hypergrid Business*. Retrieved May 27, 2012, from http://www.hypergridbusiness.com/2011/07/virtual-world-usage-accelerates/

Krause, K.-L. (2005). *Understanding and promoting student engagement in university learning communities.* http://www.deakin.edu.au/itl/student-engagement/Resources/StudengKrause.pdf.

Kzero. (2008). Research. *Resident experts in virtual worlds.* Retrieved September 1, 2009, from http://www.kzero.co.uk/blog/?page_id=2092

Lemon, M., & Kelly, O. (2009). *Laying second life foundations: Second chance learners get first life skills.* Retrieved from http://www.ascilite.org.au/conferences/auckland09/procs/lemon.pdf

Linden Lab. (2008). *Second life.* Retrieved July 19, 2008, from http://www.secondlife.com

McLoughlin, C., & Lee, M. J. W. (2008). Future learning landscapes: Transforming pedagogy through social software. *Innovate, 4*(5), 1–8.

Raeburn, P., Muldoon, N., & Bookallil, C. (2009). *Blended spaces, work based learning and constructive alignment: Impacts on student engagement.* Retrieved from http://www.ascilite.org.au/conferences/auckland09/procs/raeburn.pdf

Reading, C. E. (2008). *Recognising and measuring engagement in ICT-rich learning environments.* Paper presented at the ACEC2008. Canberra, Australia.

Russell, V. J., Ainley, M., & Frydenberg, E. (2005). Schooling issues digest: Student motivation and engagement. Retrieved March 9, 2009, from http://www.dest.gov.au/sectors/school_education/publications_resources/schooling_issues_digest/schooling_issues_digest_motivation_engagement.htm

Schaufeli, W., Bakker, A., & Salanova, M. (2006). The measurement of work engagement with a short questionnaire: A cross-national study. *Educational and Psychological Measurement, 66*(n), 701–716. doi:10.1177/0013164405282471

Schutt, S., & Martino, J. (2008). *Virtual worlds as an architecture of learning.* Retrieved from http://www.ascilite.org.au/conferences/melbourne08/procs/schutt-poster.pdf

Siemens, G. (2004). Connectivism: A learning theory for the digital age. *elearnspace everything elearning.* Retrieved April 24, 2009, from http://www.elearnspace.org/Articles/connectivism.htm

Siemens, G. (2008). *Connectivisim: networked learning.* Retrieved from http://www.connectivism.ca/

Tateru, N. (2012). *Second life statistical charts.* Retrieved May 25, 2012, from http://dwellonit.taterunino.net/sl-statistical-charts/

University of Southern California. (2007). Triangulation. *Institute for Global Health: Triangulation.* Retrieved July 31, 2008, from http://www.igh.org/triangulation/

Wood, D., & Hopkins, L. (2008). 3D virtual environments: Businesses are ready but are our 'digital natives' prepared for changing landscapes? In *Proceedings Ascilite Melbourne 2008,* (pp. 1136–1146). Retrieved from http://www.ascilite.org.au/conferences/melbourne08/procs/wood-2.pdf

ADDITIONAL READING

Dalgarno, B., Lee, M. J. W., Carlson, L., Gregory, S., & Tynan, B. (2010). 3D immersive virtual worlds in higher education: An Australian and New Zealand scoping study. In C. Steel, M.J. Keppell, & P. Gerbic (Eds.), *Curriculum, Technology & Transformation for an Unknown Future: Proceedings ascilite Sydney 2010,* (pp. 269-280). Retrieved from http://www.ascilite.org.au/conferences/sydney10/Ascilite%20conference%20proceedings%202010/Dalgarno-full.pdf

Dalgarno, B., Lee, M. J. W., Carlson, L., Gregory, S., & Tynan, B. (2011). Institutional support for and barriers to the use of 3D immersive virtual worlds|in higher education. In G. Williams, P. Statham, N. Brown, & B. Cleland (Eds.), *Changing Demands, Changing Directions: Proceedings ascilite Hobart 2011,* (pp. 316-330). Retrieved from http://www.leishman-associates.com.au/ascilite2011/downloads/papers/Dalgarno-full.pdf

Dalgarno, B., Lee, M. J. W., Carlson, L., Gregory, S., & Tynan, B. (2011). An Australian and New Zealand scoping study on the use of 3D immersive virtual worlds in higher education. *Australasian Journal of Educational Technology, 27*(1), 1-15. Retrieved from http://www.ascilite.org.au/ajet/ajet27/dalgarno.html

Dron, J., Reiners, T., & Gregory, S. (2011). Manifestations of hard and soft technologies in immersive spaces. In *Proceedings of the World Conference on E-Learning in Corporate, Government, Healthcare & Higher Education,* (pp. 1895-1905). Hawaii, HI: IEEE.

Gregory, B., Gregory, S., Wood, D., Masters, Y., Hillier, M., & Stokes-Thompson, F. ... Yusupova, A. (2011). How are Australian higher education institutions contributing to change through innovative teaching and learning in virtual worlds? In G. Williams, P. Statham, N. Brown, & B. Cleland (Eds.), *Changing Demands, Changing Directions: Proceedings ascilite Hobart 2011,* (pp. 475-590). Retrieved from http://www.leishman-associates.com.au/ascilite2011/downloads/papers/Gregory-full.pdf

Gregory, S. (2009). Innovative tutorial model using second life - Through weekly tutorials with national and international guests. In M. Docherty & Rosin (Eds.), *Mobile Me: Creativity on the Go,* (pp. 43-49). Retrieved from http://www.auc.edu.au/myfiles/uploads//Training/CW09/CW09-final.pdf

Gregory, S. (2011a). Rethinking teaching and learning through machinima professional development on sloodle. In P. Jerry & L. Lindsey (Eds.), *Experiential Learning in Virtual Worlds: Opening an Undiscovered Country,* (pp. 221-232). Oxford, UK: Inter-Disciplinary Press. Retrieved from https://www.interdisciplinarypress.net/online-store/ebooks/digital-humanities/experiential-learning-in-virtual-worlds

Gregory, S. (2011b). Teaching higher education students with diverse learning outcomes in the virtual world of second life. In Hinrichs, R., & Wankel, C. (Eds.), *Transforming Virtual World Learning, Cutting-edge Technologies in Higher Education* (*Vol. 4*, pp. 333–362). Teynampet, India: Emerald Group Publishing Limited.

Gregory, S. (2012). Learning in a virtual world: Student perceptions and outcomes. In Moyle, K., & Winjnaards, G. (Eds.), *Student Reactions to Learning with Technologies: Perceptions and Outcomes* (*Vol. 1*, pp. 91–116). Hershey, PA: IGI Global.

Gregory, S., Dalgarno, B., Campbell, M., Reiners, T., Knox, V., & Masters, Y. (2011). *Changing directions through VirtualPREX: Engaging pre-service teachers in virtual professional experience*. Retrieved from http://www.leishman-associates. com.au/ascilite2011/downloads/papers/GregoryS-full.pdf

Gregory, S., & Gregory, B. (2011). Do virtual worlds have a role in increasing student engagement as measured by their higher academic grades? In Docherty, M., & Hitchcock, M. (Eds.), *Create-World 2011 Pre-Publication Proceedings* (pp. 34–44). Brisbane, Australia: Griffith University.

Gregory, S., & James, R. (2011). *VirtualPREX: Open and distance learning for pre-service teachers*. Paper presented at the 24th ICDE World Conference on Open & Distance Learning. Bali, Malaysia.

Gregory, S., & Masters, Y. (2010). Virtual classrooms and playgrounds - Why would anyone use them? In *Proceedings of the 4th Annual Postgraduate Research Conference*. Brisbane, Australia: University of New England.

Gregory, S., & Masters, Y. (2012). Real thinking with virtual hats: A role-playing activity for pre-service teachers in second life. *Australasian Journal of Educational Technology, 28*(3), 420-440. Retrieved from http://www.ascilite.org.au/ajet/ajet28/gregory.html

Gregory, S., Reiners, T., & Tynan, B. (2010). Alternative realities: Immersive learning for and with students. In Song, H. (Ed.), *Distance Learning Technology, Current Instruction, and the Future of Education: Applications of Today, Practices of Tomorrow* (pp. 245–271). Hershey, PA: IGI Global.

Gregory, S., & Smith, H. (2009). Virtual worlds: Can virtual worlds promote a higher level of collaboration, engagement and deeper thinking for students than traditional Web 2.0 tools? In *Proceedings of the 3rd Annual Postgraduate Research Conference*, (pp. 85-92). Brisbane, Australia: University of New England.

Gregory, S., & Smith, H. (2010). How virtual classrooms are changing the face of education: Using virtual classrooms in today's university environment. In W. Halloway & Maurer (Eds.), *International Research in Teacher Education: Current Perspectives*, (pp. 239:252). Armidale, Australia: University of New England.

Gregory, S., & Tynan, B. (2009). *Introducing Jass Easterman: My second life learning space*. Retrieved from http://www.ascilite.org.au/conferences/auckland09/procs/gregory.pdf

Gregory. S., Lee, M.J.W., Ellis, A., Gregory, B., Wood, D., Hillier, M., McKeown, L. (2010). Australian higher education institutions transforming the future of teaching and learning through virtual worlds. In C. Steel, M.J. Keppell, & P. Gerbic (Eds.), *Curriculum, Technology & Transformation for an Unknown Future: Proceedings ascilite Sydney 2010,* (pp. 399-415). Retrieved from http://www.ascilite.org.au/conferences/sydney10/Ascilite%20conference%20proceedings%202010/Gregory-full.pdf

Hearns, M., Diener, S., Honey, M., Cockeram, J., Parsons, D., & Champion, E. … Gregory, S. (2011). He ara hou ka tu mai: NZ institutions of higher learning unpacking demands and facilitating change. In G. Williams, P. Statham, N. Brown, & B. Cleland (Eds.), *Changing Demands, Changing Directions: Proceedings ascilite Hobart 2011,* (pp. 571-579). Retrieved from http://www.leishman-associates.com.au/ascilite2011/downloads/papers/Hearns-concise.pdf

Masters, Y., & Gregory, S. (2010). *Second life: Harnessing virtual world technology to enhance student engagement and learning.* Paper presented at the Rethinking Learning in Your Discipline. Armidale, Australia. Retrieved from http://www.une.edu.au/altc/ult-futures/documents/ULT-Futures-2010-Masters.pdf

Masters, Y., & Gregory, S. (2011a). *Second life and higher education: New opportunities for teaching and learning.* Retrieved from http://www.interdisciplinary.net/wp-content/uploads/2011/02/mastersepaper.pdf

Masters, Y., & Gregory, S. (2011b). *Second life and higher education: New opportunities for teaching and learning.* Retrieved from https://www.interdisciplinarypress.net/online-store/ebooks/digital-humanities/experiential-learning-in-virtual-worlds

Reiners, T., Gregory, S., & Dreher, H. (2011). *Educational assessment in virtual world environments.* Retrieved from http://otl.curtin.edu.au/atna2011/files/ATNA_2011_Proceedings.pdf

KEY TERMS AND DEFINITIONS

Beliefs: How someone views things and believes them to be true depending on the perception of the world.

Engagement: Immersed in learning.

Feelings: How one feels about a situation, circumstance, depending on their perceptions, beliefs, values and current state.

Observations: Watching and listening to things happening around you.

Off-Campus Students: Distance education, not on campus, studying through learning management system resource materials.

Perceptions: How someone sees things depending on their view of the world.

Second Life: One of over 200 virtual worlds available.

Virtual Worlds: A virtual world is "an online electronic presence that imitates real life in the form of a personal presence through someone's avatar (the alter ego which is a graphical representation of themselves in the virtual world).

Chapter 10
Gaming in School:
Factors Influencing the Use of Serious Games in Public Schools in Middle Germany

Daniel Schultheiss
Ilmenau University of Technology, Germany

Maike Helm
Ilmenau University of Technology, Germany

ABSTRACT

As the impact of media on society steadily increases, schools need to teach their students media skills. In this regard, the usage of computers is an inherent part of everyday school life. The recent integration of serious games and their future potential in Middle German general educational schools is the subject of this chapter. With the aid of interviews held with experts the usage and potential of serious games in Middle German schools are examined, and the barriers to integrate computers and serious games into lessons are discussed. Serious game usage has clear potential for development. Games are applied in different subjects and for different age groups, but not all teachers are aware of their existence. The interviewees disagree about factors hindering integration of computers and serious games in school. As a qualitative study, this chapter constitutes a basis for further research and enlarges knowledge about serious games in schools.

INTRODUCTION

In today's media-oriented and constantly evolving information and knowledge society the use of multimedia technologies is a vital requirement for participation in political, economic and social life. Media literacy is becoming more and more important and therefore needs to be taught in schools. In recognition of this, in 2002 a media studies course was introduced for Thuringian grades five to seven but the use of computers today is an important part of all school education (Thuringian Ministry of Education, Research and Culture 2008).

DOI: 10.4018/978-1-4666-3673-6.ch010

Computers mean new teaching media, such as digital games, can be used in the classroom. A subtype of digital games is the so-called digital serious game which imparts knowledge in real conditions. Teaching duties normally carried out with a variety of equipment can now be managed virtually with a standard computer, so the traditional jam-packed preparation rooms of biology, physics or chemistry, for instance, could be partially be replaced by computers. Additionally, experiments which could not be done before because of non-existent or hard-to-deliver materials can be performed virtually with the help of serious games. Digital learning games demonstrably contain more benefits. Among other things they can be used as a safe alternative to dangerous experiments (such as those with corrosive materials); they can show invisible but important operations, such as the flow of electric energy. Despite these and other advantages few studies have been carried out so that the effects of serious games on students are not precisely known and many teachers are skeptical about their use in school education.

This chapter delivers a short overview of the current state of research on educational digital serious games. As their usage in schools requires the use of computers in the classroom, this is also considered in that research. Also the main constraining and fostering factors for the integration of computers and serious games in Middle German classrooms are identified. Finally, the results are discussed and directions of further research are given.

SERIOUS GAMES

Digital serious games are typically computer and video games (Ritterfeld & Weber 2006). A large variety of serious game genres is available. Among others, military-based games like 'America's Army' – designed to recruit soldiers for military service – are well known. Thanks to its free delivery over the Internet it received considerable attention and gave the genre's development and research a real boost (Gudmundsen 2006). Yet military serious games are only a small part of the whole repertoire of serious games. A study of 650 serious games and their genres documented that only 5 per cent of the tested games were of a military nature, 8 per cent were concerned with medicine and health and 14 per cent of the games focused on social issues. The biggest part (65 per cent) was in the school and educational context (Wang et al. 2009). In this context, we define the object of investigation in this chapter:

Serious games are understood as digital games, 'with a purpose beyond entertainment' (Heeter et al. 2010, Sherry & Dibble 2009) to strive for real learning goals in natural sciences, health, social and political areas (Bente & Breuer 2009).

For several years, schools have been equipped with computer labs. Those labs could also be used for educational serious games. According to Prensky (2000), today's students are a real 'game generation' that can no longer be motivated by a purely traditional teaching style. Indeed, a British study from 2006 shows that 85 per cent of all students use computer games at least once every two weeks. In contrast, 72 per cent of all teachers have never used any computer games at all. Despite this fact 36 per cent of primary and 27 per cent of secondary school teachers have used digital educational games in class (Sandford et al. 2006). This shows not just a generational difference in media use, but also the influence of media change on school education, so a trend towards an increasing use of computer games, including serious games, in educational contexts can be found, which obviously requires changes in the teacher's role. Needless to say that this is not just an issue in education, it is more a societal one. Studies indicate that similar problems exist for example in the field of therapy, where lacks of familiarity also lead to barriers regarding their usage (Ceranoglu 2010).

Using serious games in lessons means their role changes from that of a pure knowledge broker to a kind of guide, the so-called 'in-game coach' or player with expert knowledge, who assists students during self-discovery and learning (Shute et al. 2009).

SERIOUS GAMES IN SCHOOL EDUCATION

Serious games make use of the known fact that humans learn easiest during play. Games are an interactive multimedia product and the best paradigm for entertainment-education. This means that entertaining packages which include education content result in motivation to learn and learning success (Singhal & Rogers 1999, Ritterfeld & Weber 2006). As it is known that children instinctively collect their first knowledge by playful exploring their environment, games in general can be seen as a basis for human learning processes (Ritterfeld et al. 2009). Especially in digital games continuous learning is necessary to find the solution. Goals in a game can usually only be achieved with practice and understanding (Gee 2009). The possibilities to find the final solution are almost unlimited and gamers experiment by learning and applying the specific rules of each game (Sherry & Dibble 2009).

The more the game world and its specific rules equal the real world's rules, the more the knowledge and skills learned can be used in real life as well (Gee 2009). Hence, serious games which reflect real circumstances are particularly suited for educational purposes. In certain cases learning can be made easier, and gaming reality is extended by certain 'unreal' factors (Sherry & Dibble 2009). Thus, for example, the illustration of the (invisible) electric flow by arrows in a fictive physics lab can increase learning effects. Additionally, through the fun and the entertainment of serious games any lack of interest in teaching contents could be addressed (Ritterfeld & Weber

2006). To meet the challenge, reach the next level or conclude with a high score is the main motivation of play for children and young adults (Sherry et al. 2006). Because game levels can be passed only by learning and applying the specific rules of the game, which in serious games relate to real teaching contents, this motivation is helpful for the overall learning process (Gee 2009).

Serious games fulfil numerous didactic demands. They are interactive, give feedback and performance review, create experience-based learning, and promote problem- and action-oriented learning. Additionally, by immersion in the game world a very high and positive concentration is built up. In the end, pleasure, reward, structure, creativity and community complete the picture of the motivating learning medium, the serious game (Prensky 2005). Regardless of all learning effects it has to be noted that the use of modern media at school can also advance media competence.

It has been indicated empirically that serious games are most effective when they treat very specific, limited problems as are typical, for example, of mathematics, physics, art or language courses (Griffiths 2002). Complicated problems, however, can also be solved excellently with the help of computer games. The use of multiplayer games can motivate people to work in cooperation, which trains team ability. Their application in school lessons also raises the discussion readiness of children, so training their social skills (McFarlane et al. 2002).

Success at school can be increased by computer games and motivation, attention and concentration can be raised thereby. Thus positive effects in the areas of reading, spelling and grammar, as well as the development of complicated thinking and strategic planning, have been observed as a result of the use of computer games in school education (Kirriemuir 2005). In general, information and communication technologies can increase the independence of children and contribute to the individual support of both the highly gifted and under-achievers. Moreover, it is proved that positive attitudes about computer games directly affect attitudes to learning contents (Kulik et al. 1983) and the time spent on learning processes can be considerably shortened by the use of computers (Kulik & Kulik 1991). Nevertheless, up to now computer games have been seldom used in the German education system and only then if they make aims accessible which are otherwise inaccessible.

STATUS QUO OF COMPUTER AND SERIOUS GAME USAGE

Only a little research on serious game usage in German schools exists, because presently games are rarely used in the context of school education. Additionally, their potential as a teaching medium has been overlooked, partly because of their association with acts of violence such as the school shootings which have occurred in the past decade. Even though there is scientific proof that there is no connection between such acts of violence and games (Ferguson et al. 2011), social debates can influence the usage of games in teaching matters.

Serious game usage in school assumes as a base the use of computers, and study results in this area can also explain serious games usage. A closer look at this topic is therefore warranted. Computer games in general and serious games, according to UNICEF president David Puttnam (2006), are undoubtedly important for the education and development of the next generation 'digital citizens', who need experience in dealing with interactive media and communication networks if an educated and critical society is to be created.

In Germany computer applications and the usage of serious games in lessons are important components of school life and will be promoted more and more (Thuringian Ministry of Education, Research and Culture 2008). A survey of the initiative D21 (2010) was able to prove that about 35 per cent of all scholars already use a computer in lessons other than computer science at least once a week. Some 30 per cent of the scholars reported, however, that computers are not used at all outside computer science courses. At an average 74 per cent of European teachers indicated in 2006, however, regardless of school type, that they use information and communication technologies in their lessons (Korte & Hüsing 2006). Nevertheless, development of computer usage is not to be compared with the usage of serious games in terms of teaching means. Their use has hardly spread (Michael & Chen 2006) and, as mentioned earlier, only a few studies exist on the usage of serious games and their effects in educational contexts.

Even though there are several games and frameworks for usage in schools (e.g. Annetta 2010) it also has to be mentioned that serious games in many cases are designed especially for higher education (Westera et al. 2008, Rooney et al. 2009, Younis & Loh 2010) and compared to schools, usage in higher education is more common. Serious games, game like learning spaces and online courses already play a bigger role in academics. It is also expected that such technologies and environments will grow extremely in the next ten years (Anderson et al. 2012).

CONSTRAINTS

We now want to have a look at factors which hinder the integration of computers in school life. This can ultimately affect serious game usage. Schaumburg (2002) provided a systematization of such constraints. Four main factors are the school's organization (e.g. strict separation of courses, short courses, strong connection to curricula, etc.), the lack of accessible computers, insufficient computer knowledge and the negative attitude of teachers who prefer to offer conventional lessons and cannot deliver support in technical terms. These four constraints, school organization, equipment, teachers' attitude, and know-how apply in the present work as well as constraints on serious game usage, because serious game application, as already explained, depends on the usage of computers. Hence, in the following all four constraints are introduced. Teachers' attitude and their know-how are summarized as one factor, as the constraining factor is the teacher.

School Organization

On the one hand, computer games are a time-consuming teaching medium, because many take over ten hours to play through. On the other hand, there are timetables, strict course separation and single hour courses. Not all computer games are suitable for every type of lecture, except those specifically designed for school usage. Also the curriculum for German teachers limits computer usage in lessons (Schaumburg 2002). Nevertheless, in this connection the relatively new course of media studies has to be mentioned; its implementation makes it clear that media competence and usage which cover the use of computer games in lessons – is important to the Thuringian Ministry of Education, Research and Culture (2008), which is responsible for school education.

Equipment

In a study by the European Commission (2006) which questioned teachers as well as school principals throughout Europe, 49 per cent of the interviewees said that the very low use of computers in education is a result of the lack of equipment in schools, although in 2006 78 per cent of German teachers were – theoretically – able to use computers in school. About half of these (56 per cent) used them in less than 10 per cent of their lessons. Only 6 per cent used them in a large part of their teaching. The frequency was clearly higher at vocational schools than in general (European Commission 2006).

Therefore, the statements about the availability of computers do not mean automatically that they are used in lessons. Though it has been proved that bad equipment hampers the use of modern technology in education (OECD 2009), nevertheless, good equipment does not lead immediately

to an increased use of the technology (Pelgrum 2008). Additionally, only a few German schools permit the use of private laptops to increase the number of available computers in school lessons. Nonetheless, it is assumed that a growth in the computer equipment of schools took place in the past years.

Teachers' Attitude and Know-How

In 2005 about half of the German teachers in primary and secondary schools were more than 50 years old (OECD 2009). Only 25 per cent of the teachers had not yet reached the age of 40. The Commodore 64 (C64) was the beginning of the computer game phenomenon as recently as the 1980s, so today's 50-year-old teachers would not be familiar with digital games and computers from childhood. The result may be a lack of understanding of the digital game and insufficient know-how in dealing with the technology.

Several projects in Germany are trying to solve this problem. Workshops are offered in which teachers and administrators are qualified for the use of information technology in lessons (D21, 2010). The ThILLM (Thuringian Institute for Teacher Training, Curriculum Development and Media), which promotes media competence in school life also organizes advanced training and workshops.

RESEARCH QUESTIONS

In the light of the above, the main research question is as follows:

RQ: How can serious games be integrated into lessons of Middle German schools?

This question can be divided into more detailed questions. The first dimension deals with the choice of teaching material which can influence serious games as a teaching medium.

RQ1: By whom and according to what criteria is teaching material chosen for lessons in Middle German schools?

Furthermore, the present use and suitability of serious games in school lessons will be examined for an overview of the situation in middle German schools and to extend or to concretize the research state as described earlier.

RQ2: How are serious games used in Middle German schools and for which age groups or subjects are they suitable?

Finally, factors of influence on serious game usage will be examined: both factors which restrain the usage of computers and serious games and those which can increase their usage. RQ3 is built on the constraints which we discussed above. RQ4 asks for further usage.

RQ3: What are the attitudes of media pedagogues and teachers in Middle German schools regarding the use of serious games in lessons and how do they assess the constraints of computer and serious game usage in lessons?

RQ4: Which conditions must be fulfilled from the point of view of media pedagogues and teachers to increase the usage of computers and serious games in lessons?

The answers to these research questions will give a clear picture of the current integration of computers and serious games in Middle German schools, the impediments and how use can be increased.

METHOD

Data Collection

Personal assessments and views can be validated only on the basis of experiments, physiological measurements or observations. Questioning can examine certain research aspects directly or indirectly, however, and can be applied quantitatively or qualitatively. In this research, we decided on a qualitative method. There are few available studies about the usage of serious games in school educational contexts so a quantitative measuring model was not appropriate. Qualitative expert interviews were used because of the sparse research available on serious game usage in education. To prevent large excurses during the interviews and to make clear the special knowledge of the interviewer, a guide with open questions is used in the present work. The procedure can therefore be called half-structured and qualitative. Because the questions are not repeated, one can talk about a non-experimental cross-section study design.

Sample and Realization

In qualitative investigation designs the relevance of the interviewees is essential to the research subject. Generalization is also aimed here; however, it is not the main goal. Because the research questions are already concrete in this study pre-sampling was applied. On this occasion, the population was divided into types to which representative experts could be assigned. This research project examines the usage of serious games in lessons in Middle German schools so first we needed to know who decides which teaching materials are used in lessons. The ThILLM (Thuringian Institute for Teacher Training, Curriculum Development and Media) is responsible for decisions like this in a general context, which means they provide advice for schools and teachers. Every teacher, however, chooses his/her teaching materials personally. Only coarse learning targets are defined in the curriculum, so teachers were the main experts for this investigation. School principals could be more informative, because they should have the best overview about the activities of other teachers. To reach principals who could make statements about as many teachers as possible, the Thuringian schools with the highest number of personnel were selected: the largest

Thuringian high schools, junior high schools, and elementary schools. The schools were determined with the help of federal statistics. Finally, we were able to include the principal of a big state elementary school in Thuringia (P1, with 23 teachers), the principal of a big state junior high school (P2, with 58 teachers) and the principal of a big state high school (P3, with 86 teachers) for expert interviews. As the interviewees want to remain anonymous we simply describe their affiliation and competence. Because principals or teachers could nevertheless lack an overview about the overall situation and have insufficient knowledge on the subject of serious games, we decided to include context experts as well. They know the object of investigation and are informed about the use of computers and serious games in schools. We were able to include the director of an institute of educational computer game research (C1), who has a PhD in pedagogics. He examines computer games critically in the educational context and provides workshops on their usage to teachers. As a media pedagogue he works in Middle Germany. The second context expert was an employee (C2) of the ThILLM. He deals with media competence in schools and was involved in the process of development of the media studies course which was implemented for grades five to seven, as described earlier. This sample of directly affected persons and context experts was expected to deliver qualitative results for a comprehensive overview of serious game usage in Middle German schools, the constraints and the possibilities of increased use. It was impossible to provide a representative sample of the whole population of teachers and experts, however.

To check survey and method a pretest of the interview guide with a principal from a different state high school was performed. The expert interviews were carried out in March, 2010 by phone and were taped by software. The interview duration amounted to an average of 35 minutes. Afterwards the questions and answers were transcribed into text and evaluated.

RESULTS

In the following section the results of all interviews are shown according to the numerical order of the research questions. A description of the common statements of the interviewees is provided first, followed by differences between the expert statements, if any.

Selection of Teaching Materials (RQ1)

The first research question referred to the process of teaching material choice. Interviewees said that teachers are personally responsible for the choice of teaching material and their decisions are taken independently of ThILLM. ThILLM can influence teachers, however, merely by the presentation of certain materials in workshops attended. The principal of the junior high school told us about a democratic selection procedure and pointed to teacher conferences which influenced, for example, the choice of school books. The criteria according to which teachers choose their teaching material are subject-specific. In general, teaching material must correspond to the level of the courses, as well as didactic and methodical principles, to fulfill the particular teaching aim.

Serious Game Usage in Middle German Schools (RQ2)

Research question 2 examines the present usage of serious games in Thuringian schools and their suitability for certain age groups or subjects. The usage of computers and serious games is still very low in Thuringian schools, so there are currently no strong effects on education or the school system in general. In the high school, serious games are not used at all, according to the information supplied by its principal. Because technical development is ongoing, however, the usage of new media in lessons is becoming more and more important for him, and computers as well as multimedia use will inevitably become part of media education. The principal of the elementary school thought computer use beyond learning groups or classes should be obligatory, as well as in the normal lessons. Nevertheless, he highlighted that one cannot force teachers to use computers. The principals of the junior high school and the high school spoke of high demand, no pressure, and excellent usage. Computers and serious games are already used in the lessons of Thuringian schools, not only in computer science lessons, but in other different fields. The elementary school principal reported the usage of computers and computer games in ecological courses, mathematics and foreign language lessons and enthused about the game 'Nutrikid', which was used in dietetics and home economics courses. In the junior high school computers and computer games are used in the fields of economics, law, technology, geography, the natural sciences and language courses. The principal of the high school explained that the available computers of his school are used almost every school hour. Nevertheless, the usage must be always planned well and often seems superficial because of more time-consuming computer games. Hence, project days and project weeks are popular in terms of computers and computer games, according to all experts questioned. Outside the lessons other possibilities arise. Parents could promote serious game use while they play with their children after class. This is often easier than in school.

Regarding the suitability of serious games it must be said that suitability must be assessed for every game and subject by the concerning teacher. The junior high school principal pointed out gender-specific patterns of utilization. Whereas boys would rather test things and like to learn from mistakes, girls are rather creative, and this has to be taken into account in decisions on the suitability of a serious game for school lessons. According to the school type serious games are suited for use in certain fields. In elementary school their usage would be possible in nearly all fields like ecology, English, German, mathematics, local history, geography and even ethics. Also usage is conceivable later in sports, physics and social studies if the teachers identify aspects of the game which are similar to real life. Therefore not only are tailor-made serious games suitable, but also popular mainstream games. In junior high school serious games could be used in courses which take place several times a week, as for example the elective course offered in ninth grade. All interviewees considered serious games as suitable for the mediation of key competences and topics which are neither too concrete nor too complicated. Additionally, serious games are especially suitable for certain user groups, whose age is in accord with the game specification. In elementary schools serious games can be used at the earliest in third grade, because of the reading ability required, as well as the difficulty of computer usage. There are many children who do not have a computer at home and need to learn the usage of this technology first. If one thinks that serious games are useful not only because of pure technology use, but above all because of the reflection of their content, actually, from a media-educational view, more complex computer games seem to be appropriate at the earliest in grades five and above. Then children are able to reflect their own playing, which is something that one is not able to do at a very young age. In addition, serious games are only suitable for classes, which know how to handle gaming-educational methods.

Finally, expert 1 thought that not all serious games are educationally suitable. Thus, for example, it is unhelpful if game manufacturers try to smuggle a little bit of educational theory into the game or even worse if only pedagogues develop games. Rather, one can try to develop popular games which children also play in their social environment, and to transfer aspects of the games into reality. Serious games are suitable for lessons when they are not too complicated and still contain the relevant subject as well as the necessary fun. They need to be relevant, draw the attention to a certain problem in the learning context and have a long-lasting learning effect. This is possible when recompensing learning is integrated and neither too concrete nor too complicated subjects are treated. Above all, however, games must be designed so that children are willing to get involved in the area between learning and gaming.

Attitudes and Constraints Regarding Serious Game Usage (RQ3)

To answer research question 3, all constraints of computer and serious games use in school described by Schaumburg (2002) are examined more closely in the following with the help of the expert statements.

School organization. With regard to school organization the curricula, which may be too tight for the integration of computers in lessons (according to Schaumburg, 2002), were selected as the first topic during interviews. In the opinion of all interviewees curricula are designed in such a way that they leave free spaces for the teachers in terms of content, but there is little temporal space. Thus, every kind of media integration requires first a specific plan. Context expert 2, who has insights into the creation of curricula as an adviser for media in ThILLM, observed that curricula have to be geared up for more media use in schools. Nevertheless, computer game use is to be seen in the context of all media use at school, and hence still has to take place beyond lessons at home. Context expert 1 noted that general school organization can influence the use of computers and computer games in a negative way. Thus, one is thrown as a young teacher every now and then into a scenario, which does not allow one to form innovative projects. He refers to the attitudes of teachers who already teach several years at their schools. They have a certain influence and, however, often are not openly with new computer games compared to younger teachers.

Equipment. Computer equipment in schools was rated by most experts as ranging from sufficient to good. The elementary school principal rated the equipment as insufficient and unsuitable for use in lessons. The junior high school principal

described the computer equipment of his school as satisfactory, because it is fully used and as the demand from teachers for more computers is not increasing, the existing technology is sufficient. Computers are accessible, centralized, as well as decentralized, in the form of computer cabinets, learning corners and transportable devices. Additionally, devices belonging to school are complemented by the school's close associates, for example, youth clubs. Context expert 2 refers, in this context, to the equipment recommendations of the Thuringian Ministry of Education, Research and Culture which not all schools can adopt. The available technology mostly has to be renewed. All interviewees agree, besides, that it could be expanded. The principal of the elementary school excludes improvements, nevertheless, for financial reasons. According to context expert 1, equipment (computers and teaching material) is in general always dependent on the cooperation of the respective schools with their school authority. To assess the equipment factor properly, computer game context expert 2 warns against equating the pure availability of computers with the usage of computers. Finally, it would seem that every now and then computer cabinets equate to the storeroom, because the operators fear viruses or other problems.

Teachers' attitude and know-how. Here the interviewees' statements differed. Firstly all interviewees believed that teachers are obliged to use computers in lessons, nevertheless, many teachers have doubts because of lacking qualification and prejudices. Furthermore, the interviewees said uniformly that younger generations of teachers are more open regarding computer use than older ones. When teachers are approaching pensionable age, they are not open to new teaching methods, not willing to learn and hostile to new media in terms of content as well as technical knowledge. The elementary school principal spoke of colleagues lack of interest in computers and serious games and their reluctance to use them, insisting that children must concentrate on books. Discussions about old and new teaching methods are exhausting. In spite of some more open and positively minded teachers the perception of most colleagues is not satisfactory.

In contrast are the statements of context expert 1. There is considerable interest among teachers in computer use at school and there are those who look for ways to integrate computers and serious games into lessons. The judgements of teachers' attitudes are different but all are increasingly positive. Computers are a necessary teaching medium, working medium and aid, so attitudes towards them improve and their usage is seen more and more as a natural part of lessons. According to the context experts, however, they are to be seen in the context of media use and they are not necessary for the curriculum fulfilment.

All interviewees described a developing potential of computer and computer game use in lessons. The fact that teachers still dislike the application of computers and serious games to lessons, is based, inter alia, on the age of Thuringian teachers. In the case of the elementary school teachers have an average age of 57, in the high school most are in their 50s as well and the junior high school principal told us that the youngest teacher in the school was forty.

The knowledge of the teachers regarding computers is described as improvable by all experts. Fifteen years ago no knowledge existed, but now computer know-how is a condition for work in the school system. Today a certain pressure exists according to the interviewees to use online applications, which are necessary for lessons, so that teachers must deal with computers. Hence, their know-how with regard to information technology is sufficient. In some cases – e.g. in the elementary school – the knowledge of teachers is insufficient, and they have less know-how than the children have.

Workshops and advanced training for teachers are seldom requested according to all the experts and hence are rarely offered, so that the basics have to be learnt in self-study or in adult education programmes. The elementary principal noted that

advanced training registration is often possible only on the Internet. Because many of her colleagues do not know how they can deal with it, advanced trainings are used seldom at this school or substituted by teachers who explain how the online registration works.

Future Usage of Serious Games in Middle German Schools (RQ4)

A future increase of the computer and serious game usage in school education in Middle Germany could succeed according to all interviewees if certain conditions are fulfilled. At this point, the constraints of computer and serious game usage described before emerge once more. The school organization would have to change in terms of curriculum relaxation. According to the computer game context expert one must think about whether learning has changed in itself and, if this is the case, the school must also change. This is a long-term project and not compulsory, however. Also the lack of equipment was mentioned. If not enough work stations exist and this cannot be changed for financial or other reasons, more supervisors must be available to split classes and to use the computers in groups. The elementary school principal added that games with sound may be unsuitable for use in pairs, as usually there is only one earphone per computer.

Experts said unanimously that above all teachers must change their attitude to computer and serious game usage in lessons, so that an increased usage can occur. Thus, they have to deal with computer games, get to know different genres and also try to integrate games which children like in their lessons. To be more confident about computer use and to weaken the constraint of poor know-how they must qualify further in the use of computers and serious games. Thus, today's advanced training must introduce concrete games, discuss them and give the chance to the teachers to play independently, to gain experience and to improve computer usage. Furthermore, computers and serious games need to constitute a main focus in school development and be valued positively by school and professional conference leaders. In this connection the elementary school principal reported on presentations of learning games by some colleagues and their enthusiasm as soon as they experienced the effect the games could have on the children. In addition, more suitable serious games and methods were requested several times by the experts, methods which demanded neither too much of the teachers nor too many resources and contained a good combination of gaming and learning.

DISCUSSION

Teachers put together their teaching materials independently for their lessons and therefore have the biggest influence on the use of computers and serious games in Middle German school education. Their attitude to computers and games is therefore vital.

Computer and serious game applications according to the experts already exist in almost all fields and for most different purposes of education. Computers are seen by many as essential for today's school system. Serious games are viewed with some scepticism, however, because their playing duration is often too time-consuming for teaching use. In general they are applicable in all fields and to nearly every age group. The findings of Sherry and Dibble (2009), who recommend an adequate combination of play and learning and recompensing learning e.g. in the form of point scales, are supported.

A basic condition for the usage of serious games is the willingness to use computers in lessons. This willingness according to the questioned experts can be found in some of the Thuringian teachers. The general interest in integrating computers and serious games into school lessons is low, because it means additional expenditure for teachers to change teaching plans, to get involved in new

projects and to improve their computer skills. Older teachers who predominate in Thuringia tend to be averse to computer use.

To sum up, it can be said that the principals of the junior high school and the high school believed the constraints school organization, equipment, teachers' attitude and know-to have little influence on the computer and serious game usage in their schools. The elementary school principal confirmed, however, all constraints.

Regarding an increase in the present use of serious games the experts looked once more at the conviction of the teachers as an important factor of influence for the success of games. The elementary school principal reported that the aim could be fulfilled if one brought the games directly into the class to skeptical teachers and allowed them to observe the effects on children themselves. The computer game context expert similarly recommended that everyone can play and experiment with computers and games together. He stressed that media competence in education is not only found through the games, but also and above all with active reflection of their usage.

The increase of serious game usage in Thuringian public schools seems to be likely in the light of these statements. Political support already exists by the plans for media competence development even if this does not aim explicitly at serious game usage. Changes in the school system are also to be seen as essentially longer-term and on no account to be made compulsory in the opinion of the experts.

Limitations and Outlook

There are two main limitations in this study that need to be addressed. The first one is the method. The generalization of qualitative research is doubtful, because samples cannot be chosen randomly and the representativity cannot be proven by significance tests as it can in quantitative research. Rather, an exemplary generalization process can occur and be strengthened if the sample is of typical representatives of a group of similar cases. The sample arrangement of the study was discussed in the methodological part of this chapter and comprised typical media pedagogues and principals of different school types. Nevertheless, the statements of the principals showed considerable differences, although these may not be related to the different school types but could be of a purely accidental nature. Therefore, the generalization of all results should be checked by subsequent quantitative research.

The second limitation is the geographical one. As we only examined Thuringian school principals it is not possible to talk about the German, European or worldwide situation, although one could probably act on the assumption that the situation throughout the rest of Germany is very similar. For other geographical areas other studies have to be conducted.

As a third limitation the selection of interviewees has to be mentioned. On the one hand the interviewees in school did probably not gain their experience from class, as principles have less teaching duties. Even though it could be expected that principals have a very good insight into their teaching staff. This limitation does also apply to the context experts. On the other hand interviewees may have an own point of view regarding serious games in class which they want to promote or they could have other interests to influence our results. We tried to prevent such habits in all interviews to generate objective data.

Concluded can be said that most limitations were rooted in the method of this study. As it is important to gain qualitative results for further examination of the usage of serious games in school all limitations are acceptable.

Finally, for a first stocktaking to indicate the possibilities of the integration of computers and serious games in the lessons of Middle German schools, the method used seems eminently suitable. The experts' statements deliver a varied picture of the present situation in Middle German schools; therefore, this study can serve as a base for further research in different countries and motivate subsequent quantitative studies.

REFERENCES

Anderson, J. Q., Boyles, J. L., & Rainie, L. (2012). The future impact of the internet on higher education: experts expect more efficient collaborative environments and new grading schemes: They worry about massive online courses, the shift away from on-campus life. *Pew Internet & American Life Project*. Retrieved October 8, 2012, from http://pewinternet.org/~/media/Files/Reports/2012/PIP_Future_of_Higher_Ed.pdf

Annetta, L. A. (2010). The "I's" have it: A framework for serious educational game design. *Review of General Psychology, 14*(2), 105–112. doi:10.1037/a0018985.

Bente, G., & Breuer, J. (2009). Making the implicit explicit: Embedded measurement in serious games. In Ritterfeld, U., Cody, M., & Vorderer, P. (Eds.), *Serious Games: Mechanisms and Effects* (pp. 322–343). New York, NY: Routledge.

Ceranoglu, T. A. (2010). Video games in psychotherapy. *Review of General Psychology, 14*(2), 141–146. doi:10.1037/a0019439.

European Commission. (2006). *Benchmarking access and use of ICT in European schools 2006: Key findings*. Retrieved February 13, 2011, from http://ec.europa.eu/information_society/newsroom/cf/itemlongdetail.cfm?item_id=2888

Ferguson, C. J., Coulson, M., & Barnett, J. (2011). Psychological profiles of school shooters: Positive directions and one big wrong turn. *Journal of Police Crisis Negotiations, 11*(2), 141–158. doi:10.1080/15332586.2011.581523.

Gee, J. P. (2009). Deep learning properties of good digital games: How far can they go? In Ritterfeld, U., Cody, M., & Vorderer, P. (Eds.), *Serious Games: Mechanisms and Effects* (pp. 67–83). New York, NY: Routledge.

Griffiths, M. D. (2002). The educational benefits of videogames. *Education for Health, 20*(3), 47–51.

Gudmundsen, J. (2006). Movement gets serious about making games with purpose. *Gannett News Service*. Retrieved February 13, 2011, from http://pressconnects.gns.gannettonline.com/apps/pbcs.dll/article?AID=/20060518/TECH05/602150620/1001/TECH

Heeter, C., Winn, B., & Fleck, L. (2010). Deliberative games: Games for entertainment and learning lab. *Michigan State University*. Retrieved October 8, 2012, from http://www.gel.msu.edu/tism/deliberative-games

Initiative D21. (2010). *Website*. Retrieved February 13, 2011, from http://www.initiatived21.de

Kirriemuir, J. (2005). *Computer and videogames in curriculum-based education*. London, UK: Department for Education and Skills.

Korte, W. H., & Hüsing, T. (2006). Benchmarking access and use of ICT in European schools 2006. In *Empirica* (pp. 1–120). Bonn, Germany: Empirica.

Kulik, C. L. C., & Kulik, J. A. (1991). Effectiveness of computer-based Instruction: An updated analysis. *Computers in Human Behavior, 7*, 75–94. doi:10.1016/0747-5632(91)90030-5.

Kulik, J. A., Bangert, R. L., & Williams, G. W. (1983). Effects of computer-based teaching on secondary school students. *Journal of Educational Psychology, 75*, 19–26. doi:10.1037/0022-0663.75.1.19.

McFarlane, A., Sparrowhawk, A., & Heald, Y. (2002). Report on educational use of games. *TEEM (Teachers Evaluating Educational Multimedia)*. Retrieved February 13, 2011, from http://www.teem.org.uk/publications/teem_gaesined_full.pdf

Michael, D., & Chen, S. (2006). *Serious games: Games that educate, train and inform*. Boston, MA: Thomson Course Technology.

Organisation for Economic Co-operation and Development. (2009). *Creating effective teaching and learning environments*. Paris, France: OECD Publishing.

Pelgrum, W. J. (2008). School practices and conditions for pedagogy and ICTs. In Law, N., Pelgrum, W., & Plomp, T. (Eds.), *Pedagogy and ICT Use in Schools around the World: Findings from the IEA SITES 2006 Study* (pp. 67–122). Hong Kong, Hong Kong: CERC-Springer. doi:10.1007/978-1-4020-8928-2_4.

Prensky, M. (2000). *Digital game-based learning*. New York, NY: McGraw Hill.

Prensky, M. (2005). Computer games and learning: Digital game-based learning. In Raessens, J., & Goldstein, J. (Eds.), *Handbook of Computer Game Studies* (pp. 97–122). Cambridge, MA: MIT Press.

Puttnam, D. (2006). Foreword. In H. Ellis, S. Heppell, J. Kirriemuir, A. Krotoski, & A. McFarlane (Eds.), *Unlimited Learning: Computer and Video Games in the Learning Landscape,* (p. 1). London, UK: ELSPA (Entertainment and Leisure Software Publishers Association). Retrieved February 13, 2011, from http://www.elspa.com/assets/files/u/unlimitedlearningtheroleofcomputerandvideogamesint_344.pdf

Ritterfeld, U., Cody, M., & Vorderer, P. (2009). *Serious games: Mechanisms and effects*. New York, NY: Routledge.

Ritterfeld, U., & Weber, R. (2006). Video games for entertainment and education. In Vorderer, P., & Bryant, J. (Eds.), *Playing Video Games: Motives, Responses and Consequences* (pp. 399–413). Mahwah, NJ: Lawrence Erlbaum.

Rooney, P., O'Rourke, K., Burke, G., MacNamee, B., & Igbrude, C. (2009). Cross-disciplinary approaches for developing serious games. In *Proceedings of IEEE VS-Games'09*. IEEE.

Sandford, R., Ulicsak, M., Facer, K., & Rudd, T. (2006). *Teaching with games: Using commercial off-the-shelf computer games in formal education*. Bistrol, UK: Futurelab.

Schaumburg, H. (2002). Besseres lernen durch computer in der schule? Nutzungsbeispiele und einsatzbedingungen. [Improved learning in school? Examples of utilisation and application.] In Issing, L., & Klimsa, P. (Eds.), *Information und Lernen mit Multimedia* [Information and learning with multimedia]. (pp. 335–344). Weinheim, Germany: PVU.

Sherry, J. L., & Dibble, J. L. (2009). The impact of serious games on childhood development. In Ritterfeld, U., Cody, M., & Vorderer, P. (Eds.), *Serious Games: Mechanisms and Effects* (pp. 145–166). New York, NY: Routledge.

Sherry, J. L., Lucas, K., Greenberg, B. S., & Lachlan, K. (2006). Video game uses and gratifications as predictors of use and game preference. In Vorderer, P., & Bryant, J. (Eds.), *Playing Video Games: Motives, Responses and Consequences* (pp. 214–224). Mahwah, NJ: Lawrence Erlbaum.

Shute, V. J., Ventura, M., Bauer, M., & Zapata-Rivera, D. (2009). Melding the power of serious games and embedded assessment to monitor and foster learning: Flow and grow. In Ritterfeld, U., Cody, M., & Vorderer, P. (Eds.), *Serious Games: Mechanisms and Effects* (pp. 295–321). New York, NY: Routledge.

Singhal, A., & Rogers, E. M. (1999). *Entertainment education: A communication strategy for social change*. Mahwah, NJ: Lawrence Erlbaum.

Thuringian Ministry of Education, Research and Culture. (2008). *Framework agreement to promote media literacy in the free state of Thuringia*. Retrieved February 13, 2011, from http://www.thueringen.de/imperia/md/content/tkm/schuleonline2/rahmenvereinbarung_tkm_mit_tlm_medienkompetenzentwicklung.pdf

Wang, H., Shen, C., & Ritterfeld, U. (2009). Enjoyment in games. In Ritterfeld, U., Cody, M., & Vorderer, P. (Eds.), *Serious Games: Mechanisms and Effects* (pp. 25–47). Mahwah, NJ: Routledge/LEA.

Westera, W., Nadolski, R. J., Hummel, H. G. K., & Wopereis, I. G. J. H. (2008). Serious games for higher education: A framework for reducing design complexity. *Journal of Computer Assisted Learning*, 24(5), 420–432. doi:10.1111/j.1365-2729.2008.00279.x.

Younis, B., & Loh, C. S. (2010). *Integrating serious games in higher education programs*. Paper presented at Academic Colloquium 2010: Building Partnership in Teaching Excellence. Ramallah, Palestine.

Chapter 11
Quantitative Analysis of Voice and Keyboard Chat in a Paper Presentation Seminar in a Virtual World

Michael Gutjahr
Technische Universität Darmstadt, Germany

Wolfgang Bösche
University of Education Karlsruhe, Germany

ABSTRACT

To investigate the possibilities that are offered to improve teaching within a virtual environment, chat recordings from a paper presentation seminar in a virtual world were analyzed. A total of 9 sessions with more than 500 minutes of recordings from 19 participants were classified in diverse categories by two independent coders. The channel used (voice or keyboard) as well as other attributes of the contributions, the contributors, and the sessions were coded. Results show that the voice channel was mainly used for relevant contributions, while the keyboard channel contained mainly irrelevant contributions. The longer a session was the lower was the percentage of irrelevant contributions, p < .05. Gender and previous experience with digital games are both highly correlated with the percentage of irrelevant contributions, p < .01. Technical and personal factors are related to the rate of irrelevant contributions, while situational and relational factors seem to have a minor impact.

INTRODUCTION AND BACKGROUND

Educational games and game-based learning are becoming more and more relevant for instructional design and formal education (for example, see Prensky, 2001; Squire, 2003; Felicia, 2011). When a classical paper presentation seminar is held in a virtual classroom or virtual world, new communication options can arise. In the present chapter (for an in-depth description of the approach, see Bösche & Kattner, 2011), oral paper presentations and discussions in a university seminar were carried

DOI: 10.4018/978-1-4666-3673-6.ch011

out using a digital game that allowed for voice and keyboard chat simultaneously over the internet. The course topic was the psychological impact of violent video games and included learning in virtual environments. An internet multiplayer game was applied encompassing comprehensive communication features and both violent and non-violent interactivity of the players with each other as well as the environment. Except for the scientific background literature that was downloadable from a learning management system, all content was delivered through the game itself: All presentations and discussions took place in the game, and many phenomena discussed were directly demonstrated to and were experienced by the students in the game itself. The game served as a virtual classroom for all these matters.

Beyond the classical paper presentations held via voice chat, accompanying missions for the game were designed to demonstrate the crux of the matter in a playful style (called "action-oriented exams"). This included both real world procedures well known to the participants such as map reading and vehicle driving as well as rather uncommon ones like flying a helicopter and complex missions with different roles needed like emergency rescues or freeing hostages. This way, participants were able to compare their known real world experiences with virtual ones and directly evaluate the relevant psychological theories that were told to them in the lessons in a comprehensive virtual world. Furthermore, participants could reflect on learning in general and especially on the perception and learning of aggressive associations, thoughts, and behavior in a virtual environment in a depth that would hardly have been possible without the interactive experience. This was in order to give all participants, also those without prior experience in digital games, the opportunity to reflect the rather abstract theoretical principles of learning in digital games with lucid experiencing for themselves directly within the medium.

Whilst in a classical classroom setting, there is only one shared communication channel: The voice. Typically, this channel is explicitly or im-

plicitly moderated, especially in discussions, such that the channel isn't overloaded, and most of the time only one speaker is talking. This resembles - especially in the virtual world and the settings used (only one voice communication channel that is equally shared by all participants alike, but moderated by the lecturer) – a centralized communication structure called a "star" (Leavitt, 1951). Mainly, the lecturer monitored, moderated and therefore decided who was allowed to speak to the class in which situation. However, technically it was possible for everyone to start speaking (or yelling) while another had the floor. Therefore, the student that had the floor could decide to stop talking or go on talking, producing a collision in the voice channel. All speakers that pressed the corresponding key were heard in the channel simultaneously (but it was very hard to understand anything if multiple persons spoke at the same time). Though it never occurred, it was clear to the participants that destructive behaviors like filling the voice channel with unwanted noise would result in sanctions. The communication guidelines given out in advance clearly stated that disturbing or abusive behavior would result in being "kicked out of the session and maybe even banned from the server". Such a communication structure is most satisfying for the leader of the group (the lecturer), but not for the other participants. On the contrary, a fully interconnected circle structure where anyone can address everyone without having to request for permission to talk and being admitted to the floor, raises satisfaction levels for all participants (Leavitt, 1951).

The voice channel of the virtual world was used like it is used in a traditional classroom setting, and corresponding communication protocols like signaling if someone wants to be admitted to the floor were applied to the voice channel in the virtual world. Rules of communication were given out in advance, which addressed the gestures and communicative possibilities of the game.

Additionally to the voice channel, a keyboard channel was available for all participants. When such an additional and independent channel is introduced to a classroom scenario, several different uses can be applied. One could think of using that channel to discuss something in parallel, or to use this channel to help moderating the voice channel, or to drop messages that are not meant to disrupt the voice channel. We introduced such a channel by additionally switching on keyboard chat that was displayed onto the screen, and were interested if and how students make use of this. The keyboard channel was not moderated, so the students could use them as they liked. However, that additional keyboard channel was visible to all participants logged into the server including the lecturer. The students were told that the channel would be monitored by tutors, so that they could detect and solve technical issues and the like.

Theoretically, being able to communicate freely in a second (in this case text based) channel enable participants to share their thoughts and exchange opinions about the presented paper. Therefore, the lesson was no longer restricted to one given vantage point. Participants could explain difficult theses given by the lecturer to each other and discuss implications of new theories. By allowing a free exchange of their opinions, lessons became more interactive and in the end more democratic compared to ex-cathedra teaching, as it contains cues towards fairness, respect, and free expression, and can be theoretically classified as a fully interconnected communication circle. This feeling of being respected and recognized is a very important part of a good session (Syvertsen, Flanagan, & Stout, 2009). Therefore, one should expect also substantial contributions in the second channel.

A quantitative analysis of the students' use of both the voice and the text channel will be presented in this chapter, distinguishing relevant channel use for the topic of the seminar from irrelevant contributions or misuse. For the time being, since no satisfactory standardized quantitative in-depth coding system for multi-user virtual environments exist of yet, the aim is for a rather superficial and preliminary analysis of the data. We are aware of

Wright, Boria and Breidenbach (2002) as well as Yee, Ducheneaut, Nelson and Likarish (2011), however we find these approaches not applicable to our data, because it focuses on speech, communication and behavior that occurs in a "pure" gaming situation, and not in an educational or edutainment situation in which there is a special interweaving of learning goals and gaming that might or might not compete against pure gaming. Also we are aware of Mazur (2004), which however is a mainly qualitative approach that focuses on theoretical and methodological issues, but does not propose a ready-to-apply structure for coding online-talk in an educational settings.

For educational settings at university level teaching, Wang, Newlin and Tucker (2001) applied discourse analysis to an electronic chat in a university course, and correlated students' use of the channel with performance data from homework, mid-term and final exams. The high-level-categories they used were:

1. Remarks concerning lecture problems/examples discussed in chat lecture
2. Homework-related remarks
3. Remarks concerning course administration
4. Social remarks

Only the number of contributions in category 1 (contributions concerning the lecture problems and examples) correlated with students' performance. In our coding scheme, we adapted Wang, Newlin and Tucker (2001) to the situation in the seminar analyzed in this study.

Our recordings were coded into four categories: Relevant, irrelevant, technical issues and unclassifiable. We defined a contribution as relevant if it extends knowledge or appreciation of the topic in any way (for details and examples see the Methods section). In respect to Yee (2006) we included not only a technical aspect (voice or keyboard chat), but also personal factors as possible reasons for participation or making irrelevant contributions to the topic or the educational situation.

So the main purpose of this study is to present data from a paper presentation seminar in a virtual world which help to identify technical (e.g. used communication chat: voice versus keyboard), personal (e.g. prior experience with or interest in the topic, gender), situational (e.g. length or number of the session) and relational (e.g. number of participants present) factors that help to understand what causes relevant and irrelevant contributions in such a setting.

Since this is the recount of an explorative data collection, we aim to report results that help to create input for further research. At this intermediate point a first conceptual approach would be to analyze the technical, personal, situational and relational factors. Unlike an experimental setting we do not intend to prove specific hypothesis, but inspect these four categories as research questions:

1. Is there a difference between the use of the keyboard chat that is free for all and the voice chat that is monitored by the lecturer?
2. Are there personal factors (e.g. interest in the topic) that predict the percentage of relevant contributions to the topic?
3. Are there situational factors (e.g. length of a session) that predict the percentage of relevant contributions?
4. Are there relational factors (e.g. number of participants present) that predict the percentage of relevant contributions?

METHOD

Participants

Additionally to being listed briefly in the university calendar, a poster was displayed in the Department of Psychology and in the Department of Computer Science including an extended abstract on the course objective. An e-mail was sent to all applicants shortly before the beginning of the course informing them that the seminar would take place in a virtual world, and that online participation using the internet would be possible. The hardware requirements of the game were listed for the ones interested in participating from home, and it was noted that seats had been booked in the on-site computer pool if one could not or did not want to connect from home. A total of 13 students enlisted for the seminar. Females were 46 percent; psychology majors 38 percent. Previous digital game experience was 62 percent. Gender and previous digital game experience were correlated, $r = .69, p < .01$.

Materials and Apparatus

The software used as virtual classroom was a multiplayer online game (Armed Assault by Bohemia Interactive). The game mechanics are based on the 3D first-person shooter genre. However, avatars could be steered both in the first-person perspective as well as via a third person view. The game featured a 400 km^2 world landscape with towns, villages and streets connecting them, along with a map, different climate zones, and a built-in editor with lots of objects to place, and a scripting language to control or trigger events. The game could be played online, and featured up-to-date graphics effects like HDR lightning. Participants without the necessary hardware to install and run the game could join the server by using a prepared onsite pool where the game and necessary hardware like headsets was installed.

The virtual world featured two independent communication channels: voice and keyboard. The voice channel allowed for multiple speakers (like in real classroom settings), but it was said it was difficult to follow even if only two speakers were speaking at the same time. Though this might be somewhat comparable to a real classroom setting, the voice channel in the game and the perspicuity of multiple speakers speaking at the same time was definitely below real world voice channel fidelity. The frequency range in the game was limited and positional information was not modeled using the voice channels of the game that sounded like radio talk. In contrast to this, the keyboard channel messages were superimposed onto the screen, consisted of multiple lines, and allowed scrolling back and reviewing past contributions, therefore allowed multiple chatting at the same time, see Figure 1.

Though the game featured several independent levels and scopes of voice and keyboard chat channels (a message could be sent to all players logged into the server, to all players in the same group, to all players in the vicinity, to all players in the same vehicle et cetera), to ease things for the participants, all avatars were programmed to belong to the same group, and the oral paper presentation missions typically gathered all players on foot near each other. In this manner, everyone received all messages independent of the channel chosen by the participant within the software. Therefore, both channels - voice and chat - were public, synchronized, and available to all participants.

A dedicated server running specially designed missions for holding the communications provided the place for the participants to meet virtually by connecting over the internet. For the oral paper presentations, missions were made in the in-built editor of the game. Typically, for every presentation a pleasant and interesting place in the virtual world was selected, like a beach with palms, an old castle with a great view of the surrounding mountains, or a lovely little town market place. The dress of the avatars in the game reflected the status. The students played civilian avatars that wore T-shirts and jeans or boxer shorts. The tutors wore a battledresses with a distinct blue beret and the lecturer wore a dress uniform with a peaked cap. Participants playing on a computer used for recording the session appeared in clothes of a combat reporter. The lecturer was defined as the group leader allowing participants to easily recognize him or receive direct commands from him through the game's interface (e.g. where to walk is shown by a marker displaying "move here"). For the talks, a ramp served as a seating area for the audience.

Figure 1. Example of keyboard chat (on the bottom of the screen)

All other materials, for example the literature for preparing the talk, were identical to a real world seminar, and were downloadable in an e-learning system that was compatible to run on the same computer along with the virtual world.

Measurement/Coding

Adapting the categories used by Wang, Newlin, and Tucker (2001), we either code laxed or only use the categories that were applicable to our data:

1. A category for "homework related contributions" was not coded, because the course did not generally include homework in a classical sense. Homework, if given, consisted of replaying a training mission to acquire the game mechanics, and therefore was not related to learning the course topic.
2. Wang et al. (2001) subsumed in the category "remarks concerning course administration" both "technical issues" as well as "administrative policy." We dropped the latter subcategory, because all of this was already sorted out in advance of the sessions and was not part of the recordings. However, we kept their subcategory "technical issues" as is, but as a main category.
3. Remarks and contributions concerning the lecture problems and examples are counted here in the category "relevant," to distinguish it from.
4. "Irrelevant" contributions. We define irrelevance in the sense that it is not related to the course topic and does not help the situation concerning a learning progress. Wang et al. (2001) called this category "social remarks", however we stress by our labeling that such remarks are not beneficial for the course topic: Discussing today's menu in the Mensa or the weather isn't beneficial the learning process, because it consumes time and cognitive resources that are needed

to follow the session. According to Wang et al. (2001), communicating in this category does not predict students' performance.

So concerning the content of a contribution we divide the contributions in four categories: relevant, irrelevant, technical issues and unclassifiable.

Relevant contributions are connected to the lessons topic. A relevant contribution provides information to the topic of the lesson, attracts attention to a special point of view of the topic of the lesson, asks questions on the topic of the lesson or extends knowledge or appreciation of the topic in any way (e.g. "Didn't Sigmund Freud say that ...", or "Is this definition of aggression applicable to violent video games?", or "I was very immersed during the last action-oriented exam", or "What games use this kind of feature to guide attention?").

Irrelevant contributions are not directly connected to the topic of the lesson and not suitable to extend knowledge or appreciation of the topic (e.g. "I used to play the mentioned game, but I always failed in the same level," or "If you think this game is difficult, you have to use the following trick: ...", or "It's raining outside").

Technical issues are all contributions which help to run the game adequate for a participant or the whole group concerning technology as well as control (e.g. "How can I stand up," or "How do I optimize the graphic settings of the game for my system," or "My system is lagging very hard").

Unclassifiable are contributions that cannot be attached to the stream of arguments or are too vague to understand. Sometimes the chat – especially the keyboard chat – runs so fast, that it is not possible to attach a contribution to the string of topic related or topic unrelated comments. And sometimes the contributions are so vague that it is impossible to say if this is a statement on the topic (as seen in Table 1, unclassifiable contributions were seldom).

Table 1. Types of contributions in the different channels (as percentage of channel use)

Channel	Contributions classified as				
	Relevant	Irrelevant	Unclassifiable	Technical Issues	Total
Voice	65	17	4	14	100
Keyboard	11	83	2	5	100

Additionally, data on the channel used, characteristics of the session, and characteristics of the contributor were coded. Thus, the following attributes of a contribution were coded: The channel used could be either (1) the voice or (2) the keyboard channel. The relevance was classified as either (1) relevant to the talk, (2) a technical issue, (3) irrelevant or (4) unclassifiable. The source of the contribution was the corresponding speaker or typist, and information on the contributor's gender, previous experience with digital games, and attendance rate of this student to the sessions were coded as well. If the contribution addressed someone specifically by her/his name or by explicitly referencing to the content of someone's earlier contribution, that person was coded as target, otherwise the target was classified as unspecified. Characteristic of the session and situation coded were either (1) during or (2) during a discussion, the number of the session, the length of the session, the number of attending students in that session, and if the session was followed by a pre-announced action-oriented exam adjacent to the oral presentation.

RESULTS

A total of nine paper presentations sessions consisting of more than 500 minutes of action recordings of 19 participants ($n = 13$ students, $n_2 = 5$ tutors, $n_3 = 1$ instructor) were analyzed. During the seminar, some drop outs occurred. The overall student completion rate of the course was 77%, and the completion rate for students applying for course credit was 90%. Most of the drop outs happened during the Christmas break, meaning that some participants simply did not come back after the break. However, independent of the completion status all student contributions were coded. This does not distort the general results, because most of the results presented here are based on percentages using an adequate measure for standardization. For example, the absolute number of contributions in a session was used for calculating relative percentages of contribution types.

In all of the following, for reporting statistical significance we use the conventional alpha-error levels. That means we report and use $p < .01$ for highly statistically significant results, $p < .05$ for statistically significant results, and $p > .20$ for statistically insignificant and therefore not attestable results. For anything in between statistically significant and insignificant results, we report the exact p-value.

Two independent coders coded and classified student participant's ($n = 13$) contributions during the paper presentations talks and their subsequent discussion. Communication and contributions in the playful action-oriented exams were not coded. Therefore, the data presented here are somehow comparable to classical classroom presentations and discussions and at the same time presentations and discussion happening in a virtual classroom in general. To average the raters, each rater's data received a weight of 0.5 for the subsequent analyses. Only spontaneous contributions from student participants were analyzed. A spontaneous contribution is defined as a voice or keyboard message that is not provoked by direct invitations or inquiries. For example, the contributions as a part of a referee giving her/his talk on the main subject is not coded because it is a direct requirement to pass the seminar and therefore it is not spontaneous. Same is true for contributions based on politeness (e.g. "Hello" or "Goodbye") or answering a direct question of the referee (e.g. "Who thinks that...?" or "Who agrees?"). Also, answering typical comprehension questions posed by the lecturer are not coded. This finally led to a selection of 479 contributions that were analyzed. To analyze what causes irrelevant contribution, we tested (1) technical factors, (2) personal factors, (3) situational factors, and (4) relational factors.

Technical Factors

21% of the contributions were classified as relevant to the talk, 6% as technical issues, 70% as irrelevant, and 2% could not be classified into one of these types. 81% of the contributions were made in the keyboard channel and 19% in the voice channel. Table 1 shows the types of contributions in the different channels.

The number of contributions on resolving technical issues became less from session to session ($r = -.67$, $p < .05$). The top 3 contributors make up to 49.3%, the top 5 up to 76.3% of all contributions. Table 2 shows the distribution of the contributions of all student participants.

From all student contributions, 70.9% were made by participants with prior experience with digital games, students without prior experience with digital games contributed less ($p < .01$), but their relative usage of the voice and keyboard channel did not differ from the students with prior experience, $p > .20$.

Subsequently, only relevant and irrelevant contributions of students were analyzed. Excluding technical issues and unclassifiable contributions, the total number of contributions were reduced from 479 to 437. Given this selection, the mean percentage of irrelevant contributions was $M = 77\%$.

Table 2. Distribution of contributions

Student Rank	% of all contributions	Cumulated % of all contributions
1	19.3	19.3
2	15.7	35.0
3	14.3	**49.3**
4	14.0	63.3
5	13.0	**76.3**
6	7.3	83.6
7	6.1	89.7
8	4.9	94.6
9	2.6	97.2
10	1.7	98.9
11	0.9	99.8
12	0.1	99.9
13	0.1	100.0

Personal Factors

Table 3 summarizes the main results and statistical tests conducted for personal factors. To begin with possible effects of gender should be investigated. Previous studies have shown that, though males and females consume about the same amount of media in general, boys play digital games more than girls (for example, see Gentile, Lynch, Linder & Walsh, 2004). In turn this might lead to gender differences in the behaviors shown in the virtual world used for this study. In our sample, male students contribute more in the average ($M = 48.29$; $SD = 27.59$) than female students ($M = 16.67$; $SD = 23.47$), $p < .05$. The rate of irrelevant contributions is descriptively higher for male students ($M = 71.49\%$; $SD = 23.71\%$) than for female students ($M = 34.70\%$; $SD = 38.8\%$), this difference is bordering statistical significance, $p = .06$. Remarkably, with the exception of one, male students had more than 74% irrelevant contributions, female students on the other hand, seem to split into two groups: One group ($n = 3$) – comparable to the males – shows over 60%

Table 3. Relation of personal factors to relevant and irrelevant contributions

Factor	Level(s)	Result	Statistic
Gender	Males	Contribute more	$p < .05$
Gender	Males	Higher percentage of irrelevant contributions	$p = .06$
Gender	Both	Attendance rate is comparable	$p > .20$
Game experience	Both	Contribution level is comparable	$p = .12$
Game experience	Yes	Higher rate of irrelevant contributions	$p = .07$
Attending to every session	Yes	Contribute more	$p < .05$
Attending to every session	Yes	Higher rate of irrelevant contributions	$p < .05$

irrelevant contributions, and another group ($n = 3$) that did not make any irrelevant contributions at all. Attendance rates are comparable between males ($M = 85.71\%$; $SD = 24.07\%$) and females ($M = 70.83\%$; $SD = 34.93\%$), $p > .20$. An explanation for such a pattern that is independent on gender might be that there are some students who are interested in talking on matters that do not relate to the seminar, while other students are simply not interested in this and concentrate on the seminar content. But contrarily to this assumption, the correlation between the number of relevant and irrelevant contributions of a student is statistical significant, $r(13) = .58$, $p < .05$. Correlating the overall number of contributions a person made and the percentage of irrelevant contribution she/he produces, it turned out, that the more someone is contributing the higher the percentage of irrelevant contributions she/he produces, $r(13) = .76$, $p < .01$. Those who drive the session ahead by adding good ideas are the same who disturb the sessions with irrelevant contributions. Another obvious speculation may be that students who are familiar to digital games are more interested in the topic and more activated generally overall, so they produce more contributions and at the same moment are more at risk to start irrelevant discussions. Taking a closer look on the prior experience with digital games, no difference in the number of contributions between those with prior game experience ($n = 7$; $M = 45.57$; $SD = 24.86$) and those without ($n = 6$; $M = 19.83$; $SD = 30.67$) could been found, $p = .12$. But those having prior game experience produce a higher percentage of irrelevant contributions ($M = 70.99\%$; $SD = 23.45\%$) than those having no prior game experience ($M = 35.29\%$; $SD = 39.34\%$), $p = .07$. Also, we tested if the department a student was enlisted in made a difference. Of $N=13$ participants, 38.46% ($n=5$) were majoring in psychology. This variable does not correlate with or predicts any of the other variables, all $ps > .15$. The last personal based presumption is that those who were present at every session must be highly topic motivated and therefore have a high risk of producing irrelevant contributions. Truly, those who attended all sessions were not only contributing more ($n = 6$, $M = 51.83$; $SD = 26.60$) than those who did not attend to at least one session ($n = 7$, $M = 18.14$; $SD = 23.62$), $p < .05$. This could be explained by the amount of time they talked, because they were always present. Students who attended all sessions produced a higher rate of irrelevant contributions ($M = 76.63\%$; $SD = 11.70\%$) than those who did not attend to at least one session ($M = 35.55\%$; $SD = 38.77\%$). Attendance rate and prior experience are both indicators of a topic based motivation, but they are uncorrelated, $r(13) = .26$; $p > .20$. So we used attendance and prior game experience as independent factors for an ANOVA to predict the percentage of the produced irrelevant contributions. Both factors were found to influence the percentage of irrelevant contributions, $p < .01$, and in addition an interaction shows that those who had no prior experience with digital games *and* are not always attending produce a very low percentage of irrelevant contributions, while those who were always present and had prior experience to digital games produced the highest percentage of irrelevant contributions, $p < .05$, see Figure 2. This could be understood that if someone is interested in the topic and also has prior experience and therefore background knowledge, she/he is highly at the risk of talking. But those who had no interest in the topic and no background knowledge do not disturb. Unfortunately, gender and prior experience with digital games are correlated, $r(13) = .69$, $p < .01$, therefore, it is not possible to finally differentiate the effect of prior game experience from gender.

Situational Factors

Viewing the characteristics of the sessions, the first guess is that because of the limited ability to hold attention longer session could trigger more irrelevant contributions. However, surprisingly, the longer a session was, the lower was the percentage of irrelevant contributions, $r(9) = -.56$,

Figure 2. Mean percentage of irrelevant contributions as a function of the student attending to all session and her/his previous experience with digital games

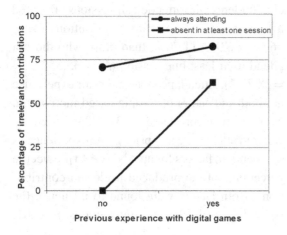

$p = .12$. Speculating that the nature of irrelevant contributions is commenting and not informing, it could be supposed that most irrelevant contributions appear in free discussions and not while the talks were held. On the other hand, free discussions allows stating one's own opinion and could prevent irrelevant contributions by giving the space for free speech. So we tested the role of free discussions on irrelevant contributions. The relative percentage of irrelevant contributions is much higher while the talk was held (87%) than while the talk was discussed after it had been completed (65%), $p < .01$. As explained to the students in the first session, the keyboard channel is open for questions and it is self-evident that the voice channel could be overburdened very easy, simply by having some people use it on at same time. So the keyboard channel was used more for irrelevant contributions (88%) than the voice channel (20%), $p < .01$. The percentage of irrelevant contributions differ a lot (range is from 40% to 97%) between the sessions, $p < .01$, however, it is not a linear function of the session number, $r(9) = .25$, $p > .20$, see Figure 3. So some more characteristics of the sessions might be relevant. Something that provoked irrelevant contributions might have been the expectance of weapon use later in that session. But neither is there a difference in irrelevant contributions between the sessions with

Figure 3. Relative percentage of irrelevant contributions over the several sessions

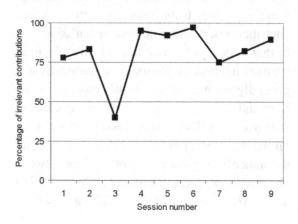

the notification of a weapon use ($M = 87.29\%$; $SD = 7.09\%$) and no weapon use ($M = 77.38\%$; $SD = 19.36\%$), nor is there a difference between sessions with action-oriented exams ($M = 80.88\%$; $SD = 15.06\%$) and no action-oriented exams ($M = 80.30\%$; $SD = 22.77\%$), p > .20.

Relational Factors

Relations subsume all parameters that are dependent not only on one person or situation, but on the whole group. So the number of students present and the percentage of females or students with prior experience with digital games may trigger irrelevant contributions, just because a situation with more people present possesses more potential targets for irrelevant talks. Given that irrelevant talk might be used as an option to produce status in the peer group, there must simply be someone to talk to. Surprisingly there is no correlation between the percentage of irrelevant contributions and the number of students present, the percentage of females, and the percentage of students present with prior game experience.

DISCUSSION

Research Questions

In general, the data – especially the substantial number of relevant contributions – show that it is indeed possible to realize a paper presentation seminar in a virtual world, even when most of the participants and the lecturer are only virtually present.

Technical problems became less from session to session, and the voice channel had been mostly used for relevant or technical contributions (79%), only 17% of the contributions in this channel did not bring the seminar forward (4% unclassified contributions). But in contrast, 83% of all con-

tributions being posted in the keyboard channel had been irrelevant – so the proportion of relevant to irrelevant contribution is very different in the two channels.

Surprisingly, irrelevant contributions made by each student is correlated with the number of relevant contributions that the student made, $r(13) = .58, p < .05$, and the more someone contributes in general, the higher was the percentage of irrelevant contributions, $r(13) = .76, p < .01$. This means that the students discussing the relevant topics and the producers of irrelevant content are not distinct groups. Those who benefit the seminar with relevant contributions are the same who deliver irrelevant contributions. More surprisingly, while males have a high percentage of irrelevant contributions in general, females split in two groups, one spamming like males and one that does not spam at all. Furthermore it turned out, that the attendance rate of a student and her/his prior experience with digital games both raise the percentage of irrelevant contributions produced, $p < .05$. Those who have prior experience with digital games and always attend have the highest percentage of irrelevant contributions, while those who have no prior experience with digital games and are not always present do not spam at all. This could be caused by reasons of motivation. Specifically, the highest percentage of irrelevant contributions is produced by students with interest and knowledge of the topic, while those who are neither interested nor have any knowledge of the topic do not spam at all. However, there are characteristics of a person (knowledge, gender, motivation on the topic) that predict the percentage of irrelevant contributions she/he will produce during the sessions. While we have discussed the effects of the characteristic of the person, the question arises if the percentage of irrelevant contribution may also be caused by characteristics of the situation. Neither notification of weapon use, nor the notification of action-oriented exams, nor the number of the session, nor the number of present students are correlated to the percentage of irrelevant contributions.

To conclude, the research question made at the introduction, about the impact of technical, personal, situational and relational factors, we can say in summary, that the technical factors (the kind of chat) as well as personal factors (gender, motivation, and topic knowledge) influence the rate of relevant contributions. Situational factors (e.g. length of the session) and relational factors (e.g. number of students present) have no (significant) impact.

Theoretical Implications

The relative percentage of irrelevant contributions differ enormously among the sessions and is much higher while the talks were held than during the discussion afterwards. Therefore, the percentage of irrelevant contributions is not only caused by the person, but by cues of the situation. This underlines that the "social context is a crucial element of discourse analysis" Mazur (2004, p. 1076). Consequentially, the option of restricting or even switching off the keyboard channel needs to be discussed. But "the principle of turn-talking [...] is the basic component of all conversation" (Mazur, 2004, p. 1078), and it is hard to imagine how a fair and open lesson (as it is strongly suggested by Syvertsen, Flanagan, & Stout, 2009) could be realized by switching off the opportunity of free speech.

As opposed to Wang, Newlin and Tucker (2001) we labeled socializing remarks as irrelevant, or maybe even detrimental to the topic and the learning process. We still believe that it might be relevant to or influence learning in a meditational way over variables of well-being and satisfaction, as discussed by Levitt (1951). However at the moment, we can only suppose such a link, because our data lack students' performance data that could be analyzed to answer this question.

On the one hand, an additional keyboard channel enables the participants to deepen text based discussion, solve technical problems and increase the feeling of being a community with democratic structures by giving the opportunity of free speech. This helps to actively make the participants part of the lesson, instead of condemning them to be mere listeners. On the other hand, this independence allows for irrelevant discussions, which might be detrimental for the learning process - especially if the irrelevant chat is competing for attention with the relevant topics. Moreover, structural properties and affordances of the channel (as the possibility of easy turn-talking) may be a decisive situative cue to increase both relevant and irrelevant contributions. Before finally judging on the use of the advantages and disadvantages of a virtual seminar, the main task is to identify which cues reinforce relevant contributions.

Shortcomings of this Study

Like in every study there are some shortcomings that have to be discussed. First, the seminar was not obligatory for all students, but optional and especially appealing to those who were interested in the topic. In respect to those who were interested in the topic (always being present and engaging in digital games at home) produce the highest rate of irrelevant contributions, the reported overall rate of irrelevant contributions might be an overestimate compared to a situation in that attending the seminar would be obligatory to all students regardless of their personal preferences. This could explain why there is such a high percentage of irrelevant contributions, namely 77%. Another important point is that more males had prior experiences with digital games than females, $p < .01$. To be explicit, there was only one male that had no prior experience with digital games and one female that had prior experience with digital games. Therefore, the gender effects reported here are confounded with prior game experiences, and that could be seen as an aspect of interest in the topic. So, it is impossible to say which one of these two factors caused the irrelevant contributions. But it is obvious that gender, interest in the topic, and the rate of irrelevant contributions are highly correlated in this case. Therefore, it has to be systematically checked in further lessons with other content if interest in the topic or gender causes the irrelevant contributions.

One might suggest that the usage of the chat channel mainly for irrelevant contributions might be due to the fact that some students were not used to a keyboard chat channel from their real life. Therefore, when more accustomed to it, the rate of irrelevant contributions might decrease when they realize the channel should be used for vital information, or when the novelty of the keyboard channel wears off. Such a conjecture could be checked if the students were observed over a longer period of time, for example in following courses in virtual worlds. However, from the observations presented here, it is not expected. About half of the participants already had prior experience with digital games. Neither their rate of irrelevant contributions nor their relative channel choice (voice or keyboard) differed from the students to which gaming was new. Also, the keyboard channel was generally used much more than the voice channel, so the argument of "not known from real life" does not apply. Additionally, there is no indication that the rate of irrelevant contributions significantly changed as a function of time (session number) within our period of observation.

Further Work

This study presented a first analysis of data collected in a paper presentation seminar that was conducted in a virtual world. In focus was the question if there are potential benefits of a free keyboard chat enabling students to communicate freely. But having a virtual classroom setting opens up farther and new options compared to what classical teaching can offer. Working together in

ideally matched, fittable, and changing groups, exchange opinions in a free way without disturbing others, integrate presentation and sharing of audio-visual material, monitoring the learning progress and adapting the challenge's difficulty to the students' skill are only a few options that could be realized and guarded in a virtual setting in the future. Specially designed software may not only allow the execution to be optimized of those tasks more successfully than in classical classrooms, it also allows the mentor to monitor the ongoing work process. Using an immersive virtual setting (Nacke, 2009) to present the exercises may also advance the emotional state of the students and enables them to experience some kind of flow by having ideal matched, adaptive challenges as it is submitted as an basic concept for an flow experience by Csikszentmihalyi (1975). Further there is a great potential to increase the quality of assistance for students by using virtual tutors, which are available for every student. Autonomous agents monitoring the state of a virtual world, help students learn to perform, manipulating the virtual world and be able to adopt the role of a tutor or teammate are already available (Rickel & Johnson, 1998).

Also, our data could be compared to traditional classroom settings in the real world. One problem of such comparison would be that the channels for communication used in our virtual classroom (and even generally in any virtual environment existing at the moment) do not match perfectly the channels and their ease of use and their ability to be recorded in the real world. Though in digital games and virtual worlds, nonverbal channels from the real world like gestures, mimics, eye contact, body positions and behavior (like standing up, running around in the classroom, filling the voice channel with noise, or leaving the virtual classroom) exist, they are in most cases something that must be explicitly controlled by the player, instead of implicitly produced by the participant. In the near future, there will generally be no situation where data from real and virtual classrooms could be mapped 1:1 for comparison. Concerning the ability to record data, virtual classrooms offer better possibilities: Everything has to be processed by a machine, and this can be recorded easily. While in a traditional classroom setting, whispering to the neighbor, handing her/him a note or other "side channel" communication can be at best perceived to exist, but what was communicated is nearly impossible to analyze unless a traditional classroom would be filled up with much recording equipment, probably changing the traditional setting.

CONCLUSION AND FUTURE RESEARCH DIRECTIONS

This study is based on the data collected from a paper presentation seminar with action-oriented exams which are intended to have the students getting familiar with the topic of virtual worlds. So the main target was to have the students learn something in the lessons, not to conduct an experimental designed and methodically planned study. Following from this decision, there were some limitations of the framework used and the data collected. Analyzing some key data like number of relevant contributions and the rate of irrelevant contributions, and personal and situational factors are just a first explorative approach. Further studies should include some more elements to evaluate. Additional to the behavior (relevant and irrelevant contributions, attendance of the students), emotion (questionnaire), and cognition (for example, achievement in the final exam) as dependent measurements as well as age and interest in the topic as important variables could be recorded and analyzed. Characteristics of the session (like length and action-oriented exams) could be explicitly varied under the experimental control of the lecturer. By that, it is possible to systematically test for the effects that had been found here by using correlational approaches.

REFERENCES

Bösche, W., & Kattner, F. (2011). Using a violent multiplayer game as a virtual classroom for a course on violent video games. In Felicia, P. (Ed.), *Handbook of Research on Improving Learning and Motivation through Educational Games: Multidisciplinary Approaches* (pp. 777–805). Hershey, PA: IGI Global. doi:10.4018/978-1-60960-495-0.ch035.

Csikszentmihalyi, M. (1975). *Beyond boredom and anxiety*. San Francisco, CA: Jossey-Bass Publishers.

Felicia, P. (2011). *Handbook of research on improving learning and motivation through educational games: Multidisciplinary approaches*. Hershey, PA: IGI Global. doi:10.4018/978-1-60960-495-0.

Gentile, D. A., Lynch, P. J., Linder, J. R., & Walsh, D. A. (2004). The effects of violent video game habits on adolescent hostility, aggressive behaviors, and school performance. *Journal of Adolescence*, 27, 5–22. doi:10.1016/j.adolescence.2003.10.002 PMID:15013257.

Leavitt, H. (1951). Some effects of certain communication patterns on group performance. *Journal of Abnormal and Social Psychology*, 46, 38–50. doi:10.1037/h0057189 PMID:14813886.

Mazur, J. (2004). Conversation analysis for educational technologists: Theoretical and methodological issues for researching the structures, processes and meaning of on-line talk. In Jonassen, D. (Ed.), *Handbook of Research for Educational Communications and Technology*. New York, NY: McMillian.

Nacke, L. E. (2009). *Affective ludology: Scientific measurement of user experience in interactive entertainment*. Karlskrona, Sweden: Belkinge Institute of Technology.

Prensky, M. (2001). Digital natives, digital immigrants. *Horizon*, *9*, 1–6. Retrieved from http://www.marcprensky.com/writing/Prensky%20-%20Digital%20Natives,%20Digital%20Immigrants%20-%20Part1.pdf.

Rickel, J., & Johnson, W. L. (1998). STEVE: A pedagogical agent for virtual reality. In K.P. Sycara & M. Wooldridge (Eds.), *Proceedings of the Second International Conference on Autonomous Agents (AGENTS '98)*. New York, NY: ACM.

Squire, K. (2003). Video games in education. *International Journal of Intelligent Simulations and Gaming*, *2*(1).

Syvertsen, A. K., Flanagan, C. A., & Stout, M. D. (2009). Code of silence: Students' perception of school climate and willingness to intervene in a peer's dangerous plan. *Journal of Educational Psychology*, *101*, 219–232. doi:10.1037/a0013246 PMID:20126300.

Wang, A. Y., Newlin, M. H., & Tucker, T. L. (2001). A discourse analysis of on-line classroom chats: Predictors of cyber-student performance. *Teaching of Psychology*, *28*, 222–226. doi:10.1207/S15328023TOP2803_09.

Wright, T., Boria, E., & Breidenbach, P. (2002). Creative player actions in FPS online video games. *The International Journal of Computer Game Research*, *2*. Retrieved from http://www.gamestudies.org/0202/wright/

Yee, N. (2006). The demographics, motivations and derived experiences of users of massively-multiuser online graphical environments. *Presence (Cambridge, Mass.)*, *15*, 309–329. doi:10.1162/pres.15.3.309.

Yee, N., Ducheneaut, N., Nelson, L., & Likarish, P. (2011). Introverted elves and conscientious gnomes. The expression of personality in World of Warcraft. In *Proceedings of CHI 2011*, (pp. 753-762). ACM.

KEY TERMS AND DEFINITIONS

Irrelevant Contributions: Are not directly connected to the topic of the lesson and not suitable to extend knowledge or appreciation of the topic.

Personal Factors: Subsume all factors that are dependent on the person (e.g. gender).

Relational Factors: Subsume all parameters that are dependent not only on one person or situation, but on the whole group.

Relevant Contributions: Are connected to the lessons topic. A relevant contribution provides information to the topic of the lesson, attracts attention to a special point of view of the topic of the lesson, asks questions on the topic of the lesson or extends knowledge or appreciation of the topic in any way.

Situational Factors: Subsume all parameters that are dependent on the lesson (e.g. length of the lesson).

Technical Factors: Subsume all parameters that are dependent on the technic used (e.g. voice or keyboard chat).

Technical Issues: Are all contributions which help to run the game adequate for a participant or the whole group concerning technology as well as control.

Chapter 12

Serious Games as an Instrument of Non-Formal Learning:
A Review of Web-Based Learning Experiences on the Issue of Renewable Energy

Steffen Winny
University of Augsburg, Germany

ABSTRACT

This chapter contains a systematic overview of various didactic designs, which are used to provide learning experiences via the Internet. Using the example of renewable energy, the development and status quo of Web-didactic offers is reconstructed on the basis of concrete cases ranging from simple replication of classical teaching materials to different kinds of serious games. This bottom-up approach provides a practical introduction on how to evaluate serious games or other digital learning offers by identifying the most essential criteria for a didactic game analysis, but can also be used for benchmarking as some of the examples might also be inspiring for actual game design. Furthermore, this review indicates a significant gap between the high didactic standards for designing self-administrated learning environments and the factual realization as it is shown in most of the examined cases. A basic understanding of the requirements of different learning settings is given in the introduction.

INTRODUCTION

From a didactic point of view, games are an interesting phenomenon: In general, games are very popular because needs of affection, attention and recognition may be fulfilled as well as needs for prestige, strength, achievement, independence or freedom (cp. Maslow, 1943). Because of the high intrinsic motivation of the gamers to meet these needs, gaming becomes an end in itself with the single purpose of performing the playing activity.

Although learning processes are usually neither intended nor reflected by the gamers, a major part of cognitive, motoric, and social development

DOI: 10.4018/978-1-4666-3673-6.ch012

takes part within the context of games. The easiness of acquiring knowledge, skills, or cognition while playing arouses interest in using this kind of learning for different intentions. In this case, games are designed or transformed in such a way that they pursue at least one further purpose other than the pure pleasure of the game as specified by the initiator of the respective game. Games become more serious because they now take on functions which are perceived to be relevant beyond the borders of the game.

The player's motivating force – the pursuit of satisfaction – does not become less important but is in fact exploited in terms of the additional purpose because the motivated engagement in the game represents the prior condition for imparting transferable knowledge. On the other hand, it is this very exploitation which may adversely affect the motivation of the player because it is precisely the stepping out of "real" life which constitutes the game situation (Huizinga, 1950, p. 35f).

Each attempt to influence the gamer from outside the game causes a serious intervention into the games world and runs the risk of reducing the gaming pleasure of the players. Nevertheless, gamers may accept non-game-related purposes under the following conditions:

1. The gamer does not recognize the manipulation and appreciates just the game itself (Ignorance).
2. The gamer recognizes the manipulation but rates the (expected) satisfaction by the game higher than the possibility of being affected adversely (tolerance).
3. The gamer recognizes the purposes of the game provider and endorses his intention in principle or trusts his reputation (acceptance).
4. The aims of the gamer correspond with the intention of the game provider (agreement).
5. The game setting is integrated within an institutionalized context and – at least in part – is extrinsically motivated (commitment).

In case of the behavioral patterns ignorance, tolerance and acceptance, the gamer's interest is focused on the game itself, while learning processes occur, at best, incidentally.

According to Kirchhöfer (2002) Incidental Learning is neither goal-oriented nor reflected, but arises simultaneously to another performed activity which means that Incidental Learning is always situational and linked to a certain problem. Typical examples from the area of Serious Games are Advergames, Recruitment Games, but also some News Games, Games for Change or Games from the genre of Edutainment or Infotainment.

In contrast, there are also a number of Serious Games, which are used by the gamer with the intention of learning, training, acquiring or creating something, that endure beyond the game. Relating to learning aspects, this means that being engaged in the game requires inherent time for learning processes which might be either self-organized (4) or externally-organized (5). In this case, gaming describes just one among many other methods to deal with the learning content.

Kirchhöfer (2003, p. 32) differentiates goal-orientated learning between (4) Informal and (5) Formal Learning. However, he defines Formal Learning not categorically as learning in formal educational institutions, like Dohmen (2001), Livingstone (2001) or the EC (2001, p. 33ff), but rather qualitative through characteristics such as external structure, curricular learning targets and independence from a specific problems. Accordingly, Informal Learning is marked by its own problem-oriented construction of learning targets and a self-determined learning rhythm.

According to Kirchhöfer´s definition, the differentiation between Formal and Informal Learning is not always clear cut due to the relative reference, but it is always focused on the learner, which makes his approach most suitable for didactic considerations - especially in cases of Non-Formal Learning. While games for Informal or Incidental Learning purposes can be easily integrated into Formal Learning contexts, games for Informal or Incidental Learning have to be adapted to suit the substantial requirements of a leisure-oriented Learning environment.

The differences between Formal, Informal and Incidental Learning environments for media-didactic considerations can be illustrated by the example of the genre Games for Health. Games for Health can be classified as games for therapeutic purpose and those for prevention. Therapeutic Games are often used within a framework which is more or less characterized by

- A defined target group (e.g. persons in re-habilitation for a specific illness).
- Concrete goals, which can easily be opera-tionalized (e.g. recovery, coping or behav-ior modification).
- Formalized settings (e.g. therapeutic sessions.)
- A personal introduction and/or support (e.g. by a therapist).
- An evaluation of the outcome by professionals.

In contrast, prevention and health promotion is not only targeted at affected parties or high-risk-groups, but also at major parts of the total population. Even large-scale prevention programs in schools or companies will not be able to reach the whole target group.

Thus, the target group is not only unequally larger than the one of therapeutic games, but also remains unspecific and therefore eludes direct control due as the obligation of formal education is no longer present. The commitment continues to decrease depending on how far the learning setting is anonymized and how easily the learner may opt out of the situation - as is typical for the personal usage of websites.

This makes clear that digital learning in non-formal environments requires a media-didactic approach that vitally focuses on the learner as it is up to him or her whether a learning setting occurs at all and for how long it will last. Instead

of obligation, the learning setting will be con-stituted by the self-interest of the learner which might refer to the attractiveness of the respective subject's content (Informal Learning) as well as the motivation for playing the game (Incidental Learning).

In general, however, these are two differing approaches which require different game designs, placements and promotion. Nevertheless, this does not exclude the possibility of cross-linking or combining both together. In an ideal situation, a serious game incidentally raises awareness of a problem which is usually a precondition to reading up on further information or being engaged in the subject in another way of Non-Formal Learning.

A case-related overview of existing online offers of Formal, Informal and Incidental Learn-ing will be given in the following sections. The presented selection results from a systematic review of websites and games on the issue of (renewable) energy, which has been documented in a Serious Game Database with approximately 72 categorized and commented entries.

FROM BOOK PAGE TO WEB PAGE

Many providers consider the internet mainly as a cheap opportunity to spread knowledge and other kinds of content. Thus, websites as well as seri-ous games sometimes become quite text-laden, because text, from a technical point of view, is easy to produce and may already exist in other contexts. And so the former children's-website of the German Federal Ministry for the Environment, Nature Conversation and Nuclear Safety (Figure 1) appears to have been copied from the brochure "Perspective – what everyday life has to do with the environment?" [1] (Jensen, 2003, p. 14).

Text and illustrations were identical but had been arranged differently. The current version of *bmu-kids* still contains the characters although they have become less important as they do not perform an active part any more.

Figure 1. Former version of the children's-website www.bmu-kids.de (2004-2010) and booklet (2003)

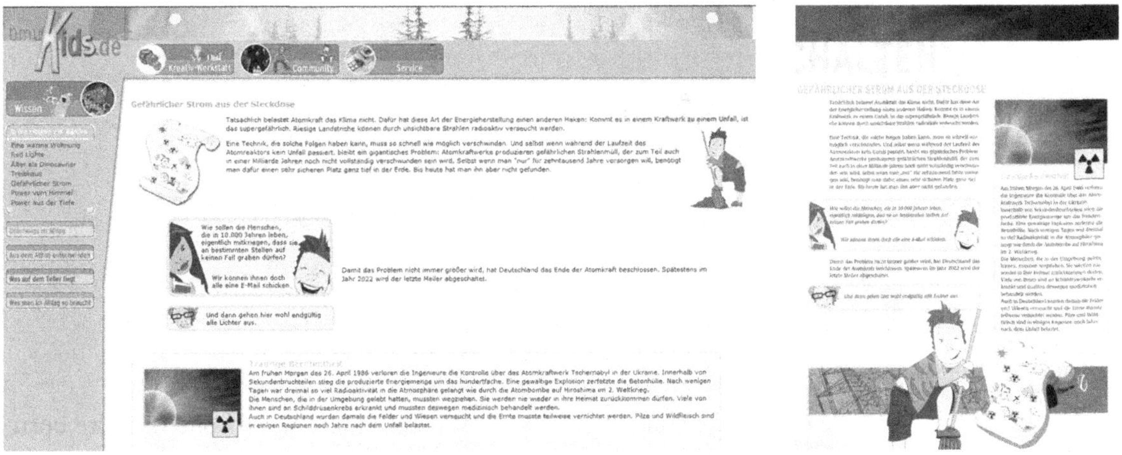

At the same time, the text has been completely replaced and has become more businesslike and, primarily, more extensive: with about 1000 words per page, the proportion of text has quadrupled. This is insofar remarkable, as it is shown in our studies (Fromme & Winny, 2007a, 2012a, 2012b), that children below the age of twelve are hardly willing to read text (within games) when they do not have to. Nevertheless, instructions and information in written form are common even on websites for younger children although fluent reading capability cannot be assumed before the age of eight.

In principle, extensive (factual) texts are rather an instrument for (In)Formal learning environments. Regarding children, Kirchhöfer (2002, p. 32) points out that children have – in the absence of self-determined free time – rarely occasions for Informal Learning. Nevertheless, out-of-school learning often appears very instructional, which is probably due to the learning comprehension of the developers and providers, which is usually geared to own experiences during school education.

The reviewed websites also included cloze texts or matching tasks, similar to work sheets in school education. Within experimental settings, children liked such tasks probably because they were familiar with it from school. Whether they would choose them also at home, where other activities and games are available, is at least questionable.

The digital work sheets are also interesting for another reason, as they use – unlike pure text websites – a special characteristic of digital media, namely interactivity. Thus, in addition to target group orientation, the media-specific potential can be identified as another quality criterion of media design.

Figure 2 shows two interactive tasks for two different target groups (teens/pre-teens). Whereas the task and the handling are quite similar, the attributing items of the second screenshot are illustrated. Through this visualization, the task obtains an additional value that can hardly be achieved outside of digital environments e.g with paper and pencil. Hence, multimedia belongs – as well as interactivity – to the media-specific characteristics of digital media. A third one, (social) communication, will be given attention in the following sections.

QUIZ: BETWEEN ASSESSMENT TOOL AND GAME ENTERTAINMENT

A popular method of spreading information is a quiz. On the part of the initiator quizzes are easy to generate and, due to corresponding authoring tools, not even programming skills are required. On the part of the users, quizzes are often popular, because:

Figure 2. Digital work sheets by drag-and-drop: strom-online and VWEW

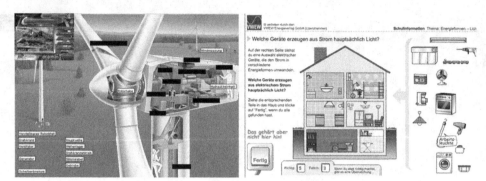

- They are easy to handle even if the content changes.
- They provide the opportunity to test one's own knowledge and possibly find out something about one's own abilities.
- It is fun to succeed at a quiz even if the correct answers have been given by chance instead of knowledge.

The attractiveness of quizzes is often based on reconsidering latent knowledge bases or rather on the capability to find proper answers due to plausibility checks and speculations without knowing the answer in advance. This process might be quite entertaining as, for instance, demonstrated by the quiz show "Who Wants to Be a Millionaire?" which has substantially increased the popularity of quizzes. From a didactic point of view, quizzes seem to be less an effective method of knowledge transfer than a test about what someone knows about a certain subject.

The simplest form of a quiz is a questionnaire with a list of several multiple-choice questions for instance in case of the *Environmental Quiz* of BBC England. Due to usability aspects such as orientation and navigation, a limitation of just one question per page seems to be more comfortable and is in accordance with central didactic principles like the structuring of content or the focusing on content. Further variations of quizzes depend on the following points:

- Whether there is just one or more correct answers possible.
- Whether feedback is given directly after each response, after each question or cumulatively at the end of the quiz.
- Whether a wrong response causes hard consequences (game over) or soft ones (no limitation of attempts) or something in between.
- Whether support or help is given (e.g. jokers).
- Whether the solution is displayed (during the quiz or at the end).
- Whether additional information is given such as remarks, explanations or illustrations.

Quizzes do not usually belong to the category of games, but they can include game elements so that the entertainment aspect comes to the fore. Figure 3 shows two examples of such quiz-games. The first screenshot shows a quiz, which is integrated in a virtual board game. The second one is a typical quiz but with an elaborated graphic design and characteristic game technology like (high)scores, time pressure and the opportunity to challenge other players.

Another notable feature of the quiz-game *Blue Planet* is the illustration of the questions through appropriate photos. These not only have the function of creating a certain atmosphere but also to

Figure 3. Quiz games: board game treibhauseffekt and blue planet

build up a connection between the content of the quiz and its equivalent in reality for encouraging knowledge transfer.

Nevertheless, the expectations of learning effects due to quizzes are not particularly high (Fromme & Russler, 2005). Firstly, questions in quizzes constitute just selective extracts of a subject and imply almost exclusive context-independent factual knowledge. Though some quizzes provide further explanations within the feedback to the answers, the possibilities are restricted to a few lines, so that the presented information remains to a large extend isolated.

Without an appropriate context, there is the danger that knowledge resulting from the quiz might not display any educational substance. In the *Board Game Treibhauseffekt²* (Figure 3), a benefit for the learner appears neither current nor prospective, nor does it refer to a higher issue, as e.g. Klafki (1991, p. 272) demands for appropriate learning content.

Another objection concerning learning theories applies to the presentation of several answers, which also contain – according to the intention of the quiz – wrong answers. Reading all response options including the wrong one impedes the mental association of the correct answer to the corresponding question.

FOOTPRINT SIMULATIONS: QUIZZES ON PERSONAL BEHAVIOR

Footprint simulations can be seen as a special form of quiz which does not ask for universal knowledge but for individual consumer behavior. Based on the user's responses, footprint simulations generate a personal carbon dioxide balance as a feedback for the user. These digital footprints should demonstrate the relationship between every day (buying) decisions and global warming and indicate alternative behavior patterns.

Footprint simulations may have different focus points. Quite common are inquiries about current consumption, wastage and lifestyle. The footprint *KonsuManiac* (Figure 4), which also relates to younger users, limits itself to food, clothing and products from do-it-yourself stores as well as drugstores. Other footprints additionally ask about travel and mobility habits, heating and water consumption, thermal insulation and leisure time activities.

I'm Alright Jack differs from other footprints insofar as the user has to make the decisions in the name of Jack over his entire lifetime. At the end, when Jack is retired, the impact of these decisions regarding to climate change will be pointed out (See Figure 4). The advantage of the

Figure 4. Footprint simulations: KonsuManiac and I´m Alright Jack

climate-simulation is due to the visualization of the consequences of a - usually inconsiderate - consumer's behavior. Therefore the abstract term of climate change is made tangible by concrete illustrations of climate-damages.

In the case of the footprint *Klimacheck* (Figure 5) for instance, the impact of the player's behavior can be shown after 10, 20 or 50 years. By subsequently changing the parameters or after restarting, other results can be achieved until the best modes of behavior are identified, which do not adversely affect the environment.

Incidentally, most footprint simulations do not target children who would be utterly overextended by questions about electric power consumption, thermal insulation of buildings or mobility.

Besides the *KonsuManiac* of Figure 4, which targets teens between 15 and 19 years (Weninger, 2010, p. 1), there is - according to the research - just one other footprint that focus directly on children.

The *Footprint Game* is made for preteens aged 5 to 12 years and follows the same principles as the other footprint simulations with the additional use of audio response for the written text as well as more basic questions. One of these questions suggests forgoing a shower as a best practical environment option[3] - a statement which is obviously not intended. As in this case, games as well as other media may contain non-intended statements as more examples in the following sections will demonstrate.

Figure 5. Visualization of the climate impact within the former Klimacheck footprint of the WWF Switzerland

CASUAL GAMES: INCIDENTAL LEARNING WITHIN FIVE MINUTES

As the previous examples show the preliminary evolution, this chapter now comes to serious games themselves. The majority of the reviewed games have been casual games, which are indeed the most popular games played on a PC (Nielsen, 2009). Casual games are characterized by an easy-entry into the game as well as the possibility to opt out quickly without the risk of losses in future games.

This is also noticeable in the daily gaming time: this amounts to approximately 30 minutes per day, which is less than the half of the time for games of other genres (Nielsen, 2009). Many casual games take just a few minutes to play, but are often played several time in a row. In addition, there are also casual games which continue uninterrupted, so that the player may get in or out at any time while the game goes on.

Regarding games research on the subject of renewable energy, there have also been some games which use the issue of energy or electricity as a narrative framework for mostly abstract games like arcade, puzzle or other skill games. These games do not belong to serious games as the thematic reference is limited to ornamental or rather atmospheric purposes.

Nevertheless, it is quite interesting that these games used the topic of Energy/Electricity to make them more attractive while others, namely the powerado research projects, are developed to enhance the emotional tie to renewable energy. At any rate, learning effects regarding renewable energy through these games are neither expected nor are they intended.

In the next group of games, learning effects are indeed intended, but the learning content is – similar to the games before – merely part of the graphical design. Figure 6 shows two digital clones of the children´s memory game "concentration," which are both part of a bigger game environment. The *Planet Green Game* contains a classic version of the memory game except that the pictures on the cards have been replaced by photos of objects from the field of energy.

Regarding learning effects, this is problematic as the pictures on the cards are not relevant to the game. The task of these games is to find pairs by turning two cards over. Although the player has to check whether both cards will match to each other, it is not necessary for him or her to deal with the items that are shown on these cards.

The right-hand screenshot in Figure 6 shows the memory variant *Fridge Frenzy*. Although the player's task within this game is the same as in the game before, this time it is integrated into a narrative which presents the task within a new context in order to tie it to the subject of energy. Thus, the player does not have cards anymore but fridges which he has to look into in order to find two similar pieces of food.

However, he or she has to be quick as each time the player opens the door, the coldness leaks from the fridge. Therefore, the intention of the game is to find all matches before too much energy dwindles away and causes a game over. The key message which fits to the game situation as well as to real life could be: "If you are wasting too much energy by opening the fridge again and again, you will lose."

The integration of learning content into the game design constitutes the basic prerequisite for implementing learning processes via serious games. If the content is merely superficial, meaning that the content is exchangeable as in the *Planet Green Game* (Figure 6), the learning potential remains low due to a lack of real involvement with the content. The same applies if the thematic reference has to be established first in an artificial way.

The *Energy Champions* (Figure 7) for instance comes with the task of catching garbage and separating it into the appropriate refuse containers. The relationship to energy results exclusively from the carbon dioxide indicator in form of a

Figure 6. Memory variations: planet green game and energy hog

footprint which becomes bigger whenever the garbage has been sorted into the wrong bin. If this happens too many times, the game is ended. The initiator of the game, incidentally, is E.ON, the worldwide biggest non-governmental energy company, which, in the meantime, has removed the game from their website.

Another example is the game *Polar Ranger* (Figure 7). In the role of a penguin ranger, the player has to fight against greenhouse gas. His task is to shoot down tons of greenhouse gas from the sky with his harpoon so that they explode before they hit the ground. The task becomes more difficult through bear traps, huskies and penguin-hunting Eskimos.

This example shows an attempt to concretize and depict the subject matter of greenhouse gases. However, the game design deviates so far from reality that the benefit of potential learning effects beyond the game itself seems to be very improbable.

Generally there are two different kinds of worlds within Serious Games: The imaginative game world on the one hand and the "serious" world on the other, which should be represented in the game with all relevant qualities so that an immediate association to reality is possible at any time to support the transfer of cognition and knowledge.

In the game *Beat the CO$_2$ Monster* there is, for instance, a reality-based environment with exhaust gas pollution by planes and cars as well as a fairy from a fantasy world who wants to clean up the air by a vacuum cleaner. One can debate whether a vacuum cleaner is an appropriate tool to fight air pollution, but as long as the intention of the game is to raise attention to the problem of air pollution itself or rather to sensitize without focusing on certain methods, this does not necessarily constitute a breach of the world.

This would have been different if the fairy had used a magic wand instead of a vacuum cleaner as environmental pollution cannot be solved by

Figure 7. Energy champions and polar ranger

magic. Of course, these are very metaphoric interpretations which are nevertheless important to make clear as it was certainly not the intention of the initiator (the Greens/European Free Alliance in the European Parliament) to trivialize the problem of air pollution.

The effect of non-intended messages becomes even more conspicuous in the case of *Jiffy*, an online game provided by the European Commission. *Jiffy* was a part of a larger website which offered information, quizzes and mini games according to the issues of air, water, garbage and nature.

Within the wind generator game *Jiffy* (Figure 8), the player had to click as many times as possible on the four windmills in the game for a duration of five (5) minutes to make Jiffy blow the rotor blades so that they would rotate and generate energy. Looking at what players may learn by playing this game, it seems initially trivial that wind generators require wind to turn. As the windmills in the game are not powered by nature but by Jiffy, the players may learn that generating energy by windmills is very exhausting - by blowing as well as by clicking.

EXCURSUS: GAMES ON THE ISSUE OF ENERGY SAVING

There are a lot of games from different genres which deal with the issue of energy saving. Especially for children, this topic is much closer to their living environment and much more tangible than renewable energy. The task is almost always the same: Identifying Energy-wasting appliances in a room or a house which need to be switched off or replaced should be identified.

On the website *Solar is future* there is such a game where power eaters have to be disconnected from the network by mouse click. Apart from small animations, the game design is static and is more an interactive website than a game. It is comparable to a digital worksheet, even though the task – seek and discover - is a little bit more playful.

In case of the comic-adventure *Lolly vs. The Energy Monkeys* the player has to do much the same as in the game *Solar is future* except that now the task is imbedded into a story about energy wasting space monkeys. Due to the narrative, the application gains not only the greater involvement of the players but also a stronger appearance as a game even though the interactive parts do not increase.

As in *Solar is future*, the visualization of the rooms is static and the interaction is limited to the localization of power eaters per mouse click. The story itself is presented linearly as a non-stop animation without the possibility for the player to influence the sequence. Although the story is clearly instructional, it fulfills an important function as it introduces the fictional world of the game as well as creating a meaningful context which consequently adds legitimization of the game task, even if this framework is fictional.

Figure 8. Point and click games: Beat the CO2 Monster and Jiffy

The next game, *Powerscout*, is a classical Jump & Run game and provides more interaction and more freedom to interact. As the game generates time pressure, there is little opportunity to intensively deal with the issue of energy saving while playing. As feedback is mainly given through the awarding of scores, the game activities are exchangeable, which means that it makes no difference to playing the game whether a TV set has to be switched off or coins or jewels have to be collected.

Another game that runs under comparable conditions to *Powerscout* is *Energuy*. As before, playing takes place under time pressure but *Energuy* provides a better solution for the feedback. Firstly there is in-game feedback (the cheering of *Energuy*) whenever a new item is discovered and secondly, all items are listed once more including additional information after the game is over.

The comparable realistic representation of the *Energuy* and the premises encourage the transfer between game world and reality. Yet, the gaming fun remains unwaning due to the extraordinary control of *Energuy* as well as his extroverted reactions, which is precisely not matching to reality.

Figure 9 also shows a screenshot of the mobile phone game *Energybuster* which is provided as a free download by the German Federal Environment Agency. In relation to distribution aspects, games for cell phones or Apps for smartphones and tablet-PCs are quite interesting and have a high potential for serious games in non-formal contexts. Within the serious games review, *Energybuster* was the only example of a mobile game on the issue of Energy (Saving). The research, however, was limited to websites and did not include App-Stores.

Another genre, which generally provides good conditions for the combination of game tasks and learning content, is that of the Adventure Game. These games usually assign the player the task of readjusting a disarranged world. The solution process is predetermined by the game architecture and has to be reconstructed by the players who have been allocated a broad scope of (inter)action to do so. Hence, adventure games represent an ideal-typical environment for cognitivist learning.

Furthermore, the narrative structure provides good opportunities to integrate real problems into fictional contexts, as it is shown in the example of the game *Climate House of Horror*. As before, the player´s task consists of seeking and stopping energy wastage, but this time it is a little bit more tricky. In order to fix a dripping water tap, for instance, the player requires a sealing ring which cannot be found until the lawn has been mown.

Figure 9. Energuy and the mobile phone game Energybuster

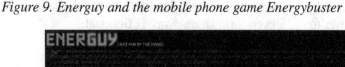

COMPLEX GAMES = SUSTAINABLE LEARNING?

Beside the games introduced previously, there are also some games which are more elaborately designed and therefore are expected to enable a deeper or maybe a more intensive learning experience. In most cases, these games are simulations or management games.

As simulations are usually geared to reality, they provide a good initial position to integrate (reality-related) learning content into the game. In this respect, there can be different key aspects and approaches as the research has discovered. *Windfall Tycoon* (Figure 10), for instance, is an English language economy simulation with the task to build wind powered stations next to a city in order to produce as much green electricity as possible. In so doing, the player has to consider the profitability as well as the satisfaction of the residents who may otherwise start to demonstrate.

While the goal of economy simulations is usually focused on profit maximization, the Japanese life simulation *Eco-Ego* (Figure 10) aims for balance between the needs of the individual and those of the environment. Similar to the Tamagotchi in the late nineties, the player has to "care" for the needs of a character and to make decisions concerning the daily routine and recreational activities of this character.

As in the footprint simulations before, each decision influences, to some extent, the environment but now the impacts are visible within the game. Both the little man as well as nature may die if the player neglects one of them. In the case of the little man, this might also happen if he is very bored. Thus, it is not sufficient to abstain from TV and game consoles, the player must also provide further options like playing with the butterflies in front of the house. At the end, there is feedback including tips on environmental behavior.

The game is playable in English and Japanese, but the game is controlled generally without written texts due to graphic user interfaces like pictured menus which might appear at first somewhat odd (for Europeans). Apart from that, *Eco-Ego*, which was awarded the Japanese Yahoo!-Internet Gold Creative Award in 2006, manages to reduce the subject of climate safety to the elementary conflicts of needs and to present it in a very playful and vivid way. Regarding the design and setting of tasks (e.g. caring), the game may be rather more appealing to girls who tend more towards simulation games than boys[4].

The games in Figure 11 are policy simulations and target teens above 16 years, a clearly older target group than most of the previous games. Both policy simulations aim to provide an insight into the structures and procedures of decision making in the context of environmental and climate policy. Learning is now no longer related to knowledge of

Figure 10. Economy simulation Windfall Tycoon and life simulation Eco-Ego

environmental behavior, but to the understanding of the political system – perhaps for one's own environmental political purpose.

The game *Keep Cool Online* is an adaption of the board game Keep Cool, which was developed by Gerhad Petschel-Held and Klaus Eisenack as an instrument for science communication. The online-version is a multiplayer game for three to six players, which represent different states and their specific interests. In addition to general economic interests, each player has an agenda with his own economic and/or political aims. While one of the players takes over the moderation, the other players have to negotiate to achieve the country-specific, as well as the common, purposes.

The online game is implemented by Schulen ans Netz e.V., a German association to support IT development in school education. Indeed, the game is in the first instance intended for use in schools and therefore represents an instrument of Formal Education.

Although *Climate Challenge* (Figure 11) is quite similar to *Keep Cool Online*, it is developed as a game for Non-Formal Learning. Thus, it is interesting to focus on the dissimilarity as the context determines the requirements of the game. While in Formal Education the creation of several teams as well as to appoint someone as a moderator is quite easy, it is very difficult to do so within Non-Formal Learning contexts.

Such demanding preconditions lead, in leisure-oriented game settings, in the majority of cases, to an exit of the game. An easy-entry to the game is in this context a basic requirement which is inherently problematical in cases of complex games like *Climate Challenge*, because the willingness to become acquainted with the game has to exist as well as the motivation to invest sufficient time into the game.

Consequently, the BBC as the initiator of the game, names fun as the primary aim of the game on its website. As a further learning purpose *Climate Challenge* aims to provide (1) an understanding of some of the causes of climate change, (2) an awareness of policy options available to governments and (3) a sense of the challenges facing international climate change negotiators (BBC, 2006).

Therefore, the player takes over the role of the President of the European Nations and may play certain policy cards which influence climate safety as well as the finance of the EU. Each intervention causes positive and negative impacts. In addition, the member states have to be convinced to invest in climate safety.

Developing the game, the BBC attached great importance to authenticity: Thus, the calculation of the carbon dioxide emissions is based widely on one of the scenarios of the Special Report on Emissions Scenarios (SRES) by the Intergovernmental Panel on Climate Change (IPCC). Further,

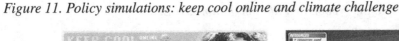

Figure 11. Policy simulations: keep cool online and climate challenge

the measures of the policy cards originate from former actual government policy documents, except for some futuristic ones that appear at the end of the game (BBC, 2006).

However, the impact of the measures in the game is boosted so that the consequences of the political decisions become visible within the next move to keep the going of the game. In this case, the game deliberately sets functional correctness aside in order to make the correlations clearer for the learner. The same is also the case in the next game (Figure 12).

Oiligarchy appears at first like an ordinary manager/economy simulation. However, in principle, it criticizes the behavioral pattern which is at first required in order to manage the game. Antigames like *Oiligarchy* appear like ordinary games and tie in with the existing game experiences and strategies of the players, but these do not lead, as expected, to success. The opportunity to win the game is usually highly restricted or missing completely. The following examples may give an idea of how antigames work (Winny, 2011):

- The simulation *September 12th* allows the dropping of bombs onto an Iraqi town to eliminate Taliban terrorists. As every bomb causes the death of militants or citizens, some of the bereaved become Taliban so that the number of enemies increases.

- *Against all Odds* is a game in which the player assumes the role of a refugee who escapes from his homeland. Because of the rigid game structure, the player is forced to permanently act against his or her own ideals and moral convictions.

- In the *McDonalds Video Game* the player has to manage an American fast food store including production, sales and PR. As the natural resources are not able to supply an unlimited demand for hamburgers, there is no way to win this game.

In the game *Oiligarchy*, the player has to build up an oil company and to satisfy the market. To be successful, he has to destroy the environment, kill animals, get rid of natives and demonstrators and manipulate elections and political decisions such as the invasion of Iraq or the abolition of the ban on oil production in Alaska. If the player is not successful, he will be fired and the game is over.

Thus, it is because the player is forced to act against social norms and values that the immoral behavior of the oil companies is revealed. But this strategy is just successful as long as there is enough oil resources left. If the player continues like this when the resource is depleting then the increasing oil price will cause an atomic war and the game is over. To finish the game in a positive way the player has to change his strategy by reducing output as well as his influence on political

Figure 12. Antigame: oiligarchy and virtual worlds – power-up

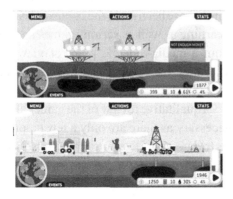 

decisions so that necessary environmental laws (such as for the development of renewable energies) are not blocked.

Such a change of strategy within a game is extremely unusual and leads to player irritation and frustration. This is also reflected by the online-feedback of *Oiligarchy* which is summarized by the developer as follows: "The debasement and relativization of the binary win/lose formula seems to be the most shocking part for the habitual gamers" (Molleindustria, n.d.).

From a constructivist point of view, this shocking-experience is a matter of perturbation, which means a perceived interruption that indicates that the previous imagination of the world is no longer valid enough to explain it and therefore has to be modified. This learning process is quite similar to that of the oil industry which, due to declining resources, is also forced to adapt and re-think.

The multiplayer online game *Power-Up* (Figure 12) is, just as *Keep Cool Online* (Figure 11), primarily envisaged for school education and provides a curriculum for six lessons on the corresponding website (TryScience, 2008, p. Teachers). Although it is possible to play the game, which first has to be downloaded and installed, in single-player-mode, playing in a team with up to eight players is recommended "for the best possible gaming experience" (TryScience, 2008, p. FAQ).

The virtual 3D-environment of the game is exclusively provided for each team. The members of the team can move around freely, talk to virtual agents/Non-Player-Characters (NPCs) and receive tasks from them which they have to perform such as collecting and assembling modules for a wind engine. The team members can communicate among each other via chat which is restricted to pre-set phrases due to youth protection issues.

IBM principally attached importance to parental and pedagogical acceptance for example regarding data privacy and alternative interfaces for handicapped people. Moreover, the technical

arrangement reflects the company's high level of capability and know-how. Nevertheless, Power-up is not necessarily among the best practice examples for serious games.

The question arises, not only from a didactic point of view, as to whether the quite simple learning tasks of the three missions justify the elaborate realization. Immersion, which is often an aspired benefit of virtual environments, is hindered here by game-intrinsic restrictions such as the limited numbers of multiplayers or the stereotypical communication.

Furthermore, the players rarely get the opportunity to make their own contributions to the virtual world as they can merely choose whether to fulfill the integrated tasks or not. The free moving space of the 3D-world becomes, especially within the single-player-mode, a restriction because the spacious rooms and landscapes of the game world have to be overcome before the player reaches the settings, which allows one of the few interactions.

CONCLUSION

The games presented here are a systematic selection of the games which are documented within the serious games database on the issue of renewable energy. Neither this selection nor the database makes the claim to be complete.

Nevertheless, it provides a good overview of existing learning offers in the World Wide Web starting from simple websites up to complex and elaborate games. Through the commentation, the games have been set in the context of Non-Formal Learning as well as serious games and evaluated from a media-didactic point of view including an estimation of potential learning effects (See Figure 13).

A qualitative review of the games also appears necessary as there are only a few empirical studies to date on the learning effects of serious games

Figure 13. Websites and games on renewable energy by learning purpose (including best practice)

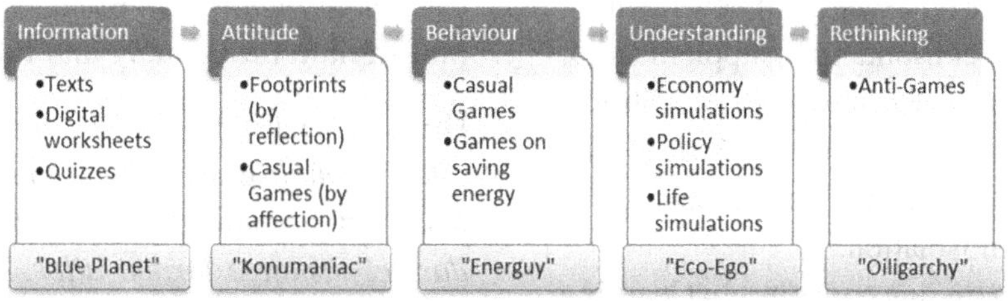

(Gee, 2007, p. 332; Ritterfeld et al., 2009, p. 6) which are, due to the heterogeneity of the research field, only marginally comparable.

In relation to a secondary analysis of existing impact studies on games for health, Lampert, Schwinge and Tolks (2009, p. 12) come at the conclusion that "serious games are particularly suitable in those areas in which a narrow scope of action is given: The more precise the goal setting and the adaption toward the target group is, the higher the efficacy regarding the learning success might be rated."[5]

Such a narrow scope of action is usual in the first instance constituted by a formalized context, which, by definition, does not exist in cases of games in non-formal settings. By comparison, the suitability of serious games outside Formal Learning settings is rather defined by the potential to transfer learning content beyond the borders of controllable learning environments.

Accordingly, the impact of a serious game is not restricted only by the (lesser) learning effect, but moreover through the range of distribution which has to be considered as an additional criterion of success, especially if target groups should be reached, which are difficult to address within formal education. Even casual games that mostly allow just minor complexity of learning content might be interesting in this context as they provide a higher potential for a wide reception than complex games.

Although many researchers assume that digital games provide good conditions for learning experiences (Gee, 2009, p. 67; Wilson et al., 2009; Habgood, Ainsworth, & Benford, 2005), this seri-

ous games research has shown that many of the reviewed games do not tap this potential. Essential to achieving learning effects is ultimately how the games are designed and created. This means that the didactic consideration becomes a key role in terms of the game development.

Accordingly, the following basic requirements can be formulated for serious games in leisure-oriented learning settings: First, serious games have to meet all the quality criteria of an ordinary game which means it must be fun, should offer easy entry regarding usability and should be tailored to the target group. Secondly, the learning content should be integrated into the game task.

It becomes obvious that learning issues are subordinated to the game issues insofar as the willingness of the gamer to spend time on the game is an essential condition for the formation of learning processes.

In the context of an evaluation study (Fromme & Russler, 2007b), we attempted to verify significant learning effects for a game which had been developed within the Powerado research projects. In this case, objective evidence could not be provided but it appeared from the collected data that children between the ages of eight to twelve already have previous knowledge concerning renewable energy at their command that they are able to distinguish between "good" and "bad" energies very well and to name preferences on demand.

However, the cognitive, affective, and conative pattern of this age-group (8-12 years) has not yet been consolidated as several cluster analyses have indicated high fluctuations between the clusters at different points of time.

If the function of such or similar serious games[6] is not necessarily the conveyance of new learning content but rather of consolidation, supplementing and reactivating existing (knowledge) constructs then the question arises as to whether these effects are still measurable and whether it makes sense to examine them in isolation.

Either way, this finding confirms that learning is not a singular incident but instead a process which is characterized by varied experiences of learning - and that in formal as well as in non-formal contexts. Serious Games may provide one of many possibilities to support learning and development processes and they do so in a variety of ways.

In informal contexts, they provide the opportunity to constitute low-threshold learning environments that complement established learning settings with functions that may not be available within classic school education.

ACKNOWLEDGMENT

The previous selection of Non-Formal Learning offers on the Internet results from a systematic review of websites and games on the issue of (renewable) energy, which has been conducted at the chair of Media Research in Educational Science at the University of Magdeburg (Germany) in 2009/2010. The data originates from an investigation on Serious Games within the research project "Renewable Energy Experience," which was funded by the Federal Ministry for the Environment, Nature Conversation, and Nuclear Safety.

REFERENCES

BBC. (2006). *Climate challenge: Background information of the game.* Retrieved from http://www.bbc.co.uk/sn/hottopics/climatechange/climate_challenge/aboutgame.shtml

Dohmen, G. (1999). *Weiterbildungsinstitutionen, medien, lernumwelten.* Bonn, Germany: Bundesministerium für Bildung und Forschung.

Dohmen, G. (2001). *Das informelle lernen – Die internationale Erschließung einer bisher vernachlässigten grundform menschlichen lernens für das lebenslange lernen aller.* Bonn, Germany: Bundesministerium für Bildung und Forschung.

Dohmen, G. (2002). Informelles lernen in der freizeit. *Spektrum Freizeit, 24*(1), 18–27.

EC. (2001). *Making a European area of lifelong learning a reality.* Brussels, Belgium: Commission of the European Communities. Retrieved from http://eur-lex.europa.eu/LexUriServ/LexUriServ.do?uri=COM:2001:0678:FIN:EN:PDF

Erikson, E. H. (1966). *Identität und lebenszyklus.* Frankfurt am Main, Germany: Suhrkamp.

Feil, C., Decker, R., & Gieger, C. (2004). *Wie entdecken kinder das internet?* Wiesbaden, Germany: VS Verlag für Sozialwissenschaften. doi:10.1007/978-3-531-90143-5.

Fromme, J., & Russler, S. (2005). *Mediendidaktische beratung zum online-spiel und projektlogo: Ergebnisbericht PC1.* Magdeburg, Germany: Chair of Educational Media Research.

Fromme, J., & Russler, S. (2007a). *Ergebnisse der zwischenevaluation zum computerspiel powerado: Ergebnisbericht PC5.* Magdeburg, Germany: Chair of Educational Media Research.

Fromme, J., & Russler, S. (2007b). *Ergebnisse der hauptevaluation zum computerspiel powerado: Ergebnisbericht PC8.* Magdeburg, Germany: Chair of Educational Media Research.

Fromme, J., & Winny, S. (2012a). *Konzeptevaluation für das online-spiel 5x5: Ergebnisbericht OS6.* Magdeburg, Germany: Chair of Educational Media Research.

Fromme, J., & Winny, S. (2012b). *Prozessevaluation des online-spiels 5x5: ergebnisbericht OS8*. Magdeburg, Germany: Chair of Educational Media Research.

Gee, J. P. (2007). *What video games have to teach us about learning and literacy*. New York, NY: Palgrave Macmillan.

Habgood, M. P. J., Ainsworth, S. E., & Benford, S. (2005). Endogenous fantasy and learning in digital games. *Simulation & Gaming, 36*(4), 483–498. doi:10.1177/1046878105282276.

Huizinga, J. (1950). Homo ludens: Proeve eener bepaling van het spel-element der cultuur. In L. Brummel (Ed.), *Johan Huizinga, Verzamelde werken V (Cultuurgeschiedenis III),* (pp. 26-246). Haarlem, The Netherlands. Retrieved from http://www.dbnl.org/tekst/huiz003homo01_01/

Jensen, A. (2003). *Durchblick – Was hat unser alltag mit der umwelt zu tun*. Nürnberg, Germany: Westermann. Retrieved from http://www.apug.de/archiv/pdf/broschuere_durchblick.pdf

Kirchhöfer, D. (2002). Informelles lernen in der freizeit der kinder. *Spektrum Freizeit, 24*(1), 28–43.

Klafki, W. (1991). *Neue studien zur bildungstheorie und didaktik*. Weinheim, Germany: Beltz.

Lampert, C., Schwinge, C., & Tolks, D. (2009). *Der gespielte ernst des lebens: Bestandsaufnahme und potenziale von serious games (for health)*. Retrieved from http://www.medienpaed.com/15/lampert0903.pdf

Livingstone, D. W. (2001). *Adults' informal learning: Definitions, findings, gaps and future research*. NALL Working Paper, No. 21. Toronto, Canada: Centre for the Study of Education and Work, OISE/UT.

Maslow, A. H. (1943). A theory of human motivation. *Psychological Review, 50*, 370–396. Retrieved from http://psychclassics.yorku.ca/Maslow/motivation.htm doi:10.1037/h0054346.

Meder, N. (2006). *Webdidaktik: Eine neue didaktik webbasierten lernens*. Bielefeld, Germany: Bertelsmann.

Medienpädagogischer Forschungsverbund Südwest. (2010). *KIM-studie 2010*. Retrieved from www.mpfs.de

Medienpädagogischer Forschungsverbund Südwest. (2011). *JIM-studie 2011*. Retrieved from www.mpfs.de

Molleindustria. (n.d.). *Oiligarchy postmortem: Background information of the game*. Retrieved from http://www.molleindustria.org/oiligarchy-postmortem#11

Nielsen Research. (2009). *Insights on casual games analysis of casual games for the PC*. Retrieved from http://www.scribd.com/doc/20232878/Insights-on-Casual-Games-Analysis-of-Casual-Games-for-the-PC-Nielsen-Research-2009

O'Reilly, T. (2006). *Web 2.0 – Principles and practices*. Oreilly & Assoc Inc..

Petschel-Held, G. (n.d.). *Keep cool – Gambling with the climate: The scientific background of the game*. Potsdam, Germany: Potsdam Institute for Climate Impact Research.

Piaget, J. (1978). *Das weltbild des kindes*. München, Germany: dtv/Klett-Cotta.

Ritterfeld, U., Cody, M., & Vorderer, P. (2009). *Serious games: Mechanisms and effects*. New York, NY: Routledge/LEA.

TryScience. (2008). *PowerUP: Background information of the game*. Retrieved from http://www.poweruptthegame.org

Weninger, E. (2010). *KonsuManiac: Didaktische materialien zum online-tool konsumaniac.at*. Wien, Austria: Forum Umweltbildung.

Wilson, K. A., Bedwell, W. L., Lazzara, E. H., Salas, E., Burke, C. S., & Estock, J. L. et al. (2009). Relationships between game attributes and learning outcomes: Review and research proposals. *Simulation & Gaming, 40*(2), 217–266. doi:10.1177/1046878108321866.

Winny, S. (2011). *Anti games*. Retrieved from http://www.winnyswelt.de/2011/06/anti-games/

KEY TERMS AND DEFINITIONS

Advergames: Games which are designed for the purpose of Advertisement.

Antigames: Games which initiate learning processes by breaking with common game experiences and strategies, e.g. by game immanent restrictions or missing opportunities to win the game.

Games for Change: Games which deal with social issues and/or social change.

Games for Health: Games which are designed for therapeutic use or health prevention.

Footprint Simulations: Simulations, which generate an individual carbon dioxide balance based on personal information. Footprint Simulations are used to demonstrate the relationship between every day (buying) decisions and global warming.

Formal Learning: Learning which is characterized by an external structure, curricular learning targets and independence from a specific problem. Formal Learning, like e.g. school education, is mostly extrinsic motivated.

Incidental Learning: Learning which arises simultaneously to another performed activity which means that it is always situational and linked to a certain problem. Incidental Learning is neither goal-oriented nor reflected, but can change to Informal Learning if reflection occurs.

Informal Learning: Learning which is characterized by its own problem-oriented construction of learning targets and a self-determined learning rhythm. Informal Learning is intrinsic motivated and requires inherent time for learning purpose.

News Games: Games which deal with journalistic issues/news.

Non-Formal Learning: Learning which does not belong to Formal Learning. Non-Formal Learning is a collective term for Informal and Incidental Learning.

Recruitment Games: Games which should acquire members or followers.

Serious Games: Games that are designed for at least one further purpose other than the pure pleasure of the game.

ENDNOTES

[1] Translated from German: "Durchblick – was hat der Alltag mit Umwelt zu tun" (Jensen, 2003, p. 14).

[2] The quiz question is: What should the night setting of a heating system be?
The answers included the following options: 5 kelvin, 10 kelvin, or 15 kelvin.

[3] Question: How long was your shower today? Answers: "no shower," "2 minutes," "5 minutes," "+10 minutes".

[4] Within the KIM-Study, 973 children in Germany aged between 6 and 13 Years were asked about their three favorite games. The girl's top answer was the SIMS (12%), whereas boys named this game in just in 4% of the cases (MPFS, 2010).

[5] Translated from German: "Die Ergebnisse der empirischen Studien deuten allerdings darauf hin, dass Serious Games insbesondere in den Bereichen geeignet sind, in denen ein enger Handlungsrahmen vorliegt: Je präziser die Zielformulierung und die Ausrichtung

an der Zielgruppe ist, desto höher ist die Wirksamkeit bzw. der Lernerfolg dieser Spiele einzuschätzen" (Lampert, Schwinge & Tolks, 2009, p. 12).

[6] The set of problems is to a large extend comparable to other subjects like e.g. nicotine and alcohol consumption, HIV prevention, nutrition advice, etc.

[7] All links were proofed in August 2012.

APPENDIX

LIST OF PRESENTED WEBSITES/GAMES[7]

- **Websites**
  - **Bmu-kids.de (Federal Ministry for the Environment, Nature Conversation and Nuclear Safety, Germany):**
    - **Current Version:** www.bmu-kids.de
    - **Former Version:** http://web.archive.org/web/20060302173922/
    - **Booklet:** http://www.bmu-kids.de/wissen/index_wissen.htm
  - **Strom Online (Joint Website of Several Electric Energy Suppliers, Switzerland):** http://www.strom-online.ch/windkraftwerk_interaktiv.html
  - **VWEW (EnBW, Germany):** No longer online.
- **Quizzes**
  - **BBC Environmental Quiz (BBC England, UK):** http://news.bbc.co.uk/cbbcnews/hi/newsid_4120000/newsid_4123400/4123441.stm
  - **Quiz by Volker Quaschning (Volker Quatschning, Germany):** http://www.volker-quaschning.de/quiz/index.php
  - **Board game "Treibhauseffekt" (energydesign, Germany):** http://www.treibhauseffekt.com/game/game.htm
  - **Quiz Game "Blue Planet" (Federal Ministry for the Environment, Nature Conversation and Nuclear Safety, Germany):** http://www.klima-sucht-schutz.de/mitmachen/klima-quiz/quiz-spielen.html
- **Footprints**
  - **Konsumaniac (Environmental Education FORUM - an Initiative of the Austrian Federal Ministry of Agriculture, Forestry, Environment and Water Management and the Austrian Federal Ministry for Education, the Arts and Culture, Austria):** http://www.umweltbildung.at/konsumaniac/index.html
  - **I´m Alright Jack/Climate Challenge (BBC England, UK):** http://www.bbc.co.uk/climate/adaptation/jack.shtml
  - **Klimacheck (WWF – World Wide Fund for Nature, Switzerland):** No longer online. Documentation at http://www.ucs.ch/ref/refklimacheck.html
  - **The Footprint Game (Kids Stories International, Canada):** http://www.littleanimation-4kids.com/footprint/
- **Casual Games**
  - **Planet Green Game (Global Green/Starbucks, USA):** No longer online
  - **Energy Hog/Fridge Frenzy (Alliance to save Energy, USA):** http://www.energyhog.org/childrens.htm
  - **Energy Champions (E.ON, UK):** http://flashgames.de/onlinespiel/energy-champions
  - **Polar Ranger (Federal Ministry for the Environment, Nature Conversation and Nuclear Safety, Germany):** http://envizone.de/klimaspiel

- ◦ **Beat the CO2 Monster (the Greens/European Free Alliance in the European Parliament, EU):** http://greens-efa-service.eu/medialib/media/flash/climate_game
  - ◦ **Jiffy (European Commission, EU):** No longer online
- **Games on Saving Energy**
  - ◦ **Solar is Future (SMA Solar Technology AG):** http://www.solar-is-future.de/kids/
  - ◦ **Lolly vs. the Energy Monkeys (National Grid of Learning, UK):** http://www.cwndesign.co.uk/funergy/game/index.html
  - ◦ **Powerscout (Initiative Energieeffizienz, Germany):** http://www.stromeffizienz.de/fileadmin/powerscout/index.htm
  - ◦ **Energuy (Ministry of Natural Resources and Wildlife, Quebec, Canada):** http://www.aee.gouv.qc.ca/en/energuy/game
  - ◦ **Energybuster (Federal Environment Agency, Germany):** Download for mobile phones: http://www.energybuster.de
  - ◦ **Climate House of Horror (Office of the Federal State Government of Upper Austria, Austria):** http://www.klimarettung.at/de/91
- **Economic Simulation Game**
  - ◦ **Windfall Tycoon (Persuasive Games, Atlanta, USA):** http://flashgames.de/index.php?onlinespiele=10371&todo=play
- **Life Simulation Game**
  - ◦ **Eco-Ego (Marukin Ad Co. Ltd., Japan):** www.marukin-ad.co.jp/ecoego
- **Policy Simulation Games**
  - ◦ **Keep Cool Online (Schulen ans Netz e.V., Germany):** http://www.keep-cool-online.de
  - ◦ **Climate Challenge (BBC England, UK):** http://www.bbc.co.uk/sn/hottopics/climatechange/climate_challenge/index_1.shtml
- **Antigames**
  - ◦ **Oiligarchy (la Molleindustria, Italy):** http://www.molleindustria.org/en/oiligarchy/
  - ◦ **September the 12th (Newsgaming.com, Uruguay):** http://www.newsgaming.com/games/index12.htm
  - ◦ **Against all Odds (UNHCR - The UN Refugee Agency, Switzerland):** http://www.playagainstallodds.com/
  - ◦ **McDonald Video Game (la Molleindustria, Italy):** http://www.mcvideogame.com/
- **3D Role-Playing Video Game**
  - ◦ **Power-Up (Tryscience/IBM, USA):** http://www.powerupthegame.org/

Section 4
Games and Virtual Worlds in Health Care

Chapter 13
Serious Games and Motor Learning:
Concepts, Evidence, Technology

Josef Wiemeyer
Technische Unversität Darmstadt, Germany

Sandro Hardy
Technische Unversität Darmstadt, Germany

ABSTRACT

Digital games in general require fine motor skills, i.e., operating the computer mouse, the keyboard, the touch-screen, or a joystick. With the development of new gaming interfaces, the performance of whole-body movements became possible to control a game. This opens up new lines of application, e.g. improving motor skills and motor abilities. The most important question is whether and how virtual game-based perceptual-motor training transfers to real motor tasks. Theory distinguishes between specific motor skill learning and generic motor ability improvement. Existing evidence shows that the improvement of motor abilities (e.g., balance) is possible by particular exergames while the improvement of motor skills (e.g., basketball throw) depends on several moderators like accuracy of the interface and correspondence of virtual and real tasks. The authors conclude that there are two mechanisms of transfer, located at the elementary and fundamental perceptual-motor level and at the cognitive level. Current issues for technology comprise adaptivity, personalization, game mastering, accuracy of interfaces and sensors, activity recognition, and error detection.

INTRODUCTION

Digital games, i.e., games that are played on electronic devices including microprocessors, have become a widely spread leisure activity attracting not only children and youth but also younger and older adults (e.g., ESA, 2012). When playing digital games, players normally improve their performance, i.e. game score. As a 'secondary effect', players enhance their competencies demanded by the game. For example, Green and Bavelier (2007) showed that playing an ego-shooter game, i.e., a

DOI: 10.4018/978-1-4666-3673-6.ch013

game where the player acts from a first-person perspective and has to fight against other players by using a gun, improved spatial resolution of visual perception. This was not the case for participants playing Tetris.

In Figure 1 competency areas relevant to digital games are illustrated. Gaming can affect five dimensions of competencies:

- Cognitive competencies.
- Motivational, emotional and volitional competencies.
- Perceptual-motor competencies.
- Social competencies.
- Media competencies.

Considering these game-specific effects on competencies the idea seems likely to develop and construct digital games that do not only elicit fun and entertainment but are intentionally and systematically designed to improve selected competencies. Therefore, Serious Games (SG) can be defined as digital games explicitly serving additional purposes beyond mere fun and entertainment. Beginning in the 1980s, SG have been

Figure 1. Competencies potentially enhanced by playing digital games (adapted with modifications from Wiemeyer & Kliem, 2012, p. 42)

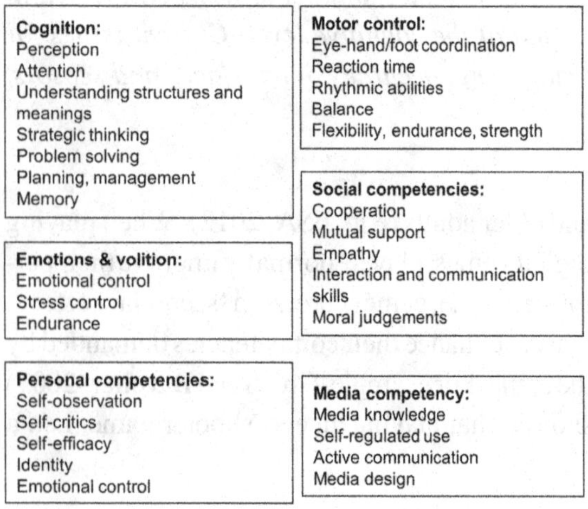

Cognition: Perception Attention Understanding structures and meanings Strategic thinking Problem solving Planning, management Memory	Motor control: Eye-hand/foot coordination Reaction time Rhythmic abilities Balance Flexibility, endurance, strength
Emotions & volition: Emotional control Stress control Endurance	Social competencies: Cooperation Mutual support Empathy Interaction and communication skills Moral judgements
Personal competencies: Self-observation Self-critics Self-efficacy Identity Emotional control	Media competency: Media knowledge Self-regulated use Active communication Media design

developed for and applied to numerous fields like vocational training, academic and school education, health and rehabilitation, solving scientific issues, and sports (e.g., Ratan & Ritterfeld, 2009). SG promise to offer unique options for learning meeting the requirements posed by theories of learning: "Modern theories of effective learning suggest that learning is most effective when it is active, experiential, situated, problem-based and provides immediate feedback" (Connolly, Boyle, McArthur, Hainey, & Boyle, 2012, p. 661).

In this chapter, we focus on the application of SG to motor learning.

The objective of this chapter is to address the following questions: Can motor learning be enhanced by SG? If so, which mechanisms are responsible for the learning effects? For further applications, which are the prerequisites for establishing strong and sustainable motor learning effects?

As a first step, theories of motor learning and transfer are discussed in order to deal with the possible mechanisms relevant to the impact of SG on motor competencies. Then existing evidence is analyzed testing the influence of SG on motor learning. Finally, the chances and limits of applying SG to motor learning are discussed.

SERIOUS GAMES FOR MOTOR LEARNING: THEORY

Motor learning can be defined as the more or less permanent change of the capability to show observable behavior (i.e., movements) as a consequence of experience (i.e., mental or physical practice).

In principle motor learning can take two forms (See Figure 2): On the one hand *specific motor skills* like operating a surgical instrument or throwing a javelin can be acquired or improved. On the other hand *domain-specific general motor abilities* can be improved. General abilities are differentiated into conditional and coordinative abilities.

Figure 2. Motor learning between specificity and generality

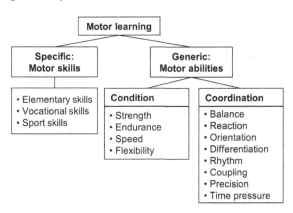

Figure 3. General framework of motor learning

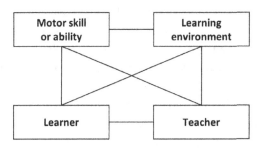

information processing approach and the dynamic systems approach will be discussed in more detail in the following two sections.

Information Processing Approach

For SG the information processing approach is of particular relevance. This approach considers the human as an entity that takes up, processes, and produces information. Sensory input is delivered by the senses, i.e., vision, audition, proprioception, etc. Information processing takes place at several stages including various memory functions like sensory, short-term and long-term memory. Information production can be established by speech, gestures, mimics, and other movements.

Basic Assumptions

One key issue for the information processing approach is how to enhance motor learning by supporting information processing. This approach has generated valuable knowledge concerning instruction, feedback, and arrangement of practice. Motor learning comprises various explicit and implicit processes. Whereas *explicit learning* means that the learner is aware of his or her own learning (including the intention of learn), *implicit learning* means that awareness or intention to learn are not present. Explicit learning concerns explicit or declarative memory, for instance, of facts and events, whereas implicit learning concerns procedural memory, for instance, non-aware processes

Conditional abilities denote motor abilities where energy is the most important limiting factor. This category comprises strength, endurance, speed, and flexibility. Whereas in strength, endurance, and speed performance metabolic energy is most important, in flexibility features of active and passive transfer of (bio)mechanical energy within and between the joints are the limiting factor.

Coordinative abilities denote motor abilities where information processing is the most important limiting factor. These generic features of perceptual-motor control include balance, reaction, rhythm, proprioceptive differentiation or spatial orientation. Perceptual-motor abilities are considered important conditions enhancing the control, adaptation, and learning of motor skills (e.g., Fleishman & Rich, 1963).

Motor learning comprises complex interactions of learner(s), teacher(s), motor skill or ability (task), and the learning environment (See Figure 3). Numerous theoretical approaches to the issue of motor learning have been proposed focusing on specific aspects of these complex interactions (e.g., Magill, 2010; Schmidt & Wrisberg, 2008). There are three main streams of theory: behaviorism, information processing (or cognitivism), and dynamic systems theory (or constructivism). Due to their great importance for motor learning, the of motor control. Although the application of SG to motor learning can support both types of learning, the main advantage seems to be the enhancement of implicit motor learning: Within SG players may forget about learning and just try to successfully master the in-game motor tasks.

Another fundamental contribution of the information processing approach is the finding that in motor learning explicit processes are particularly important at an early stage of motor learning. Initially, a cognitive representation of the motor skill to be learned has to be established. At later stages of motor learning the influence of cognitive representations decreases but does not totally vanish. Furthermore, the *crucial role of instruction, feedback, and practice schedule* has been confirmed.

Guidelines and Principles

For the issue of enhancing motor learning by the application of SG the following guidelines and principles can be derived from the information processing approach (see also Wiemeyer, 2004):

Instructions should be short, clear, and understandable. In this regard, *verbal cues*, i.e., 'concise phrases, often just one or two words, that either direct a student's attention to relevant task stimuli or prompt key movement pattern elements of a motor skill' (Landin, 1994, p. 299) have been proven successful.

Instructions should take into account existing memory structures (e.g., preliminary knowledge, skills, etc.). Therefore, instructions should make use of appropriate *metaphors, comparisons*, and *analogies* in order to establish a connection between the task to be learned and existing knowledge or experiences (e.g., Tielemann, Raab, & Arnold, 2008).

Instructions can define the problem (e.g., 'clear the bar'), deliver the solution to the problem (e.g., run-up, take-off, flight, and landing) or activate or convey knowledge relevant to the solution (e.g., biomechanical basics).

Instructions should direct attention to the *external effects* of movement (Wulf, 2007) or to effects that are easily perceivable and closely related to the quality of movement.

Instructions should be delivered as a *combination of visual and auditory information*. In this regard, sonification and music can support learning (e.g., Karagheorgis & Priest, 2012; Effenberg, 2005).

Extrinsic Feedback, i.e., feedback delivered by a teacher or a technical device, must be presented within certain *time limits*. If the time interval between movement and feedback is too short, processing of intrinsic information is blocked or diminished, and if the interval is too long movement-related information may be forgotten. Depending on the type of learning a pre-feedback interval of 5 to 45 seconds and a post-feedback interval of 20 to 120 seconds should be deployed (e.g., Blischke, Marschall, Müller, & Daugs, 1999).

The *accuracy* of extrinsic feedback must fit the control capacities of the system. There is an optimal level of accuracy, favoring feedback that is not too accurate (i.e., including tolerances) and not too vague to be useful for movement corrections.

The *frequency* of extrinsic feedback has to follow a specific schedule: Feedback delivered too often will lead to a 'guidance effect' (Marschall, Bund, & Wiemeyer, 2007), i.e., resulting in neglecting intrinsic feedback delivered by the own senses and maladaptive short-term corrections causing instable motor control. In many cases, feedback is more important at the beginning of learning favoring a *fading schedule* of feedback presentation.

Informational support in motor learning should take into consideration the various *types of learners*, e.g., learners preferring haptic, visual, or verbal information processing.

Variable practice will enhance learning and particularly transfer. Variability of practice can be established by changing perceptual demands, time pressure, accuracy and precision demands, complexity demands, physical load etc. of the task to be performed or applying different tasks. Concerning the improvement of motor abilities several different tasks belonging to the same perceptual-motor domain (e.g., balance) should be applied. Variable practice can be structured in numerous ways ranging from blocked to alternating or random order of trials. For novices a blocked order (low contextual interference) is more effective whereas advanced learners benefit from random order (high contextual interference; Porter & Magill, 2010). Recently support for a strategy of systematically increasing contextual interference, i.e., starting with blocked practice and ending with random practice, has proved superior to pure low or high contextual interference (Porter & Magill, 2010).

Transfer in motor learning is subject to the complex interplay of learning design, learner's characteristics and transfer environment. The information processing required by the learning task(s) should match the transfer task as closely as possible ('transfer surface'; Osgood, 1949). The most critical source of interference is a coupling of similar situations and opposing or antagonistic actions or reactions. This should be avoided.

Distribution or spacing of practice is another important issue of motor learning. On the one hand single practice trials should be separated by appropriate inter-trial intervals (a few seconds to one minute; Lee & Genovese, 1988; Donovan & Radosevich, 1999) and on the other hand practice sessions comprising more than one trial should be separated by one day rather than a few minutes or hours (Shea, Lai, Black, & Park, 2000). An interesting finding reported in a meta-analysis (Donovan & Radosevich, 1999) is that learning video games and other tasks of average complexity (e.g., slide bar task, voice recognition, verbal discrimination, and maze learning) is enhanced by comparatively long inter-trial intervals (10 minutes to 1 hour). This poses a serious problem for SG because players prefer to immediately repeat

an activity that has been completed, particularly when they failed to achieve the desired goal. This immediate repetition behavior should be avoided by the control of SG.

A great challenge for motor learning is the issue that many motor skills are too complex to be immediately learned as a whole. An often-practiced strategy is to divide the skills into functional parts that are first exercised in isolation as single parts and subsequently re-composed to the whole skill according to specific principles or rules, for example 'from the simple to the more difficult' or 'from the functional core to the functional margin' (Wiemeyer, 2003). The main question is where to divide the skill without destroying the whole structure. In long and high jump, for example, a 'cut' between run-up and take-off phase would be dysfunctional because there is a close interrelation of these two phases. Another problem is to determine how long a specific partial exercise should be practiced before transition to the next stage.

Dynamic Systems Approach

Basic Assumptions

Of course, every approach has its strengths and limits. Another approach which has been opposed to the information processing approach is the ecological or dynamic systems approach. This approach emphasizes the fact that in complex systems like the human order, e.g., skillful behavior, is establish by self-organization. This means that there is not a central intelligence establishing order; rather order emerges by a complex interplay of different control levels influenced by certain constraints.

One important result of research based on this approach is that transfer of learning needs to take into account the complex interrelation of the human and the environment imposing specific constraints on the dynamic perception-action coupling. From an ecological perspective, motor learning always has to take place in authentic contexts. For the application of SG to motor learning, this means that the respective digital game should present the learning environment as close to the real environment as possible or at least pose functionally similar perceptual-motor demands.

Differential Learning

A second interesting approach based on the dynamic systems perspective is the 'differential learning' approach proposed by Schöllhorn, Beckmann, and Davids (2010) and Schöllhorn, Beckmann, Janssen, and Drepper (2010). This approach contends that systematically increasing fluctuations and stochastic perturbations in motor learning will lead to more stable and more flexible motor skills. The basic rule 'never train the "right way"' means to vary the constraints of learning as much as possible, e.g., the kinematics, dynamics, and rhythm of the movement, and to avoid repetitions of similar movements in order to fully explore the 'perceptual-motor workspace' constrained by learner, task and environment for stable and unstable regions of solutions. This approach is very similar to the contextual interference approach, which also posits that variable practice enhances learning and transfer of motor skills. Variable practice is also the most important principle for improving coordinative abilities. For the application of SG to motor learning this means to offer variable practice by changing tasks, task conditions etc. as much as possible.

SERIOUS GAMES FOR MOTOR LEARNING: EVIDENCE

In this section, the application of SG to motor learning in different domains is analyzed.

To study the impact of SG in motor learning numerous methodological requirements have to be considered:

- An ideal research design will comprise a structured acquisition period followed by early and late retention and transfer periods, respectively.
- The research design should comprise at least a SG treatment group, a traditional learning group and a no-treatment control group.
- Assignment to the groups should be randomized or pseudo-randomized based on preliminary performance or initial level of experience, skills, or abilities.
- Pre-tests, acquisition tests, as well as early and late retention and transfer tests should be administered.
- Moderating or mediating variables like motivation, initial skill level or previous experience should be either controlled or assessed.
- An important requirement is the assessment of game experience. SG do not deserve the label 'game' if the players do not show any game experience like fun, enjoyment, challenge, flow, curiosity, immersion, and positive or negative emotions.

According to the classification scheme presented in the previous section (Figure 2), the existing studies concerning the application of SG to the domain of motor learning can be categorized into the acquisition and improvement of vocational skills in medicine, sport skills, the (re-)learning of motor skills in rehabilitation and the improvement of (coordinative and conditional) motor abilities. Whereas studies addressing vocational skills are mainly correlational studies, experimental studies have been published addressing sport skills and motor abilities. The published papers dealing with motor learning in rehabilitation are predominantly case reports or small sample studies. In the following section existing evidence will be discussed with respect to three questions:

1. Do the studies support the hypothesis that SG enhance learning of motor skills and motor abilities?
2. Which learning mechanisms and principles mentioned in the previous section are deployed?
3. Which game and interface technology is used?

Issues of motor learning in clinical contexts, i.e., with patients, are addressed in a more general way, because every disease poses specific problems for the appropriate treatment of the perceptual-motor system that cannot be addressed within the limits of this chapter.

Surgical (or Vocational) Motor Skills

Evidence

Grantcharov, Bardram, Funch-Jensen, and Rosenberg (2003) showed that 10 surgeons in training (mean age: 35 years) with game experience committed significantly less errors than 15 non-gamers when performing a complex task on a virtual surgical training device (10 repetitions). Gamers also showed a tendency toward shorter movement time, whereas the number of unnecessary movements did not differ between groups. Unfortunately, the authors do not give information how game experience was assessed.

Enochsson et al. (2004) found that 5 medical students with video game experience (criteria: daily or occasional use) performed significantly better (endoscopy time and efficiency) on a simulated gastroscopy (1 trial) than a group of 12 non-players. Furthermore, the authors found a positive correlation between endoscopic performance (relative time with clear vision) and the Pictorial Surface Orientation test, i.e., a test for three-dimensional spatial perception.

Shane, Pettitt, Morgenthal, and Smith (2008) showed that video game experience (i.e., regular gaming of more than 3 hours per week) significantly shortened time for acquiring two surgical skills in a sample of 26 surgical novices. The 11 gamers (average game activity: 4.5 hrs per week) reached proficiency in both tasks earlier (task 1: 0 versus 6 trials; task 2: 0 versus 4 trials) than the 15 non- gamers (average game activity: 0.27 hrs per week).

Badurdeen et al. (2010) correlated performance of 20 medical students and junior doctors in three Wii games (Pose Mii, Shooting range, Charge!) with performance in three virtual laparoscopic tasks (one trial per task and game, respectively). They found a significant positive correlation of 0.82 between aggregated game score and laparoscopic score. Total gaming experience (mean: 1,255 hours; range: 0 to 9,360 hours) also correlated significantly with laparoscopic score ($r=0.578$, $2p=0.01$).

Lynch, Aughwane, and Hammond (2010) discuss existing evidence for the impact of video games on laparoscopic, gastrointestinal endoscopic, endovascular, and robotic surgery. Analysis of 12 studies led to the conclusion that experience with and training on video games improves endoscopic but not robotic techniques.

In a recent study, Dongen, Verleisdonk, Schijven, and Broeders (2011) analyzed the performance of schoolchildren (mean age: 12.5 years) and adult students (mean age: 24 years) with and without video game experience on a virtual reality simulation device for endoscopic surgery. The authors found a significant advantage of the adult group with video game experience concerning efficiency and speed, but not precision of endoscopy.

Discussion

Most of the studies on the impact of video game experience on surgical skills cannot be considered as learning experiments in a strict sense because an acquisition period and/or appropriate control conditions were missing and no (delayed) retention or transfer tests were applied. Therefore the results can mainly be interpreted as short-term performance effects.

The existing evidence indicates that video game performance and surgical skills may share a common factor enhancing performance of basic surgical skills. Due to the well-documented positive impact of video gaming on spatial perception (e.g., Green & Bavelier, 2007; Lager & Bremberg, 2005) and the correlation of spatial perception and endoscopic performance (Enochsson et al., 2004) spatial abilities are the most likely candidate for this factor. On the other hand, the adaptability of eye-hand control may be also a promising candidate. Unfortunately, the kind of game interfaces used in the video games is not clear. Another possible explanation is the role of elementary reaction abilities. In some studies on the impact of video game experience, the speed of surgical operations is significantly higher in video game users. Improvement of elementary reaction time is also a well-known effect of video games (e.g., Lager & Bremberg, 2005). Finally, due to the fact that most studies use a virtual simulator the correlation of video game experience and (virtual) surgery performance may also just be caused by a general familiarization effect to virtual environments.

The studies of Green and Bavelier (2007) and Dongen et al. (2011) provide some evidence that learning mechanisms rather than selection based on innate differences may play a dominant role.

Sport Skills

Evidence

Table 1 provides an overview of studies examining the impact of SG on sport skill learning.

Studies have been published analysing learning tasks in golf (Fery & Ponserre, 2001; Heinen et al., 2009), table tennis (Sohnsmeyer, 2011), sailing (Hebbel-Seeger, 2008), and basketball (Wiemeyer & Schneider, 2012).

Most of the studies do not find a specific perceptual-motor effect of games but rather a conceptual transfer of (strategic) knowledge.

This is indicated by the increase of knowledge (Sohnsmeyer, 2011) or symbolic transfer (Fery & Ponserre, 2001). Furthermore, specific learning effects in the 'virtual' game task can be found that only transfer to the 'real' task if there is a close similarity (Heinen et al., 2009). Another effect is the improvement of elementary perceptual functions like anticipation (Sohnsmeyer, 2011, studies 2 and 3).

Discussion

Taken together, the existing studies support the assumption that learning sport or sport-relevant motor skills can be enhanced by the application of SG. However, evidence is sparse and the mechanisms seem to involve either elementary or basic perceptual-motor processes (e.g., reaction) or cognitive transfer (knowledge and strategy). Improvement of the specific coordination in motor skills has rarely been assessed and could not be confirmed. Specific effects on motor skills seem to depend on the biomechanical or physical correspondence of game movement and sport movement requiring accurate measuring devices and classification algorithms. Furthermore, research designs and research methods are rather heterogeneous. Concepts and findings of movement science and biomechanics seem not to be included explicitly in the SG.

Children and youth have rarely been examined. Existing studies focus almost exclusively on the outcome of the movements rather than the quality of the movements. Furthermore, game experience is also widely neglected.

The interface technologies mostly used are the computer mouse and remote (motion) controllers. Concerning the application of contactless visual sensors only a proposed design is known (di Tore, D'Elia, Aiello, Carlomagno, & Sibilio, 2012).

Table 1. Overview of experimental studies on motor skill learning in sport

Authors (year) Sport skill	Sample size age	Instruction	Feedback	Practice	Interface technology	Tests	Results
Fery & Ponserre (2001) Golf (putting)	$N = 62$ $M = 19.7$ y Male students	2 factors: Attention (scale vs. swing), intention (transfer vs. fun) Additional information in the pre- and post-test (posture & alignment)	Concurrent & terminal	Virtual practice: 10 sessions of 20 trials	mouse	Pre-test Post-test (real putting, 10 trials)	Post-test: • AE & VE: scale > control • AE: scale & transfer > scale & fun • CE: no effects
Hebbel-Seeger (2008) Sailing	$N = 21$ NA Interested people	No specific 2 groups: game vs. no instruction	Concurrent (audiovisual) and terminal (verbal, visual)	Virtual practice, variable duration (criteria: finishing all tasks, sailing licence)	mouse	Post-test (real sailing)	Post-test: game > control No effects of session time and distribution
Heinen, Velentzas, Walter, & Goebel (2009) Golf (putting)	$N = 27$ 26 ± 2 y Sport students	Instructions: putting technique	Concurrent (audiovisual, haptic) and terminal (visual)	Virtual vs. real practice: 6 sessions of 25 minutes within 3 weeks (50 puts per session) Variable practice (distance, slope)	Wii remote controller (attached to a golf club)	Pre-test Post-test Retention test (real putting; 30 trials)	Post & retention test: • Virtual & real > control • Virtual & real improve, control not
Sohnsmeyer (2011) Table tennis	$N = 48/52/$ 69 16-18 y (Study 1) 12-14 y (Study 2) 20-24 y (Study 3)	Studies 1 & 2: No specific instructions Study 3: attention (gaming vs. shot technique)	Concurrent (visual, haptic) and terminal (visual)	Virtual vs. real practice: 4 sessions of 90 minutes (#1) 8 sessions of ≥ 20 minutes (#2) or 30 minutes (#3)	Wii remote controller	Pre-test Post-test Retention (anticipation, knowledge)	All studies: knowledge↑ (Wii) Studies 2 to 3: anticipation↑ (Wii)
Wiemeyer & Schneider (2012) Basketball (throws)	$N = 23$ $10.5 \pm$ y 1.1 Basketball players	No specific instructions	Concurrent (visual, haptic) and terminal (visual)	Virtual vs. real practice: 10 sessions within 5 weeks (75 throws per session)	Wii remote controller	Pre-test Post-test (performance, technique, transfer, self-efficacy, emotions)	Real & virtual post-tests: specific effects Technique: - Emotions: real > game

(Re-)Learning Motor Skills in Rehabilitation

Evidence

In rehabilitation, patients suffering from perceptual-motor impairments, for instance after stroke incidents, often have to perform repetitive movements with or without the assistance of a human or a technical device to regain perceptual-motor functions. Motivation and sometimes ability of the patients to perform these movements is either low because of their disease or negative experiences like pain or boredom or vanishes gradually because of missing incentives. Furthermore, depending on the stage of recovery, assistance has to be gradually removed.

Therefore, numerous game applications have been developed in perceptual-motor rehabilitation to enhance motivation by meaningful and functional movements, immediate and personalized feedback, and incentives (recent review: Wiemeyer

& Kliem, 2012) and to support personalized rehabilitation. The majority of the published papers are either technical reports (e.g., Schönauer, Pintaric, & Kaufmann, 2011), pilot studies or case reports (e.g., Betker, Desai, Nett, Kapadia, & Sztum, 2007). Randomized Controlled Trials (RCT) are rarely to be found (e.g., Yavuzer, Senel, Atay, & Stam, 2008).

Existing evidence shows that the quality of movements increases substantially when video games are applied to (motor) therapy. The respective studies also report a considerable increase of motivation and enjoyment.

Discussion

The interfaces used in the interventions range from off-the shelf game interfaces (e.g., joysticks, game controllers, balance board, or Kinect camera) to self-developed simple sensors (e.g., pressure mat; Betker et al., 2007) and highly sophisticated robots (e.g., ARMin; Nef, Guidali, Klamroth-Marganska, & Riener, 2009).

Looking at the existing studies, explicit reference to theories or principles of motor learning can be found (e.g., van Wijk et al., 2011). In the published papers, the issues of motivation, feedback, (visual and acoustic) cueing, adaptive physical guidance and functional movement (task-specific practice) are addressed.

Different to motor learning in sport, where skill training is added to games, in rehabilitation games are rather added to therapy. However, high-quality RCT studies are missing. Therefore existing evidence is preliminary and gives rise of hope that the application of SG to motor therapy may enhance efficiency, personalization, and sustainability.

Motor Abilities

As has been stated in the first section, motor abilities are differentiated into conditional and coordinative abilities. Concerning coordinative abilities particularly the acquisition and improve-

ment of balance and reaction abilities has been addressed by experimental studies. Whereas many studies deal with the influence of exergames, i.e., SG combining exercising (or exertion) and gaming, on energy expenditure and endurance training, only one study is known that addressed the improvement of strength as a conditional ability.

Balance Abilities

Brumels, Blasius, Cortright, Oumedian, and Solberg (2008) compared a traditional program to a Wii group and a Dance Dance Revolution (DDR) group (age of the participants: 18 to 24 years). All training programs consisted of 15 sessions (3 sessions per week over 5 weeks) and balance exercise of 12 to 15 minutes per session. The traditional training program comprised five different balance exercises, whereas the DDR group performed different dancing games while standing on one leg. The Wii group had to play three balance games (Ski Slalom, Table Tilt, and Balance Bubble) while standing on the Wii Balance Board. The authors applied two tests: Star Excursion Balance Test (SEBT) and postural stability using a force plate. Brumels et al. (2008) showed that all three programs improved balance, but the game groups had specific benefits concerning postural sway. Furthermore the game-based training was more motivating than the traditional training program.

Using a similar design (i.e., 3 weeks, 3 sessions per week, and 10 to 12 minutes of balance training per session), Kliem and Wiemeyer (2010) compared a traditional and a Wii group within a recreation centre (age: 18 to 67 years). The traditional training group performed four different levels of balance exercises whereas the Wii group played exactly the games applied by Brumels et al. (2008). Three kinds of tests were applied (two traditional tests: SEBT, ball handling; two Wii game tests: balance bubble, ski slalom; four dynamic balance tests). As a general result, the training program elicited specific effects: Whereas the traditional group improved predominantly in the traditional tests, the Wii group improved in the

Wii test. Furthermore, there was also a transfer from traditional to game experience and vice versa. The most important result is that both training programs transferred to dynamic balance tests. Because of a missing no-treatment control group it is not clear whether these results just represent a test repetition effect. Contrary to the results of Brumels et al. (2008) the participants of the Wii group did not report a more motivating experience. The Wii program was rated more difficult and less enjoyable compared to the traditional program. These differences in motivation may be either due to the age of the participants or the training context.

Vernadakis, Gioftsidou, Antoniou, Ioannidis, and Giannousi (2012) also compared a traditional program to a Wii training (duration: 8 weeks, two times per week, and 24 min per session). The Wii training included five Yoga exercises and three to four balance games per session, whereas the traditional program comprised exercises on a mini trampoline and an inflated rubber hemisphere. Each training group consisted of 16 undergraduate PE students. Before and after the training intervention a dynamic postural stability test was applied: The students had to maintain balance on an unstable balance platform. As a result, both groups improved significantly, but no group differences appeared. Again, a missing no-treatment control group makes the interpretation of true treatment effects difficult. The authors discuss the motivational and informational function of feedback as one possible reason for the learning effects in the Wii group.

Three further studies reviewed by Vernadakis et al. (2012) indicate that Wii-based balance training can enhance balance and reduce fear of falling in older people. Unfortunately, the studies are either of poor quality or not well documented. Furthermore, they do not consider game experience. Therefore it is not clear whether the results proposed by Kliem and Wiemeyer (2010) can be generalized.

Reaction Abilities

Three experimental studies have been published which all find a significant improvement of reaction times immediately after playing video games.

Clark, Lanphear, and Riddick (1987) compared the impact of a 7-week period of video gaming (at least 2 hours per week; two games: Pac Man and Donkey Kong) on the two-choice visual reaction performance of elderly subjects ($N = 7$; mean age: 65 years) to a no-treatment control group ($N = 7$; mean age: 74 years). Reaction time was assessed under high and low stimulus-response compatibility. The results show that the gaming group significantly improved reaction performance under both compatibility conditions. Furthermore, the gaming group could significantly reduce reaction time differences due to compatibility.

Dustman, Emmerson, Steinhaus, Shearer, and Dustman (1992) compared the influence of an 11-week period of either gaming or movie viewing (game group: three 1-hour sessions per week; movie group: two 1.5-hour sessions per week) on flicker sensitivity, cognition, mood, and reaction time (Sternberg test) to a no-treatment control group. The game group could choose between 12 video games. Each group consisted of 20 elderly persons (age: 60 to 79 years). The authors found significant improvements of reaction time in the game group, but neither in the movie nor in the control group. Cognitive and emotional functions did not change.

Goldstein et al. (1997) compared the impact of a five-week period of video gaming (SuperTetris; minimum duration of playing: five hours per week) on reaction time (Sternberg test), cognitive adaptability (Stroop test), and emotional well-being of elderly people ($N = 10$; age: $M = 76.5$ years; $SD = 3.8$) to a no-treatment control group ($N = 12$; age: $M = 78.7$ years; $SD = 6.4$). The only significant result was the improvement of reaction times in the game group.

Due to large variety of games and the lack of differences in other cognitive and emotional measures these effects seem to be unspecific and elementary speeding-up effects on central-nervous information processing.

Energy Expenditure and Endurance

As mentioned before, there are numerous studies (recent reviews and meta-analyses: Peng, Lin, & Crouse, 2011; Peng, Crouse, & Lin, 2012) indicating that playing exergames raises energy expenditure above a critical threshold of 3 METs (Metabolic Equivalents) or kcal per hour and kg body weight (i.e., three times rest energy expenditure). This may elicit small or moderate endurance training effects, but energy expenditure in these exergames is considerably lower than in the respective real sports activities (e.g., Graves et al., 2010). To reach the minimum volume of 500 to 1000 kcal per week recommended by the ACSM (2011), playing activities ranging from 2.5 to 5 hours per week are required. Existing longitudinal studies (reviews: Biddiss & Irwin, 2010; Peng, Crouse, & Lin, 2012) show inconclusive results indicating that under certain conditions endurance increases moderately after exergame-based training.

Strength Abilities

Sohnsmeyer, Gilbrich, and Weisser (2010) compared the impact of a 6-week gaming period (Wii bowling; 2 sessions of 20 minutes per week) on strength performance of 20 elderly participants (age: M = 76.95 years, SD = 4.84) to a no-treatment control group (N = 20; M = 77.75 years; SD = 8.69). Whereas the game group improved maximum strength of the knee extensors (m. quadriceps) significantly, the control group only showed a small improvement due to a test repetition effect.

Discussion

Existing evidence shows that improvement of coordinative or conditional abilities is possible by applying SG. Balance, reaction, endurance, and strength abilities can be improved particularly in samples with a low ability level, like older people. However, in some studies comparing game and conventional programs the latter seem to be slightly more effective.

Virtually all studies included untrained subjects who started at a comparatively low initial level. Therefore, it remains unclear whether the positive effects of gaming also hold for target groups with higher initial levels. Furthermore, dose-response relationships are not addressed. Motivation, fun, and other components of game experience have rarely been addressed.

A great variety of games and game interfaces have been used. Due to the general nature of abilities the game genre as well as the game interface does not seem to be as important as in motor skill learning.

In some studies, the basic principle of variable practice has been adopted by offering various games or physical exercises.

Discussion of Evidence

There is a considerable difference concerning the application of games and game interfaces in the different domains of motor learning. Whereas Off-The Shelf Games (OTSG) and game interfaces (i.e., mouse, joystick, remote controllers, contact mat, and balance board) were used in the domains of vocational skills, sport skills, and motor abilities, self-developed games and game interfaces are dominant in the area of motor (re-) learning in rehabilitation. This may be due to the fact that OTSG overload most patients concerning speed and complexity of motor actions as well as appropriate adaptation. Furthermore, the type and the accuracy of game interfaces do not seem to play an important role in the improvement of conditional and coordinative abilities (with the exception of balance). At a low initial level, reaction, endurance, and strength abilities can be improved by gaming activities that just require movements exceeding certain critical thresholds, whereas specific learning of motor skills requires accurate feedback for appropriate corrections.

Concepts of movement and training science have rarely been considered explicitly in the areas of vocational training, sport skill learning, and motor ability learning, whereas they are more often addressed in the area of rehabilitation.

On the other hand, studies of high quality can predominantly be found in the areas of sport skill learning and motor abilities.

SERIOUS GAMES FOR MOTOR LEARNING: TECHNOLOGY

Generally speaking, the application of SG to motor learning adds an additional degree of freedom to the complex interaction of learners, teachers, learning environment and learning matter, i.e. motor skill or ability (See Figure 3). In other words: SG technology has to fulfill all the functions and tasks characterizing high-quality 'traditional' learning and teaching of motor skills and abilities without compromising game experience or – to use a positive expression – with the additional challenge of establishing game experience like (intrinsic) motivation, fun, flow, challenge, immersion, tension, etc. (e.g., Nacke, 2009). Various scenarios are possible: SG may be part of the learning environment or/and they may also complement or substitute the teacher. They may be integrated into single-learner or cooperative learning scenarios.

According to the first section the following requirements have to be met be an effective SG:

- Appropriate instructions.
- Appropriate feedback.

- Appropriate practice schedule.
- Individualised information for different types of learners and different stages of learning.

The following technological solutions have been proposed to ensure "seamless learning":

- Micro and macro adaptivity.
- Adaptation and personalisation.
- Game mastering.
- Activity recognition and error detection (motion sensors & computer vision).

Micro and Macro Adaptivity

The concepts of *micro and macro adaptability* denote different 'educationally intelligent' techniques for flexible accommodation of SG according to the specific situation of the learner. Macro adaptation comprises 'traditional' techniques like adaptive presentation, navigation, curriculum sequencing, and problem solving support based on static learner's features. Due to the great challenge that adaptation must not compromise gaming experience, dynamic in-game (or 'stealth') real-time assessment of cognitive, perceptual-motor, emotional and motivational states is indispensable in order to provide appropriate non-disruptive micro adaptations, i.e., non-invasive adaptations like adaptive hinting, adaptive feedback, or an adaptive adjustment of the environment. The theory of micro-adaptability includes the following concepts (Kickmeier-Rust, Mattheis, Steiner, & Albert, 2011; Kickmeier-Rust & Albert, 2012): Competence-Based Knowledge Space Theory (CbKST) separates observable behavior from non-observable constructs causing this behavior, i.e., skills or competencies. To solve a particular problem, the player needs a specific set of skills or competencies. The skill function assigns a particular subset of competencies to the particular skill. To cover the dynamic process of problem solving as a meaningful sequence of problem solution states, a problem space model was developed, i.e., probabilistic models to estimate the likelihood of state transitions and the likelihood of reaching the solution state. This problem space model is:

Segmented into a set of possible problem solution states, each mapped to one of a set of possible competence states. By this means, the educational AI of a game can interpret the behaviour of the learner in terms of available knowledge, un-activated knowledge, or missing knowledge simply by matching the actions of the learner to competence states (Kickmeier-Rust & Albert, 2012, p. 18).

The technical implementation of micro adaptability comprises three components: assessment, educational reasoner, and adaptation realization. The assessment component provides a robust, meaningful, and simple estimation of skill and motivational states based on the observable variables like performance and psychophysiological indicators. Based on educational rules and meta-rules, the educational reasoner provides recommendations for appropriate adaptive interventions to the adaptation realization component, which implements the adaptive interventions, i.e., competency activation, competency acquisition, motivation, assessment clarification, or feedback. A challenge for the future is to include more subtle indicators of motivational and emotional states like gestures, mimics, force exerted on game controllers, etc.

Applied to the issue of motor learning, the relevant competencies, abilities, and skills can be assigned to specific tasks or groups of tasks of the game based on different concepts of movement and game structure. An example for a sport game (handball or basketball) is given in Table 2.

In Table 2 the first four task groups are comparatively simple because just one motor skill has to be performed based on appropriate motor abilities like orientation. Task groups 5 and 6 combine two skills which have to be executed in succession and which are based on more complex perceptual demands. Task groups 7 to 9 require the successive combination of three skills based on complex perceptual demands. Starting with task group 10 simultaneous and successive combinations of skills are required based on increasingly complex perceptual and adaptation demands. In the final task, all relevant skills and abilities are required.

Figure 4 illustrates a state transition model that was vertically structured according to the assignments of skills and abilities to tasks in Table 2. On the bottom level, the skills are performed in isolation, whereas the second level of task groups combines two skills. The third level contains three skills, which have to be executed in successive order, whereas the fourth level of task groups requires the simultaneous execution of two skills. On the fifth level five or six skills are combined in successive and simultaneous ways and on the sixth level all skills and abilities are required by the respective task group.

Task groups 1 to 4 serve as possible starting points. The transition between these task groups is allowed. From task group 1 and 2 the transition to task group 5 is allowed as well as the step back if the accomplishment of task group 5 is too difficult. The same holds for the transition from task groups 1 and 3 to task group 6. From task group 4 a direct transition to task group 9 is permitted, which results in a step back to task groups 5 or 6.

Due to comprehensiveness, the proposed model is very simple. The principle of arrangement of task groups is to systematically combine all skills and abilities in order to get clear information which skill or ability is already available and which skill(s) or abilities have to be addressed in isolation or appropriate combination with the available skills and abilities. Furthermore, in case of difficulties with the accomplishment of one task appropriate instructions, feedback, and change of practice schedule will be presented according to the rules and principles discussed in the first section.

Table 2. Example of assignment of abilities, or skills to specific task groups in a sport game

Task group (TG) Skill (S) Ability (A)	TG 1	TG 2	TG 3	TG 4	TG 5	TG 6	TG 7	TG 8	TG 9	TG 10	TG 11	TG 12	TG 13	TG 14	TG 15
S1 – Catch	x				x	x	x	x	x			x	x	x	x
S2 – Throw		x			x				x	x	x		x	x	x
S3 – Pass			x			x	x	x				x		x	x
S4 – Dribble				x			x	x	x		x		x	x	x
S5 – Jump										x	x		x	x	x
S6 – Run												x	x	x	x
A1 – Find a gap									x				x	x	x
A2 – Find a receiver			x			x	x	x				x		x	x
A3 – Avoid obstruction							x	x					x		x
A4 – Orientation	x	x			x	x	x	x	x	x	x		x	x	x
A5 – Be available					x	x	x	x	x			x	x	x	x
A6 – Adapt speed								x	x	x	x				x

Legend: S – skill; A – ability; TG – task group

Of course the assignment and transition models look different when a complex sport skill or perceptual-motor ability is the learning objective like pole vaulting or balance, respectively. In this case, different functional components like sub-skills or elementary perceptual-motor operations will be assigned to different tasks and exercises or numerous exercise variations assigned to the respective sub-abilities.

Adaptation and Personalization

Technology-enhanced games support further adaptation methodologies by directly measuring the reactions, movements, and behavior of the user. This potential is limited by the costs and possibilities, especially the accuracy and precision, of currently available sensors. These sensors need to be seamlessly integrated into the game setting and the gameplay to allow non-obstructive measurements and adaptation. In general, numerous different sensors allow the measurement and therefore the accurate and precise recording of performance parameters. This procedure is already applied in professional sports training and competitive sports. In these application fields, the heart rates of team members are recorded or the movements are captured with high-speed cameras and force platforms in order to analyze detailed aspects of movements, e.g., to optimize

Figure 4. Admissible task transitions according to Table 2. TG – task group; S – skill; A – ability; {} – set of skills and abilities required for the solution of the task.

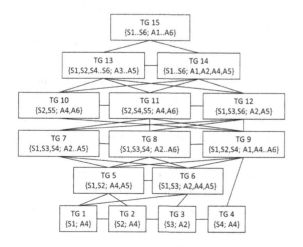

the ground reaction forces in sprint or high jump. The respective technology is very precise but often not portable, complex, time-consuming, and expensive. For the use in playful training scenarios, beyond comparably low costs, other minimum requirements for the applied sensors and actuators must be fulfilled.

To embed movement information in real-time in a game and in order to provide appropriate movement control and feedback, the used sensors need to work at high accuracy and precision, low delay and sufficient sampling rates. Depending on the training goals, measuring devices from professional or amateur sports can be used (cycling ergometer, chest belt). Independent of the specific sensors and their features, the adaptation process itself needs to be considered separately with respect to the application field. The proposed model, based on the model published by Hardy, Göbel, Gutjahr, Wiemeyer, and Steinmetz (2011) for the use of sensors to adapt exergames to a specific use (training goal), consists of three levels (See Figure 5): Constitutional Adaptation, User Experience Adaptation, and Physiological Adaptation. These levels need to be considered separately, but there are also interrelations between the three levels. The term 'adaptation' describes that a system can be modified in order to fulfill a specified goal. The term 'personalization' denotes adaptations that take into account individual attributes of multiple users. Figure 5 sketches the interdependencies among the different levels and the workflow within the levels.

The *Constitutional Adaptation* level describes the adaptation of the exergames to the physical constitution of the user. This includes the stature, physical limitations, and performance parameters such as maximum strength. The goal of the Constitutional Adaptation is to adapt the whole system according to the physical preconditions of the user. The adaptation of the hardware means adjusting the hardware to the body size, e.g. adjusting the saddle height on a cycling ergometer or providing a frame for balance training or by ex-

changing the hardware partly (e.g., the handles) or completely (small bike for small children). This allows the usage of a game for children and young adults as well as for full-grown adults, independent of their body size. The Constitutional Adaptation Layer therefore enforces a modular hardware design which allows the extension and modification of the hardware. Beyond the hardware, the minimum and maximum performance parameters are also important if the system is designed for different player types. Depending on age, gender, and physical condition, players vary strongly in their maximum performance capacity. Training at low performance levels and at a low cadence must offer the same control precision as training with high cadence and high performance. The adaptation control itself is realized by an adaptive game engine which alters the relation between sensor inputs, game objects and corresponding feedback.

The Constitutional Adaptation level also includes the accessibility aspects. The utilization of a game for a broad range of users, ranging from fully capable healthy persons to more or less impaired persons, can be realized by the adaptation of different types of feedback: visual, auditory, and haptic. Accessibility is not necessarily a hardware issue. Changing contrast, colors, and object size can help people with amblyopia. People with perceptual-motor impairments may need a higher delay and decelerated reactions of the game. In a balance training game, e.g., the sensitivity of the force sensors of the controller and the virtual weight of the ball can be adjusted. Consequently, the game can be played independently of the maximum strength of the player. This allows wheelchair drivers, people with gait impairments as well as healthy people to play at their individual performance limit, which ensures the most effective training load.

The *User Experience (UX) Adaptation* level describes the adaptation of a game according to the personal preferences of a user and according to the increasing cognitive skills of a user. The

Figure 5. Adaptation levels and their interactions

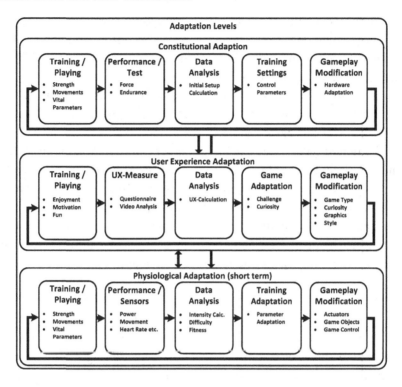

UX Adaptation takes into account different UX attributes, such as immersion or arousal. A direct or indirect measurement of the player experience by the use of sensors is challenging and a still unresolved current research issue. An adaptation is possible by incorporating the player in the adaptation process. This is possible by using questionnaires as shown for multiplayer online games. The first step in the UX adaptation process is the selection of an appropriate game from a set of games which meet the specified training goal. The selection can be determined based on a matching of specified characteristics (game type, style) or by testing a game for a short time. The definition and matching of such characteristics is a challenging task in UX research (Nacke, 2009).

A precise analysis and differentiation of the attributes relevant to UX is suggested. To measure fun a video analysis of facial expressions can be used. For the UX aspect of challenge, the gained points per time unit can be taken into account, but this is not necessarily corresponding to the experienced challenge or success level. Based on the measurements or on user ratings (perceived User Experience) another game can be suggested or the game can be adapted in a previously defined manner. The game 'BalanceFit', a balance training game for elderly people, e.g., allows modifying the amount of game objects or obstacles to change the (cognitive) challenge. Additionally, one or more game objects can be added to enhance the curiosity. A second option is the modification of physical parameters (resistance, sway area) in order to adjust the physical challenge. The adaptation is possible in real-time while playing the game or by the usage of an external tool (Mehm, Hardy, Göbel, & Steinmetz, 2011). Modifying the physical challenge also affects the perceived or cognitive challenge and vice versa.

The *Physiological Adaptation* (goal-specific adaptation) level describes the adaptation of the game to the requirements of sport science. This level consists of two adaptation loops, one short-term loop (real-time, during the runtime of a game) and one long-term loop (adaptation between two training sessions). Sensors in exergames measure positions (movements) or force of human limbs or the full body. This data is sampled with relation to the behavior of virtual objects inside a game. The behavior of virtual objects in a game can be used to communicate different types of feedback (visual, auditory, haptic) about body movements to a player. Training adaptation can be performed by the modification of parameter values, more specifically by changing the relations between game objects and therefore their behavior. These parameters are called Training Control parameters.

Game Mastering

The concept of *game mastering* addresses the issue that the in-game assessment of cognitive, perceptual-motor, motivational and emotional states might not be able to detect all possible individual combinations and constellations. Particularly, creative and innovative solutions that have not been foreseen by the game developers pose great challenges. Therefore, a game master is introduced as a complement:

A game master is a person who participates in the game in a meta role. The game master can observe, adjudicate, and influence the game. Being a human person, the game master has much more freedom in evaluating the performance of a player and giving useful feedback. Such a game master can evaluate innovative player solutions which the game itself cannot recognize (Wendel, Göbel, & Steinmetz, 2011, p. 222).

Thus, a flexible integration of gaming technology and human capabilities is established taking the advantages of both. However, several challenges have to be taken into account as shown in Wendel, Göbel, and Steinmetz (2012). These challenges include the design of a game master

interface for the respective game or application in order for the game master to be able to access all necessary information and to have all necessary means of adaptation available.

Activity Recognition and Error Detection

A very important issue in motor learning is the correction of errors. In order to correct errors they have first to be detected in real-time. As has already been mentioned in the previous sections, the automated and accurate detection of movement errors in real-time is a big challenge to game technology: First, the sensors that are used need to be very accurate and precise concerning spatial and temporal resolution because perceptual-motor skills are often very fast and show very small deviations from the correct movement. Second, error detection algorithms have to be very fast and robust. And third, every motor skill and ability has specific and often inter- and intraindividually different tolerances depending on the individual coordinative and conditional capabilities and the particular stage of the learning process. Therefore, error detection must be very flexible and adaptive.

Despite considerable progress in the domains of sensor-based and vision-based activity recognition, existing game controllers (e.g., Wii remote controllers and Sony move controllers) as well as cameras (e.g., the IR camera of the Kinect system) including the movement recognition algorithms still lack the required accuracy both from a biomechanical and from a perceptual-motor point of view (e.g., Bailey & Bodenheimer, 2012; Dutta, 2012; Martin & Wiemeyer, 2012).

SUMMARY AND CONCLUSION

In this chapter we addressed the issue of motor learning with SG. In the first section we introduced theoretical concepts discussed in movement and sport science that are relevant to the appropriate learning of motor skills and abilities. Numerous guidelines and principles for instruction, feedback, and organization of practice have been proposed. Therefore, theory and empirical research on motor learning offer elaborate possible solutions to many issues of motor learning.

In the second section we analyzed existing evidence concerning effectivity and efficiency of SG in motor learning. Existing evidence is promising, but still sparse. Research design and methods are extremely heterogeneous and do not follow a commonly agreed standard. Concepts of motor learning are not considered and included systematically. Many studies just prove the impact of SG on the respective motor skills or abilities without dealing with the issue of true game experience. A SG deserves its label only if both effects can be proved: achievement of the 'serious' goal and preservation of game experience.

In the third section we introduced selected technological solutions to main issues of motor learning with SG.

For the future numerous issues have to be addressed:

- Systematic inclusion of theoretical concepts of motor learning.
- Increasing accuracy and precision of game interfaces.
- Improving real-time algorithms for movement classification – including errors and tolerances.
- Enhancing adaptability and personalization.
- Evaluation studies including both detailed assessment of achievement of the serious goal as well as true gaming experience.
- Standards for high-quality experimental designs.

Finally, there is still a long way to go for SG. Quality has its price, and usually research programs do not establish the required sustainability. Rather successful interdisciplinary projects and examples of good practice in the domain of game-based motor learning may work as a motivation for commercial game industry to enhance engagement in SG in order to offer new motivating forms of acquiring and improving competencies in the various areas mentioned in the introduction. Particularly games addressing a broader audience (e.g., sport clubs, fitness studios, rehabilitation facilities or school) are promising candidates for commercial success. Furthermore, including other stakeholders like possible players, health and rehabilitation networks, engineering sciences, sport science, (neuro-)physiology and psychology may help promoting the idea of a more effective and efficient motor learning with Serious Games.

REFERENCES

ACSM. (2011). Quantity and quality of exercise for developing and maintaining cardiorespiratory, musculoskeletal, and neuromotor fitness in apparently healthy adults: Guidance for prescribing exercise. *Medicine and Science in Sports and Exercise*, *43*(7), 1334–1359. doi:10.1249/MSS.0b013e318213fefb PMID:21694556.

Badurdeen, S., Abdul-Samad, O., Story, G., Wilson, C., Down, S., & Harris, A. (2010). Nintendo Wii video-gaming ability predicts laparoscopic skill. *Surgical Endoscopy*, *24*, 1824–1828. doi:10.1007/s00464-009-0862-z PMID:20108147.

Bailey, S. W., & Bodenheimer, B. (2012). A comparison of motion capture data recorded from a Vicon system and a Microsoft Kinect sensor. In *Proceedings of SAP 2012,* (p. 121). New York, NY: ACM.

Bavelier, D., Levi, D. M., Li, R. W., Dan, Y., & Hensch, D. K. (2010). Removing brakes on adult brain plasticity: From molecular to behavioral interventions. *The Journal of Neuroscience*, *30*(45), 14964–14971. doi:10.1523/JNEUROSCI.4812-10.2010 PMID:21068299.

Betker, A. L., Desai, A., Nett, C., Kapadia, N., & Sztum, T. (2007). Game-based exercises for dynamic short-sitting balance rehabilitation of people with chronic spinal cord and traumatic brain injuries. *Physical Therapy, 87,* 1389–1398. doi:10.2522/ptj.20060229 PMID:17712036.

Biddiss, E., & Irwin, J. (2010). Active video games to promote physical activity in children and youth: A systematic review. *Archives of Pediatrics & Adolescent Medicine, 164*(7), 664–672. doi:10.1001/archpediatrics.2010.104 PMID:20603468.

Blischke, K., Marschall, F., Müller, H., & Daugs, R. (1999). Augmented information in motor skill acquisition. In Auweele, Y. V., Baker, F., Bidle, S., Durand, D., & Seiler, R. (Eds.), *Psychology for Physical Educators* (pp. 257–287). Champaign, IL: Human Kinetics.

Brumels, K. A., Blasius, T., Cortright, T., Oumedian, D., & Solberg, B. (2008). Comparison of efficacy between traditional and video game based balance programs. *Clinical Kinesiology: Journal of the American Kinesiotherapy Association, 62*(4), 26–31.

Clark, J. E., Lanphear, A. K., & Riddick, C. C. (1987). The effects of videogame playing on the response selection processing of elderly adults. *Journal of Gerontology, 42*(1), 82–85. doi:10.1093/geronj/42.1.82 PMID:3794204.

Connolly, T. M., Boyle, E. A., MacArthur, E., Hainey, T., & Boyle, J. M. (2012). A systematic literature review of empirical evidence on computer games and serious games. *Computers & Education, 59,* 661–686. doi:10.1016/j.compedu.2012.03.004.

Dongen, K. W., van Verleisdonk, E.-J., Schijven, M. P., & Broeders, I. A. M. J. (2011). Will the Playstation generation become better endoscopic surgeons? *Surgical Endoscopy, 25,* 2275–2280. doi:10.1007/s00464-010-1548-2 PMID:21416186.

Donovan, J. J., & Radosevich, D. J. (1999). A meta-analytic review of the distribution of practice effect: Now you see it, now you don't. *The Journal of Applied Psychology, 84*(5), 795–805. doi:10.1037/0021-9010.84.5.795.

Dustman, R. E., Emmerson, R. Y., Steinhaus, L. A., Shearer, D. E., & Dustman, T. J. (1992). The effects of videogame playing on neuropsychological performance of elderly individuals. *Journal of Gerontology, 47*(3), 168–P171. doi:10.1093/geronj/47.3.P168 PMID:1573200.

Dutta, T. (2012). Evaluation of the Kinect sensor for 3-D kinematic measurement in the workplace. *Applied Ergonomics, 43,* 645–649. doi:10.1016/j.apergo.2011.09.011 PMID:22018839.

Effenberg, A. O. (2005). Movement sonification: Effects on perception and action. *IEEE MultiMedia, 12*(2), 53–59. doi:10.1109/MMUL.2005.31.

Enochsson, L., Isaakson, B., Tour, R., Kjellin, A., Hedman, L., Wredmark, T., & Tsai-Felländer, L. (2004). Visuospatial skills and computer game experience influence the performance of virtual endoscopy. *Journal of Gastrointestinal Surgery, 8*(7), 874–880. doi:10.1016/j.gassur.2004.06.015 PMID:15531242.

ESA. (2012). *Essential facts about the computer and video game industry*. Retrieved from http://www.theesa.com/facts/pdfs/ESA_EF_2012.pdf

Fery, Y.-A., & Ponserre, S. (2001). Enhancing the control of force in putting by video game training. *Ergonomics, 44*(12), 1025–1037. doi:10.1080/00140130110084773 PMID:11780726.

Fleishman, E. A., & Rich, S. (1963). Role of kinesthetic and spatial-visual abilities in perceptual-motor learning. *Journal of Experimental Psychology, 66*(1), 6–11. doi:10.1037/h0046677 PMID:13945480.

Goldstein, J. H., Cajko, L., Oosterbroek, M., Michielsen, M., van Houten, O., & Salverda, F. (1997). Video games and the elderly. *Social Behavior and Personality*, *25*(4), 345–352. doi:10.2224/sbp.1997.25.4.345.

Grantcharov, T.P., Bardram, L., Funch-Jensen, P., & Rosenberg, J., J. (2003). Impact of hand dominance, gender, and experience with computer games on performance in virtual reality laparoscopy. *Surgical Endoscopy*, *17*, 1082–1085. doi:10.1007/s00464-002-9176-0 PMID:12728373.

Graves, L. E., Ridgers, N. D., Williams, K., Stratton, G., Atkinson, G., & Cable, N. T. (2010). The physiological cost and enjoyment of wii fit in adolescents, young adults, and older adults. *Journal of Physical Activity & Health*, *7*(3), 393–401. PMID:20551497.

Green, C. S., & Bavelier, D. (2007). Action-video-game experience alters the spatial resolution of vision. *Psychological Science*, *18*(1), 88–94. doi:10.1111/j.1467-9280.2007.01853.x PMID:17362383.

Hardy, S., Göbel, S., Gutjahr, M., Wiemeyer, J., & Steinmetz, R. (2012). Adaptation model for indoor exergames. *International Journal of Computer Science in Sport*, *11*(1), 73–85.

Hebbel-Seeger, A. (2008). Videospiel und sportpraxis - (k)ein widerspruch. [Video gaming and sport practice – no contraction]. *Zeitschrift für e-Learning, 3*(4), 9-20.

Heinen, T., Velentzas, K., Walther, M., & Goebel, R. (2009). (Video-)Spielend bewegungen lernen?! Einsatz und erforschung der effekte digitaler sportspiele. [Learning movements by video games?! Application of and research on the effects of digital sport games]. *F.i.t.*, *14*(2), 4-7.

Karageorghis, C. I., & Priest, D.-L. (2012). Music in the exercise domain: A review and synthesis (part I). *International Review of Sport and Exercise Psychology*, *5*(1), 44–66. doi:10.1080/1750984X.2011.631026 PMID:22577472.

Kickmeier-Rust, M., & Albert, D. (2012). Educationally adaptive: Balancing serious games. *International Journal of Computer Science in Sport*, *11*(1), 15–28.

Kickmeier-Rust, M. D., Mattheiss, E., Steiner, C. M., & Albert, D. (2011). A psycho-pedagogical framework for multi-adaptive educational games. *International Journal of Game-Based Learning*, *1*(1), 45–58. doi:10.4018/ijgbl.2011010104.

Kliem, A., & Wiemeyer, J. (2010). Comparison of a traditional and a video game-based balance training program. *International Journal of Computer Science in Sport*, *9*, 78–89.

Lager, A., & Bremberg, S. (2005). *Health effects of video and computer game playing: A systematic review*. Stockholm: Swedish National Institute of Public Health.

Landin, D. (1994). The role of verbal cues in skill learning. *Quest*, *46*, 299–313. doi:10.1080/00336297.1994.10484128.

Lee, T. D., & Genovese, E. D. (1988). Distribution of practice in motor skill acquisition: Learning and performance effects reconsidered. *Research Quarterly*, *59*, 277–287.

Lynch, J., Aughwane, P., & Hammond, T. M. (2010). Video games and surgical ability: A literature review. *Journal of Surgical Education*, *67*(3), 184–189. doi:10.1016/j.jsurg.2010.02.010 PMID:20630431.

Magill, R. A. (2010). *Motor learning and control: Concepts and applications* (8th ed.). Boston, MA: McGraw Hill.

Marschall, F., Bund, A., & Wiemeyer, J. (2007). Does frequent augmented feedback really degrade learning? A meta-analysis. *Bewegung und Training, 1*, 74–85.

Martin, A. L., & Wiemeyer, J. (2012). The impact of different gaming interfaces on spatial experience and spatial presence – A pilot study. In Göbel, S., Müller, W., Urban, B., & Wiemeyer, J. (Eds.), *E-Learning and Games for Training, Education, Health and Sports* (pp. 177–182). Berlin, Germany: Springer. doi:10.1007/978-3-642-33466-5_20.

Mehm, F., Hardy, S., Göbel, S., & Steinmetz, R. (2011). Collaborative authoring of serious games for health. In *Proceedings of the 19th ACM International Conference on Multimedia,* (pp. 807-808). New York, NY: ACM.

Nacke, L. E. (2009). *Affective ludology: Scientific measurement of user experience in interactive entertainment.* (Doctoral Dissertation). Blekinge Institute of Technology. Belkinge, Sweden.

Nef, O., Guidali, M., Klamroth-Marganska, V., & Riener, R. (2009). ARMin - Exoskeleton robot for stroke rehabilitation. In Dössel, O., & Schlegel, W. C. (Eds.), *WC 2009, IFMBE Proceedings 25/ IX* (pp. 127–130). Berlin, Germany: Springer.

Osgood, C. E. (1949). The similarity paradox in human learning: A resolution. *Psychological Review, 56*(3), 132–143. doi:10.1037/h0057488 PMID:18139121.

Peng, W., Crouse, J. C., & Lin, J.-H. (2012). Using active video games for physical activity promotion: A systematic review of the current state of research. *Health Education & Behavior.* Retrieved from http://heb.sagepub.com/content/early/2012/07/06/1090198112444956

Porter, J. M., & Magill, R. A. (2010). Systematically increasing contextual interference is beneficial for learning sport skills. *Journal of Sports Sciences, 28*(12), 1277–1285. doi:10.1080/02640414.2010.502946 PMID:20845219.

Ratan, R., & Ritterfeld, U. (2009). Classifying serious games. In Ritterfeld, U., Cody, M., & Vorderer, P. (Eds.), *Serious Games: Mechanisms and Effects* (pp. 10–24). New York, NY: Routledge.

Schmidt, R. A., & Wrisberg, C. A. (2008). *Motor learning and performance: A situation-based approach* (4th ed.). Champaign, IL: Human Kinetics.

Schöllhorn, W. I., Beckmann, H., & Davids, K. (2010). Exploiting system fluctuations: Differential training in physical prevention and rehabilitation programs for health and exercise. *Medicina, 46*(6), 365–373. PMID:20944444.

Schöllhorn, W. I., Beckmann, H., Janssen, D., & Drepper, J. (2010). Stochastic perturbations in athletics field events enhance skill acquisition. In Renshaw, I., Davids, K., & Savelsbergh, G. J. P. (Eds.), *Motor Learning in Practice: A Constraints-Led Approach* (pp. 69–82). London, UK: Routledge.

Schönauer, C., Pintaric, T., & Kaufmann, H. (2011). Full body interaction for serious games in motor rehabilitation. In *Proceedings of the 2nd Augmented Human International Conference.* New York, NY: ACM.

Shane, M. D., Pettitt, B. J., Morgenthal, C. B., & Smith, C. D. (2008). Should surgical novices trade their retractors for joysticks? Videogame experience decreases the time needed to acquire surgical skills. *Surgical Endoscopy, 22*, 1294–1297. doi:10.1007/s00464-007-9614-0 PMID:17972136.

Shea, C. B., Lai, Q., Black, C., & Park, J.-H. (2000). Spacing practice session across days benefits the learning of motor skills. *Human Movement Science, 19*, 737–760. doi:10.1016/S0167-9457(00)00021-X.

Sohnsmeyer, J. (2011). *Virtuelles spiel und realer sport – Über transferpotenziale digitaler sportspiele am beispiel von tischtennis* [Virtual games and real sport – About the transfer potentials of sport games using the example of table tennis]. Hamburg, Germany: Czwalina.

Sohnsmeyer, J., Gilbrich, H., & Weisser, B. (2010). Effect of a six-week-intervention with an activity-promoting video game on isometric muscle strength in elderly subjects. *International Journal of Computer Science in Sport, 9*(3), 75–79.

Tielemann, N., Raab, M., & Arnold, A. (2008). Effekte von instruktionen auf motorische lernprozesse: Lernen durch analogien oder bewegungsregeln? [Effects of instructions on motor learning: Learning by analogies or movement rules?]. *Zeitschrift für Sportpsychologie, 15*(4), 118–128. doi:10.1026/1612-5010.15.4.118.

Tore, S., di D'Elia, F., Aiello, P., Carlomagno, N., & Sibilio, M. (2012). Didactics, movement and technology: New frontiers of the human-machine interaction. *Journal of Human Sport & Exercise, 7*(1), S178–S183. doi:10.4100/jhse.2012.7.Proc1.20.

van Wijk, F., Knox, D., Dodds, C., Cassidy, G., Alexander, G., & MacDonald, R. (2011). Making music after stroke: Using musical activities to enhance arm function. *Annals of the New York Academy of Sciences, 1252*, 305–311. doi:10.1111/j.1749-6632.2011.06403.x.

Vernadakis, N., Gioftsidou, A., Antoniou, P., Ioannidis, D., & Giannousi, M. (2012). The impact of Nintendo Wii to physical education students' balance compared to the traditional approaches. *Computers & Education, 59*, 196–205. doi:10.1016/j.compedu.2012.01.003.

Wendel, V., Göbel, S., & Steinmetz, R. (2011). Seamless learning in serious games - How to improve seamless learning-content integration in serious games. In *Proceedings of the CSEDU 2011,* (vol. 1, pp. 219-224). SciTePress - Science and Technology Publications.

Wendel, V., Göbel, S., & Steinmetz, R. (2012). Game mastering in collaborative multiplayer serious games. In Göbel, S., Müller, W., Urban, B., & Wiemeyer, J. (Eds.), *E-Learning and Games for Training, Education, Health and Sports* (pp. 23–34). Berlin, Germany: Springer. doi:10.1007/978-3-642-33466-5_3.

Wiemeyer, J. (2003). Function as constitutive feature of movements in sport. *International Journal of Computer Science in Sport, 2*(2), 113–115.

Wiemeyer, J. (2004). Beyond representation and self-organisation: What is required in motor control and learning? In M. Bugdol, M. Kapica, & J. Pospiech (Eds.), Pogranicza Edukacji, (S.320-328). Raciborz: Scriba.

Wiemeyer, J., & Kliem, A. (2012). Serious games and ageing - A new panacea? *European Review of Aging and Physical Activity, 9*(1), 41–50. doi:10.1007/s11556-011-0093-x.

Wulf, G. (2007). *Attention and motor skill learning.* Champaign, IL: Human Kinetics.

Yavuzer, G., Senel, A., Atay, M. B., & Stam, H. J. (2008). Playstation eyetoy games improve upper extremity-related motor functioning in subacute stroke: A randomized controlled clinical trial. *European Journal of Physical and Rehabilitation Medicine*, *44*(3), 237–244. PMID:18469735.

KEY TERMS AND DEFINITIONS

Activity Recognition: Identification and classification of (game) actions.

Adaptation: Customization of (game) features depending on the prerequisites, needs, reactions or behaviour of the users and the gaming process.

Dynamic Systems Approach: Approach to motor control and learning that emphasizes the important role of dynamics and self-organisation within the complex interaction of organism, task, and environment.

Error Detection: Identification of movement errors.

Feedback: (Intrinsic and extrinsic) information delivered by the senses during the execution of the movement.

Game Mastering: Participation of a person fulfilling a meta-role, i.e., being able to control the gaming process by feedback, advice, or other interventions.

Information Processing: Approach to human learning and performance emphasizing the fundamental role of acquisition, analysis, and presentation of information including memory.

Instruction: All (informational) means of supporting (motor) learning.

Motor Learning: All (hypothetical and real) processes causing a permanent change of the ability to perform and transfer motor skills.

Serious Games: Digital game serving two purposes, i.e., game experience (fun, challenge, etc.), and additional purpose like learning, health-related behavior, or training.

Chapter 14
Clinical Virtual Worlds:
The Wider Implications for Professional Development in Healthcare

LeRoy Heinrichs
Stanford University, USA

Li Fellander-Tsai
Karolinska Institutet, Sweden

Dick Davies
Ambient Performance, UK

ABSTRACT

The deployment of virtual worlds into clinical practice is gradually becoming an accepted if innovative approach. This chapter offers an overview of the application of virtual worlds in a healthcare settings with specific focus on the application of virtual worlds in clinical practice. When combined with dynamic patient data models, facilitators are able to customize and deliver real time immersive clinical training experiences in a range of contexts. Given that virtual worlds are now being implemented in some of the more complex areas of healthcare, this chapter then explores how the lessons being learnt in this context could be applied more widely to other areas of professional development in the healthcare sector and concludes that direct and valuable lessons from mainstream clinical practice with virtual worlds are ready to be applied now more widely in the healthcare sector.

INTRODUCTION

Virtual worlds are increasingly accepted as part of the toolset for training in clinical practice. This chapter focuses on virtual worlds as a platform for training in the field of medicine and more widely in the field of professions allied to healthcare. The application of virtual worlds ranges from basic medical training to the professional development of full clinical practioners. Originally steming from text-based multiplayer games, virtual worlds enable scenario-based training for multiple users

DOI: 10.4018/978-1-4666-3673-6.ch014

– a key reality in today's team-based working environments. (See Graafland 2012) The deployment of virtual worlds for professional development in medical training is dependent on context and wider aspects. Today's stake holders range from traditional medical professions to allied health care professionals i.e. health care professions distinct from medicine, dentistry, nursing, and also emerging medical professions. The current generation of students and practitioners in health care are no longer naive regarding web based communication. Frequent exposure and use of these techniques during childhood and adolescence creates new demands and sets the scene for a new educational and training paradigm. Virtual worlds for development of both technical- and non technical skills as well as basic cognitive training are discussed. A review of ongoing projects using virtual worlds for professional development in general including different platforms and case studies is presented as well as lessons learned based on delivered attributes (Hew, 2010; Peterson, 2010; Wiecha, 2010).

Current aims in healthcare to reduce error in clinical practice has led to a recognition of simulated training in managing crisis situations (Knudson, 2008; Wallin, 2007). Serious games represent an emerging asset in view of this trend (Knight, 2010). Linked to this, virtual world technology is emerging in medical training and is a result of technology-supported, individualized teaching and training originally inspired from established and widespread leisure and entertainment games. Interactive and visualization based modes of learning are increasingly advocated. Virtual worlds have the capacity to engage and activate the learner by means of visualization even where the focus is on simple procedures or on scenario based training. Clinical virtual worlds enable role-playing serious games or multiuser virtual environments that are related to gaming technologies in which the users are represented in virtual worlds by avatars.

Serious games provide judgement-free environments in which the player(s) can safely "trial and error". In many ways this is comparable to game-play in childhood and adolescence. The ability to be 'good' at a game is not innate; skills are acquired and developed through repetitive practice (Ericsson,1993). One of the commonly assumed strengths using serious games is the capacity to engage and thus motivate the "player" i.e. learners who are represented in the virtual world by an avatar.

Virtual worlds allow teams of professionals to train cases simultaneously, i.e. implicitly training collaboration and single professionals to train on multiple cases i.e. training multitasking. Training these non-technical skills are recognized as critical in reducing medical errors in dynamic high risk environments, like the operating room or the emergency department. Serious games also present training environments for complex disaster situations and mass casualty incidents, including combat care (Heinrichs, 2010).

Game-designers agree that optimal design of serious games focuses on engagement and thus motivation of the player and not primarily on educational content. Learning objectives must be well integrated and embedded into the design in advance. Realistic virtual surroundings, in which sights, sounds, and confusion are mimicked, provide a complete experience and improve preparation. On the other hand, the main current pedagogical approaches emphasize the need for self-regulated learning. This requires an active and constructive process wherein learners need to define goals for their learning and then, aim at controlling their performance and behavior in a specific context, e.g. virtual worlds enabling procedure - and/or scenario based training by means of visualization (See Section 3 of this chapter).

In summary, the primary objective of this chapter is to show how a diverse range of virtual worlds have and are being applied in clinical settings. In particular, it aims to demonstrate that a sub-set of virtual worlds, namely clinical virtual worlds, have differentiated from all purpose virtual worlds and are maturing into a specific category that can play a valuable part in the education of clinical professionals. The secondary objective of the chapter is to investigate how professional development in other healthcare professions is being assisted by the use of virtual worlds. Associated with this objective this chapter concludes by arguing that the generic lessons learnt from the use of virtual worlds in educating clinical professionals could be applied profitably as an educational tool in many of the professions allied to healthcare.

CLINICAL VIRTUAL WORLDS: CATEGORIZED OVERVIEW OF VIRTUAL WORLDS IN CLINICAL PRACTICE

Over time, the language describing virtual worlds is becoming more descriptive and precise. A decade ago, a Virtual Medical Centre could mean an online aggregation of medical literature, such as in a virtual library on a webpage (Wikipedia, 2012). More recently, the term Virtual Worlds (VWs) has come to indicate online, 3-dimensional spaces containing one or more interactive avatars and objects/medical devices, much like a video game, e.g. World of WarCraft. Earlier virtual worlds, especially those for entertainment use were 'single-player', but recently many are now 'multiplayer'. Developers in the entertainment and gaming sector often prefer the acronyms MUVEs (multi-user virtual environments), MMOVEs (massively, multi-player, online, virtual environments), MMORPGs (*massively, multiplayer, online role-playing games),* or VLEs (Virtual Learning Environments) to describe Multiplayer Virtual Worlds that accommodate teams.

This section:

1. Surveys free-to-use or low cost multiplayer virtual worlds identifying, where known, current or past clinical or health-related uses.
2. Explores examples of commercial virtual worlds being deployed in clinical contexts: Clinical Virtual Worlds.

3. Finally, touches briefly on new developments in the deployment of clinical virtual worlds, notably on mobile platforms.

Free-to-Use and Low Cost Virtual Worlds

An important technical consideration in choosing a virtual world software program/platform on which these environments are built; most are not interchangeable. The most widely popular platform is Second Life (Linden Labs, San Francisco, CA) that sells 'islands' on which tens of thousands of users have built customized facilities and avatars using primatives ('prims') as the development language. Estimates are of 30 million users registered in Second Life, and that 30-50,000 are in-world at any time (Gridsurvey, 2012). Users include international corporations such as IBM and Cisco, which may regularly conduct online staff meetings for dispersed personnel, or educational institutions that build facilities that simulate established buildings with familiar objects/devices used by students for learning and practicing procedures see University of Arkansas's list of studies (2012). As an example of institutional applications, the University of Kansas (2012) exhibits art dynamically in its Spencer Hall Museum.

An outstanding, medically related contribution by the Department of Biosurgery and Surgical Technologies at Imperial College London is its' scenario-based, medical simulation in the 3D virtual world of Second Life where four Second Life islands are occupied. NanoDave (Taylor, 2011) states in his blog, "Our research illustrated the use of Second Life as a novel platform for immersive clinical training. Participants were able to learn and practice in a complex but safe environment where they could make mistakes without risk to any real patients. The project was awarded a 'Special Mention' by Linden Lab as an innovative virtual world project that improves the way people work, learn, and communicate in their daily lives outside of the virtual world."

Another source of information about Second Life is the Webicina reviews by Mesko (2012) His website offers medical community sites, pharmaceutical companies, research groups and clinics advice about how to create a properly designed online presence and reach their target audience effectively through social media platforms. An example of one of these Second Life sites is the Ann Myers Medical Clinic supported by Sprott-Shaw College in Canada, whose nursing students use the Clinic for developing skills in initial exam history and physicals, focusing upon listening skills, teaching them that they can heal simply by listening and caring, assisting students to become more proficient in the analysis of MRIs, CTs and X-rays, and in learning about psychoimmunobiology, the body's ability to heal itself through the stimulation of the immune system to fight disease (Anne Myers Medical Centre, 2012). The Clinic uses a group of volunteering professionals who meet online with scheduled groups and drop-ins. An informative, if controversial critique of Second Life has been published by Young (2010).

A recent entry into the group of virtual worlds is OpenSimulator (OpenSim, 2012), an open-source, community-based platform developed using libsl (a BSD open source library for creating custom clients that can connect to Second Life). The original idea behind OpenSimulator was the goal of creating a proof of concept server that the Second Life client could connect to, offering some basic functions. OpenSim continues pursuing innovative directions towards becoming the "bare bones, but extensible, server of the 3D Web, ultimately independent of Second Life." At The Journal (2011) one can find a good comparison of the advantages and disadvantages of Second Life and OpenSim. Applications in healthcare topics are slim in OpenSim with a notable exception, biomechanics. Groups at Stanford and Knoxville, TN, USA have used OpenSim to model components of the musculo-skeletal system (Delp, 2012) A team at the VA Hospital in San Diego, USA has developed a virtual hospital at which they have conducted a decontamination drill (Greci, 2011). This team has also used Second Life.

ActiveWorlds (2012) is another product that offers over 1000 virtual environments useful for holding meetings, chatting, shopping, etc. No medical environments are identified. Another platform, Open Cobalt, (Open Cobalt, 2012) is designed to enable the deployment of secure virtual world spaces that support education, research, and the activities of virtual organizations. By leveraging OpenGL-based 3D graphics, Open Cobalt supports highly scalable collaborative data visualization, virtual learning and problem solving environments, 3D wikis, online gaming environments (MMORPGs), as well as privately and securely maintained multi-user virtual environments. This innovative platform, designed by Duke University, USA using Squeak, Sketchup and Blender software, is a tool for accessing and interacting with virtual workspaces that can exist anywhere on the Internet (rather than a virtual world in itself) in the same way that one thinks of a web browser as a tool for accessing and interacting with web pages. Open Cobalt's ability to leverage peer-to-peer technology as a way of supporting interactions within virtual worlds is a major point of difference from commercial multi-user virtual world systems such as Second Life where all in-world interactions are managed by central servers. Open Cobalt is in early development.

The original technology behind Teleplace—and its' OpenQwaq—was Open Croquet (OpenQwaq, 2012). It was a basic tool set, not a complete virtual world platform, and it was distributed under the MIT license—that permits reuse in proprietary applications. Teleplace was a virtual world platform built on top of the Open Croquet components. By comparison, the OpenSim server software is released under the BSD license, which allows vendors to create derivative works, keep them proprietary, and profit from them. RealXtend, a mesh-enabled branch of OpenSim that's been rebuilt from the ground up as a game development platform, is released under the Apache 2 license, which also allows proprietary works. OpenWonderland (Open Wonderland, 2012), a Java-based virtual world platform originally launched by Sun Microsystems, but spun off after the acquisition by Oracle, is licensed under GPL 2 with a "Classpath" exception, allowing vendors to distribute proprietary add-on modules. Another member of this group is ProtoSphere 2.0, a sophisticated business collaboration software platform that can easily be deployed within any organization through either a Cloud/SaaS offering or a traditional on-premise install. It is built on Microsoft's *Lync,* a browser-based software (Protonmedia, 2012). TheraSim, a Web-based knowledge assessment tool that offers virtual patients (Therasim, 2012), TheraSim's Metrics captures and tracks with its' TheraSim 360 technology the decisions and actions that users make throughout the courses provided by the 2D system for medicine, nursing, pharmacy, and allied-health. Jibe, developed by ReactionGrid (Reaction Grid, 2012), is a multiuser 3D virtual world platform accessible via a web browser or standalone client. Jibe allows one to design and manage their own virtual world that can either be hosted by ReactionGrid or fully installed on remote servers.

The penchant is great for low-cost or free tools developed by computer scientists working with open source platforms. Potential users seek spatial assets that can be implemented and extended to include diverse assets on many topics such as for marine life, mining, biology, etc. Open source platforms also work well for educational institutions where instructors seek design and development experience for students, and as well as for individuals who enjoy the experience of creative design and development of VWs as a hobby, or 'side-interest'. Thus, most open-source programs grow slowly or in unpredictable directions that do not serve well the focused user. An exception is the Imperial College group—mentioned earlier in this section—that has subsisted with sustained government grants/awards.

Commercial Virtual Worlds in Clinical Contexts: Clinical Virtual Worlds

In contrast, the creation of fully functional Virtual Worlds requires a dedicated design effort and platform development team which can advance the software as new capabilities are recognized, a technical team with skills in graphical representations, lighting, movement, and even behavior, to enable the creation and maintenance of Virtual Worlds with the quality needed for incorporation as learning tools, and finally, managers with a vision for different applications. This requirement for multiple collaborators usually necessitates funding over time to sustain the endeavor as a business. Medicine is a 'business sector' that justifies such an investment, or as is also common, game companies seeking to expand into new markets, target healthcare as offering multiple and diverse opportunities in which to begin creating new and useful virtual world products.

An example of an award-winning virtual world is ARA's Virtual Heroes, created by a North Carolina, USA -based company that has licensed the Epic Games' Unreal Engine 3, for developing simulations based upon its' HumanSim platform for medical education and training (ARA, 2012). An example of the products available from ARA is *Pamoja Mtaani,* an open-world game focused on HIV infections that allows up to five players in selected youth centers throughout Nairobi to work together through a collection of 'twitch mini-games'. Each player takes on the role of a unique character and plays through a quest that has been developed to be both fun and educational. In its 3DiT product, a high-fidelity, virtual field hospital, the player begins a scenario awaiting the patient's arrival. Players act in their pre-assigned role as a doctor, nurse, technician, or observer as the instructor begins a briefing for the upcoming patient interaction. Upon the patients' arrival, the team enters and begins to assess and treat the patient. The instructor's user interface allows manual control over the patient's vital signs in response to the player actions or allows the embedded physiology engine to control patient's response. Once the patient is stabilized, a telephone handoff takes place between the care team and the receiving care team. The team then reassembles outside the patient care area to perform a debriefing (Virtual Heroes, 2012). Duke University is said to be developing an anesthesia simulation on this platform.

From 2003-2004, two of the authors (WLH, L-FT) and their teams, developed using a beta version of *Atmosphere* from Adobe Systems' a virtual emergency medical environment suitable for team learning. In an international collaboration, they conducted a study comparing learning by medical students using scenarios developed on a high-fidelity mannequin in a simulated emergency medical department, with the same scenarios presented in the virtual environment that had an elementary physiology model. With a pre-test, post-test design with four interval cases, the 'real' and the virtual environments produced equivalent results. This platform ceased being supported in 2006, but realizing these unexpected but beneficial findings led these teams to subsequent experiences with further virtual worlds.

Subsequently, in their early entry into developing virtual worlds for applications in medical education in 2004, WLH and his colleagues at SUMMIT (Stanford University Medical Media and Information Technologies) developed a beta version copy of a virtual world designed on *Atmosphere* (Adobe Systems, Inc.) in which virtual trauma victims could be managed in a very elementary, 3D virtual emergency department (Heinrichs, 2008b; Youngblood, 2008). The unexpected result was that the same scenarios simulated in a simulation laboratory with high-fidelity mannequins yielded equivalent results among 30 graduating medical students exposed to either of these training environments. Efforts to publish these before and after design experimental study results were resisted during three submissions to clinical practice journals.

Another early entry into the field of virtual worlds was OLIVE (On-Line Interactive Learning Environment), developed by Forterra Systems, USA, after the company 'spun-off' *There*, a 'social entertainment environment'. That virtual world was billed as ". . . an online getaway where you can hang out with your friends and meet new ones . . ." (Wikipedia, 2012) In contrast, OLIVE was developed to serve up private and secure MMO virtual worlds for corporate, government, defense, medical and educational clients which launched them in their private IT networks (Wikipedia – Forterra Systems, 2012) Another differentiating feature of OLIVE environments is that real-world locations are replicated in OLIVE virtual worlds, as opposed to fantasy-based worlds or hypothetical "islands." One of the authors (WLH) and his colleague at Stanford, Parvati Dev, PhD, were recruited by Forterra to build a medical environment in OLIVE. Using anonymysed photos of clinical environments in the Stanford University Medical Center, this new component offered opportunity to evaluate virtual worlds for their benefit in medical education. With US government funding focusing on training First Responders and civilian caregivers for terrorist attacks and requiring the triage of potential victims, emergency facilities were created that enabled users to learn and practice emergency management skills needed in mass casualty events. Two situations were simulated; exposure to a nerve gas (sarin) that produces asphyxia in victims, and exposure to an explosion that produced traumatic hemorrhage with subsequent hypovolemic shock. The avatars' physiology models reflected these lethal conditions that were a consequence unless remediation was instituted. Research conducted among practicing emergency providers indicated a strong endorsement of training in OLIVE (Heinrichs, et al., 2010).

Given the availability of the OLIVE training environment, and funding from the Wallenberg Global Learning Network (WGLN, 2005), another medical application (Simergency, 2006) was trialled in another international collaboration with the Karolinska Institutet in Stockholm, Sweden. (Creuzefelt, In press) Anticipating the use of this immersive environment by the general public, the gestures of Cardio-Pulmonary Resuscitation (CPR) were created by the Forterra OLIVE development team, and studies were conducted among high school students in both countries, and among medical students in Sweden, by two of the authors (WLH, L-FT) and their teams. The results show that students at both levels of education enjoy the training exercise, and want more examples. The latest studies confirm that repetitive training is required to maintain proficiency beyond six months (Creutzfeldt, 2009). It has also been demonstrated however, that repetitive virtual world training of CPR seems to prevent learning decay regarding CPR guidelines (Creutzfeldt, 2010).

Another application of the OLIVE platform has been developed by InWorld Solutions, LLC. The InWorld product supports the delivery of on-line role-playing and therapeutic assessments via the OLIVE virtual world.(Frenkel, 2012) [Note: The OLIVE virtual world platform and Forterra Solutions has been purchased by SAIC – Systems Applications International Coorporation, a fortune 500 company that services US military modeling and simulation needs (Koskovich, 2009). SAIC is working on a browser-based version of OLIVE, hosted on the UNITY platform.] InWorld has worked with SAIC to conduct Operational Assessments for the US Air Force on the potential use of the OLIVE Virtual World for behavioral healthcare within the US Department of Defence. "Virtual reality avatars give you space for direct experience and emotional impact," said Ivana Steigman, project director. "It gives people space not to just talk about things and imagine them, but to actually do them" (Steigman, 2011).

BreakAway, USA, is another leading developer of entertainment games and game-based technology products that create entertainment experiences enabling people to master skills and concepts in virtual worlds, preparing them to transfer this game-based expertise for real world problems (Breakaway Games, 2012). Using the mōsbē™ desktop development studio, BreakAway located in Maryland, USA, designs strategy-based platforms to enable military, homeland security, medical, and corporate customers to solve real-world problems with the situational realism and experiential engagement of game-based simulation. Powered by BreakAway's Pulse!! technology, the company provides a unique Dental Implant Training Simulation that provides engaging, distributable, game-based learning. In this 3D, virtual environment students guide their avatar and interact with virtual patients to practice the proper decision- making protocol to determine if the patients are physically and mentally prepared for dental implant procedures. If surgery is required, the student then practices the procedure in a safe, realistic environment.

In the behavioral medicine arena, Albert "Skip" Rizzo at the University of Southern California's Institute for Creative Technologies, USA, co-developed Virt*ual Iraq,* a simulation program the Department of Defense is hoping can help Iraq veterans suffering from post-traumatic stress disorder, commonly known as PTSD. In collaboration with the Naval Medical Center-San Diego Virtually Better Inc. (Virtually Better, 2012) and the Geneva Foundation, they used a modified version of the video game *Full Spectrum Warrior* to recreate traumatic events from combat veterans' lives.

In a final example Clinispace is an example of an emergent sub-type of focused virtual worlds, in this case what the authors have termed a 'Clinical Virtual World.' CliniSpace™, CliniSpace Nursing™, and BattleCare™, are products of Innovation in Learning, Inc. a California-based company co-founded by an author – WLH and his long-time collaborator, Parvati Dev, PhD. (Dev, 2011) The newest of the examples of virtual worlds described in this chapter, each of IIL's products has won awards in competitions: two have been Grand Champion awards in the U.S. Army's most-recent, annual GameTech Challenges, and the third was awarded 2nd place at INACSL, an international organization of simulation nurses. Built upon the Unity3D platform by Indusgeeks Solutions, Limited in Mumbi, India for IIL, Inc., CliniSpace offers several virtual environments comprising most of a virtual hospital, including a medical clinic, hospital ward, intensive care unit, a neonatal resuscitation space, and a conference room where briefings with Second Life sets or videos are available, and where the action log can be accessed for debriefing after the 'training exercise.' As users enter a selected learning space using passwords for security, they assume assigned roles for learning and practicing clinical assessment and management. Two virtual patient avatars are in each Virtual Learning Environment, offering clinical challenges in topics of acute traumatic hemorrhage or sepsis. An interactive physiology model operates either continuously, or in state-based scenarios set with authoring tools (Heinrichs, 2008a).

The advanced features of the CliniSpace products, going beyond their very realistic graphical fidelity, are the set of interactive objects and devices that are integrated with the virtual patient's physiology model. Only after identifying the virtual patient using a barcoder available in the electronic medical record machine, is it possible to attach blood pressure cuffs to register the systolic and diastolic pressures, finger-clips are attached to measure the SpO_2, and a urethral catheter enables recording of urine secretion rates reported by selecting the virtual patient. (See Figure 1) The ability for users to select washing their hands is optional. The avatars are dynamic, exhibiting different appearances, including skin rashes, paleness or flushing with a fever, and petechiae (minute blood clots in the skin), different motions including shivering, coughing, vomiting, or seizures, and different behaviors such as fatigue, anxiety, sluggish responsiveness, or coma.

Interactive objects selected with the cursor deliver intravenous, resuscitative fluids of five types selected from a 'pop-up' menu, a pharmacopeia with 12 categories of medications that change the medical model, i.e., stopping a seizure from excessive blood loss using an anti-convulsant medication, and an ultrasound or a monitor for displaying video clips or images appropriate to the scenario (See Figure 2). A training facilitator can access the Web pages for each team member whose performance has been automatically recorded for individual review and discussion. This description indicates the wisdom of Steigman's comment (Steigman, 2012), that virtual worlds are indeed *places* in which to 'talk about' and 'imagine things',... and as mentioned with *There*, to 'hang out', but they accommodate 'doing stuff', which in healthcare means assisting patients. CliniSpace provides the needed interactive objects/devices and virtual patients needed to accomplish the goal of providing an immersive learner experience in simulated medical care.

Figure 1. Virtual patients in Clinispace

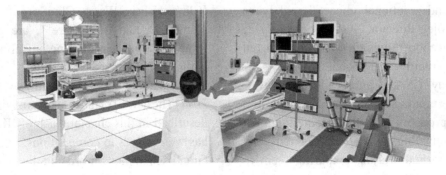

Figure 2. Virtual patient in Clinispace showing real time physiological model in operation via vital signs monitor

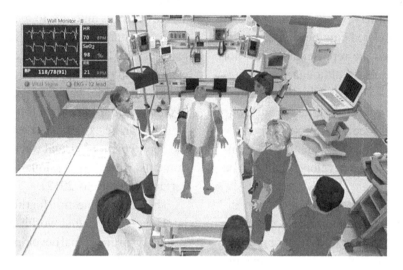

Mobile Platforms for the Delivery of Clinical Virtual Worlds

Mobile platforms offer at least two benefits to users. The first is the convenience of displaying applications on a device that is conveniently used by those 'on-the-move.' Several of the above platforms and products have been deployed on mobile devices, including mobile phones. The second benefit is intrinsic to the interface of the iPad – and similar 'pads'. Its touch-screen enables a new experience for users, the ability of interacting digitally with virtual patients, similarly as they do with 'real' patients. At this time, the authors are unaware of any virtual world beyond BattleCare that applies the second benefit.

In the BattleCare simulation of an Acute Traumatic Life Support (ATLS) scenario, a single-user interacts, using the touch screen of an iPad, with a virtual wounded warrior who has 'taken-a-shot' in the chest. The victim is delivered to the field hospital in an ambulance from which the user extracts the stretcher by grasping and pulling it out.

As the ABC procedures are applied, the user opens the victims mouth to insert, from a supplies bag, the suction syringe to aspirate the oropharynx, followed by listening to both sides of the chest and the central chest with a stethoscope (Virtual sounds are gratis Lipmann Stethoscopes), also pulled from the supplies bag.(See Figure 3) Thereafter, the user cleans the wound with a sponge from the supplies bag, followed by inserting a chest tube, (also secured from the supplies bag), that aspirates the chest cavity to re-inflate the injured lung. The iPad enables a new concept in medical simulation, the intuitive application of the caregivers' touch for producing beneficial change, simulating 'real-life' experiences.

Figure 3. Clinispace BattleCare simulation on Apple iPad

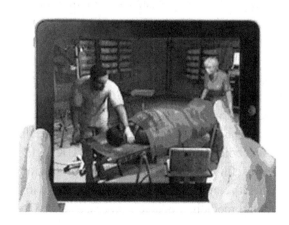

In summary, a clear message from the above descriptions of virtual worlds is that the genre comprises a wide variety of designs, topics, and scope, and that more are being developed by the day. Those described are representative but not exhaustive; for an extensive, although a 'not-quite-up-to-date' listing – *There,* in the discontinued category, has been reactivated, and *CliniSpace* has not been listed (see Metaverse Standards, 2012). At Health Games Research (2012), another list of serious games developers can also be viewed.

Current applications of virtual worlds for medical education suggest that the future is bright, as they seem to be maturing beyond infancy into childhood with the arrival of focussed specialist virtual worlds such as Clinispace. Many new opportunities for healthcare applications will challenge their future sophistication and development. We encourage users to determine their value for learning and practicing clinical skills by conducting and publicizing assessment studies.

CLINICAL VIRTUAL WORLDS: WIDER IMPLICATIONS FOR PROFESSIONAL DEVELOPMENT IN HEALTHCARE

Looking through the recruitment websites for healthcare professionals and then surfing the numerous educational institutional sites offering healthcare professional inhouse or online courses, one cannot be other than amazed by the variety of professions, other than for physicians and nurses, that now exist. Here is a limited sample: Respiratory Therapist; Health Educator; Medical Technician; Cardiographer; ECG Technologist; Cytotechnologist; Perfusionist; Phlebotomist; Sonographer; etc. For a UK example of health career choice, see NHS Careers (NHS UK, 2012). As a useful definition, allied health professions are health care professions distinct from dentistry, nursing, medicine, podiatry and pharmacy. One

estimate reported allied health professionals make up 60 percent of the total health workforce. Worldwide this amounts to many, many millions of professionals (Wikipedia – Allied Health Professions, 2012). In the context of this chapter's examination of the application of clinical virtual worlds into wider healthcare professional areas: "Whilst technology development [for virtual worlds] can be extrapolated with some certainty, the deployment of virtual worlds in specific sub-domains within professional healthcare is less certain" (Heinrichs 2012).

The framing question for this section therefore is, 'How might virtual worlds be exploited more widely for professional development in healthcare beyond the clinical practice provided by physicians and nurses?' It has already been demonstrated in this chapter that there a range of examples of the innovative implementation of virtual worlds primarliy in clinical care, so the focus in this section is on their application to that wide range of allied healthcare professions listed above.

To link back to the title of this section, a number of questions can be asked about deployment of virtual worlds more widely in healthcare:

1. What lessons can be drawn about professional development from the deployment of Virtual Clinical Worlds (VCWs)? What is particular about learning in clinical settings that VCWs can deliver and that other delivery methods cannot/cannot do as well?
2. Of these lessons which are specific to the clinical practice context and which are more generic? (What criteria would you use to decide which are clinical practice dependant and which are not?)
3. How might these more generic lessons be applied more widely in other healthcare areas? (What criteria would you use from these other healthcare areas to see if these generic lessons might be applicable?)

Taking these questions in turn:

What Lessons Can be Drawn About Professional Development in Clinical Virtual Worlds?

Previously it has been argued (Heinrichs, 2012) that in **clinical practice** VWs are being deployed because they offer the following attributes:

- Presence
- Immersion i.e. engagement
- Team based activities
- Real workplace settings
- Safe 'play spaces'
- Relatively low cost (compared to custom healthcare game development)

The important question is that, given these attributes, "Why are VWs being deployed for professional development"? LInked to this question and in the context of clinical professional development: "Becoming a skilled professional requires the acquisition of theoretical knowledge and the practice of skills under the guidance of an expert. The idea of learning-through- apprenticeship is long accepted in medicine, and, more generally, in the health sciences, where practicum courses are an essential part of most curricula" (Chodos, 2010).

If we address this practicum requirement directly and unpack what we are offering from a theoretical perspective in the educational context then:

1. Virtual worlds are offered both as simulated environments and environments for simulation.
2. Simulation-based learning is supported by Situated Cognition Theory (Brown, 1989).
3. Situated Cognition Theory is underpinned by Social Constructivism (Wertsch, 1995).
4. Social Constructivism is underpinned by a Theory of Knowledge that says that knowledge is a social construction..

Constructivism views the learner as active not passive. Social constructivism understands that we do not construct knowledge ('our view of the world') alone, but that we always do it with others. From this perspective, learning should be embedded in an appropriate context. Instruction should be of an authentic activity where the learner actively participates. In practice this leads to the ideas of modelling, scaffolding and reflection. Modelling – an expert 'shows how it is done' in a realistic context. Scaffolding – the 'expert' (this may include a fellow student working at higher level of expertise) actively supports the student as they move to the next level of expertise. Reflection – the learner reviews their efforts in the context of peer review (Palincsar, 1998).

Virtual worlds, like the real world they strive to emulate, are social not individual. However, they are not exclusively social in the sense that others are always co-present as in the real world, so individual activities can take place within them. In these virtual worlds experience, and hence knowledge construction is always social, be it 'alone', one-to-one or many-to-many. These virtual experiences are 'authentic' in that participants are deeply and socially intimately immersed.

In the context of healthcare, we can therefore say that virtual worlds can be places for authentic, participatory experiences where experts can support learners and other learners can support other learners in moving to their next level in learning and practice.

The key differentiators of virtual worlds are their social i.e. team and immersive, aspects. So, whereever the co-operative and visually realistic aspects of healthcare need to be introduced, virtual worlds may then have a role. "Further, as immersive spaces capable of exhibiting 'real work place' characteristics, they will increasingly be developed as a 'safe play space' for the modelling and testing of complex team-based health related activities" (Heinrichs, 2012).

Of These Lessons Which are Specific to the Clinical Practice Context and Which are More Generic?

Classically skills in healthcare settings are divided into:

- Technical skills
- Non-technical skills
- Cognitive skills

Technical and cognitive medical skills have been shown to be only a part of the delivery of clinical practice. It has been shown that non-technical skills play an equally important part. (Flin, 2004). These non-technical skills have been identified (Reader, 2006) as:

- Task management
- Team working
- Decision making
- Situation awareness
- Stress management

It has been suggested that these non-technical 'soft skills' are of a different category of learning, in the sense of a higher logical level i.e. learning about learning, than learning technical skills and so should be regarded as a meta-level of learning. This concept has implications in that these 'skills' have to be learnt through experience and as such cannot simply be 'taught' (Bateson, 1972). It would therefore seem to follow that the near real working environments offered by virtual worlds could be a platform for initially experiencing these soft skills.

A pragmatic word of warning, however, is pertinent at this stage. Owens (2011) looking at the operation of teams in *non-clinical settings* identified 'behaviours of interest' in their study of virtual world project teams. These were: Co-ordination – 'where people and technology resources work together to carry our specified activities in order to accomplish stated goals'; Role Clarity – 'state of understanding individual roles…knowing ones responsibilities and knowing what is expected' and Shared Understanding – 'mutual knowledge, mutual beliefs, and mutual assumptions that team members develop'. These behaviours are one part of a three-part model of interaction in virtual worlds that consists of the Technical Components – virtual world visualisation and communication capabilities; the Social Components – the Behaviours listed above by people controlled avatars and the Outcomes – group effectiveness in terms of both task and team-related outcomes.

In an earlier study (Davis, 2009) which deployed the same model as Owens (2011) the authors conclude that virtual worlds have a richness that can 'enhance team-building and cohesiveness' but that 'positive outcomes are never guaranteed.' Importantly, 'Managers should not assume that people will behave and look like their real world counterparts … Teams in these environments should not be managed just like traditional virtual teams, as people and behaviours may be fundamentally different.'

From the above and in the context of the allied healthcare professions, then non-technical skills and learning are clearly the more generic. That however, does not imply that learning technical and cognitive skills for the allied healthcare professions could not also be delivered using virtual worlds. Importantly, it is beyond the expertise of the authors to say how this might happen in practice and so would have to be explored on a profession by profession basis.

How Might These More Generic Lessons be Applied More Widely in Other Healthcare Areas?

It has been demonstrated that there are sets of skills that are not specifically clinical technical task dependent. In addition, it is posited that VWs offer a set of general attributes for learning in clinical and possibly other healthcare settings. Taking the non-technical skills and cross matching them to VW attributes should therefore give us some indication of where VWs might be applied more widely in healthcare.

What this cross matching exercise demonstrates (See Figure 4) is that there is a potential congruence between the generic set of non-technical skills in healthcare and the attributes offered by virtual worlds. This congruence holds whether or not there is full agreement on the exact lists of non-technical skills or virtual world attributes. On this basis, this chapter would therefore advocate that the deployment of virtual worlds should be strongly considered for the allied healthcare professions.

Examples of Wider Professional Development in Virtual Worlds

How virtual worlds might be deployed in practice for specific professions allied to healthcare is beyond the scope of this chapter as that would require the input of specialists from those domains to design the relevant immersive experiences together with virtual world engineers.

To illustrate that activity is very evident, this section closes with a diverse set of examples of the deployment of virtual worlds in allied healthcare professions:

- **Virtual Worlds in Health Education Project at Centre for Education Excellence, CIT, Australia:** Here Allied Health Assistants work alongside healthcare professionals such as physiotherapists, occupational therapists and speech pathologists to observe and learn from these professionals in the real work place. 'In an ideal world, practicum places would be available for all students in their choice of workplace however unfortunately this is not the case. Only limited numbers of students are allowed in any workplace at

Figure 4. Non-technical skills in healthcare cross matched to virtual world attributes

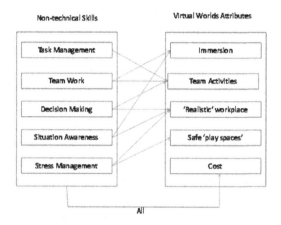

a given time and supervisors in the workplace need free time to train and guide the students. A serious lack of health professionals in the health industry locally means that current practicum locations are understaffed and very busy. Simulation Centres within educational institutions which replicate these physical environments are very expensive to build and still require professionals to leave their workplace. To overcome these issues, we decided to use a Virtual World platform to simulate a health workplace that would familiarise students with some of the environments and situations that they would encounter in professional practice' (Neuendorf, 2010).

- **University of North Carolina's (UNC) School of Pharmacy:** UNC's Information Technology Services have replicated parts of UNC's pharmacy school in Second Life. They have also built replicas of hospitals and practice sites in which their students visit during their experiential rotations. Students, as avatars, can visit these places in Second Life to familiarize themselves with the environment before actually going in real life (UNC School of Pharmacy, 2012).

- **Virtual World Interview Skills for Health Professionals:** The project will evaluate health professional interview skills training via a virtual world, in comparison to interview skills training undertaken via case study review. The Health Science Faculties at University of Sydney and University of Canberra will engage their students in the disciplines of psychology, physiotherapy and the general community health care sector, with simulated interview skills training via MyCosm Virtual World software. Ethical care situations within these environments will be created in collaboration with Faculty of Law at The Australian National University (Australian National University, 2012).

- **Health Science Interprofessional Education:** Health science students enrolled in an interdisciplinary course were assigned to interprofessional teams drawn from nine different health science disciplines. With the guidance of a facilitator, students planned and enacted a patient admission conference and a discharge conference with a standardized patient and family member in a virtual world (Boechler, 2010).

- **Virtual Worlds Demand Innovative Roles and Skills from Medical Librarians:** 'An academic medical library collaborated with local health sciences schools and programs on developing a Second Life space. The librarians initiated training sessions on Second Life skills; organized a seminar series; developed resources and exhibits that bridged the virtual world and online environments; collaborated with local, national and international partners; and broadly served as community managers for the Second Life community and space' (Anderson, 2012).

The examples above show that a diverse use of virtual worlds in wider healthcare professional development is emerging. Given the vast numbers in these allied healthcare professions, the increasing global demand for healthcare and the accessibility of virtual worlds, it can be assumed that their use will only grow. This growth will give rise to a number of important questions, both around educational issues and the virtual world technologies being deployed. These are explored in the final part of this chapter.

CONCLUSION

Clinical virtual worlds are here to stay. This chapter has shown that virtual worlds are being deployed widely and innovatively in a range of clinical settings. What has also been described is a range of specific and relevant innovations in the clinical domain. Two particular technical innovations stand out: the development of 'virtual patients' driven by underlying physiological data models and the very recent move to mobile platforms with novel touch and position sensitive interfaces. At the same time the resources needed for platform and scenario development in clinical virtual worlds has increased. It has been proposed that this is developing as a 'business sector' that is able to attract investment.

The chapter has also demonstrated that virtual worlds are being deployed innovatively by a small number of professions allied to healthcare such as pharmacy, care assistants, medical librarians, and physiotherapy. This is an interesting if gradual development, but given the vast numbers in the professions allied to healthcare not at all unexpected.

Given these developments this concluding section now explores what factors will influence the deployment of virtual worlds for professional development more widely in healthcare.

Internal and External Drivers to Deployment

There are a number of drivers both external and internal that will influence the deployment of virtual worlds in the wider healthcare professions. Internal drivers include: increased tempo of healthcare change; constrained budgets; introduction of new equipment and techniques; diminishing training times; a rising interest in simulation by healthcare professionals with the subsequent development of an evidence base. The main external drivers will be the falling cost of the technologies and the increasing size, leading to lower resource costs, of the virtual world development community.

Coupled with this at the same time however, is the emergence of an increasing confusing virtual world landscape as technologies and services multiply. It has been recently noted by the authors (WLII/DD) that: 'Differentiation is a classic feature of the development of technologies and the services they provide....A reasonable expectation is that clusters of domain expertise will develop on certain platforms, and as these develop, then these platforms will become de facto hubs for the development of specialist virtual world applications in a given domain' (Heinrichs, 2012). An example of this kind of differentiation in healthcare is the emergence of the focused Clinispace platform described earlier in this chapter. Clinispace is a first mover in this space. It can only be expected that further focused applications will emerge.

From the perspective of the healthcare professional looking at deploying a virtual world platform however, the description above does not offer much guidance. Clearly, any decision process should be informed by a set of relevant factors. In this context, these factors should be primarily educational. The final section explores what some of these factors might be.

Educational Factors in Virtual World Deployment in Healthcare

These are early days in the deployment of virtual worlds for educational use. Unsurprisingly Kim et al. (2012) whilst researching the educational use of virtual worlds found, 'While doing the literature review and coding the articles included in the sample, we realized that in many of the studies, the authors did not explain why they used a certain virtual world platform for the specific contexts.' The early implementation of new technologies in organisations is often carried out by enthusiastic 'intrepreneurs' who simply use what they can get their hands on at zero or little cost – hence the widespread use of Second Life in education.

Delwiche (2006), starting from the practical basis of introducing different virtual worlds into different courses, points out that 'All virtual environments are not created equal.' He advocates that when choosing a virtual world the key factors to consider are accessibility, genre, and extensibility.

- **Accessibility:** Is the world easy to use and understand. If not, is the additional investment in time learning to use the world appropriate to the intended use and outcomes?
- **Genre:** is the world theme appropriate? Some virtual worlds are fantastical game-like environments. These are unlikely therefore to be suitable for professional healthcare education. Other worlds are dull virtual office suites for corporate meetings. Again, these may be unsuitable for certain professional uses.
- **Extensibility:** Can the world be developed to design and add new scenarios? If yes, who could add those new scenarios? In other words what level of skills and access

are needed? Can the student or instructor modify the world or does it need a sophisticated C++ programmer?

In the context of professional environments in healthcare a further factor should be added, and that is security.

- **Security:** Can the virtual world be made private? Notice that this is an option, but the fact that non-public professional conversations and activities may be observed in a public virtual world is not acceptable to many healthcare organisations – and in fact to most organisations.

Prior to this selection process however, the basic educational question raised earlier needs to be flagged again in this conclusion in order to answer the question 'Why deploy a virtual world for professional development?' Virtual worlds are deployed because they can be places for authentic, participatory experiences where experts can support learners and other learners can support other learners in moving to their next level in learning and practice. They offer complex, immersive, co-operative, engaging experiences, but this is not a sufficient educational reason by itself to deploy them. Given the often heavy resource requirements to design and run them, then there has to be some further driving factors that enable them to deliver a special value in learning.

In conclusion this chapter posits that in clinical practice and in the wider healthcare professions both the internal drivers: healthcare change; constrained budgets; new equipment and techniques; diminishing training times; a rising interest in simulation; and the external drivers: lowered costs; emerging specialist development communities, will drive the adoption of virtual worlds in two ways. Firstly, to semi-replace high cost participatory activities, in particular those involving real workplace settings and team activities i.e. to of-fer safe 'play-workspaces'. Secondly, as secure spaces for innovation where novel methods of practice, service delivery, etc can be developed and tested prior to their possible roll out to their target constituencies. In both cases the exploitation of virtual worlds now offer a set of extraordinary opportunities for professional development in healthcare.

ACKNOWLEDGMENT

Prof. Wm. LeRoy Heinrichs is the Executive Medical Director for 'Innovation in Learning,' the developers of Clinispace. Dick Davies is the Executive Producer for Ambient Performance Ltd., the distributors in Europe for the SAIC OLIVE virtual world platform. Li Felländer-Tsai has received research grants from the Wallenberg Foundations, the Stockholm County Council and the Swedish Research Council.

REFERENCES

Active Worlds. (2012). *Website*. Retrieved 2 October 2012 from http://activeworlds.com/

Allied Health Professions. (2012). *Wikipedia*. Retrieved from http://en.wikipedia.org/wiki/Allied_health_professions

Anne Myers Medical Centre. (2012). *Second life*. Retrieved from http://ammc.wordpress.com/

ARA. (2012). *Website*. Retrieved 2 October 2012 from http://www.ara.com/Newsroom_Whatsnew/press_releases/unreal-network.htm

Australian National University. (2012). *Website*. Retrieved from http://www.olt.gov.au/project-virtual-world-interview-skills-health-professionals-2011

Bateson, G. (1972). *Steps to an ecology of mind*. San Francisco, CA: Aronson.

Boechler, P., King, S., Stroulia, E., Carbonaro, M., deJong, E., Wasniewski, E., & Chodos, D. (2010). Managing virtual world sessions for health science interprofessional education. In J. Sanchez & K. Zhang (Eds.), *Proceedings of World Conference on E-Learning in Corporate, Government, Healthcare, and Higher Education 2010*, (pp. 610-615). Chesapeake, VA: AACE.

Breakaway Games. (2012). *Website.* Retrieved from http://www.breakawaygames.com/about/overview/

Brown, J. S., Collins, A., & Duguid, S. (1989). Situated cognition and the culture of learning. *Educational Researcher, 18*(1), 32–42.

Chodos, D., Stroulia, E., Boechler, P., King, S., Kuras, P., Carbonaro, M., & De Jong, E. (2010). Healthcare education with virtual-world simulations. In *Proceedings of the 2010 ICSE Workshop on Software Engineering in Health Care.* ICSE.

Creutzfeld, J., Hedman, L., Medin, C., Heinrichs, W. L., & Tsai, L. (2010). Virtual worlds for scenario based repeated team training of cardiopulmonary resuscitation in medical students. *Journal of Medical Internet Research, 12*(3), e38. doi:10.2196/jmir.1426 PMID:20813717.

Creutzfeldt., et al. (2009). *Website.* Retrieved from http://www.ncbi.nlm.nih.gov/pubmed/19377114

Creutzfeldt, J., Hedman, L., Heinrichs, W. L., Youngblood, P., & Felländer-Tsai, L. (2012). An international study of digital natives training CPR in virtual worlds. *Journal of Medical Internet Research, 15*(1). PMID:23302475.

Davis, A., Murphy, J., Owens, D., Khzaanchi, D., & Zigurs, I. (2009). Avatars, people, and virtual worlds: Foundations for research in the metaverse. *Journal of the Association for Information Systems, 10*(2), 90–117.

Delp, S., Arnold, A., & Hammer, S. (2012). *Neuromuscular biomechanics laboratory, Stanford University.* Retrieved from http://www.scribd.com/doc/56096401/OpenSim-Tutorial1/

Delwiche, A. (2006). Massively multiplayer online games (MMOs) in the new media classroom. *Journal of Educational Technology & Society, 9*(3), 160–172.

Dev, P., Heinrichs, W. L., & Youngblood, P. (2011). CliniSpace™: A multiperson 3D online immersive training environment accessible through a browser. In *Proceedings of MMVR2011.* Long Beach, CA: IOS Press.

Ericsson, K. A., Krampe, R. T., & Tesch-Romer, C. (1993). The role of deliberate practice in the acquisition of expert performance. *Psychological Review*, (3): 363–406. doi:10.1037/0033-295X.100.3.363.

Flin, R., & Maran, N. (2004). Identifying and training non-technical skills in acute medicine. *Quality & Safety in Health Care, 13*(Suppl I), i180–i184. doi:10.1136/qshc.2004.009993 PMID:15465960.

Forterra Systems. (2012). *Wikipedia.* Retrieved from http://en.wikipedia.org/wiki/Forterra_Systems

Frenkel. (2012). *Therapists use virtual worlds to address real problems.* Retrieved from http://www.inworldsolutions.net/news/articles

Graafland, M., Schraagen, J. M., & Schijven, M. P. (2012). Systematic review of serious games for medical education and surgical skills training. *British Journal of Surgery, 99*, 1322–1330. doi:10.1002/bjs.8819 PMID:22961509.

Greci, L. S., Hurst, S., Garman, K., Huang, R., Hoffman, H., & Cardenas, M. et al. (2011). Multi-User virtual environment boot camp and patient surge triage practice. *Medicine Meets Virtual Reality, 18*, 16–17.

Gridsurvery. (2012). *Website*. Retrieved from http://gridsurvey.com/index.php

Health Games Research. (2012). *Website*. Retrieved from http://www.healthgamesresearch. org/db/search/tab=organizations~~keywords= Virtual%20Worlds#

Heinrichs, W.L., Kung, S.-Y., & Dev, P. (2008a). Design and Implementation of rule-based medical models: An in silico patho-physiological trauma model for hypovolemic shock. In *Proceedings of MMVR2008*. Long Beach, CA: IOS Press.

Heinrichs, W. L., Davies, D., & Davies, J. (2012). Virtual worlds in healthcare: Applications and implications. In Arnab, S., Dunwell, I., & Debattista, K. (Eds.), *Serious Games in Healthcare* (pp. 1–22). Hershey, PA: IGI Global. doi:10.4018/978-1-4666-1903-6.ch001.

Heinrichs, W. L., Harter, P., Youngblood, P., Kusumoto, L., & Dev, P. (2010). Training healthcare personnel for mass casualty incidents in a virtual emergency department: VED II. *Prehospital and Disaster Medicine, 25*(5), 422–434. PMID:21053190.

Heinrichs, W. L., Youngblood, P., Harter, P. M., & Dev, P. (2008b). Simulation for team training and assessment: Case studies of online training with virtual worlds. *World Journal of Surgery, 32*, 161–170. doi:10.1007/s00268-007-9354-2 PMID:18188640.

Hew, K. F., & Cheung, W. S. (2010). Use of three-dimensional (3D) immersive virtual worlds in K-12 and higher education settings: A review of the research. *British Journal of Educational Technology, 41*(1), 33–55. doi:10.1111/j.1467-8535.2008.00900.x.

Journal. (2012). *Article*. Retrieved from http://thejournal.com/articles/2011/01/11/next-stop-open-sim.aspx

Kim, S. H., Bangmok, L., & Thomas, M. K. (2012). Between purpose and method: a review of educational research on 3D virtual worlds. *Virtual Worlds Research, 5*(1).

Knight, J. F., Carley, S., Tregunna, B., Jarvis, S., Smithies, R., & de Freitas, S. et al. (2010). Serious gaming technology in major incident triage training: A pragmatic controlled trial. *Resuscitation, 81*(9), 1175–1179. doi:10.1016/j.resuscitation.2010.03.042 PMID:20732609.

Knudson, M., Khaw, L., Bullard, M. K., Dicker, R., Cohen, M. J., & Staudenmayer, K. et al. (2008). Trauma training in simulation: TranSecond lifeating skills from SIM time to real time. *The Journal of Trauma Injury Infection and Critical Care, 64*(2).

Koskovich, M. (2009). *Website*. Retrieved from http://www.prnewswire.com/news-releases/saic-purchases-simulation--collaboration-product-line-from-forterra-systems-inc-83237277.html

Mesko, B. (2012). *Website*. Retrieved from http://www.webicina.com/about/

Metaverse Standards. (2012). *Website*. Retrieved from http://www.metaversestandards.org/index.php?title=Virtual_Worlds

Neuendorf, P., & Simpson, C. (2010). Redesigning role plays for a virtual world in health education. In *Proceedings of Global Learn 2010*. Global Learn.

NHS UK. (2012). *Website*. Retrieved from http://www.nhscareers.nhs.uk/atoz.shtml

Open Cobalt. (2012). *Website*. Retrieved from http://www.opencobalt.org/home

Open Wonderland. (2012). *Website*. Retrieved from http://openwonderland.org/

OpenQwaq. (2012). *Website*. Retrieved from http://code.google.com/p/openqwaq/

OpenSim. (2012). *Website.* Retrieved from http://opensimulator.org/wiki/Main_Page

Owens, D., Mitchell, A., Khazanchi, D., & Zigurs, I. (2011). An empirical investigation of virtual world projects and metaverse technology capabilities. *The Data Base for Advances in Information Systems, 42*(1).

Palincsar, A. (1998). Social constructivist perspectives on teaching and learning. *Annual Review of Psychology, 49,* 345–373. doi:10.1146/annurev.psych.49.1.345 PMID:15012472.

Peterson, M. (2010). Computerized games and simulations in computer-assisted language-learning: A meta-analysis of research. *Simulation & Gaming, 41*(1), 72–93. doi:10.1177/1046878109355684.

Protonmedia. (2012). *Website.* Retrieved from www.protonmedia.com/.../ProtoSphere_Product_Datasheet.pdf

Reaction Grid. (2012). *Website.* Retrieved from http://www.reactiongrid.com

Reader, T., Flin, R., Lauche, K., & Cuthbertson, B. H. (2006). Non-technical skills in the intensive care unit. *British Journal of Anaesthesia, 96*(5). doi:10.1093/bja/ael067 PMID:16567346.

Rizzo, A. A., Graap, K., Perlman, K., McLay, R. N., Rothbaum, B. O., & Reger, G. et al. (2008). Virtual Iraq: Initial results from a VR exposure therapy application for combat-related PTSD. *Studies in Health Technology and Informatics, 132,* 420–425. PMID:18391334.

Simergency. (2006). *Website.* Retrieved from http://simergency.stanford.edu/

Steigman, I. (2011). *A virtual way to go clean.* Retrieved from http://www.nbcbayarea.com/news/local/A-Virtual-Way-To-Go-Clean-122980713.html

Taylor, D. (2011). *Website.* Retrieved from http://knowledgecast.wordpress.com/

Therasim. (2012). *Website.* Retrieved from http://therasim.com/about/

There. (2012). *Wikipedia.* Retrieved from http://en.wikipedia.org/wiki/There_28virtual_world29

UNC School of Pharmacy. (2012). *Website.* Retrieved from http://www.pharmacy.unc.edu/news/features/using-second-life-to-help-students-in-real-life

University of Arkansas. (2012). *Everything is alive project.* Retrieved from http://vw.ddns.uark.edu/index.php?page=docs

University of Kansas. (2012). *Website.* Retrieved from http://www.spencerart.ku.edu/exhibitions/secondlife.shtml

Virtual Heroes. (2012). *Website.* Retrieved from http://virtualheroes.com/projects/3diteams

Virtual Medical Centre. (2012). *Wikipedia.* Retrieved from http://en.wikipedia.org/wiki/Virtual_Medical_Centre

Virtually Better. (2012). *Website.* Retrieved from http://www.virtuallybetter.com/portfolio/virtual-iraq-intense/

Wallin, C.-J., Meurling, L., Hedman, L., & Hedegard, J., & Fellander-Tsai, Li. (2007). Target-focused medical emergency team training using a human patient simulator: Effects on behaviour and attitude. *Medical Education, 41,* 173–180. doi:10.1111/j.1365-2929.2006.02670.x PMID:17269951.

Wertsch, J. V., & Sohmer, R. (1995). Vygotsky on learning and development. *Human Development,* (38): 332–337. doi:10.1159/000278339.

WGLN. (2005). *Website.* Retrieved from http://wgln.stanford.edu/projects/2005-2006.html

Wiecha, J., Heyden, R., Sternthal, E., & Merialdi, M. (2010). Learning in a virtual world: Experience with using second life for medical education. *Journal of Medical Internet Research*, *12*(1), e1. doi:10.2196/jmir.1337 PMID:20097652.

Young, J. R. (2010). After frustrations in second life, colleges look to new virtual worlds. The Chronicle of Higher Education. Retrieved from http://chronicle.com/article/After-Frustrations-in-Second/64137/

Youngblood, P., Harter, P., Srivastava, S., Wallin, C.-J., Fellander-Tsai, L., Moffet, S., & Heinrichs, W. L. (2008). Design, development and evaluation of an online virtual emergency department for training trauma teams. *Simulation in Healthcare*, *3*(3), 146–153. doi:10.1097/SIH.0b013e31817bedf7 PMID:19088658.

Chapter 15
Play Yourself Fit:
Exercise + Videogames = Exergames

Hannah R. Marston
German Sport University, Germany

Philip A. McClenaghan
Augsburg University, Germany

ABSTRACT

Exergames and Exergaming have become a new phenomenon in recent years due to the release of the Nintendo Wii console and more recently the Microsoft Kinect. Videogames are categorized into genres based upon the actions that gamers are expected to execute to achieve goals and overcome challenges. However, with the development of new technology, and this notion of exergaming, is it actually activity or gameplay that defines the notion of exergames as a genre into current categories? This chapter reviews several genre/taxonomy theories to gain a greater understanding of exergames within the serious games arena, with several facets proposed by the authors to provide a more succinct progress within this sector.

INTRODUCTION

Defining videogame genres has been helpful over recent years in attempting to provide a comprehensive understanding for researchers and users alike (Botte, Matera, & Sponsiello, 2009; Kickmeier-Rust, 2009; Mueller, Gibbs, & Vetere, 2008; Bogost 2007, 2005; Jantke, 2006).

During its short lifespan, the games industry has witnessed many peaks and troughs, which has resulted in a variety of hardware and software developments. The 1990's saw the advent of games becoming more realistic, for example *Unreal* (1998), part of the first person shooter (FPS) genre. This development occurred with the release of the Sony PlayStation® (1995) console,

DOI: 10.4018/978-1-4666-3673-6.ch015

which enabled developers to create games in high contrast, providing a more superior collection of graphics than previous consoles on the market. From the mid-1990 to the release of the Nintendo Wii™ (2006) console there were several hardware developments and consoles released by Nintendo, Sony and Microsoft. These developments produced higher specifications and delivered greater memory and additional features, such as CD-ROM, storage for music and Downloadable Content (DLC).

Traditionally, the nature of interaction on these consoles was via a game pad, held in the hands of the gamer and a series of multiple buttons were pressed to execute one move. This changed with the release of the Nintendo Wii™ (2006) which enabled gamers to hold a remote in one hand and, via a motion swing, execute a move in a more natural form with a single button press.

This approach is not necessarily new as a similar piece of hardware was available from Sony – the Eyetoy® (1999), which utilized natural gesture movement via a webcam situated on top of the television. Consequently, this interactive approach has led to some researchers to recognize the opportunities that game technology has in benefiting a wider audience such as older adults and for additional implementation within the field of health, primarily focusing on rehabilitation.

In recent years the term exergaming was coined by Sawyer (2003) 'Serious Games: Improving Public Policy through Game-based Learning and Simulation,' and can be found within the field of serious games. However, the notion of integrating games for a particular purpose originated from the book *Serious Games* by Clark C. Abt (1975), who defines this concept by stating: 'We are concerned with serious games in the sense that these games have an explicit and carefully thought out educational purpose and are not intended to be played primarily for amusement' (Abt, 1975, p. 9).

Equally, additional terms have being conceived, for example: "A serious game is a game in which education (in its various forms) is the primary goal, rather than entertainment" (Michael, &

Chen, 2006, p. 17). "Serious games have more than just story, art and software, however. [...] They involve pedagogy: activities that educate or instruct, thereby imparting knowledge or skill. This addition makes games serious" (Zyda, 2005, p. 26).

In contrast Sawyer (2007) presented, 'The "Serious Games" Landscape' in which the topic related to understanding what 'serious games' are, the purpose of such games, what one can do with games and the different sectors in which these games can be utilized. The notion of serious games derives from solutions to problems (Sawyer, 2007). Several examples of serious games were provided and are listed as follows:

- Any meaningful use of computerized game/game industry resources whose chief mission is not entertainment;
- Serious games are simply solutions to problems that utilize assets developed by the modern day computer and videogame industry;
- The serious in serious games refers to the purpose and nothing else; and
- Many serious game projects do not result in the creation of a game.

Although there have been several studies focusing upon the use and implementation of game technologies for health aimed at an ageing society, there remains little understanding about the software employed. In particular, the configuration of game genres/taxonomies and where the exergame genre corresponds with preconceived models. The term 'exergaming' was first coined by the media, the "combination of exercise and videogames" (Lawrence, 2005).

The aims of this chapter are: to provide an overview of literature focusing upon the utilization of game technology within the field of health rehabilitation, to discuss the existing literature of game genre theory in order to provide a clearer understanding of the exergame genre and thus to build upon this information and to propose series of recommendations relating to future exergames.

BACKGROUND

It has become popular to combine gaming with exercise, emerging with the term 'exergaming' to describe software such as *Your Shape: Fitness Evolved 2012* (Ubisoft). The turning point for the genre of exergaming appeared with the release of the Nintendo Wii/Balance board in conjunction with the *WiiFit*™ software. There are similarities between these games (See Table 1), enabling users to interact or exercise to enhance their health and physical strength. The games have incorporated several exercises such as Tai Chi, Yoga, and training exercises which enable the user to build-up their strength and balance through a series of training programs.

The notion of exergaming is not a new phenomenon. According to Noah Falstein (Orland, & Remo, 2008) the idea of bringing video games and exercise together can be traced back to the early 1980s with the game *Sinister* (1982, Williams Electronics).

Further attempts were made throughout the 1990s to enable gamers to lead a less sedentary lifestyle. These were largely unsuccessful, because "Nobody wants to go to an arcade to work up a sweat" (Orland, & Remo, 2008) until the release of *Dance Dance Revolution* (DDR) (Konami, 1999). The DDR comprised a dance pad set on a stage and users were required to press a series of coloured arrows with their feet, to coincide with the music. Additionally, the DDR was released for use within the home environment in which, the 'stage' was set within a game pad controller held in the hands of the user with interaction being via fingers rather than the user's feet.

The release of the DDR was the turning point in gaming which combined entertainment with exercise, although it is speculative as to whether the primary intention was to provide an exercise game: "This is a rare example of something that was designed purely as a fun game that has become successful as an exercise game" (Orland, & Remo, 2008).

The combination of gaming and physical activity has become a phenomenon due to the increase in ageing population, not solely in Europe but worldwide (UN, 2011; i2010 Independent Living for the Ageing Society, 2007). Identifying suitable, innovative approaches to aid older adults in maintaining a healthy lifestyle and enhance their Quality of Life (QoL) via the integration of technology is crucial for future technologies within the market place. The notion of easier game play was initially recognized with the release of the Nintendo Wii™ console (2006), and in conjunction with clever marketing campaigns, and randomized control trials; it has demonstrated the positive elements of videogames. This has illustrated that games are not solely for young audiences but older adults too. It is suggested that the popularity of exergames and exergaming has emerged since the release of the Nintendo Wii™, and gained in popularity with peripherals such as the Wii Balance Board (WBB) and software such as Wii Fit™ which enables users to execute a series of exercises within the comfort of their own home.

Table 1. Displays the characteristics of Wii Fit/Plus and Yourshape

Wii Fit/Plus	**Your shape**
Personal Trainer	Personal Training
Strength and balance training (mini games, comprising of slalom skiing, snowboarding, tightrope walking)	Sport Games (mini games, coordinative (balance, reaction time skills)
Yoga, Aerobic exercises	Zen/Aerobic Exercises
Body Test (BMI, balance control, Wii Fit Age – physical strength)	
Calorie counter (Wii Fit+)	

Although primarily designed for use in the home environment, exergames are increasingly being utilized within the field of health (see Marston, & Smith, 2012) which provides an overview of commercial and purpose-built technologies, utilized for stroke and fall prevention. Several recommendations were proposed by Marston and Smith (2012) in a bid to enhance and build-upon existing knowledge within this field of research.

However, there is still uncertainty regarding the definition of exergaming (Oh & Yang, 2011) and how this recently created 'genre' can be utilized. Marston & Smith (2012) proposed several recommendations for the implementation of commercial and purpose built virtual reality technology to be utilized for fall and stroke rehabilitation. Subsequently, Greenleaf (Ruppert, 2011) indicates there are no clinical guidelines for using this type of technology in the appropriate manner to achieve the necessary results which would be acceptable from a health perspective. Greenleaf suggests this type of technology may be suitable to initiate general exercise however, substantial damage may occur if one is recovering from an injury or there is little monitoring of the exercise regime (Ruppert, 2011). Furthermore, Greenleaf reports he is aware of clinicians who have been inclined to suggest using the Nintendo Wii™ console to aid their patients motivations to exercise. However at present, the available software is not sufficiently precise to manage an exercise program for use within the home environment and act as a clinical application. Greenleaf has proposed the notion that validation studies are crucial for this technology to be accepted and used within clinical practice, stating:

When companies skip this step, no one buys the technology, because it has not been validated. If we want this to be a more cost-effective way of providing health care by, say, 2015, we need to start appropriate trials now; that will make the difference between technology that is a laboratory curiosity and technology that has become the standard of care (Ruppert, 2011, p. 279).

What Defines a Video Game Genre?

The concept of genre can assist in the discussion of games and help users to identify their preferred type of game. Genre has the ability to identify an individual within a group and can provide an automatic relationship between users/viewers, forming an initial common interest (Fencott, Lockyear, Clay, & Massey, 2012). There is, however, considerable debate as to how a game genre is defined.

According to Chandler (2000), defining a clear distinction between genres is not easy due to overlap, resulting in 'mixed genres', as categorization by one theme may result in alignment with another group based upon added characteristics. For example, Neale (1980, pp. 22-23) contends that the distinction of genre is the 'relative prominence, combination and functions which are distinctive' whereas Todorov (cited in Swales 1990, p. 36) argues; "a new genre is always the transformation of one or several old genres." Fencott *et al.* (2012) suggests genres can be identified through the types of activities which take place within games and Schiffler (2006) describes six game genre classifications: Action, Strategy, Adventure, Simulation, Puzzle and Education, which can be further divided into sub-genres such as 2-D platform, Real-time strategy and Massively Multiplayer Online Role-Playing (MMORPG).

A case study which illustrates the fluidity and perceived relationships between genres but also the complexity of attempting to integrate genre and activity mapping was a project undertaken by students at Teesside University while studying on a third year 'Games Futures' course (See Figure 1), which explored how genre(s) could be understood through the activities performed within them (Fencott *et al.* 2012). Figure 2 illustrates how there is an over-lap on a number of genres identified by Fencott, *et al.* (2012) which differ significantly with regard to genre definition and highlights the different perceptions of what should and what should not be classified as a genre.

For the purpose of this chapter, Figure 2 will be used to build on the notion of integrating additional genres and sub-categories of serious games.

Adams (2009b), on the other hand, prefers to 'sort out the genre muddle' by suggesting that Setting, Audience, Theme and Purpose are also important elements to consider when categorizing games. Genre, in his opinion, is just one of a number of dimensions along which games can be categorized. According to Adams, video game genres are determined by gameplay—the challenges the player faces and the actions performed to overcome these challenges. Adams identifies eight 'traditional' genres: Action, Strategy, Role-Playing, Sports, Vehicle Simulations, Construction and Management, Adventure and Puzzle which can, he suggests, be further divided into sub-genres such as the specific type of sport in the Sport genre or type of vehicle in a Vehicle Simulation genre (2009). Adams acknowledges, however, that genres are fluid and increasingly form hybrids of traditional genres such as role-playing games incorporating physical co-ordination challenges, those which are typical of fighting games.

Adams (2009b) proposes that the game setting is independent of its genre: "a shooter is a shooter whether it's set in the Old West or on Mars" and indeed, different genres can be found in the same setting such as a shooter or a management game set in the Old West. The participants, he states, is similarly genre independent, citing the range of games marketed as 'Games for Girls' as having various types of gameplay. Adams also indicates that a particular theme, such as those games categorized as 'Christian Games', can also contain various types of games with differing gameplay and thus genres. To conclude, Adams tells us that the purpose of the game - the reason it was made, does not define the genre. Therefore games created to solve a problem or 'Serious Games' dealing with healthcare or education for example, do not constitute a genre in their own right.

Thus, the Action genre noted by Adams appears the most useful when viewing Exergames in terms

Figure 1. Displays a genre map created by students at Teesside University

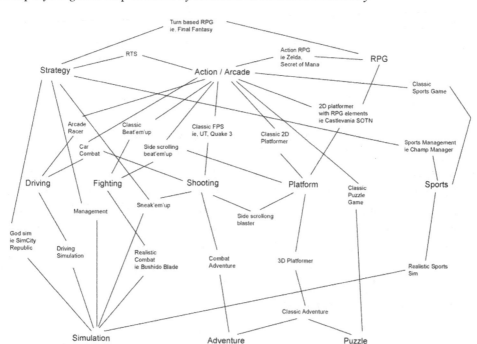

Figure 2. Displays a genre map created by Fencott et al. (2012) (courtesy of Clive Fencott, used with permission)

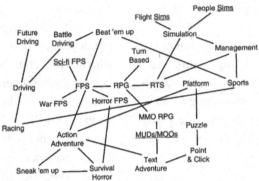

of genre. Adams (2009) defines an action game as one in which "the majority of challenges presented are tests of the player's physical skills and coordination. Puzzle-solving, tactical conflict, and exploration challenges are often present as well".

Defining the Exergame Genre

The concept of exercise pertains to repetitive movements executed over a period of time and includes an increase of difficulty to build-up one's muscle and strength (Carpensen, Powell, & Christenson, 1985). Exercise, however, is a subcategory of physical activity, which is "planned, structured, repetitive and purposive in the sense that improvement or maintenance of one or more components of physical fitness is an objective" (Carpensen *et al.* 1985). There are several elements which make-up physical activity (See Table 2).

Oh and Yang (2011) identified a variety of terms for the same meaning from 23 articles (Oh & Yang, 2011). A matrix illustrated the different terms including exertainment, dance simulation video game, interactive video game, and activity promoting video game, physical gaming, and (kin) aesthetic video game. Exergaming was identified as the most popular terminology. Referring back to Adams (2009), "a sports game simulates some

aspect of a real or imaginary athletic sport whether it is playing in matches, managing a team or career, or both. Match play uses physical and strategic challenges; the management challenges are chiefly economic". The employment of the term 'athletic sport' and the implication of competitive game play in this definition would appear to exclude exercise. Indeed, it is also debatable whether the Stack-em-Up game can in fact be termed a sport game.

The inclusion of, and focus on, physical exercise and thus exertion in these games differs from other games in the sports genre such as FIFA 12 (2011), which require little physical exertion except from controlling a character via a console, mouse or keyboard. Therefore, defining exertion as "the act of exerting, involving skeletal muscles, which results in physical fatigue, often associated with physical sport." Mueller, Gibbs, and Vetere (2008) devised a taxonomy of 'exertion' games where "An exertion game has an input mechanism in which the user is intentionally investing physical exertion." Mueller *et al.* (2008) attempted to define what exertion games are in order to distinguish them from other 'computationally augmented games' and proposed four taxonomic units (See Figure 3):

Table 2. Elements of physical activity and exercise

Physical Activity	Exercise
Body movement via skeletal muscles	Body movement via skeletal muscles
Results in energy expenditure	Results in energy expenditure
Energy expenditure varies continuously from low to high	Energy expenditure varies continuously from low to high
Positively correlated with physical fitness	Very positively correlated with physical fitness
	Planned, structured and repetitive bodily movement
	An objective is to improve or maintain physical fitness component(s)

- **Exertion vs. Non-exertion:** Where attaining the goal of an exertion game requires gross motor competency.
- **Competitive vs. Non-Competitive:** Whereby a competitive game contains at least one opponent, resulting in the ability to compare results.
- **Parallel vs. Non-Parallel:** Which differ in terms of the presence of an opponent who functions as an obstacle to attaining the goal of the non-parallel game, thus creating offensive and defensive gameplay and the absence of an opponent resulting in independent activities performed by the player in parallel games.

Figure 3. Displays the proposed taxonomy by Mueller et al (2008) (courtesy of Floyd Mueller, used with permission)

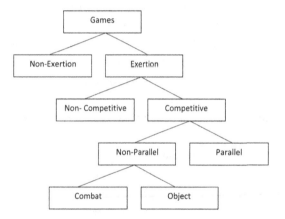

Figure 4. Displays the 'serious games' genre to the genre map created by Fencott et al. (2012)

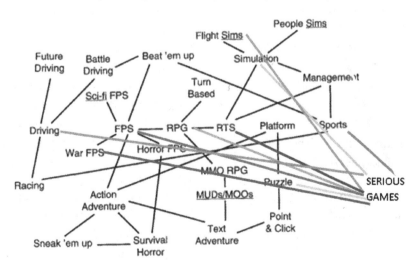

- **Combat vs. Object:** Where the player tries to control either the opponent as in boxing or an object such as a tennis ball.

Conversely, this taxonomy helps to define exertion games and demonstrates that not all such games are the same. However, it provides a means of identifying the differences between the games and thus enabling categorization.

Likewise, Lindley (2008) proposes an approach composed of a series of 'classification planes'. Starting with a 2-Dimensional (2-D) plane comprising of ludology, narratology and simulation, Lindley implements gambling to create a 3-D classification space, before introducing two additional sets of distinctions in the form of fiction/non-fiction and virtual/physical. In this context, 'virtual' relates to games primarily comprising of their mechanics processed within a computer and all audio visual content provided by computer peripherals. Whereas 'physical' means games played within the physical world such as soccer in a stadium.

Alternatively, Sawyer and Smith (2008) have composed a taxonomy of serious games, which takes the approach of genre and sector. The taxonomy outlines several types of genres (games for health, advergames, games for training, education, science and research, product and games for work) and sectors (government/NGO, defense, healthcare, marketing and communication, education, corporate and industry).

Video games such as *Wii Fit* (2008a) and *My Fitness Coach* (2008b), were initially viewed as self-improvement games (Dring, 2009 a/b) and thus lie within the category of games which included *Dr Kawashima's Brain Training* (2006) and *Big Brain Academy* 2006). The notion of self-improvement games has continued to develop within the games sector (Dring, 2009a, 2009b) and moreover, Marston (2010) suggested that the implementation of self-improvement within established brands could transform gaming into a different format from what was currently being experienced.

Adams (2009b) stated 'self improvement' can be identified as a purpose which can contain differing games with various gameplay and thus genres. The gameplay in *My Fitness Coach* (2008c) is significantly different to that of *Dr Kawashima's Brain Training* (2006) and thus could be said to belong to separate genres. In the *YourShape* (2008b) game, for example, the user can choose from 'personal trainer', 'sport games' and 'zen/aerobic exercises'. Within the sport games section the player is offered a variety of options to aid the development of strength, balance and coordinative skills. The 'Stack-em-Up' game, for example, expects the users to hold their arms out in front of them in order to catch a series of falling boxes. At different intervals one of two ditches opens up, giving the user the option to store the boxes in a trough or to continue stacking the falling boxes in the quest to gain higher points. These games, therefore, may be more appropriately attributed to the sports genre.

Recalling Adams (2009b), we can see that genre is only one of a number of dimensions by which a game can be measured. Therefore, does the term 'exergame' accurately describe the purpose of these games and not, in fact, a genre? Is it instead a collective term for a diverse range of games, which can be assigned to several genres with the commonality of focused exertion to perform exercise? Are Exergames therefore, in fact, genre independent? It would certainly appear so. Exercise can be a by-product of, for example, a sports game but does not need to be a sports game (within the definition provided by Adams) to offer exercise. Depending on the game play, exergames could be categorized as for example: dance games, sports games, fighting games or hybrids of several genres.

The authors have attempted to illustrate how the genre 'serious games' may fit within the genre map presented by Fencott *et al.* (2012), based upon activity profiles featured within each genre. Figure

4 illustrates how it may be possible to integrate the genre serious games into the existing concepts initially displayed in Figure 2.

As previously outlined by Sawyer and Smith, (2008), serious games have the ability to incorporate anything which requires problem solving. To illustrate this notion, and attempt to categorize games within the serious game genre (self-improvement, DDR, and exergames), the authors have contemplated how Figures 2 and 4 would aid greater understanding of individual sub-genres within serious games into Figure 5, utilizing the map by Fencott *et al.* (2012).

On the contrary, Figures 4 and 5 are solely suggestions and initial grounding for future work to be conducted. However, it may provide an initial basis to understand how sub-categories within the serious games genre may be integrated. Rather than trying to shoehorn exergames solely into a genre, it is perhaps more conducive to understand the nature of exergames by viewing them in terms of other dimensions such as those suggested by Adams (2009b), Mueller *et al.* (2008) and Sawyer & Smith (2008). With this in mind, future genre maps may take on a different perspective, depending upon how one chooses to devise exergames and self-improvement.

SOLUTIONS AND RECOMMENDATIONS

The objective of this chapter was to provide a greater understanding of the exergame genre/taxonomy. Conversely, it has become evident in recent years that alternative forms of user interaction have been facilitated via natural physical movement due to enhanced technology hardware. This has enabled game playing to move from a sedentary pastime to an activity with potentially positive effects for health and fitness.

There have been several taxonomies presented by the authors, illustrating a variety of approaches to classifying games. This approach has been employed by the authors in an attempt to understand the characteristics of exergaming taking into consideration the elements that make up exercise and physical activity.

The matrix developed by Oh and Yang (2011) facilitated the base of understanding of respective researchers notions of this genre, enabling the authors to build upon and attempt to identify where the exergame genre fits within the current concepts. However, Oh and Yang (2011) stated that there is a problem calling games 'exergames', due to the notion of exercise. Subsequently, the perception of videogames is of having fun and the concept of exercise is a subdivision of physical activity, which contains explicit condi-

Figure 5. Displays sub-categories of the serious games genre to the Fencott et al. (2012) genre map

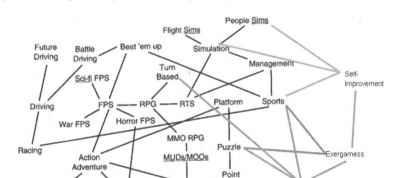

tions that differentiates this sub-category from physical activity. Caspersen *et al.* (1985, p. 126), defines exercise as a form of physical activity: "intentionally to improve or maintain physical fitness with a planned, repetitive, and structured format". Therefore, implementing 'exergames' into one's life for the purpose of exercise, one would have to maintain and improve their physical fitness, ensuring all movements are repeated and structured. Consequently, a user choosing *Wii Fit Yoga* for the purpose of exercise and fitness would need to follow a structured program on a regular basis, following the information presented by the program. If we take on board the argument posed by Oh and Yang (2011), playing games such as *Wii Sports Bowling*, then it is suggested that this game may not necessarily be classed as an exergame but a sports game with the intention of having fun within a social environment.

Taking into account the maps created by Fencott *et al.* (2012), the integration of exergames with the notion of self-improvement (Dring 2009a, 2009b, 2009c), incorporating the game elements and activities has been taken into consideration, for example: dance, sports, puzzle, simulation. The authors have identified that these elements can be linked to the existing genres on the maps (See Figures 4 and 5). The figures do not necessarily show an in-depth detail; however, they do illustrate the relationships between the different genres.

The taxonomy proposed by Mueller *et al.* (2008) integrates game elements into four groups. Integrating the exergame genre into this taxonomy is not straightforward. It is suggested that games such as *Wii Sports* would have to be analysed individually and then categorized into one or more of the four groups identified. If we take the *Wii Sports boxing* and *bowling* as examples; based upon the definitions outlined by Mueller *et al.* (2008), it is suggested that the bowling game would be placed within the 'Parallel/Non-parallel', 'Competitive/Non-Competitive' and the 'Exertion/Non-Exertion' groups. The boxing game could be categorised into the 'Combat/Non-Combat', 'Ex-ertion/Non-Exertion', 'Parallel/Non-parallel', and the 'Competitive/Non-Competitive'. Conversely, for games to be categorized under this taxonomy it is proposed games would have to be identified under the exergame genre and then individually analysed, enabling the researchers to appropriately place the games into the taxonomy. Moreover, the notion of identifying specific game elements may aid clinicians in choosing appropriate games for utilization within health rehabilitation, within the specified groups and thus specifically outlining which games may be suitable for stroke, fall prevention, or obesity.

The taxonomy presented by Lindley (2008) has shown a series of classification planes. It is suggested that exergames could be categorized under the 'physical' plane in conjunction with ludology. Again using the example of *Wii Sports*, the games have the ability to be single or multiplayer with very little narrative. Furthermore, it is suggested that the games on the *Wii Sports* may have a form of narrative via the players' scores and, within a social environment whereby users are in a bowling league, a story could be formed by the players themselves. With this in mind it has been suggested that exergames could fit on to the physical plane, situated between ludology and narrative.

Finally, the taxonomy created by Sawyer & Smith (2008) has taken a different approach to the former proposed taxonomies, having taken the perspective of sector and the sub-categories of serious games, offering an alternative and conducive method. This taxonomy doesn't actually define game elements or suggest suitable games for that particular area. Conversely, it doesn't suggest which kind of games could be played; for example 'advergames and government/NGOs' would relate to political games such as *President Forever 2008+ Primaries* (TheorySpark, 2006), a simulation game which incorporates realism and fiction. Furthermore, the genre games for health and the defence sector align themselves with rehabilitation and wellness. Second Life has already been implementing strategies which could aid service personnel returning from tours of duty and suffering with Post-Traumatic Stress Disorder (PTSD) and provide their families with support, enabling users to identify the symptoms of the condition from an outsider's perspective (ESA, 2012).

Adams (2009a, 2009b) contends that genre is based upon the gameplay to be experienced by users and Lazzaro (2004) indicates that users play games for a challenge or to overcome an obstacle. Games can include a number of obstacles to be conquered and goals to be attained, resulting in enjoyment and the sense of achievement from playing the game (Lazzaro, 2004). For example, the objective of playing the *Wii Sports*™ golf game is to hit the ball around the course in as few shots as possible. If the player holds the ball, they have overcome the challenges and obstacle set by the rules of the game, thus resulting in the user experiencing the pleasure of enjoyment and achievement. It is noted that players will play games that they may not necessarily enjoy or like because of the social element provided by gaming, which is perceived as more important than personal preference (Lazzaro, 2004).

Games, such as *Wii Fit, Brain Training,* and *Cooking with Mama,* have become popular amongst wider audiences because of the varied gaming experience (Dring, 2009a). The objective of exergames is to provide physical activity to audiences via entertainment but with the underlying aim of facilitating and improving the user's physical activity. It is suggested that this approach may be particularly attractive to older adults who are interested in maintaining physical exercise but who can't, for example, go to a gym or who are more interested in the results of exercise rather than the activity of exercise. Therefore, gameplay could provide the motivation to exercise in such cases and increase exercise amongst audiences who would not necessarily take-up traditional forms of physical activity.

Video games are proving to be an advantage within a variety of settings, such as the classroom or clinical environments. "The games that people are using as part of their everyday enjoyment are far from dumbing them down. They can enhance the educational experience" (Dring, 2009c). Additional encouragement and motivation to users such as older adults via easy interaction (IJsselsteijn, de Kort, Midden, Eggen, & van den Hoven, 2006; IJsselsteijn, Nap, de Kort, & Poels, 2007) is imperative for success across a variety of fields. However, it is suggested that the role of, and user interaction with, the technology plays an important role within the genre of exergaming. The majority of studies to date have utilized various combinations of commercial exergames such as *Wii Sports*, purpose built software, commercial hardware products such as the Nintendo Wii™ console and purpose built virtual reality technology (see Marston, & Smith, 2012). As noted by Ruppert (2011) and Marston & Smith (2012), implementing this technology into health environments is still in its infancy and what seems to be a reccurring comment is the need for substantial clinical and longitudinal studies to fully establish the effects of this technology on patient health/rehabilitation.

With this in mind, consoles such as the Nintendo Wii™ and Microsoft Kinect™ enable users to interact with the environment using natural movements via a remote or gesture move. It is suggested that this form of natural interaction could be more enticing to older adults who want to take-up exercise and play games which they used to play in their earlier years.

FUTURE RESEARCH DIRECTIONS

The utilization of exergames is fast becoming a popular sub-category of the serious games genre within the medium of interactive entertainment. Exergames potentially offer several health benefits to users, clinicians, and scientists alike, while the future appears bright within the fields of gerontology and game studies. Taking into account the taxonomies presented in this chapter, there is no clear or significant taxonomy which the authors can state is the most appropriate for exergames. Readers should consider the initial ground work undertaken by Oh and Yang (2011) and Fencott *et al.* (2012), who have taken different routes to establish a definition of exergames and design a genre map based upon film categories.

However, the taxonomy by Sawyer and Smith (2008) provides researchers and professionals with a different perspective which does not confine current games into a particular category and thus primarily focuses upon the actual sector in which potential games could be utilized. Additionally; Mueller *et al.* (2008) taxonomy takes on the premise of game elements that are categorized into four sections which may also prove useful to understanding this growing area in greater detail and future studies.

Consequently, the authors would like to propose steps for future work and consideration with the purpose of expanding and utilizing the notion of serious games, in particular exergaming, into health rehabilitation. The proposed recommendations are:

- A conducive methodology which would result in a taxonomy to suit the sectors within which serious games are categorized (Sawyer, & Smith, 2008).
- Game analysis and examination of off-the-shelf games and online games, resulting in the exact identification of game elements to fit into a unified classification system, building-upon previous work (Mueller *et al.,* 2008).

- Establish a series of guidelines for utilization within the serious game arena (Ruppert, 2011), which would facilitate clinician/user recommendation to service users.
- Consider and revise the current video game classification system, which would include 'games for health', for users and clinicians who are unfamiliar with the suitability of games for a particular health purpose.
- To conduct longitudinal studies to fully understand the positive effects of commercial and purpose-built technologies for rehabilitation. This could potentially enhance this sub-category under the umbrella of serious games and provide researchers, clinicians, industry professionals and service users with the confidence of to recommend such technologies for future clinical use.

The proposed recommendations have been outlined to build upon previous work by researchers in addition to those presented by Marston and Smith (2012), and to raise awareness of the importance of future studies, such as, longitudinal studies which would provide the community with a greater in-depth knowledge of technology use for rehabilitation. Taking these recommendations on board, it is suggested that substantial progress could be made in this area, bringing together researchers from a variety of backgrounds, in addition to industry professionals. Initial work has already started with international games for health conferences being held in the United States of America and Europe. Additionally, social networking sites such as Facebook have facilitated users who have interest in this area to join groups such as 'Games for Health Australasia' where knowledge, resources, and experience can be shared amongst researchers.

In conclusion, this chapter has identified several approaches taken by researchers to taxonomies. The authors have attempted to provide a greater understanding of the so-called exergame genre within the area of serious games and games for health, both areas of which are still relatively new with little understanding from a clinical and game perspective. To fully comprehend this area of serious games and understand the full use and benefit, further study is required in the field of game and gerontology studies. Additionally, taking on board the recommendations proposed by the authors in this chapter, this could provide and result in greater comprehension adding substantial progress within this segment of game studies. Furthermore, the utilization of different games from different genres may provide researchers to assess the feasibility, usability, and learnability of exergames for prospective users.

REFERENCES

i2010: Independent Living for the Ageing Society. (2007). *Information society and media, European communities*. Retrieved from http://ec.europa.eu/information_society/activities/policy_link/brochures/documents/independent _living.pdf

Abt, C. C. (1975). *Serious games*. New York, NY: Viking Compass.

Adams, E. (2009a). *Fundamentals of game design* (2nd ed.). Berkeley, CA: New Riders.

Adams, E. (2009b). *The designer's notebook: Sorting out the genre muddle*. Retrieved July 9, 2009, from http://www.gamasutra.com/view/feature/4074/the_designers_notebook_sorting_.php

Bogost, I. (2005). *The rhetoric of exergaming*. Paper presented at the Digital Arts and Cultures conference. Copenhagen, Denmark. Retrieved from http://www.bogost.com/writing/the_rhetoric_of_exergaming.shtml

Bogost, I. (2007). *Persuasive games*. Cambridge, MA: MIT Press.

Botte, B., Matera, C., & Sponsiello, M. (2009). Serious games between simulation and game: A proposal of taxonomy. *Journal of e-Learning and Knowledge Society, 5*(2), 11-21.

Caspersen, C. J., Powell, K. E., & Christenson, G. M. (1985). Physical activity, exercise, and physical fitness: Definitions and distinctions for health-related research. *Public Health Reports (Washington, D.C.), 100*(2), 126–131. PMID:3920711.

Chandler, D. (2000). *An introduction to genre theory*. Retrieved from http://www.aber.ac.uk/media/Documents/intgenre/intgenre1.html

Chang, Y. J., Chen, S. F., & Huang, J. D. (2011). A kinect-based system for physical rehabilitation: A pilot study for young adults with motor disabilities. *Research in Developmental Disabilities, 32*, 2566–2570. doi:10.1016/j.ridd.2011.07.002 PMID:21784612.

Clark, R., & Kraemer, T. (2009). Clinical use of Nintendo Wii bowling simulation to decrease fall risk in an elderly resident of a nursing home: A case report. *Journal of Geriatric Physical Therapy, 32*, 174–180. doi:10.1519/00139143-200932040-00006 PMID:20469567.

Dring, C. (2009a). *The I-generation*. Retrieved from http://issuu.com/intentmedia/docs/mcv_issue530

Dring, C. (2009b). *Nintendo DS – Retail biz*. Retrieved from http://issuu.com/intentmedia/docs/mcv_issue531

Entertainment Software Association. (2012). *Games: Improving health*. Retrieved from http://www.theesa.com/games-improving-what-matters/health.asp

Fencott, C., Lockyer, M., Clay, J., & Massey, P. (2012). *Game invaders, the theory and understanding of computer games*. Hoboken, NJ: John Wiley & Sons, Inc. doi:10.1002/9781118347584.

Flynn, S., Palma, P., & Bender, A. (2007). Feasibility of using the Sony PlayStation 2 gaming platform for an individual poststroke: A case report. *Journal of Neurologic Physical Therapy; JNPT, 31*, 180–189. PMID:18172415.

Gaggioli, A., Meneghini, A., Morganti, F., Alcaniz, M., & Riva, G. (2006). A strategy for computer-assisted mental practice in stroke rehabilitation. *Neurorehabilitation and Neural Repair*, *20*, 503–507. doi:10.1177/1545968306290224 PMID:17082506.

Hartman, M. (2011). Wii remote accidents: The dangers of console gaming. *Altered Gamer*. Retrieved from http://www.alteredgamer.com/wii-gear/42586-wii-remote-accidents-the-dangers-of-console-gaming/

IJsselsteijn, W., de Kort, Y. K., Midden, C., Eggen, B., & van den Hoven, E. (2006). *Persuasive technology for human well-being: Setting the scene*. Berlin, Germany: Springer-Verlag. doi:10.1007/11755494_1.

IJsselsteijn, W., Nap, H. H., de Kort, Y., & Poels, K. (2007). *Digital game design for elderly users*. Retrieved from http://alexandria.tue.nl/openaccess/Metis215142.pdf

Janke, K. P. (2006). *Eine taxonomie für digitale spiele*. Ilmenau, Germany: Technical University of Ilmenau, Institute for Media and Communication Science.

Kickmeier-Rust, M. D. (n.d.). *Talking digital educational games*. Retrieved from http://www.eightydays.eu/Paper/01%20Graz%20Workshop.pdf

Kizony, R., Weiss, P. L., Shahar, M., & Rand, D. (2006). TheraTitle—A home based virtual reality rehabilitation system. In *Proceedings of the 6th International Conference on Disability, Virtual Reality and Associated Technologies*, (pp. 209-214). Esbjerg, Denmark: International Society for Virtual Rehabilitation. Retrieved from www.icdvrat.rdg.ac.uk/2006/papers/ICDVRAT2006_S06_N03_Kizony_et_al.pdf

Lange, B., Flynn, S., & Rizzo, A. (2009). Initial usability assessment of off the-shelf video title consoles for clinical title-based motor rehabilitation. *The Physical Therapy Review*, *14*, 355–363. doi:10.1179/108331909X12488667117258.

Laver, K., Ratcliffe, J., George, S., Burgess, L., & Crotty, M. (2011). Is the Nintendo Wii Fit really acceptable to older people? A discrete choice experiment. *BMC Geriatrics*, *11*, 64. doi:10.1186/1471-2318-11-64 PMID:22011360.

Lawrence, S. (2005, January 18). Exercise, lose weight with 'exergaming'. *Fox News*.

Lazzaro, N. (2004). *Why we play games: Four keys to more emotion without story*. Technical Report. XEO Design Inc..

Lindley, C. (2003). Game taxonomies: A high level framework for game analysis and design. *Gamasutra*. Retrieved from http://www.gamasutra.com/view/feature/131205/game_taxonomies_a_high_level_.php?page=2

Marston, H. R. (2010). *Wii like to play too: Computer gaming habits of older adults*. (PhD Thesis). Teesside University. Middlesbrough, UK.

Marston, H. R., & Smith, S. T. (2012). Interactive videogame technologies to support independence in the elderly: A narrative review. *Games for Health Journal: Research, Development, and Clinical Application*, *1*(2), 139–159. doi: doi:10.1089/g4h.2011.0008.

Michael, D., & Chen, S. (2005). *Serious games: Games that educate, train, and inform*. Course Technology PTR.

Mueller, F., Gibbs, M. R., & Vetere, F. (2008). *Taxonomy of exertion games*. Paper presented at OZCHI 2008. Cairns, Australia.

Neale, S. (1980). *Genre*. London, UK: British Film Institute.

Nintendo. (2008a). *Website.* Retrieved from http://www.nintendo.com/games/detail/hoiNtus-4JvIcPtP8LQPyud4Kyy393oep

Nintendo. (2008b). *Website.* Retrieved from http://www.nintendo.com/games/detail/4g1xoYv-pBuBjGBqCS-nGN1GKR4OLQEc

Nintendo. (2008c). *Website.* Retrieved from http://www.nintendo.com/games/detail/4g1xoYv-pBuBjGBqCS-nGN1GKR4OLQEc

Oh, Y., & Yang, S. (2010). *Defining exergames and exergaming.* Retrieved from http://meaningfulplay.msu.edu/proceedings2010/mp2010_paper_63.pdf

Orland, K., & Remo, C. (2008). *Games for health: Noah Falstein on exergaming history.* Retrieved from http://www.gamasutra.com/phpbin/news_index.php?story=18561

Radford, C. (2009). Nintendo Wii injuries: It's not Wii, it's us. *The Telegraph.* Retrieved from http://blogs.telegraph.co.uk/news/ceriradford/100019260/nintendo-wii-injuries-its-not-wii-its-us/

Rand, D., Kizony, R., & Weiss, P. L. (2004). Virtual reality rehabilitation for all: Vivid GX versus Sony PlayStation II EyeToy. In *Proceedings of the 5th International Conference on Disability, Virtual Reality and Associated Technologies,* (pp. 87-94). Oxford, UK: International Society for Virtual Rehabilitation. Retrieved from http://www.gesturetek.com/gesturetekhealth/pdfs/research/Enjoyment_VR.pdf

Rand, D., Kizony, R., & Weiss, P. T. L. (2008). The Sony PlayStation II EyeToy: Low-cost virtual reality for use in rehabilitation. *Journal of Neurologic Physical Therapy; JNPT, 32,* 155–163. PMID:19265756.

Ruppert, B. (2011). New directions in virtual environments and gaming to address obesity and diabetes: Industry perspective. *Journal of Diabetes Science and Technology, 5*(2), 277–282. PMID:21527094.

Sawyer, B. (2007). *The "serious games" landscape.* Paper presented at the Instructional & Research Technology Symposium for Arts, Humanities and Social Sciences. Camden, MA.

Sawyer, B., & Smith, P. (2008). *Serious games taxonomy.* Paper presented at the Game Developers Conference 2008. Retrieved from http://www.dmill.com/presentations/serious-games-taxonomy-2008.pdf

Sports, E. A. (2011). *Fifa 2012.* Retrieved from http://www.ea.com/soccer/fifa12

Swales, J. M. (1990). *Genre analysis.* Cambridge, UK: Cambridge University Press.

United Nations. (2011). *World population prospects.* Retrieved from http://esa.un.org/unpd/wpp/Documentation/pdf/WPP2010_Press_Release.pdf

Yong, J. L., Soon, Y. T., Xu, D., Thia, E., Pei Fen, C., Kuah, C. W., & Kong, K. H. (2010). A feasibility study using interactive commercial off-the-shelf computer gaming in upper limb rehabilitation in patients after stroke. *Journal of Rehabilitation Medicine, 42,* 437–441. doi:10.2340/16501977-0528 PMID:20544153.

Zyda, M. (2005). From visual simulation to virtual reality in games. *Computer, 38*(9), 25–32. doi:10.1109/MC.2005.297.

ADDITIONAL READING

Allen, J. S. (2010). *The effects of a Wii Fit exercise program on balance in a female elderly population.* (M.Ed Thesis). Austin State University. Austin, TX. Retrieved from http://gradworks.umi.com/14/81/1481978.html

Annema, J. H., Verstraete, M., Abeele, V. V., Desmet, S., & Geerts, D. (2010). *Videogames in therapy: A therapist's perspective.* Paper presented at the Fun and Games '10. New York, NY.

Axelrod, L., Fitzpatrick, G., Harley, D., McAllister, G., & White, G. (2010). Making the Wii at home: Game play by older people in sheltered housing. *Lecture Notes in Computer Science, 6389*, 156–176. doi:10.1007/978-3-642-16607-5_10.

Beale, I. L. (2011). *Video games for health, principles and strategies for design and evaluation.* New York, NY: Nova Science Publishers, Inc..

Berthouze, N., Kim, W. W., & Darshak, P. (2007). Does body movement engage you more in digital game play? And Why? In *Proceedings of the International Conference of Affective Computing and Intelligent Interaction,* (pp. 102-113). Lisboa, Portugal: Springer.

Bogost, I. (2007). Persuasive games. In *The Expressive Power of Videogames.* Cambridge, MA: MIT Press.

Bongers, A. J., & Smith, S. T. (2010). *Interactivated rehabilitation device.* Paper presented at the Conference of the Computer-Human Interaction Special Interest Group of Australia on Computer-Human Interaction. Brisbane, Australia.

Bouwhuis, D. G. (2003). Design for person-environment interaction in older age: A gerontechnological perspective. *Gerontechnology (Valkenswaard), 2*, 232–246. doi:10.4017/gt.2003.02.03.002.00.

de Bruin, E. D., Schoene, D., Pichierri, G., & Smith, S. T. (2010). Use of virtual reality technique for the training of motor control in the elderly. *Zeitschrift für Gerontologie und Geriatrie, 43*, 229–234. doi:10.1007/s00391-010-0124-7 PMID:20814798.

de Kort, Y.A.W., & IJsselsteijn, W.A. (2008). People, places and play: Player experience in a socio-spatial content. *ACM Computing Entertainment, 6*(2). doi:/10.1145/1371216.1371221

de Schutter, B. (2010). Never too old to play: The appeal of digital games to an older audience. *Games and Culture, 6*(2), 155–170. doi:10.1177/1555412010364978.

de Schutter, B., & Vanden Abeele, V. (2010). Designing meaningful play within the psychosocial context of older adults. In *Proceedings of Fun & Games 2010.* Leuven, Belgium: ACM. doi:10.1145/1823818.1823827.

Demris, G., Charness, N., Krupinski, E., Ben-Arieh, D., Washington, K., Wu, J., & Farberow, B. (2010). The role of human factors in telehealth. *Telemedicine Journal and e-Health, 16*, 446–453. doi:10.1089/tmj.2009.0114 PMID:20420540.

Fozard, J. L., & Kearns, W. D. (2006). Persuasive GERONtechnology: Reaping technology's coaching benefits at older age. *Lecture Notes in Computer Science, 3962*, 199–202. doi:10.1007/11755494_30.

Gamberini, L., Alcaniz, M., Barresi, G., Fabregat, M., Prontu, L., & Seraglia, B. (2008). Playing for a real bonus: Videogames to empower elderly people. *Journal of Cybertherapy and Rehabilitation, 1*, 37–47.

Gamberini, L., Barresi, G., Majer, A., & Scarpetta, F. (2008). A title a day keeps the doctor away: A short review of computer titles in mental healthcare. *Journal of Cybertherapy and Rehabilitation, 1*, 127–145. Retrievedd from http://htlab.psy.unipd.it/uploads/Pdf/Publications/Papers/Cyber_rehab08.pdf

Guderian, B., Borreson, L. A., Sletten, L. E., Cable, K., Stecker, T. P., Probst, M. A., & Dalleck, L. C. (2010). The cardiovascular and metabolic responses to Wii Fit video game playing in middle-aged and older adults. *The Journal of Sports Medicine and Physical Fitness, 50*, 436–442. PMID:21178930.

Play Yourself Fit

Higgins, H. C., Horton, J. K., Hodgkinson, B. C., & Muggleton, S. B. (2010). Lessons learned: Staff perceptions of the Nintendo Wii as a health promotion tool within an aged-care and disability service. _Health Promotion Journal of Australia_, _21_, 189–195. PMID:21118065.

Kato, P. M. (2010). Video titles in health care: Closing the gap. _Review of General Psychology_, _14_, 113–121. doi:10.1037/a0019441.

Khoo, E. T., & Cheok, A. D. (2006). Age invaders: Inter-generational mixed reality family game. _The International Journal of Virtual Reality_, _5_(2), 45–50.

Koay, J. L., Ng, J. S., & Wong, G. L. (2009). _Nintendo Wii as an intervention: Improving the well-being of elderly in long-term care facilities_. Nanyang Technological University Digital Repository. Retrieved from http://dr.ntu.edu.sg/handle/10220/6217

Mattke, S., Klautzer, L., Mengistu, T., Garnett, J., Hu, J., & Wu, H. (2010). Health and wellbeing in the home: A global analysis of needs, expectations, and priorities for home health care technology. _Rand Corporation_. Retrieved form www.rand.org/pubs/occasional_papers/OP323.html

Nitz, J. C., Kuys, S., Isles, R., & Fu, S. (2010). Is the Wii Fit™ a new-generation tool for improving balance, health and well-being? A pilot study. _Informa Healthcare_, _13_(5), 487–491. PMID:19905991.

Voida, A., & Greenberg, S. (2010a). _Console gaming across generations: Exploring intergenerational interactions in collocated console gaming_. Berlin, Germany: Springer.

Voida, A., & Greenberg, S. (2010b). _A gameroom of our own: Exploring the domestic gaming environment_. Retrieved 12 October 2010, from http://grouplab.cpsc.ucalgary.ca/grouplab/uploads/Publications/Publications/2010-Gameroom.Report2010-961-10.pdf

Wollersheim, D., Merkes, M., Shields, N., Liamputton, P., Wallis, L., Reynolds, F., & Koh, L. (2010). Physical and psychosocial effects of Wii video title use among older women. _International Journal of the Emerging Technology Society_, _8_, 85–98.

KEY TERMS AND DEFINITIONS

Advergames: Relates to the practice of utilizing video games to advertise a product, organization, or perspective.

Exergaming: Is the term used when video-games are used as a form of exercise.

Genre: Is a term used to categorize literature, film, television programs, and video games.

Gerontechnology: Is an interdisciplinary study of ageing and technology, encompassing aspects such as assistive technology, inclusive design, bringing together individuals from a variety of fields such as; health, engineering, psychology, education, architecture and science.

Gerontology: Is the study of ageing, encompassing social, psychological, and biological aspects.

Taxonomy: Is the concept, classification of groups.

Video Game: Is an electronic games involving human interaction with a user interface, which provides feedback during interaction.

Chapter 16
Exergames for Elderly Persons:
Physical Exercise Software Based on Motion Tracking within the Framework of Ambient Assisted Living

Oliver Korn
KORION Simulation and Assistive Technology GmbH, Germany

Klaus Hauer
Agaplesion Bethanien-Hospital Heidelberg, Germany

Michael Brach
University of Muenster, Germany

Sven Unkauf
Wohlfahrtswerk für Baden-Württemberg, Germany

ABSTRACT

This chapter introduces the prototype of a software developed to assist elderly persons in performing physical exercises to prevent falls. The result—a combination of sport exercises and gaming—is also called "exergame." The software is based on research and development conducted within the "motivotion60+" research project as part of the AAL-program (Ambient Assisted Living). The authors outline the use of motion recognition and analysis to promote physical activity among elderly people: it allows Natural Interaction (NI) and takes away the conventional controller, which represented a hurdle for the acceptance of technical solutions in the target group; it allows the real-time scaling of the exergame's difficulty to adjust to the user's individual fitness level and thus keep motivation up. The authors' experiences with the design of the exergame and the first results from its evaluation regarding space, interaction, design, effort, and fun, as well as human factors, are portrayed. The authors also give an outlook on what future exergames using motion recognition should look like.

DOI: 10.4018/978-1-4666-3673-6.ch016

INTRODUCTION

In 2008 the German Federal Ministry of Education and Research (BMBF) introduced a program for research and development in the framework of ambient assisted living (AAL) focusing on solutions that empower the elderly. The framework and its more recent developments like the integration of work contexts have been described elsewhere (Brach & Korn, 2012).

Within the AAL-framework the project "motivotion60+" was funded by the BMBF. The basic idea of this project was using mechanism from gaming to both motivate senior citizens to perform health exercises and assist and support them while doing so. This process of using game mechanics in order to promote real-world activities is called "gamification". Accordingly a major outcome of the project was an exergame (Bogost, 2005) designed to support elderly persons in performing preventive physical exercises based on the principles of sports science.

Life concepts, experiences as well as physical and cognitive abilities of elderly persons are more heterogeneous than in comparable younger groups (Bundesministerium des Innern, 2012; Jian et al., 2011). Thus appropriate exercise-oriented solutions for this group are scarce and scalability is a paradigm for new approaches. The use of motion detection as the primary controller in the exergame is a comparatively new technical path to reach this required scalability.

We describe our experiences from studying the users' perspective and lay out the consequences for the iterative design and development of the exergame regarding space, interaction, design, effort and fun as well as human factors.

BACKGROUND: THE ELDERLY

Elderly people face the prospect of increased morbidity and mortality as part of the natural aging process. They experience a gradual loss in muscle mass, muscle strength, muscle power, balance, flexibility and cardio-respiratory function. This decline is highly interlinked and causal relations with a lack of physical training or detraining have been shown (Nelson et al., 2007). However, all these performances can significantly be improved by physical training without increased risk of clinical adverse events at old age.

The demographic change in Europe and other parts of the industrialized world leads to a relative increase of elderly persons. This calls for the development and implementation of solutions for health promotion and prevention with the aim of preserving the physical, mental and social health of the elderly. Their main concern is to live independently as long as possible. Hence, older people need to be supported to preserve their health and mobility and to guarantee for security in home life and the living environment (Meyer & BMBF-VDE-Innovationspartnerschaft AAL, 2010, p. 124). Physical activity is one of the main measures seniors can take to prevent immobility.

Despite of this potential, the actual physical activity decreases continuously during lifetime. Only 10% of the seniors aged 65-74 meet the recommendations given by official health care institutions. At old age, physical activity declines even more. However, 30 minutes of moderate physical activity at five days or more per week is recommended (e.g. NHS Health Scotland, 2008, p. 25). More specified guidelines suggest different training targets such as improvement of strength, flexibility, endurance or postural control and coordination and give information of training intensity. As described in the ACSM guidelines (American College of Sports Medicine) intensity recommendations are crucial as they relate to the risks in endurance training, especially for persons at risk like as patients with heart disease (Haskell et al., 2007).

In order to meet the guidelines or recommendations, more than 90% of the seniors need to increase the frequency and duration of physical activities. At this point, motivation and the project motivotion60+ come into play: It offers a scalable and fun solution supporting both indoor and outdoor activities.

REQUIREMENTS

Although the adult recommendation defines aerobic intensity in absolute terms (e.g. expressed in METS), a different definition of aerobic intensity is appropriate for older adults, because the fitness level can be low. Moderate-intensity aerobic activity involves a moderate level of effort relative to an individual's aerobic fitness. Thus, for some older adults, a moderate-intensity walk will be a slow walk, whereas for others it will be a brisk walk.

Therefore the perception of different needs and the inclusion of the elderly's diversity into the development is an important success factor: Products and services should not exclude anyone but correspond to the concept of universal design. For this reason, the context-sensitive and user-centered scalability (CSUCS) of the motivotion system can be considered the central requirement (Korn, Brach, Schmidt, Hörz, & Konrad, 2012). A similar requirement called "open system" also implies a modular design (Van Den Broek, Cavallo, & Wehrmann, 2010, p. 17). In a more detailed specification of the requirements for preventive exercises (Hinrichs & Brach, 2012) these are required to be:

- Appropriate, individualized and scalable.
- Attractive to beginners and supports motivating for sustainers.
- Based on modern training principles.
- Within reach even with impaired mobility.

Scalability and openness on the module level have to be complemented on the activity level: exercise configurations based on the principles of training science should be provided for each individual player. If this cannot be managed by automatic rules, a possibility for experts to intervene "manually" has to be implemented.

Another important aim of motivotion60+ is establishing a "good value" solution, so that the tight budgets of social organizations like nursing homes are not over-stretched. The technical system used for the exergame has to be kept to a minimum both in size and complexity so that it can be easily installed in a social facility.

Since the success of new products and services depends on the users' acceptance, the Wohlfahrtswerk for Baden-Wuerttemberg – one of the largest agencies for elderly care in the German state Baden-Wuerttemberg – took an important the role as the link to the end users. With regard to the project this means that everything associated with the exergame was checked whether it met the demands of the potential users regarding space, interaction, graphic design, effort and fun as well as human factors.

SOLUTION AND PROTOTYPE

The aim of the project motivotion60+ is to establish a suitable training and exercise framework for elderly people. The exergame exercises have been developed in co-operation with experts from sports science and sports medicine. In the coordination/strength training sector ("indoor") focused here, the user plays an exergame consisting of several mini-games. Each mini-game is played by performing a certain exercise with motor and cognitive affordances, thus gaining score points and achievements. More details on the exercise conception, training configuration, time scales and quality control have already been published (Brach et al., 2012).

The mini-games are based on exercises developing better abilities in the three areas balance, strength and complex (= balance plus strength) – areas helping to prevent the elderly from falls. In total seven mini-games have been developed which are allocated to the categories above in Table 1.

The strategy was to identify a set of exercises both suited to the medical task and the high age of the users, and to design the games around these

Table 1. Overview of the minigames

Game	Flying	Football	Chariot Race	Dove Hunt	Stair Climbing	Bell Ringing	Dancing
Place	Plane	Rio	Rome	Venice	Paris	Paris	Athens
Focus	Balance	Complex	Balance	Complex	Strength	Strength	Complex

exercises. The first task was to establish a narrative framework integrating the interests of the elderly and thus increasing their motivation to carry out the physical exercises. The resulting game concept was a never-ending journey to interesting places around the world. While this stage was easy to set up, the technical realization of computer-based sports games or exergames was demanding because a central requirement for acceptance was the establishment of Natural Interaction (NI) and thus the use of motion recognition as a primary input device.

Technical Implementation

Since an important requirement was a "good value" solution the system used was kept to a minimum both in size and complexity, so it can be easily installed in a social facility. This led to the decision of using off-the-shelve-hardware, i.e. Microsoft's Kinect in combination with a Zotac mini-PC based on AMD's fusion processors using Windows and automatically launching the game client.

The games are controlled by the motion tracking system Kinect, which records the player's movement and extracts a skeleton by using algorithms based on the combined data of two video cameras and the depth image obtained by an infrared sensor. Traditionally, the form of video analysis used by the Kinect required expensive equipment. Thanks to a compact design and the price effects of mass production, the Kinect allows an inexpensive way to track human body movements with quantifiable results.

Although the Kinect's abilities excel those of Sony's EyeToy or Nintendo's Wii, there are still limitations: Depending on the quality of the implementation and the camera setup, the Kinect can currently only detect changes in angle above ten degrees and resolve objects with a minimum of three centimeters in size. Nevertheless this allows the analysis of complex movements required for sports exercises. Another challenge was the latency of the system: for real-time feedback and context-sensitive scaling (Korn, Brach, et al., 2012) the latency should be below 200 ms.

Motion recognition as a game controlling mechanic had been pre-tested in 2010 (six months before Microsoft's Kinect was released) by playing motion-based games with the target group using Sony's EyeToy. Based on these early tests we chose to avoid 3D-space in the motivotion exergames because orientation then became too demanding for most of the elderly players.

User Experience

To give an insight in the current user experience, we provide a description of the user activities involved playing the game "goal keeping," a complex exercise set in a football arena in Rio de Janeiro.

At first the user has to log into the system so the corresponding set of parameters is selected. The player then might take a look at his current statistics, showing not only the games played but also the distribution of effort among the three areas power, balance and complex.

To start an exergame, the player selects it from the games menu. While moving through the menu the corresponding destinations are pinpointed on the world map. In-between the place-specific exercises (e.g. stair-climbing the Notre Dame in Paris) there is always a virtual flight sequence. This flight is realized as a short balance game, where the player has to avoid hitting birds while steering the plane with his arms. This feature emphasizes the importance of balance exercises and guarantees their frequent use. Once the plane arrives at its destination, a start screen provides the following information about the upcoming game and the corresponding exercise:

- Duration and level.
- An exercise instruction text.
- An animation of the "personal trainer" (i.e. the avatar) showing the correct exercise movement.
- A historical or geographical fact about the destination under the headline "did you know?" which might later come up as a quiz question.

When a user starts a game for the first time, the set of training parameters is either a standard set or has been individually adapted to the user by the caretakers. Some cases will require manual adaptations of the parameters, e.g. if the subject has problems to move the arms up to shoulder level.

The results of each exercise in every game are continuously stored and analyzed, so substantial improvements or degradations of the player's performance are recognized immediately. After only a few minutes this continuous record of training data allows to adjust the game and thus the exercises' challenge level according to the user's performance – so the most important requirement, the user-centered scalability can be met. Since every game starts at the lowest difficulty level, the challenge can be slightly increased if the results show potential for more advanced exercises. On the other hand the challenge level can be quickly lowered if the results show that the user has a "bad day." Thus, the requirement of being attractive to beginners and motivating for sustainers is met.

The user has access to most of the data collected (scores, times, achievements) in a statistics screen designed for intuitive understanding (Figure 1).

Given the consent of the user, these training results can also be transferred to a web-based health-platform and then be assessed by medical experts who can also be consulted for training advices.

The goal keeping game is a good example for this adaptation of parameters: The size of the area which the goalkeeper can cover and thus the effort needed to catch a ball can be adapted. Another parameter with a direct impact on difficulty is the frequency of balls and their flight characteristics. Although all balls are shot at a random angle, the height of their flight path or even the option to bounce can be edited. The visual feedback is obvious and motivating: When the ball is caught, the screen flashes in green and the crowd cheers. When the ball enters the goal the screen flashes red (See Figure 2).

After each game a results screen shows the performance and the score gained. It also informs the player if a new level has been reached (in case of exceptionally good or bad performance) and displays achievements.

Rather than concentrating on a comparison of performances between different individuals as in current social games, the motivotion exergame highlights individual progress and motivates by positive feedback and achievements. These achievements are gained if certain thresholds are met (e. g. 100 caught balls) and serve the sole purpose of keeping the players motivated. To prevent the abstract lists of achievements known from game platforms like X-Box Live, we implemented a visual representation for each medal or cup. To scale the training time covered by achievements, each achievement is realized in four grades (bronze, silver, gold and diamond). These cups and medals are automatically put on display in a trophy board (Figure 3) that is directly accessible from the main menu – so like in real life, the players can "brag" about their accomplishments.

After the physical exercise each game is followed by a quiz question randomly drawn from the set of facts displayed on the start screen. Thus,

Figure 1. Intuitive statistics showing the user's scores in monthly periods

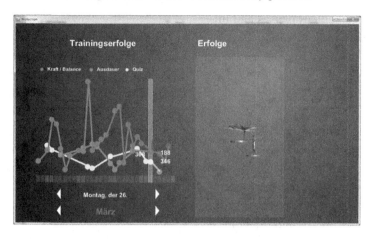

Figure 2. Screenshot of the goal keeping game

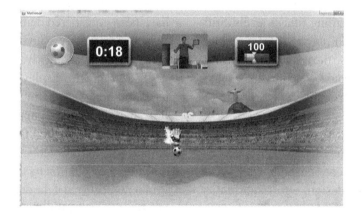

Figure 3. Trophy board with achievements visualized by cups and medals

cognitive and physical activities are combined, a blended strategy that guarantees pauses and improves performance on both levels.

EVALUATION

The evaluation of the motivotion system with potential users at the the Wohlfahrtswerk for Baden-Wuerttemberg is ongoing. Nineteen players aged 60-93 with an average age of 76 have been using the motivotion system at least three times a week. The usage times and training data have been recorded and in addition questionnaires were used at irregular intervals. The strong variation in scores (Figure 4) is a direct result of the high individual variance regarding fitness levels. Still eleven players (ca. 58%) played at least six out seven days (Figure 4) – so the usage of the system was higher than anticipated which indicates that the scalability of the exergame was suitable to keep the motivation up.

Although the evaluation is not complete, it has brought the following findings and consequences for the future development of exergames regarding space, interaction, design, effort and fun as well as human factors:

Space

Rooms or areas (outside of their own domesticity) in which the exergame is used need to be directly accessible by public transport and provide accessibility. Cables become stumbling blocks and adequate lighting must be provided. The users need sufficient moving space: since it uses the Kinect's sensor, the required space exceeds the corresponding requirements of established systems like the Nintendo Wii (Harley, Fitzpatrick, Axelrod, White, & McAllister, 2010). The use of a projection instead of a television has proven to be beneficial in the field of visual representation because the area covered is much larger.

Interaction

The usability and ergonomics of input devices are often not suitable for persons not used to new technology or who are cognitively and/or physically impaired – especially the proper usage of a controller. Since the exergame developed in motivotion could be operated without classical input devices, the usage was intuitive. Using Natural Interaction (NI) can be strongly recommended.

Design

Small and hard-to-read texts and graphics can lead to the exclusion of users. Foreign words or references to recent movies and music bands have been considered demotivating by the users. If such elements were involved in quiz questions, resignation enters quickly ("That's not my field").

The graphical display should appeal to the users but not overwhelm them with complexity. It is helpful if they encounter representations known from everyday life. Abstraction leads to comprehension problems. This was clearly shown during pre-evaluation by the response to avatars: Problems occurred if the degree of abstraction was too high so users did no longer identify. Hence the avatar was designed to resemble an abstract human body instead of a cartoon character.

Effort and Fun

For quizzes or other assignments it is important to keep in mind that time pressure, which for instance is visualized by using an hourglass, creates pressure and nervousness. Similar experiences have been made with games that punish errors of the player in a way that the game is stopped. The evaluation showed that scoring and winning the game is rather secondary for the player while having fun is in the foreground (See Figure 5).

Figure 4. Daily score rate of the 19 users recorded in the current evaluation period

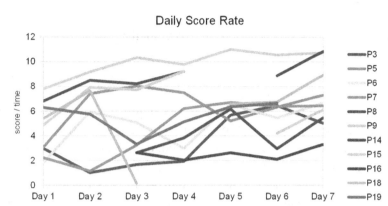

Figure 5. Impressions from the user experience evaluation of the indoor games

Human Factors

Whether an activity is considered to be "fun" also depends on how the system is introduced. According to the principle of universal design, it is essential that potential users are not stigmatized, so names like "old" or "retirees" should be avoided completely. Research has clearly shown that the combination of fun and play with physical and mental training is particularly appreciated (Lager & Bremberg, 2005) – but the acceptance also rises if these potential benefits are communicated from the very beginning. During the evaluation we could also establish a relationship between the acceptance of the system and the appearance and the "charisma" of the introducing person. It

is important that this person appears positively, motivates the participants, plays the game and explains new concepts such as the avatar.

These findings are consistent with the observation that the willingness to engage with computer games is mainly connected to the extent in which intrinsic motivation is addressed by means of easy access, suitable requirement-levels and known game content (Jäger & Weiniger, 2010). At the same time concerns and reservations expressed by the participants should be taken seriously. Skeptical attitudes towards new technologies in general and especially against computer games can be overcome if participants get the opportunity to observe other players at the beginning and join the game at a later point of time.

FUTURE RESEARCH

With the success of the Kinect and other motion recognition sensors like the Asus Xtion or the SoftKinetic exergames are becoming more frequent. However, games especially designed for the needs of the elderly are still rare. Although this group highly benefits from the security and the medical data collection resulting from the use motion sensors, there are several problems:

- The users' technical affinity often is so low, that small problems like an unplugged cable lead to service requests.
- The combination of a small income, high diversity and a high service demand results in unattractive business models, so many companies prefer developing for different audiences.

Obviously, the robustness of the systems has to be increased even further. Currently the placement and also the look of the motivotion system (including a visible camera/sensor) create technical and emotional barriers. A vision for the future is a system of independent motion sensors which automatically calibrates through wireless communication. These sensors would only need a power supply and a place in the living room to work. The motion data could be analyzed by a small computer directly connected to the user's TV-set.

Another research scenario recently addressed by the AAL program is the development of systems which support the elderly while they are still at the workplace. Such systems could decrease ergonomic problems and increase motivation in the last years of professional life. A framework for Assistive Systems in Production Environments (ASiPE) using motion recognition and gamification has already been introduced (Korn, Schmidt, & Hörz, 2012).

CONCLUSION

Within the research and development project motivotion60+ an exergame for elderly persons was developed. The aim was to motivate the users to perform prevention exercises. The solution was significantly improved by the implementation of Natural Interaction (NI) based on motion recognition. The real-time analysis of the user's performance in the exercises allows a quick adaption of the challenge level according to the current physical or cognitive state of the user.

Our findings regarding space, interaction, design, effort and fun as well as human factors can help future exergame development. However, the steps of studying requirements and adapting the solution should be considered a circular repeating process, with each iteration leading to a more useful and accepted solution. In this process real user feedback should be integrated as soon as possible.

The propagation of exergames depends on their robustness and their ease of use. Future systems both in homes and at the workplace will need to take Natural Interaction (NI) to the next level by configuring autonomously and assisting discretely from the background.

REFERENCES

Bogost, I. (2005). *The rhetoric of exergaming*. Paper presented at the Digital Arts and Cultures (DAC) Conference (December 2005). Copenhagen, Denmark.

Brach, M., Hauer, K., Rotter, L., Werres, C., Korn, O., Konrad, R., & Göbel, S. (2012). Modern principles of training in exergames for sedentary seniors: Requirements and approaches for sport and exercise sciences. *International Journal of Computer Science in Sport, 11*, 86–99.

Brach, M., & Korn, O. (2012). Assistive technologies at home and in the workplace—A field of research for exercise science and human movement science. *European Review of Aging and Physical Activity*, 9(1), 1–4. doi:10.1007/s11556-012-0099-z.

Bundesministerium des Innern. (2012). *Demografiebericht*. Berlin, Germany: Bundesministerium des Innern.

Harley, D., Fitzpatrick, G., Axelrod, L., White, G., & McAllister, G. (2010). Making the Wii at home: Game play by older people in sheltered housing. In *Proceedings of the 6th International Conference on HCI in Work and Learning, Life and Leisure: Workgroup Human-Computer Interaction and Usability Engineering*, (pp. 156–176). Berlin, Germany: Springer-Verlag. Retrieved from http://dl.acm.org/citation.cfm?id=1917789.1917802

Haskell, W. L., Lee, I.-M., Pate, R. R., Powell, K. E., Blair, S. N., & Franklin, B. A. et al. (2007). Physical activity and public health: Updated recommendation for adults from the American College of Sports Medicine and the American Heart Association. *Medicine and Science in Sports and Exercise*, 39(8), 1423–1434. doi:10.1249/mss.0b013e3180616b27 PMID:17762377.

Health Scotland, N. H. S. (2008). Energising lives: A guide to promoting physical activity in primary care. Edinburgh, UK: Glasgow.

Hinrichs, T., & Brach, M. (2012). The general practitioner's role in promoting physical activity to older adults: A review based on program theory. *Current Aging Science*, 5(1), 41–50. doi: 10.2174/1874609811205010041 PMID:21762090.

Jäger, K. W., & Weiniger, R. (2010). Silver gaming–Ein zukunftsträchtiger baustein gegen altersbedingte Isolation. *Ambient Assisted Living-AAL*. Retrieved from http://www.vde-verlag.de/proceedings-en/453209058.html

Jian, C., Sasse, N., von Steinbüchel-Rheinwall, N., Schafmeister, F., Shi, H., Rachuy, C., & Schmidt, H. (2011). Towards effective, efficient and elderly-friendly multimodal interaction. In *Proceedings of the 4th International Conference on Pervasive Technologies Related to Assistive Environments*, (pp. 45:1–45:8). New York, NY: ACM. doi:10.1145/2141622.2141675

Korn, O., Brach, M., Schmidt, A., Hörz, T., & Konrad, R. (2012). Context-sensitive user-centered scalability: An introduction focusing on exergames and assistive systems in work contexts. In S. Göbel, W. Müller, B. Urban, & J. Wiemeyer (Eds.), *E-Learning and Games for Training, Education, Health and Sports*, (Vol. 7516, pp. 164–176). Berlin, Germany: Springer. Retrieved from http://www.springerlink.com/index/10.1007/978-3-642-33466-5_19

Korn, O., Schmidt, A., & Hörz, T. (2012). Assistive systems in production environments: Exploring motion recognition and gamification. In *Proceedings of the 5th International Conference on Pervasive Technologies Related to Assistive Environments*. New York, NY: ACM. 2012, doi: 10.1145/2413097.2413109

Lager, A., & Bremberg, S. (2005). *Health effects of video and computer game playing: A systematic review*. Retrieved from https://xn--folkhlsostmman-9hbf.se/PageFiles/4170/R200518_video_computer_game(1).pdf

Meyer, S., & BMBF-VDE-Innovationspartnerschaft AAL. (2010). *AAL in der alternden gesellschaft : Anforderungen, akzeptanz und perspektiven : Analyse und planungshilfe*. Berlin, Germany: VDE-Verl.

Nelson, M. E., Rejeski, W. J., Blair, S. N., Duncan, P. W., Judge, J. O., & King, A. C. et al. (2007). Physical activity and public health in older adults. *Medicine and Science in Sports and Exercise*, 39(8), 1435–1445. doi:10.1249/mss.0b013e3180616aa2 PMID:17762378.

Van Den Broek, G., Cavallo, F., & Wehrmann, C. (2010). *AALIANCE ambient assisted living roadmap*. Amsterdam, The Netherlands: IOS Press.

ADDITIONAL READING

Bailey, R. W. (1989). *Human performance engineering using human factors/ergonomics to achieve computer system usability* (2nd ed.). Englewood Cliffs, NJ: Prentice Hall.

Deterding, S., Sicart, M., Nacke, L., O'Hara, K., & Dixon, D. (2011). Gamification: Using game design elements in non-gaming contexts. In *Proceedings of the 2011 Annual Conference on Human Factors in Computing Systems*. ACM.

Ilmarinen, J. (2006). *Towards a longer worklife: Ageing and the quality of worklife in the European Union*. Helsinki, Finland: FIOH.

Korn, O. (2012). Industrial playgrounds: How gamification helps to enrich work for elderly or impaired persons in production. In *Proceedings of the ACM EICS '12*. New York, NY: ACM. doi: 10.1145/2305484.2305539

McGonigal, J. (2011). *Reality is broken: Why games make us better and how they can change the world*. London, UK: Random House.

Nunes, F., Silva, P. A., & Abrantes, F. (2010). Human-computer interaction and the older adult: An example using user research and personas. In *Proceedings of PETRA '10*. ACM.

Reeves, B., & Read, J. L. (2009). *Total engagement: Using games and virtual worlds to change the way people work and businesses compete*. New York, NY: ACM.

Satre, D., Knight, B. G., & David, S. (2006). Cognitive behavioral interventions with older adults: Integrating clinical and gerontological research. *Professional Psychology, Research and Practice*, (37): 489–498. http://escholarship.org/uc/item/1qg446xk doi:10.1037/0735-7028.37.5.489.

Wiemeyer, J. (2010). Gesundheit auf dem spiel? Serious games in prävention und rehabilitation. *Deutsche Zeitschrift fur Sportmedizin, 61*(11), 252–257.

Chapter 17
Social Inclusion through Virtual Worlds

Hein de Graaf
Social Psychologist, The Netherlands

ABSTRACT

In this chapter, the theoretical foundation of the use of virtual worlds (3D environments) to strengthen the personal social network of people who are challenged in that area, especially the elderly, is described. The psychological (bordering on sociological and anthropological) aspects of "living" in a virtual "world," such as Second Life, are described. Opportunities and threats of those aspects regarding the possibilities of strengthening the personal network and quality of life are indicated. The chapter is based on a 5-year research project. The concrete outcome of which is translated into real life projects under the name VayaV. VayaV is described in this chapter as a case study. The Dutch municipalities all agree that the main social problems facing their citizens are exclusion, feeling lonely, passivity, and lack of friends and an adequate personal social network. In the latest figures, more than a third of the people who were interviewed (a cross section of the whole Dutch population) said: I am often lonely and I am suffering because of it. With their consent, a virtual environment is developed based on the research project in Second Life, in such a way that people who do not like computers and know nothing about digital social networks can meet and have fun and form a community of friends and acquaintances. In this case, there is more to the VayaV approach than playing a game in which someone has set the rules and goals for you. It is more like everyday life where people set their own goals and rules, according to their own values and norms.

INTRODUCTION

More and more presenters start their presentation with: "I am a Baby boomer, 65 years of age...." This is a strange way of introducing themselves, as if their age is defining them. But more and more people come to realise that this a relevant introduction in presentations, even in very serious circles. Age has become a defining characteristic. And admitting that somebody is part of the increasing group of 'elderly citizens, seniors' or whatever euphemism is used, seems to become more and more important.

DOI: 10.4018/978-1-4666-3673-6.ch017

There is a lingering and pervasive stigma toward older people: we are seen as a burden, instead of as an opportunity. We seem to be a problem in the future years, increasing the 'Crisis', because we are often sick, disabled and in constant need of expensive care. My answer to this stigma is: of course we are human and therefor fragile. But most of us will be able to handle it, even in a future when we will be even more challenged, with a little help from our friends. But we would be lost without those friends. And a characteristic of growing old is, as we all know, losing friends and the ability to make new ones. Dorothy Field is cited in an article about friendship in encyclopedia.com (1999):

Older adulthood, usually considered to begin when a person reaches about sixty-five years of age, is marked by two kinds of changes that affect friendships. On the one hand, increasing health concerns, reduced mobility, and declining vigor reduce opportunities for contact with friends and the energy the individual has to devote to them. On the other hand, retirement and reduced social and family obligations increase the free and uncommitted time the individual has to nurture existing friendships and to develop new ones. Social networks are a must for us, not a choice. The challenge lies there: how to strengthen our social networks, even the more challenged among us 'elderly'.

Until the end of 2011, I worked for the Dutch Association of Municipalities (VNG). The municipalities must assist their citizens, especially the elderly, to live their life to the full, using their experience, talents and possibilities where possible and giving them a hand where needed. In The Netherlands, there is now a law for this: Wmo (Wet maatschappelijke ondersteuning: the Societal support Act). The municipalities found out that their citizens to a large extend were suffering from the same 'disease': loneliness. Van Tilburg and Gierveld found out that approximately 30% of the Dutch population feels lonely often. One third of them to such extend that they are suffering from it. They feel sick, often literally.

There is more evidence that lonely, isolated people have more health problems than active persons. Several papers from a recent meeting of the IFA (International Federation on Aging) in May 2012 in Prague confirmed this to be the case all over the world. Paoletti (2012) wrote participation in social activities and social network is important for the quality of life of older people, but also it has preventive effects on mental and physical functioning. Dobson and McLaughlin (2012) stated that high levels of social support and engagement may in fact help sustain good health and functional ability. Baecker et al. (2012) discussed that isolation may lead to feelings of loneliness and depression, which tends to reinforce loneliness and isolation. Both conditions are connected to poor physical health and to increased mortality.

Hong (2012) found that elderly who worried more about social isolation tended to have poor health, whereas those who had more positive image about themselves who participated more in social activities and who went out more often showed higher level of health.

Finally, Schwarz-Woelzl (2012) stated that to be embedded in social networks contributes significantly to older people's quality of life. It leads to lower rates of depression, decreased risk of dementia and lower mortality rates.

So, for social and for health reasons it is very important for the municipalities to support and facilitate their citizens to be active and have a strong social network. Imagine the very unpleasant surprise for the municipalities as they realized that for those 30%, loneliness and lack of social connections are at the heart of many problems they have. At the same time they realised that it is very hard to fight loneliness with the old methods of information, advice and training they used before. This traditional methods did not work!

Therefore, as it is often the case, they were more than willing to hear about other innovative methods, even ICT based and including very alien concepts like 'virtual worlds'. But they asked me: will it work? To answer that, I needed to analyse the phenomenon of 'loneliness' and the role ICT social networks (can) play.

Loneliness is the subjective experience of an unpleasant or inadmissible lack of (quality of) certain social relationships (de Jong-Gierveld, 1987). People who feel lonely, say that they are especially bothered by it because they no longer feel able to participate in their social environment. If in trouble they can only fall back on the 'government' and ask them for formal professional care providers.

If those formal carers are able to help them to solve their problems in the future themselves, remains to be seen. The new law in The Netherlands Wmo (Wet maatschappelijke ondersteuning: the Societal Support Act) has a new role for the local authorities: listening to the citizens and making a plan together to solve immediate problems and help them solve their future problems themselves. The best approach turns out to be: helping them strengthen their social networks.

But some people are challenged more than others combined with too few resources (and motivation) to do something about it. This is often associated with certain characteristics that make them vulnerable to setbacks as well as missing the ability to do something about it themselves. This is the target group of the VayaV approach I am about to describe. The goal of our strategy in VayaV is first to encourage interaction in a community. Then follows activation and participation in their everyday social environment.

An important question to answer is: why not offer them the existing successful social networks on the market, like Facebook?

It turns out that virtual social networks like Facebook are hardly used by our target group. The reason is mainly this: Facebook-like social networks do not enable each other to 'meet' and interact as a group/community. Facebook is actually still boils down to the exchange of (not always reliable) information.

There are still significant digital divisions in the use of Internet according to age and life-stage, with retired Internet users being particularly unlikely to access social networking sites, write a blog, or participate in chat rooms (Dutton,

Helsper and Gerber, 2009). However, previous research shows that in the context of increased geographical mobility, older age groups value the Internet for maintaining family, friendship, and support networks, and reducing social isolation (Blit-Cohen and Litwin, 2004).

While participants valued the use of email and Skype to communicate with family and friends, few respondents, according to Buse (2012), used social networking sites such as Facebook or MySpace. However, social networking sites such as Friends Reunited or Genes Reunited were more frequently used, and enabled participants to maintain existing offline friendship and family networks, reawaken dormant relationships, and establish new connections.

The decision makers from the dutch municipalities had another problem with ICT and elderly people. And this is a stigma that is often heard around the world: older people cannot and do not want to use new technology. Half of the people aged 75 to 79 years believe that new technology could be beneficial and helpful in handling their daily activities (Sternberg, 2012).

Research carried out in Australia showed that older people are keen to embrace new technologies and that newer, user friendly technologies combined with reliable, fast internet connections and on-going localised, personalised support enhance access to general information, social networks and community services. Pilot participants reported improved self-rated health, better community involvement, and positive changes to their social networks, in particular communication with dispersed family ties improved (Feist, 2012).

We run the risk that elderly people are again on the verge of being excluded. They avoid the ICT solutions that are on offer because they do not fit their expectations, life style, and needs. But they are excluded from the increasingly important digital resources that they need in view of their situation.

The problem is not the older person; the problem is the way ICT solutions are designed and presented. The experts all agree on that. There are some conditions the ICT solution should meet. The following conditions were verbally presented at the IFA conference May 2012, as a result of one of the workshops (no author):

1. Co-creation, tailor made
2. Simple technology
3. High volume, low costs
4. Local-regional
5. Human contacts
6. Suppliers and vendors and elderly plus carers, service providers, hobbyists of all ages
7. Sustainable (also after investments)
8. User centred
9. Government now facilitating, stimulating (not financing)
10. Standardized, proven and open technology
11. Mobile devices, like pads
12. Living lab approach

As my research approach aimed at concrete activities and projects in the municipalities I tried to incorporate all these conditions in the VayaV Metaverse project that will be described in the last part of this chapter.

BACKGROUND

LaMendola (2010, pp. 108-119) emphasizes that 'there is nowadays a commonplace recognition that the online world is, in part, a world of social networks that promote community'. He goes on to say that "computer networks" have become "social institutions" integrated into "everyday lives". Wellman (2001, pp. 2031-2034) stated:

Computer networks are inherently social networks, linking people, organizations and knowledge... The proliferation of computer networks has facilitated a de-emphasis on group solidarities at work and in the community and afforded a turn to networked societies that are loosely bounded and sparsely knit.

LaMendola (2010) discussed the implication of digital social networks for social work practice and as a social worker he takes this conclusion as a charge to social work. This means a challenge to use social psychology notions to analyze the possibilities of these 'virtual social institutions' for people who are struggling in their everyday life to maintain or establish adequate personal social networks they can depend on when needed. In other words: to help them fight social exclusion and loneliness.

Castells (2009) is very optimistic about the possibilities of the new information age for all of us:

Citizens of the Information Age become able to invent new programs for their lives with the materials of their suffering, dreams, fears and hopes. They build their projects by sharing their experience. They subvert the practice of communication as usual by squatting in the medium and creating their message. They overcome the powerlessness of their solitary despair by networking their desire. They fight the powers that be by identifying the networks that are... if you think differently, communication networks will operate differently (p. 431).

Almost poetic, this quote, but challenging. However, there are a lot of people out there who would love to be like those new citizens because of their 'suffering' but are unable to do so on their own. Therefor the study became the basis for a concrete action programme called VayaV (VirtuAlly Young Again in a Virtual world) about which more information is given later.

In this article, I describe some of my 4-year Second Life research (2008-2012) and the VayaV program itself. As this is not a detective story I can afford to give away the clue already at the beginning: Second Life is not the best place for people socially challenged! However a specially developed virtual world based on the OpenSimulator platform can be, if the designing is done by the intended users (residents) themselves.

MAIN FOCUS OF THE CHAPTER[1]

Issues, Controversies, Problems

Psychological, Sociological, and Anthropological Aspects of the Virtual World

In this chapter, I describe the characteristics of a virtual world (or metaverse) using the only long time established Virtual World called 'Second Life' as example. Jillian Sherwin (2007) describes in an internet article Second Life as a Massive Multiplayer Online Role-Playing 'Game' (MMORG)... A world of endless possibilities, where if you can imagine it, it can happen. Avatars, the digital representations of human gamers, can do everything that people can do and more; they eat, sleep, buy houses, form relationships, and also fly and teleport.

In 1999, Philip Rosedale formed Linden Lab, the company behind Second Life, with the goal of creating a revolutionary three-dimensional shared experience. Second Life was launched to the public in June 2003. It has grown exponentially as inhabitants of the world constantly build and add to it.

Unlike many MMORGs, there is no specific objective or mission that denizens of Second Life must achieve. In that respect, Second Life is not really a 'game'. The residents/avatars set their own rules and goals. Avatars act like regular people. They go shopping, go out on dates and get married, attend concerts, have jobs. With chat and instant messaging capabilities, Second Life avatars can communicate in several ways. Users can also control the movement of their avatar, from basic gestures like a handshake, to more complicated moves, like dancing.

Just for fun and out of curiosity I entered Second Life (a 3D virtual world) early 2007 as an avatar named Hannes (last name Breda). After a lot of confusion I discovered real communities in a virtual environment. I even started a group with 150 members called: Second and First Life Confusion. We were wearing virtual T-shirts with the text: 'I am confused, or wait, maybe not'. Later I went to the Dutch SL quarters and started a Dutch community called Doggersbank on a 'region' I bought with the name 'Nederland' (it still remains to this day).

Being a social psychologist by trade and by nature I started my own personal research, action research. Kurt Lewin's (1946) description of "action research" (a phrase he coined) is that it is a process of change involving three steps: *Unfreezing*: the individual or group become aware of a need to change. *Changing*: The situation is diagnosed and new models of behavior are explored and tested. *Refreezing*: Application of new behavior is evaluated, and if reinforcing, adopted (pp. 34-46).

More or less, I started to feel like an anthropologist, especially after reading a book by Tom Boellstorff, associate professor of anthropology, University of California, Irvine, who did the same as I did: participate as an avatar in everything that Second Life has to offer. He wrote it down in his book *Coming of Age in Second Life*. I refer to his book for references from literature on these issues. The reason I always recommend this book, is that there is hardly anything written about Second Life at an empirical level.

I also started to give weekly psychology 'classes' to Dutch 'residents' of Second Life in my very own regions (Nederland and Noordzee) that I bought (looking like a medieval village and surroundings, that I designed and build together with some knowledgeable friends). In those classes I commented on psychological issues regarding living in a virtual environment as Second Life. Some of the analyses in this chapter are from these classes.

Second life residents are all playing roles and disguised as avatars they themselves have chosen. So, anonymity is the rule. However, during the years I lead this Dutch community I discovered that a lot of those residents were older than 60 and one way or another challenged by their Real Life circumstances. Second Life was for them a possibility to 'forget' about those challenges for a while.

My findings in short: the psychological, socio-logical, and anthropological aspects of a virtual world as Second Life are very much 'real'. People have fun, are frustrated, are excited and even 'in love'. The emotions they feel are real. The feeling of belonging to a group are real. The successes and failures are experienced as real. It is known that people can experience 'virtual' experiences as real.

An important concept here is: 'suspended disbelief'. You know something is 'not real', but having fun and liking it, you suspend your disbelief. Everyone who likes reading fiction knows this feeling: for a short while you are 'in the story'. So, if the effect of living in a virtual world and meeting people there and expanding your social network into the realms of 'make belief' are having real effect on your real life, what an opportunity this is for others.

In my work (until the end of 2011) for the As-sociation of Netherlands Municipalities I visited a lot of policymakers on a local level. They all agreed that the main social problem facing their citizens was: exclusion, feeling lonely, passivity, lack of friends and an adequate personal social network. The latest figures: more than a third of the people who were interviewed (a cross section of the whole Dutch population) said: I am often lonely and I am suffering because of it.

In view of my action research aspirations I started to unfreeze and change things based on the experiences and analysis of my Second Life. My mission: develop a virtual environment in such a way that people who don't like computers and know nothing about digital social networks, can meet and have fun and form a community of friends and acquaintances. I called this VayaV (from the Spanish word meaning: come on! And the V of Virtual. Also an acronym: Virtually Young again).

VayaV Could be Described as a Case Study for Avatar-Based Communication as an Instrument for Socializing and Community Building

The challenges are: how can you explain the sunset to a blind man and how can you develop a market when there is none? Outside the users of virtual environments it is very hard to convince people that they can use this to their advantage. And if convinced, how can we start sustainable communities that will be able to use this virtual 3D environment in the foreseeable future?

Before coming back to these issues and answer-ing these questions and describing VayaV I will first give you the theoretical foundation of VayaV.

Feelings of friendship, fears, worries, arousal, love, and hate, being happy, having fun are im-portant human emotions. They are always real, also in a virtual world like Second Life. Reality is what your mind makes of it. It is important to be serious about emotions even if they are aroused in a 'game' environment as Second Life. Because people experience these emotions in their real (First) Life. And at that moment Second Life is part of their First Life.

Social behaviour is dealing with people. Your actions are based on your perceptions of people surrounding you and on the norms and values of the society you live in (the rules as you see them and are willing to follow).

Second Life is almost an anarchy. There are some basic rules, but there are also areas in Sec-ond Life where they do not apply. Moreover, the rules are there because the residents themselves have chosen to make them and follow them (and enforce them upon others). Also, the residents of Second Life base their actions on their perceptions of the people (avatars) around them.

Suspended Disbelief

Books, movies, games, and SL have something in common: you can be 'submerged' (immersed) in it - even without tricks as helmets and goggles.

Most writers emphasise the technological aspects of immersion. Steuer (1992, pp. 73-93) for example mentions as the two main sources of immersion: depth and breadth of information. This depth is a function of the resolution of the display, i.e. of the amount of data encoded in the transmission channel. Breadth of information is defined as "the number of sensory dimensions simultaneously presented". Breadth of information is achieved through the collaboration of multiple media: image, sound, olfactory signals, as well as through the use of technical devices allowing tactile sensations. VR is not so much a medium in itself, as a technology for the synthesis of all media.

I am emphasizing the psychological aspects of immersion, or 'presence' as it is also often called.

Werner Wirth et al. (2007) have tried to combine the existing research into one unified theory.

Immersion or spatial presence can be described as follows: media contents are perceived as 'real' in the sense that media users experience a sensation of being spatially located in the mediated environment (Wissmath, 2009). The 'real world sensory experiences' are muted and your virtual experiences are 'real'. The Americans have invented a nice term for it: suspended disbelief, disbelief postponed. A rough version of the explanation of this phenomenon is this: Our primitive brain

(where the primal instincts lurk) is always there in the background: Watch out! A snake! Danger! Flee or kill! Our modern brain then says: It's just a picture, relax!

When we are in a virtual environment the primitive brain tells us it is 'real' and also 'fun'. Our modern brain postpones calling out: it's just a picture! Why? Because we have fun and we want to keep it so. We put our disbelief (modern brain) on hold, just because we have fun (primitive brain) (See Figure 1).

LaMendola (2010) discussed the human presence in an online (virtual) world. He argues that human presence is a fundamental consideration of social work practices and that we should elaborate this notion using research into social presence. I am not focusing on social work in this chapter, but human and social presence is an important aspect of 'living in a virtual world'. I refer the readers to LaMendola's article for an elaborate discussion of the relationship between Social Work and Social presence in an Online World.

Suspended disbelief makes us organizing our sensory information in such a way as to create a psychological state in which we perceive ourselves as being present in a virtual world (or in a game, book, play or film, for that matter). From

Figure 1. Immersive environment Nederland on SL

psychology we know that people only need very few incentives (stimuli) to create your own reality. My own experience with reading books proves that. When I read Tolkien when I was 16 for half a day I was saving the world. And later in the Lord of the Rings movies it was reduced to only 2 hours, but with a deeper impact.

Being present means associating with others, the experience of the encounter. Social presence is the key issue here. Biocca et al. (2003, 456-480) argue that social presence might include your perception of the degree to which you feel you are:

1. Being there, with others, together;
2. Being involved and known;
3. Being immediately engaged in joint activities.

These three degrees of presence are very much consistent with my findings about Second Life. Every resident I met is still there in Second Life because all three degrees are met. If not, they quickly disappear, frustrated with the lack of interaction with the 'others' (See Figure 2).

There is a way of analysing the chances that Second Life residents will keep on being present in their virtual community. It is based on the classification scheme of Garrison and Anderson (2007) in "Online community of inquiry review: Social, cognitive and teaching presence issues". The chance they will not drop out are higher if they display:

- Affective responses, such as expressions of emotions, use of humour and self-disclosure;
- Open communication responses, such as asking questions, expressing agreement and complimenting others;
- Cohesive responses, such as referring to others by name, addressing the group as 'we', and personal greetings.

It is interesting to see how much these social presences cues have become part of the informal set of norms in Second Life, much more so than in real life. My conclusion is that in Second Life the residents know by experience that these cues are deciding if their friends will remain in their community and not drop out into the unreachable real world and therefore be lost to them.

Figure 2. Engaged in joint activities: marriage on SL

Dell (2008) describes how close to everyday 'real' life Second life can be. She quotes Jeremy Bailenson, head of the lab at Stanford University and an assistant professor of communication at Stanford, who studied the way self-perception affects behaviour. In a personal conversation with Dell he said:

What we think about ourselves affects the confidence with which we approach the world, also the virtual world. The qualities you acquire online—whether it's confidence or insecurity—can spill over and change your conduct in the real world, often without your awareness. We found that even 90 seconds spent chatting it up with avatars is enough to elicit behavioural changes offline—at least in the short term. When we cloak ourselves in avatars, it subtly alters the manner in which we behave. It's about self-perception and self-confidence.

The possibilities are—virtually—endless. Inhabit buffed-up versions of yourself to lose weight, cuter versions of yourself to gain confidence, or older versions to start putting money away for the future. The most stunning part is how subtle the manipulations are and how difficult they are to detect, but how much it affects real life later on (http://www.time.com/time/health/article/0,8599,1739601,00.html).

For most residents in Second Life this virtual life becomes real for the time they are spending there. In a 18th century novella from China there was a sign on the Gateway to the country of illusions: Truth is fiction when fiction turns out to be true.

All emotions, feelings, thoughts, knowledge and experiences that SL provides us with, are real. Our real life culture influences in SL our choice of appearance, dress, behaviour, kind of contacts, interaction, and behaviour.

Second Life is just a new opportunity to live your 'real' life; just as a vacation in an exotic country will change your life at home. And even more so than in such a faraway land, SL will confuse you. And we need confusion to be able to see things with different eyes. Thus we are able and willing to change towards more opportunities to live a fulfilling and happy life.

Self-confidence increases when you are successful in SL. A whole world reshaped? Then that little garden you have around your home is no problem. Popular in your SL group? That is good for your ego, the same ego that determines your role at work.

Issues to be Discussed

Psychology, sociology, and anthropology offer us a wealth of knowledge that can be applied to the experiences people have participating in a virtual world. I have chosen the following subjects to be described in the article:

- **Identity:** How do I want people to perceive me?
- **Confusion and Trust:** Anonymity and role playing.
- **Community:** Social networking in communities. Who can I depend on in times of need?
- **Friendship and Intimacy:** Weak ties and disappointments.
- **Gender:** Women and men in the virtual world.
- **Playing and Well-Being**
- **Compensation:** For physical and 'personality' challenges.

Social networks are for meeting friends, making new friends, some of them are providers of services and advice or experts on issues relevant to you. We need them, especially when we get older and lose friends and the ability to make new ones. Since 2003 the world has seen the astonishing quick rise of virtual social networks. Millions of users joined them, but only a small percentage of those are senior citizens. Roughly speaking the analyses tell us that the relatively successful areas where the senior citizens are active are the ones that are closest to their 'lifestyle', their everyday experiences: email (reminding us of writing letters), search engines (looking up facts). But the 3D environment to meet people almost as in the physical world, has been ignored until now. This is a feature Facebook cannot deliver: the possibility to meet in groups and interact in groups (See Figure 3).

Identity

Snow (2001) distinguishes between personal, social and collective identity: personal identities are the attributes and meaning attributed to oneself by the actor; they are self-designations and self-attributions regarded as personally distinctive. Social identities are the identities attributed or imputed to others in an attempt to situate them in social space. They are grounded in established social roles.

In this paragraph, I am referring to personal identity to avoid confusion.

In Second Life the residents (as they are called) are presenting a 'functional display of the self to each other'. Unlike in real life they can create themselves from scratch thinking about the effect it will have on the 'others'. They want to send out a message through the characteristics of their avatar. And the message turns out to be in most cases: I am sexually attractive, come to me!

In real life identity is a powerful but vague concept. It is formed by how you see yourself and how you think others see you (image and mirror image). A 'person' in the Western Culture is seen as a unique, dynamic mix of emotions, judgements, knowledge, actions, feelings. If you see a friend again you know beforehand what 'mix' you can expect in any specific set of circumstances and environment.

In Second Life everyone is interacting with each other as if this 'foreknowledge' is the same as in real life. Moreover, I have often heard people say in Second Life: here I can find the real me, here I can at last be myself. While in reality they are saying: here I can be who I want to be.

I developed a *typology* to describe the Second Life residents:

- **Achievers:** Wanting to better themselves, gain.
- **Explorers:** Drifters individually, not within a group, looking for new exciting things, fun.
- **Hippies:** Called hobo's in Second Life. Want to be different and oppose any social rule
- **Socializers:** Looking for friendship.
- **Controllers:** Laying down rules and enforcing them.

Figure 3. Meeting at the Imbuss in SL

- **Creators:** Making things for fun and gain, for others. Everything you see in Second Life is made by residents, who like to create and build.
- **Organisers:** Buying land and starting communities.
- **'Grievers':** As they are called in Second Life, looking for mischief.

In this Second Life is different from games. In a game you don't need to create an identity, you can chose out of different fixed roles. From that moment on you are stuck in that role. A good example is: World of Warcraft.

Still, in Second Life you are also stuck to the role that is inherent to the kind of avatar you have chosen to create. But you can have multiple avatars, using them depending on your mood and intentions. The following picture depicts two of my avatars, one of them intentionally ugly (called Potter) to find out how people would react to that in SL. It turns out that they turn away without acknowledging Potter and reacting hostile to him saying hello to them (See Figure 4).

And do not forget: Second Life is all about role playing and not letting people know who 'you really are in real life'.

Confusion and Trust: Anonymity and Role Playing

In everyday life, it is a constant challenge to understand each other well. The answer to the question: 'what does she/he means with that' can only be given when you have sufficient data. The most important tool you have is knowing the man or woman in question from before.

If in a virtual world like Second Life the avatar standing before you is hiding behind a role and giving you 'false' data to keep up his or hers anonymity, you are in trouble. Confusion about what he means to say to you is almost unavoidable. In my study, I have seen this again and again.

Several friendships were destroyed by misinterpretation of the behaviour and words of the virtual loved one.

- **Language:** Most of the time only typed text (chat) without intonation and 'body and face signals'.
- **Social Cues:** Is he joking or serious? Is he tired and distracted? In what context is he saying those things to me? Very important is the lack of eye contact ('eyes are the windows to the soul').
- **Culture, Norms and Values:** More on those later on. But we underestimate the influence of seeing from what cultural background someone is and what norms and values go with that background.
- **Confusing Body Language = Animations:** In the virtual world the avatars are animated by software embedded in their so called 'AO= Animation override'. All those animated movements are unwillingly interpreted while 'listening' to his text. For instance, in my AO there was a moment that I looked at my virtual watch. This is a powerful signal in real life of wanting to end the conversation and to go looking for more important meetings.
- **Lack of Trust:** Trust is essential for a group to be a real community. But how can you trust each other if everyone is playing a role in such a way as not to give away your 'real self'?

An example of confusion is the following picture where you see President Obama visiting IJsselmonde-Rotterdam in SL (See Figure 5).

Community

There are all kind of social networks around a person. One could describe a social network as people who live in a certain area sharing com-

Figure 4. Two avatars of the author in SL

Figure 5. Obama visits IJsselmonde?

mon interests. The particular area is the virtual world in our case. The common interest mainly is a shared passion or shared fun followed by gain (learning from each other and joined actions to find information needed).

I use the term 'community' for the kind of social network in which people believe that they can depend on each other in times of need. So I am talking more or less about a community of 'friends', which means that next to instrumental reasons for meeting each other, there are also emotional reasons.

The challenges to keep such a community alive and kicking are manifold: continuity, reliability, fulfilling mutual obligations, boredom, other priorities, group dynamics (fights, disagreements, leadership issues). And most of all: having fun together, sharing exciting experiences, making jokes, playing games, dancing and creating things together and sharing mutual passions and hobbies.

Nobody wants to meet on a regular basis if they are not having fun and find pleasure in those meetings. But how to provide that if people have so different opinions about what fun is? I tried the following:

1. My community is self-selected. People look for people they liked and stayed with them.
2. Secondly, together with my co-organisers, we had to provide 'opportunities to have fun'. On a weekly base there are musical performances, club and DJ dancing parties, celebrations, virtual sports events, hobby meetings, small scale games, trips to interesting virtual places, discussion groups and real life event related festivities (Christmas, New year, winning the Champions League, which we did not do often, and such) translated to SL.
3. Thirdly we organised events that will gain the participants more insight, knowledge and experience, like a popular course on the psychological aspects of meeting people in a virtual environment (given by myself, every week already for more than 2 years).

Our aim was to implement what we called in Dutch the 3 G's: Genot, Gewin and Gezelligheid. Roughly translated: Pleasure, Gain and the feeling of belonging. Also feeling secure (in Dutch the 4th G, Geborgenheid, turned out to be important.

After and during the 'fun' the members could share questions, challenges and problems they had in their daily life in RL (Real Life as opposed to SL Second Life). Together they could find answers and solutions and advice from each other. This strengthened the mutual ties.

Also they got the opportunity for 'blended learning'. To get insights and knowledge they thought they needed in view of those RL questions and challenges.

It turned out that despite these efforts the community was a small hard core of maximum 5 people and a floating group of 20 more or less active members (only participating in certain fun-events). Around 50 members we saw now and again when they had a problem they wanted solved. The group officially had 150 subscribed members.

The amount of visitors joining the Dutch community on SL-Nederland is very large (almost 18000 in 2 years), as seen in Figure 6.

Communities are important for people. But why look for social contacts in such a confusing world as SL? As we all know Aristotle describes Man as by nature a social animal, while Spinoza once said: "Man is scarcely able to live a solitary life". So the need is irrefutable. Man is looking for: mutual ties through which people can depend on each other in troubled times. Mutual rewards and advantages, trust, continuity, safety and the feeling to be needed/loved/respected by people who matter to you. And also clarity of the intentions of all concerned.

Figure 6. Amount of visitors to the Dutch community on SL

This will cost you investments of energy and time, active outreaching attentive behaviour towards your friends, participating in common activities and fitting yourself into a 'organisation' to which you both belong.

In SL those are difficult requirements. You are there for selfish reasons (fun and recreation), no need for social contacts per se, anonymity and role playing is accepted and even expected, hindering trust and safety and above all clarity. SL is often called 'the land of confusion'.

This is a problem because the characteristics of a community are, as I found during my research:

- Willing to share personal feelings
- Being available when others need you
- Keeping appointments and acknowledge arrangements
- Being sincere
- Being 'real', not playing games that can hurt another group member
- While getting to know each other's weak points, refraining from using those in arguments and jokes
- Honour the expectations they have about you
- Participate in group activities actively

And, moreover, in fun oriented informal groups these characteristics cannot be enforced by formal rules, protocols, punishment, control and monitoring. They should be 'spontaneous' (See Figure 7).

Friendship and Intimacy

Friendship in SL can be described as: weak ties and disappointments. Not so different from many 'real life' friendships, perhaps.

Real friendship is possible on SL, but only if there is a proven respect for each other (more important than 'a nice person'). Also there must be some openness about the real characteristics of the other person. However, we are there 'to play roles' for fun. There are rules, but no rule forbids disguising yourself and hiding your real characteristics.

'Friend' in Second Life is a label, a tag. In real life, it is a process continuously subject to change, but with a certain presence and depth. During my observations in SL I discovered that this is one of the most common forms of confusion and misunderstanding: the meaning of the term 'friend' is seen as identical in RL and SL. The result is that there is real pain, frustration, anger, and sadness about the behaviour of SL friends (See Figure 8).

Figure 7. Group lunch on SL

This is nothing new. In the 19th century, there were many 'pen pals' friendship through exchange of letters. Same frustrations and challenges were experienced such as: "You don't write often enough." "Should we meet in the flesh, will the friendship continue to exist?"

Obviously there are strong 'RL-like' friendships in SL. But often there are weak ties. The connection is there as long as both parties find that they gain from it. Many residents of SL invest little in such a relationship. It starts quickly and easily (click and send out a request that is rarely refused). But it also ends too easily, even if the 'tag' remains on your friends list.

I once did a kind of social experiment in the first year I was in SL. I invited all my friends on the SL list (about 200) to a party. I made a preliminary estimate how many would actually come. I came to 20 names. Indeed all those came (or excused themselves). That turned out to be a lot, compared to the experiences of others. A SL resident: "I recently sent out a notecard to all my SL friends. In it, I said that I would be away from SL for a few weeks and I gave them my email address to stay in touch. Only 2 responded. Now I know who my real SL friends are."

Figure 8. Love in SL

My hypothesis, based on social psychology findings and my own research is that if you manage to meet 150 people, you discover that you want to meet 50 of them again to share a mutual problem to solve, but only once or twice. 20 you want to meet more often to have fun together. And in the end, if you are lucky, you have 1 or 2 real friends left, that you can depend on. These figures coincide with the numbers I mentioned about my Dutch community.

In SL it is very easy to meet 150 people, but don't expect them all to be real friends.

Gender: Women and Men in the Virtual World

Martine Delfos (2004), a famous Dutch psychologist, claims that the new virtual environment is the beginning of a new emancipation process: men and women are not afraid to be 'different'. And at the same time it makes the real differences between men and women clearer.

Men build things to compete and to impress. Women build things for others to enjoy. Men 'click and go' and women want first understand where they go. Men want action, women need words first. Men use short sharp phrases. Women want to make themselves clear through coherent well-worded phrases to avoid misunderstandings. Men want form, women content.

It is a fact that women are the champions of the blog-world. They are around thirty, blogging from home and well trained. They greatly appreciate their anonymity and privacy. They are (therefore?) very free in their expressions of feelings and opinions, and use more and better phrases than men. Delfos (2004) states, their alias means that they can do whatever they want without being judged, as in RL. They behave wilder, more free and sexier. In a personal conversation she once quoted a woman who was an active 'chatter' on internet (See Figure 9):

I chat away with lot of men, knowing they lie about everything. But I lie also about myself. I am leading them on for my own pleasure. Girls just want to have fun! I am not chatting to be serious, I want to make those men mad in any respect, also lust!

Playing and Well-Being

Second Life is a social scene, an artistic medium, a place where one can play, but it is not 'a game' as such. A Play is more than a Game.

Following Huizinga (1938), playing is choosing freedom. You step out of real life in a temporary environment you have chosen and sometimes formed yourself including its limits of time and place. He calls it the magic circle of the game.

SL is not an escape from reality, it is complementary. There is not such a big difference with reading an exciting book, seeing an emotional play, watching a romantic movie. You get lost in another world. For centuries, we are warned against such an escape into unreality. Plato even warned against writing as a substitute for speaking (in his writings he called it inhuman, pretending that something can exist outside your mind, regardless of your mind).

Second Life is as good or bad for you as your daily life can be. It is what you make of it. But the chances that it works out well for you, are larger in Second Life, since you have more control over your environment than in Real Life. You have the power to mute and ban people, to teleport to friends and of course ... the 'on-off' button.

Lastly, you can play and have fun in SL doing all the things that were not possible in RL. For example musical performances. Here you see me playing guitar and singing together with my RL wife for a large audience (See Figure 10).

Here the Dutch community on SL is playing the arrival of 'Sinterklaas', a typical Dutch occasion on every 5th of December (See Figure 11).

Compensation for Physical and Personality Challenges

The virtual life is a known and highly praised method for people to present themselves without their personal physical and 'personality' challenges. They can compensate in this way the 'real life' problems they face every day, due to their 'handicaps'.

In Second Life I met many people who turned out to have considerable 'challenges' in their everyday life. The ones who gained most were suffering from mobility issues. They told me: for the first time I meet people who are not immediately focusing on my 'handicap'. They accept me the way I see myself, the way I present myself to them as an avatar I created. It makes accepting my real life challenges easier (See Figure 12).

Figure 9. Lust on SL

Figure 10. Playing for an audience in SL

Figure 11. Saint Nicolas on SL

Mobility is not only 'to be able to move around', but more importantly: 'to be able to meet people and go to places'. In the years to come, when growing older, some and eventually almost all, will only be able to 'move' with some help.

One of the most important preparations for that time is to establish, strengthen or to expand their social network, so it will be sustainable and always there when they want to meet people and go to places (mobility), to have fun and share their passions, hobbies and talents and need some help (assistive technology and devices) to do that.

In SL it is possible to assess your mobility challenges by discussing the possibilities with experts from the 'assistive technology' sector. I

contacted them in The Netherlands and it turned out that they were keen on future involvement in our communities because they themselves have a problem.

The assistive technology industry want to be able to reach their (potential) customers directly. At the moment they have to deal with intermediary institutions, like insurance companies and (local) authorities. This is confirmed by the Dutch mobility/assistive technology and devices SME's and their branch organisation *Firevaned*. This means they lack the direct feedback from their (potential) customers about their needs. Services turn out to be a much more important product they want than only a 'device'. The innovations

Figure 12. Dancing regardless of handicap in SL

the end users need are coming to the industry as a surprise: more communication and interaction, not only new ways of being able to move around.

In their eyes that is the best solution to their problem: reaching the potential consumers of their product as a group in a (virtual) community and in an early stage. Their approach until now has not been a success: organising those groups amongst their existing clientele. The rationale: people do not want to meet each other regularly on a problem-centric base but only when 'fun' is the focus. And they do not want to go to meetings which they see as the industrial providers wanting to sell them more of their product.

SUMMARY OF FINDINGS

Virtual life is not so different from real life. Misunderstandings and confusion among those participating in a virtual environment as Second Life are the result of them forgetting this simple statement. Even when they are playing roles and hiding their real identity, they must keep on 'behaving' as in real world social networks. If not, they are rejected in and sometimes ejected from Second Life.

A very important conclusion I came to was: Second Life is not for everyone. In this it is more or less like 'games: either you like it or you don't understand what the fun in it is.

After the 4 year research in and about Second Life my conclusion based on the analysis of all the data was: not fit to be used in real life projects aiming at fighting social exclusion and loneliness.

The main reason is the confusion about everyone you meet in Second Life. Anonymity and role playing are very destructive to trust in each other and sharing fun and emotions. Second Life communities come and go. And in most instances they end in tears, fights and frustration leading to more real life challenges than before.

Therefor I started VayaV Metaverse, based on the Second Life platform, but fully in our control.

SOLUTIONS AND RECOMMENDATIONS: THE VAYAV METAVERSE

The core of the project VayaV is the exchange of knowledge and experience between those who have the advantages of knowing what virtual social networks are about and those who may find that interesting. All available local care and service providers in the field will be invited, too: professionals and volunteers. And finally, provide through a helpdesk appropriate technical infrastructure, including maintenance and services, so the frustrations of using 'computers' will be minimal or absent.

In The Netherlands, to describe the steps people are taking towards finding a job, professionals are using a concept often called 'the participation ladder'. The objectives of VayaV are based on the first 4 steps of this participation ladder, Step 1: isolated life, step 2: socializing outdoors, step 3: participation in organized activities; step 4. unpaid work/voluntary work. VayaV wants people to go from 1 to 4.

Social benefits of the VayaV Metaverse are: at any you can invite group members (eg by mail, or old fashioned way: by phone) in order to come together for something fun/useful to do. One can easily spontaneously organise subgroups to undertake a specific activity that fits that subgroup.

My findings in Second Life convinced me that it was not a suitable environment (platform) for the target group I described before. The main problem was the anonymity and role playing of the SL residents. You never can trust the people you meet (even in your community) to be what they said they were. Age, gender, looks, the users can create their avatar to be whatever they want to be. This makes it very difficult to establish strong ties.

Therefore I started to research and develop the VayaV approach. VayaV turned out to be a combination of a strategy, an ICT product *(VayaV Metaverse)* and a blueprint for a project structure. From now on I will speak of 'we', because I now have a team of co-workers, partly from my own network and partly from my SL communities.

VayaV is a digital social network environment like Facebook, but with a feature Facebook cannot deliver: the possibility to meet in groups and interact in groups. VayaV will be a 3D 'world' designed and build according to the specifications

our target groups will provide *(VayaV Metaverse)*. VayaV will also have its own interface to this Metaverse *(VayaV Viewer)*.

The VayaV Community Service is the third part of our product. We will start and maintain local VayaV communities, together with municipalities and their partners.

These groups will start out by meeting each other in *the physical, real world* locally. Mainly for pleasure and fun, but also for gain, training, increased experience and knowledge about their possibilities and challenges. Specific topics will be provided. The communities will be a mix of our target group with (local) service and product providers, computer hobbyists and experts in certain relevant fields. During the physical meetings the participants will be demonstrated what a 3D world looks like and how people have fun in there. They will then provide us with feedback in what kind of virtual environment they would like to meet. We have builders, designers and ICT experts that we met in our 4 year SL research, who will translate this feed back into our own VayaV world running on our own servers, based on the existing open source Open Sim platform.

The participants will actively adapt or even help build the environment.

As an example I give you a short description of the VayaV groups set up in Kerkrade in 2012:

The VayaV groups are organised by the local authorities in Kerkrade and their partners, through the usual channels. The venue will be the Public Library. The groups meetings are divided in three parts: first informal conversation among each other about their latest daily activities. Secondly a learning session with a mix of technology solutions relevant to their needs. Thirdly an entertaining demonstration of the possibilities of meeting in a virtual environment, using our existing Second Life simulations and communities.

By showing in the third part of the meetings what is possible in Second Life the participants will be made familiar with virtual worlds. When the curiosity about the opportunities for the participants themselves is high enough, we facilitate hands on experiences. The VayaV world is offered as virtual environment to meet. This VayaV world is build according to the specifications and ideas of the participants themselves.

In short: the VayaV groups in Kerkrade mainly meet in the form of physical gatherings of people. Step by step, they will get used to the possibilities and requirements of meetings in a virtual environment. First by looking at what is possible and by talking about it. Then, still in physical groups, they will start using it themselves guided by expert users off and on line.

Both in the physical and virtual meetings we have the following main goals:

- Sharing of experiences
- Learning from each other
- Individual and collective learning through the training opportunities offered
- The joy of having social contacts, sharing fun

Everything takes place in a safe environment. There will be a mix of interaction methods: voice, images, text (which while typing in your own language can be translated in another language through Google translate). It is also possible to group members in the virtual environment and private comments to exchange messages without to let the whole group noticing.

Our main general target group at first will be the *baby boomers (age group 59 – 69)*. The target groups will be offered the use of VayaV Metaverse and Viewer to meet each other and start VayaV communities, for free. The will be enticed to subscribe to the VayaV Community Service, however, through which they will be able to get services, support, extra facilities and influence in the development of the updates to VayaV Metaverse. By becoming a VayaV member their contribution also will be used for the VayaV

communities themselves (costs of organisation and logistics, organising activities, trips and collective buying of products needed).

VayaV Metaverse Specifications

The specifications will be decided upon by the users in the test groups. Based on our study we predict that these specifications will be asked for:

- Chose and adapt 'In world' (running within the VayaV Metaverse) applications to help the users preserve the level of privacy they have chosen and to defend themselves against possible threats to their virtual wellbeing;
- Choice between using voice and typing or combine both. While typing, a fast and relatively accurate translation module can be activated with a choice of almost all major languages. This is already available on the market for free;
- One can describe one's self in a personal profile all can see adding anything you want to share. Just clicking on a person is enough to see that profile. An easy way of introducing yourself. You can also add a personal comment to anyone's profile only readable by yourself, to remind you what you need to remember about him or her;
- One can find which friends are on line, but one can also chose to be on line anonymous. One can send notices and surveys to the members of the group one belongs to and one can start sub groups for any purpose;
- Messages people sent to you within the simulation can be send to you by regular email services if you are not on line;
- You can decide on any given moment who you will allow to speak to you privately or publicly, who you will allow to meet you and whom you will chose to be your friend.

- In the 3D virtual environment you can play any game you like together with your friends (chess, mah-jong, checkers etc.) or share hobby or educational activities (going to classes and discussions on any subject) or visit recreational or cultural events in the virtual environment (music, films, dancing, performances on a virtual stage or by opening websites for all to see and share);
- One can adapt their own virtual personal space (furniture, style of building, garden). You can have a pet to raise and feed.

Virtual VayaV Metaverse facilities

- Voice driven movement and action.
- One can teleport or invite friends to teleport to any place in the simulation in an instant, or chose to 'walk'. Any form of mobility is available: horse riding, bicycle, cars, airplanes etc, all animated and menu driven;
- There is on line help, training and explanations available when needed. There are 'in world' guides, volunteers who are there to help you find your way;
- Links to any website can be opened on screens for all to see and discuss.
- It is possible for end users to exchange virtual products among themselves as gifts or to trade;
- Users can make 'films' of all their activities (screen grabbing);
- Users can make photo's in real life and use them in the VayaV Metaverse to show them to friends or to use them on structures they build themselves;
- Users can start subgroups around these facilities, e.g. starting a Photo- or Film group.

Immersive Surroundings

- The virtual surroundings are 'lifelike', day and night cycles are there, everything takes on a different light when the sun is rising or setting, there are seasonal changes, the weather can change.
- Participants chose their appearance. VayaV will provide a ready-made avatar to begin with, but that is adaptable for the user. The virtual body is animated, it is standing and moving as in real life, even when passive. The lips move when speaking, your eyes blink.

Fun in VayaV

- Together play games chosen from the wide array of games available on the Internet. Board games (checkers, chess, MahYong ed.), simulations, games, shooting games, adventure etc.
- Virtual activities not possible (anymore) in the "real world" such as: horse riding, flying, swimming, car racing, dancing, exotic (simulated) places to visit. Physical barriers and constraints play no role.
- Internet videos, websites, facebook profiles, photos can be shared in the virtual world by showing them on a screen that everyone can see and jointly enjoy and learn from by discussing the contents.
- Under the expert guidance to build and create yourself (art, music, clothing, objects, houses, nature). To distribute your products to group members to enjoy and use.
- Organise festivities as a group (e.g. birthdays).
- Simulations 'role play' of (old) trades.
- Performances, presentations, for the group in the virtual environment.
- Virtual 'lessons' to follow on relevant topics such as health and relationships.

Practical Approach of the VayaV Groups

The VayaV groups will carry out the 'hands on' testing and trials as a group, while meeting in one physical environment (public library, schools, providers of assistive technology and devices buildings etc.). Those environments will be chosen also because of optimal broadband connections they already have. The available equipment will be adapted to meet the VayaV requirements.

The users will form pairs: first time user plus an experienced computer user, both from our target group. The equipment that will be used by them is state of the art, using large flat screens. Hardware interface will be mouse and keyboard, but also touch screen if possible and any alternative to the mouse that is available on the market and easy to use by senior citizens for the purpose of moving around in a 3D world.

In case a group member is unable to leave his or her house, a special connection will be set up in the house, with equipment and interfaces adapted to the need of the said user. He or she will be able to take part in the physical group meetings through video or through the virtual 3 D environment when that will be available. All group members are also free to test and try out VayaV Metaverse from their homes, but they have to meet the minimum requirements we will provide. They will be facilitated by the local VayaV group organisers and online by the VayaV volunteers (students and old time users of 3D environments).

VayaV Groups Developed in DISCOVER Project

On April 2012 a European project called *DISCOVER* (aiming at informal carers caring for the elderly) has started. This project is partially funded under the ICT Policy Support Programme (ICT-PSP) as part of the Competitiveness and Innovation Programme by the European Commission.

DISCOVER is piloted in 4 testbeds in Thessaloniki, several locations across the Netherlands, Zamora and Valladolid and Birmingham. 400 informal and formal carers will receive digital skills training. Carers will be facilitated to become mentors for their peers and for the older people they care for, thus increasing the initial reach of the project.

DISCOVER is about using digital technologies to enable carers to access the information they need, when they need it, in mediums that facilitate knowledge and information sharing, fostering well-being of carers, older people and the development of ICT skills.

Currently, over a 100 million people in Europe care for a family member, partner, relative or friend and this figure will rise sharply with ongoing population ageing. The increase in demand for care will have implications for public services, families, and health care providers, with families increasingly expected to take on more complex care tasks and healthcare professionals experiencing increased workloads.

The DISCOVER project aims to challenge existing training practices and create a technical solution for the provision of better care now and into the future. The DISCOVER platform will develop new digital skills training content and will use the most appropriate technology and innovative forms of learning to reach and engage with carers. Participants will use a variety of channels including computer, mobile phones, and digital television. The project will also maximise value through repurposing and improving existing content. The DISCOVER platform will become the single point of entry for carers.

Expected benefits are improved digital skills, better communication, and support for carers, i.e. less isolation through virtual and real social networks, increased confidence and thus a better quality of life. The benefits for the older people will include improvements in quality of care and levels of independent living.

In The Netherlands we are able to set up the first VayaV groups as part of the DISCOVER project aiming at communities of formal and informal carers.

We are using the virtual environment of Second life and the Second Life viewer for testing purposes. We have built a virtual simulation of the city of Kerkrade as demo for the VayaV groups and also started a Dutch social community mainly consisting of older persons in the sim Nederland, called Doggersbank burgers. Both are available for on line visitors through downloading the Viewer and starting a new avatar through de website of Second Life (www.secondlife.com).

There are videos on YouTube available showing the Virtueel Kerkrade simulation and a midwinter gathering on Doggersbank in Second Life:

- http://www.youtube.com/watch?v=ZNxIfvKHsSg
- http://www.youtube.com/watch?v=nExXbU10ag0

Next to the VayaV community members we will also involve local community leaders and others who represent diverse interests in the community such as community service organizations and the local authorities. They will provide input into the process of assessing changes in the social environment of the end-users that may occur as a result of the VayaV communities activities and experience.

Also the effects of the VayaV communities will be evaluated in the context of the target group attitudes. Is a 'fear of change' bias inherent in their attitudes towards this new form of communities? How can this potential fear of change be overcome? Information about these attitudes and perceptions will also be gathered from community leaders because their attitudes are important and may give insight into the overall attitudes of our target group if community leaders are perceptive and sensitive to community concerns and interests.

CONCLUSION

VayaV Metaverse is the development of a 3D virtual world especially designed and constructed for the elderly, based on the open source platform Open Sim, on which already several 'Open Grid' environments are running. In this VayaV Metaverse simulated 3D environments will be shaped and built based on the look and feel of the local municipalities the elderly are living in.

In the virtual world, there is a place for video, for photo realism, for verbal or written representation of oneself and instrumented avatars. We can look at virtual worlds as being able to reach and communicate with one another by new means that are not so different from the old trusted ones. Much of this is dependent on individual preferences. Some people like audio, some like text, some like 'real' faces, other respond to cartoon creativity. All these are available in the 3D world we will develop. In the VayaV Metaverse we will provide to each user a view and interaction that makes them feel comfortable, but not at the expense of others comfort.

In the localised VayaV projects like Discover, older persons are meeting in the 'real world', together with enthusiastic (elderly) virtual world users and computer hobbyists and professional service providers, with the aim of getting acquainted with the possibility of meeting also in the virtual world. A large percentage of the elderly are interested in this combination of virtual and real.

REFERENCES

Baecker, R., et al. (2012). *Social support technology for those at risk of social isolation.* Paper presented a the IFA, 11th Global Conference on Aging. Prague, Czech Republic.

Biocca, F., Harms, C., & Burgoon, J. (2003). Toward a more robust theory and measure of social presence: Review and suggested criteria. *Presence (Cambridge, Mass.)*, *12*(5), 456–480. doi:10.1162/105474603322761270.

Blit-Cohen, E., & Litwin, H. (2009). *Elder participation in cyberspace: A qualitative analysis of Israeli retirees*. Jerusalem, Israel: Hebrew University.

Boellstorff, T. (2008). *Coming of age in second life*. Princeton, NJ: Princeton University Press.

Buse, C. E. (2012). *It's a way of bringing families together that was never possible before: Connecting generations across the digital divide*. Paper presented at the IFA 11th Global Conference on Aging. Prague, Czech Republic.

Castells, M. (2009). *Communication power*. Oxford, UK: Oxford University Press.

de Jong-Gierveld, J. (1987). Developing and testing a model of loneliness. *Journal of Personality and Social Psychology*, *53*, 119–128. doi:10.1037/0022-3514.53.1.119 PMID:3612484.

Delfos, M. (2004). *De schoonheid van het verschil*. San Diego, CA: Harcourt Book Publishers.

Dell, K. (2008). How second life affects real life. *TIME Science*. Retrieved October 2012 from http://www.time.com/time/health/article/0,8599,1739601,00.html

Dobson, A., & McLaughlin, D. (2012). *Social support and disability: It's not the size of the network that counts*. Paper presented at IFA 11th Global Conference on Aging. Prague, Czech Republic.

Dutton, W. H., Helsper, E. J., & Gerber, M. M. (2009). *Oxford internet survey 2009 report: The internet in Britain*. Oxford, UK: University of Oxford Press.

Feist, H. (2012). *Social spaces, rural places: Ageing in place in rural South Australia*. Paper presented at IFA 11th Global Conference on Aging. Prague, Czech Republic.

Field, D. (1999). Continuity and change in friendships in advanced old age: Findings from the Berkeley older generation study. *International Journal of Aging & Human Development*, *48*(4). doi:10.2190/J4UJ-JAU6-14TF-2MVF PMID:10498019.

Garrison, D. R., & Anderson, T. (2007). Online community of inquiry review: Social, cognitive and teaching presence issues. *Journal of Asynchronous Learning Networks*, *11*(1), 61–72.

Hong, J. (2012). *Multidimensional evaluation of the health status of elderly people in the context of social relationship networks*. Paper presented at IFA 11th Global Conference on Aging. Prague, Czech Republic.

Huizinga, J. (1938). *Homo ludens*. Boston, MA: Beacon Press.

LaMendola, W. (2010). Social presence in an online world. *Journal of Technology in Human Services*, *28*, 108–119. doi:10.1080/15228831003759562.

Lewin, K. (1946). Action research and minority problems. *The Journal of Social Issues*, *2*(4), 34–46. doi:10.1111/j.1540-4560.1946.tb02295.x.

Paoletti, P. (2012). The dimension of future in old age: Promoting healthy and active aging with older women in Portugal. *Personality and Social Psychology*, *53*, 119–128.

Schwarz-Woelzl, M. (2012). *Older people, social networks, online social network platforms – Mythe and practice*. Paper presented at IFA 11th Global Conference on Aging. Prague, Czech Republic.

Sherwin, J. (2007). Get a (second) life. *APS Observer, 20*(6). Retrieved October 2012 from http://www.psychologicalscience.org/index.php/publications/observer/2007/june-july-07/get-a-second-life.html

Snow, D. (2001). *collective identity and expressive forms.* Retrieved from www.democracywww.csd.bg

Stenberg, L. (2012). *Attitudes to and usage of technology among the elderly in Finland.* Paper presented at IFA 11th Global Conference on Aging. Prague, Czech Republic.

Steuer, J. (1992). Defining virtual reality: Dimensions determining telepresence. *The Journal of Communication, 42*(4), 73–93. doi:10.1111/j.1460-2466.1992.tb00812.x.

van Tilburg, T., & de Jong-Gierveld, J. (2007). *Zicht op eenzaamheid: Achtergronden, oorzaken en aanpak.* Amsterdam, The Netherlands: Vrije Universiteit Press.

Wellman, B. (2001). Computer networks as social networks. *Science, 293,* 2031–2034. doi:10.1126/science.1065547 PMID:11557877.

Wirth, W., Hartmann, T., Bocking, S., Vorderer, P., Klimmt, C., & Holger, S. et al. (2007). A process model for the formation of spatial presence experiences. *Media Psychology, 9,* 493–525. doi:10.1080/15213260701283079.

Wissmath, B., Weibel, D., & Groner, R. (2009). Dubbing or subtitling? Effects on spatial presence, transportation, flow, and enjoyment. *Journal of Media Psychology, 21*(3), 114–125. doi:10.1027/1864-1105.21.3.114.

ADDITIONAL READING

Boellstorff, T. (2008). *Coming of age in second life.* Princeton, NJ: Princeton University Press.

LaMendola, W. (2010). Social presence in an online world. *Journal of Technology in Human Services, 28,* 108–119. doi:10.1080/15228831003759562.

KEY TERMS AND DEFINITIONS

Open Simulator: Open source platform based on the Linden Lab owned Second Life. Here also the rules and goals are determined by the users themselves.

Real Life (Abbreviated as RL): As opposed to Second Life, used to describe our everyday life.

Second Life (Abbreviated as SL): Multiplayer online role-playing environment based on a 3D platform mostly Open Source and with Viewers installed on the clients computers. The difference with games is that the rules and goals are not prefixed, but determined by the users themselves.

VayaV Metaverse: The name of the new product being developed for mainly the elderly users. VayaV is a digital social network environment with the possibility to meet in groups and interact in groups. VayaV will be a 3D 'world' designed and build according to the specifications our target groups will provide (*VayaV Metaverse*). VayaV will also have its own interface to this Metaverse (*VayaV Viewer*). The participants/users of VayaV will get *VayaV Community Services* where wanted and needed.

Chapter 18
Massively Multiplayer Online Role Playing Games for Health Communication in Brazil

Marcelo Simão de Vasconcellos
Oswaldo Cruz Foundation, Brazil

Inesita Soares de Araújo
Oswaldo Cruz Foundation, Brazil

ABSTRACT

Video games' potential for gathering interest from children and adults originated many serious games to communicate, inform, teach, and train. MMORPGs may have even more potential, since they create a shared communication space where players can interact with each other. In Brazil, public Health Communication is a major area of concern, since there is a large population who needs information about health. Much of the communication initiatives come from dated models and are too normative, unable to attend population adequately. This chapter presents first reflections about the main advantages of applying MMORPGs for public Health Communication, using Mediations Theory as a starting point to look into these games' characteristics. This perspective reveals that, in addition to engagement created by their interactive nature, MMORPGs' social characteristics are particularly useful for building Brazilian Health Communication current aspirations: creating instances for hearing population, granting them active voice and enhancing their participation in developing public health policies.

INTRODUCTION

The video game industry has grown intensively lately, topping film industry revenue since 2007 (Growth, 2008). Massively Multiplayer Online Role Playing Games (hereafter called just MMOR-PGs), are a kind of game that gained popularity over the last years, creating many online communities and currently account for $11 billion of the video game industry's worldwide revenue of $44 billion (Analyst, 2009). In parallel, video games surpassed the entertainment sphere and games

DOI: 10.4018/978-1-4666-3673-6.ch018

known as serious games are used in employee training, as supplements to formal education, means of awareness and even political activism (Jones, 2008; Purdy, 2007).

A recent survey ranked Brazil as the fourth world market for video games, with approximately 35 million people (of the country's current population of 195 million inhabitants) playing routinely (Gap Closing, 2011). Video games are not restricted to privileged social classes, but are popular also in poor urban neighborhoods and in rural areas of the country. Another survey interviewed 2516 children focusing in their use of communication technologies and reported that ninety percent of children from 5 to 9 years had their first experiences on Internet playing games (Barbosa, Cappi, & Jereissati, 2011).

However, despite the increasingly widespread use of video games for serious applications, Brazilian public communications, particularly the Health Communication field, have not yet realized their potential. The aim of this chapter is to present the main benefits MMORPGs could bring to Brazilian public Health Communication strategies, considering Brazilian government current aspirations for population's participation and understanding of collective health issues. For this, there is an explanation of the Brazilian health situation, the current concept of Health Communication and then the advantages that could arise from use of MMORPGs designed for public Health Communication. We also present the main challenges for their application. Despite the peculiarities of Brazilian health system, some ideas described in this chapter can possibly be useful for other countries and cultures.

BACKGROUND

SUS: Brazil's Unified Health System

Brazil's huge territory and population of nearly 200 million inhabitants foster a great variety of cultures and worldviews, but also inequalities that present unique challenges to Brazilian government administration and make very hard the planning of adequate health policies (Victora et al., 2011b). Health in Brazil have had great progress in the last years, but some difficulties still persist, with new health problems arising from increased urbanization and social and environmental change (Buss, 2011).

The Brazilian Health Sector Reform occurred at the same time as democratization, in the mid-1970s, and was a movement that brought together initiatives in multiple sections of society. Its political and ideological viewpoint was of health not as an exclusively biological issue to be resolved by medical services, but as a social and political issue to be addressed in public policies. This reform would originate Brazil's current health system and showed since its beginnings great concern with the reduction of social inequalities, equal access to health and the idea of health as a set of factors broader than just the physical well-being of the population (Paim, Travassos, Almeida, Bahia, & Macinko, 2011).

Brazil's public health system, SUS (Unified Health System), is one of the largest public health systems in the world, created in 1988 to serve Brazil's entire population under the belief that health is a right for every person and a duty of the state. SUS follows an expanded concept of health, encompassing not only physical and mental well-being but all social, economic, cultural, ethnic, psychological and behavioral factors that influence the occurrence of health problems and their risk factors in the population (Buss & Pellegrini Filho, 2007). It aims to provide comprehensive, universal preventive and curative care, provision of health services to the entire population and promotion of community participation at all administrative levels (Victora et al., 2011a). SUS principles for Health Promotion are closely related to those presented by World Health Organization in the "Ottawa Charter for Health Promotion" (World Health Organization, 1986) encompassing biomedical, environmental, lifestyle, social and community aspects. As such, they are not a unique responsibility of the health sector, but require the establishment of public policies favorable to health, development of personal skills, creation of supportive environments, developing collective actions for the population, promoting participation of community and the reorientation of the health services. These actions are considered fundamental elements for the success of any health policy (Paim, et al., 2011).

Health Communication

As expected, Brazilian government places much importance in Health Communication strategies, using printed information (leaflets, brochures, books, posters and billboards), large health campaigns on radio and television and, lately, online media like websites, blogs and online social networks. They include information about disease prevention, epidemics, and guidelines for a better quality of life (Victora et al., 2011b).

Meanwhile, the Health Communication campaigns typically have centralized production, unable to cater to particular contexts. They have an impersonal style, without cultural references, which is not adequate to the needs of a country as large and diversified as Brazil. They also tend to be highly prescriptive, using imperative tone, focusing on diffusion of norms and behaviors for people's adoption. As a result, Health Communication initiatives do not properly address many groups and population segments. This approach, as most large-scale media communication, is unidirectional, with no place for dialogue with the public, which greatly limits its expected benefits (Araújo, 2009).

The ideas behind most of these misguided communication efforts come from the association of behaviorist ideas with the model of communication proposed by Claude Shannon and Warren Weaver (1949). This model presented communication with eight key elements: *source* (origin of the communication), *message* (content), *encoder* (which formats the message), *channel* (message's route),

decoder (which interprets the message), *receiver* (message's recipient), *feedback* (receiver's answer back to the source). The last element, *noise*, is undesirable in the communication process since it interferes and distorts the original message. Under this view, adequate Health Communication strategies would modify public's health behavior to follow a desirable model by precise use of the right stimuli (Araújo & Cardoso, 2007).

However, this theory was developed for application in telecommunications and its appropriation by the social sciences to describe human communication raised problems: the roles (source and receiver) in the communication process were stationary, it purported communication as a unidirectional linear event, based on technical aspects and showing only two points, all external influences were classified as harmful and their elimination supposedly would guarantee a perfect transference of the knowledge through the message and, lastly, it assumed a perfect control of the language by source and receiver, disregarding the many ambiguities and language mutations that occur in a dialogue (Araújo, 2000)

Nonetheless, despite its deficiencies to take into account the complexity of society's communication practice, Shannon and Weaver's model was simple and objective, which facilitated its adoption in large scale. This effect was intensified by the economic theory of Developmentalism, which influenced Brazilian public administration since 1950 and considered communication as a key factor for social and economic growth, believing that plenty of information would change behaviors and improve conducts.

Although the Developmentalism gradually has given way to other economic theories, its communication practices continued for the following decades. Even today, they have great influence over many of Brazilian government's public Health Communication policies (Araújo, 2002). Consequently, many communication theories that account for the social dimension of communication took too long to influence the scenario in Brazil. This way, the semiological current started by Roland Barthes (1977, 1994); the Foucault's lineage of discourse analysis; Mikhail Bakthin's polyphony (1986); Pierre Bourdieu's symbolic power theory (1999); Cultural Studies' contributions for understanding the implications of culture and power relations in social practice; Paulo Freire's "Pedagogy of the oppressed" (1993) and Eliseo Verón theory of social semiosis (1980) as well as many other theoretical developments only much more recently (since the 1990s) began to resonate in the Brazilian Health Communication field.

The Mediations Theory arrived in Brazil in this period, emphasizing the importance of culture in human communication, since it influences the reception, recognition and appropriation of messages by the public. According to this theory, the public is never a passive receptor of messages, even under the most hegemonic mass media, since these alleged receptors also create culture. Mediations are the exchanges between communication processes, politics and culture, where the meaning of messages is continually negotiated, adapted and reconfigured. They include appropriation, encoding and reframing processes exercised by receivers on a given message, creating their particular meanings and as a consequence, generating new content. Thus, meaning is not anymore inherent to the message, but something produced by the receptor, and this process is dynamic, continuous and culturally shaped. The technology, in turn, materializes new arrangements in communication processes, acting as a mediator for them (Martín-Barbero, 1993).

These theoretical developments are significant to the Health Communication in Latin America and the related public policies. Since the first communication models required a centralization of the communication process, electing an authorized source, they tended to foster communication practices that favored the voice of science, ignoring other kinds of knowledge and adopting a normative attitude. Mediations Theory in turn allowed a

model with room for dialogue with the population, expression of multiple voices occupying public space and a practice of Health Communication able to adapt to the diverse contexts that make up society. Under this view, communication would be a process of continuous transformation of reality, not limited to institutional communication to the population, but instead multiplying itself at different levels through the actions of different actors, who will appropriate, change, and disseminate messages (Araújo, 2009).

As SUS is an all-inclusive health policy, the objective now is not only to offer educational messages to the population, but also to turn them into speakers able to express themselves. This ideal requires dealing with different forms of social participation, cultural expression and politics, and a continuous search for new methods of intervention and action for public health policies (Inesita Soares Araújo & Cardoso, 2007). Video games and particularly MMORPGs could have an important role in this regard.

MMORPGS FOR HEALTH COMMUNICATION

Games for Health

The popularity of video games raised interest to use them for training, awareness and communication, the so-called serious games. Many educators consider that the video games' problem-solving approach makes students more active in knowledge acquisition. In addition, games create a dynamic environment where learning does not occur in a static way, but through the player's actions over time (Gee, 2007; Klawe, 1999; Malone, 1980; Oblinger, 2004; Papastergiou, 2009; Prensky, 2004). Besides training and education, some serious games also try to raise players' awareness for social and political causes: in *Food Force* (2005) developed by United Nations' World Food Program, players manage resources and perform missions to help refugees; in *Darfur is Dying* (Darfur, 2006), the objective is to protect refugee camps from the militias that terrorize Darfur, in Sudan.

The first serious games aiming at Health Communication and Health Promotion launched in the nineties for the Super Nintendo Entertainment System (SNES). *Captain Novolin*'s objective was diabetes education, *Rex Ronan: Experimental Surgeon*'s was smoking prevention and *Bronkie the Bronchiasaurus*, and *Packy and Marlon* aimed to improve self-care in kids with asthma and diabetes respectively (Lieberman, 2001). *Captain Novolin*'s sponsors were the makers of the Novolin brand of insulin, while the other games were developed through research grants (Brown et al., 1997). These games were sold by mail order or by a doctor's prescription and apart from the evaluating academic studies attesting their success in Health Communication, there is not much information about how was their reception by the wider public (Brown, et al., 1997; Managing Ailments, 1999).

More recently, the game Re-Mission became an emblematic example of the potential of games for health. Aiming at increasing young cancer patients' knowledge about cancer treatment, its creation included detailed health information obtained from oncologists, nurses, and cancer patients. In *Re-Mission,* the player controls a miniaturized robot that fights cancer cells in the human body using weapons inspired by treatments for the disease, such as radiation gun, antibiotic rockets and chemical explosives. It is provided free from Hopelab's website that reports more than 185000 downloads of the game, distributed to 81 countries worldwide (Re-Mission, 2009). Research about the patients' use of the game reported improvements in knowledge about cancer, self-esteem and treatment compliance (Kato, Cole, Bradlyn, & Pollock, 2008).

Today, the use of video games for health encompasses of training courses for health practitioners in game format (Reiner & Siegel, 2008) up to use of motion controlled games (like those of Microsoft Kinect and Nintendo Wii) in

rehabilitation (Chang, Chen, & Huang, 2011; Staiano, Abraham, & Calvert, 2012) In academic literature it is possible to find several cases of health-related behavior change after use of serious games (Baranowski, Buday, Thompson, & Baranowski, 2008).According to these findings, video games' advantages over traditional Health Communication methods include more interest in health content, fostered by interaction with the game, a flexible space for rehearsing self-care and prevention strategies and the immediate feedback of players' actions in game. Their main effects were improvements in self-esteem, knowledge and self-efficacy, confirming games as a valid strategy for prevention, care and health promotion (Lieberman, 2001).

Massively Multiplayer Online Role Playing Games (MMORPGs)

In MMORPGs, thousands (or millions) of players interact simultaneously within a fictional virtual world, sometimes competing with each other in battles and duels, sometimes collaborating to face computer-controlled enemies like monsters. Typically, they create individual characters (avatars) that live in a world with specific history and geography. The settings include fantasy kingdoms, superhero cities, post-apocalyptic wastelands, and science fiction universes. In comparison with other game types, MMORPGs have a wider age range public, from early teens to senior citizens (12 to 65 years) (Williams, Yee, & Caplan, 2008). They have a strong social component and players have several ways to communicate and negotiate with others across the game-world (Barnett & Coulson, 2010). For many players this immersive complex array of online relationships is one of the main attractions of MMORPGs (Williams, Yee, & Caplan, 2008).

Most MMORPGs share six characteristics that set them apart from other games: *persistence* (the game world and community keep going even in player's absence), *physicality* (there are internally coherent physical rules, typically in a 3D environment), *avatar-mediated play* (a player uses a particular character to interact with the game world and other players), *vertical game play* (there is progression of a character's power and/or abilities), *perpetuity* (there is no "finish line" and players can continue in the game world indefinitely) and *social interaction* (players act in several communication networks through many channels) (Barnett & Coulson, 2010).

Although the high costs of MMORPG production make less frequent their use as serious games, there are projects in progress, looking for new collaborative learning models (Herz, 2002). Quest Atlantis, designed for learning and teaching, has more than 50000 participants worldwide and reports success in engaging children with their game-based activities (Barab, Thomas, Dodge, Carteaux, & Tuzun, 2005). Recently, MIT Education Arcade received a $3 million grant to develop a MMORPG to enhance math and biology learning of high school students ("MIT's Education," 2012) and Yale School of Medicine announced in 2009 that a grant of almost $4 million would allow them to develop a game with MMORPG characteristics designed to prevent sex, drugs and alcohol abuse in teenagers, playable in several devices including smartphones (Video Game, 2009).

However, maybe the first association between MMORPGs and Health occurred by accident. In 2005, game developers of MMORPG *World of Warcraft* designed a mission where players should conquer a fortress called "Zul'Gurub". Its main villain, "Hakkar," a huge winged serpent, could infect players with a magical disease called "Corrupted Blood" that weakened and could potentially kill them. It was highly contagious but had short duration. In addition, "Zul'Gurub" was designed for experienced and powerful characters and far from other cities, so "Corrupted Blood" would be just a way to bring challenge to the battle. However, the developers could not foresee that, against all odds, some infected victims of Corrupted Blood reached cities, causing an uncontrolled virtual

epidemic. This outbreak revealed many similarities between players' behavior inside the game and behaviors observed in the physical world during great epidemics: characters fled from the quarantine areas created by the game developers; many others kept themselves away from the cities to avoid contamination; others yet started to kill contaminated characters on sight. While some characters tried to help the affected areas, others tried to spread the contagion on purpose (Lofgren & Fefferman, 2007). Even the *Centre for Disease Control* (CDC) contacted the game designer Jeffrey Kaplan asking for information about the outbreak ("Looking Back," 2005). The only solution for the crisis was restarting all game servers. Epidemiologists who studied the case afterward suggested that the similarities between the virtual epidemic and historical outbreaks could provide insights about the behavior of human populations during the turmoil of real world epidemics. Therefore, even fantasy MMORPGs like *World of Warcraft* could be potential spaces for research in collective health (Balicer, 2007).

Avatar and Self-Care

The realistic aspect in *Corrupted Blood* epidemics that puzzled epidemiologists showed the attachment that most players have with their characters in game. Inside the MMORPG, the avatar becomes the digital "body" of the player and not by chance, MMORPGs' avatars tend to be humans or humanoids, like elves and orcs. This eases the identification between player and avatar and therefore adaptation to the game world. Many customizations for avatar's appearance allows players to choose different costumes, equipment, weapons, armor, skin colors, hair colors, hair styles and even jewelry, which further enhances identification (Klastrup & Tosca, 2009; Turkaya & Adinolf, 2010). Of course, the MMORPG does not erase the "real" self of the player, but the avatar becomes a new ramification of player's personality. It is possible to say that a player has multiple selves; a superposition of a person´s many facets, manifested in different online interactions through several channels of expression, sometimes overlapping each other (Turkle, 1995). Thus, the MMORPG would superimpose over the "common" world a layer of expanded experience.

However, connections between avatar and player can be deep and complex. Yee and Bailenson (2007) found bidirectional influences between offline world and MMORPG, showing that even aesthetical aspects of avatars could have measurable impact over players "real" lives: players with attractive characters had more chances to reveal personal information inside the game, while players with created taller characters started to be more assertive when dealing with people, inside and outside the MMORPG.

In the same way that people worry about keeping their health and physical prowess, MMORPG players undertake great efforts to improve their characters, becoming stronger, quicker, and more resistant, aiming to increase their chances of victory in game. Some players mathematically analyze game mechanics in order to improve their chances, while others look for loopholes to cheat and circumvent the rules (Karlsen, 2011; Kücklich, 2009). In parallel, players are always vigilant to potential dangers around them, be it the form of enemies or environmental hazards. The traditional "health bar" is a convention in MMORPGs that illustrates how they use the threat of loss of health to change the strategies and tactics of players (Brooksby, 2008). Assessing risks to health and well-being is already a dominant convention in video games and that enhances their ability to highlight risky behaviors to players.

Both aspects could be used to Health Promotion through teaching self-care practices to players. This way, their protection and improvement actions in favor of their avatars inside the game would make them grasp health promotion concepts that could be applied into the physical world, becoming part of their daily lives even when they are not playing the MMORPG. Their participation

in the game could turn into habits and strategies, flowing into the offline world as a more active stance in maintaining their own physical health.

Interaction and Feedback

Significant part of the engagement video games create is due to their interactive qualities that require and reward player's active participation. In MMORPGs, this participation entails from the exploration of the vast open territory to the many options a player has to create a character and advance it through the game, developing specific skills and abilities. The player constructs freely the path for advancement of his/her avatar, choosing from a plethora of classes, roles, professions, missions, and activities. These choices deepen even more the link between player and avatar and enhance enjoyment of the game's virtual world. In parallel, game developers can block some pathways or options until some condition are met, customizing the experience for each player (Barnett & Coulson, 2010). In these games, health content could be tailored to individual characteristics and limitations, allowing players to absorb it at their own pace. The very act of making choices within the game would make players more involved in the process of learning about health issues, avoiding the passive posture before normative content so typical of most of the traditional initiatives of Health Communication (Lieberman, 2001).

In addition, every game interaction generates feedback, making the players constantly aware of their performance. Scores, levels and other attributes of progress enrich players' experience and provide a sense of continuous improvement and development, becoming an incentive for continuous learning. Moreover, acting as a hero in a virtual world boosts self-esteem and self-efficacy, especially when players are young. This sense of empowerment is a crucial element to health promotion (World Health Organization, 1998). Unlike in real life, where often a risky behavior promoting health vulnerabilities only becomes apparent as health problems much later, a MMORPG can clearly show cause and effect relationships between actions of avatars and changes in their health. This way, links between events that would be too subtle to draw attention in the physical world, could be emphasized in a MMORPG to enhance players' comprehension of the whole dynamic chain of events that surround health issues.

Lastly, although a MMORPG presents challenges to players, it is implicit that there are viable solutions to each problem or obstacle. This reinforces players' perception that their efforts are relevant and teaches them that the right amount of skill, dedication, team collaboration and experience can overcome such challenges. Video games in general encourage an approach of problem solving, trial and error, strategic thinking and other behaviors very valuable both in online and in offline life (Gee, 2008). This is particularly true concerning Health Promotion.

Communication, Community, and Participation

MMORPGs' strong social component and players' many ways to communicate and negotiate with others from across the game-world allow the emergence of a complex network of communication between the video game and players and among players themselves (Barnett & Coulson, 2010). MMORPGs' content does not follow a linear route from top to bottom only, but developers can create methods to contact the players and monitor their participation and enjoyment in the game. The players in turn communicate among themselves seeking help for questions, making alliances, trading, racing, dueling, entering into wars of factions, and even putting together a government (Schiesel, 2008). They receive game content, but also continuously contextualize, question, transform and redistribute it, taking part in a rich social process immersed in the cultural context of their society (Araújo, 2002).

Because of these mediation processes, often the MMORPG becomes a venue for expression of players' creativity and its fictional setting inspires many stories, illustrations, comic books, videos and *machinima* created by the players (Jenkins, 2008; Silveira, 2009). These participatory culture initiatives are common in regular video games, but in MMORPGs, they reach a greater number of people, due to their multiplayer characteristics. It is possible to say that an entire cultural ecosystem develops around a particular game, considerably broadening its area of influence and its effect on culture, even among non-players. In a MMORPG applied to Health Communication, this could greatly reinforce the health content for the players and make health issues present in their minds.

Furthermore, MMORPGs could be invaluable to teach the importance of collective actions in favor of a greater cause. Cooperating together to achieve some goal in the game, the players could see by themselves the benefits of technical collaboration to win obstacles and battles, the need of social interaction to settle disputes and disagreements and the importance of political action to fight for their interests before the game developers. This way, players could understand that personal health choices often affect other individuals and communities and that public health is a collective issue (Paim, 2010). Features already present in commercial games can inspire innovative approaches to enhance this communal sense for health, like public quests and raids (missions requiring the cooperation of many players for completion) and player owned houses and neighborhoods. In commercial MMORPGs, players have already organized protests, awareness campaigns, civil movements, created militias and even political parties (Koster, 1998; Schiesel, 2008). Applying these ideas for Health Communication would give society another public space where they could demand their rights and present their ideas.

MMORPGs as a Public Health Strategy in Brazil

Thus, fostering collective action and promoting participatory culture could be unique contributions of MMORPGs to public Health Communication strategy in Brazil, given SUS objectives of fostering civil society engagement in health policies (Paim, et al., 2011). This approach could be an innovative way to enhance population's understanding about individual and collective participation in building a healthier society. Therefore, differently from the previous health games mentioned, probably the best approach for MMORPG initiatives for public Health Communication in Brazil would not be focusing on specific conditions like cancer, asthma, or diabetes. Instead, in accordance with the expanded concept of health promoted by SUS, these games could try to reach larger groups, promoting healthy behavior and ideas that were meaningful for broader sections of population. From this approach, a number of benefits could arise.

A MMORPG for Health Communication would allow distributing health content in multiple formats, including text, infographics, images, video, and animation. Customizable game content could give each player access to an appropriate subset of the full content, at same time accommodating his previous knowledge, interpretations, and specific existential and situational contexts (Araújo, 2009). In addition, online distribution would overcome distances (an important consideration, given the huge size of Brazilian territory) and allow timely corrections and updates to the MMORPG content. Even with their high initial costs of production and deployment, their maintenance would be probably cheaper than most media used today in most of Brazilian Health Communication initiatives such as brochures, educational books, posters, billboards, and campaigns on radio and TV.

Besides being an effective way to distribute engaging content to the players, a MMORPG for Health Communication would be a new space for discussing health related themes. Since the health content would be intrinsic part of the game, players' talk about game objectives would also be a talk about health. As previously mentioned, the communication network of players would allow continuous circulation of the health content and this dialogic process between the player base and the game system would lead to a full utilization of such information. As mentioned, such game could also become another public space where players could interact and organize themselves for action. A recent study reported that leadership in MMORPGs could reflect beneficially on the subject's leadership skills at work (Xanthopoulou & Papagiannidis, 2012). In a similar way, if players have opportunities for taking decisive action related to health policies inside the game, there is a chance that they start to be more active in their offline lives too. Thus, a MMORPG for Health Communication would be more than a mere distribution channel for content, but could also become a space for political participation and citizenship.

Such communication processes and actions would be not restricted to the virtual world. In Brazil it is very common the meeting of youth and adolescents to play MMORPGs in lan-houses (very simple cyber cafes), that provide Web access, e-mail and access to online games. There, the MMORPG of choice becomes the starting point of a social network, where players apprehend its content both individually and in groups, forging bonds of fellowship and sharing experiences. Websites, mailing lists, chat rooms, social network posts and other spaces where the video game content can be discussed, appropriated, and reframed further enhance this effect (Jeanneret, 2009; Pereira, 2008). These communication processes would enhance the reverberation of the game content in players' minds and conversations, even when they are out of the game.

The use of MMORPGs for Health Communication could also be enlightening to health managers, showing them the forms of appropriation of the content by the public. In-game contact forms, surveys, quizzes and chat sessions, both collective and individual, would multiply the means for health managers to gather information and get into dialogue with the audience. This way, they would be able to better understand the player base of the MMORPG and identify what health themes and doubts require more explanation, revision, or extra content. In addition, a MMORPG for Health Communication could include features for measuring and analyzing online behavior, which would provide invaluable information to assess the effectiveness of health content portrayed in game. There could be even exchange of places between population members and health practitioners, so each one could understand better the other side. This approach could compensate for the current tendency of centralized and prescriptive health campaigns previously mentioned.

Finally, when used for health communication, MMORPGs may reveal themselves as a fertile area of research, since they bring together a network of social mediations and a valuable source of data about the audience behavior, especially if this behavior relates to health. This potential was particularly evident in the previously cited "Corrupted Blood" event as described by epidemiologists Lofgren and Fefferman (2007) and Balicer (2007). Health managers and health researchers could use feedback from a MMORPG for health to evolve their communication models and public policies in order to improve population's quality of life.

Challenges

In Brazil, MMORPGs for public Heath Communication would probably be free, to reach as much public as possible. As such, they must be feasible through support of public agencies, since the Brazilian government is the largest investor in the field of health. The first problem in this case is to persuade health managers to consider MMORPGs a possible strategy for health com-

munication. However, currently in Brazil there is a good will from government to try new technologies. Brazilian Ministry of Culture launched in 2005 the program Games BR, which aimed to encourage local game developers to make products able to compete in the international market. Other government funding programs are expanding their scope to include video games and similar interactive products (BR Games, 2007).

Even with such good news, video games are complex cultural and technical products, requiring a broad range of financial, technological, and creative resources for their design, production and distribution. MMORPGs in particular are in the top of the complexity scale of game development and there is not a consolidated method to their production yet. More than once a well-known game company invested much money in a MMORPG only to cancel it after release due to low number of players. The problems that afflicts most academically developed games are infrastructural ones, like the lack of any distribution mechanism, the lack of product discoverability, the prohibitive expense of content creation, the dearth of meaningful assessment (and therefore of consumer confidence in the product), and the lack of sustainable business models (Mayo, 2009).

Three main challenges for MMORPGs' use for Public Health Communication in Brazil can be named at first glance: the access by the public, since the computers needed to run a MMORPG may be too expensive for the poorer population, their complexity and lastly their high costs of production. While these are real difficulties, we would like to point possible strategies to minimize such problems.

As previously mentioned, lan-houses play an important role in Brazil. They are very simple cyber cafés, often operating without legal permits, present in all kinds of neighborhoods, especially in low-income areas. Despite their commercial activity deeply rooted in informality, sometimes using pirated software, they allow poor population to access internet for very cheap fees. Because of this important social benefit that they bring to their customers, Brazilian Internet Steering Committee urged government managers to encourage their permanence (Survey, 2010). Furthermore, the constant drop in computer prices combined with increasingly credit lines to their acquisition by the public has led to considerable progress in digital inclusion. Projects like "Banda Larga Popular" (Popular Broad Brand), a partnership between Brazilian government and telecommunications companies for cheapening internet access to population further contribute to this growing potential public for MMORPGs ("Banda larga," 2012).

Concerning the complexity factor, game development for public Health Communication would be particularly challenging, especially considering the typical bureaucracy and slowness that cripples creative projects in the public sector. Of course, MMORPGs for Health Communication would not be comparable to the big entertainment games like *World of Warcraft*. Probably the best way to start this initiative would be partnerships between government agencies and private game studios to design and develop MMORPGs highly focused in specific target groups. Judicious use of game engines (as detailed below) would also make technical aspects more manageable. These first experiences could provide more insights about the production process and further improve chances of success for subsequent more ambitious projects. Although the adoption of a MMORPG is a difficult thing to ensure, a possible solution would be starting such game as part of supplementary activities in public schools. Such projects could start with specific classrooms and age groups in particular regions and later grow to encompass broader groups. This way, the MMORPG would be in constant refinement to assure that it would have adequate population and at same time be relevant to them. Other possibility would be the inclusion of health themes in regular games already established. One example of this approach (although not in a typical MMORPG) is the current partnership of Brazilian Ministry of

Health with the browser game "Mundo do Sítio" (World of the Farm), which often exhibits health care content mixed with the game activities (Zé Gotinha, 2012).

Concerning the costs of production, it is worth mentioning that there are an increasing number of virtual world development platforms, which greatly reduces production costs and at same time eases the more daunting technical challenges of developing a MMORPG. Some of these platforms like OpenSimulator (2012) are free, others charge very low fees, like the HeroEngine (used in Bioware's recent published MMORPG Star Wars: The Old Republic) which combines game engine, MMO server and billing platform (HeroEngine, 2012). Game engines' prices are also becoming more accessible to limited budget teams and they can be adapted to support MMORPGs. Unity, Unreal Development Kit (UDK) and CryEngine are examples of fully featured game engines that are very cheap or even free to non-commercial use (CryENGINE, 2012; UDK, 2012; Unity3D, 2012). As a MMORPG designed for public Health Communication probably would be free to the public, it would benefit from these conditions. That would make costs with game engines and similar tools much smaller than equivalent commercial ventures. In addition, it is reasonable to presume that maybe MMORPGs' development process will have an evolution similar to the single user game development, where the emergence of cheaper and more powerful tools allowed the growing of the indie game developers sector (Irwin, 2008). A possible first example of this trend is the MMORPG Project Gorgon whose creator, programmer and game designer Eric Heimburg, works alone using Unity as main tool. Concerning overcoming distribution costs and obstacles, there is a growing trend of browser MMORPGs, which eases access to people who plays from lan-houses, cyber cafes and other public computers (Heimburg, 2011).

Lastly, although not classified strictly as MMORPGs, other successful online initiatives perhaps may offer some insights about engaging people while keeping reduced costs. *Whyville,* for example, started in 1999 as an education space for children and it was one of the first virtual spaces to have a virtual economy and to accept user submitted content. In 2009, it had five millions players and its user base is still growing (Whyville Demographics, 2009). Several companies sponsor educational activities and events in game, including Whypox, a recurring virtual epidemic that requires players' search for a cure (Kafai, Quintero, & Feldon, 2010). This, in combination with *Whyville's* promotion of user created content, guarantee a constant influx of new elements in the game. Some of these strategies could possibly be adapted to a MMORPG for Health Communication.

FUTURE RESEARCH DIRECTIONS

This chapter summarizes our very first insights and efforts to understand how MMORPGs could be useful for Health Communication in Brazil. Other ongoing projects will help to develop and supplement these ideas.

As a way to understand what are the main engagement factors of MMORPGs over players, and the real possibilities of using them for Health Communication, we are conducting interviews with four main groups. We conducted interviews with Brazilian MMORPG players in the first months of 2012, with the objective of assessing their motives for playing, likes, dislikes and relationships with other players inside and outside the virtual world. We are currently interviewing key health managers from Brazilian Ministry of Health, trying to assess their knowledge about MMORPGs and video games in general and their interest in using games in Health Communication. The third group will be health researchers and health communication professionals, to assess how they see the use of MMORPGs in Health Communication. Lastly, we will conduct interviews with Brazilian game developers, trying to discover their opinions about

venues to make these games financially feasible and capable of combining Health Communication aspirations with the day-to-day logistics of game development in a country whose game industry is still in its infancy.

Although not exactly related to MMORPGs, but still dealing with games, our research group is at the early stages of development of a board game about sex, STDs and health issues for teenagers for which a prototype should be ready on the second quarter of 2013. Currently we are researching the ways these boys and girls make sense of health information about STDs. After that, we should start the first sketches of the game rules. This project spanned a digital counterpart, which will allow players to interact with each other using a regular web browser, therefore serving also as a starting point to online initiatives. Our aim is to use these small projects as a means of developing and testing ideas about Health Communication and game design, while at same time gathering a group of like-minded professionals with varied capabilities seeking to research and apply games for Health Communication.

In addition, we are about to start a study on health board games created in Brazil. Although they are in small number and typically made by amateurs, our aim is to analyze how such board games present the health content and what kind of participation they allow to the player, looking if it is possible to build upon their strengths.

Future steps for research include further studies about the possible ways for funding and implementation of MMORPGs in Brazil, more in depth evaluations of technological and logistical alternatives to facilitate video games' adoption as a valid medium for Health Communication, research on the use of these games in mobile platforms, development of a set of guidelines to help young game developers willing to create video games directed to health themes and definition of reliable metrics and measurement methods for analysis of video games' impact on Health Communication.

CONCLUSION

For years, video games have been extensively present in serious projects. Their multimedia capabilities and power to engage the public, especially youngsters, make them invaluable as a means for Health Communication. This is particularly true in the case of MMORPGs, since the Internet makes very easy to distribute, maintain, correct, update, and expand such games. In addition, as previously mentioned, games are a gateway for the technologies of information and communication for a huge number of people. It is important to harness their potential to improve their health and well-being.

Health Communication in Brazil, despite still shaped in great part by dated communication theories that tried to model behaviors by prescriptive norms and arbitrary authority, is increasingly changing to embrace theories that consider the importance of culture and social contexts. These changes reflect in the new media approaches by Ministry of Health, like use of websites and social networks. This willingness to try new media in general opens way for using also video games and MMORPGs.

Despite MMORPGs high cost and technical complexity, they may be more effective and economically viable than traditional media campaigns. New tools and techniques for game development are continuously reducing production costs and there are great chances that this trend continues even further. It is reasonable to expect that some of these advances will be applicable to MMORPGs as well. In parallel, Brazilian government makes large investments in Health Communication campaigns and these resources could be oriented to attract professional game developers for creating MMORPGs with health content. At the same time, access and digital inclusion are growing in Brazil. As more people start playing games and internet access increase, there will be more potential players to interact in these virtual worlds.

Nonetheless, mere technology does not make miracles and it is important to focus also on the social aspects of these initiatives. MMORPGs are shared worlds where the players interact between themselves and one's action often has effects over other players. As such, they create a useful environment to show players important concepts about self-care, prevention, and collective health, while at the same time allowing them to act in favor of themselves and others. In addition, the vast range of activities typical of MMORPGs and the constant social interaction also foster a participatory culture, visible in all kinds of fan created art and culture in and around the MMORPG.

Therefore, MMORPGs could be not only a way to distribute content, but mainly a space where health managers could hear and interact with the population, granting them social and political agency and fostering dialogue between government and citizens, health managers and public.

REFERENCES

Araújo, I. S. (2000). *A reconversão do olhar* [The Reconversion of Looking]. São Leopoldo, Brazil: Unisinos.

Araújo, I. S. (2002). *Mercado simbólico: Interlocução, luta, poder - Um modelo de comunicação para políticas públicas* [Symbolic Market: Dialogue, struggle, power - A communication model for public policies]. Rio de Janeiro, Brazil: Universidade Federal do Rio de Janeiro.

Araújo, I. S. (2009). Contexts, mediations and production of meanings: A conceptual and methodological approach for communication and health. *RECIIS*, *3*(3), 42–50. doi:10.3395/reciis. v3i3.280en.

Araújo, I. S., & Cardoso, J. M. (2007). *Comunicação e saúde* [Communication and health]. Rio de Janeiro, Brazil: Editora Fiocruz.

Ars Technica. (2008). *Growth of gaming in 2007 far outpaces movies, music.* Retrieved 07 jan 2010, from http://arstechnica.com/gaming/news/2008/01/growth-of-gaming-in-2007-far-outpaces-movies-music.ars

Bakthin, M. (1986). *Speech genres and other late essays.* Austin, TX: University of Texas Press.

Balicer, R. D. (2007). Modeling infectious diseases dissemination through online role-playing games. *Epidemiology (Cambridge, Mass.)*, *18*(2), 260–261. doi:10.1097/01.ede.0000254692.80550.60 PMID:17301707.

Barab, S., Thomas, M., Dodge, T., Carteaux, R., & Tuzun, H. (2005). Making learning fun: Quest Atlantis, a game without guns. *Educational Technology Research and Development*, *53*(1), 86–107. doi:10.1007/BF02504859.

Baranowski, T., Buday, R., Thompson, D. I., & Baranowski, J. (2008). Playing for real: Video games and stories for health-related behavior change. *American Journal of Preventive Medicine*, *34*(1), 74–82. doi:10.1016/j.amepre.2007.09.027 PMID:18083454.

Barbosa, A., Cappi, J., & Jereissati, T. (2011). *Pesquisa TIC crianças 2010: Pesquisa sobre o uso das tecnologias de informação e comunicação no brasil.* [Research ICT Children 2010: Survey on the Use of Information and Communication Technologies in Brazil]. Retrieved from http://www.cetic.br/usuarios/criancas/2010/apresentacao-tic-criancas-2010.pdf

Barnett, J., & Coulson, M. (2010). Virtually real: A psychological perspective on massively multiplayer online games. *Review of General Psychology*, *14*(2), 167–179. doi:10.1037/a0019442.

Barthes, R. (1977). *Elements of semiology.* New York, NY: Hill and Wang.

Barthes, R. (1994). *The semiotic challenge.* Berkeley, CA: University of California Press.

Blog do Sitio. (2012). *Zé gotinha na campanha nacional de vacinação.* [The droplet in the national vaccination campaign]. Retrieved 4 May 2012, from http://blog.mundodositio.globo.com/2012/05/04/ze-gotinha-na-campanha-nacional-de-vacinacao/

Bourdieu, P. (1999). *Language and symbolic power.* Cambridge, MA: Harvard University Press.

Brazilian Internet Steering Committee. (2010). *Survey on the use of information and communication technologies in Brazil - ICT LANHOUSES - 2010.* São Paulo, Brazil: Brazilian Internet Steering Committee.

Brooksby, A. (2008). Exploring the representation of health in videogames: A content analysis. *Cyberpsychology & Behavior*, *11*(6), 771–773. doi:10.1089/cpb.2007.0007 PMID:18954269

Brown, S. J., Lieberman, D. A., Gemeny, B. A., Fan, Y. C., Wilson, D. M., & Pasta, D. J. (1997). Educational video game for juvenile diabetes: Results of a controlled trial. *Informatics for Health & Social Care*, *22*(1), 77–89. doi:10.3109/14639239709089835 PMID:9183781.

Buss, P. (2011). Brazil: Structuring cooperation for health. *Lancet*, *377*(9779), 1722–1723. doi:10.1016/S0140-6736(11)60354-1 PMID:21561654.

Buss, P. M., & Pellegrini Filho, A. (2007). A saúde e seus determinantes sociais. [The Health and its Social Determinants]. *PHYSIS: Rev. Saúde Coletiva*, *17*(1), 77–93.

Chang, Y.-J., Chen, S.-F., & Huang, J.-D. (2011). A kinect-based system for physical rehabilitation: A pilot study for young adults with motor disabilities. *Research in Developmental Disabilities*, *32*(6), 2566–2570. doi:10.1016/j.ridd.2011.07.002 PMID:21784612.

Computer and Videogames. (2005). *Looking back... World of Warcraft*. Retrieved 07 jan 2010, from http://www.computerandvideogames.com/article.php?id=131791

CryDev.net. (2012). *CryENGINE 3 free SDK*. Retrieved 11 Oct 2012, from http://www.crydev.net/dm_eds/download_detail.php?id=4

Darfur Is Dying. (2006). *Website*. Retrieved 27 jan 2011, from http://www.darfurisdying.com/

Freire, P. (1993). *Pedagogy of the oppressed*. New York, NY: Continuum Publishing Company.

Gamasutra. (2009). *Analyst: Online games now $11B of $44B worldwide game market*. Retrieved from http://www.gamasutra.com/view/news/114898/Analyst_Online_Games_Now_11B_Of_44B_Worldwide_Game_Market.php

Gee, J. P. (2007). *What video games have to teach us about learning and literacy*. New York, NY: Palgrave Macmillan.

Gee, J. P. (2008). Video games and embodiment. *Games and Culture*, *3*(3-4). doi:10.1177/1555412008317309.

Heimburg, E. (2011). Project gorgon, an indie MMO in development. *Elder Game*. Retrieved 15 Sep 2012, from http://www.eldergame.com/2011/10/early-prep-for-newbies/

HeroEngine. (2012). *Website*. Retrieved 5 Oct 2012, from http://www.heroengine.com/

Herz, J. C. (2002). Gaming the system: What higher education can learn from multiplayer online worlds. In The Internet and the University, Forum, (pp. 169-191). EDUCAUSE.

Irwin, M. J. (2008). Indie game developers rise up. *Forbes.com*. Retrieved 22 Sep 2012, from http://www.forbes.com/2008/11/20/games-indie-developers-tech-ebiz-cx_mji_1120indiegames.html

Jeanneret, Y. (2009). The relation between mediation and use in the research field of information and communication in France. *RECIIS*, *3*(3), 25–34.

Jenkins, H. (2008). *Convergence culture: Where old and new media collide*. New York, NY: NYU Press.

Jones, R. (2008). Saving worlds with videogame activism. In Ferdig, R. E. (Ed.), *Handbook of Research on Effective Electronic Gaming in Education* (pp. 970–988). Hershey, PA: IGI Global. doi:10.4018/978-1-59904-808-6.ch056.

Kafai, Y. B., Quintero, M., & Feldon, D. (2010). Investigating the ''why'' in whypox: Casual and systematic explorations of a virtual epidemic. *Games and Culture*, *5*(1), 116–135. doi:10.1177/1555412009351265.

Karlsen, F. (2011). *Theorycrafting: From collective intelligence to intrinsic satisfaction*. Paper presented at the DiGRA 2011 Conference: Think Design Play. Hilversum, The Netherlands.

Kato, P. M., Cole, S. W., Bradlyn, A. S., & Pollock, B. H. (2008). A video game improves behavioral outcomes in adolescents and young adults with cancer - A randomized trial. *Pediatrics*, *122*(2), e305–e317. doi:10.1542/peds.2007-3134 PMID:18676516.

Klastrup, L., & Tosca, S. (2009). Because it just looks cool! Fashion as character performance: The case of WoW. *Journal of Virtual Worlds Research*, *1*(3), 4–17.

Klawe, M. (1999). *Computer games, education and interfaces: The E-GEMS project*. Paper presented at the Graphics interface conference. Ontario, Canada.

Koster, R. (1998). The man behind the curtain. *Raph Koster's Website*. Retrieved 13 Oct 2012, from http://www.raphkoster.com/gaming/essay5.shtml

Kücklich, J. (2009). A techno-semiotic approach to cheating in computer games. *Games and Culture*, *4*(2), 158–169. doi:10.1177/1555412008325486.

Lieberman, D. A. (2001). Management of chronic pediatric diseases with interactive health games: Theory and research findings. *The Journal of Ambulatory Care Management*, *24*(1), 26–38. PMID:11189794.

Lofgren, E. T., & Fefferman, N. H. (2007). The untapped potential of virtual game worlds to shed light on real world epidemics. *The Lancet Infectious Diseases*, *7*(9), 625–629. doi:10.1016/S1473-3099(07)70212-8 PMID:17714675.

Malone, T. (1980). *What makes things fun to learn? A study of intrinsically motivating computer games*. Technical report no. CIS-7 (SSL-80-11). Palo Alto, CA: Xerox Palo Alto Research Center.

Martín-Barbero, J. (1993). *Communication, culture and hegemony: From the media to mediations*. London, UK: Sage Publications.

Mayo, M. J. (2009). Video games: A route to large-scale STEM education? *Science*, *323*, 79–82. doi:10.1126/science.1166900 PMID:19119223.

Ministerio da Cultura. (2007). *BR games: Objetivo, público e diretrizes*. [BR Games: Purpose, Audience and Guidelines]. Retrieved 23 jan 2010, from http://www.cultura.gov.br/site/2007/09/25/jogos-br/

MIT. (2012). *MIT's education arcade uses online gaming to teach science*. Retrieved from http://education.mit.edu/blogs/louisa/2012/pressrelease

New York Times. (1999, April 6). *Managing ailments through video games*. Retrieved from http://www.nytimes.com/1999/04/06/health/managing-ailments-through-video-games.html

Newzoo. (2011). *Gap closing between emerging and western game markets*. Retrieved 01 jun 2011, from http://www.newzoo.com/ENG/1504-Detail.html&id=79

Oblinger, D. (2004). The next generation of educational engagement. *Journal of Interactive Media in Education*, *8*, 1–18.

OpenSimulator. (2012). *Website*. Retrieved from http://opensimulator.org

Organization. (1998). *Health promotion evaluation: Recommendations to policymakers*. Copenhagen, Denmark: European Working Group on Health Promotion Evaluation.

Paim, J., Travassos, C., Almeida, C., Bahia, L., & Macinko, J. (2011). The Brazilian health system: History, advances, and challenges. *Lancet*, *377*(9779), 1778–1797. doi:10.1016/S0140-6736(11)60054-8 PMID:21561655.

Paim, J. S. (2010). *O que é o SUS* [What is the SUS]. Rio de Janeiro, Brazil: Editora Fiocruz.

Papastergiou, M. (2009). Exploring the potential of computer and video games for health and physical education: A literature review. *Computers & Education*, *53*(3), 603–622. doi:10.1016/j.compedu.2009.04.001.

Pereira, V. A. (2008). *Na lan house, "porque jogar sozinho não tem graça": Estudo das redes sociais juvenis on- e off-line*. [In the lan house, "because it's no fun playing alone": A study of juvenile social networks online and offline]. (PhD Thesis) Universidade Federal do Rio de Janeiro. Rio de Janeiro, Brazil.

Portal Brasil. (2012). *Banda larga popular já chegou a quase 1.400 municípios*. [Popular broadband has reached almost 1,400 cities]. Retrieved 10 Oct 2012, from http://www.brasil.gov.br/noticias/arquivos/2012/06/14/banda-larga-popular-ja-chegou-a-quase-1.400-municipios

Prensky, M. (2004). *Digital game-based learning*. New York, NY: McGraw-Hill.

Purdy, J. (2007). Serious games: Getting serious about digital games in learning. *Corporate University Journal*, 3-6.

0

Re-Mission. (2009). *A game for young people with cancer*. Retrieved 26 jan 2011 from http://www.re-mission.net/

Reiner, B., & Siegel, E. (2008). The potential for gaming techniques in radiology education and practice. *Journal of the American College of Radiology*, *5*(2), 110–114. doi:10.1016/j.jacr.2007.09.002 PMID:18242526.

Schiesel, S. (2008). Face to face - A council of eve online gamers. *New York Times*. Retrieved from http://www.nytimes.com/2008/06/28/arts/television/28eve.html?_r=1&ref=arts&pagewanted=all

Shannon, C. E., & Weaver, W. (1949). *The mathematical theory of communication*. Champaign, IL: University of Illinois Press.

Silveira, S. A. (2009). Game-ativismo e a nova esfera pública interconectada. *Líbero*, *12*(24), 131–138.

Staiano, A., Abraham, A., & Calvert, S. (2012). The WII club: Promoting weight loss, psychosocial health, and sports involvement through an exergaming intervention for overweight and obese youth. *The Journal of Adolescent Health*, *50*(2), S9–S10. doi:10.1016/j.jadohealth.2011.10.038.

Turkaya, S., & Adinolf, S. (2010). Free to be me: A survey study on customization with World of Warcraft and City of Heroes/Villains players. *Procedia Social and Behavioral Sciences*, 1840-1845. doi: 10.1016/j.sbspro.2010.03.995

Turkle, S. (1995). *Life on the screen: Identity in the age of the internet*. New York, NY: Simon & Schuster.

UDK. (2012). *Unreal engine*. Retrieved 28 Sep 2012, from http://www.unrealengine.com/udk/

UN. (2005). *Food force: The first humanitarian video game*. Retrieved 29 jun 2012, from http://www.wfp.org/how-to-help/individuals/food-force

Unity3D. (2012). *Website*. Retrieved 29 Sep 2012, from http://unity3d.com/

Verón, E. (1980). *A produção do sentido*. São Paulo, Brazil: Cultrix / USP.

Victora, C. G., Aquino, E. M. L., do Carmo Leal, M., Monteiro, C. A., Barros, F. C., & Szwarcwald, C. L. (2011). Maternal and child health in Brazil: Progress and challenges. *Lancet*, *377*(9780), 1863–1876. doi:10.1016/S0140-6736(11)60138-4 PMID:21561656.

Victora, C. G., Barreto, M. L., do Carmo Leal, M., Monteiro, C. A., Schmidt, M. I., & Paim, J. et al. (2011). Health conditions and health-policy innovations in Brazil: The way forward. *Lancet*, *377*(9782), 2042–2053. doi:10.1016/S0140-6736(11)60055-X PMID:21561659.

Whyville. (2009). Whyville demographics. *Whyville.Net*. Retrieved from http://b.whyville.net/smmk/top/gatesInfo?topic=pdf_library

Williams, D., Yee, N., & Caplan, S. E. (2008). Who plays, how much, and why? Debunking the stereotypical gamer profile. *Journal of Computer-Mediated Communication*, *13*(4), 993–1018. doi:10.1111/j.1083-6101.2008.00428.x.

World Health Organization. (1986). *The Ottawa charter for health promotion*. Ottawa, Canada: World Health Organization.

Xanthopoulou, D., & Papagiannidis, S. (2012). Play online, work better? Examining the spillover of active learning and transformational leadership. *Technological Forecasting and Social Change*, *79*(7), 1328–1339. doi:10.1016/j.techfore.2012.03.006.

Yale. (2009). *Video game to help urban teens avoid HIV infection focus of nearly $4 million grant to Yale*. Retrieved from http://news.yale.edu/2009/09/24/video-game-help-urban-teens-avoid-hiv-infection-focus-nearly-4-million-grant-yale

Yee, N., & Bailenson, J. (2007). The proteus effect: The effect of transformed self-representation on behavior. *Human Communication Research, 33*, 271–290. doi:10.1111/j.1468-2958.2007.00299.x.

ADDITIONAL READING

Almeida Filho, N. (2011). Higher education and health care in Brazil. *Lancet, 377*(9781), 1898–1900. doi:10.1016/S0140-6736(11)60326-7 PMID:21561653.

Bainbridge, W. S. (2010). *The warcraft civilization: Social science in a virtual world*. Cambridge, MA: The MIT Press.

Barreto, M. L., Teixeira, M. G., Bastos, F. I., Ximenes, R. A. A., Barata, R. B., & Rodrigues, L. C. (2011). Successes and failures in the control of infectious diseases in Brazil: Social and environmental context, policies, interventions, and research needs. *Lancet, 377*(9780), 1877–1889. doi:10.1016/S0140-6736(11)60202-X PMID:21561657.

Beale, I., Kato, P., Martin-Bowling, V., Guthrie, N., & Cole, S. (2007). Improvement in cancer-related knowledge following use of a psychoeducational video game for adolescents and young adults with cancer. *The Journal of Adolescent Health, 41*(3), 263–270. doi:10.1016/j.jadohealth.2007.04.006 PMID:17707296.

Buss, P. M. (2011). Brazil: Structuring cooperation for health. *Lancet, 377*(9779), 1722–1723. doi:10.1016/S0140-6736(11)60354-1 PMID:21561654.

Caillois, R. (2001). *Man, play and games*. Champaign, IL: University of Illinois Press.

Campello de Souza, B., Lima e Silva, L. X. D., & Roazzi, A. (2010). MMORPGS and cognitive performance: A study with 1280 Brazilian high school students. *Computers in Human Behavior, 26*, 1564–1573. doi:10.1016/j.chb.2010.06.001.

De Castell, S., & Jenson, J. (2003). Serious play. *Journal of Curriculum Studies, 35*(6), 649–665. doi:10.1080/0022027032000145552.

De Castell, S., & Jenson, J. (2007). Digital games for education: When meanings play. *Intermediality: History and Theory of the Arts. Literature and Technologies, 9*, 113–132.

Flanagan, M. (2009). *Critical play: Radical game design*. Cambridge, MA: The MIT Press.

Fleury, S. (2011). Brazil's health-care reform: Social movements and civil society. *Lancet, 377*(9779), 1724–1725. doi:10.1016/S0140-6736(11)60318-8 PMID:21561650.

Gee, J. P. (2007). *What video games have to teach us about learning and literacy*. New York, NY: Palgrave Macmillan.

Huizinga, J. (1971). *Homo ludens: A study of the play-element in culture*. Boston, MA: The Beacon Press.

Kent, S. L. (2001). *The ultimate history of video games: From Pong to Pokémon and beyond - The story behind the craze that touched our lives and changed the world*. New York, NY: Three Rivers Press.

Kleinert, S., & Horton, R. (2011). Brazil: Towards sustainability and equity in health. *Lancet, 377*(9779), 1721–1722. doi:10.1016/S0140-6736(11)60433-9 PMID:21561652.

McGonigal, J. (2011). *Reality is broken: Why games make us better and how they can change the world*. New York, NY: Penguin Press.

Nardi, B. (2010). *My life as a night elf priest: An anthropological account of World of Warcraft.* Ann Arbor, MI: University of Michigan Press.

Peng, W. (2009). Design and evaluation of a computer game to promote a healthy diet for young adults. *Health Communication, 24,* 115–127. doi:10.1080/10410230802676490 PMID:19280455.

Raessens, J. (2005). Computer games as participatory media culture. In Raessens, J. F. F., & Goldstein, J. (Eds.), *Handbook of Computer Game Studies* (pp. 373–389). Cambridge, MA: The MIT Press.

Raessens, J. (2006). Playful identities, or the ludification of culture. *Games and Culture, 1*(52), 52–57. doi:10.1177/1555412005281779.

Raessens, J. (2010). *Homo ludens 2.0: The ludic turn in media theory.* Utrecht, The Netherlands: Utrecht University.

Ratan, R., & Ritterfeld, U. (2009). Classifying serious games. In Ritterfeld, U., Cody, M., & Vorderer, P. (Eds.), *Serious Games: Mechanisms and Effects* (pp. 10–24). London, UK: Routledge.

Salen, K., & Zimmerman, E. (2004). *Rules of play: Game design fundamentals.* Cambridge, MA: The MIT Press.

Schmidt, M. I., Duncan, B. B., Silva, G. A., Menezes, A. M., Monteiro, C. A., & Barreto, S. M. et al. (2011). Chronic non-communicable diseases in Brazil: Burden and current challenges. *Lancet, 377*(9781), 1949–1961. doi:10.1016/S0140-6736(11)60135-9 PMID:21561658.

Singhal, A., & Rogers, E. M. (2002). A theoretical agenda for entertainment-education. *Communication Theory, 12*(2), 117–135.

Turkle, S. (2011). *Alone together: Why we expect more from technology and less from each other.* New York, NY: Basic Books.

Uauy, R. (2011). The impact of the Brazil experience in Latin America. *Lancet, 377*(9782), 1984–1986. doi:10.1016/S0140-6736(11)60437-6 PMID:21561651.

Vasconcellos, M. S., & Araújo, I. S. (2011). Uses of ethnography in image-based virtual worlds. *RECIIS, 5*(2), 75–85. doi:10.3395/reciis.v5i2.496en.

KEY TERMS AND DEFINITIONS

Avatar: Digital customizable agent operated by a player to act in a virtual environment.

Health Communication: A field of research and practice concerned with sharing health-related information to individuals, institutions and public audiences.

Machinima: Animation technique that uses primarily in-game animations as raw footage.

Massively Multiplayer Online Role Playing Games (MMORPGs): Sometimes called simply MMOs, games where large numbers of players interact simultaneously inside online fictional virtual worlds using avatars.

Serious Game: Any form of interactive digital game software, on any platform, usable for one or more players, developed with the intention to be more than entertainment.

Video Game: A game in which the player operates a user interface and receives feedback thanks to a video device.

Virtual World: A computer-based simulated environment. Normally the use of this term implies an online virtual world. Not all virtual worlds are games, but all MMORPGs happen in online virtual worlds.

Compilation of References

Abt, C. C. (1975). *Serious games*. New York, NY: Viking Compass.

ACSM. (2011). Quantity and quality of exercise for developing and maintaining cardiorespiratory, musculoskeletal, and neuromotor fitness in apparently healthy adults: Guidance for prescribing exercise. *Medicine and Science in Sports and Exercise, 43*(7), 1334–1359. doi:10.1249/MSS.0b013e318213fefb

Active Worlds. (2012). *Website*. Retrieved 2 October 2012 from http://activeworlds.com/

Adachi, P. C., & Willoughby, T. (2011). The effect of video game competition and violence on aggressive behavior: Which characteristic has the greatest influence? *Psychology Of Violence, 1*(4), 259–274. doi:10.1037/a0024908

Adamovich, S., Fluet, G., Tunik, E., & Merians, A. (2009). Sensorimotor training in virtual reality: A review. *NeuroRehabilitation, 25*, 29–44.

Adams, E. (2009). *The designer's notebook: Sorting out the genre muddle*. Retrieved July 9, 2009, from http://www.gamasutra.com/view/feature/4074/the_designers_notebook_sorting_.php

Adams, E. (2009). *Fundamentals of game design* (2nd ed.). Berkeley, CA: New Riders.

Albert, D., & Lukas, J. (1999). *Knowledge spaces: Theories, empirical research, and applications*. London, UK: Routledge.

Allied Health Professions. (2012). *Wikipedia*. Retrieved from http://en.wikipedia.org/wiki/Allied_health_professions

Alsina-Jurnet, I., Gutierrez-Maldonado, J., & Rangel-Gomez, M. (2011). The role of presence in the level of anxiety experienced in clinical virtual environments. *Computers in Human Behavior, 27*, 504–512. doi:10.1016/j.chb.2010.09.018

Anderson, J. Q., Boyles, J. L., & Rainie, L. (2012). The future impact of the internet on higher education: experts expect more efficient collaborative environments and new grading schemes: They worry about massive online courses, the shift away from on-campus life. *Pew Internet & American Life Project*. Retrieved October 8, 2012, from http://pewinternet.org/~/media/Files/Reports/2012/PIP_Future_of_Higher_Ed.pdf

Anderson, C. (2004). An update on the effects of playing violent video games. *Journal of Adolescence, 27*, 113–122. doi:10.1016/j.adolescence.2003.10.009

Anderson, C. A., & Bushman, B. J. (2001). Effects of violent video games on aggressive behavior, aggressive cognition, aggressive affect, physiological arousal, and prosocial behavior: A meta-analytic review of the scientific literature. *Psychological Science, 12*(5), 353–359. doi:10.1111/1467-9280.00366

Anderson, C., & Dill, K. (2000). Video games and aggressive thoughts, feelings and behavior in the laboratory and in life. *Journal of Personality and Social Psychology, 78*, 772–790. doi:10.1037/0022-3514.78.4.772

Anderson, C., & Ford, C. (1987). Affect of the game player: Short term effects of highly and mildly aggressive video games. *Personality and Social Psychology Bulletin, 12*(4), 390–402. doi:10.1177/0146167286124002

Anne Myers Medical Centre. (2012). *Second life*. Retrieved from http://ammc.wordpress.com/

Annetta, L. A. (2010). The "I's" have it: A framework for serious educational game design. *Review of General Psychology*, *14*(2), 105–112. doi:10.1037/a0018985

ARA. (2012). *Website*. Retrieved 2 October 2012 from http://www.ara.com/Newsroom_Whatsnew/press_releases/unreal-network.htm

Araújo, I. S. (2000). *A reconversão do olhar* [The Reconversion of Looking]. São Leopoldo, Brazil: Unisinos.

Araújo, I. S. (2002). *Mercado simbólico: Interlocução, luta, poder - Um modelo de comunicação para políticas públicas* [Symbolic Market: Dialogue, struggle, power - A communication model for public policies]. Rio de Janeiro, Brazil: Universidade Federal do Rio de Janeiro.

Araújo, I. S. (2009). Contexts, mediations and production of meanings: A conceptual and methodological approach for communication and health. *RECIIS*, *3*(3), 42–50. doi:10.3395/reciis.v3i3.280en

Araújo, I. S., & Cardoso, J. M. (2007). *Comunicação e saúde* [Communication and health]. Rio de Janeiro, Brazil: Editora Fiocruz.

Ars Technica. (2008). *Growth of gaming in 2007 far outpaces movies, music*. Retrieved 07 jan 2010, from http://arstechnica.com/gaming/news/2008/01/growth-of-gaming-in-2007-far-outpaces-movies-music.ars

Australian National University. (2012). *Website*. Retrieved from http://www.olt.gov.au/project-virtual-world-inter-view-skills-health-professionals-2011

Azevedo, R., Moos, D., Winters, F., Greene, J., Cromley, J., Olson, E., & Godbole Chaudhuri, P. (2005). Why is externally-regulated learning more effective than self-regulated learning with hypermedia? In *Proceeding of the 2005 Conference on Artificial Intelligence in Education: Supporting Learning through Intelligent and Socially Informed Technology*, (pp. 41–48). IEEE.

Badurdeen, S., Abdul-Samad, O., Story, G., Wilson, C., Down, S., & Harris, A. (2010). Nintendo Wii video-gaming ability predicts laparoscopic skill. *Surgical Endoscopy*, *24*, 1824–1828. doi:10.1007/s00464-009-0862-z

Baecker, R., et al. (2012). *Social support technology for those at risk of social isolation*. Paper presented a the IFA, 11th Global Conference on Aging. Prague, Czech Republic.

Bailenson, J. N., Beall, A. C., Blascovich, J., Loomis, J., & Turk, M. (2005). Transformed social interaction, augmented gaze, and social influence in immersive virtual environments. *Human Communication Research*, *31*, 511–537. doi:10.1111/j.1468-2958.2005.tb00881.x

Bailenson, J. N., & Yee, N. (2006). A longitudinal study of task performance, head movements, subjective report, simulator sickness, and transformed social interaction in collaborative virtual environments. *Presence (Cambridge, Mass.)*, *15*(6), 699–716. doi:10.1162/pres.15.6.699

Bailey, S. W., & Bodenheimer, B. (2012). A comparison of motion capture data recorded from a Vicon system and a Microsoft Kinect sensor. In *Proceedings of SAP 2012*, (p. 121). New York, NY: ACM.

Bainbridge, W. S. (2007). The scientific research potential of virtual worlds. *Science*, *317*(5837), 472–476. doi:10.1126/science.1146930

Baker, M., & Lund, K. (1997). Promoting reflective interactions in a computer-supported collaborative learning environment. *Journal of Computer Assisted Learning*, *13*, 175–193. doi:10.1046/j.1365-2729.1997.00019.x

Bakthin, M. (1986). *Speech genres and other late essays*. Austin, TX: University of Texas Press.

Balicer, R. D. (2007). Modeling infectious diseases dissemination through online role-playing games. *Epidemiology (Cambridge, Mass.)*, *18*(2), 260–261. doi:10.1097/01.ede.0000254692.80550.60

Banos, R., Botella, C., Garcia-Palacious, A., Villa, H., Perpina, C., & Gallardo, M. (1999). Psychological variables and reality judgements in virtual environments: The role of absorption and dissociation. *Cyberpsychology & Behavior*, *2*, 135–142. doi:10.1089/cpb.1999.2.143

Barab, S., Thomas, M., Dodge, T., Carteaux, R., & Tuzun, H. (2005). Making learning fun: Quest Atlantis, a game without guns. *Educational Technology Research and Development*, *53*(1), 86–107. doi:10.1007/BF02504859

Baranowski, T., Buday, R., Thompson, D. I., & Baranowski, J. (2008). Playing for real: Video games and stories for health-related behavior change. *American Journal of Preventive Medicine, 34*(1), 74–82. doi:10.1016/j.amepre.2007.09.027

Barbosa, A., Cappi, J., & Jereissati, T. (2011). *Pesquisa TIC crianças 2010: Pesquisa sobre o uso das tecnologias de informação e comunicação no brasil.* [Research ICT Children 2010: Survey on the Use of Information and Communication Technologies in Brazil]. Retrieved from http://www.cetic.br/usuarios/criancas/2010/apresentacao-tic-criancas-2010.pdf

Barfield, W., & Hendrix, C. (1995). The effect of update rate on the sense of presence within virtual environments. *Virtual Reality: The Journal of the Virtual Reality Society, 1*, 3–16. doi:10.1007/BF02009709

Barnett, J., & Coulson, M. (2010). Virtually real: A psychological perspective on massively multiplayer online games. *Review of General Psychology, 14*(2), 167–179. doi:10.1037/a0019442

Barthes, R. (1977). *Elements of semiology.* New York, NY: Hill and Wang.

Barthes, R. (1994). *The semiotic challenge.* Berkeley, CA: University of California Press.

Bartle, R. (1996). Hearts, clubs, diamonds, spades: Players who suit MUDS. *Journal of Virtual Environments, 1*(1), 19.

Bates, B. (2004). *Game design* (2nd ed.). Boston, MA: Thomson Course Technology.

Bateson, G. (1972). *Steps to an ecology of mind.* San Francisco, CA: Aronson.

Bavelier, D., Levi, D. M., Li, R. W., Dan, Y., & Hensch, D. K. (2010). Removing brakes on adult brain plasticity: From molecular to behavioral interventions. *The Journal of Neuroscience, 30*(45), 14964–14971. doi:10.1523/JNEUROSCI.4812-10.2010

Bayrhuber-Habeck, M. (2009). *Konstruktion und evaluation eines kompetenzstrukturmodells im bereich mathematischer repräsentationen: Psychologie schweizerische zeitschrift für psychologie und ihre andwendungen.* PH Freiburg.

Bayrhuber, M., Leuders, T., Bruder, R., & Wirtz, M. (2010). *Pedocs - Repräsentationswechsel beim umgang mit funktionen – Identifikation von kompetenzprofilen auf der basis eines kompetenzstrukturmodells: Projekt HEUREKO.* BELTZ Pädagogik.

BBC. (2006). *Climate challenge: Background information of the game.* Retrieved from http://www.bbc.co.uk/sn/hottopics/climatechange/climate_challenge/aboutgame.shtml

Becker, B., & Mark, G. (2002). Social conventions in computer-mediated communication: a comparison of three online shared virtual environments. In Schroeder, R. (Ed.), *The Social Life of Avatars: Presence and Interaction in Shared Virtual Environments* (pp. 19–39). London, UK: Springer. doi:10.1007/978-1-4471-0277-9_2

Beldarrain, Y. (2006). Distance education trends: Integrating new technologies to foster student interaction and collaboration. *Distance Education, 27*(2), 139–153. doi:http://dx.doi.org/10.1080/01587910600789498

Bell, M. W., Castronova, E., & Wagner, G. G. (2009). *Surveying the virtual world - A large scale survey in second life using the virtual data collection interface (VDCI).* German Council for Social and Economic Data (RatSWD) Research Notes No. 40. Retrieved from http://ssrn.com/abstract=1480254

Bennerstedt, U., Ivarsson, J., & Linderoth, J. (2012). How gamers manage aggression: Situating skills in collaborative computer games. *Computer Supported Collaborative Learning, 7*, 43–61. doi:10.1007/s11412-011-9136-6

Bente, G., & Breuer, J. (2009). Making the implicit explicit: Embedded measurement in serious games. In Ritterfeld, U., Cody, M., & Vorderer, P. (Eds.), *Serious Games: Mechanisms and Effects* (pp. 322–343). New York, NY: Routledge.

Betker, A. L., Desai, A., Nett, C., Kapadia, N., & Sztum, T. (2007). Game-based exercises for dynamic short-sitting balance rehabilitation of people with chronic spinal cord and traumatic brain injuries. *Physical Therapy, 87*, 1389–1398. doi:10.2522/ptj.20060229

Biddiss, E., & Irwin, J. (2010). Active video games to promote physical activity in children and youth: A systematic review. *Archives of Pediatrics & Adolescent Medicine, 164*(7), 664–672. doi:10.1001/archpediatrics.2010.104

Biocca, F., Harms, C., & Burgoon, J. (2003). Toward a more robust theory and measure of social presence: Review and suggested criteria. *Presence (Cambridge, Mass.)*, *12*(5), 456–480. doi:10.1162/105474603322761270

Birkenbusch, J. (2012). *Measuring immersive tendencies: Conception of a German language questionnaire.* (Unpublished Master Thesis). Technische Universität Darmstadt. Darmstadt, Germany.

Blascovich, J., Loomis, J., Beall, A. C., Swinth, K. R., Hoyt, C. L., & Bailenson, J. (2002). Immersive virtual environment technology as a methodological tool for social psychology. *Psychological Inquiry*, *13*(2), 103–124. doi:10.1207/S15327965PLI1302_01

Blischke, K., Marschall, F., Müller, H., & Daugs, R. (1999). Augmented information in motor skill acquisition. In Auweele, Y. V., Baker, F., Bidle, S., Durand, D., & Seiler, R. (Eds.), *Psychology for Physical Educators* (pp. 257–287). Champaign, IL: Human Kinetics.

Blit-Cohen, E., & Litwin, H. (2009). *Elder participation in cyberspace: A qualitative analysis of Israeli retirees.* Jerusalem, Israel: Hebrew University.

Block, J., & Crain, B. (2007). Omissions and errors in media violence and the American public. *The American Psychologist*, *62*, 252–253. doi:10.1037/0003-066X.62.3.252

Blog do Sitio. (2012). *Zé gotinha na campanha nacional de vacinação.* [The droplet in the national vaccination campaign]. Retrieved 4 May 2012, from http://blog.mundodositio.globo.com/2012/05/04/ze-gotinha-na-campanha-nacional-de-vacinacao/

Bloom, B. S., Engelhart, M. D., Furst, E. J., Hill, W. H., & Krathwohl, D. R. (1956). Taxonomy of educational objectives: The classification of educational goals. In Handbook, I. (Ed.), *Cognitive Domain*. New York, NY: McKay.

Boechler, P., King, S., Stroulia, E., Carbonaro, M., deJong, E., Wasniewski, E., & Chodos, D. (2010). Managing virtual world sessions for health science interprofessional education. In J. Sanchez & K. Zhang (Eds.), Proceedings of World Conference on E-Learning in Corporate, Government, Healthcare, and Higher Education 2010, (pp. 610-615). Chesapeake, VA: AACE.

Boellstorff, T. (2008). *Coming of age in second life.* Princeton, NJ: Princeton University Press.

Bogost, I. (2005). *The rhetoric of exergaming.* Paper presented at the Digital Arts and Cultures (DAC) Conference (December 2005). Copenhagen, Denmark.

Bogost, I. (2007). *Persuasive games.* Cambridge, MA: MIT Press.

Bopp, M. (2005). Immersive didaktik: Verdeckte lernhilfen und framingprozesse in computerspielen. *kommunikation@gesellschaft, 6.*

Bösche, W., & Kattner, F. (2011). Using a violent multiplayer game as a virtual classroom for a course on violent video games. In Felicia, P. (Ed.), *Handbook of Research on Improving Learning and Motivation through Educational Games: Multidisciplinary Approaches* (pp. 777–805). Hershey, PA: IGI Global. doi:10.4018/978-1-60960-495-0.ch035

Botte, B., Matera, C., & Sponsiello, M. (2009). Serious games between simulation and game: A proposal of taxonomy. *Journal of e-Learning and Knowledge Society*, *5*(2), 11-21.

Bourdieu, P. (1999). *Language and symbolic power.* Cambridge, MA: Harvard University Press.

Brach, M., Hauer, K., Rotter, L., Werres, C., Korn, O., Konrad, R., & Göbel, S. (2012). Modern principles of training in exergames for sedentary seniors: Requirements and approaches for sport and exercise sciences. *International Journal of Computer Science in Sport*, *11*, 86–99.

Brach, M., & Korn, O. (2012). Assistive technologies at home and in the workplace—A field of research for exercise science and human movement science. *European Review of Aging and Physical Activity*, *9*(1), 1–4. doi:10.1007/s11556-012-0099-z

Brazilian Internet Steering Committee. (2010). *Survey on the use of information and communication technologies in Brazil - ICT LANHOUSES - 2010.* São Paulo, Brazil: Brazilian Internet Steering Committee.

Breakaway Games. (2012). *Website.* Retrieved from http://www.breakawaygames.com/about/overview/

Bredl, K., & Groß, A. (2012). Gestaltung und bewertung von lernszenarien in immersiven virtuellen welten. *Zeitschrift für E-Learning*, *7*(1), 36–46.

Brewer, B., McDowell, S., & Worthen-Chaudhari, L. (2007). Poststroke upper extremity rehabilitation: A review of robotic systems and clinical results. *Topics in Stroke Rehabilitation*, *14*, 22–44. doi:10.1310/tsr1406-22

Brochard, S., Robertson, J., Médée, B., & Rémy-Néris, O. (2010). What's new in new technologies for upper extremity rehabilitation? *Current Opinion in Neurology*, *23*, 683–687. doi:10.1097/WCO.0b013e32833f61ce

Brooksby, A. (2008). Exploring the representation of health in videogames: A content analysis. *Cyberpsychology & Behavior*, *11*(6), 771–773. doi:10.1089/cpb.2007.0007

Brown v EMA. (2011). *Website*. Retrieved 7/1/11 from http://www.supremecourt.gov/opinions/10pdf/08-1448.pdf

Brown, J. S., Collins, A., & Duguid, P. (1989). Situated cognition and the culture of learning. *Educational Researcher*, *18*(1), 32–42.

Brown, S. J., Lieberman, D. A., Gemeny, B. A., Fan, Y. C., Wilson, D. M., & Pasta, D. J. (1997). Educational video game for juvenile diabetes: Results of a controlled trial. *Informatics for Health & Social Care*, *22*(1), 77–89. doi:10.3109/14639239709089835

Brumels, K. A., Blasius, T., Cortright, T., Oumedian, D., & Solberg, B. (2008). Comparison of efficacy between traditional and video game based balance programs. *Clinical Kinesiology: Journal of the American Kinesiotherapy Association*, *62*(4), 26–31.

Buchanan, R., & Csikszentmihalyi, M. (1991). Flow: The psychology of optimal experience. *Design Issues*, *8*(1), 80. doi:10.2307/1511458

Bundesministerium des Innern. (2012). *Demografiebericht*. Berlin, Germany: Bundesministerium des Innern.

Burke, J., McNeill, M., Charles, D., Morrow, P., Crosbie, J., & McDonough, S. (2009). Optimising engagement for stroke rehabilitation using serious games. *The Visual Computer*, *25*, 1085–1099. doi:10.1007/s00371-009-0387-4

Burridge, J., & Hughes, A. (2010). Potential for new technologies in clinical practice. *Current Opinion in Neurology*, *23*, 671–677. doi:10.1097/WCO.0b013e3283402af5

Buse, C. E. (2012). *It's a way of bringing families together that was never possible before: Connecting generations across the digital divide*. Paper presented at the IFA 11th Global Conference on Aging. Prague, Czech Republic.

Bushman, B., & Anderson, C. (2001). Media violence and the American public. *The American Psychologist*, *56*, 477–489. doi:10.1037/0003-066X.56.6-7.477

Buss, P. (2011). Brazil: Structuring cooperation for health. *Lancet*, *377*(9779), 1722–1723. doi:10.1016/S0140-6736(11)60354-1

Buss, P. M., & Pellegrini Filho, A. (2007). A saúde e seus determinantes sociais. [The Health and its Social Determinants]. *PHYSIS: Rev. Saúde Coletiva*, *17*(1), 77–93.

Butler, D. (2008). *Air gondwana: Teaching negotiation skills by utilising virtual worlds for an authentic learning experience*. Paper presented at the ascilite 2008. Melbourne, Australia. Retrieved from http://www.ascilite.org.au/conferences/melbourne08/procs/butler-d-poster.pdf

Calonge, C. (2007). *A view from second life's trenches: Are you a pioneer or a settler?* Paper presented at the New Media Consortium. Berkeley, CA.

Campbell, M. (2009). *Using 3D-virtual worlds to teach decision-making*. Retrieved from http://www.ascilite.org.au/conferences/auckland09/procs/filename.pdf

Campbell, J. (1949). *The hero with a thousand faces*. London, UK: Bollingen Foundation.

Carr, D., Oliver, M., & Burn, A. (2008). *Learning, teaching and ambiguity in virtual worlds*. Retrieved from http://www.open.ac.uk/relive08/

Caspersen, C. J., Powell, K. E., & Christenson, G. M. (1985). Physical activity, exercise, and physical fitness: Definitions and distinctions for health-related research. *Public Health Reports (Washington, D.C.)*, *100*(2), 126–131.

Castells, M. (2009). *Communication power*. Oxford, UK: Oxford University Press.

Castronova, E., & Falk, M. (2008). *Virtual worlds as petri dishes for the social and behavioral sciences*. Retrieved from http://ssrn.com/abstract=1313161

Cavazza, M., Champagnat, R., & Leonardi, R. (2009). The IRIS network of excellence: Future directions in interactive storytelling. In *Proceedings of the 2nd Joint International Conference on Interactive Digital Storytelling: Interactive Storytelling* (pp. 8-13). ICIDS.

Ceranoglu, T. A. (2010). Video games in psychotherapy. *Review of General Psychology, 14*(2), 141–146. doi:10.1037/a0019439

Chandler, D. (2000). *An introduction to genre theory*. Retrieved from http://www.aber.ac.uk/media/Documents/intgenre/intgenre1.html

Chang, Y.-J., Chen, S.-F., & Huang, J.-D. (2011). A kinect-based system for physical rehabilitation: A pilot study for young adults with motor disabilities. *Research in Developmental Disabilities, 32*(6), 2566–2570. doi:10.1016/j.ridd.2011.07.002

Chen, J. (2007). Flow in games (and everything else). *Communications of the ACM, 50*(4), 31–34. doi:10.1145/1232743.1232769

Chesnevar, C. I., Maguitman, A. G., Gonzalez, M. P., & Cobo, M. L. (2004). Teaching fundamentals of computing theory: A constructivist approach. *Journal of Computer Science & Technology, 4*(2).

Childstats.gov. (2012). *America's children: Key national indicators of wellbeing*. Retrieved 9/26/12 from http://www.childstats.gov/americaschildren/beh.asp

Chodos, D., Stroulia, E., Boechler, P., King, S., Kuras, P., Carbonaro, M., & De Jong, E. (2010). Healthcare education with virtual-world simulations. In *Proceedings of the 2010 ICSE Workshop on Software Engineering in Health Care*. ICSE.

Clark, J. E., Lanphear, A. K., & Riddick, C. C. (1987). The effects of videogame playing on the response selection processing of elderly adults. *Journal of Gerontology, 42*(1), 82–85. doi:10.1093/geronj/42.1.82

Clark, R., & Kraemer, T. (2009). Clinical use of Nintendo Wii bowling simulation to decrease fall risk in an elderly resident of a nursing home: A case report. *Journal of Geriatric Physical Therapy, 32*, 174–180. doi:10.1519/00139143-200932040-00006

Cohen, G. E. (1994). *Designing groupwork: Strategies for the heterogeneous classroom* (2nd ed.). New York, NY: Teachers College Press.

Collins, A., Brown, J. S., & Newman, S. E. (1987). *Cognitive apprenticeship: Teaching the craft of reading, writing, and mathematics* (Tech. Rep. No. 403). Urbana-Champaign, IL: Center for the Study of Reading, University of Illinois.

Collins, C. (2008). *AVWW 2008: Australasian virtual worlds workshop*. Brisbane, Australia: Swinburne University of Technology.

Colwell, J., & Kato, M. (2003). Investigation of the relationship between social isolation, self-esteem, aggression and computer game play in Japanese adolescents. *Asian Journal of Social Psychology, 6*, 149–158. doi:10.1111/1467-839X.t01-1-00017

Computer and Videogames. (2005). *Looking back... World of Warcraft*. Retrieved 07 jan 2010, from http://www.computerandvideogames.com/article.php?id=131791

Connolly, T. M., Boyle, E. A., MacArthur, E., Hainey, T., & Boyle, J. M. (2012). A systematic literature review of empirical evidence on computer games and serious games. *Computers & Education, 59*, 661–686. doi:10.1016/j.compedu.2012.03.004

Conrad, F. G., Shober, M. F., & Coiner, T. (2007). Bringing features of human dialogue to web surveys. *Applied Cognitive Psychology, 21*, 165–187. doi:10.1002/acp.1335

Constant, D., Sproull, L., & Kiesler, S. (1996). The kindness of strangers: The usefulness of electronic weak ties for technical advice. *Organization Science, 7*(2), 119–135. Retrieved from http://www-2.cs.cmu.edu/~kiesler/publications/PDFs/Constantkindness.pdfdoi:10.1287/orsc.7.2.119

Cook, D. (2000). *Testimony of the American academy of pediatrics on media violence before the U.S. senate commerce committee.* Elk Grove Village, IL: American Academy of Pediatrics. Retrieved from http://www.aap.org/advocacy/releases/mediaviolencetestimony.pdf

Cooper, J., & Mackie, D. (1986). Video games and aggression in children. *Journal of Applied Social Psychology, 16*, 726–744. doi:10.1111/j.1559-1816.1986.tb01755.x

Costa, P., & McCrae, R. (1992). *Revised NEO personality inventory (NEO-PI-R) and NEO five- factor inventory (NEO-FFI) professional manual.* New York, NY: Psychological Assessment Resources.

Couper, M. P. (2008). Technology and the survey interview/questionnaire. In Conrad, F. G., & Schober, M. F. (Eds.), *Envisioning the Survey Interview of the Future* (pp. 58–76). Hoboken, NJ: John Wiley & Sons, Inc.

Cowley, B., Charles, D., Black, M., & Hickey, R. (2008). Toward an understanding of flow in video games. *Computers in Entertainment, 6*(2), 1. doi:10.1145/1371216.1371223

Cranton, P., & Tisdell, E. J. (2008). Transformative learning. In J. Athanasou (Ed.), *Adult Education and Training,* (pp. 35–50). Terrigal: David Barlow Publishing.

Cranton, P. (1992). *Working with adult learners.* Montreal, Canada: Wall & Emerson, Inc.

Crawford, C. (2005). *Chris Crawford on interactive storytelling.* Berkeley, CA: New Riders Games.

Creutzfeld, J., Hedman, L., Medin, C., Heinrichs, W. L., & Tsai, L. (2010). Virtual worlds for scenario based repeated team training of cardiopulmonary resuscitation in medical students. *Journal of Medical Internet Research, 12*(3), e38. doi:10.2196/jmir.1426

Creutzfeldt., et al. (2009). *Website.* Retrieved from http://www.ncbi.nlm.nih.gov/pubmed/19377114

Creutzfeldt, J., Hedman, L., Heinrichs, W. L., Youngblood, P., & Felländer-Tsai, L. (2012). An international study of digital natives training CPR in virtual worlds. *Journal of Medical Internet Research, 15*(1).

Crowder, N. A., & Martin, G. C. (1960). *Adventures in algebra.* Garden City, NY: Doubleday.

Crumlish, C., & Malone, E. (2009). *Designing social interfaces: Principles, patterns, and practices for improving the user experience (animal guide)* (p. 520). New York, NY: Yahoo Press.

CryDev.net. (2012). *CryENGINE 3 free SDK.* Retrieved 11 Oct 2012, from http://www.crydev.net/dm_eds/download_detail.php?id=4

Csikszentmihalyi, M. (1975). *Beyond boredom and anxiety.* San Francisco, CA: Jossey-Bass Publishers.

Csikszentmihalyi, M. (2004). *Flow: The psychology of optimal experience.* Paris, France: Robert Laffont.

Dahms, M., Geonnotti, K., Passalacqua, D., Schilk, J. N., & Wetzel, A. (2008). *The educational theory of Lev Semenovich Vygotsky: An analysis.* Retrieved April 24, 2009, from http://www.newfoundations.com/GALLERY/Vygotsky.html

Damon, W. (1984). Peer education: The untapped potential. *Journal of Applied Developmental Psychology, 5*(4), 331–343. doi:10.1016/0193-3973(84)90006-6

Darfur Is Dying. (2006). *Website.* Retrieved 27 jan 2011, from http://www.darfurisdying.com/

Davis, A., Murphy, J., Owens, D., Khzaanchi, D., & Zigurs, I. (2009). Avatars, people, and virtual worlds: Foundations for research in the metaverse. *Journal of the Association for Information Systems, 10*(2), 90–117.

de Freitas, S., & Oliver, M. (2006). How can exploratory learning with games and simulations within the curriculum can be most effectively evaluated. *Computers & Education, 46*(3), 249–264. doi:10.1016/j.compedu.2005.11.007

de Jong-Gierveld, J. (1987). Developing and testing a model of loneliness. *Journal of Personality and Social Psychology, 53*, 119–128. doi:10.1037/0022-3514.53.1.119

de Jong, T., & van Joolingen, W. R. (1998). Scientific discovery learning with computer simulations of conceptual domains. *Review of Educational Research, 68*(2), 179–201.

de Leeuw, E., & Van der Zouwen, J. (1988). Data quality in telephone and face-to-face surveys: A comparative meta-analysis. In Groves, R., Biemer, P., Lyberg, L., Massey, J., Nicholls, W. II, & Waksberg, J. (Eds.), *Telephone Survey Methodology* (pp. 283–300). New York, NY: John Wiley.

de Nood, D., & Attema, J. (2006). *Second life, the second life of virtual reality*. The Hague, The Netherlands: Electronic Highway Platform. Retrieved from: http://www.epn.net/interrealiteit/EPN-REPORT-The_Second_Life_of_VR.pdf

Delfos, M. (2004). *De schoonheid van het verschil*. San Diego, CA: Harcourt Book Publishers.

Dell, K. (2008). How second life affects real life. *TIME Science*. Retrieved October 2012 from http://www.time.com/time/health/article/0,8599,1739601,00.html

Delp, S., Arnold, A., & Hammer, S. (2012). *Neuromuscular biomechanics laboratory, Stanford University*. Retrieved from http://www.scribd.com/doc/56096401/OpenSim-Tutorial1/

Delwiche, A. (2006). Massively multiplayer online games (MMOs) in the new media classroom. *Journal of Educational Technology & Society, 9*(3), 160–172.

Desai, R., Krishnan-Sarin, S., Cavallo, D., & Potenza, M. (2010). Video-gaming among high school students: health correlates, gender differences, and problematic gaming. *Pediatrics, 126*(6), e1414–e1424. doi:10.1542/peds.2009-2706

Dev, P., Heinrichs, W. L., & Youngblood, P. (2011). CliniSpace™: A multiperson 3D online immersive training environment accessible through a browser. In *Proceedings of MMVR2011*. Long Beach, CA: IOS Press.

Dewey, J., & Dewey, E. (1915). *Schools of tomorrow*. New York, NY: Dutton.

Dillenbourg, P., Järvelä, S., & Fischer, F. (2009). The evolution of research on computer-supported collaborative learning. *Technology-Enhanced Learning*, 3–19.

Dillenbourg, P. (1999). What do you mean by collaborative learning? In Dillenbourg, P. (Ed.), *Collaborative Learning: Cognitive and Computational Approaches* (pp. 1–19). Oxford, UK: Elsevier.

Dillman, D. A. (2000). *Mail and internet surveys: The tailored design method* (2nd ed.). New York, NY: John Wiley & Sons.

Dobson, A., & McLaughlin, D. (2012). *Social support and disability: It's not the size of the network that counts*. Paper presented at IFA 11th Global Conference on Aging. Prague, Czech Republic.

Dohmen, G. (1999). *Weiterbildungsinstitutionen, medien, lernumwelten*. Bonn, Germany: Bundesministerium für Bildung und Forschung.

Dohmen, G. (2001). *Das informelle lernen – Die internationale Erschließung einer bisher vernachlässigten grundform menschlichen lernens für das lebenslange lernen aller*. Bonn, Germany: Bundesministerium für Bildung und Forschung.

Dohmen, G. (2002). Informelles lernen in der freizeit. *Spektrum Freizeit, 24*(1), 18–27.

Doignon, J.-P., & Falmagne, J.-C. (1985). Spaces for the assessment of knowledge. *International Journal of Man-Machine Studies, 23*(2), 175–196. doi:10.1016/S0020-7373(85)80031-6

Dongen, K. W., van Verleisdonk, E.-J., Schijven, M. P., & Broeders, I. A. M. J. (2011). Will the Playstation generation become better endoscopic surgeons? *Surgical Endoscopy, 25*, 2275–2280. doi:10.1007/s00464-010-1548-2

Donovan, J. J., & Radosevich, D. J. (1999). A meta-analytic review of the distribution of practice effect: Now you see it, now you don't. *The Journal of Applied Psychology, 84*(5), 795–805. doi:10.1037/0021-9010.84.5.795

Dormans, J. (2011). *Integrating emergence and progression*. Paper presented at the 5th DiGRA Conference on Games and Play. Utrecht, The Netherlands.

Dreyfus, H. L., & Dreyfus, S. E. (1986). *Mind over machine*. New York, NY: The Free Press.

Dreyfus, H. L., & Dreyfus, S. E. (2004). The ethical implications of the five-stage skill-acquisition model. *Bulletin of Science, Technology & Society, 24*(3), 251–264. doi:10.1177/0270467604265023

Dring, C. (2009). *The I-generation*. Retrieved from http://issuu.com/intentmedia/docs/mcv_issue530

Dring, C. (2009). *Nintendo DS – Retail biz*. Retrieved from http://issuu.com/intentmedia/docs/mcv_issue531

Druin, A. (2002). The role of children in the design of new technology. *Behaviour & Information Technology, 21*(1), 1–25. doi:10.1080/01449290110108659

Durkin, K. (2010). Videogames and young people with developmental disorders. *Review of General Psychology, 14*(2), 122–140. doi:10.1037/a0019438

Dustman, R. E., Emmerson, R. Y., Steinhaus, L. A., Shearer, D. E., & Dustman, T. J. (1992). The effects of videogame playing on neuropsychological performance of elderly individuals. *Journal of Gerontology, 47*(3), 168–P171. doi:10.1093/geronj/47.3.P168

Dutta, T. (2012). Evaluation of the Kinect sensor for 3-D kinematic measurement in the workplace. *Applied Ergonomics, 43*, 645–649. doi:10.1016/j.apergo.2011.09.011

Dutton, W. H., Helsper, E. J., & Gerber, M. M. (2009). *Oxford internet survey 2009 report: The internet in Britain*. Oxford, UK: University of Oxford Press.

Dyer, R., Matthews, J., Stulac, J., Wright, C., & Yudowitch, K. (1976). *Questionnaire construction manual, annex literature survey and bibliography*. Palo Alto, CA: Operations Research Associates.

EC. (2001). *Making a European area of lifelong learning a reality*. Brussels, Belgium: Commission of the European Communities. Retrieved from http://eur-lex.europa.eu/LexUriServ/LexUriServ.do?uri=COM:2001:0678:FIN:EN:PDF

Effenberg, A. O. (2005). Movement sonification: Effects on perception and action. *IEEE MultiMedia, 12*(2), 53–59. doi:10.1109/MMUL.2005.31

Egenfeldt-Nielsen, S. (2005). *Beyond edutainment: Exploring the educational potential of computer games*. Copenhagen, Denmark: IT-University Copenhagen.

Egenfeldt-Nielsen, S. (2007). Third generation educational use of computer games. *Journal of Educational Multimedia and Hypermedia, 16*(3), 263–281.

Einsiedler, W. (1981). *Lehrmethoden*. Baltimore, MD: Urban & Schwarzenberg.

El Saddik, A. (2001). *Interactive multimedia learning - Shared reusable visualization-based modules*. Heidelberg, Germany: Springer.

Ellis, S. (1996). Presence of mind: A reaction to Thomas Sheridan's "further musing on the psychology of presence". *Presence (Cambridge, Mass.), 5*, 247–259.

Enochsson, L., Isaakson, B., Tour, R., Kjellin, A., Hedman, L., Wredmark, T., & Tsai-Felländer, L. (2004). Visuospatial skills and computer game experience influence the performance of virtual endoscopy. *Journal of Gastrointestinal Surgery, 8*(7), 874–880. doi:10.1016/j.gassur.2004.06.015

Entertainment Software Association. (2012). *Games: Improving health*. Retrieved from http://www.theesa.com/games-improving-what-matters/health.asp

Ericsson, K. A., Krampe, R. T., & Tesch-Romer, C. (1993). The role of deliberate practice in the acquisition of expert performance. *Psychological Review*, (3): 363–406. doi:10.1037/0033-295X.100.3.363

Erikson, E. H. (1966). *Identität und lebenszyklus*. Frankfurt am Main, Germany: Suhrkamp.

ESA. (2012). *Essential facts about the computer and video game industry*. Retrieved from http://www.theesa.com/facts/pdfs/ESA_EF_2012.pdf

European Commission. (2006). *Benchmarking access and use of ICT in European schools 2006: Key findings*. Retrieved February 13, 2011, from http://ec.europa.eu/information_society/newsroom/cf/itemlongdetail.cfm?item_id=2888

Farley, H., & Steel, C. (2009). *A quest for the holy grail: Tactile precision, natural movement and haptic feedback in 3D virtual spaces*. Retrieved from http://www.ascilite.org.au/conferences/auckland09/procs/farley.pdf

Feil, C., Decker, R., & Gieger, C. (2004). *Wie entdecken kinder das internet?* Wiesbaden, Germany: VS Verlag für Sozialwissenschaften. doi:10.1007/978-3-531-90143-5

Feinstein, B. A., Bhatia, V., Hershenberg, R., & Davila, J. (2012). Another venue for problematic interpersonal behavior: The effects of depressive and anxious symptoms on social networking experience. *Journal of Social and Clinical Psychology, 31*(4), 356–382. doi:10.1521/jscp.2012.31.4.356

Feist, H. (2012). *Social spaces, rural places: Ageing in place in rural South Australia*. Paper presented at IFA 11th Global Conference on Aging. Prague, Czech Republic.

Felicia, P. (2011). *Handbook of research on improving learning and motivation through educational games: Multidisciplinary approaches*. Hershey, PA: IGI Global. doi:10.4018/978-1-60960-495-0

Fencott, C., Lockyer, M., Clay, J., & Massey, P. (2012). *Game invaders, the theory and understanding of computer games*. Hoboken, NJ: John Wiley & Sons, Inc. doi:10.1002/9781118347584

Ferguson, C. J. (2009). Is psychological research really as good as medical research? Effect size comparisons between psychology and medicine. *Review of General Psychology, 13*(2), 130–136. doi:10.1037/a0015103

Ferguson, C. J. (2010). Blazing angels or resident evil? Can violent video games be a force for good? *Review of General Psychology, 14*(2), 68–81. doi:10.1037/a0018941

Ferguson, C. J. (2011). Video games and youth violence: A prospective analysis in adolescents. *Journal of Youth and Adolescence, 40*(4), 377–391. doi:10.1007/s10964-010-9610-x

Ferguson, C. J., Coulson, M., & Barnett, J. (2011). Psychological profiles of school shooters: Positive directions and one big wrong turn. *Journal of Police Crisis Negotiations, 11*(2), 141–158. doi:10.1080/15332586.2011.581523

Ferguson, C. J., Munoz, M. E., & Medrano, M. R. (2012). Advertising influences on young children's food choices are only marginally reduced by parental influence: A randomized controlled experiment. *The Journal of Pediatrics, 160*(3), 452–455. doi:10.1016/j.jpeds.2011.08.023

Ferguson, C. J., Rueda, S., Cruz, A., Ferguson, D., Fritz, S., & Smith, S. (2008). Violent video games and aggression: Causal relationship or byproduct of family violence and intrinsic violence motivation? *Criminal Justice and Behavior, 35*, 311–332. doi:10.1177/0093854807311719

Fery, Y.-A., & Ponserre, S. (2001). Enhancing the control of force in putting by video game training. *Ergonomics, 44*(12), 1025–1037. doi:10.1080/00140130110084773

Fetter, S., Berlanga, A., & Sloep, P. (2009). Enhancing the social capital of learning communities by using an ad hoc transient communities service. *Advances in Web Based Learning, (1)*, 150–157. doi:10.1007/978-3-642-03426-8_19

Field, D. (1999). Continuity and change in friendships in advanced old age: Findings from the Berkeley older generation study. *International Journal of Aging & Human Development, 48*(4). doi:10.2190/J4UJ-JAU6-14TF-2MVF

Field, S. (2005). *Screenplay*. New York, NY: Delta.

Finger, M., & Asun, J. M. (2001). *Adult education at the crossroads: Learning our way out*. New York, NY: Zed Books Ltd.

Fleishman, E. A., & Rich, S. (1963). Role of kinesthetic and spatial-visual abilities in perceptual-motor learning. *Journal of Experimental Psychology, 66*(1), 6–11. doi:10.1037/h0046677

Flin, R., & Maran, N. (2004). Identifying and training non-technical skills in acute medicine. *Quality & Safety in Health Care, 13*(Suppl I), i180–i184. doi:10.1136/qshc.2004.009993

Flynn, S., Palma, P., & Bender, A. (2007). Feasibility of using the Sony PlayStation 2 gaming platform for an individual poststroke: A case report. *Journal of Neurologic Physical Therapy; JNPT, 31*, 180–189.

Forterra Systems. (2012). *Wikipedia*. Retrieved from http://en.wikipedia.org/wiki/Forterra_Systems

Freeman, J., Avons, S., Meddis, R., Pearson, D., & IJselsteijn, W. (2000). Using behavioral realism to estimate presence: A study of the utility of postural responses to motion stimuli. *Presence (Cambridge, Mass.), 9*, 149–164. doi:10.1162/105474600566691

Freire, P. (1993). *Pedagogy of the oppressed*. New York, NY: Continuum Publishing Company.

Frenkel. (2012). *Therapists use virtual worlds to address real problems*. Retrieved from http://www.inworldsolutions.net/news/articles

Fromme, J., & Russler, S. (2005). *Mediendidaktische beratung zum online-spiel und projektlogo: Ergebnisbericht PC1*. Magdeburg, Germany: Chair of Educational Media Research.

Fromme, J., & Russler, S. (2007). *Ergebnisse der zwischenevaluation zum computerspiel powerado: Ergebnisbericht PC5*. Magdeburg, Germany: Chair of Educational Media Research.

Fromme, J., & Winny, S. (2012). *Konzeptevaluation für das online-spiel 5x5: Ergebnisbericht OS6*. Magdeburg, Germany: Chair of Educational Media Research.

Fromme, J., & Winny, S. (2012). *Prozessevaluation des online-spiels 5x5: ergebnisbericht OS8.* Magdeburg, Germany: Chair of Educational Media Research.

Gaggioli, A., Meneghini, A., Morganti, F., Alcaniz, M., & Riva, G. (2006). A strategy for computer-assisted mental practice in stroke rehabilitation. *Neurorehabilitation and Neural Repair, 20,* 503–507. doi:10.1177/1545968306290224

Gamasutra. (2009). *Analyst: Online games now $11B of $44B worldwide game market.* Retrieved from http://www.gamasutra.com/view/news/114898/Analyst_Online_Games_Now_11B_Of_44B_Worldwide_Game_Market.php

Gamberini, L., Barresi, G., Majer, A., & Scarpetta, F. (2008). A game a day keeps the doctor away: A short review of computer games in mental healthcare. *Journal of Cyber Therapy & Rehabilitation, 1,* 127–145.

Garrison, D. R., & Anderson, T. (2007). Online community of inquiry review: Social, cognitive and teaching presence issues. *Journal of Asynchronous Learning Networks, 11*(1), 61–72.

Gee, J. P. (2007). *What video games have to teach us about learning and literacy.* New York, NY: Palgrave Macmillan.

Gee, J. P. (2008). Video games and embodiment. *Games and Culture, 3*(3-4). doi:10.1177/1555412008317309

Gee, J. P. (2009). Deep learning properties of good digital games: How far can they go? In Ritterfeld, U., Cody, M., & Vorderer, P. (Eds.), *Serious Games: Mechanisms and Effects* (pp. 67–83). New York, NY: Routledge.

Gennari, J. H., Musen, M. A., Fergerson, R. W., Grosso, W. E., Crubezy, M., & Eriksson, H. (2003). The evolution of Protege: An environment for knowledge-based systems development. *International Journal of Human-Computer Studies, 58*(1), 89–123. doi:10.1016/S1071-5819(02)00127-1

Gentile, D. A., Lynch, P. J., Linder, J. R., & Walsh, D. A. (2004). The effects of violent video game habits on adolescent hostility, aggressive behaviors, and school performance. *Journal of Adolescence, 27,* 5–22. doi:10.1016/j.adolescence.2003.10.002

Gillies, R. (2004). The effects of cooperative learning on junior high school students during small group learning. *Learning and Instruction, 14*(2), 197–213. doi:10.1016/S0959-4752(03)00068-9

Glogger, I., Holzäpfel, L., Schwonke, R., Nückles, M., & Renkl, A. (2009). Activation of learning strategies in writing learning journals. *Zeitschrift fur Padagogische Psychologie, 23*(2), 95–104. doi:10.1024/1010-0652.23.2.95

Göbel, S., Gutjahr, M., & Steinmetz, R. (2011). What makes a good serious game - Conceptual approach towards a metadata format for the description and evaluation of serious games. In D. Gouscous & M. Meimaris (Eds.), *5th European Conference on Games Based Learning,* (pp. 202-210). Reading, UK: Academic Conferences Limited.

Göbel, S., Mehm, F., & Radke, S. (2009). 80Days: Adaptive digital storytelling for digital educational games. In Y. Cao, A. Hannemann, & B. F. Manjon (Eds.), *International Workshop on Story-Telling and Educational Games: CEUR Workshop Proceedings.* CEUR.

Göbel, S., Wendel, V., Ritter, C., & Steinmetz, R. (2010). Personalized, adaptive digital educational games using narrative game-based learning objects. In *Proceedings of Entertainment for Education: Digital Techniques and Systems,* (pp. 438–445). IEEE.

Göbel, S., Becker, F., & Feix, A. (2005). INSCAPE: Story-models for interactive storytelling and edutainment applications. In *Proceedings of Virtual Storytelling - Using Virtual Reality Technologies for Storytelling* (pp. 168–171). Berlin, Germany: Springer. doi:10.1007/11590361_19

Göbel, S., Konrad, R., Salvatore, L., Sauer, S., & Osswald, K. (2007). U-CREATE: Authoring tool for the creation of interactive storytelling based edutainment applications. In *Proceedings of Eva 2007 Florence: Electronic Imaging and the Visual Arts: Conference, Training and Exhibition* (pp. 53–58). Bologna, Italy: Pitagora Editrice.

Göbel, S., Malkewitz, R., & Becker, F. (2006). *Story pacing in interactive storytelling. Technologies for E-Learning and Digital Entertainment* (Vol. 3942, pp. 419–428). Heidelberg, Germany: Springer. doi:10.1007/11736639_53

Göbel, S., Mehm, F., & Wendel, V. (2012). Adaptive digital storytelling for digital educational games. In Kickmeier-Rust, M. D., & Albert, D. (Eds.), *An Alien's Guide to Multi-Adaptive Educational Computer Games* (pp. 89–104). Santa Rosa, CA: Informing Science Press.

Golbeck, J. A. (2005). *Computing and applying trust in web-based social networks*. University Park, MD: University of Maryland.

Goldstein, J. H., Cajko, L., Oosterbroek, M., Michielsen, M., van Houten, O., & Salverda, F. (1997). Video games and the elderly. *Social Behavior and Personality*, 25(4), 345–352. doi:10.2224/sbp.1997.25.4.345

Graafland, M., Schraagen, J. M., & Schijven, M. P. (2012). Systematic review of serious games for medical education and surgical skills training. *British Journal of Surgery*, 99, 1322–1330. doi:10.1002/bjs.8819

Granovetter, M. S. (1973). The strength-of-weak-ties perspective on creativity: A comprehensive examination and extension. *American Journal of Sociology*, 78(6), 1360–1380. doi:10.1086/225469

Grantcharov, T.P., Bardram, L., Funch-Jensen, P., & Rosenberg, J., J. (2003). Impact of hand dominance, gender, and experience with computer games on performance in virtual reality laparoscopy. *Surgical Endoscopy*, 17, 1082–1085. doi:10.1007/s00464-002-9176-0

Graves, L. E., Ridgers, N. D., Williams, K., Stratton, G., Atkinson, G., & Cable, N. T. (2010). The physiological cost and enjoyment of wii fit in adolescents, young adults, and older adults. *Journal of Physical Activity & Health*, 7(3), 393–401.

Greci, L. S., Hurst, S., Garman, K., Huang, R., Hoffman, H., & Cardenas, M. (2011). Multi-User virtual environment boot camp and patient surge triage practice. *Medicine Meets Virtual Reality*, 18, 16–17.

Green, J. (1998). Andragogy: Teaching adults. *Encyclopedia of Educational Technology*. Retrieved April 7, 2009, from http://coe.sdsu.edu/eet/Articles/andragogy/index.htm

Green, C. S., & Bavelier, D. (2007). Action-video-game experience alters the spatial resolution of vision. *Psychological Science*, 18(1), 88–94. doi:10.1111/j.1467-9280.2007.01853.x

Greene, B., A., & Miller, R., B. (1996). Influences on achievement: Goals, perceived ability and cognitive engagement. *Contemporary Educational Psychology*, 21(15), 181–192. doi:10.1006/ceps.1996.0015

Gregory, B., Gregory, S., Wood, D., Masters, Y., Hillier, M., Stokes-Thompson, F., et al. (2011). How are Australian higher education institutions contributing to change through innovative teaching and learning in virtual worlds? Retrieved from http://www.leishman-associates.com.au/ascilite2011/downloads/papers/Gregory-full.pdf

Gregory, S. (2007). *Virtual classrooms: Learning in a virtual environment*. Retrieved October 9, 2007, from http://www.virtualclassrooms.info

Gregory, S., & Smith, H. (2008). *How virtual classrooms are changing the face of education: Using virtual classrooms in today's university environment*. Paper presented at the ISTE. Armidale, Australia.

Gregory, S., Lee, M. J. W., Ellis, A., Gregory, B., Wood, D., Hillier, M., et al. (2010). Australian higher education institutions transforming the future of teaching and learning through virtual worlds. In C. Steel, M. J. Keppell, & P. Gerbic (Eds.), *Curriculum, Technology & Transformation for an Unknown Future,* (pp. 399–415). Retrieved from http://www.ascilite.org.au/conferences/sydney10/Ascilite%20conference%20proceedings%202010/Gregory-full.pdf

Gregory, S., Reiners, T., & Tynan, B. (2010). Alternative realities: Immersive learning for and with students. In Song, H. (Ed.), *Distance Learning Technology, Current Instruction, and the Future of Education: Applications of Today, Practices of Tomorrow* (pp. 245–271). Hershey, PA: IGI Global.

Gridsurvey. (2012). *Website*. Retrieved from http://gridsurvey.com/index.php

Griffiths, M. D. (2002). The educational benefits of videogames. *Education for Health*, 20(3), 47–51.

Griffiths, M. D., Davies, M. N. O., & Chappell, D. (2004). Online computer gaming: A comparison of adolescent and adult gamers. *Journal of Adolescence*, 27(1), 87–96. doi:10.1016/j.adolescence.2003.10.007

Grossman, D. (1996). *On killing: The psychological cost of learning to kill in war and society*. Boston, MA: Back Bay Books.

Group, N. P. D. (2012). *Research shows $2.88 billion spent on video game content in the US for second quarter, 2012.* Retrieved 9/26/12 from https://www.npd.com/wps/portal/npd/us/news/press-releases/pr_120809/

Gudmundsen, J. (2006). Movement gets serious about making games with purpose. *Gannett News Service.* Retrieved February 13, 2011, from http://pressconnects.gns.gannettonline.com/apps/pbcs.dll/article?AID=/20060518/TECH05/602150620/1001/TECH

Habgood, M. P. J., Ainsworth, S. E., & Benford, S. (2005). Endogenous fantasy and learning in digital games. *Simulation & Gaming, 36*(4), 483–498. doi:10.1177/1046878105282276

Hallford, N., & Hallford, J. (2001). *Sword & circuitry: A designer's guide to computer role-playing games.* Roseville, CA: Prima Tech.

Hall, R., Day, T., & Hall, R. (2011). Reply to Murray et al. (2011) and Ferguson (2011). *Mayo Clinic Proceedings, 86*(6), 821–823. doi:10.4065/mcp.2011.0357

Hämäläinen, R. (2006). Designing and evaluating collaboration in a virtual game environment for vocational learning. *Computers & Education, 50*(1), 98–109. doi:10.1016/j.compedu.2006.04.001

Hämäläinen, R., Manninen, T., Järvelä, S., & Häkkinen, P. (2006). Learning to collaborate: Designing collaboration in a 3-D game environment. *The Internet and Higher Education, 9*(1), 47–61. doi:10.1016/j.iheduc.2005.12.004

Hämäläinen, R., & Oksanen, K. (2012). Challenge of supporting vocational learning: Empowering collaboration in a scripted 3D game - How does teachers' real-time orchestration make a difference? *Computers & Education, 59*, 281–293. doi:10.1016/j.compedu.2012.01.002

Handler Miller, C. (2004). *Digital storytelling: A creator's guide to interactive entertainment.* Burlington, MA: Focal Press.

Hardy, S., Göbel, S., Gutjahr, M., Wiemeyer, J., & Steinmetz, R. (2012). Adaptation model for indoor exergames. *International Journal of Computer Science in Sport, 11*(1), 73–85.

Harley, D., Fitzpatrick, G., Axelrod, L., White, G., & McAllister, G. (2010). Making the Wii at home: Game play by older people in sheltered housing. In *Proceedings of the 6th International Conference on HCI in Work and Learning, Life and Leisure: Workgroup Human-Computer Interaction and Usability Engineering,* (pp. 156–176). Berlin, Germany: Springer-Verlag. Retrieved from http://dl.acm.org/citation.cfm?id=1947789.1947802

Harr, R., Buch, T., & Hanghøj, T. (2008). Exploring the discrepancy between educational goals and educational game design. In *Proceedings of the 2ⁿᵈ European Conference on Games Based Learning (ECGBL 2008),* (pp. 165–174). Reading, MA: Academic Publishing.

Hartman, M. (2011). Wii remote accidents: The dangers of console gaming. *Altered Gamer.* Retrieved from http://www.alteredgamer.com/wii-gear/42586-wii-remote-accidents-the-dangers-of-console-gaming/

Haskell, W. L., Lee, I.-M., Pate, R. R., Powell, K. E., Blair, S. N., & Franklin, B. A. (2007). Physical activity and public health: Updated recommendation for adults from the American College of Sports Medicine and the American Heart Association. *Medicine and Science in Sports and Exercise, 39*(8), 1423–1434. doi:10.1249/mss.0b013e3180616b27

Health Games Research. (2012). *Website.* Retrieved from http://www.healthgamesresearch.org/db/search/tab=organizations~~keywords=Virtual%20Worlds#

Health Scotland, N. H. S. (2008). *Energising lives: A guide to promoting physical activity in primary care.* Edinburgh, UK: Glasgow.

Hearns, M., Diener, S., Honey, M., Cockeram, J., Parsons, D., Champion, E., et al. (2011). He ara hou ka tū mai: NZ institutions of higher learning unpacking demands and facilitating change. In G. Williams, P. Statham, N. Brown, & B. Cleland (Eds.), *Changing Demands, Changing Directions: Proceedings Ascilite Hobart 2011,* (pp. 571–579). Retrieved from http://www.leishman-associates.com.au/ascilite2011/downloads/papers/Hearns-concise.pdf

Hebbel-Seeger, A. (2008). Videospiel und sportpraxis - (k) ein widerspruch. [Video gaming and sport practice – no contraction]. *Zeitschrift für e-Learning, 3*(4), 9-20.

Heeter, C., Winn, B., & Fleck, L. (2010). Deliberative games: Games for entertainment and learning lab. *Michigan State University*. Retrieved October 8, 2012, from http://www.gel.msu.edu/tism/deliberative-games

Heimburg, E. (2011). Project gorgon, an indie MMO in development. *Elder Game*. Retrieved 15 Sep 2012, from http://www.eldergame.com/2011/10/early-prep-for-newbies/

Heinen, T., Velentzas, K., Walther, M., & Goebel, R. (2009). (Video-)Spielend bewegungen lernen?! Einsatz und erforschung der effekte digitaler sportspiele. [Learning movements by video games?! Application of and research on the effects of digital sport games]. *F.i.t., 14*(2), 4-7.

Heinrichs, W. L., Kung, S.-Y., & Dev, P. (2008). Design and Implementation of rule-based medical models: An in silico patho-physiological trauma model for hypovolemic shock. In *Proceedings of MMVR2008*. Long Beach, CA: IOS Press.

Heinrichs, W. L., Davies, D., & Davies, J. (2012). Virtual worlds in healthcare: Applications and implications. In Arnab, S., Dunwell, I., & Debattista, K. (Eds.), *Serious Games in Healthcare* (pp. 1–22). Hershey, PA: IGI Global. doi:10.4018/978-1-4666-1903-6.ch001

Heinrichs, W. L., Harter, P., Youngblood, P., Kusumoto, L., & Dev, P. (2010). Training healthcare personnel for mass casualty incidents in a virtual emergency department: VED II. *Prehospital and Disaster Medicine, 25*(5), 422–434.

Heinrichs, W. L., Youngblood, P., Harter, P. M., & Dev, P. (2008). Simulation for team training and assessment: Case studies of online training with virtual worlds. *World Journal of Surgery, 32*, 161–170. doi:10.1007/s00268-007-9354-2

Hellmig, L., & Martens, A. (2010). Blended learning– Ein sinnloser begriff? In S. Hambach, A. Martens, D. Tavangarian, & B. Urban (Eds.), *eLearning Baltics 2010: Proceedings of the 3rd International eLBa Science Conference,* (pp. 215–224). Stuttgart, Germany: Fraunhofer.

HeroEngine. (2012). *Website*. Retrieved 5 Oct 2012, from http://www.heroengine.com/

Herz, J. C. (2002). Gaming the system: What higher education can learn from multiplayer online worlds. In *The Internet and the University, Forum*, (pp. 169-191). EDUCAUSE.

Hew, K. F., & Cheung, W. S. (2010). Use of three-dimensional (3D) immersive virtual worlds in K-12 and higher education settings: A review of the research. *British Journal of Educational Technology, 41*(1), 33–55. doi:10.1111/j.1467-8535.2008.00900.x

Hilbert, T., Renkl, A., Schworm, S., Kessler, S., & Reiss, K. (2008). Learning to teach with worked-out examples: A computer-based learning environment for teachers. *Journal of Computer Assisted Learning, 24*(4), 316–332. doi:10.1111/j.1365-2729.2007.00266.x

Hindmarsh, J., Heath, C., & Fraser, M. (2006). (Im) materiality, virtual reality and interaction: Grounding the 'virtual' in studies of technology in action. *The Sociological Review, 54*(4), 795–817. doi:10.1111/j.1467-954X.2006.00672.x

Hinrichs, T., & Brach, M. (2012). The general practitioner's role in promoting physical activity to older adults: A review based on program theory. *Current Aging Science, 5*(1), 41–50. doi:doi:10.2174/1874609811205010041

Hinz, J. (2001). *Facetten der kreativität: Entwicklungsprozesse in natur, kultur und persönlichkeit* (2nd ed.). Aachen, Germany: Shaker.

Hoermann, S., Hildebrandt, T., Rensing, C., & Steinmetz, R. (2005). Resource center - A digital learning object repository with an integrated authoring tool set. In P. Kommers & G. Richards (Eds.), *World Conference on Educational Multimedia, Hypermedia and Telecommunications,* (pp. 3453–3460). IEEE.

Hoffmann, A., Göbel, S., Schneider, O., & Iurgel, I. (2005). Storytelling-based edutainment applications. In Tan, L., & Subramaniam, R. (Eds.), *E-Learning and Virtual Science Centers* (pp. 190–212). Hershey, PA: IGI Global. doi:10.4018/978-1-59140-591-7.ch009

Hollins, P., & Robbins, S. (2008). *The educational affordances of multi user virtual environments (MUVE).* Retrieved from http://www.open.ac.uk/relive08/

Honey, M., Diener, S., Connor, K., Veltman, M., & Bodily, D. (2009). *Teaching in virtual space: An interactive session demonstrating second life simulation for haemorrhage management.* Retrieved from http://www.ascilite.org.au/conferences/auckland09/procs/honey-interactivesession.pdf.

Hong, J. (2012). *Multidimensional evaluation of the health status of elderly people in the context of social relationship networks.* Paper presented at IFA 11th Global Conference on Aging. Prague, Czech Republic.

Horton, W., & Horton, K. (2003). *E-learning tools and technologies: A consumer's guide for trainers, teachers, educators, and instructional designers.* Hoboken, NJ: Wiley.

Houlette, R. (2004). Player modelling for adaptive games. [IEEE.]. *Proceedings of AI Game Programming Wisdom, II,* 557–566.

Howard, J. (2008). *Quests: Design, theory, and history in games and narratives.* Wellesley, MA: A K Peters.

Hübner, S., Nückles, M., & Renkl, A. (2007). Lerntagebücher als medium des selbstgesteuerten lernens: Wie viel instruktionale unterstützung ist sinnvoll? *Empirische Pädagogik, 21*(2), 119–137.

Huizinga, J. (1950). Homo ludens: Proeve eener bepaling van het spel-element der cultuur. In L. Brummel (Ed.), *Johan Huizinga, Verzamelde werken V (Cultuurgeschiedenis III),* (pp. 26-246). Haarlem, The Netherlands. Retrieved from http://www.dbnl.org/tekst/huiz003homo01_01/

Huizinga, J. (1938). *Homo ludens.* Boston, MA: Beacon Press.

Hu, S., & Kuht, G., D. (2002). Being (dis)engaged in educationally purposeful activities: The influences of student and institutional characteristics. *Research in Higher Education, 43*(5), 555–575. doi:10.1023/A:1020114231387

i2010: Independent Living for the Ageing Society. (2007). *Information society and media, European communities.* Retrieved from http://ec.europa.eu/information_society/activities/policy_link/brochures/documents/independent_living.pdf

Ijsselsteijn, W. (2002). *Elements of a multi-level theory of presence: Phenomenology, mental processing and neural correlates.* Paper presented at Presence 2002: International Workshop on Presence. Porto, Portugal.

Ijsselsteijn, W., de Ridder, H., Freeman, J., & Avons, S. (2000). Presence: Concept, determinants and measurement. In *Proceedings of the SPIE, Human Vision and Electronic Imaging,* (pp. 520-529). SPIE.

IJsselsteijn, W., Nap, H. H., de Kort, Y., & Poels, K. (2007). *Digital game design for elderly users.* Retrieved from http://alexandria.tue.nl/openaccess/Metis215142.pdf

IJsselsteijn, W., de Kort, Y. K., Midden, C., Eggen, B., & van den Hoven, E. (2006). *Persuasive technology for human well-being: Setting the scene.* Berlin, Germany: Springer-Verlag. doi:10.1007/11755494_1

Initiative D21. (2010). *Website.* Retrieved February 13, 2011, from http://www.initiatived21.de

Irwin, M. J. (2008). Indie game developers rise up. *Forbes.com.* Retrieved 22 Sep 2012, from http://www.forbes.com/2008/11/20/games-indie-developers-tech-ebiz-cx_mji_1120indiegames.html

Ivory, J., & Kalyanaraman, S. (2009). Video games make people violent - Well, maybe not that game: Effects of content and person abstraction on perceptions of violent video games' effects and support of censorship. *Communication Reports, 22*(1), 1–12. doi:10.1080/08934210902798536

Jäger, K. W., & Weiniger, R. (2010). Silver gaming–Ein zukunftsträchtiger baustein gegen altersbedingte Isolation. *Ambient Assisted Living-AAL.* Retrieved from http://www.vde-verlag.de/proceedings-en/453209058.html

Janke, K. P. (2006). *Eine taxonomie für digitale spiele.* Ilmenau, Germany: Technical University of Ilmenau, Institute for Media and Communication Science.

Jeanneret, Y. (2009). The relation between mediation and use in the research field of information and communication in France. *RECIIS, 3*(3), 25–34.

Jeffery, C. (2008). *Using non-player characters as tutors in virtual environments.* Retrieved from http://www.open.ac.uk/relive08/

Jenkins, H. (2008). *Convergence culture: Where old and new media collide.* New York, NY: NYU Press.

Jennett, C., Cox, A., Cairns, P., Dhoparee, S., Epps, A., Tijs, T., & Walton, A. (2008). Measuring and defining the experience of immersion in games. *International Journal of Human-Computer Studies*, *66*, 641–661. doi:10.1016/j.ijhcs.2008.04.004

Jensen, A. (2003). *Durchblick – Was hat unser alltag mit der umwelt zu tun*. Nürnberg, Germany: Westermann. Retrieved from http://www.apug.de/archiv/pdf/broschuere_durchblick.pdf

Jian, C., Sasse, N., von Steinbüchel-Rheinwall, N., Schafmeister, F., Shi, H., Rachuy, C., & Schmidt, H. (2011). Towards effective, efficient and elderly-friendly multimodal interaction. In *Proceedings of the 4th International Conference on Pervasive Technologies Related to Assistive Environments*, (pp. 45:1–45:8). New York, NY: ACM. doi:10.1145/2141622.2141675

Jimerson, S. R., Campos, E., & Greif, J. L. (2003). Toward an understanding of definitions and measures of school engagement and related terms. *California School Psychologist*, *8*, 7–27.

Johns, C., Nunez, D., Daya, M., Sellars, D., Casanueva, J., & Blake, E. (2000). The interaction between individuals' immersive tendencies and the sensation of presence in virtual environments. In J. Mulder & R. van Liere (Eds.), *Virtual Environments 2000: Proceedings of the Eurographics Workshop*. London, UK: Springer.

Johnson, R. T., & Johnson, D. W. (1988). Cooperative learning: Two heads learn better than one. *Transforming Education: In Context*, *18*, 34. Retrieved from http://www.context.org/ICLIB/IC18/Johnson.htm

Jones, R. (2008). Saving worlds with videogame activism. In Ferdig, R. E. (Ed.), *Handbook of Research on Effective Electronic Gaming in Education* (pp. 970–988). Hershey, PA: IGI Global. doi:10.4018/978-1-59904-808-6.ch056

Journal. (2012). *Article*. Retrieved from http://thejournal.com/articles/2011/01/11/next-stop-open-sim.aspx

Julien, J. (2011). Social media interaction pattern library. *The Jordan Rules*. Retrieved May 8, 2012, from http://thejordanrules.posterous.com/social-media-interaction-pattern-library

Kafai, Y. B., Quintero, M., & Feldon, D. (2010). Investigating the "why" in whypox: Casual and systematic explorations of a virtual epidemic. *Games and Culture*, *5*(1), 116–135. doi:10.1177/1555412009351265

Karageorghis, C. I., & Priest, D.-L. (2012). Music in the exercise domain: A review and synthesis (part I). *International Review of Sport and Exercise Psychology*, *5*(1), 44–66. doi:10.1080/1750984X.2011.631026

Karlsen, F. (2011). *Theorycrafting: From collective intelligence to intrinsic satisfaction*. Paper presented at the DiGRA 2011 Conference: Think Design Play. Hilversum, The Netherlands.

Kato, P. M., Cole, S. W., Bradlyn, A. S., & Pollock, B. H. (2008). A video game improves behavioural outcomes in adolescents and young adults with cancer: A randomized trial. *Pediatrics*, *122*(2), 305–317. doi:10.1542/peds.2007-3134

Kawalsky, R. (2000). *The validity of presence as a reliable human performance metric in immersive environments*. Paper presented at Presence 2000: International Workshop on Presence. Delft, The Netherlands.

Kearsley, G. (2009). *Explorations in learning & instruction: The theory into practice database; transformative learning (J. Mezirow)*. Retrieved September 8, 2009, from http://tip.psychology.org/bruner.html

Kelly, G. A. (1955). *The psychology of personal constructs*. New York, NY: Norton.

Kennedy, R., Lane, N., Berbaum, K., & Lilienthal, M. (1993). Simulator sickness questionnaire: An enhanced method for quantifying simulator sickness. *The International Journal of Aviation Psychology*, *3*, 203–220. doi:10.1207/s15327108ijap0303_3

Kickmeier-Rust, M. D. (2009). Talking digital educational games. In M. D. Kickmeier-Rust (Ed.), *Proceedings of the First International Open Workshop on Intelligent Personalization and Adaptation in Digital Educational Games*, (pp. 7–16). Graz.

Kickmeier-Rust, M., Göbel, S., & Albert, D. (2008). 80Days: Melding adaptive educational technology and adaptive and interactive storytelling in digital educational games. In R. Klamma Nalin, N.Sharda, B. Fernández-Manjón, H. Kosch, & M. Spaniol (Eds.), *Proceedings of the First International Workshop on Story-Telling and Educational Games (STEG'08)*, (p. 8). STEG.

Kickmeier-Rust, M. D., Mattheiss, E., Steiner, C. M., & Albert, D. (2011). A psycho-pedagogical framework for multi-adaptive educational games. *International Journal of Game-Based Learning*, *1*(1), 45–58. doi:10.4018/ijgbl.2011010104

Kickmeier-Rust, M., & Albert, D. (2007). The ELEKTRA ontology model: a learner-centered approach to resource description. In *Advances in Web Based Learning–ICWL 2007* (pp. 78–89). Springer.

Kickmeier-Rust, M., & Albert, D. (2012). Educationally adaptive: Balancing serious games. *International Journal of Computer Science in Sport*, *11*(1), 15–28.

Kim, S. H., Bangmok, L., & Thomas, M. K. (2012). Between purpose and method: a review of educational research on 3D virtual worlds. *Virtual Worlds Research*, *5*(1).

Kim, T., & Biocca, F. (1997). Telepresence via television: Two dimensions of telepresence may have different connections to memory and persuasion. *International Journal of Computer-Mediated Communication*, *3*.

Kim, Y., Kim, H., Kim, E., & Ko, H. (2005). Characteristic changes in the physiological components of cybersickness. *Psychophysiology*, *42*, 616–625.

Kirchhöfer, D. (2002). Informelles lernen in der freizeit der kinder. *Spektrum Freizeit*, *24*(1), 28–43.

Kirriemuir, J. (2005). *Computer and videogames in curriculum-based education*. London, UK: Department for Education and Skills.

Kizony, R., Weiss, P. L., Shahar, M., & Rand, D. (2006). TheraTitle—A home based virtual reality rehabilitation system. In *Proceedings of the 6th International Conference on Disability, Virtual Reality and Associated Technologies*, (pp. 209-214). Esbjerg, Denmark: International Society for Virtual Rehabilitation. Retrieved from www.icdvrat.rdg.ac.uk/2006/papers/ICDVRAT2006_S06_N03_Kizony_et_al.pdf

Klabbers, J. H. G. (2003). Gaming and simulation: Principles of a science of design. *Simulation & Gaming*, *34*(4), 569–591. doi:10.1177/1046878103258205

Klafki, W. (1991). *Neue studien zur bildungstheorie und didaktik*. Weinheim, Germany: Beltz.

Klastrup, L., & Tosca, S. (2009). Because it just looks cool! Fashion as character performance: The case of WoW. *Journal of Virtual Worlds Research*, *1*(3), 4–17.

Klawe, M. (1999). *Computer games, education and interfaces: The E-GEMS project*. Paper presented at the Graphics interface conference. Ontario, Canada.

Klawe, M., & Phillips, E. (1995). A classroom study : Electronic games engage children as researchers. In *Proceedings of the First International Conference on Computer Support for Collaborative Learning*, (pp. 209–213). doi:10.1.1.47.9799

Kliem, A., & Wiemeyer, J. (2010). Comparison of a traditional and a video game-based balance training program. *International Journal of Computer Science in Sport*, *9*, 78–89.

Knight, J. F., Carley, S., Tregunna, B., Jarvis, S., Smithies, R., & de Freitas, S. (2010). Serious gaming technology in major incident triage training: A pragmatic controlled trial. *Resuscitation*, *81*(9), 1175–1179. doi:10.1016/j.resuscitation.2010.03.042

Knowles, M. S. (1984). *Andragogy in action: Applying modern principles of adult learning*. San Francisco, CA: Jossey-Bass.

Knudson, M., Khaw, L., Bullard, M. K., Dicker, R., Cohen, M. J., & Staudenmayer, K. (2008). Trauma training in simulation: TranSecond lifeating skills from SIM time to real time. *The Journal of Trauma Injury Infection and Critical Care*, *64*(2).

Kollar, I. (2012). *The classroom of the future: Orchestrating collaborative learning spaces*. Sense.

Konert, J., Göbel, S., & Steinmetz, R. (2012). Towards social serious games. In T. Connolly, P. Felicia, G. Neville, & S. Tabirca (Eds.), *Proceedings of the 6th European Conference on Games Based Learning (ECGBL)*, (Vol. 1). Cork, Ireland: Academic Bookshop.

Korn, O., Brach, M., Schmidt, A., Hörz, T., & Konrad, R. (2012). Context-sensitive user-centered scalability: An introduction focusing on exergames and assistive systems in work contexts. In S. Göbel, W. Müller, B. Urban, & J. Wiemeyer (Eds.), *E-Learning and Games for Training, Education, Health and Sports,* (Vol. 7516, pp. 164–176). Berlin, Germany: Springer. Retrieved from http://www.springerlink.com/index/10.1007/978-3-642-33466-5_19

Korn, O., Schmidt, A., & Hörz, T. (2012). Assistive systems in production environments: Exploring motion recognition and gamification. In *Proceedings of the 5th International Conference on Pervasive Technologies Related to Assistive Environments.* ACM Press.

Korolov, M. (2011). Virtual world usage accelerates. *Hypergrid Business.* Retrieved May 27, 2012, from http://www.hypergridbusiness.com/2011/07/virtual-world-usage-accelerates/

Korossy, K. (1999). Modelling knowledge as competence and performance. In Albert, D., & Lukas, J. (Eds.), *Knowledge Spaces Theories Empirical Research Applications* (pp. 103–132). Springer.

Korte, W. H., & Hüsing, T. (2006). Benchmarking access and use of ICT in European schools 2006. In *Empirica* (pp. 1–120). Bonn, Germany: Empirica.

Koskovich, M. (2009). *Website.* Retrieved from http://www.prnewswire.com/news-releases/saic-purchases-simulation--collaboration-product-line-from-forterra-systems-inc-83237277.html

Koster, R. (1998). The man behind the curtain. *Raph Koster's Website.* Retrieved 13 Oct 2012, from http://www.raphkoster.com/gaming/essay5.shtml

Krause, K.-L. (2005). *Understanding and promoting student engagement in university learning communities.* http://www.deakin.edu.au/itl/student-engagement/Resources/StudengKrause.pdf

Kreijns, K., Kirschner, P. A., Jochems, W., & Van Buuren, H. (2007). Measuring perceived sociability of computer-supported collaborative learning environments. *Computers & Education, 49*(2), 176–192. doi:10.1016/j.compedu.2005.05.004

Kretschmann, R., Dittus, I., Lutz, I., & Meier, C. (2010). Nintendo Wii sports: Simple gadget or serious "measure" for health promotion? A pilot study according to the energy expenditure, movement extent, and student perceptions. In *Proceedings of the GameDays 2010 – Serious Games for Sports and Health,* (pp. 147-159). GameDays.

Kriegel, M., & Aylett, R. (2008). Emergent narrative as a novel framework for massively collaborative authoring. In *Intelligent Virtual Agents* (pp. 73–80). Berlin, Germany: Springer. doi:10.1007/978-3-540-85483-8_7

Krijn, M., Emmelkamp, P., Biemond, R., & Ligny, C., de Wilde, Schuemi, M., & van der Mast, C. (2004). Treatment of acrophobia in virtual reality: The role of immersion and presence. *Behaviour Research and Therapy, 42,* 299–239. doi:10.1016/S0005-7967(03)00139-6

Kücklich, J. (2009). A techno-semiotic approach to cheating in computer games. *Games and Culture, 4*(2), 158–169. doi:10.1177/1555412008325486

Kulik, C. L. C., & Kulik, J. A. (1991). Effectiveness of computer-based Instruction: An updated analysis. *Computers in Human Behavior, 7,* 75–94. doi:10.1016/0747-5632(91)90030-5

Kulik, J. A., Bangert, R. L., & Williams, G. W. (1983). Effects of computer-based teaching on secondary school students. *Journal of Educational Psychology, 75,* 19–26. doi:10.1037/0022-0663.75.1.19

Kutner, L., & Olson, C. (2008). *Grand theft childhood: The surprising truth about violent video games and what parents can do.* New York, NY: Simon & Schuster.

Kzero. (2008). Research. *Resident experts in virtual worlds.* Retrieved September 1, 2009, from http://www.kzero.co.uk/blog/?page_id=2092

Laarni, J., Ravaja, N., Saari, T., & Hartmann, T. (2004). Personality-related differences in subjective presence. In Alcaniz Raya, M., & Rey Solaz, B. (Eds.), *Proceedings of Presence 2004* (pp. 88–95). Valencia, Spain: Presence.

Lager, A., & Bremberg, S. (2005). *Health effects of video and computer game playing: A systematic review.* Retrieved from https://xn--folkhlsostmman-9hbf.se/PageFiles/4170/R200518_video_computer_game(1).pdf

Lager, A., & Bremberg, S. (2005). *Health effects of video and computer game playing: A systematic review.* Stockholm: Swedish National Institute of Public Health.

LaMendola, W. (2010). Social presence in an online world. *Journal of Technology in Human Services, 28,* 108–119. doi:10.1080/15228831003759562

Lampert, C., Schwinge, C., & Tolks, D. (2009). *Der gespielte ernst des lebens: Bestandsaufnahme und potenziale von serious games (for health).* Retrieved from http://www.medienpaed.com/15/lampert0903.pdf

Landin, D. (1994). The role of verbal cues in skill learning. *Quest, 46,* 299–313. doi:10.1080/00336297.1994.10484128

Lange, B., Flynn, S., & Rizzo, A. (2009). Initial usability assessment of off the-shelf video title consoles for clinical title-based motor rehabilitation. *The Physical Therapy Review, 14,* 355–363. doi:10.1179/108331909X12488667117258

Langer, H. (2012). *Entwicklung eines gesprächsmodells für interactive geschichten in computerspielen.* (Bachelor's Thesis). University of Rostock, Rostock, Germany.

Larusson, J. A., & Alterman, R. (2009). Wikis to support the "collaborative" part of collaborative learning. *International Journal of Computer-Supported Collaborative Learning, 4*(4), 371–402. doi:10.1007/s11412-009-9076-6

Laver, K., Ratcliffe, J., George, S., Burgess, L., & Crotty, M. (2011). Is the Nintendo Wii Fit really acceptable to older people? A discrete choice experiment. *BMC Geriatrics, 11,* 64. doi:10.1186/1471-2318-11-64

Law, E. L.-C., Kickmeier-Rust, M., Albert, D., & Holzinger, A. (2008). Challenges in the development and evaluation of immersive digital educational games. *Lecture Notes in Computer Science, 5289.*

Lawrence, S. (2005, January 18). Exercise, lose weight with 'exergaming'. *Fox News.*

Lazzaro, N. (2004). *Why we play games: Four keys to more emotion without story.* Technical Report. XEO Design Inc.

Leavitt, H. (1951). Some effects of certain communication patterns on group performance. *Journal of Abnormal and Social Psychology, 46,* 38–50. doi:10.1037/h0057189

LeBel, E. P., & Peters, K. R. (2011). Fearing the future of empirical psychology: Bem's (2011) evidence of psi as a case study of deficiencies in modal research practice. *Review of General Psychology, 15*(4), 371–379. doi:10.1037/a0025172

Lee, K. M. (2004). Presence, explicated. *Communication Theory, 14*(1), 27–50. doi:10.1111/j.1468-2885.2004.tb00302.x

Lee, T. D., & Genovese, E. D. (1988). Distribution of practice in motor skill acquisition: Learning and performance effects reconsidered. *Research Quarterly, 59,* 277–287.

Leitert, A. (2011). *Graphenbasierte überprüfung unvollständiger lösungen in modellierungsaufgaben.* (Student Thesis). University of Rostock, Rostock, Germany.

Lemon, M., & Kelly, O. (2009). *Laying second life foundations: Second chance learners get first life skills.* Retrieved from http://www.ascilite.org.au/conferences/auckland09/procs/lemon.pdf

Lenhart, A., Kahne, J., Middaugh, E., MacGill, A., Evans, C., & Mitak, J. (2008). *Teens, video games and civics: Teens gaming experiences are diverse and include significant social interaction and civic engagement.* Retrieved 10/2/08 from http://www.pewinternet.org/PPF/r/263/report_display.asp

Lessiter, J., Freeman, J., Keogh, E., & Davidoff, J. (2000). *Development of a cross-media presence questionnaire: The ITC-sense of presence.* Paper presented at Presence 2000: International Workshop on Presence. Delft, The Netherlands.

Lewin, K. (1946). Action research and minority problems. *The Journal of Social Issues, 2*(4), 34–46. doi:10.1111/j.1540-4560.1946.tb02295.x

Lieberman, D. A. (1992). *Learning: Behavior and cognition.* Pacific Grove, CA: Brooks/Cole.

Lieberman, D. A. (2001). Management of chronic pediatric diseases with interactive health games: Theory and research findings. *The Journal of Ambulatory Care Management, 24*(1), 26–38.

Lim, Q. (2008). Global citizenship education, school curriculum and games: Learning mathematics, English and science as a global citizen. *Computers & Education, 51,* 1073–1093. doi:10.1016/j.compedu.2007.10.005

Linden Lab. (2008). *Second life*. Retrieved July 19, 2008, from http://www.secondlife.com

Lindley, C. (2003). Game taxonomies: A high level framework for game analysis and design. *Gamasutra*. Retrieved from http://www.gamasutra.com/view/feature/131205/game_taxonomies_a_high_level_.php?page=2

Linn, M. C. (1990). Summary: Establishing a science and engineering of science education. In Gardner, M., Greeno, J. G., Reif, F., Schoenfeld, A. H., diSessa, A., & Stage, E. (Eds.), *Toward a Scientific Practice of Science Education* (pp. 323–341). Hillsdale, NJ: Lawrence Erlbaum.

Lisak, A., & Erez, M. (2009). Leaders and followers in multi-cultural teams. In *Proceeding of the 2009 International Workshop on Intercultural Collaboration - IWIC '09,* (p. 81). New York, NY: ACM Press. doi:10.1145/1499224.1499238

Livingstone, D. W. (2001). *Adults' informal learning: Definitions, findings, gaps and future research*. NALL Working Paper, No. 21. Toronto, Canada: Centre for the Study of Education and Work, OISE/UT.

Lofgren, E. T., & Fefferman, N. H. (2007). The untapped potential of virtual game worlds to shed light on real world epidemics. *The Lancet Infectious Diseases, 7*(9), 625–629. doi:10.1016/S1473-3099(07)70212-8

Lombard, M., & Jones, M. T. (2007). Identifying the (tele) presence literature. *PsychNology Journal, 5*(2), 197–206.

Loreto, I. D., & Gouaïch, A. (2004). *Social casual games success is not so casual*. Word Journal of the International Linguistic Association.

Louchart, S., & Aylett, R. (2003). Solving the narrative paradox in VEs – Lessons from RPGs. In T. Rist, R. Aylett, D. Bellin, & J. Rickel (Eds.), *Intelligent Virtual Agents: 4th International Workshop, IVA 2003, Proceedings,* (pp. 244–248). Berlin, Germany: Springer.

Louchart, S., & Aylett, R. (2003). Solving the narrative paradox in VEs – Lessons from RPGs. In Rist, T., Aylett, R., Ballin, D., & Rickel, J. (Eds.), *Intelligent Virtual Agents* (Vol. 2792, pp. 244–248). Berlin, Germany: Springer. doi:10.1007/978-3-540-39396-2_41

Louchart, S., & Aylett, R. (2004). Narrative theory and emergent interactive narrative. *International Journal of Continuing Engineering Education and Lifelong Learning, 14*, 506–518. doi:10.1504/IJCEELL.2004.006017

Lynch, J., Aughwane, P., & Hammond, T. M. (2010). Video games and surgical ability: A literature review. *Journal of Surgical Education, 67*(3), 184–189. doi:10.1016/j.jsurg.2010.02.010

Maciuszek, D., & Martens, A. (2009). Virtuelle labore als simulationsspiele. In S. Fischer, E. Maehle, & R. Reischuk (Eds.), *INFORMATIK 2009 – Im Focus das Leben: Beiträge der 39. Jahrestagung der Gesellschaft für Informatik,* (pp. 1965–1979). Bonn, Germany: GI.

Maciuszek, D., & Martens, A. (2011). Cognitive tasks and collaborative agents for microadaptive game activities. In A. Dittmar & P. Forbrig (Eds.), *Designing Collaborative Activities. ECCE 2011: European Conference on Cognitive Ergonomics 2011,* (pp. 271–272). Rostock, Germany: Universitätsdruckerei Rostock.

Maciuszek, D., & Martens, A. (2011). Computer role-playing games as an educational game genre: Activities and reflection. In D. Gouscos & M. Meimaris (Eds.), *Proceedings of the 5th International Conference on Games-Based Learning (ECGBL 2011),* (pp. 368–377). Reading, MA: Academic Publishing.

Maciuszek, D., Ladhoff, S., & Martens, A. (2011). Content design patterns for game-based learning. *International Journal of Game-Based Learning, 1*(3), 65–82. doi:10.4018/ijgbl.2011070105

Maciuszek, D., & Martens, A. (2011). A reference architecture for game-based intelligent tutoring. In Felicia, P. (Ed.), *Handbook of Research on Improving Learning and Motivation through Educational Games: Multidisciplinary Approaches* (pp. 658–682). Hershey, PA: IGI Global. doi:10.4018/978-1-60960-495-0.ch031

Maciuszek, D., Martens, A., Lucke, U., Zender, R., & Keil, T. (2013). Second life as a virtual lab environment. In Hebbel-Seeger, A., Reiners, T., & Schäffer, D. (Eds.), *Synthetic Worlds: Emerging Technologies in Education and Economics*. Berlin, Germany: Springer.

Magerko, B., Heeter, C., Fitzgerald, J., & Medler, B. (2008). Intelligent adaptation of digital game-based learning. In *Proceedings of the 2008 Conference on Future Play: Research, Play, Share*, (pp. 200–203). New York, NY: ACM.

Magic, L. (2011). *Facebook depression: A nonexistent condition*. Retrieved 5/20/12 from http://www.huffingtonpost.com/larry-magid/facebook-depression-nonexistent_b_842733.html

Magill, R. A. (2010). *Motor learning and control: Concepts and applications* (8th ed.). Boston, MA: McGraw Hill.

Magnussen, R., & Holm Sørensen, B. (2010). Designing intervention in educational game research: Developing methodological approaches for design-based participatory research. In B. Meyer (Ed.), *Proceedings of the 4th European Conference on Games-Based Learning (ECGBL 2010)*, (pp. 218–225). Reading, MA: Academic Publishing

Malone, T. (1980). *What makes things fun to learn? A study of intrinsically motivating computer games*. Technical report no. CIS-7 (SSL-80-11). Palo Alto, CA: Xerox Palo Alto Research Center.

Malone, T. W., & Lepper, M. R. (1987). Making learning fun: A taxonomy of intrinsic motivations for learning. In Snow, R. E., & Farr, M. J. (Eds.), *Aptitude, Learning and Instruction: Conative and Affective Process Analyses* (pp. 223–253). Hillsdale, NJ: Erlbaum.

Ma, M., & Zheng, H. (2011). Virtual reality and serious games in healthcare. In Brahnam, S., & Jain, L. C. (Eds.), *Advanced Computational Intelligence Paradigms in Healthcare* (pp. 169–192). Berlin, Germany: Springer. doi:10.1007/978-3-642-17824-5_9

Mandl, H., & Kopp, B. (2006). *Blended learning: Forschungsfragen und perspektiven* (Tech. Rep. No. 182). München, Germany: Department Psychologie, Institut für Pädagogische Psychologie, Ludwig-Maximilians-Universität.

Mandryk, R. L., Aktins, M. S., & Inkpen, K. M. (2006). A continuous and objective evaluation of emotional experience with interactive play environments. In *Proceedings of CHI'06*. ACM.

Mania, K., & Chalmers, A. (2000). *A user-centered methodology for investigating presence and task performance*. Paper presented at Presence 2000: International Workshop on Presence. Delft, The Netherlands.

Marschall, F., Bund, A., & Wiemeyer, J. (2007). Does frequent augmented feedback really degrade learning? A meta-analysis. *Bewegung und Training, 1*, 74–85.

Marston, H. R. (2010). *Wii like to play too: Computer gaming habits of older adults*. (PhD Thesis). Teesside University. Middlesbrough, UK.

Marston, H. R., & Smith, S. T. (2012). Interactive videogame technologies to support independence in the elderly: A narrative review. *Games for Health Journal: Research, Development, and Clinical Application, 1*(2), 139–159. doi:doi:10.1089/g4h.2011.0008

Martens, A. (2004). *Ein tutoring prozess modell für fallbasierte intelligente tutoring systeme*. Berlin, Germany: Aka.

Martin, A. L., & Wiemeyer, J. (2012). The impact of different gaming interfaces on spatial experience and spatial presence – A pilot study. In Göbel, S., Müller, W., Urban, B., & Wiemeyer, J. (Eds.), *E-Learning and Games for Training, Education, Health and Sports* (pp. 177–182). Berlin, Germany: Springer. doi:10.1007/978-3-642-33466-5_20

Martín-Barbero, J. (1993). *Communication, culture and hegemony: From the media to mediations*. London, UK: Sage Publications.

Maslow, A. H. (1943). A theory of human motivation. *Psychological Review, 50*, 370–396. Retrieved from http://psychclassics.yorku.ca/Maslow/motivation.htm doi:10.1037/h0054346

Mateas, M., & Stern, A. (2005). Structuring content in the Facade interactive drama architecture. In M. Young & J. Laird (Eds.), *Proceedings of the First Artificial Intelligence and Interactive Digital Entertainment Conference*, (pp. 93-98). Palo Alto, CA: AAAI Press

Maturana, H. R. (1970). *Biology of cognition (Tech. Rep. No. BCL 9.0)*. Urbana, IL: Biological Computer Laboratory, University of Illinois.

Mayo, M. J. (2009). Video games: A route to large-scale STEM education? *Science*, *323*, 79–82. doi:10.1126/science.1166900

Mazur, J. (2004). Conversation analysis for educational technologists: Theoretical and methodological issues for researching the structures, processes and meaning of on-line talk. In Jonassen, D. (Ed.), *Handbook of Research for Educational Communications and Technology*. New York, NY: McMillian.

McFarlane, A., Sparrowhawk, A., & Heald, Y. (2002). Report on educational use of games. *TEEM (Teachers Evaluating Educational Multimedia)*. Retrieved February 13, 2011, from http://www.teem.org.uk/publications/teem_gaesined_full.pdf

McGonigal, J. (2011). *Reality is broken: Why games make us better and how they can change the world*. New York, NY: Penguin Press.

McLoughlin, C., & Lee, M. J. W. (2008). Future learning landscapes: Transforming pedagogy through social software. *Innovate*, *4*(5), 1–8.

Meder, N. (2006). *Webdidaktik: Eine neue didaktik webbasierten lernens*. Bielefeld, Germany: Bertelsmann.

Medienpädagogischer Forschungsverbund Südwest. (2010). *KIM-studie 2010*. Retrieved from www.mpfs.de

Mehm, F., Göbel, S., & Steinmetz, R. (2011). Introducing component-based templates into a game authoring tool. In M. M. Dimitris Gouscos (Ed.), *5th European Conference on Games Based Learning*, (pp. 395–403). Reading, UK: Academic Conferences Limited.

Mehm, F., Göbel, S., Radke, S., & Steinmetz, R. (2009). Authoring environment for story-based digital educational games. In M. D. Kickmeier-Rust (Ed.), *Proceedings of the 1st International Open Workshop on Intelligent Personalization and Adaptation in Digital Educational Games*, (pp. 113–124). IEEE.

Mehm, F., Hardy, S., Göbel, S., & Steinmetz, R. (2011). Collaborative authoring of serious games for health. In *Proceedings of the 19th ACM International Conference on Multimedia*, (pp. 807-808). New York, NY: ACM.

Mehm, F., Hardy, S., Göbel, S., & Steinmetz, R. (2011). Collaborative authoring of serious games for health. In *Proceedings of the 19th ACM International Conference on Multimedia*, (pp. 807–808). New York, NY: ACM.

Mehm, F., Wendel, V., Göbel, S., & Steinmetz, R. (2010). Bat cave: A testing and evaluation platform for digital educational games. In B. Meyer (Ed.), *Proceedings of the 3rd European Conference on Games Based Learning,* (pp. 251–260). Reading, UK: Academic Conferences International.

Mehm, F. (2010). Authoring serious games. [New York, NY: ACM.]. *Proceedings of Foundations of Digital Games*, *2010*, 271–273.

Mesko, B. (2012). *Website*. Retrieved from http://www.webicina.com/about/

Metaverse Standards. (2012). *Website*. Retrieved from http://www.metaversestandards.org/index.php?title=Virtual_Worlds

Meyer, S., & BMBF-VDE-Innovationspartnerschaft AAL. (2010). *AAL in der alternden gesellschaft : Anforderungen, akzeptanz und perspektiven : Analyse und planungshilfe*. Berlin, Germany: VDE-Verl.

Michael, D., & Chen, S. (2006). *Serious games: Games that educate, train and inform*. Boston, MA: Thomson Course Technology.

Mietzel, G. (2007). *Pädagogische psychologie des lehrens und lernens* (8th ed.). Göttingen, Germany: Hogrefe.

Ministerio da Cultura. (2007). *BR games: Objetivo, público e diretrizes*. [BR Games: Purpose, Audience and Guidelines]. Retrieved 23 jan 2010, from http://www.cultura.gov.br/site/2007/09/25/jogos-br/

Minsky, M. (1980). Telepresence. *Omni (New York, N.Y.)*, *2*, 45–51.

MIT. (2012). *MIT's education arcade uses online gaming to teach science*. Retrieved from http://education.mit.edu/blogs/louisa/2012/pressrelease

Mitchell, A., Savill-Smith, C., & Britain, G. (2004). *The use of computer and video games for learning: A review of the literature*. London, UK: Learning and Skills Development Agency.

Mitchell, S. N., Reilly, R., Bramwell, F. G., & Lilly, F. (2012). Friendship and choosing groupmates: Preferences for teacher-selected vs. student- selected groupings in high school science classes. *Journal of Instructional Psychology*, *31*(1), 1–6.

Mohammad, A. L. S., Guetl, C., & Kappe, F. (2009). PASS: Peer-assessment approach for modern learning settings. In *Proceedings of the Advances in Web Based Learning-ICWL 2009: 8th International Conference*, (p. 44). Springer-Verlag. doi:10.1007/978-3-642-03426-8_5

Mohan, A., Lemenager, E., & McCracken, M. (2006). Targeting areas of improvement in intra-group dynamics using a participative approach - A case study. In *Proceedings of the 2006 IEEE International Engineering Management Conference*, (pp. 110–115). IEEE. doi:10.1109/IEMC.2006.4279828

Molleindustria. (n.d.). *Oiligarchy postmortem: Background information of the game*. Retrieved from http://www.molleindustria.org/oiligarchy-postmortem#11

Moses, A. (2011). *From fantasy to lethal reality: Breivik trained on modern warfare game*. Retrieved 5/22/12 from http://m.smh.com.au/digital-life/games/from-fantasy-to-lethal-reality-breivik-trained-on-modern-warfare-game-20110725-1hw41.html

Mueller, F., Gibbs, M. R., & Vetere, F. (2008). *Taxonomy of exertion games*. Paper presented at OZCHI 2008. Cairns, Australia.

Murray, C., Fox, J., & Pettifer, S. (2007). Absorption, dissociation, locus of control and presence in virtual reality. *Computers in Human Behavior, 23*, 1347–1354. doi:10.1016/j.chb.2004.12.010

Nacke, L. E. (2009). *Affective ludology: Scientific measurement of user experience in interactive entertainment*. (Doctoral Dissertation). Blekinge Institute of Technology. Belkinge, Sweden.

Nacke, L., Drachen, A., & Göbel, S. (2010). Methods for evaluating gameplay experience in a serious gaming context. *International Journal of Computer Science in Sport, 9*.

Nacke, L. E. (2009). *Affective ludology: Scientific measurement of user experience in interactive entertainment*. Karlskrona, Sweden: Belkinge Institute of Technology.

Nass, C., Moon, Y., & Green, N. (1997). Are machines gender neutral? Gender-stereotypic responses to computers with voices. *Journal of Applied Social Psychology, 27*(10), 864–876. doi:10.1111/j.1559-1816.1997.tb00275.x

Neale, S. (1980). *Genre*. London, UK: British Film Institute.

Neff, J., & Klaassen, A. (2007). Web research could gain clout via virtual currency. *Advertising Age, 78*(50), 4–34.

Nef, O., Guidali, M., Klamroth-Marganska, V., & Riener, R. (2009). ARMin - Exoskeleton robot for stroke rehabilitation. In Dössel, O., & Schlegel, W. C. (Eds.), *WC 2009, IFMBE Proceedings 25/IX* (pp. 127–130). Berlin, Germany: Springer.

Nelson, B., & Ketelhut, D. (2008). Exploring embedded guidance and self-efficacy in educational multi-user virtual environments. *International Journal of Computer-Supported Collaborative Learning, 3*(4), 413–427. Retrieved from http://dx.doi.org/10.1007/s11412-008-9049-1

Nelson, M. E., Rejeski, W. J., Blair, S. N., Duncan, P. W., Judge, J. O., & King, A. C. (2007). Physical activity and public health in older adults. *Medicine and Science in Sports and Exercise, 39*(8), 1435–1445. doi:10.1249/mss.0b013e3180616aa2

Neuendorf, P., & Simpson, C. (2010). Redesigning role plays for a virtual world in health education. In *Proceedings of Global Learn 2010*. Global Learn.

New York Times. (1999, April 6). *Managing ailments through video games*. Retrieved from http://www.nytimes.com/1999/04/06/health/managing-ailments-through-video-games.html

Newzoo. (2011). *Gap closing between emerging and western game markets*. Retrieved 01 jun 2011, from http://www.newzoo.com/ENG/1504-Detail.html&id=79

Neyer, F., Felber, J., & Gebhardt, C. (2012). Entwicklung und validierung einer kurzskala zur erfassung von technikbereitschaft. *Diagnostica, 58*, 87–99. doi:10.1026/0012-1924/a000067

NHS UK. (2012). *Website*. Retrieved from http://www.nhscareers.nhs.uk/atoz.shtml

Nicovic, S., Boller, G., & Cornwell, T. (2005). Experienced presence within computer-mediated communications: Initial explorations on the effects of gender with respect to empathy and immersion. *Journal of Computer-Mediated Communication, 10*, 1–17.

Nielsen Research. (2009). *Insights on casual games analysis of casual games for the PC*. Retrieved from http://www.scribd.com/doc/20232878/Insights-on-Casual-Games-Analysis-of-Casual-Games-for-the-PC-Nielsen-Research-2009

Nintendo. (2008). *Website*. Retrieved from http://www.nintendo.com/games/detail/hoiNtus4JvIcPtP8LQPyud-4Kyy393oep

Norman, D., & Bobrow, D. (1975). On data-limited and resource-limited processes. *Cognitive Psychology, 7*, 44–64. doi:10.1016/0010-0285(75)90004-3

Nückles, M., Hübner, S., & Renkl, A. (2008). Enhancing self-regulated learning by writing learning protocols. *Learning and Instruction, 19*, 259–271. doi:10.1016/j.learninstruc.2008.05.002

O'Neill, N. (2008). What exactly are social games? *Social Times*. Retrieved January 18, 2011, from http://www.socialtimes.com/2008/07/social-games/

Oblinger, D. (2004). The next generation of educational engagement. *Journal of Interactive Media in Education, 8*, 1–18.

Oh, Y., & Yang, S. (2010). *Defining exergames and exergaming*. Retrieved from http://meaningfulplay.msu.edu/proceedings2010/mp2010_paper_63.pdf

Olson, C. K. (2010). Children's motivations for video game play in the context of normal development. *Review of General Psychology, 14*(2), 180–187. doi:10.1037/a0018984

Olson, C., Kutner, L., Warner, D., Almerigi, J., Baer, L., Nicholi, A., & Beresin, E. (2007). Factors correlated with violent video game use by adolescent boys and girls. *The Journal of Adolescent Health, 41*, 77–83. doi:10.1016/j.jadohealth.2007.01.001

Onrubia, J., & Engel, A. (2009). Strategies for collaborative writing and phases of knowledge construction in CSCL environments. *Computers & Education, 53*(4), 1256–1265. doi:10.1016/j.compedu.2009.06.008

Open Cobalt. (2012). *Website*. Retrieved from http://www.opencobalt.org/home

Open Wonderland. (2012). *Website*. Retrieved from http://openwonderland.org/

OpenQwaq. (2012). *Website*. Retrieved from http://code.google.com/p/openqwaq/

OpenSim. (2012). *Website*. Retrieved from http://opensimulator.org/wiki/Main_Page

OpenSimulator. (2012). *Website*. Retrieved from http://opensimulator.org

O'Reilly, T. (2006). *Web 2.0 – Principles and practices*. Oreilly & Assoc Inc.

Organisation for Economic Co-operation and Development. (2009). *Creating effective teaching and learning environments*. Paris, France: OECD Publishing.

Organization. (1998). *Health promotion evaluation: Recommendations to policymakers*. Copenhagen, Denmark: European Working Group on Health Promotion Evaluation.

Orland, K., & Remo, C. (2008). *Games for health: Noah Falstein on exergaming history*. Retrieved from http://www.gamasutra.com/phpbin/news_index.php?story=18561

Osgood, C. E. (1949). The similarity paradox in human learning: A resolution. *Psychological Review, 56*(3), 132–143. doi:10.1037/h0057488

Owens, D., Mitchell, A., Khazanchi, D., & Zigurs, I. (2011). An empirical investigation of virtual world projects and metaverse technology capabilities. *The Data Base for Advances in Information Systems, 42*(1).

Paim, J. S. (2010). *O que é o SUS* [What is the SUS]. Rio de Janeiro, Brazil: Editora Fiocruz.

Paim, J., Travassos, C., Almeida, C., Bahia, L., & Macinko, J. (2011). The Brazilian health system: History, advances, and challenges. *Lancet, 377*(9779), 1778–1797. doi:10.1016/S0140-6736(11)60054-8

Palincsar, A. (1998). Social constructivist perspectives on teaching and learning. *Annual Review of Psychology, 49*, 345–373. doi:10.1146/annurev.psych.49.1.345

Paoletti, P. (2012). The dimension of future in old age: Promoting healthy and active aging with older women in Portugal. *Personality and Social Psychology, 53*, 119–128.

Papastergiou, M. (2009). Exploring the potential of computer and video games for health and physical education: A literature review. *Computers & Education, 53*(3), 603–622. doi:10.1016/j.compedu.2009.04.001

Papert, S. (1980). *Mindstorms: Children, computer and powerful ideas*. New York, NY: Basic Books.

Peinado, F., Gómez-Martín, P. P., & Gómez-Martín, M. A. (2005). A game architecture for emergent story-puzzles in a persistent world. In *Proceedings of DiGRA 2005 Conference: Changing Views – Worlds in Play*. Vancouver, Canada: DiGRA.

Pelgrum, W. J. (2008). School practices and conditions for pedagogy and ICTs. In Law, N., Pelgrum, W., & Plomp, T. (Eds.), *Pedagogy and ICT Use in Schools around the World: Findings from the IEA SITES 2006 Study* (pp. 67–122). Hong Kong, Hong Kong: CERC-Springer. doi:10.1007/978-1-4020-8928-2_4

Peng, W., Crouse, J. C., & Lin, J.-H. (2012). Using active video games for physical activity promotion: A systematic review of the current state of research. *Health Education & Behavior*. Retrieved from http://heb.sagepub.com/content/early/2012/07/06/1090198112444956

Pereira, V. A. (2008). *Na lan house, "porque jogar sozinho não tem graça": Estudo das redes sociais juvenis on- e off-line*. [In the lan house, "because it's no fun playing alone": A study of juvenile social networks online and offline]. (PhD Thesis) Universidade Federal do Rio de Janeiro. Rio de Janeiro, Brazil.

Peterson, M. (2010). Computerized games and simulations in computer-assisted language-learning: A meta-analysis of research. *Simulation & Gaming, 41*(1), 72–93. doi:10.1177/1046878109355684

Petróczi, A., Nepusz, T., & Bazsó, F. (2006). Measuring tie-strength in virtual social networks. *Connections, 27*(2), 39–52.

Petschel-Held, G. (n.d.). *Keep cool – Gambling with the climate: The scientific background of the game*. Potsdam, Germany: Potsdam Institute for Climate Impact Research.

Pew Research Center. (2012). *Digital divides and bridges: Technology use among youth*. Retrieved 5/22/12 from http://pewinternet.org/Presentations/2012/Apr/Digital-Divides-and-Bridges-Technology-Use-Among-Youth.aspx

Piaget, J. (1978). *Das weltbild des kindes*. München, Germany: dtv/Klett-Cotta.

Pollard Sacks, D., Bushman, B. J., & Anderson, C. A. (2011). Do violent video games harm children? Comparing the scientific amicus curiae "experts" in Brown v. Entertainment Merchants Association. *Northwestern University Law Review: Colloquy, 106*, 1-12.

Pörksen, B. (2011). Schlüsselwerke des konstruktivismus: Eine einführung. In Pörksen, B. (Ed.), *Schlüsselwerke des Konstruktivismus* (pp. 13–28). Wiesbaden, Germany: VS-Verlag. doi:10.1007/978-3-531-93069-5_1

Portal Brasil. (2012). *Banda larga popular já chegou a quase 1.400 municípios*. [Popular broadband has reached almost 1,400 cities]. Retrieved 10 Oct 2012, from http://www.brasil.gov.br/noticias/arquivos/2012/06/14/banda-larga-popular-ja-chegou-a-quase-1.400-municipios

Porter, J. M., & Magill, R. A. (2010). Systematically increasing contextual interference is beneficial for learning sport skills. *Journal of Sports Sciences, 28*(12), 1277–1285. doi:10.1080/02640414.2010.502946

Prediger, S., Selter, C., & Dortmund, U. (2008). Diagnose als grundlage für individuelle förderung im mathematikunterricht. *Schule NRW, 6*(3), 113–116.

Prensky, M. (2001). Digital natives, digital immigrants. *Horizon, 9*, 1–6. Retrieved from http://www.marcprensky.com/writing/Prensky%20-%20Digital%20Natives,%20Digital%20Immigrants%20-%20Part1.pdf

Prensky, M. (2004). *Digital game-based learning*. New York, NY: McGraw-Hill.

Prensky, M. (2005). Computer games and learning: Digital game-based learning. In Raessens, J., & Goldstein, J. (Eds.), *Handbook of Computer Game Studies* (pp. 97–122). Cambridge, MA: MIT Press.

Prothero, J., & Hoffman, H. (1995). *Widening the field-of-view increases the sense of presence within immersive virtual environments*. Human Interface Technology Laboratory Technical Report R-95-4. Seattle, WA: University of Washington.

Protonmedia. (2012). *Website*. Retrieved from www.protonmedia.com/.../ProtoSphere_Product_Datasheet.pdf

Przybylski, A. K., Rigby, C. S., & Ryan, R. M. (2010). A motivational model of video game engagement. *Review of General Psychology, 14*(2), 154–166. doi:10.1037/a0019440

Przybylski, A., Ryan, R., & Rigby, C. (2009). The motivating role of violence in video games. *Personality and Social Psychology Bulletin, 35,* 243–259. doi:10.1177/0146167208327216

Purdy, J. (2007). Serious games: Getting serious about digital games in learning. *Corporate University Journal,* 3-6.

Puttnam, D. (2006). Foreword. In H. Ellis, S. Heppell, J. Kirriemuir, A. Krotoski, & A. McFarlane (Eds.), *Unlimited Learning: Computer and Video Games in the Learning Landscape,* (p. 1). London, UK: ELSPA (Entertainment and Leisure Software Publishers Association). Retrieved February 13, 2011, from http://www.elspa.com/assets/files/u/unlimitedlearningtheroleofcomputerandvideogamesint_344.pdf

Radford, C. (2009). Nintendo Wii injuries: It's not Wii, it's us. *The Telegraph.* Retrieved from http://blogs.telegraph.co.uk/news/ceriradford/100019260/nintendo-wii-injuries-its-not-wii-its-us/

Raeburn, P., Muldoon, N., & Bookallil, C. (2009). *Blended spaces, work based learning and constructive alignment: Impacts on student engagement.* Retrieved from http://www.ascilite.org.au/conferences/auckland09/procs/raeburn.pdf

Rand, D., Kizony, R., & Weiss, P. L. (2004). Virtual reality rehabilitation for all: Vivid GX versus Sony PlayStation II EyeToy. In *Proceedings of the 5th International Conference on Disability, Virtual Reality and Associated Technologies,* (pp. 87-94). Oxford, UK: International Society for Virtual Rehabilitation. Retrieved from http://www.gesturetek.com/gesturetekhealth/pdfs/research/Enjoyment_VR.pdf

Rand, D., Kizony, R., & Weiss, P. T. L. (2008). The Sony PlayStation II EyeToy: Low-cost virtual reality for use in rehabilitation. *Journal of Neurologic Physical Therapy; JNPT, 32,* 155–163.

Rasch, G. (1981). *Probabilistic models for some intelligence and attainment tests.* Chicago, IL: University of Chicago Print (Tx). Retrieved from http://www.amazon.com/Probabilistic-Models-Intelligence-Attainment-Tests/dp/0226705544

Ratan, R., & Ritterfeld, U. (2009). Classifying serious games. In Ritterfeld, U., Cody, M., & Vorderer, P. (Eds.), *Serious Games: Mechanisms and Effects* (pp. 10–24). New York, NY: Routledge.

Rauterberg, G. W. M. (2002). Determinantes for collaboration in networked multi-user games. In *Proceedings of Entertainment Computing: Technologies and Applications.* IEEE.

Reaction Grid. (2012). *Website.* Retrieved from http://www.reactiongrid.com

Reader, T., Flin, R., Lauche, K., & Cuthbertson, B. H. (2006). Non-technical skills in the intensive care unit. *British Journal of Anaesthesia, 96*(5). doi:10.1093/bja/ael067

Reading, C. E. (2008). *Recognising and measuring engagement in ICT-rich learning environments.* Paper presented at the ACEC2008. Canberra, Australia.

Reeves, B., & Nass, C. (2006). *The media equation.* Cambridge, UK: Cambridge University Press.

Regenbrecht, H., Schubert, T., & Friedman, F. (1998). Measuring sense of presence and its relation to fear of heights in virtual environments. *International Journal of Human-Computer Interaction, 10,* 233–249. doi:10.1207/s15327590ijhc1003_2

Reich, K. (2005). *Systemisch-konstruktivistische Pädagogik* (5th ed.). Weinheim, Germany: Beltz.

Reiner, B., & Siegel, E. (2008). The potential for gaming techniques in radiology education and practice. *Journal of the American College of Radiology, 5*(2), 110–114. doi:10.1016/j.jacr.2007.09.002

Reinkensmeyer, D., & Boninger, M. (2012). Technologies and combination therapies for enhancing movement training for people with a disability. *Journal of Neuroengineering and Rehabilitation, 9,* 17. doi:10.1186/1743-0003-9-17

Re-Mission. (2009). *A game for young people with cancer.* Retrieved 26 jan 2011 from http://www.re-mission.net/

Renaud, P., Chartier, S., Albert, G., Décarie, J., Cournoyer, L.-G., & Bouchard, S. (2007). Presence as determined by fractal perceptual-motor dynamics. *Cyberpsychology & Behavior, 10,* 122–130. doi:10.1089/cpb.2006.9983

Reuter, C., Wendel, V., Göbel, S., & Steinmetz, R. (2012). Multiplayer adventures for collaborative learning with serious games. In *Proceedings of the 6th European Conference on Games Based Learning,* (pp. 416–423). Reading, UK: Academic Conferences International.

Reuter, C., Wendel, V., Göbel, S., & Steinmetz, R. (2012). Towards puzzle templates for multiplayer adventures. In S. Göbel, W. Müller, B. Urban, & J. Wiemeyer (Eds.), *3rd International Conference on Serious Games for Training, Education and Health,* (pp. 161–163). Berlin, Germany: Springer.

Reynolds, C. W. (1999). Steering behaviors for autonomous characters. In *Proceedings of Game Developers Conference 1999,* (pp. 763–782). San Francisco, CA: Miller Freeman Game Group.

Rice, J. (2007). New media resistance: Barriers to implementation of computer video games in the classroom. *Journal of Educational Multimedia and Hypermedia, 16,* 249–261.

Rickel, J., & Johnson, W. L. (1998). STEVE: A pedagogical agent for virtual reality. In K.P. Sycara & M. Wooldridge (Eds.), *Proceedings of the Second International Conference on Autonomous Agents (AGENTS '98).* New York, NY: ACM.

Rieber, L. R. (1992). Computer-based microworlds: A bridge between constructivism and direct instruction. *Educational Technology Research and Development, 40*(1), 93–106. doi:10.1007/BF02296709

Ritterfeld, U., Cody, M., & Vorderer, P. (2009). *Serious games: Mechanisms and effects.* New York, NY: Routledge.

Ritterfeld, U., & Weber, R. (2006). Video games for entertainment and education. In Vorderer, P., & Bryant, J. (Eds.), *Playing Video Games: Motives, Responses and Consequences* (pp. 399–413). Mahwah, NJ: Lawrence Erlbaum.

Ritter, S., Anderson, J. R., Koedinger, K. R., & Corbett, A. (2007). Cognitive tutor: Applied research in mathematics education. *Psychonomic Bulletin & Review, 14*(2), 249–255. doi:10.3758/BF03194060

Rizzo, A. A., Graap, K., Perlman, K., McLay, R. N., Rothbaum, B. O., & Reger, G. (2008). Virtual Iraq: Initial results from a VR exposure therapy application for combat-related PTSD. *Studies in Health Technology and Informatics, 132,* 420–425.

Robillard, G., Bouchard, S., Fournier, T., & Renaud, P. (2003). Anxiety and presence during VR immersion: A comparative study of the reactions of phobic and non-phobic participants in therapeutic virtual environments derived from computer games. *Cyberpsychology & Behavior, 6,* 467–476. doi:10.1089/109493103769710497

Rollings, A., & Adams, E. (2003). *Andrew Rollings and Ernest Adams on game design.* Berkeley, CA: New Riders Games.

Rooney, P., O'Rourke, K., Burke, G., MacNamee, B., & Igbrude, C. (2009). Cross-disciplinary approaches for developing serious games. In *Proceedings of IEEE VS-Games'09.* IEEE.

Roschelle, J., & Teasley, S. (1995). The construction of shared knowledge in collaborative problem solving. In O'Malley, C. (Ed.), *Computer-Supported Collaborative Learning* (pp. 69–97). Berlin, Germany: Springer-Verlag. doi:10.1007/978-3-642-85098-1_5

Rosen, G. M., & Davison, G. C. (2001). Echo attributions and other risks when publishing on novel therapies without peer review. *Journal of Clinical Psychology, 57*(10), 1245–1250. doi:10.1002/jclp.1092

Rotter, J. (1966). Generalized expectancies for internal versus external locus of reinforcement. *Psychological Monographs, 33,* 300–303.

Ruppert, B. (2011). New directions in virtual environments and gaming to address obesity and diabetes: Industry perspective. *Journal of Diabetes Science and Technology, 5*(2), 277–282.

Russell, V. J., Ainley, M., & Frydenberg, E. (2005). Schooling issues digest: Student motivation and engagement. Retrieved March 9, 2009, from http://www.dest.gov.au/sectors/school_education/publications_resources/schooling_issues_digest/schooling_issues_digest_motivation_engagement.htm

Sander, F. N. (2008). *Linear interactive storytelling.* (Master's Thesis). Stuttgart Media University. Stuttgart, Germany.

Sandford, R., Ulicsak, M., Facer, K., & Rudd, T. (2006). *Teaching with games: Using commercial off-the-shelf computer games in formal education.* Bistrol, UK: Futurelab.

Sas, C., & O'Hare, G. (2003). Presence equation: A investigation into cognitive factors underlying presence. *Presence (Cambridge, Mass.), 12,* 523–537. doi:10.1162/105474603322761315

Sawyer, B. (2007). *The "serious games" landscape.* Paper presented at the Instructional & Research Technology Symposium for Arts, Humanities and Social Sciences. Camden, MA.

Sawyer, B., & Smith, P. (2008). *Serious games taxonomy.* Paper presented at the Game Developers Conference 2008. Retrieved from http://www.dmill.com/presentations/serious-games-taxonomy-2008.pdf

Schaar, A., & Ziefle, M. (2011). What determines the public perception of implantable medical technology: Insights in cognitive and affective factors. In Holzinger, H., & Simonic, K.-M. (Eds.), *Human-Computer Interaction: Information Quality in eHealth* (pp. 513–532). Berlin, Germany: Springer. doi:10.1007/978-3-642-25364-5_36

Schanda, F. (1995). *Computer-lernprogramme.* Weinheim, Germany: Beltz.

Schaumburg, H. (2002). Besseres lernen durch computer in der schule? Nutzungsbeispiele und einsatzbedingungen. [Improved learning in school? Examples of utilisation and application.] In Issing, L., & Klimsa, P. (Eds.), *Information und Lernen mit Multimedia* [Information and learning with multimedia]. (pp. 335–344). Weinheim, Germany: PVU.

Schiefele, U., & Pekrun, R. (1996). Psychologische modelle des fremdgesteuerten und selbstgesteuerten lernens. In Weinert, F. E. (Ed.), *Psychologie des Lernens und der Instruktion* (pp. 249–278). Göttingen, Germany: Hogrefe.

Schiesel, S. (2008). Face to face - A council of eve online gamers. *New York Times.* Retrieved from http://www.nytimes.com/2008/06/28/arts/television/28eve.html?_r=1&ref=arts&pagewanted=all

Schleicher, A. (1999). *Measuring student knowledge and skills: A new framework for assessment.* Organization for Economic.

Schmidt, R. A., & Wrisberg, C. A. (2008). *Motor learning and performance: A situation-based approach* (4th ed.). Champaign, IL: Human Kinetics.

Schöllhorn, W. I., Beckmann, H., & Davids, K. (2010). Exploiting system fluctuations: Differential training in physical prevention and rehabilitation programs for health and exercise. *Medicina, 46*(6), 365–373.

Schöllhorn, W. I., Beckmann, H., Janssen, D., & Drepper, J. (2010). Stochastic perturbations in athletics field events enhance skill acquisition. In Renshaw, I., Davids, K., & Savelsbergh, G. J. P. (Eds.), *Motor Learning in Practice: A Constraints-Led Approach* (pp. 69–82). London, UK: Routledge.

Schönauer, C., Pintaric, T., & Kaufmann, H. (2011). Full body interaction for serious games in motor rehabilitation. In *Proceedings of the 2nd Augmented Human International Conference.* New York, NY: ACM.

Schrader, P. G., & Lawless, K. A. (2011). Research on immersive environments and 21st century skills: An introduction to the special issue. *Journal of Educational Computing Research, 44*(4), 385–390. doi:10.2190/EC.44.4.a

Schroeder, R., & Bailenson, J. (2008). Research uses of multi-user virtual environments. In Fielding, N., Lee, R. M., & Blank, G. (Eds.), *The SAGE Handbook of Online Research Methods.* Thousand Oaks, CA: SAGE. doi:10.4135/9780857020055.n18

Schubert, T., Friedmann, F., & Regenbrecht, H. (2001). The experience of presence: factor analytic insights. *Presence (Cambridge, Mass.), 10,* 266–281. doi:10.1162/105474601300343603

Schuemi, T., Bruynzeel, M., Drost, L., Brinckman, M., de Haan, G., Emmelkamp, P., et al. (2000). Treatment of acrophobia in virtual reality: A pilot study. In F. Broeckx & L. Pauwels (Eds.), *Conference Proceedings Euromedia 2000,* (pp. 271-275). Antwerp, Belgium: Euromedia.

Schulmeister, R. (2003). Taxonomy of multimedia component interactivity: A contribution to the current metadata debate. *Studies in Communication Sciences, 3*(3), 61–80.

Schutt, S., & Martino, J. (2008). *Virtual worlds as an architecture of learning.* Retrieved from http://www.ascilite.org.au/conferences/melbourne08/procs/schutt-poster.pdf

Schwan, S., & Buder, J. (2002). Lernen und wissenserwerb in virtuellen realitäten. In Bente, G., Krämer, N. C., & Petersen, A. (Eds.), *Virtuelle Realitäten* (pp. 109–132). Göttingen, Germany: Hogrefe.

Schwarz-Woelzl, M. (2012). *Older people, social networks, online social network platforms – Mythe and practice*. Paper presented at IFA 11th Global Conference on Aging. Prague, Czech Republic.

Shane, M. D., Pettitt, B. J., Morgenthal, C. B., & Smith, C. D. (2008). Should surgical novices trade their retractors for joysticks? Videogame experience decreases the time needed to acquire surgical skills. *Surgical Endoscopy, 22*, 1294–1297. doi:10.1007/s00464-007-9614-0

Shannon, C. E., & Weaver, W. (1949). *The mathematical theory of communication*. Champaign, IL: University of Illinois Press.

Shea, C. B., Lai, Q., Black, C., & Park, J.-H. (2000). Spacing practice session across days benefits the learning of motor skills. *Human Movement Science, 19*, 737–760. doi:10.1016/S0167-9457(00)00021-X

Shen, C., Wang, H., & Ritterfeld, U. (2009). Serious games and seriously fun games. In Ritterfeld, U., Cody, M., & Vorderer, P. (Eds.), *Serious Games: Mechanisms and Effects*. New York, NY: Routledge.

Sheridan, T. (1992). Musings on telepresence and virtual presence. *Presence (Cambridge, Mass.), 1*, 120–125.

Sheridan, T. B. (2002). *Humans and automation: System design and research issues*. Hoboken, NJ: Wiley.

Sherry, J. (2001). The effects of violent video games on aggression: A meta-analysis. *Human Communication Research, 27*, 409–431.

Sherry, J. L., & Dibble, J. L. (2009). The impact of serious games on childhood development. In Ritterfeld, U., Cody, M., & Vorderer, P. (Eds.), *Serious Games: Mechanisms and Effects* (pp. 145–166). New York, NY: Routledge.

Sherry, J. L., Lucas, K., Greenberg, B. S., & Lachlan, K. (2006). Video game uses and gratifications as predicators of use and game preference. In Vorderer, P., Bryant, J., Vorderer, P., & Bryant, J. (Eds.), *Playing Video Games: Motives, Responses, and Consequences* (pp. 213–224). Hoboken, NJ: Lawrence Erlbaum.

Sherwin, J. (2007). Get a (second) life. *APS Observer, 20*(6). Retrieved October 2012 from http://www.psychologicalscience.org/index.php/publications/observer/2007/june-july-07/get-a-second-life.html

Shute, V. J., Ventura, M., Bauer, M., & Zapata-Rivera, D. (2009). Melding the power of serious games and embedded assessment to monitor and foster learning: Flow and grow. In Ritterfeld, U., Cody, M., & Vorderer, P. (Eds.), *Serious Games: Mechanisms and Effects* (pp. 295–321). New York, NY: Routledge.

Siemens, G. (2004). Connectivism: A learning theory for the digital age. *elearnspace everything elearning*. Retrieved April 24, 2009, from http://www.elearnspace.org/Articles/connectivism.htm

Siemens, G. (2008). *Connectivisim: networked learning*. Retrieved from http://www.connectivism.ca/

Silveira, S. A. (2009). Game-ativismo e a nova esfera pública interconectada. *Líbero, 12*(24), 131 138.

Silvern, S. B., & Williamson, P. A. (1987). The effects of video game play on young children's aggression, fantasy and prosocial behavior. *Journal of Applied Developmental Psychology, 8*, 453–462. doi:10.1016/0193-3973(87)90033-5

Simergency. (2006). *Website*. Retrieved from http://simergency.stanford.edu/

Simmons, J. P., Nelson, L. D., & Simonsohn, U. (2011). False-positive psychology: Undisclosed flexibility in data collection and analysis allows presenting anything as significant. *Psychological Science, 22*(11), 1359–1366. doi:10.1177/0956797611417632

Singhal, A., & Rogers, E. M. (1999). *Entertainment education: A communication strategy for social change*. Mahwah, NJ: Lawrence Erlbaum.

Slater, M., Linakis, V., Usoh, M., & Kooper, R. (1996). *Immersion, presence and performance in virtual environments: An experiment with tri-dimensional chess*. Paper presented at the 1996 Virtual Reality and Software and Technology Conference. Hong Kong, Hong Kong.

Slater, M., Steed, A., & Usoh, M. (1993). The virtual treadmill: A naturalistic metaphor for navigation in immersive virtual environments. In M. Goebel (Ed.), *First Eurographic Workshop on Virtual Reality Environments*, (p. 71-83). Barcelona, Spain: IEEE.

Slater, M. (1999). Measuring presence: A response to the Witmer and Singer presence questionnaire. *Presence (Cambridge, Mass.)*, *3*, 130–144.

Slater, M. (2004). How colorful was your day? Why questionnaires cannot assess presence in virtual environments. *Presence (Cambridge, Mass.)*, *13*, 484–493. doi:10.1162/1054746041944849

Slater, M., Usoh, M., & Chrysanthou, Y. (1995). The influence of dynamic shadows on presence in immersive virtual environments. In Goebel, M. (Ed.), *Virtual Environments* (pp. 8–21). New York, NY: Springer Computer Science. doi:10.1007/978-3-7091-9433-1_2

Slater, M., Usoh, M., & Steed, A. (1994). Depth of presence in virtual environments. *Presence (Cambridge, Mass.)*, *6*, 130–144.

Slater, M., & Wilbur, S. (1997). A framework for immersive virtual environments (five): Speculations on the role of presence in virtual environments. *Presence (Cambridge, Mass.)*, *6*, 603–616.

Snow, D. (2001). *collective identity and expressive forms*. Retrieved from www.democracywww.csd.bg

Sohnsmeyer, J. (2011). *Virtuelles spiel und realer sport – Über transferpotenziale digitaler sportspiele am beispiel von tischtennis* [Virtual games and real sport – About the transfer potentials of sport games using the example of table tennis]. Hamburg, Germany: Czwalina.

Sohnsmeyer, J., Gilbrich, H., & Weisser, B. (2010). Effect of a six-week-intervention with an activity-promoting video game on isometric muscle strength in elderly subjects. *International Journal of Computer Science in Sport*, *9*(3), 75–79.

Sports, E. A. (2011). *Fifa 2012*. Retrieved from http://www.ea.com/soccer/fifa12

Squire, K. (2003). Video games in education. *International Journal of Intelligent Simulations and Gaming*, *2*(1).

Squire, K. D. (2006). From content to context: Videogames as designed experience. *Educational Researcher*, *35*, 19–29. doi:10.3102/0013189X035008019

Stahl, G., Koschmann, T., & Suthers, D. (2006). *Cambridge handbook of the learning sciences*. Cambridge, UK: Cambridge University Press.

Staiano, A., Abraham, A., & Calvert, S. (2012). The WII club: Promoting weight loss, psychosocial health, and sports involvement through an exergaming intervention for overweight and obese youth. *The Journal of Adolescent Health*, *50*(2), S9–S10. doi:10.1016/j.jadohealth.2011.10.038

Steigman, I. (2011). *A virtual way to go clean*. Retrieved from http://www.nbcbayarea.com/news/local/A-Virtual-Way-To-Go-Clean-122980713.html

Steinkuehler, C. A. (2013). Cognition and literacy in massively multiplayer online games. In Leu, D., Coiro, J., Lankshear, C., & Knobel, K. (Eds.), *Handbook of Research on New Literacies*. Mahwah, NJ: Erlbaum.

Steinkuehler, C., & Duncan, S. (2008). Scientific habits of mind in virtual worlds. *Journal of Science Education and Technology*. doi:10.1007/s10956-008-9120-8

Steinkuehler, C., & Williams, D. (2006). Where everybody knows your (screen) name: Online games as "third places". *Journal of Computer-Mediated Communication*, *11*(4). doi:10.1111/j.1083-6101.2006.00300.x

Stenberg, L. (2012). *Attitudes to and usage of technology among the elderly in Finland*. Paper presented at IFA 11th Global Conference on Aging. Prague, Czech Republic.

Stepanyan, K., Mather, R., Jones, H., & Lusuardi, C. (2009). Student engagement with peer assessment: A review of pedagogical design and technologies. In *Proceedings of the Advances in Web Based Learning–ICWL 2009*, (pp. 367–375). ICWL. doi:10.1007/978-3-642-03426-8_44

Sternberg, R. J., & Grigorenko, E. L. (1997). Are cognitive styles still in style? *The American Psychologist*, *52*(7), 700–712. doi:10.1037/0003-066X.52.7.700

Steuer, J. (1992). Defining virtual reality: Dimensions determining telepresence. *The Journal of Communication*, *42*(4), 73–93. doi:10.1111/j.1460-2466.1992.tb00812.x

Stolovitch, H. D., & Thiagarajan, S. (1980). *Frame games*. Englewood Cliffs, NJ: Educational Technology Publications.

Sutcliffe, A. G., & Mehandjiev, N. (2004). End user development. *Communications of the ACM*, *47*(49), 33–37.

Swales, J. M. (1990). *Genre analysis*. Cambridge, UK: Cambridge University Press.

Swartjes, I., & Theune, M. (2006). A fabula model for emergent narrative. In S. Göbel, R. Malkewitz, & I. Iurgel (Eds.), *Technologies for Interactive Digital Storytelling and Entertainment, Third International Conference, TIDSE 2006,* (pp. 49–60). Berlin, Germany: Springer.

Sweetser, P. (2005). *An emergent approach to game design – Development and play.* (Dissertation). University of Queensland. Brisbane, Australia.

Syvertsen, A. K., Flanagan, C. A., & Stout, M. D. (2009). Code of silence: Students' perception of school climate and willingness to intervene in a peer's dangerous plan. *Journal of Educational Psychology, 101,* 219–232. doi:10.1037/a0013246

Szilas, N. (1999). *Interactive drama on computer: Beyond linear narrative.* Paper presented at AAAI 1999 Fall Symposium on Narrative Intelligence. Cape Cod, MA.

Tateru, N. (2012). *Second life statistical charts.* Retrieved May 25, 2012, from http://dwellonit.taterunino.net/sl-statistical-charts/

Taylor, D. (2011). *Website.* Retrieved from http://knowledgecast.wordpress.com/

Tellegen, A., & Atkinson, G. (1974). Openness to absorption and self-altering experiences ("absorption"), a trait related to hypnotic susceptibility. *Journal of Abnormal Psychology, 83,* 267–277. doi:10.1037/h0036681

Therasim. (2012). *Website.* Retrieved from http://therasim.com/about/

There. (2012). *Wikipedia.* Retrieved from http://en.wikipedia.org/wiki/There_28virtual_world29

Thornson, C., Goldiez, B., & Le, H. (2009). Predicting presence: Constructing a tendency towards presence inventory. *International Journal of Human-Computer Studies, 67,* 62–78. doi:10.1016/j.ijhcs.2008.08.006

Thue, D., & Bulitko, V. (2008). PaSSAGE: A demonstration of player modeling in interactive storytelling. In *Proceedings of the Fourth Artificial Intelligence and Interactive Digital Entertainment Conference,* (pp. 226–227). IEEE.

Thuringian Ministry of Education, Research and Culture. (2008). *Framework agreement to promote media literacy in the free state of Thuringia.* Retrieved February 13, 2011, from http://www.thueringen.de/imperia/md/content/tkm/schuleonline2/rahmenvereinbarung_tkm_mit_tlm_medienkompetenzentwicklung.pdf

Tielemann, N., Raab, M., & Arnold, A. (2008). Effekte von instruktionen auf motorische lernprozesse: Lernen durch analogien oder bewegungsregeln? [Effects of instructions on motor learning: Learning by analogies or movement rules?]. *Zeitschrift für Sportpsychologie, 15*(4), 118–128. doi:10.1026/1612-5010.15.4.118

Tomasello, M. (2003). The key is social cognition. In Gentner, D., & Goldin-Meadow, S. (Eds.), *Language in Mind: Advances in the Study of Language and Thought* (pp. 47–57). Cambridge, MA: MIT Press.

Tore, S., di D'Elia, F., Aiello, P., Carlomagno, N., & Sibilio, M. (2012). Didactics, movement and technology: New frontiers of the human-machine interaction. *Journal of Human Sport & Exercise, 7*(1), S178–S183. doi:10.4100/jhse.2012.7.Proc1.20

Toro-Troconis, M. (2008). Designing game-based learning activities for virtual patients in second life. *Journal of Cyber Therapy & Rehabilitation, 1*(3), 225–238.

Torrente, J., Blanco, Á. D., Cañizal, G., Moreno-Ger, P., & Fernandéz-Manjón, B. (2008). <e-Adventure3D>: An open source authoring environment for 3D adventure games in education. In *Proceedings of the 2008 International Conference on Advances in Computer Entertainment Technology,* (pp. 191-194). New York, NY: ACM.

Tourangeau, R., & Smith, T. W. (1996). Asking sensitive questions: The impact of data collection mode, question format and question context. *Public Opinion Quarterly, 60,* 275–304. doi:10.1086/297751

Tourangeau, R., & Yan, T. (2007). Sensitive questions in surveys. *Psychological Bulletin, 133*(5), 859–883. doi:10.1037/0033-2909.133.5.859

Trogemann, G. (2002). Augmenting human creativity: Virtuelle realitäten als design-aufgabe. In Bente, G., Krämer, N. C., & Petersen, A. (Eds.), *Virtuelle Realitäten* (pp. 275–297). Göttingen, Germany: Hogrefe.

TryScience. (2008). *PowerUP: Background information of the game*. Retrieved from http://www.powerupthegame. org

Turkaya, S., & Adinolf, S. (2010). Free to be me: A survey study on customization with World of Warcraft and City of Heroes/Villains players. *Procedia Social and Behavioral Sciences*, 1840-1845. doi: 10.1016/j.sbspro.2010.03.995

Turkle, S. (1995). *Life on the screen: Identity in the age of the internet*. New York, NY: Simon & Schuster.

Turner, C. F., Forsyth, B. H., O'Reilly, J. M., Cooley, P. C., Smith, T. K., Rogers, S. M., & Miller, H. G. (1998). Automated self-interviewing and the survey measurement of sensitive behaviors. In Couper, M. P., Baker, R. P., Bethlehem, J., Clark, C. Z. F., Martin, J., Nichols, W. L. II, & O'Reilly, J. M. (Eds.), *Computer Assisted Survey Information Collection* (pp. 455–474). New York, NY: Wiley and Sons.

Tychsen, A., Hitchens, M., Brolund, T., & Kavakli, M. (2005). The game master. In *Proceedings of the Second Australasian Conference on Interactive Entertainment*, (pp. 215–222). IEEE.

UDK. (2012). *Unreal engine*. Retrieved 28 Sep 2012, from http://www.unrealengine.com/udk/

UN. (2005). *Food force: The first humanitarian video game*. Retrieved 29 jun 2012, from http://www.wfp.org/ how-to-help/individuals/food-force

UNC School of Pharmacy. (2012). *Website*. Retrieved from http://www.pharmacy.unc.edu/news/features/using-second-life-to-help-students-in-real-life

United Nations World Food Program. (2008). *Food force*. Retrieved 10/7/08 from http://www.food-force.com/

United Nations. (2011). *World population prospects*. Retrieved from http://esa.un.org/unpd/wpp/Documenta-tion/pdf/WPP2010_Press_Release.pdf

Unity3D. (2012). *Website*. Retrieved 29 Sep 2012, from http://unity3d.com/

University of Arkansas. (2012). *Everything is alive project*. Retrieved from http://vw.ddns.uark.edu/index. php?page=docs

University of Kansas. (2012). *Website*. Retrieved from http://www.spencerart.ku.edu/exhibitions/secondlife. shtml

University of Southern California. (2007). Triangulation. *Institute for Global Health: Triangulation*. Retrieved July 31, 2008, from http://www.igh.org/triangulation/

Usoh, M., Catena, E., Arman, S., & Slater, M. (2000). Using presence questionnaires in reality. *Presence (Cambridge, Mass.)*, *9*, 497–503. doi:10.1162/105474600566989

Van Den Broek, G., Cavallo, F., & Wehrmann, C. (2010). *AALIANCE ambient assisted living roadmap*. Amsterdam, The Netherlands: IOS Press.

van Tilburg, T., & de Jong-Gierveld, J. (2007). *Zicht op eenzaamheid: Achtergronden, oorzaken en aanpak*. Amsterdam, The Netherlands: Vrije Universiteit Press.

van Wijk, F., Knox, D., Dodds, C., Cassidy, G., Alexander, G., & MacDonald, R. (2011). Making music after stroke: Using musical activities to enhance arm function. *Annals of the New York Academy of Sciences*, *1252*, 305–311. doi:10.1111/j.1749-6632.2011.06403.x

VanDeventer, S., & White, J. (2002). Expert behavior in children's video game play. *Simulation & Gaming*, *33*(1), 28–48. doi:10.1177/1046878102033001002

Venkatesh, V. (2000). Determinants of perceived ease of use: Integrating control, intrinsic motivation, and emotion into the technology acceptance model. *Information Systems Research*, *11*, 342–365. doi:10.1287/ isre.11.4.342.11872

Venkatesh, V., & Davis, F. (2012). A theoretical extension of the technology acceptance model: Four longitudinal field studies. *Management Science*, *46*, 186–204. doi:10.1287/mnsc.46.2.186.11926

Vernadakis, N., Gioftsidou, A., Antoniou, P., Ioannidis, D., & Giannousi, M. (2012). The impact of Nintendo Wii to physical education students' balance compared to the traditional approaches. *Computers & Education*, *59*, 196–205. doi:10.1016/j.compedu.2012.01.003

Verón, E. (1980). *A produção do sentido*. São Paulo, Brazil: Cultrix/USP.

Victora, C. G., Aquino, E. M. L., do Carmo Leal, M., Monteiro, C. A., Barros, F. C., & Szwarcwald, C. L. (2011). Maternal and child health in Brazil: Progress and challenges. *Lancet*, *377*(9780), 1863–1876. doi:10.1016/ S0140-6736(11)60138-4

Victora, C. G., Barreto, M. L., do Carmo Leal, M., Monteiro, C. A., Schmidt, M. I., & Paim, J. (2011). Health conditions and health-policy innovations in Brazil: The way forward. *Lancet, 377*(9782), 2042–2053. doi:10.1016/S0140-6736(11)60055-X

Virtual Heroes. (2012). *Website.* Retrieved from http://virtualheroes.com/projects/3diteams

Virtual Medical Centre. (2012). *Wikipedia.* Retrieved from http://en.wikipedia.org/wiki/Virtual_Medical_Centre

Virtually Better. (2012). *Website.* Retrieved from http://www.virtuallybetter.com/portfolio/virtual-iraq-intense/

Vogler, C. (1992). *The writer's journey: Mythic structures for storytellers and screenwriters.* New York, NY: M. Wiese Productions.

von Salisch, M., Vogelgesang, J., Kristen, A., & Oppl, C. (2011). Preference for violent electronic games and aggressive behavior among children: The beginning of the downward spiral? *Media Psychology, 14*(3), 233–258. doi:10.1080/15213269.2011.596468

Voulgari, I., & Komis, V. (2008). Massively multi-user online games: The emergence of effective collaborative activities for learning. In *Proceedings of the 2008 Second IEEE International Conference on Digital Game and Intelligent Toy Enhanced Learning,* (pp. 132–134). IEEE Computer Society. doi:http://dx.doi.org/10.1109/DIGITEL.2008.20

Walber, M. (2007). *Selbststeuerung im lernprozess und erkenntniskonstruktion: Eine empirische studie in der weiterbildung.* Münster, Germany: Waxmann.

Wallach, H., Safir, M., & Samana, R. (2010). Personality variables and presence. *Virtual Reality (Waltham Cross), 14*, 3–13. doi:10.1007/s10055-009-0124-3

Wallin, C.-J., Meurling, L., Hedman, L., & Hedegard, J., & Fellander-Tsai, Li. (2007). Target-focused medical emergency team training using a human patient simulator: Effects on behaviour and attitude. *Medical Education, 41*, 173–180. doi:10.1111/j.1365-2929.2006.02670.x

Wang, A. Y., Newlin, M. H., & Tucker, T. L. (2001). A discourse analysis of on-line classroom chats: Predictors of cyber-student performance. *Teaching of Psychology, 28*, 222–226. doi:10.1207/S15328023TOP2803_09

Wang, H., Shen, C., & Ritterfeld, U. (2009). Enjoyment in games. In Ritterfeld, U., Cody, M., & Vorderer, P. (Eds.), *Serious Games: Mechanisms and Effects* (pp. 25–47). Mahwah, NJ: Routledge/LEA.

Weibel, D., & Wissmath, B. (2011). Immersion in computer games: The role of spatial presence and flow. *International Journal of Computer Games Technology.* Retrieved from http://www.hindawi.com/journals/ijcgt/2011/282345/

Weibel, D., Wissmath, B., & Mast, F. (2010). Immersion in mediated environments: The role of personality traits. *Cyberpsychology, Behavior, and Social Networking, 13*, 251–256. doi:10.1089/cyber.2009.0171

Weibel, D., Wissmath, B., & Stricker, D. (2011). The influence of neuroticism on spatial presence and enjoyment in films. *Personality and Individual Differences, 51*, 866–869. doi:10.1016/j.paid.2011.07.011

Weicht, M., Maciuszek, D., & Martens, A. (2012). Designing virtual experiments in the context of marine sciences. In *Proceedings of the 2012 12th IEEE International Conference on Advanced Learning Technologies (ICALT 2012), Workshop Go-Lab.* Rome, Italy: ICALT.

Welch, R., Blackman, T., Liu, A., Mellers, B., & Stark, L. (1996). The effects of pictorial realism, delay of visual feedback and observer interactivity on the subjective sense of presence. *Presence (Cambridge, Mass.), 5*, 263–273.

Wellman, B. (2001). Computer networks as social networks. *Science, 293*, 2031–2034. doi:10.1126/science.1065547

Wendel, V., Göbel, S., & Steinmetz, R. (2011). Seamless learning in serious games - How to improve seamless learning-content integration in serious games. In *Proceedings of the CSEDU 2011,* (vol. 1, pp. 219-224). SciTePress - Science and Technology Publications.

Wendel, V., Gutjahr, M., Göbel, S., & Steinmetz, R. (2012). Designing collaborative multiplayer serious games for collaborative learning. In *Proceedings of the CSEDU 2012.* CSEDU.

Wendel, V., Babarinow, M., Hörl, T., Kolmogorov, S., Göbel, S., & Steinmetz, R. (2010). *Transactions on edutainment IV.* Springer.

Wendel, V., Göbel, S., & Steinmetz, R. (2012). Game mastering in collaborative multiplayer serious games. In Göbel, S., Müller, W., Urban, B., & Wiemeyer, J. (Eds.), *E-Learning and Games for Training, Education, Health and Sports* (pp. 23–34). Berlin, Germany: Springer. doi:10.1007/978-3-642-33466-5_3

Weninger, E. (2010). *KonsuManiac: Didaktische materialien zum online-tool konsumaniac.at*. Wien, Austria: Forum Umweltbildung.

Wertham, F., & Legman, G. (1948). The psychopathology of comic books. *American Journal of Psychotherapy*, *2*(3), 472–490.

Wertsch, J. V., & Sohmer, R. (1995). Vygotsky on learning and development. *Human Development*, (38): 332–337. doi:10.1159/000278339

Wesener, S. (2004). *Spielen in virtuellen welten: Eine untersuchung von transferprozessen in bildschirmspielen*. Wiesbaden, Germany: VS-Verlag. doi:10.1007/978-3-322-80655-0

Westera, W., & Wagemans, L. (2007). Help me! Online learner support through the self- organised allocation of peer tutors. *Abstracts of the 13th International Conference on Technology Supported Learning & Training*, (pp. 105–107). Berlin, Germany: ICEW GmbH. Retrieved from http://hdl.handle.net/1820/2075

Westera, W., Nadolski, R. J., Hummel, H. G. K., & Wopereis, I. G. J. H. (2008). Serious games for higher education: A framework for reducing design complexity. *Journal of Computer Assisted Learning*, *24*(5), 420–432. doi:10.1111/j.1365-2729.2008.00279.x

WGLN. (2005). *Website*. Retrieved from http://wgln.stanford.edu/projects/2005-2006.html

Whitehead, A., Johnston, H., Nixon, N., & Welch, C. (2010). *Exergame effectiveness: What the numbers can tell us*. New York, NY: Academic Press. doi:10.1145/1836135.1836144

Whyville. (2009). Whyville demographics. *Whyville. Net*. Retrieved from http://b.whyville.net/smmk/top/gatesInfo?topic=pdf_library

Wiecha, J., Heyden, R., Sternthal, E., & Merialdi, M. (2010). Learning in a virtual world: Experience with using second life for medical education. *Journal of Medical Internet Research*, *12*(1), e1. doi:10.2196/jmir.1337

Wiederhold, B., Davis, R., & Wiederhold, M. (1998). The effects of immersiveness on physiology. In Riva, G., Wiederhold, B., & Molinari, E. (Eds.), *Virtual Environments in Clinical Psychology and Neuroscience*. Amsterdam, The Netherlands: IOS Press.

Wiemeyer, J. (2004). Beyond representation and self-organisation: What is required in motor control and learning? In M. Bugdol, M. Kapica, & J. Pospiech (Eds.), *Pogranicza Edukacji*, (S.320-328). Raciborz: Scriba.

Wiemeyer, J. (2003). Function as constitutive feature of movements in sport. *International Journal of Computer Science in Sport*, *2*(2), 113–115.

Wiemeyer, J., & Kliem, A. (2012). Serious games and ageing - A new panacea? *European Review of Aging and Physical Activity*, *9*(1), 41–50. doi:10.1007/s11556-011-0093-x

Wikipedia. (2012). *Poetics*. Retrieved May 2, 2012, from http://en.wikipedia.org/wiki/Poetics_(Aristotle)

Williams, D., Caplan, S., & Xiong, L. (2007). Can you hear me now? The impact of voice in an online gaming community. *Human Communication Research*, *33*, 427–449. doi:10.1111/j.1468-2958.2007.00306.x

Williams, D., Yee, N., & Caplan, S. E. (2008). Who plays, how much, and why? Debunking the stereotypical gamer profile. *Journal of Computer-Mediated Communication*, *13*(4), 993–1018. doi:10.1111/j.1083-6101.2008.00428.x

Wilson, K. A., Bedwell, W. L., Lazzara, E. H., Salas, E., Burke, C. S., & Estock, J. L. (2009). Relationships between game attributes and learning outcomes: Review and research proposals. *Simulation & Gaming*, *40*(2), 217–266. doi:10.1177/1046878108321866

Winny, S. (2011). *Anti games*. Retrieved from http://www.winnyswelt.de/2011/06/anti-games/

Winteler, A. (2004). *Professionell lehren und lernen: Ein praxisbuch*. Darmstadt, Germany: Wissenschaftliche Buchgesellschaft.

Wirth, W., Hartmann, T., Bocking, S., Vorderer, P., Klimmt, C., & Holger, S. (2007). A process model for the formation of spatial presence experiences. *Media Psychology, 9*, 493–525. doi:10.1080/15213260701283079

Wissmath, B., Weibel, D., & Groner, R. (2009). Dubbing or subtitling? Effects on spatial presence, transportation, flow, and enjoyment. *Journal of Media Psychology, 21*(3), 114–125. doi:10.1027/1864-1105.21.3.114

Witmer, B., & Singer, M. (1998). Measuring presence in virtual environments: A presence questionnaire. *Presence (Cambridge, Mass.), 7*, 225–240. doi:10.1162/105474698565686

Wood, D., & Hopkins, L. (2008). 3D virtual environments: Businesses are ready but are our 'digital natives' prepared for changing landscapes? In *Proceedings Ascilite Melbourne 2008,* (pp. 1136–1146). Retrieved from http://www.ascilite.org.au/conferences/melbourne08/procs/wood-2.pdf

Woolley, J., & Van Reet, J. (2006). Effects of context on judgments concerning the reality status of novel entities. *Child Development, 77*, 1778–1793. doi:10.1111/j.1467-8624.2006.00973.x

World Health Organization. (1986). *The Ottawa charter for health promotion.* Ottawa, Canada: World Health Organization.

Wouters, P., van Oostendorp, H., & van der Spek, E. D. (2010). Game design: The mapping of cognitive task analysis and game discourse analysis in creating effective and entertaining serious games. In M. Neerincx & W.-P. Brinkman (Eds.), *Proceedings of the 28th Annual European Conference on Cognitive Ergonomics (ECCE 2010),* (pp. 287–293). New York, NY: ACM.

Wright, T., Boria, E., & Breidenbach, P. (2002). Creative player actions in FPS online video games. *The International Journal of Computer Game Research, 2.* Retrieved from http://www.gamestudies.org/0202/wright/

Wulf, G. (2007). *Attention and motor skill learning.* Champaign, IL: Human Kinetics.

Xanthopoulou, D., & Papagiannidis, S. (2012). Play online, work better? Examining the spillover of active learning and transformational leadership. *Technological Forecasting and Social Change, 79*(7), 1328–1339. doi:10.1016/j.techfore.2012.03.006

Yale. (2009). *Video game to help urban teens avoid HIV infection focus of nearly $4 million grant to Yale.* Retrieved from http://news.yale.edu/2009/09/24/video-game-help-urban-teens-avoid-hiv-infection-focus-nearly-4-million-grant-yale

Yannakakis, G. N., & Maragoudakis, M. (2005). Player modeling impact on player's entertainment in computer games. [Springer.]. *Proceedings of User Modeling, 2005,* 74–78.

Yavuzer, G., Senel, A., Atay, M. B., & Stam, H. J. (2008). Playstation eyetoy games improve upper extremity-related motor functioning in subacute stroke: A randomized controlled clinical trial. *European Journal of Physical and Rehabilitation Medicine, 44*(3), 237–244.

Yee, N., Ducheneaut, N., Nelson, L., & Likarish, P. (2011). Introverted elves and conscientious gnomes. The expression of personality in World of Warcraft. In *Proceedings of CHI 2011,* (pp. 753-762). ACM.

Yee, N. (2006). The demographics, motivations and derived experiences of users of massively-multiuser online graphical environments. *Presence (Cambridge, Mass.), 15*, 309–329. doi:10.1162/pres.15.3.309

Yee, N., & Bailenson, J. (2007). The proteus effect: The effect of transformed self-representation on behavior. *Human Communication Research, 33*, 271–290. doi:10.1111/j.1468-2958.2007.00299.x

Yee, N., Bailenson, J. N., Urbanek, M., Chang, F., & Merget, D. (2007). The unbearable likeness of being digital: The persistence of nonverbal social norms in online virtual environments. *Cyberpsychology & Behavior, 10*(1), 115–121. doi:10.1089/cpb.2006.9984

Yong, J. L., Soon, Y. T., Xu, D., Thia, E., Pei Fen, C., Kuah, C. W., & Kong, K. H. (2010). A feasibility study using interactive commercial off-the-shelf computer gaming in upper limb rehabilitation in patients after stroke. *Journal of Rehabilitation Medicine, 42*, 437–441. doi:10.2340/16501977-0528

Young, J. R. (2010). After frustrations in second life, colleges look to new virtual worlds. *The Chronicle of Higher Education.* Retrieved from http://chronicle.com/article/After-Frustrations-in-Second/64137/

Youngblood, P., Harter, P., Srivastava, S., Wallin, C.-J., Fellander-Tsai, L., Moffet, S., & Heinrichs, W. L. (2008). Design, development and evaluation of an online virtual emergency department for training trauma teams. *Simulation in Healthcare*, *3*(3), 146–153. doi:10.1097/SIH.0b013e31817bedf7

Younis, B., & Loh, C. S. (2010). *Integrating serious games in higher education programs*. Paper presented at Academic Colloquium 2010: Building Partnership in Teaching Excellence. Ramallah, Palestine.

Zagal, J. P., Nussbaum, M., & Rosas, R. (2000). A model to support the design of multiplayer games. *Presence: Teleoperating Virtual Environments*, *9*(5), 448–462. doi:10.1162/105474600566943

Zagal, J. P., Rick, J., & Hsi, I. (2006). Collaborative games: Lessons learned from board games. *Simulation & Gaming*, *37*(1), 24–40. doi:10.1177/1046878105282279

Zahorik, P., & Jenison, R. (1998). Presence as being-in-the-world. *Presence (Cambridge, Mass.)*, *7*, 78–89. doi:10.1162/105474698565541

Zea, N. P., Sanchez, J. L. G., & Gutierrez, F. L. (2009). Collaborative learning by means of video games: An entertainment system in the learning processes. In *Proceedings of the 2009 Ninth IEEE International Conference on Advanced Learning Technologies*, (pp. 215–217). Washington, DC: IEEE Computer Society. doi:http://dx.doi.org/10.1109/ICALT.2009.95

Zimmerli, L., Duschau-Wicke, A., Riener, R., Mayr, A., & Lunenburger, L. (2009). Virtual reality and gait rehabilitation: Augmented feedback for the Lokomat. In *Proceedings of the IEEE Virtual Rehabilitation International Conference*, (pp. 150-153). IEEE.

Zimmermann, B., Rensing, C., & Steinmetz, R. (2008). Experiences in using patterns to support process experts in wizard creation. In *Proceedings of EuroPLoP 2008*. EuroPLoP.

Zyda, M. (2005). From visual simulation to virtual reality in games. *Computer*, *38*(9), 25–32. doi:10.1109/MC.2005.297

About the Contributors

Klaus Bredl is Professor for Digital Media at the Institute for Media and Educational Technologies at Augsburg University. Before this, he held a Professorship for Social Informatics/Technology in Human Services at Neubrandenburg University of Applied Sciences. He started as an Assistant Professor in the Institute for Information Systems at the University of Regensburg, where he worked on a nationally funded interdisciplinary research project on the competence development of consultants. In Augsburg, his team is focused on research and teaching in the field of Digital Social Media, especially Virtual Worlds, Media Literacy, and Technology-Enhanced Learning.

Wolfgang Bösche (born 1971) was Research Assistant and Lecturer at the Department of Psychology, Technische Universität Darmstadt, Germany. He received his Doctorate in 2002 for his dissertation on adaptive network models of classification learning. In 2011, he habilitated on cognitive and motivational effects of violent video games. His research and teaching interests encompass multimedia learning and media psychology (with focus on the effects of violent video games), cognitive and mathematical psychology, and methodology. At the moment, he is Interim Professor at the Institute of Psychology at the University of Education Karlsruhe.

* * *

Jana Birkenbusch, born in April 1989, earned her Master of Science degree in Psychology from Technical University Darmstadt in September 2012, after four years of study, and started her Doctoral studies in October 2012. In her dissertation, which is supervised by Ph.D. Wolfgang Ellermeier, she investigates the perception of time by means of axiomatic measurement theory. Further research interests include the experience of presence in virtual environments, concepts of affective learning, language perception, and memory. While pursuing her degree, Jana Birkenbusch worked as Research Assistant for Applied Cognitive Psychology at the Institute of Psychology and the Fraunhofer-Institut für Graphische Datenverarbeitung IGD in Darmstadt, where she gained experience in current research on working memory and software evaluation, as well as in interdisciplinary team work.

Michael Brach is General Manager of the Institute of Sport and Exercise Science (University of Muenster, Germany). Before, he worked as a researcher at the universities of Bonn and Bochum. His research interests include mobility and ageing, and implementation and evaluation of ageing-related exercise programs in different settings, especially on the individual and on the institutional level. He studied sport science, mathematics, and psychology at the universities in Bochum, Duisburg, and Hagen. After conducting research on EEG and motor control, he received a Ph.D. in Human Movement Science from the University of Potsdam. He is an Outside Lecturer (Privatdozent) at the Karlsruhe Institute of Technology (KIT), and he leads the standardization group on mobility in ambient assisted living on behalf of the German Commission for Electrical, Electronic, and Information Technologies (DKE).

Oliver Christ works as a Post-Doc Researcher and Lecturer in the Psychological Department of the Technische Universität Darmstadt, Germany. Additionally he is the CEO of the Blue Flower Company founded in 2011 together with Sebastian Ohlmes. The main focus of his research can be divided in human-related advantageous and disadvantageous learning factors during work with human machine interfaces. This includes pain research, sensory motor incongruence, visual search, ergonomics, prosthesis technology evaluation, human-computer interaction, creativity and serious games, and computer-based trainings. Beside the work as a consultant and researcher, he plays guitar in several projects and as a solo artist.

Sarah Cook is a Survey Methodologist at RTI International. She has been involved in survey research for 8 years and specializes in instrument design and in-depth interviewing for cognitive and usability testing purposes. She is particularly interested in developing data collection methods for new technologies, including mobile devices, social media, and virtual worlds. She focuses her research on gathering user experience and cognition to improve data validity and reduce respondent burden in both self- and interviewer-administered surveys. Her research also concentrates on improving instrument design and usability testing methods of data collection on mobile devices.

Dick Davies started his career as a Clinical Scientist working in hospitals across the globe before 'settling down' and retraining into the social sciences and taking an academic career path. Discovering IT in the early 1980s and then on finding that IT innovation had moved from the university sector into the commercial space with the rise of the Internet, he moved into the corporate sector in the 1990s and then into start ups during the dot.bust era of 2000s, developing technology-based learning environments. Not losing his taste for innovation, he co-founded Ambient Performance in 2005 to introduce serious virtual worlds and ambient mobile applications into Europe. Recognising that, as technologies and the markets for them mature and differentiate, he is now working on developing a focused service for 3D immersive environments for clinical professionals.

Elizabeth Dean is a Survey Methodologist at RTI International. She has over 14 years' experience designing and pretesting surveys for social research, including topics such as health behaviors, exposure registration, social and family relationships, and substance abuse. She specializes in the design of surveys to be administered via emerging digital communication technologies. Her research focuses on developing and testing innovative applications of pretesting methods, including cognitive testing, questionnaire appraisal, and usability assessment. She has published research on conducting surveys in virtual worlds, conducting cross-cultural questionnaire appraisals, improving usability test methods, and using cognitive interviews to test consent forms.

Hein de Graaf, Social Psychologist (University of Amsterdam, 1974), started out as a Social Researcher (1974-1986). Fellow for the Council of Europe in 1980 on client records, Hein wrote a report based on an empirical study: "Computers in Social Services" in 1986. He wrote a paper called "The Senior Citizens after 2000" in 1995 and "Senior Citizens on the Electronic Highway" in 1995. Hein was chairman of the DG XIII workgroup "European Nervous System Program (ENS)" in 1991. From 1994 to 1998, Hein was evaluator for EU TIDE projects and TIDE proposals (DG XIII, IT for senior citizens and handicapped) and advisor for TIDE program 4e EU Framework and also evaluator and rapporteur for Urban and Rural Area program in 4th Frame-work EG. Hein de Graaf was founder and secretary to the European Network IT Human Services (ENITH), 1988 – 1994 and co-founder and Board member of the Human Service IT Applications (Husita). From 1996 to 2003, Hein was Project Manager for the Dutch National Program OL2000 for the social sector. 2009-2011, he worked for the Dutch Association of Municipalities (VNG). At the moment, Hein is retired but working hard as Director of his own company Astra-com (partner in the CIP-ICT project DISCOVER) and CEO of the VayaV Cooperatie UA. He is now (November 2012) starting up an EU-EIP-AHA partnership called VayaV, aiming at the use of virtual meetings in a 3D environment for senior citizens mixed with actual meetings in their local communities.

Li Felländer-Tsai was appointed Professor of Orthopaedics at Karolinska Institutet in 2006. She is the Chairman of the Department of Clinical Science, Intervention and Technology and Director of the Center for Advanced Medical Simulation. She is active in orthopedic education, training, and research as well as advanced surgical technology. She has developed and implemented a technique for monitoring of synovial tissue metabolism and inflammation with intraoperative and postoperative microdialysis. Other fields of research include virtual reality and surgical simulation. She is President of the Swedish Orthopedic Society and past registrar and Chairman of the Swedish ACL Register (quality registry for cruciate ligament reconstruction). She chaired the process of Accreditation of the Center for Advanced Medical Simulation and Training as an American College of Surgeons Level I Educational Institute and is now Director of the Center.

Christopher J. Ferguson is Department Chair of Psychology and Communication and an Associate Professor of Psychology and Criminal Justice. Most of his research work has examined the issue of media effects on behavior, including violent video game effects. His work has questioned popular beliefs linking violent media with aggression, and has taken a sociological view, examining fears and biased scholarship of video game effects in the context of historical moral panics of media. He holds a Ph.D. in Clinical Psychology from Texas A&M International University. He lives in Laredo, TX, with his wife and young son.

Stefan Göbel holds a PhD in Computer Science from TU Darmstadt and has long-term experience in Graphic Information Systems, Interactive Digital Storytelling, Edutainment Applications, and Serious Games. After five years work as Researcher at the Fraunhofer Institute for Computer Graphics, from 2002 to 2008, he was heading the Digital Storytelling Group at the Computer Graphics Center in Darmstadt. Late 2008, Dr. Göbel moved to TUD and is heading the prospering Serious Gaming group at the Multimedia Communications Lab. Stefan is the Initiator and Permanent Host of the GameDays, project leader of different research and science meets business projects on regional, national, and international level. Further, he is author of numerous papers and member of different program committees in the area of multimedia technologies, edutainment, and serious games.

Sue Gregory is a Lecturer in ICT Education and Research Fellow at the University of New England, Australia. She is a long-term adult educator and has created and manages several virtual world spaces including classrooms and a playground for students. She has been teaching in Second Life since 2008 and is focused on adult learning, engagement, immersion, and the efficacy of virtual worlds for education. In particular, Sue has been exploring student perceptions of their learning in a virtual world. Sue is the Chair of the Australian and New Zealand Virtual Worlds Working Group (VWWG) and Project Leader of an OLT-funded project on virtual professional experience: VirtualPREX: Innovative assessment using a 3D virtual world with pre-service teachers.

Michael Gutjahr studied Psychology at Technische Universität Darmstadt. In 2010, he finished his thesis on the topic of cognitive priminig effects of an interactive virtual story on perception, attribution, and behavior. Since 2012, he prepares his Ph.D. on the topic of sensor-based measurement of user experience at the Multimedia Communication Lab and the Department of Psychology at Technische Universität Darmstadt. His research interests include cognitive psychology, methodology, and user experience measurement.

Sandro Hardy finished his Master in Computer Science at Technische Universität Darmstadt in 2010 with a thesis proposing concepts and methodologies for the creation of serious games for sports and health. After that, he joined the research group at Multimedia Communication Lab (KOM) to focus on Serious Games and Physical Exertion. In his Ph.D., he focusses on the development of methodologies to measure and increase the effects of Serious Games for sports and health, also known as exergames. A major topic is the development of sensor-based interaction systems for the seamless progress measurement and adaption of exergames. His work includes the development of various prototypes such as "ErgoActive," "TheraKit," and "BalanceFit" for cardio, balance, and coordination training. He also coordinates various research projects in this field.

Klaus Hauer is the Director of the Research Department of the Bethanien Hospital Geriatric centre at the University of Heidelberg and Assistant Professor at the Medical Faculty of Heidelberg. He is also co-opted to the Faculty of Empirical Social and Behavioural Science. He studied Sport Science and Biology at the University of Heidelberg, made his PhD in Sport Science at the Institute of Sport Science at the University of Heidelberg. His research interests include mobility and ageing, biological ageing research, and methodological developments. Prof. Hauer is a member of the Prevention of Falls Network Europe (PROFANE) and the Network of ageing at the University of Heidelberg (NAR). He is reviewer in international peer reviewed journals and the author of more than a hundred scientific publications and has received numerous research prices for his scientific work.

William LeRoy Heinrichs' earned a MD w/Honors (Univ. Oklahoma), an OB/GYN Residency (Wayne State University, Detroit, MI), M.S. & Ph.D. degrees (Biochem, Univ. Oregon Health Sciences), and Ass't to Prof Appointments, Univ. Washington, Seattle, WA. He's a Josiah Macy, Jr. Faculty Fellow, an ACOG First Place Awardee for Research, and a Satava Awardee (MMVR). He served as Member & Chair of the NIH HED Study Section before arrival in 1976 at Stanford University as Professor & Chair of Obstetrics and Gynecology. There he advanced laparoscopic surgery, studying surgical simulators for enhancing surgical outcomes, and began developing Virtual Learning Environments (VLEs) for team training. Dr. H co-founded Innovation in Learning, Inc. producing two award-winning products, *CliniSpace^TM* and *BattleCare^TM*, selected as First and Grand Prize in the categories of "Artificial Intelligence in Training" and "Concept Design" in the Federal Virtual Worlds Challenge at GameTech 2011 and 2012. Dr. Heinrichs served as the 2012 President of AAGL's Council of Gynecologic Endoscopy, and as founding member of the Surgical Education Foundation begun in 2012.

Maike Helm earned a Masters' degree in Communication Research (2012) and a Bachelor of Arts degree in Applied Media Studies (2010) from Ilmenau University of Technology, Germany. In her studies, she concentrated on psychological aspects of media usage, especially on motivation and satisfaction models. Relating to this, she worked on several research projects focused on serious games and the rise of the online financing model crowdfunding. Additionally, she assisted the Department Media Management at Ilmenau University of Technology as a Graduate Student Assistant. Besides these topics, she specialized in the fields of public relations and journalism by working as a freelancer for several newspapers and PR agencies. Recently, she serves as a marketing manager for the S&S Media Group, which provides services for international IT and Web professionals.

Johannes Konert finished his Diploma in Computer Science and Attendant Studies in Cultural Studies at the Karlsruhe Institute of Technology (KIT) with a thesis proposing a Web-based knowledge management system for the integration of workflow and learnflow. After three years working on the foundation and development of the online social network Friendcafe as CEO and Senior Developer, he joined the research group at Multimedia Communication Lab (KOM) at Technische Universität Darmstadt to focus on Serious Games and Social Networks. He became a Ph.D. student of the DFG Research Training Group "Feedback-Based Quality Management in E-learning." In his research, he focusses on the development of solutions to use Social Media concepts for knowledge transfer between peers in Serious Games.

Oliver Korn studied Computational Linguistics at the University Stuttgart and at Glasgow University. Since 2001, he works in projects focusing on Human Computer Interaction (HCI), assistive systems, and simulations. From 2001 to 2005, he worked for the University Stuttgart and the Fraunhofer Institute for Industrial Engineering (IAO). In 2003, he co-founded the Fraunhofer spin-off Korion, a software company he leads as CEO. As a certified Project Manager (IHK), he led several national HCI-related projects both in research and industry. From 2006 to 2007, he was Research Associate and Lecturer for interactive systems and simulations at the Stuttgart Media University. He currently lectures "Digital Factory" at the University of Applied Sciences in Esslingen and at the Steinbeis Business Academy as well as Game Design at the Stuttgart Media University. Since 2011, he does his Doctorate at the Visualization Research Center (VISUS) at the Stuttgart University on Interactive Assistive Systems and Gamification.

Dennis Maciuszek studied Media Author (Master of Arts), Computer Science (German Diplom, Swedish Licentiate), and Psychology (minor subject). From December 2008 to November 2012, he has been a Researcher and Teacher at the University of Rostock, Germany, working mainly in the area of Game-Based Learning. Dennis is currently finishing his PhD work at the University of Education Schwäbisch Gmünd, Germany, with an interdisciplinary focus on the design of learning activities in virtual worlds. Furthermore, employing his experience in video game design and writing for different media formats, he is planning for a future as a freelancer in the media business.

Hannah R. Marston is a Post-Doctoral Fellow at the Institute of Movement and Sport Gerontology, at the German Sport University, Cologne. Currently, Hannah is working on an EU-funded project (iStoppFalls) with six additional consortium partners (Austrian Institute of Technology, Neuroscience Research Australia–Sydney, University of Siegen, Kaasa-Dusseldorf, Philips–Netherlands, and Institute of Biomechanics – Valencia). Hannah has several areas of research interests which include: gender, rural ageing, gerontology, age cohorts (baby boomers, oldest old [85+], centenarians, etc.) HCI, video games/theory/design/engagement (technology), social networking, rehabilitation, and tele-health technologies. Previously, Hannah was elected by members of the Gerontological Society of America (GSA) to represent the Emerging Scholar and Professional Organization (ESPO), the student arm of the organization as the Technology Chair. Additionally, while undertaking this role, Hannah also represented the study body on the membership committee. Furthermore, she has been an active member of the student body for the British Society of Gerontology (BSG), and at present, Hannah is working with three colleagues from University of Kentucky, Eindhoven University of Technology, and Syracuse University in setting up the student chapter for the International Society of Gerontechnology (ISG). Hannah has actively volunteered to review papers for several conferences (GSA, BSG, CHI, ISG) and is currently a member of the editorial board for the Computer Games Journal.

Alke Martens is a Professor at the University of Education Schwäbisch Gmünd, Germany, leader of the research group "Computer Science and Instructional Design," and elected Vice Rector for Research and International Affairs. She received her PhD in Computer Science from the University of Rostock, Germany, in Artificial Intelligence in the context of Intelligent Tutoring Systems. After that, she was Junior Professor at the University of Rostock and leader of the research group "eLearning and Cognitive Systems." Her current research interests are formal methods, software engineering, modeling and simulation, teaching and training systems, and a combination thereof, e.g. in Game-Based Learning.

Philip McClenaghan studied Design and worked as a Designer in London and Munich before becoming Assistant Director of a Research Lab within the Institute of Digital Innovation (IDI) at Teesside University. Philip is currently a member of the Institute of Media and Educational Technology (IMB) at the University of Augsburg and lectures at both the University of Augsburg and at Augsburg University of Applied Sciences.

Florian Mehm is a Founding Member of the Serious Games Group of the Multimedia Communications Lab (KOM) of Technische Universität Darmstadt, since 2009. He continued his work on authoring tools from his previous position at the Computer Graphics Center in Darmstadt, where he was active from 2008 to 2009. His research areas include authoring systems for storytelling-based digital educational games and serious games, personalization, and adaptation in games and technologies for games and edutainment applications. The implementation of his concepts for authoring tools is the StoryTec authoring tool along with the associated framework of software tools, including a cross-platform player for serious games.

Joe Murphy is a Survey Methodologist at RTI International with more than 15 years of experience researching the causes and solutions for issues related to survey quality and managing survey projects. His research focuses on the implementation of new data collection processes, new data sources, and analytic techniques to maximize data quality, increase response, and reduce costs. His recent work has been centered on data sources and techniques such as Internet search patterns, social media data analysis (e.g., Twitter), data visualization, crowdsourcing, and social research in virtual worlds. Mr. Murphy is the Director of the Program on Digital Technology and Society in RTI's Survey Research Division. The program investigates the role of new technologies and social media in survey and social research.

Christian Reuter studied Computer Science at Technische Universität Darmstadt and finished his Master Thesis with the topic "Development and Realization of Methods and Concepts for Multiplayer Adventures" in 2011. He then joined the Multimedia Communication Lab, where his research focus includes the concept and design of multiplayer serious games and authoring concepts for multiplayer games. He is working on an extension for the StoryTec authoring platform that allows authors to create multiplayer games in the same non-technical manner as authoring of single player games in StoryTec.

Kristina Richter received her M.A. in Sciences of Education from Technische Universität Dresden and is now doing her PhD studies in Pedagogy and Mathematics Education at Technische Universität Darmstadt. She was a Scholar in the Research-Training Group on Feedback-Based Quality Improvement in E-Learning fully funded by the German Research Foundation (DFG). Her main research interest is in the exploration of technological support for cooperative learning and teaching in classroom and academic education and the potential of games for learning. Currently, she is working at a joint research project with the focus on the method of peer review for learning and teaching and mathematics (project PEDALE).

Daniel Schultheiss earned a PhD in Media and Communication Research (2010) and a Diploma (M.A. equivalent) in Media and Communication Studies (2007) at Ilmenau University of Technology. Since 2007, he has been a Doctoral candidate, and since 2008, a Research Assistant in the Department Media Management at Ilmenau University of Technology. Since 2010, he is a Senior Researcher (Post-Doc). In his research, Schultheiss focuses the areas of online communication, knowledge management, usage of video games, online entertainment, and consumer integration through the Internet. Besides others, Schultheiss is a member of the International Communication Association (ICA), the European Communication Research and Education Association (ECREA), and the International Association of CyberPsychology, Training, and Rehabilitation (iACToR). He is on the editorial board of *Journal of Gaming & Virtual Worlds* and serves as a reviewer for ICA, Cyberpsychology, Behavior, and Social Networking, as well as other conferences and journals.

Marcelo Simão de Vasconcellos is a Designer in Rio de Janeiro, working for Oswaldo Cruz Foundation, the oldest and most important public health institution in Brazil. He has a M.A. degree in Visual Arts, and now he is a PhD Candidate, researching Massively Multiplayer Online Role-Playing Games for applications on Public Health Communication. He focuses in the use of MMORPGs' social and interactive qualities as ways to enhance population's understanding and participation in public health policies. In Oswaldo Cruz Foundation, he coordinates a small game design team, aiming to introduce the use of video games and board games in Brazilian Health Communication. He also organized the first Brazilian event about videogames applied for health, called "Saúde em Jogo" (Health in Game), which had its second installment in 2012.

Inesita Soares de Araújo is a PhD in Communication and Culture and a researcher of Oswaldo Cruz Foundation, the oldest and most important public health institution in Brazil. Her main areas of research are the fields of Communication and Public Policies, with emphasis on Collective Health. She also coordinates and teaches in the Post-Graduate Program for Information and Communication in Health (PPGICS) in the same institution. She is leader of the research group "Communication and Health" of CNPq (Brazil), coordinator of the working group "Comunicación y Salud" of the Latin American Association of Communication Researchers (ALAIC), and member of the working group "Communication and Health" of the Brazilian Association of Collective Health (ABRASCO). She is author of two books: *A Reconversão do Olhar* (The Reconversion of Looking) and *Comunicação e Saúde* (Communication and Health).

Sven Unkauf studied Social Economics at the University of Hohenheim. From 2008 to 2009, he worked for the University of Hohenheim as a Student Assistant at the Institute of Health Care & Public Management. From 2009 to 2010, he did an internship at the Department of Medical Psychology at the University Medical Center Hamburg-Eppendorf. Since 2010, he is employed at the Wohlfahrtswerk for Baden-Wuerttemberg. Initially, he worked as an Intern and a Student Assistant, after finishing his diploma thesis as a project manager. He is involved in several projects concerning technical assistance systems and games for older people. In 2012, he and his colleagues had a lectureship "Ambient Assisted Living" in general studies at the University of Applied Sciences in Esslingen.

Viktor Wendel received his Degree in Computer Science from the Julius-Maximilians-University of Würzburg in 2009. Since November 2009, he is working as a Research Assistant at the Multimedia-Communications-Lab at Technische Universität Darmstadt in the field of Serious Games. His research topics are Collaborative Learning concept development, Game Mastering concepts for instructor support in collaborative multiplayer Serious Games, and Adaptation of Serious Games for multi-user groups of learners. He is incorporated in the development of 3D multiplayer Serious Game prototypes like 'Woodment' or 'Escape From Wilson Island'. Further, he is an Editor for *ACM SIGMM Records* and a member of the committee for the European Conference on Games Based Learning (ECGBL).

Josef Wiemeyer finished his M.Ed. with the subjects Physical Education and Ancient Latin at WWU Münster (Germany) in 1985. In 1989, he gained his Doctoral degree in Sport Medicine at WWU Münster (Title of the Doctoral thesis: "Measuring Central-Nervous Activation by Means of an Improved CFF Method"). In 1996, he finished his habilitation at WWU Münster (Title of the habilitation thesis: "Motor Learning: Sensory-Motor, Cognitive, and Emotional Aspects"). Since 1996, he has been with the Institute of Sport Science at the Technische Universität Darmstadt. His current research areas comprise motor control and learning, technology-supported learning and training, and serious games. He is reviewer of many national and international journals as well as (co-)chair of numerous conferences. He has published numerous books and papers dealing with motor learning, stretching, research methods, and technology-based learning (including serious games).

Steffen Winny is a Lecturer and Research Assistant at the Chair of Digital Media at the University of Augsburg, Germany. He has graduated and worked as a qualified social educational worker within different media-pedagogical projects before he earned his degrees on Master level in educational as well as in social science. During his work as a research assistant at the Chair of Educational Media Research of the University of Magdeburg, he was involved in several third-party-funded research projects related to informal learning in exhibitions and theme parks or on the issue of serious games in the context of the education for sustainable development. His research interests are focused on informal learning, serious games, and digital media for children.

Index